TERRORISM

Documents of International and Local Control

VOLUME 93

TERRORISM

Documents of International and Local Control

VOLUME 93

THE PALESTINIAN TERRITORIES AND HAMAS

Douglas C. Lovelace Jr., Esquire
Senior National Security Strategist

Oceana®
NEW YORK

OXFORD
UNIVERSITY PRESS

Oxford University Press, Inc., publishes works that further Oxford University's objective of excellence in research, scholarship, and education.

Published by Oxford University Press, Inc.
198 Madison Avenue, New York, New York 10016

Cataloging-in-Publication information is available from the Library of Congress.

ISSN 1062-4007
Terrorism: Documents of International and Local Control

ISBN: 978-0-19-538277-8 (v. 93)

Note to Readers:

This publication is designed to provide accurate and authoritative information in regard to the subject matter covered. It is based upon sources believed to be accurate and reliable and is intended to be current as of the time it was written. It is sold with the understanding that the publisher is not engaged in rendering legal, accounting, or other professional services. If legal advice or other expert assistance is required, the services of a competent professional person should be sought. Also, to confirm that the information has not been affected or changed by recent developments, traditional legal research techniques should be used, including checking primary sources where appropriate.

(Based on the Declaration of Principles jointly adopted by a Committee of the American Bar Association and a Committee of Publishers and Associations.)

TABLE OF CONTENTS

VOLUME 93

THE PALESTINIAN TERRITORIES AND HAMAS

DOCUMENTS

B. INTERNAL PROBLEMS WITHIN THE PALESTINIAN TERRITORIES

C. THE SECURITY WALL

D. HAMAS-RELATED CASES IN U.S. COURTS

E. EUROPEAN APPROACH TO THE PALESTINIAN PROBLEM

INTRODUCTORY NOTE

The editors of *Terrorism: Documents of International and Local Control* are pleased to present in this volume a collection of English-language or translated documents pertaining to terrorism in Israel and the Palestinian territories, including recent developments in the Israeli-Palestinian conflict, such as continuing construction of Israel's West Bank security barrier, the 2006 election victory of Hamas, the 2007 Battle of Gaza between Fatah and Hamas, and the 2008 breach of the border between Egypt and the Gaza Strip. The documents included in this volume encompass a wide range of sometimes conflicting perspectives, including viewpoints from the Israeli Ministry of Foreign Affairs, from the U.S. Congressional Research Service and the U.S. Institute of Peace, and from NGOs such as Israel's Intelligence and Terrorism Information Center and Amnesty International. Also included are United Nations Security Council and General Assembly resolutions, an opinion from the International Court of Justice relating to the construction of Israel's West Bank security barrier, documents relating to European Union cooperation with the Palestinian Authority, a World Bank report on Palestinian economic recovery, U.S. federal case law relating to Hamas and the PLO, and a translation of Hamas's *Covenant of the Islamic Resistance Movement*.

Because the institutional authors of some of the documents in this volume unapologetically advocate for the objectives of the governments or organizations which they represent, it is important to note that we are providing these documents to you not as assertions of fact but rather as a tour of current positions taken by those governments and private groups. We believe that all of these documents, when evaluated together, will serve to enhance the reader's understanding of the many issues relating to terrorism in Israel and the Israeli-Palestinian conflict.

A. IN GENERAL

DOCUMENT NO. 1

THE FUTURE OF THE ISRAELI-PALESTINIAN CONFLICT: CRITICAL TRENDS AFFECTING ISRAEL

United States Institute of Peace (USIP)
Special Report 149

September 2005

ABOUT THE REPORT

The United States Institute of Peace's Project on Arab-Israeli Futures is a research effort designed to anticipate and assess obstacles and opportunities facing the peace process over the next five to ten years. Stepping back from the day-to-day ebb and flow of events in the Middle East, this project examines broader, "over-the-horizon" developments that could foreclose future options or offer new opportunities for peace. The effort brings together U.S., Israeli, and Arab researchers and is directed by Scott Lasensky of the Institute's Research and Studies program.

In this report, Yossi Alpher identifies which local, regional, and international trends will have the greatest impact on Israel's relationship with Palestinians in the coming years. Next in the series is Khalil Shikaki's study of long-term trends in Palestinian public opinion and their policy implications for the peace process.

Yossi (Joseph) Alpher is currently coeditor of the bitterlemons family of Internet-based Middle East dialogue publications. He is a former director of the Jaffee Center for Strategic Studies at Tel Aviv University. In 2000 Alpher served as a senior adviser to Israeli prime minister Ehud Barak.

The views expressed in this report do not necessarily reflect the views of the United States Institute of Peace, which does not advocate specific policy positions.

Editor's note: The original version of this document included some color images that could not be adequately reproduced in this publication. Where necessary, captions and/or headings specifically relating to any omitted images have also been left out of the version reprinted herein. The main text of the document has not been affected by these omissions.

Summary

- A broad fabric of anticipated developments and attitudes suggests only limited progress toward Israeli-Palestinian peace in the next few years.
- The elimination of the Iraqi armed forces in 2003 has minimized the danger of an all-out conventional war between Israel and its eastern neighbors, reducing the strategic value for Israel of the West Bank. At the same time, however, Israel is conscious of the danger posed by a nuclear-armed Iran, a danger that might intimidate Israel's neighbors

into taking a more aggressive stance toward Israel, exacerbating Arab-Israeli relations and escalating the Israeli-Palestinian conflict.

- U.S.-supported democratization in the Middle East may reduce inter-Arab support for the Palestinian cause but could also inspire Islamic movements, generating greater Palestinian militancy and tougher negotiating positions.
- The collapse of Oslo, the failure of Camp David, and the ensuing four years of conflict have undermined Israeli trust in a full-fledged peace process with the Palestinians. In the near term, this attitude is unlikely to change because of Palestinian leadership changes, however welcome they might be.
- Israel has opted to disengage unilaterally from the Gaza Strip and northern West Bank rather than to seek to negotiate its withdrawal. Disengagement is motivated first and foremost by a drive to ensure Israel's survival as a Jewish and democratic state rather than to reactivate the peace process. Most Israelis now support fencing off the Palestinian territories and removing isolated settlements to protect themselves and to avoid absorbing Palestinian Arabs.
- Israel's Arab population is no longer seen as a "bridge to peace" with the West Bank and Gazan Palestinian population but as yet another obstacle to achieving a two-state solution.
- Both Israel and Egypt are concerned about the emergence of a Hamas-dominated Gaza Strip after Israel withdraws from it and if ordnance is smuggled into Gaza from the Sinai Peninsula. Israel has agreed to allow enhanced Egyptian police and military forces to guard part of Sinai. Israel's need to cooperate with Egypt in order to deal with terrorism dictates an altered approach to the Egyptian military and the strategic role of the Sinai Peninsula.
- Fundamental Israeli notions regarding the strategic uses of territory are in flux. There is a growing recognition on the dominant political right that both Israel and Palestine have demographic-political needs that, at least theoretically, could be dealt with by abandoning traditional attitudes toward territory.
- The Israeli political system, far from providing a mechanism for solving Israel's conflict with the Palestinians, has become a serious obstacle to a solution. Any likely governing coalition in the coming years will probably be unable to sustain more than a partial peace process before collapsing under the weight of internal coalition contradictions.
- While the settlement movement's opposition to Prime Minister Ariel Sharon's disengagement policy failed, the settlers will continue to threaten the viability of future Israeli governments intent on dismantling additional settlements. The settlers fully intend to exact such a high price

in national trauma and delegitimization of the government that future governments will not dare to follow in Sharon's footsteps.

- International legal rulings and threats of sanctions against Israel are proliferating. These are having a growing impact on the Israeli establishment, which is actually reaching out to some multinational institutions. Measured international involvement, short of peacekeeping or mediation, could be helpful in achieving limited progress.

Introduction

This report attempts to identify critical Israel-related trends that might affect the course of the Israeli-Palestinian conflict over the next five to ten years. To the extent that this endeavor is successful, its fruits might be useful to Israeli as well as to U.S., European, and Arab policymakers and planners as they strive to understand the dynamics that could reduce tensions and generate greater stability and eventually peace.

The following discussion draws on recent strategic thinking and critical developments in Israel and extrapolates with regard to future trends. Most of these trends reflect modes of addressing the conflict inside Israel. These internal Israeli trends can be divided into the geographic/demographic (i.e., changing attitudes toward the strategic uses and advantages of populated and nonpopulated territories) and the political (i.e., the capacity of the Israeli political system to deal with the conflict and the role of the conflict and conflict fatigue in determining the strategies and the stability or lack thereof of Israeli governments). An additional set of trends is external and involves Israeli perceptions of and responses to developments in the region and to international involvement.

The trends noted here are only probabilities, of course. They could conceivably be obviated by major external events such as war or radical regime change in the region, major changes in energy prices, a Sadat-like initiative on the part of an Arab leader, and superpower intervention. Conceivably, too, they could be mitigated by alternative, hitherto unnoticed countertrends. These and similar possibilities are valid topics of analysis that go beyond the scope of this report.

All in all, the trends discussed hereunder point to the possibility of progress toward Israeli-Palestinian peace in the next few years. But that progress will be limited and will fall short of the goal of ending the conflict.

The Strategic Military Setting

From an Israeli perspective, in the coming years the regional strategic setting for Israeli-Palestinian interaction is likely to be different from that of the past. Whether or not this will benefit Israel or the cause of Israeli-Palestinian peace is not at all clear.

The elimination of the Iraqi armed forces in 2003 has, for the first time in Israel's fifty-seven-year history, minimized the danger of all-out conventional war between Israel and a coalition of its neighbors attacking from the east, thereby reducing the strategic value for Israel of the West Bank. Even before the removal of the Iraqi threat, Israel found that it could isolate a concerted Palestinian armed campaign against it—the second intifada of 2000–2005—and thwart the Palestinian goal of generating regional military escalation. Since 2003 the reality of Palestinian military isolation has become more stark than ever; it will only be compounded by the completion of the security fence being erected by the Sharon government around the West Bank with the primary goal of preventing incursion into Israel by Palestinian terrorists.

As a consequence, Palestinian bargaining power vis-à-vis Israel could be weakened in the coming years. To the extent that U.S.-supported democratic reform processes take hold in neighboring countries such as Lebanon and Syria, inter-Arab support for the Palestinian cause might be further reduced, particularly if Jerusalem can reach peace agreements with Beirut and Damascus.

At the same time, those same democratization processes could also bring Islamist movements to the fore in the region, including within the Palestinian Authority, thereby conceivably generating greater Palestinian militancy and tougher negotiating positions. The threat of Palestinian terrorism in future years should not be taken lightly.

Finally, the danger of a nuclear-armed Iran, equipped with missile-delivery systems, has replaced conventional Arab-Israeli warfare as the primary strategic military threat perceived by Israel. Insofar as a nuclearized Islamic Republic of Iran is likely to intimidate Israel's neighbors, support radical Islamist elements among them, and pressure them to take an aggressive stance toward Israel, a regional nuclear escalation or confrontation is liable to exacerbate Arab-Israeli relations and escalate the Israeli-Palestinian conflict. This constraint is often cited as a reason for Israel to offer territorial and other concessions in order to accelerate peace with its neighbors, though it could be argued that the prospect of Iranian-inspired unrest in the region justifies an Israeli decision to hold on to "strategic" territory on the Golan Heights and in the Jordan Valley. In this sense, it is difficult to say whether success in preventing Iran from developing nuclear weapons would redound positively on the prospects for Israeli-Palestinian and Arab-Israeli accommodation. In the near term, an Israeli military strike against Iran's nuclear project would certainly redound negatively, by generating intensified conflict with pro-Iranian elements such as Hezbollah and fueling anger against Israel in the Arab street.

The United States Institute of Peace and Arab-Israeli Relations

The United States Institute of Peace is a leader among U.S. institutions working toward a peaceful resolution of the Arab-Israeli conflict. Over two decades, the Institute has made contributions across many fields—from policy studies and education to professional training and interreligious dialogue. The Institute also serves as a forum for promoting new thinking about U.S. policy and bringing leading Israeli and Arab officials and policy specialists together with their U.S. counterparts. The Institute is trusted in both Washington and the region and works with all sides to operate an array of programs on the ground. For more information, see http://www.usip.org/muslimworld/arab_israeli.html.

Geographic and Demographic Trends

A discussion of geographic and demographic trends in Israeli thinking inevitably begins with a fundamental question regarding the currently dominant programs of security fence construction and unilateral disengagement: Why has Israel opted to disengage unilaterally from the Gaza Strip and northern West Bank rather than seek to negotiate its withdrawal, perhaps in return for Palestinian commitments to security? The answer is that Israeli prime minister Ariel Sharon, speaking for a large majority of Israelis, sees neither purpose nor profit in negotiating, insofar as the Palestinian Authority is perceived as impotent, corrupt, and itself terroristic, and disengagement is motivated first and foremost by a drive to ensure Israel's survival as a Jewish and democratic state rather than to reactivate the peace process.

From nearly every conceptual standpoint, disengagement and the security fence are integrated. The idea of fencing off large parts of the Palestinian territories and removing isolated Jewish settlements beyond the fence goes back some ten years. More recently, it has been very much a grassroots Israeli phenomenon, reflecting the perceived need for Israel, in the absence of an agreed-upon peace, both to protect its citizenry and to avoid at any cost absorbing the Palestinian Arabs under its sovereign rule. Polling data consistently indicate that a comfortable majority of Israelis support these objectives.

In this regard, many of the fence advocates entertain a barely hidden agenda, according to which the Gazan and West Bank fences will determine Israel's ultimate political borders with Palestine, thereby ensuring that few if any Palestinians will be annexed to Israel, which will thus retain its Jewish character whether or not it succeeds in signing a final peace agreement with the Palestine Liberation Organization (PLO). Sharon initially embraced the fence idea reluctantly. His early attempts to include large swaths of West Bank land and their Arab inhabitants on the Israeli side of the fence met with such widespread opposition—from the Israeli public, the Bush administration, and the local and international legal communities—that Sharon was obliged to alter the secondary objective (the first being antiterrorist security) of the fence from a geographic purpose—the de facto annexation of lands—to a demographic one—reducing Israeli control over much of the Palestinian population in order to ensure that Israel remains a predominantly Jewish state.

Here we encounter a parallel dynamic that has struck deep roots in Israeli public discourse since the failure of Camp David II in July 2000 and the outbreak of the second intifada in September 2000. Those events, including a week of violent rioting inside Israel in October 2000 on the part of Palestinian citizens of Israel and pronouncements by the Palestinian leadership regarding "existential" final-status issues such as the Temple Mount and the right of return, convinced most Israelis that there was no viable Palestinian partner for a process of genuine peace and reconciliation with Israel. The majority of Israelis were persuaded that most Palestinians led by Yasir Arafat, could not come to terms with the permanent existence of a Jewish state in part of historic Palestine, and that it was a long-term Palestinian strategic goal to exploit a peace process in order to undermine and "Palestinize" Israel from within.

Everything that we know about Arafat's successor, Mahmoud Abbas, indicates that—alongside his undoubted moderation and readiness to condemn violence—his political views, particularly on the right-of-return issue, will continue to nurture this Israeli reaction. The collapse of Oslo, the failure of Camp David, and the ensuing four years of conflict have had a profound effect on Israeli trust in a full-fledged peace process with the Palestinians. In the near term, this attitude may not easily be mitigated by Palestinian leadership changes, however welcome.

In the post-2000 environment, too, Israelis became aware that upward of one hundred thousand West Bank Palestinians had illegally migrated into Israel. This recognition in turn fed the separation concept and the fence-disengagement campaign, based on the contention that demographic Palestinization had already begun.

Finally, the suicide bombing campaign against Israeli civilians beginning in 2001 had a traumatic effect on Israeli attitudes toward Palestinians, underlining the perceived need for Israel to disentangle itself from Palestine and set up impenetrable barriers almost at any cost. All of these factors have also contributed to a strengthening of Israel's Jewish identity; the "post-Zionist" intellectual fringe that used to advocate concepts such as "a state of all its citizens" in order to embrace both Jews and Arabs in a secular Israeli identity has all but disappeared.

These developments explain the striking and consistent findings of Israeli opinion polling over the past three years or so: On the one hand, there exists ongoing majority support for negotiated Israeli-Palestinian peace and broad, generalized support for informal but well-publicized peace schemes such as the Geneva Accord and the Ayalon-Nusseibeh principles. But, on the other hand, there is widespread pessimism regarding the near-term prospects for peace and the credibility of the Palestinian leadership; fear lest the failure of renewed negotiations that rest on fragile foundations seriously damages long-term prospects for peace; and, therefore, growing support among a substantial majority of the Israeli public for unilateral disengagement and for a security fence. Increasingly, Israelis are opting for guarantees for their personal security (the fence) and the Jewish nature of the state (unilateral withdrawal) over the aspiration to "end the conflict," which presupposes Palestinian agreement to abandon the right of return and Palestinian acknowledgment that the Jewish people have a legitimate historic and religious claim (alongside the Muslim claim) to the Temple Mount/Haram al-Sharif in Jerusalem—concessions on Israeli/Jewish "existential" issues that for the time being seem impossible to achieve.

Thus, it is very likely that, in the coming years, Israelis will seek to continue the unilateral disengagement process—while perhaps also seeking to coordinate aspects of the withdrawal and/or to reach interim agreements—and will prefer that process to a renewed attempt to negotiate a full-fledged, comprehensive Israeli-Palestinian peace. To the extent that the Israeli public does support renewed final-status negotiations—as was the case in the aftermath of Arafat's departure from the scene—neither the Israeli nor the Palestinian political system may be up to the task (see below, "Political Trends"). Nor, for that matter, is Prime Minister Sharon, who never supported Israel's bilateral peace treaties with Egypt and Jordan (he voted against the former and abstained on the latter) and who appears to harbor a deep mistrust of Arab peace initiatives. In this regard, Sharon's leadership profile is ideally suited to the framework of unilateral efforts.

In supporting unilateral disengagement, Israelis are falling back on a classic element in pragmatic Zionist strategic thinking and opting for demography over geography. Even a veteran territorial hawk such as Sharon has felt obliged to acknowledge (in his speech of December 2004 at the strategy conference held annually in Herzliya) the primacy of "the demographic reality on the ground" over his own more traditional advocacy of occupying what he once considered to be key tactical territory in the West Bank and the Gaza Strip. Sharon has not hesitated to make indirect comparisons to the (pre-1994) South Africa–type fate awaiting Israel if it does not relinquish territory: "The alternative of one nation, where one rules over another, would be a horrible disaster for both peoples," he stated in December 2004.

True, Sharon is still striving to hold on to the settlement blocs near the "green line" (the 1949 armistice line) separating Israel from the West Bank, an objective informed by residual territorial as well as political, demographic, and water-security motives. But these areas fall within a consensus reached in 2000 by Ehud Barak and Yasir Arafat and tacitly endorsed in April 2004 and thereafter by President George Bush. Indeed, the only obvious exception to the close identity between Sharon's current fence-disengagement map and the territorial concept at the heart of the Clinton and Geneva plans is Jerusalem, where strong ideological politics still drives a fence/wall concept that is counterintuitive to Israel's demographic needs and to the map of an eventual two-state solution.

The new Israeli approach bespeaks a broader change of attitudes in Israeli strategic and political circles, including among hawkish right-wingers such as Sharon who previously energized the settlement movement in the West Bank and Gaza with regard to territory in general. Considering Israel's small dimensions, hostile regional environment, and traditional military strategy of bringing the war to enemy territory and ending wars by setting up territorial buffers between itself and its neighbors, this is a veritable revolution in Israeli strategic thinking.

Thus, the withdrawal from Gaza is paralleled by a striking revision, still within the Palestinian context, of strategy concerning the Sinai Peninsula. Traditional Israeli military thinking about Sinai held that it should be either under Israeli occupation or demilitarized and exploited as an ideal, 250-kilometer-wide, empty desert buffer that separates the Israeli and Egyptian armies. At the heart of this concept was the trauma of an Egyptian armored column moving from Sinai through Gaza and northward up the Mediterranean coast toward Tel Aviv in 1948. Since then, Israeli military victories over Egypt in 1956 and 1967 persuaded the Egyptians that their interests, too, were well served by the demilitarization of Sinai.

Now, two developments have combined to convince both Israel and Egypt to change their approach toward Sinai. One is the possible emergence, following Israeli withdrawal, of a Hamas-dominated Gaza Strip (what is sometimes referred to in Israel as "Hamastan") that could threaten Egyptian interests. The other is Israel's inability, without Egyptian cooperation on the Sinai side of the border, to stop the smuggling of ordnance into Gaza from Sinai through tunnels under the so-called Philadelphi Road that runs along the Gazan side of the border, or, for that matter, the growing wave of smuggling across the Sinai-Negev border, including quantities of arms that are transported by Israeli Bedouin to Palestinian militants in the West Bank. Terrorist attacks on Israeli vacationers in Sinai in October 2004 also contributed to the readiness of both sides to discuss the remilitarization, albeit on a small scale (two Egyptian infantry battalions), of an area of Sinai adjacent to the 12-kilometer-long Gaza border and, on a slightly larger scale (three thousand Egyptian soldiers, with armored vehicles), of the entire 250-kilometer-long Egyptian-Israeli border.

In effect, the Palestinian issue has generated a new look at Israel's traditional threat perceptions to the southwest, with the need to cooperate with Egypt in order to deal with terrorism dictating an altered approach to the Egyptian military and to the strategic role of the Sinai Peninsula. Israel, driven by unilateralism and relatively unconcerned with an Egyptian military threat, is considering withdrawing from the Philadelphi Road and allowing Egypt both to police the Rafah crossing between Sinai and Gaza—a function concerning which even the minimalistic Clinton and Geneva plans called for a three-year residual Israeli monitoring presence—and to beef up its military presence in the hitherto demilitarized overall border region.

In a more bizarre context, Israel's Palestinian dilemma has also led Israeli planners, most associated with the political right and including the prime minister's national security adviser, Major General (ret.) Giora Eiland, to examine a proposal whereby Palestinian demographic pressures in Gaza would be alleviated by Egypt ceding to Palestine the adjacent northeast corner of Sinai. Egypt would be compensated by Israel, according to this scheme, with a portion of the southern Negev and land access across the Negev to Jordan.

A parallel scheme formulated on the political right envisions an Israel-Syria peace agreement that leaves Israel in possession of 20 percent of the Golan Heights, with Syria compensated territorially by Jordan and Jordan by Israel, in both cases in less-sensitive border areas.

There is even a growing sentiment among some far-right-wing Israelis such as the politician Avigdor Lieberman that the country is better off becoming geographically smaller if this means it has fewer Palestinian Arab citizens. In this regard, Israel's Arab population is no longer seen, as it was in the 1970s,'80s, and early'90s, as a "bridge to peace" with the West Bank and Gazan Palestinian population. Rather, it is understood to be yet another obstacle to a two-state solution, insofar as Israel is called upon to rationalize the existence of a Palestinian national minority within a Jewish state. Inevitably, this dilemma too now lends itself to unilateral thinking.

Thus, the Wadi Ara region abutting the green line just north of Israel's narrow waist, with more than two hundred thousand Israeli Arab citizens, is now the subject of schemes calling for it to be included in the future Palestinian state, if necessary by Israel unilaterally moving the border. This area originally was torn by Israel from the Jordanian-controlled West Bank under threat of renewed hostilities in 1949 because Israeli security planners wanted to control a road linking central Israel to lower Galilee and to secure a hold on additional West Bank foothills that overlook the coastal plain.

Now, with no conventional military threat to the east of Israel, those geostrategic motives are beginning to pale alongside the demographic rationale. Demographic considerations also lie behind some signs of initial readiness on the part of the Israeli right, as well as the security establishment, to contemplate forsaking the religious and ideological considerations noted earlier and abandoning all or part of East Jerusalem, with its 230,000 Arab inhabitants, by moving the security barrier closer to the old green line that divided the city prior to 1967. The Sharon government took an initial step in this direction in July 2005 concerning the barrier in the northeast part of the city.

Some of the new Israeli schemes for addressing territorial and demographic issues appear to reflect a misreading of the national territorial perceptions of Israel's neighbors, or a simple refusal to countenance giving up Israeli territory. But it seems that many right-wing Israelis have reluctantly acknowledged the need to forgo territory, to the extent that they ingenuously assume a similar readiness—for the sake of peace—on the part of Egyptians, Syrians, and Jordanians.

Whether or not these schemes are practical, they reflect the fact that fundamental Israeli notions regarding the strategic uses of territory are in flux. There is a growing recognition on the dominant political right that both Israel and Palestine have demographic and political needs (Israeli settlements, Palestinian refugees) that, at least theoretically, could be dealt with by abandoning traditional attitudes toward territory.

Political Trends

The most obvious, painful, and long-lasting trend in Israeli politics that is linked to the Palestinian issue is the linkage itself: the Palestinian question has been the specific catalyst of the downfall of every governing Israeli coalition for the past twenty years. Prime ministers Rabin, Peres, Netanyahu, Barak, and Sharon have all failed to convert their popular mandate regarding the Palestinian issue into a viable coalition for change. In the course of this period, one attempt to improve the political structure—direct election of the prime minister—had to be abandoned because it merely worsened the situation, while the overall quality of Israeli politics and politicians has deteriorated.

Israel's countrywide proportional voting system (which treats the entire country as a single constituency and awards seats in the Knesset on the basis of the proportion of the popular vote won by each party slate) ensures that issues unrelated to the Palestinian problem (e.g., matters of religion and state) determine the voting patterns of adherents of some parties. In Israel's heterogeneous society, this produces complex and fragile coalitions whose members are driven by diverse and often conflicting political agendas.

As a result, the Israeli political system, far from providing a mechanism for solving Israel's conflict with the Palestinians, has become a serious obstacle to a solution insofar as government coalitions are inherently unstable and incapable of surviving dramatic peace-related moves.

Sadly, this will almost certainly continue to be the case. In the coming decades, Palestinian citizens of Israel and ultra-Orthodox Jews—sectors of the population with political agendas that differ radically from that of the Zionist mainstream—are likely to grow in Knesset representation. Israeli governments will, at best, succeed in dealing with the conflict in fits and starts, and piecemeal, before going the way of their predecessors. This means that any third party such as the U.S. government seeking to influence the course of an Israeli-Palestinian dialogue or peace process must take into account that at some early stage its efforts are likely to be thwarted by the vicissitudes of Israeli politics. During the second half of 2004, for example, Prime Minister Sharon dissolved one coalition and put together another (with Labor) in order to carry out his disengagement plan in Gaza and the northern West Bank. Whether disengagement is deemed successful or not, the new coalition is almost certain to dissolve, too, as Sharon, Labor, and the Likud hawks all seek to move in different directions on the Palestinian issue—toward additional disengagement, a renewed peace process, or no new initiatives at all. This in turn will probably provoke early elections, and these will postpone further movement and break whatever positive momentum has been achieved.

One key factor in the foundering of Israeli politics over the Palestinian issue that bears emphasis is the influence of the settlement movement. The religious-ideological settlers of the West Bank and Gaza have proved over recent decades to be the most dynamic, highly motivated, and astute political lobby in Israel. Even prime ministers intent on far-reaching territorial compromise, such as Rabin and Barak, preferred to co-opt the settlers and enable settlement expansion, thereby not only postponing confrontation with them over the territorial issue but rendering the ultimate confrontation with this minority sector that much worse in quantitative terms.

But the ideological settlers' emphasis on land as a compelling Jewish value is increasingly contradicted by the strategic realities of demography and their territorial consequences, that is, by Israeli state (as opposed to religious) considerations. From this standpoint, Sharon's disengagement effort presented a moment of truth in settler-government relations. The religious-ideological settlers realized this and sought to thwart disengagement in Gaza and the northern West Bank. While the settlement movement's opposition failed, the settlers will continue to threaten the viability of future Israeli governments intent on dismantling additional settlements. The settlers fully intend to exact such a high price in national trauma and delegitimization of the government that future governments will not dare try again to dismantle settlements in more sensitive areas such as the West Bank mountain heartland. This will leave open only the option of territorial compromise imposed by a third party—or else no solution at all, meaning the (pre-1994) South Africa–like situation even Sharon is now warning of, albeit without a (post-1994) South Africa–style binational state solution.

An additional factor of influence that will affect Israeli government decision making on Palestinian-related issues in the coming years is public fatigue with the conflict. This is not necessarily a catalyst for capitulation on the part of the public. Yasir Arafat had reportedly counted on the Israeli public's weakness and fear of losses in the current conflict to bring about Israeli acceptance of his political demands. He learned the hard way that when their backs are to the wall, and with strong leadership, Israelis rally against the toughest enemy. Yet the public, and most recently even the chief of staff of the Israel Defense Forces (IDF), are increasingly alarmed over the corrupting influence—in the form of militarily unacceptable behavior and inclinations to gratuitous violence among both the army and the public at large—of violent occupation. While the Israeli political left has long pointed to the corrupting influence of occupation, the four and a half years of warfare and "collateral damage" among the Palestinian civilian population during the second intifada moved the issue to the much larger political center. Thus, this is an additional factor mitigating in favor of unilateral withdrawal from territories in the coming years.

Political developments among the Palestinians, too, are likely to reinforce unilateralist tendencies in Israel. Assuming that Mahmoud Abbas solidifies his leadership, under the best of circumstances his rule is likely to take the form of a less centralized decision-making mechanism than under Arafat. He will hesitate to compromise over the "existential" issues of an Israeli-Palestinian final-status deal, yet be equally reticent to take unilateral steps that parallel those of Israel and that could lay the foundation for a renewed, in-depth dialogue.

While the younger, "insider" leadership supported Abbas's candidacy for leadership, his election in early 2005 nevertheless represents a delay in—or in the best case, a gradual transition to—generational change in the Palestinian leadership. This postpones the day when the insider leadership comes to the fore and, conceivably, agrees to make the concessions regarding the right of return and Jerusalem that neither Arafat nor Abbas, themselves "outsider" refugees from 1948, could make.

Meanwhile, if and as Hamas enters Palestinian politics, the possibility arises that Palestinian negotiating positions, influenced by Hamas positions, will become more rather than less demanding. This could constitute yet another impetus for Israel to abandon the aspiration to negotiate a settlement and opt for the unilateral route.

Moreover, if Palestinians draw a concerted lesson from the Israeli withdrawal from Gaza to the effect that Israelis understand only the language of force, the ensuing escalation in the West Bank could retard or delay further Israeli attempts at either unilateral disengagement or (as in the case of the Palestinian reaction to the May 2000 withdrawal from Lebanon) renewed negotiations. In response to this argument, it must be noted that Israelis are sufficiently indifferent to the negative effect of the Lebanon withdrawal—that is, they believe the benefits of leaving Lebanon outweigh the single drawback of a weakened deterrent profile encouraging Palestinian violence—to proceed, eyes open, with withdrawal from Gaza.

International Legal and Economic Trends and Multilateral Involvement

In parallel with the growing threat to the rule of law within Israel and its armed forces brought on by the violent aspects of the occupation and by widespread calls by the ideological settlers and their rabbinic leaders for soldiers to disobey orders to dismantle settlements, there appears to be a countertrend on the international scene, whereby international legal rulings and threats of sanctions against Israel are proliferating. These, in turn, are impacting more and more heavily on the Israeli establishment, which is actually reaching out to some multinational institutions. These trends were unthinkable just a few years ago, when virtually all international and multinational initiatives were looked upon with great suspicion in Israel, on the assumption that they would inevitably be biased in favor of the Arab states and would deprive Israel of its freedom of action.

One aspect of this dynamic is greater activism at the international judicial level, spearheaded by the landmark recommendations of the International Court of Justice (ICJ) at The Hague in July 2004 regarding Israel's security fence and, perhaps more significantly, the ICJ's authoritative determination that the West Bank and Gaza are occupied (and not "disputed") territories and that the green line/armistice line is effectively an international boundary.

At the Israeli judicial level, in June 2004 the Israel High Court of Justice, partly in anticipation of the ICJ ruling, mandated greater Israeli consideration for the welfare of Palestinians as Israel builds the West Bank security barrier. A month earlier, in a landmark decision, the High Court intervened in an IDF operation in Rafah to demand that army commanders take into account Palestinian humanitarian needs. Supreme Court Chief Justice Aharon Barak and Attorney General Menachem Mazuz followed by suggesting that Israel would have to deal in some way with the ICJ recommendation and could not simply dismiss it as more UN-inspired Israel bashing. Indeed, Mazuz went further, suggesting that the ICJ recommendation, which is based on the prevalent international view that the Fourth Geneva Convention applies to the West Bank and Gaza, had created "a new legal reality for Israel" whose "negative repercussions" should not be underestimated. Mazuz added that the application of the convention must now be the subject of an "in-depth examination" by Israel, which for thirty-seven years had refused to apply the convention de jure (though it claimed to apply it de facto, which in practice means selectively).

Then too, Deputy Prime Minister Ehud Olmert's acceptance, also in mid-2004, of a European Union demand that Israel label exported products produced in the settlements with their specific place of origin so that the European Union could levy an additional tax on them (in effect, apply a tax that normally is waived for Israeli products), appeared to represent a conscious decision to acquiesce in some additional international pressures on the settlements issue in the hope of allaying worse pressures. In effect, Barak, Mazuz, and Olmert were trying in 2004 to avert what was perceived as a growing danger of international sanctions on a more comprehensive level—a step Mazuz specifically warned Prime Minister Sharon about if Israel were to disregard the ICJ's recommendations.

The fear of international sanctions is linked to Israel's growing prosperity, based on integration into global markets, and consequently to its heightened vulnerability to international economic pressures that U.S. support can counter only in part. This economic reality radically differs from that of the early decades of independence, when socialist governments confronting the Arab boycott developed greater Israeli economic self-sufficiency at a huge cost in efficiency and competitiveness. Those policies have long been discredited among most Israeli politicians and economists, who have witnessed the triumph within Israeli society of Western-style individualism over socialist centralism. The public's desire for a higher standard of living, minimal inflation, and lower taxes is certain to prevail in the coming decades.

Israel's consequent sensitivity to global economic developments, incidentally, is paralleled by the sensitivity of the Palestinians' far less sophisticated economy to Israeli sanctions. During the second intifada, the economic effects of Israeli closures and roadblocks were alleviated to an extent by far-reaching international donor assistance, which in turn generated yet another field of growing international interaction with Israel. By 2005, Israeli governments and business interests wanted to continue to sell goods to the Palestinian Authority (a major source of export revenue) and were prepared to buy Palestinian gas, essentially an invisible product. But they were no longer interested (for security reasons) in employing Palestinian labor in Israel and shunned the burden of feeding impoverished Palestinians. This approach will require an enhanced international donor and developmental role in the coming decades, beginning with the Gaza disengagement, with all that this entails regarding Israeli cooperation.

There are, of course, countertrends on the Israeli political scene, that is, forces trying to reduce the influence of the legal establishment and international actors. But Sharon's very decision to begin to remove settlements and withdraw from territories—in addition to reflecting demographic realities—can be seen in this context as his own acknowledgment that Israel must take steps to neutralize international pressures. A similar concern motivated Sharon's ultimate decision to construct nearly all new sections of the security fence (primarily in the southern West Bank) more or less on the green line, as well as the effort to ensure that the Gaza Strip, after Israeli withdrawal, would no longer be deemed by the international legal community to be occupied territory.

Here Israel also took the unprecedented step of inviting the World Bank to supervise the transfer of Israeli assets in Gaza to the Palestinian Authority and to coordinate plans for economic development in the Strip. It welcomed James Wolfensohn, an envoy of the Quartet (i.e., the United States, Russia, the United Nations, and the European Union), to facilitate economic aspects of disengagement. And it asked Egypt, and possibly the Sinai-based Multinational Force and Observers (MFO) peace-monitoring force, to take over some security tasks. The World Bank, for its part, confronted Israel with reciprocal demands to desist from placing border crossing points and paving roads for exclusive settler use inside the West Bank. During the second intifada, Israel also welcomed a process of "soft internationalization" in the territories, reflected in greater openness toward international bodies such as UNRWA (the UN refugee agency for the Palestinians) and the International Red Cross.

In parallel, a number of Israeli security planners have begun to advocate that Israel find ways to enhance its association with NATO—despite Jerusalem's traditional reluctance to rely on allies in the international community for fear they will exercise undue pressure on Israel's stance toward the Arab states. Here the main impetus is the Iranian threat, which, some argue, Israel will not be able to deter on its own, coupled with the assessment that conventional warfare with the Arab world is in any case not likely in the foreseeable future—hence possible NATO pressures are not a central issue.

Clearly, U.S. dominance within NATO is seen as a comforting factor, countering possible intrusive NATO demands such as an Israeli "striptease" on nuclear issues—that is, a demand to reveal its nuclear capabilities. Indeed, many Israeli security planners would prefer a direct defense treaty relationship with the United States as a counter to Iran. Nevertheless, the move to enhance contacts with NATO dovetails with a revised and softer attitude toward multilateral institutions in general.

This new approach was first apparent in an earlier instance of Israeli unilateralism, when Prime Minister Ehud Barak opted, in early 2000, to involve the United Nations in the delineation of Israel's border with Lebanon after Israel's withdrawal from an eighteen-year occupation of parts of that country. The coming years are likely to witness an intensification of this international legal, financial, and institutional role and the pressures it occasionally entails. The PLO and the Palestinian Authority, flush with their success at the ICJ, could address the court with additional demands. Israel's growing ties with the European Union, coupled with the European Union's perception of a more intimate link with the Middle East as it deals with its own Muslim minority issues and considers admitting Turkey, are liable to lead to additional initiatives in the Palestinian context, both to apply economic pressures and to offer economic incentives to Israel. Similarly, divestment threats by U.S. universities, municipalities, church movements, and other institutions could well multiply, along with boycott initiatives by international organizations and NGOs (for example, those boycotts proposed at the Durban anti-racism conference in 2004 and by British university lecturers in 2005).

In the event of prolonged deadlock between Israel and the Palestinians, over the horizon lie possible concerted international initiatives to impose a settlement and introduce peacemaking and/or peacekeeping forces, encouraged by the assessments and activities of some prominent Israelis on the political left such as Yossi Beilin and Shlomo Ben-Ami, who project an expanded role for an international force in helping solve the conflict. Yet by and large, Israel's new and more nuanced and receptive attitude toward an international role should not be understood as welcoming international mediation or facilitation efforts. Even if confronted by such an initiative on the part of Israel's close ally, the United States, Sharon and perhaps alternative Israeli leaders as well are likely to prefer the unilateral route.

The current trend of court decisions, international pressures, and sanctions has introduced international considerations that penetrate far deeper than previously into Israel's strategic and diplomatic decision making. It has contributed to generating the disengagement plan and a largely green-line (rather than territorially intrusive) security fence. It could help ensure that disengagement does not end with the Gaza Strip and northern Samaria. In other words, limited and cautious international involvement could help pave the way for the government of Israel to move toward rational solutions of the conflict. Yet Israel has limited influence and control over the intensity of international pressures. If the international activity exhibited in 2004 and early 2005 were to intensify rather than continue at its present pace, the emerging dynamic could come to be seen by many Israelis as yet another unfair episode of ganging up on an isolated Israel that is confronting far-reaching Arab aggression while nevertheless trying to "do the right thing" by the Palestinians, the territories, and its own national demographic needs.

Conclusions and Policy Recommendations

The demographic issue has always been a factor in Israel's perceptions of its place in the region, but only recently has it entered mainstream thinking as a determinant of innovative attitudes toward territory as well as a rationale for unilateralism. Together, these developments represent an important development in Israeli thinking on the Palestinian issue. While unilateralism and new approaches to the strategic value of territory have yet to find expression as a coherent political ideology, they are nevertheless likely to constitute significant trends in Israeli thinking about the Palestinian conflict in the coming years and to generate positive new initiatives.

The conflict, in turn, continues to suffer from the failure to create a more stable and mature political process in Israel that could address conflict-related issues more rationally. In effect, Israeli political instability and the Israeli-Palestinian conflict help perpetuate one another. Meanwhile, the influence exercised by the ideological settler minority on the political scene significantly obstructs territorial progress based on removing settlements. Together, these two factors virtually guarantee that efforts in the near term to pursue peace with the Palestinians, or even unilateral measures in the Palestinian context, will at best be sporadic, lacking in continuity, and highly traumatic for Israeli society.

Finally, international legal, political, and economic pressures on Israel are likely to increase in the near future. Paradoxically from the Israeli standpoint, the unilateral route, which to some extent reflects an attempt by Prime Minister Sharon to bypass looming international pressures, may even increase the international role, and with it the potential for friction with the international community.

How might these and additional trends affect Israeli policy decisions regarding the Israeli-Palestinian conflict in the years ahead? On the one hand, some of the likely developments to which we have pointed could, understandably, generate diverse and even contradictory Israeli policies. For example, should the advent of an Iranian military nuclear capability hasten or delay Israeli territorial concessions? Should Israel welcome or oppose Arab democratization processes that bring to the fore militant Islamist movements? No recommendations are offered in these spheres.

On the other hand, assuming that future Israeli governments remain interested in ending the conflict and partitioning the territory west of the Jordan River, whether to attain a viable two-state solution or merely in order to avoid a demographic trap, the following policy recommendations would appear logical for Israel to pursue and to advocate to its neighbors and to the United States:

- The unilateral disengagement and green-line security fence projects reflect a broad Israeli consensus and should be pursued, unless a very tempting and convincing peace process with a viable and strong Palestinian partner suggests itself.

- Experience demonstrates that it is preferable from a domestic political standpoint to avoid a commitment to a comprehensive process—whether negotiated or unilateral—compacted within a short time span. The Israeli political system cannot sustain such an effort, and the outcome could be detrimental to political stability as well as to public faith in a peaceful solution.
- By the same token, it is doubtful that the Israeli political system can sustain an effort to advance on two peace tracks at once, whether Palestine and Syria, or Palestine and Lebanon. For the internal Israeli political reasons noted earlier, such a commitment should be avoided, even where the hidden agenda is to play one track against the other for tactical purposes.
- Cooperation with Egypt and Jordan may offer potential advantages, which should be examined carefully, for enhancing Israeli security and reducing its military need for territorial depth.
- The international willingness to offer enhanced assistance, particularly with regard to Palestinian economic and humanitarian needs, should be exploited, bearing in mind the possible dangers for Israel of international overinvolvement in military aspects of the conflict.

An online edition of this report can be found at our website (www.usip.org), together with additional information on the subject.

United States
Institute of Peace
1200 17th Street NW
Washington, DC 20036
www.usip.org

DOCUMENT NO. 2

PALESTINIANS AND MIDDLE EAST PEACE: ISSUES FOR THE UNITED STATES

CRS Report
IB92052

April 26, 2005

Clyde Mark Foreign Affairs,
Defense, and Trade Division

Summary

The United States began contacts with the Palestine Liberation Organization (PLO) in December 1988, after the PLO accepted Israel's right to exist, accepted U.N. Resolutions 242 and 338 that call for an exchange of land for peace, and renounced terrorism. The United States broke contact with the PLO in 1990 after a terrorist incident but reestablished contact before the 1991 Madrid conference.

Following the 1993 Israeli-PLO agreement, Congress gave the President the authority to waive previously passed legislation prohibiting U.S. contributions to the United Nations from funding any PLO activities, threatening to withdraw U.S. membership from international organizations that recognize the PLO, prohibiting U.S. government employees from negotiating with the PLO, and labeling the PLO a terrorist organization. The waiver authority was extended in P.L. 104-107 (February 12, 1996), but expired August 12, 1997. Congress also ordered closed PLO offices in Washington and New York, although the New York office serving the U.N. remains open under a U.S. court decision.

In opening remarks to the Madrid conference on October 30, 1991, the Palestinian delegation accepted confederation of a Palestinian state with Jordan, but clearly most Palestinians want an independent Palestinian state. The Israeli and Palestinian delegations did not appear to be making any progress in resolving any of the issues: elections, statehood, borders, peacekeeping, demilitarized zones, water sharing, population exchanges, economic cooperation, diplomatic relations, or Jerusalem. On August 19, 1993, Israeli and PLO representatives initialed an agreement to guide future negotiations. On September 10, the PLO and Israel exchanged letters of mutual recognition, and on September 13, they signed the Declaration of Principles calling for Israeli withdrawal from Gaza and Jericho, the election of a Palestinian Council, and negotiations for future withdrawals and a permanent settlement in five years.

A May 4, 1994, agreement provided for the Israeli withdrawal from Gaza and Jericho. The Interim Agreement signed on September 28, 1995 (also called Oslo II or the Taba Agreement), provided for elections for the 88-seat Palestinian Assembly, the release of Israeli-held prisoners, Israeli withdrawal from six West Bank cities, and other issues. The Israelis withdrew from the West Bank cities by the end of 1995, and the Palestinian Assembly was elected on January 20, 1996.

Israel and the Palestinians agreed to an Israeli withdrawal from Hebron in January 1997, and on October 23, 1998 signed the Wye agreement to meet previous commitments. The peace talks stalled at Camp David in July 2000, and remain suspended since the Palestinian uprising began in September 2000. The "Road Map" of April 2003, provides for a three-phase, three-year, peace plan, but the plan has been stalled by a series of attacks and retaliations and by stated Israeli intentions to impose unilateral actions. Also see CRS Issue Brief IB91137, *The Middle East Peace Talks*.

Most Recent Developments

On April 26, Palestine President Mahmud Abbas named Rashid Abu Shbak to head the Preventative Security Services. Shbak is one of Fatah's younger generation leaders who had been in charge of Gaza police since 2003. Earlier in April, Abbas announced that 1,150 security officials were to be retired as part of the President's police reform.

After his April 11 meeting with Israeli Prime Minister Sharon, President Bush said that there should be no expansion of settlements in the occupied territories. President Bush repeated his support for a two-state solution and his belief that Israel would retain some of the West Bank settlement areas. Palestine President Mahmud Abbas is scheduled to visit Washington to meet with the President in May.

Background and Analysis

Current Negotiations Between Israel and the Palestinians

The Road Map. According to the "road map" for the "quartet" peace proposal (Europe, Russia, U.N., U.S.A.), presented on April 30, 2003,[1] the Israelis and

[1] See "A Performance-Based Roadmap to a Permanent Two-State Solution to the Israeli-Palestinian Conflict," published by the U.S. Department of State, [http://www.state.gov/r/pa/prs/ps/2003/ 20062.htm].

Palestinians must take steps to implement the plan, but it was not clear if the steps were to be sequential (the Israeli view) or in parallel (the Palestinian view). During stage one of phase one, the Israelis were to end attacks on Palestinian cities, house demolitions, and deportations; to freeze settlement activity; and to dismantle settlements established since February 2001. The Palestinians were to name a new cabinet (approved February 24, 2005) and Prime Minister (sworn in April 30, 2003), end violence against Israelis, and consolidate the Palestinian police forces. During stage two of phase one, Israelis were to withdraw to the September 28, 2000 lines and freeze all settlement activity. The Palestinians and the Israelis were to sign a new security agreement. The Palestinians will hold elections for the Palestinian Legislative Council in the summer of 2005.

During phase two, the quartet was to establish a monitoring system to monitor compliance with the agreement and was to hold an international conference on Palestinian economic recovery. The quartet also will sponsor negotiations for a Palestinian state within provisional borders. During phase three, scheduled to begin in 2004, Israel and the Palestinians were to agree on a provisional Palestinian state and, by the beginning of 2005, were to resume negotiations for permanent borders, Jerusalem, refugees, settlements, and other issues.

Current Status. On October 6, 2004, Sharon aide Dov Weisglass told the press that the disengagement plan for an Israeli withdrawal from Gaza would prevent the establishment of a Palestinian state, which many assumed meant the end of the road map peace process.[2]

Some observers viewed Arafat's November 11, 2004, death as a possible trigger for renewed action in the peace process. The Bush Administration refused to deal with Arafat. Mahmud Abbas was elected president on January 9, 2005, and the Palestinian legislative Council approved a new cabinet under Prime Minister Ahmad Qurai on February 24. Abbas disapproves of the intifada and violence, and the new cabinet is primarily technocrats rather than Arafat loyalists.

The United States and the Palestinians

U.S. Policy Toward the Palestinians

Between World War II and the 1991 collapse of the Soviet Union, U.S. policy toward the Middle East was based on several broad goals, the most noteworthy of which were (1) stop Soviet expansion into the region; (2) keep open the Middle Eastern lines of communication and trade; (3) maintain

[2] Shavit, Ari, "Top PM Aide: Gaza Plan Aims to Freeze the Peace Process," Haaretz, Oct. 6, 2004.

Western access to Middle Eastern oil; (4) foster democracy and free market economies; and (5) protect Israel's security.

There appear to be many reasons why U.S. citizens have favored Israel: Israel and the United States espouse shared Judeo-Christian principles; both countries were "pioneering" in their early years; both countries are democracies; the United States has empathy for Israel's position as an embattled "underdog"; Israel and the United States opposed Soviet expansion during the cold war years; the United States has sympathy for the experience of European Jews in World War II; Jewish-Americans have a very effective pro-Israel political support organization; and the United States is more aware of Israel's point of view. In short, some say, Israelis "are like us." Conversely, there is less empathy among Americans for Arab viewpoints because, some say, Arabs are "not like us." Eastern Arab culture (dress, food, music, art, written and spoken language, religion) appears to have little in common with Western American culture, and Arab-Americans in the past have tended to assimilate more than some other ethnic groups and to avoid the public stage of advocacy for Arab causes.

Refugees and Terrorists. The United States, until recently, treated the Palestinians as one of the problems to be solved in ending the Arab-Israeli dispute rather than as participants in the peace process. From 1948 until the 1967 war, the United States, like many other countries, considered the Palestinian people in the context of the refugee problem and not as an independent national movement. Beginning with a series of terrorist incidents starting in 1968, most added "terrorist" to the "refugee" image of Palestinians. President Carter shifted the terrorist-refugee perception on March 16, 1977, when he said the Palestinians deserved a homeland, and on January 4, 1978, when he said that the Palestinians had legitimate rights and should participate in any deliberations about their future. The Camp David agreements of September 1978 mentioned "the legitimate rights of the Palestinian people." Early in the Reagan Administration, officials returned to referring to Palestinians as "refugees" and "terrorists" and did not mention Palestinian rights or self-determination. But in his September 1, 1982, Middle East address, President Reagan said that the Palestinian problem was more than refugees. On April 14, 2004, President Bush said the refugees should not be returned to their former homes in what is now Israel.

Recognition. In 1975, one year after the Arab League stated that the Palestine Liberation Organization (PLO) was the sole representative of the Palestinian people, Secretary of State Henry Kissinger informed Israel that the United States would not recognize or negotiate with the PLO unless and until the PLO recognized Israel and accepted U.N. Resolutions 242 and 338. Congress codified the pledge into law (Section 535, P.L. 98-473, October 12, 1984), and added that the PLO also must renounce terrorism. Secretary of State George Shultz stated on December 14, 1988, that the PLO had met the conditions stipulated by the United States, and that the United States would open a dialogue with the PLO in Tunis, Tunisia, on December 16, 1988.

President George H.W. Bush announced on March 6, 1991 (in the wake of the Gulf war), that he would pursue Arab-Israeli peace negotiations; he dispatched Secretary of State Baker to the Middle East where he met with Palestinian leaders from the occupied territories. Baker's 8 trips to the region and his contacts with the Palestinians, Jordanians, Israelis, Syrians, Egyptians, and others led to peace talks in Madrid on October 30, 1991. But at Madrid and the subsequent meetings, the United States (and Israel) treated the Palestinians as part of the Jordanian delegation, not as a separate entity.

On September 10, 1993, following the Israeli-PLO mutual recognition, President Clinton announced that the United States would resume the dialogue with the PLO. PLO leader Arafat, representing the national aspirations of the Palestinian people, shared the spotlight with Israeli Prime Minister Rabin and President Clinton at the signing of the Declaration of Principles on the White House lawn on September 13, 1993. U.S. official attitudes toward the Palestinians had evolved from seeing them only as refugees to according them a form of recognition that approached, but did not reach, nationhood. Following a pledge made at the Wye River conference, President Clinton visited Gaza to attend the December 14, 1998 meeting of the PLO National Council, at which the Council voted by show of hands to reaffirm that the PLO Covenant had been amended to remove anti-Israeli references.

Current Relations. The George W. Bush White House refused to meet with Palestinian President Yasir Arafat because, in the Administration's view, Arafat did not do enough to stop terrorism. President Bush said, in his June 24, 2002 statement, that he envisioned a two-state solution to the Israeli-Palestine problem, the first time a U.S. President advocated the formation of a Palestinian state on an equal basis to Israel. The "Quartet" of the United States, the United Nations, the European Union, and Russia presented the "road map" peace plan on April 30, the day Mahmud Abbas was sworn in as Palestinian Prime Minister. Prime Minister Abbas met with President Bush at the White House on July 25, 2003. In comments to the press after the meeting, Abbas said he raised the issues of the Israeli wall under construction in the West Bank,[3] Israeli withdrawal from Palestinian cities, the expected Israeli release of Palestinian prisoners, and other issues, and reaffirmed the Palestinian pledge to curtail terrorist attacks against Israel. President Bush said the wall was a "problem" and that he expected both

[3] See CRS Report RS21564, *Israel's Security Fences, Separating Israel from the Palestinians.*

sides to meet their obligations for peace, reaffirmed the United States support for a two-state solution, and reminded the Palestinians of their promise to end terror attacks against Israel. On April 14, 2004, President Bush endorsed the Israeli wall around Palestinian areas, approved Israel's unilateral action in Gaza and the West Bank, rejected the right of return for Palestinian refugees, and said Israel's occupied territory settlements should be recognized in final borders.

On February 21, 2005, in Brussels, President Bush said: "So Israel must freeze settlement activity, help Palestinians build a thriving economy, and ensure that a new Palestinian state is truly viable, with contiguous territory on the West Bank. A state of scattered territories will not work."

U.S. Aid for the Palestinians

(See Table 3, U.S. Assistance to the West Bank and Gaza, at the end of this report)

At an October 1, 1993, Washington meeting, 46 donor nations pledged $2.4 billion for the Palestinian entity. The U.S. Administration offered $500 million ($125 million in loans or loan guarantees and $375 million in grants) over five years for economic development of the Palestinian entity. Of the $125 million available in loan guarantees, $3 million had been drawn through April 2001. The United States provided $36 million funding for the Palestinian Authority through the Holst Fund of the World Bank. The remaining $339 million was delivered through private voluntary organizations (PVOs), and through USAID contracts. No U.S. aid went directly to the PLO.

Wye Agreement Funding. On November 30, 1998, President Clinton told the donors conference in Washington that the United States would provide $400 million in grants for the Palestinians. Congress did not include funding for the Wye Agreement in the Foreign Operations Appropriations bills for FY2000 (H.R. 2606, S. 1234). The President vetoed H.R. 2606 in part because it did not contain funding for the Wye Agreement. After negotiations with the White House, the House of Representatives passed H.R. 3196 on November 5, 1999, that included the Wye Agreement funding; $1.2 billion for Israel, $200 million for Jordan, $25 million for Egypt, and $400 million for the Palestinians. H.R. 3196 was set aside and replaced with H.R. 3422, which was included by reference in H.R. 3194, the consolidated appropriations bill passed by the House on November 18, by the Senate on November 19, and presented to the President on November 22, 1999. The $400 million Wye supplemental was in addition to annual aid levels of about $75 million.

According to a State Department report presented to Congress in late October 1999, the Wye funding for the Palestinians would be spent for infrastructure, education, community development and "Rule of Law" projects.

Other Assistance. The supplemental appropriation for FY2002 (H.R. 4775, P.L. 107-206, signed on August 2, 2002) included $50 million in disaster relief assistance for the Palestinians, primarily in response to damages inflicted during the April-May 2002 Israeli military operations in Palestinian areas, particularly the city of Jenin. The section specifically stated that the funds for the West Bank and Gaza could not be used for the Palestinian Authority. The funds were not allocated. The President requested $50 million for the Palestinians in the FY2003 supplemental appropriations, but the funds were not earmarked in the final bill (P.L. 108-11). The Department of State announced on April 21, 2003, that $50 million was allocated from the supplemental for the Palestinians. The United States announced on July 8, 2003, that it would provide $20 million of the $50 million in direct aid to the Palestinian Authority. On July 10, the State Department waived congressional restrictions against providing aid directly to the PA. The $20 million was used for water, sewers, and other infrastructure, and to pay the electric bill owed to Israel.

The Administration requested $75 million for the Palestinians for FY2005. Palestinian aid funds are not earmarked in Division D of H.R. 4818, the FY2005 appropriations act, but are mentioned in the conference report, H. Rept. 108-792. On December 8, 2004, President Bush notified Congress that $20 million of the $75 million in FY2005 foreign assistance scheduled for the Palestinians will go directly to the Palestinian Authority. The $20 million will be used to pay past-due utility bills owed to Israel, which, it was believed, would free up other PA assets to fund the January 9, 2005 presidential election. Members of Congress objected to a mid-November proposal to shift the $20 million to pay for the election because, according to the press, Congress was not satisfied with PA efforts to stop terrorism or feared that the funds would be diverted to support terrorism.

In his State of the Union message, President Bush said he would seek $350 million for the Palestinians, $200 million in supplemental FY2005 funds, and $150 million in FY2006 aid funds. The $200 million in FY2005 supplemental would include $60 million for revitalizing the economy (trade, agriculture, jobs, Gaza home construction), $90 million for development (roads, water, courts, vocational education, health care, police programs to stop terrorism), and $50 million for "building bridges" (transit points to move people and goods between Israel and the Palestinian areas). The $200 million was included in H.R. 1268, reported on March 11, 2005.

Congress and the Palestinians

Congress stated its opposition to the U.N. special committee on Palestinian rights (Section 614, P.L. 95-426, October 7, 1978), opposed U.S. participation in the International Monetary Fund if the IMF granted membership to the PLO (Section 7, P.L. 96-389, October 7, 1980), and stated that U.S. funds contributed to the U.N. could not be used to support the PLO (Section 154, P.L. 97-377, December 21, 1982). In 1984, Congress prohibited U.S. government employees from negotiating with or recognizing the PLO unless and until the PLO recognized Israel's right to exist, accepted U.N. Resolutions 242 and 338, and renounced terrorism (Section 535, P.L. 98-473, October 12, 1984).

In 1987, Congress declared the PLO to be a terrorist organization and a threat to U.S. interests, and ordered the PLO information office in Washington and the office of the PLO U.N. mission in New York to be closed (Title X of P.L. 100-204, December 22, 1987). The Department of State closed the Washington office, but the New York office remained open after a judge ruled that the office was legal under the U.N. treaty signed by the United States. The Washington office reopened in September 1993, after the PLO and Israel signed the Declaration of Principles under waiver provisions in the Middle East Peace Facilitation Act. The PLO office closed on August 12, 1997, when the Middle East Peace Facilitation Act expired because the presidential waiver expired with the act. The PLO office reopened on December 6, 1997, when the President exercised the waiver in Section 539(d) of P.L. 105118, the foreign operations appropriations law. The office remained open under subsequent presidential waivers provided in the foreign operations appropriations bills.

In 1989, Congress added Title VIII, the PLO Commitments Compliance Act (PLOCCA), to P.L. 101-246, signed into law on February 16, 1990, which repeated the prohibition against negotiating with the PLO, stated the sense of Congress that the United States should seek to prevent PLO involvement in terrorism, said the United States should obtain an accounting from the PLO of several listed incursions into Israel, required the Secretary of State to report to the Congress on the PLO explanation of the incursions, and required the President to file quarterly reports on several listed PLO activities and positions. The Secretary of State sent the first PLO Compliance Act report to Congress on January 11, 1994, stating that the PLO remained opposed to terrorism and that the United States would continue the dialogue resumed on September 10, 1993.

Following the signing of the Declaration of Principles on September 13, 1993, Congress passed the Middle East Peace Facilitation Act (MEPFA) granting the President the authority to waive sections of existing law that forbid contacts with the PLO, that prohibit the PLO from opening an office in the United States, or that constrict providing aid to the PLO through the United Nations. (The Middle East Peace Facilitation Act of 1993, P.L. 103-125, October 28, 1993; amended and renewed several times, most recently in P.L. 104-107, February 12, 1996). The most recent MEPFA and the President's waiver authority expired on August 12, 1997. The most recent combined MEPFA-PLOCCA report to Congress appeared on January 12, 1997, covered both the PLO Commitment Compliance Act and the Middle East Peace Facilitation Act, and found that the PLO was complying with its commitments.

In May 1997, some Members of Congress threatened to cut U.S. aid to the Palestinians because Palestinian leaders advocated applying a 1973 Jordanian law that called for the death penalty for Palestinians who sold land to Israelis or Jews. On June 10, 1997, the House passed by voice vote an amendment to H.R. 1757, the Foreign Relations Authorization bill, that called upon Palestinian leaders to renounce the death penalty, and stated that the President and Congress will consider Palestinian actions when considering renewal of the Middle East Peace Facilitation Act that expired on August 12, 1997. Other Members of Congress suggested cutting aid to the Palestinians because they believed that the PLO or the Palestinian Authority incited recent terror attacks against Israel. News reports that an internal PA audit released on May 25, 1997, disclosed corruption and waste prompted other Members of Congress to question U.S. aid to the Palestinians. After allowing the Middle East Peace Facilitation Act to expire on August 12, 1997, Congress added sections to the Foreign Operations Appropriations bill, H.R. 2159, and to subsequent bills, that gave the President waiver authority similar to the MEPFA waivers.

Section 584 of P.L. 105-277 of November 21, 1998, and similar sections in subsequent foreign operations appropriations bills prohibit any aid funds for the Palestine Broadcasting Corporation (PBC). The United States provided about $250,000 for training and equipment for the PBC in 1995 but withdrew the aid when it was feared that Arafat would use the public station for political purposes. The United States continues to help Palestinian journalists, but does not provide direct support to the PBC.

The House of Representatives passed H.Con.Res. 426 by a vote of 365 to 30 on October 25, 2000; the resolution expressed solidarity with Israel and condemned Palestinian Arab leaders for encouraging violence in the continuing confrontations that began following Likud Party leader Sharon's visit to the Haram al-Sharif/Temple Mount area of Jerusalem on September 28.

P.L. 107-115 (H.R. 2506), the foreign operations appropriations bill for FY2002 signed into law on January 10, 2002, requires the President to report to Congress on PLO compliance with past commitments. If not in compliance, the President may close the PLO office in Washington, designate the PLO constituents as terrorist groups, and/or limit humanitarian assistance to the Palestinians.

The House passed H.Res. 392 by a vote of 352-21 with 29 "present" on May 2, 2002. The bill stated that the Palestinian leadership incited and supported terrorism against Israel. The Administration opposed the bill because it could have hampered U.S. efforts to mediate an Israeli-Palestinian cease-fire.

The bill vowed U.S. solidarity with Israel and justified Israel's use of force against the Palestinians. The Senate passed S.Amdt. 3389 to H.R. 3009, the Andean Trade bill, the same day, also justifying Israel's actions against the Palestinians.

Title VI of the Foreign Relations Authorization Act of 2002 (P.L. 107-228, H.R. 1646), entitled the Middle East Peace Commitments Act of 2002, repeated many aspects of PLOCCA, MEPFA, and the reporting requirements in the appropriations bills mentioned above. Section 604© provided for a presidential waiver of the act's sanctions applicable to the Palestinians.

The FY2003 consolidated appropriations bill (H.J.Res. 2, P.L. 108-7, February 20, 2003) had several sections dealing with the Palestinians. Section 403 banned U.S. aid for the Palestinian Broadcast Corporation. Section 548 prohibited the use of funds to create another U.S. government office in Jerusalem. Section 552 banned funds for the Palestinian Authority but provided a presidential waiver if such aid was in the United States' national security interests. Section 563 declared that no U.S. funds could be used to support Palestinian statehood unless the Palestinians elected new leadership, agreed to co-exist with Israel, countered terrorism, resumed security cooperation with Israel, ended belligerency against Israel, and agreed to a just solution to the refugee problem. Section 563 also provided a presidential waiver if such action were in the U.S. national security interests. Section 566 banned U.S. aid for the Palestinian Broadcasting Corporation (repeating Section 403, cited above). Section 568 ensured that the U.S. Comptroller General has access to information to audit expenditure of Economic Support Funds, that the Secretary of State takes measures to ensure that U.S. funds are not used for terrorism, and that USAID conduct annual audits of Palestinian accounts.

H.R. 2673, the omnibus appropriations bill for FY2004 (P.L. 108-199,118 Stat.3, 23 January 2004), denies funding for the Palestinian Broadcasting Corporation (Sec. 403 and 565), provides $1 million in ESF for West Bank/ Gaza legal reforms, denies funds for the PLO unless certified under MEPFA (Sec. 545), denies funds to the Palestinian Authority unless waived by the President (Sec. 552), denies funds for a Palestinian state unless certified by the Secretary of State or waived by the President (Sec. 562), and stipulates that the Comptroller General should have access to financial records, that U.S. funds not be used to finance terrorism, that there will be annual audits of Palestinian aid accounts, and that $1 million is available for a USAID audit (Sec. 566).

H.R. 4818, the foreign operations appropriations act for FY2005, does not have an earmark for funds for the Palestinians but does repeat many of the restrictions on aid to the PLO, the Palestinian Authority (with a presidential waiver), and Palestinian statehood that are found in previous years' bills.

H.R. 1268, the FY2005 supplemental appropriation, includes $200 million in aid for the Palestinians and also includes in Section 2106 a requirement that the President report to the Congress information on Palestinian security services, PA actions to dismantle terrorist groups, PA actions to stop incitement, PA steps to ensure democracy, PA cooperation in investigating Yasir Arafat's finances, and a listing of aid to the Palestinians from other donors. Section 2106 set aside $5 million for an independent audit of PA accounting procedures. (It is not known if the PA would cooperate with a congressionally mandated audit.) Section 2106 also stated that the waiver in Section 550 of P.L. 108-447, the FY2005 Foreign Operations Appropriation, will not apply to funds intended for the Palestinians in the FY2005 supplemental. (The waiver permitted the President to provide funds to the PA.)

Palestinian Statehood. On November 15, 1988, the Palestine Liberation Organization National Council declared a Palestinian state with its capital in Jerusalem. Some 100 nations recognized the new state even though it did not have a government or any territory under its sovereignty. Despite the 1988 declaration, in February 1998, Palestinian leader Arafat said he would declare a state unilaterally on May 4, 1999, the date set in the 1994 Gaza-Jericho Agreement for completing the permanent status talks, but the declaration of statehood was delayed several times and has not been completed. Israeli leaders oppose the Palestinian declaration of statehood because they feel that the future status of the Palestinian entity should be a subject in the talks.

Several U.S. Administrations have decried unilateral actions that could interrupt the peace talks, and the Clinton Administration had cautioned Arafat not to declare a state unilaterally. H.Con.Res. 24, passed by the House on March 16, 1999, and the Senate on April 12, 1999, states that a unilateral declaration of Palestinian statehood would draw strong congressional opposition and that the President should assert that a statehood declaration would violate the Oslo accords. (Palestinian statehood is not mentioned in the Oslo agreements.) The House voted 385 to 27 (with four present) on September 27, 2000, to pass H.R. 5272, which would have cut off U.S. foreign assistance to the Palestinians if the Palestinians declared a state without Israeli agreement. (In the April 14, 2004, White House meeting, President Bush approved of Israel's unilateral decision to withdraw from Gaza, construct the security wall, and reject the right of return to Palestinian refugees.)

On September 24, 2002, President Bush said that a state of Palestine was part of the vision for a future resolution of the Arab-Israel problem. U.N. Security Council Resolution 1397, passed by a vote of 14-0-1 (Syria) on March 12, 2002, included the phrase "two states, Israel and Palestine," the first Security Council resolution to mention a Palestinian state. President

Bush repeated U.S. support for an independent Palestinian state at Aqaba on June 4, 2003.

Unresolved Issues in the Palestine Problem

Jerusalem

Palestinians maintain that Israel must withdraw from east Jerusalem, seized by Israel in the 1967 war along with the rest of the West Bank, and that east Jerusalem will become the capital of the Palestinian state. Israel, which has claimed Jerusalem as its capital since 1948, annexed east Jerusalem in 1967, and claims that Jerusalem's status is not negotiable. No other country recognizes Israel's annexation of east Jerusalem. Despite the Israeli claim, Israel signed the 1993 Declaration of Principles, which calls for negotiations on the future of Jerusalem.

The July 25, 1994 Jordan-Israel non-belligerency agreement states that Israel "respects . . . the special role" played by Jordan in Muslim religious shrines in Jerusalem. Arafat had stated in the past that the Palestinian entity would be responsible for non-Jewish religious shrines in the holy city. The Jordan-Israel agreement appears to set the stage for a future contest or cooperation between Jordan and Palestine over the religious sites.

The United States has maintained a policy since 1967 that the future of the city must be negotiated and cannot be decided unilaterally, and that the city should not be divided as it was between 1948 and 1967. In 1990, Congress opposed the Administration position and passed resolutions acknowledging that Jerusalem was the capital of Israel and should not be a divided city (H.Con.Res. 290, passed on April 24, 1990, and S.Con.Res. 106, passed on March 22, 1990). In 1995, Congress passed S. 1322 (P.L. 104-45, November 8, 1995) that stated that the U.S. embassy should be moved from Tel Aviv to Jerusalem. The law provides a presidential waiver if maintaining the embassy in Tel Aviv is in the U.S. national interest (Out-of-print CRS Report 94-755, *Jerusalem*, dated February 21, 1995; available by contacting Clyde Mark, 7-7681). On July 27, 2000, President Clinton told an Israeli interviewer that he favored moving the embassy to Jerusalem, but signed waivers to keep the embassy in Tel Aviv. During the 2000 campaign, George Bush said he favored moving the embassy to Jerusalem, but since becoming President has signed waivers delaying the move.

Section 214 of P.L. 107-228, the Foreign Relations Authorization Act for FY2003, states that Congress maintains its commitment to moving the U.S. embassy from Tel Aviv to Jerusalem, bans funds appropriated in the act from being used to support the Jerusalem consulate unless the U.S. ambassador to Israel has authority over the consulate, declares that publications financed under the act must list Jerusalem as the capital of Israel, and states that any U.S. citizen born in Jerusalem may request that their birthplace be listed as Israel. President Bush issued a statement on September 30, 2002, that he considered the section to be advisory, not binding, and that the section interfered with his constitutional authority to conduct the nation's foreign relations. The statement also said that U.S. policy toward Jerusalem remained unchanged, which implied that the United States holds that the future of Jerusalem must be negotiated and not be decided unilaterally, as the Israelis have done.

Boundaries

The Palestinians would prefer a return to the boundaries recommended by the United Nations in Resolution 181 of 1947, but since 1974, have accepted the 1948–1967 boundaries between the West Bank/Gaza and Israel. The Shamir government (1988–1992) claimed all of the West Bank as part of Israel and would have made the boundary the Jordan River. It is not clear what other Israeli governments would have offered or accepted. Some Israelis and most Palestinians believe that the Israeli wall/fence under construction since June 2003 to separate Israel from the Palestinians will become a permanent boundary, despite the Sharon government's claims that it will not.

The Palestinian-Israeli Interim Agreement, September 1995, partitioned the 2,200 square mile West Bank into a patchwork quilt composed of three different jurisdictions: Area A, under full Palestinian control, about 1% of the total, was comprised of the seven largest cities (excluding Jerusalem), primarily populated by Palestinian Arabs; Area B, under shared Palestinian and Israeli control, about 27% of the West Bank, was comprised of Arab villages around the cities; and Area C, under full Israeli control, about 72% of the total, was comprised of Israeli settlements, so-called "state land," highways, public areas, and Israeli military bases.

Israel withdrew from the Area A cities in December 1995-January 1996 (and Hebron February 1997) and a few of the Area B villages, leaving the Palestinian Authority in full control of about 3% of the West Bank. Israel also withdrew from 70% of the Gaza Strip, but retained four areas where there are Jewish settlements. The Netanyahu government ceded another 7% of the West Bank in November 1998, in keeping with the Wye agreement, but postponed further withdrawals until after the May 1999 election. The government of Ehud Barak, sworn in July 1999, agreed in September 1999 to further withdrawals in September and November 1999, and March 2000, that left about 18% of the West Bank in Palestinian hands, 22% under shared Israeli-Palestinian control, and 60% under full Israeli control.

According to press reports in early May 2000, Israel offered to withdraw from a total of 80% of the West Bank, withdrawing from 66% then and the remaining 14% after a couple of years. Israel would annex the remaining 20%. The Palestinians rejected the offer. The press reported on May 20 that Israel raised the offer to 90% of the West Bank, and an unconfirmed rumor circulating in August 2000 said that the United States proposed that Israel retain only 5% of the West Bank. Reports from the July 2000 Camp David talks said the figures under discussion ranged from 90% to 97%. The Palestinians rejected the Israeli Camp David offer because Israel retained sovereignty over all of Jerusalem—the Palestinians sought sovereignty over Arab east Jerusalem—and because the Israeli proposal divided the West Bank into three non-contiguous zones that would have impaired Palestinian nationalism and stymied economic growth.

Palestinians consider the Golan Heights part of Syria, not Palestine, but the Syrian-Israeli negotiations over the Golan may affect Palestinian-Israeli negotiations over the West Bank and Gaza. Persistent rumors from Israel and unconfirmed reports from Syria claim that the Rabin-Peres government agreed to withdraw from most of the Golan Heights. The Netanyahu government elected in May 1996, appeared less inclined to withdraw from Golan and not inclined to meet a commitment made by its predecessor government.

Prior to April 14, 2004, the United States stated that boundaries should be negotiated and mutually recognized, "should not reflect the weight of conquest," and that adjustments in the pre-1967 boundaries should be "insubstantial." The United States acknowledged Israel's need for defensible borders (erase some of the anomalies along the 1948-1967 armistice lines) and also acknowledged that the Palestinians desired a territorial entity separate from Israeli rule. But President Bush said, on April 14, that boundaries should reflect the realities of Israeli settlements, suggesting that Israel would establish sovereignty over Israeli settlements on the West Bank. In the same statement, the President approved Israeli unilateral action.

Israeli Settlements in the Occupied Territories

The Arab nations maintain that Israeli settlements in the occupied territories are illegal under international law, specifically paragraph 6 of Article 49 of the Fourth Geneva Convention on the Protection of Civilian Persons in Time of War, which states: "The occupying power shall not deport or transfer parts of its own civilian population into territories it occupies." Israel maintains that Jordan's 1950 annexation of the West Bank was not recognized by the international community, and therefore is illegal. Egypt never claimed the Gaza Strip. Israel maintains that the two regions are not "occupied territories," and are not subject to the Geneva Convention. Many nations, as reflected in the votes on several U.N. General Assembly and Security Council resolutions, believe that Israel is the occupying power, that the Geneva Convention applies, and that the Israeli settlements are illegal. United States' spokesmen, such as Ambassador George H. W. Bush on September 25, 1971, Ambassador William Scranton on May 26, 1976, and Secretary of State Cyrus Vance on March 21, 1980, have stated that the settlements are illegal. During a December 16, 1996 news conference, President Bill Clinton agreed with the statement that the settlements were obstacles to peace. President George W. Bush said on April 4, 2002, that Israeli settlement activity in the occupied territories must stop. On April 14, 2004, President Bush said that negotiated borders should reflect realities on the ground, meaning the Israeli settlements.

The Israeli Attorney General recommended to the Prime Minister that Israel adopt the Geneva Convention, which would be an admission by Israel that Israeli settlements in the occupied territories were against international practice.[4] The recommendation was included in a report submitted in August 2004, on the implications of the World Court decision that the wall was illegal.

Compensation/Repatriation for Palestinian Refugees

Palestinians argue that paragraph 11 of U.N.G.A. Resolution 194 of December 11, 1948, states that the Arab refugees have a choice between returning to the homes now in Israel that they left during the 1947–1948 war (the "right of return"), or receiving compensation for the lost property. Israel argues that the Arabs abandoned their property voluntarily, and that the international community should provide funding for resettling the Palestinian refugees in Arab countries. Arabs claim the Jews drove them from their homes in 1948–1949. Some Israelis counter with a claim for compensation for property abandoned by Jews who left or were driven from Arab countries in the aftermath of the 1948–1949 war. Palestinians counter that Jews who fled Arab countries should take their claims to those countries, not to the Palestinians.

Israel claims that allowing Palestinian refugees to return to homes left in 1948-1949 or 1967 will destroy the Jewish nature of Israel. Palestinians claim the right of return is a matter of justice encased in international law. The argument probably was a matter of perception rather than physically moving a number of Palestinians into Israel: by accepting the right of return, Israel would accept blame for forcing the refugees out of their homes in the first place, and the Palestinians might have been more interested in such a confession of guilt than in the actual return to abandoned properties. On April 14, 2004, President Bush said that the Palestinian refugees should be settled in a Palestinian state and not in Israel, thus

[4] King, Laura Israel Urged to Adopt Geneva Convention, Los Angeles Times, Aug. 25, 2004.

dismissing the right of return. (See CRS Report RS20616, *Middle East Peace: The Refugee Issue.*)

The Palestinian Entity

Government

On May 24, 1994, Arafat canceled all Israeli laws and reinstated pre-1967 laws in Gaza and Jericho in an attempt to erase the Israeli occupation presence. Under terms of the September 13, 1993 Declaration of Principles, the Palestinian cabinet assumed responsibility for health, education and culture, social welfare, direct taxation, and tourism. The 88-seat Palestinian Authority (also called the Palestinian Legislative Council, PLC), elected on January 20, 1996, and sworn in on March 7, 1996, and the 26-person cabinet named by President Yasir Arafat on May 9, 1996, assumed responsibility over other functions of government except for security and foreign relations, which Israel controlled through the five-year interim and into the final negotiating period. Arafat named a new 34-person cabinet on August 5, 1998, to avoid a vote of confidence in the Palestinian Legislative Council, and on June 13, 2002, reduced the cabinet to 21 members as part of his reform program. The cabinet resigned on September 19, 2002. Arafat named Mahmud Abbas to be Prime Minister on March 6, 2003. Abbas and his 24-person cabinet won a vote of confidence on April 29, 2003, and were sworn in the next day. Abbas and Arafat disagreed over control and reform of the police, and Abbas resigned on September 6. Arafat appointed PLC Speaker Ahmad Qurai as the new prime minister on September 10, 2003, but Qurai and Arafat had the same disagreement as Arafat and Abbas—who should control the police.

The PLC passed a Basic Law in 1997, but Arafat did not sign the law until May 30, 2002. The Basic Law serves as a constitution, outlining the function of the PLC, the President, the cabinet, and the electoral process. One of the reforms sought by President George W. Bush is a new Palestinian constitution.

Arafat died on November 11, 2004. Mahmud Abbas defeated six other candidates in the election held on January 9, 2005, to replace Arafat. On February 23, 2005, the Palestinian Legislative Council approved a new 24-person cabinet. Seventeen members of the new cabinet members were selected for their expertise rather than their loyalty to Arafat or Fatah, as had been the case in the past.

Police. According to negotiations following the May 4, 1994 agreement, the Palestinian enclaves were to be protected by a Palestinian police force. The Palestinian police began arriving in Gaza on May 11 and in Jericho on May 12, 1994, replacing the Israeli Defense Forces and Israeli border police. Other nations have provided training (Egypt, Jordan, Great Britain, Iraq), vehicles (the United States donated 200 light and heavy trucks, Russia donated armored vehicles, Greece donated 58 trucks), uniforms (Norway), communications equipment (Spain), anti-riot gear (Great Britain), housing and offices (Japan and Germany), and cash (the United States $5 million, European Union).

The Palestinian police are supposed to cooperate with the Israeli police in patrolling the borders and the villages, manning crossing points, and maintaining order. Paragraph 3 of Article IV of Annex I of the Interim Agreement of September 28, 1995, states that the Palestinian police force shall number 12,000 in the West Bank and 18,000 in the Gaza Strip. Israel claimed that there were between 36,000, and 40,000 Palestinian police in uniform prior to the second intifada that started in September 2000. Israel destroyed most of the Palestinian police infrastructure during the Israeli invasions of West Bank cities in April-May 2002. Arafat wants control of the police to rest in the president's office, but his two prime ministers, Abbas and Qurai, preferred that police control rest in the cabinet.

Economy

Israel's closure of the occupied territories has forced the near collapse of the Palestinian economy. Israel has closed Palestinian borders with Egypt, Israel, and Jordan, and has cordoned off Palestinian towns and villages to prevent traffic between Palestinian areas. About 100,000 Palestinian workers cannot cross into Israel to jobs; the unemployment is at 50%, and gross domestic product has fallen by 50%. In its search for terrorist infrastructure, the IDF has destroyed much of the water, electrical, telephone, and transportation systems in Ramallah, Nablus, Jenin, and other West Bank cities. The Palestinian Authority relies upon grants from the Arab states and the European Union to meet its payroll.

Other Aspects of the Palestinians

Terrorism

Individual Palestinians and Palestinian military groups, both PLO and non-PLO, have launched terror attacks against Israeli people and facilities. Palestinian terrorists also have attacked people or institutions that, in the Palestinians' view, support Israel, including U.S. citizens, property, and installations. One of the conditions set by Congress in 1984 for beginning a U.S. dialogue with the PLO was that the PLO renounce terrorism, which it did in November and December 1988. But when the PLO refused to renounce the May 30, 1990, attempted military landing near Tel Aviv, the United States broke off the dialogue. Israel maintained that the PLO is a terrorist group. Until January 1993, any contact between an Israeli or anyone under Israeli occupation and the PLO was a crime in Israel. Many Palestinians view the attacks against Israel and its supporters as part of the legitimate Palestinian armed struggle to secure Palestinian rights, and view Israeli attacks against Arab civilians as terrorism.

Palestine Refugees and UNRWA[5]

One-half of the world's almost 9 million Palestinians live in Israel or under Israeli occupation. About 1 million Palestinian Arabs live in Israel and are Israeli citizens, who may vote and are eligible to serve in the Knesset (11 Arabs were elected to the Knesset in May 1996). The 3 million Palestinians in the occupied territories are not Israeli citizens and do not vote in Israeli elections. Jordan granted citizenship to the Palestinians living in Jordan but other Arab states have not offered blanket citizenship.

Of the 9 million Palestinians, 4 million are registered with the United Nations Relief and Works Agency (UNRWA) as refugees from the 1947-1948 war. There is disagreement over why the Palestinians became refugees: Israeli sources claim the Palestinians left their homes voluntarily or because the Arab governments told them to leave; Arab sources claim the Israelis forced the Palestinians to leave. UNRWA provides shelter, food, medical and dental care, and education benefits for the 4 million Palestinian registered refugees. Not all the registered refugees receive all the benefits; some 1.3 million live in 59 refugee camps scattered across Lebanon, Syria, Jordan, the West Bank, and the Gaza Strip.

The United States contributes to UNRWA through the refugee and migration account, authorized in the State Department authorization bill and appropriated through the foreign operations appropriations bill. U.S. contributions to UNRWA have not been earmarked in past appropriations bills.

Table 1: Palestine Arab Refugees Registered with UNRWA

Countries	1950 Total Registered	2002 Total Registered	No. of Camps	No. in Camps
Lebanon	127,600	387,043	12	217,211
Syria	82,194	401,185	10	115,863
Jordan	506,200	1,679,623	10	293,215
West Bank	—	626,532	19	168,507

[5] See CRS Report RS21668, *United Nations Relief and Works Agency for the Palestine Refugees in the Near East (UNRWA).*

Countries	1950 Total Registered	2002 Total Registered	No. of Camps	No. in Camps
Gaza Strip	198,227	878,977	8	468,071
Israel	45,800	—	—	—
Total	960,021	3,973,360	59	1,262,867

Source: *Report of the Commissioner-General for UNRWA,* **Supplement 13 (A/55/13) 2002.**

Note: West Bank included in Jordan in 1950. UNRWA stopped operating in Israel in 1952, when Israel resettled its Arab refugees.

Table 2: U.S. Contributions to UNRWA, 1950–2005 (millions of dollars)

Year	Amount
Cumulative 1950–1991	1,618
1992	69
1993	68
1994	78
1995	74
1996	77
1997	79
1998	78
1999	81
2000	89
2001	101
2002	100
2003	146
2004	127
2005*	88
Cumulative 1950–2002	**2,873**

Source: Department of State.

* Regular contribution only. Before an anticipated emergency funding request.

Table 3: U.S. AID Assistance to West Bank & Gaza, FY1975-FY2004 ($ in thousands)

Fiscal Year	Expenditures	Fiscal Year	Expenditures
1975	$1,000	1991	7,663
1976	1,572	1992	7,074
1977	3,416	1993	29,557
1978	2,687	1994	56,769
1979	6,801	1995	80,263
1980	3,000	1996	63,806
1981	2,500	1997	68,680
1982	6,000	1998	60,685
1983	6,500	1999	80,092
1984	8,500	2000	118,641
1985	12,141	2001	114,292
1986	13,950	2002	181,036
1987	8,400	2003	173,907
1988	6,911	2004	84,786
1989	20,903	2005	74,400
1990	12,618	**Total**	**$1,318,550**

Source: U.S. Department of State, Agency for International Development, [http://www.usaid.gov/wbg/].

DOCUMENT NO. 3

HAMAS'S MILITARY BUILD-UP IN THE GAZA STRIP

Intelligence and Terrorism Information Center at the Israel Intelligence Heritage & Commemoration Center (IICC) Report

April 8, 2007

Overview

1. The Israeli disengagement from the Gaza Strip in August 2005 created **a new situation which accelerated the establishment of an area fully controlled by Hamas.** It was quick to use its increased military power to make political capital in internal Palestinian affairs. It won the Palestinian Legislative Council elections in January 2006 and formed the government the following March. In June 2007 Hamas carried out a putsch in the Gaza Strip, neutralized Fatah and the Palestinian Authority's military and political power and set up a radical Muslim entity in the Gaza Strip, nicknamed Hamastan. The new entity, **supported and aided by Iran and Syria,** directs its own internal and foreign affairs, conducts a terrorist campaign against Israel and has divorced itself from the PA in Judea and Samaria, led by Abu Mazen and Fatah.

2. Since the disengagement, and particularly during the past year, **Hamas has accelerated its military buildup.** The process is nurtured by a number of factors.

i) **The many difficulties faced by Hamas since it came to power, especially since its takeover of the Gaza Strip:** Hamas has been forced to struggle with a series of difficulties which include its political isolation, economic blockade, IDF activities, internal subversion, political competition with Fatah, and the unending propaganda war waged against it

---

Editor's note: The original version of this document included some color images that could not be adequately reproduced in this publication. Where necessary, captions and/or headings specifically relating to any omitted images have also been left out of the version reprinted herein. The main text of the document has not been affected by these omissions.

by Fatah and Abu Mazen's PA. All of the above have given it a sense of being menaced and present it with continual challenges, requiring it to form military-security systems which will ensure its rule in the Gaza Strip and protect it from its many enemies, internal and external.

ii) **The need to find a response to the IDF's counterterrorist activities in the Gaza Strip alongside its fear that Israel will reconquer the Strip or parts of it:** The scenario of an IDF takeover resurfaces every time Palestinian terrorism escalates and along with it increased IDF counter-terrorist activities. To that can be added Hamas's continual need to deal with the IDF's intensive activities in the Gaza Strip, including the targeted killings of terrorist operatives, attacks on bases and facilities and land activities in the northern and southern Gaza strip.

iii) **Hezbollah's success** in providing an asymmetric response to the IDF's might during the second Lebanon war made it a **role model for Hamas.** The second Lebanon war and the results of the constant rocket fire at Sderot and the western Negev population centers made it clear that rockets were strategically important with regard to Israeli civilians' vulnerability. The lessons of the second Lebanon war also illustrated the importance of having a **strong military force** which could stand fast and survive to protect Hamas's control of the Gaza Strip, like the military force Hezbollah established in south Lebanon.

3. With all of the above in mind, Hamas is **advancing its military buildup** based on two main systems: the **internal security system,** at the center of which is the **Executive Force,** its main security arm for controlling the Gaza Strip; and its **military-terrorist system,** at the center of which are the **Izzedine al-Qassam Brigades,** which deal with planning and carrying out attacks against Israel and defending the Gaza Strip from within. The operatives of the internal security system and of the other Palestinian terrorist organizations would integrate into the Izzedine al-Qassam Brigades' program for defense should the IDF enter the Gaza Strip.

4. **Hamas's military buildup includes:**

i) Increasing the size of its forces, which today are estimated at 20,000 armed operatives directly subordinate to Hamas or who can be integrated into its forces in an emergency;

ii) Reorganizing its forces into semi-military formations;

iii) Carrying out large-scale training operations both in the Gaza Strip and beyond, primarily in Iran and Syria;

iv) Supplying advanced weapons, especially improved rockets (which can reach Ashqelon and beyond) and advanced anti-tank weapons of the types used by Hezbollah (such as Konkurs and Sagger missiles);

v) Improving command and control of the forces deployed throughout the Strip;

vi) Preparing the ground for defense, including underground systems for fighting and concealment throughout the Strip;

vii) Developing powerful IEDs and placing them near roads (such as the Shawaz self-made EFP) and various locations where fighting against the IDF is expected.

5. **Hamas's military buildup is at its height and in our assessment its full implementation will take a number of years.** However, some of its components are basically ripe so that they increase the threat to the IDF and to Israel's civilian population in the western Negev. Threats include **improved capabilities to carry out complex terrorist attacks such as mass-casualty attacks and the abductions of soldiers and civilians;** an increase in the scope, accuracy, range and force of rocket fire into Israel; increasing the threat of anti-tank weapons to Israel's tanks and armored vehicles and to IDF soldiers; improved survival capabilities of Hamas forces waging most of the fighting from the densely populated areas of the Gaza Strip.

6. The military buildup is led by Hamas headquarters in Syria and relies on Iranian and Syrian support and on funds which come from Iran, the Arab-Muslim world, and even from the West. Iranian and Syrian support for Hamas's military buildup is manifested in transferring theoretical and technical knowhow, their supplies of weapons and equipment, and the training they give Hamas operatives in Iran and Syria. Weapons, money and operatives originating in Iran and Syria are smuggled into the Gaza Strip through a vast system of tunnels (and through the Rafah Crossing), exploiting the helplessness and inefficiency of the Egyptian security forces, which avoid taking effective security measures to cut off the lifeline connecting Hamas and the other terrorist organizations to the countries sponsoring and supporting them.

Part 1
Description of Hamas's Military Buildup in the Gaza Strip

Offensive and Defensive Systems

1. Hamas's military infrastructure is composed of offensive and defensive systems **which satisfy a number of the movement's basic needs:**

i) **The realization of Hamas's jihadist identity by constant terrorist activity against Israel,** manifested, since the disengagement of August 2005, **by intensive rocket and mortar fire** (more than in the past) at western Negev population centers (one of the lessons learned from Hezbollah in Lebanon). At the same time Hamas attempted, with partial success, to carry out a number of attacks using other types of methods, such as suicide bombing attacks and abductions (for example, Gilad Shalit), light weapon and anti-tank fire, laying IEDs, etc.

ii) **Coping with IDF activity in the Gaza Strip,** which became intensive especially along the border to prevent rocket fire, deal with abduction attempts and to prevent the establishment of Hamas intelligence networks. The IDF's activity heightened Hamas's sense of being threatened by an Israeli conquest of the Gaza Strip, fully or partially. **Such scenarios of both fighting limited to a specific geographic area and limited in time** (such as Operation Hot Winter during the most recent escalation, February 27–March 3, 2008), and **an extensive Israeli attack to reconquer the Gaza Strip** can be carried out. Hamas considers the full conquest of the Gaza Strip as **the main threat,** and with that in mind is promoting its military buildup.

iii) **Coping with the internal threats in the Gaza Strip:** The threats come from supporters of Abu Mazen (and Fatah) and from other groups, such as the local clans and radical Islamic networks linked to the global jihad, which are unwilling to accept Hamas authority. The strength of such opponents decreased during the past year but they are still an obstacle to Hamas's desire for complete rule of the Gaza Strip. At the same time, the Hamas government has to provide a response growing crime and the personal security needs of the residents of the Gaza Strip.

2. Hamas's military capabilities arrayed against Israel, both offensively and defensively, are based on the **Izzedine al-Qassam Brigades,** the organization's military-terrorist wing. The Brigades are currently in the process of a fast military buildup with the objective of turning into semi-military army with capabilities to both defend the Gaza Strip and continue initiating terrorist attacks against Israel as dictated by Hamas strategy.

3. The distinction between the two is **not sharply defined.** During an escalation with Israel the internal security forces are supposed to join the fighting against the IDF, as least with logistic and intelligence support. In the scenario of broader and more lengthy fighting, some of the internal security forces are supposed to reinforce the Izzedine al-Qassam Brigades fighting units and confront the IDF, even at the expense of weakening their capabilities to deal with the necessities of internal security. In effect, many Hamas operatives apparently play **two roles** by serving in the internal security forces and, at least in emergency situations, are integrated into the Izzedine al-Qassam Brigades as well.

Concept of Defense of the Gaza Strip

4. **Hamas's perception of defending the Gaza Strip provides an asymmetric response to the IDF's military supremacy and its technological**

superiority. It does that in a variety of ways: through the use of advanced weapons which were successfully used by Hezbollah in Lebanon (IEDs and anti-tank missiles); by causing large numbers of casualties to IDF forces through fighting in densely-populated built-up areas; by improving concealment tactics to preserve Hamas forces; by exhausting the Israeli home front with massive rocket attacks while the IDF is fighting inside the Gaza Strip, and if possible, at the same time carrying out suicide bombing attacks by infiltrating terrorists through the Sinai and Judea and Samaria borders; and by making extensive use of the Palestinian, Arab and international media to gain sympathy for the Palestinian cause and at the same time to limit Israel's freedom of action.

5. **That perception reflects an understanding of the relative forces between Hamas (and its supporters) and the IDF's capabilities.** Hamas is well aware of **the inequality between the sides,** which gives each side advantages and disadvantages.

i) **On the one hand,** Hamas is aware of the IDF's clear military superiority in the number of forces, protection, weapons, and air and intelligence capabilities. As a result, Hamas is aware that it will be difficult for it to stop an IDF advance and to prevent it from operating in open areas.

ii) **On the other hand, if the IDF remains in the Gaza Strip in static deployment and for an extended period of time,** Hamas is liable to have the advantage. It would wage a guerilla war of attrition, especially in **densely populated built-up areas**. According to the classic logic of asymmetric warfare, the IDF would lose its superiority, suffer many losses and harm, even if not deliberately, Palestinian civilians in a way that would lead to internal-Israeli, Arab and international pressure for the IDF to withdraw from the Gaza Strip.

6. **With that in mind Hamas developed a defensive concept according to which it would refrain from using its full military potential during the first stages of the fighting,** reduce engaging the IDF in open areas and channel the fighting into densely-populated built-up areas. Its **objective** would be to **exhaust** the IDF forces and cause its soldiers as much bloodshed as possible while continuing its attacks on the Israeli home front with rocket fire (according to the Hezbollah model in the second Lebanon war). At the same time it would preserve the survival capabilities of its operatives and military infrastructure. All of the above **would enable Hamas to represent itself as having "defeated" the IDF when it withdrew from the Gaza Strip, again, according to Hezbollah's model after the second Lebanon war.**

7. To exhaust the IDF forces and cause as many casualties as possible Hamas would seek to wage a fiercer, more determined war the deeper into the Gaza Strip the IDF advanced. **Hamas fighting is expected to include** firing light weapons at Israeli forces, including from inside houses and

roofs; digging traps in the ground at the entrances to cities and along main routes; using IEDs, mines, car bombs and camouflaged IEDs; dispatching male and female suicide bombers; the extensive use of anti-tank weapons; using civilians as human shields for terrorist operatives who are fighting from within their midst.

8. One of Hamas's tactics will be the use of suicide bombers as weapons in their guerilla campaign against the IDF. The movement has scores of explosive belts ready and apparently an established unit of suicide bombers.[1] It is also possible that other Palestinian terrorist organizations have the same plan if the IDF enters the Gaza Strip. In past fighting in the Gaza Strip there were attempts to use suicide bombers to attack IDF forces. For example, during Operation Autumn Clouds (November 6, 2006) a female suicide bomber dispatched by the Palestinian Islamic Jihad tried to attack an IDF force south of Beit Hanoun. She blew herself up near the force and slightly wounded one soldier.

Differences Between the Conditions in the Gaza Strip and Lebanon

9. Hezbollah, which acquired a great deal of experience in its years of fighting the IDF in Lebanon, **serves as a model for Hamas's military buildup and for the other terrorist organizations operating in the Gaza Strip.** However, there are a number of basic differences between the conditions in Lebanon and those in the Gaza Strip, and Hamas has taken them into consideration.

i) Topography: The Gaza Strip is small and its area is defined, while Lebanon has depth from which the terrorist organizations can operate and gives them a much longer breathing space; south Lebanon, where the hard core of Hezbollah's infrastructure is located, is mountainous and forested, while the Gaza Strip is flat and exposed. On the other hand, the Gaza Strip has **continuous, densely populated areas** which are advantageous for a defending force and difficult for regular army forces to operate in.

ii) **Access to external support:** Hezbollah enjoys massive support from Iran and Syria and easy access to supplies of weapons, which pass over the long wide-open border between Lebanon and Syria. Hamas also relies on Iranian and Syrian support, but it is more difficult to transport weapons into the Gaza Strip because of its relative distance from sources of external support and tight Israeli inspection (and not-so-tight Egyptian inspection) along the border. Thus Hamas had to develop its own weapons

[1] On March 24, 2008, the Izzedine al-Qassam Brigades Website posted the biography of Nur al-Din Jundia, a Hamas operative killed by the IDF on March 20, 2008. He was described as being a member of the suicide bombing unit.

manufacturing capabilities, bolstered by an extended system of weapons smuggling. That was done to give it capabilities to fight Israel under blockade conditions (although the Gaza Strip is not hermetically sealed), while Hezbollah receives all the standard weapons it needs from Iran and Syria.

iii) **Support from the population and local focal points of power:** Hezbollah has a determined opposition against it within the Lebanese government, the Christian camp and other sectarian groups, and it has to take them into consideration when fighting Israel. **Hamas,** on the other hand, succeeded in subduing Fatah and the Palestinian Authority security forces after its putsch in June 2007, and it enjoys much support within the Strip. That enables it to accelerate its military buildup with a great degree of freedom of action and to implement its own independent terrorist policy without bowing to meaningful internal political restraints (even when that policy, for example the rocket fire into Israel, harms Gaza Strip residents). Popular support also provides Hamas with almost unending sources of manpower for its ranks.

Part 2
Hamas Control of the Gaza Strip

The Hamas Leadership in the Gaza Strip

1. The Hamas leadership in the Gaza Strip includes the institutions and individuals responsible for the day-to-day management of the movement and for making its strategic decisions. Most of the leadership's members do not play roles in the Hamas government, although they are closely linked to its senior members (headed by Ismail Haniya).

2. The Hamas leadership in the Gaza Strip (the political bureau) directs **the movement's four main divisions: the military wing** (the Izzedine al-Qassam Brigades), **the internal security forces** (centering around the Executive Force), **the Hamas government** and its **broad civilian infrastructure** (the *da'wah* network).

3. Since the establishment of the Hamas government in March 2006, and even more so since the putsch in June 2007, the **Hamas leadership in the Gaza Strip has increased its power at the expense of the "external" leadership in Damascus.** Currently the Gaza Strip leadership makes the important decisions regarding Hamas management in the Strip. At the same time, the leadership in Damascus plays a central role in Hamas's military buildup because it has easy access to available supplies from Syria, Iran and Hezbollah. **Strength of the overall military forces in the Gaza Strip.**

4. The military force commanded by Hamas rests on the **Izzedine al-Qassam Brigades,** its military-terrorist wing. In our assessment, it has

more than 10,000 operatives. That figure may be larger because of Hamas's intense recruiting process carried out since it took over the Gaza Strip. It can be expected that the operatives will reinforce the Izzedine al-Qassam Brigades in an emergency situation with the IDF, while routinely the regular hard core is composed of **a several hundred skilled operatives.** It is currently commanded by **Ahmed Ja'abari.**[2]

5. A considerable number of the operatives expected to reinforce for the Izzedine al-Qassam Brigades normally serve in the **internal security forces.** Those forces, centering around the **Executive Force,** today number around **10,000 operatives,** most of them either Hamas members or sympathizers. Thus the total number of Izzedine al-Qassam Brigades and internal security force operatives controlled by Hamas is, in our estimation, about 15,000.[3]

6. About **3,000–4,000 operatives** belonging to the other Palestinian terrorist organizations operating in the Gaza Strip can be added to the strength of the Hamas forces. At least some of them may join the Izzedine al-Qassam Brigades in an emergency situation and accept its orders to fight the IDF. Thus the entire strength Hamas has at its command in the Gaza Strip is **about 20,000 armed men** of varying degrees of skill and professionalism.

Hamas's Military Wing (the Izzedine al-Qassam Brigades)

7. In the past few years, especially since the disengagement, Hamas's military-terrorist infrastructure has gradually transformed itself into **a hierarchical structure with semi-military patterns of action.** That change means the unification of local terrorist groups throughout the Gaza Strip into one military wing with an orderly structure which has adopted military components both in its commanding and directing the forces and support systems (manufacturing, acquiring and smuggling weapons, etc.). However, it is not a classical military organization, and under fire Hamas can be expected **to employ the principles of asymmetric warfare:** the directing of small fighting units (platoons and squads); focusing on hit and run attacks; blending in with and disappearing into the civilian population, while making extensive use of civilians as human shields, etc.

8. Hamas's military wing includes territorial brigades and designated units. It is deployed in a number of territorial brigades throughout the Gaza Strip, **each of which has more than 1,000 operatives.** Each brigade

---

[2] The status of **Muhammad Deif,** the commander of the Izzedine al-Qassam Brigades, who was badly wounded, is unclear. The Hamas media still refer to him as "the general commander of the Izzedine al-Qassam Brigades."

[3] In an interview with the London Sunday Times on March 9, 2008, a senior Hamas terrorist operative said that the Izzedine al-Qassam Brigades had **15,000** operatives. In our assessment, that figure also includes members of the internal security forces.

has a number of battalions and each battalion has several companies. Each company has three platoons composed of three combat teams (all of which have anti-tank, fighters, saboteurs and medics).

9. The brigades are deployed as follows:

i) A brigade in **northern sector,** commanded by **Ahmed Ghandour**.

ii) The **Gaza City sector,** which apparently has two brigades commanded by **Ahmed Ja'abari**.

iii) A brigade in the **central sector,** commanded by **Ayman Nawfal** (today detained by the Egyptians).

iv) A brigade in the **southern sector,** which apparently has two brigades (in accordance with geographical conditions), one in **Khan Yunis,** commanded by **Muhammad Sinwar,** and the other in Rafah, commanded by **Ra'ed al-Atar**.

10. Ordinarily, as noted above, the Izzedine al-Qassam Brigades has a few hundred skilled operatives. They carry out attacks against civilian targets in Israel (firing rockets and mortar shells) and against military targets bordering the Gaza Strip (firing mortar shells, light weapons fire, planting IEDs, attempts to kill and abduct soldiers in Israeli territory).

11. **Hamas's terrorist policy** is characterized by **treading a fine line** to defuse the tension between its governmental duties on the one hand and its belligerent jihadist identity and faith in attacks as the means of achieving its strategic objectives on the other. That means the **controlled use of terrorism** (including rocket fire) to achieve its goals seeking, at least for the time being, to avoid an overall confrontation with the IDF in the Gaza Strip. At the same time, Hamas deals with planning for an IDF attempt to conquer—fully or partially—the Gaza Strip by building up a military force as part of its emergency defense plan.

Internal Security

Overview

12. Hamas's internal security forces number **10,000 operatives,** about 6,000 of whom are police, many of them **former members of the Executive Force.**

13. In addition to the police there are the following units:

i) The **rapid response force** (an élite police force)

ii) The **security and protection force,** responsible for guarding important people and institutions.

iii) **National security** (about 400 operatives)

iv) **Internal security** (about 200 operatives)

v) **Coastal security** (about 200 operatives)

vi) **Civil defense** (about 400 operatives)

14. A short description of the various forces and units follow:

The Police Force (formerly the Executive Force)

15. The Executive Force (currently integrated into the police force) was established in April 2006. That was done because Hamas wanted to take control of the security forces in the Gaza Strip away from Abu Mazen and Fatah and to create an effective force which it could use for policing functions and to oppress Hamas's enemies. The Executive Force was subordinate to the interior ministry and became one of Hamas's most important tools for controlling the Gaza Strip. It was widely deployed during the confrontations with Fatah and played a central role in the Hamas putsch in the Gaza Strip in June 2007.

16. There are **6,000 policemen,** most of them Hamas operatives and some of them operatives of other Palestinian terrorist organizations. They are armed with Kalashnikov or M-16 assault rifles, hand grenades and a variety of anti-tank weapons. They wear uniforms and their salaries are paid by the interior ministry. When the Executive Force and police were combined, those who refused to join the new force were assigned to the **rapid response force,** which works alongside the police and helps deal with events on the ground.

17. Once the two forces had been combined, **General Tawfiq Ja'aber** was appointed police chief and his deputy was **Jamal al-Jarah,** commander of the Executive Force. Jamal al-Jarah was born in the Jabaliya refugee camp in 1965 and began his career as an operative in the Hamas security service in the Gaza Strip. In 1996 he was detained by the Palestinian security forces for a relatively long time. After his release he continued planning and executing attacks against Israel. He escaped an IDF targeted killing on December 30, 2003.

18. Since its establishment the police force **has been improving its capabilities,** expanding its deployment and increasing the scope of its activities in enforcing order. The police force is divided into five districts: the northern Gaza Strip, Gaza City, the central camps, Khan Yunis and Rafah. It keeps order, disperses demonstrations and deals with criminal activities. However, it must be taken into consideration that should there be a broad, continued IDF incursion into the Gaza Strip, its operatives and those of the other internal security forces would be extensively integrated into the ranks of the Izzedine al-Qassam Brigades fighters at the expense of performing their other internal security duties.

Coastal Security (Naval Police)

19. Coastal security was established in the summer of 2007 following a reorganization of the PA's naval force. It keeps order on the Gaza Strip beaches and carries out routine security missions along the coastline. It has about **200 operatives**.

20. Coastal security has weapons which belonged to the Palestinian security forces, including various types of boats. Its members carry light arms. In addition to keeping order, the coast guard has been involved in shooting at Israeli Navy patrol boats and can be expected to engage them if the IDF enters the Gaza Strip.

Internal Security Service

21. The internal security service was established by Hamas in August 2007. It has about **200 operatives** and is subordinate to the Hamas government's interior ministry. It replaces the Palestinian preventive security service which operated in the Gaza Strip before the Hamas putsch. Its deals with collaborators and gathers information on individuals suspected of anti-Hamas activities and is responsible for interrogating detainees.

Civil Defense

22. The force is responsible for civil defense throughout the Gaza Strip. It has about **400 operatives** and is subordinate to the Izzedine al-Qassam Brigades. It runs 18 civil defense stations, 14 of which are operative. It has 25 fire engines, four rescue vehicles and six ambulances (Al-Risala, March 18, 2008).

Other Security Units

23. There are two other units operating in the Gaza Strip

i) **Security and protection**: Responsible for responsible for guarding important Hamas people and institutions.

ii) **National security**: After Hamas took over the Gaza Strip it renewed the activities of the national security unit. Its **400 operatives** are deployed mainly along the Philadelphi route. They are responsible for routine security along the border and controlling smuggling. Some of them were formerly Fatah operatives; the others belong to Hamas.

Other Terrorist Organization Operating in the Gaza Strip

Overview

24. Hamas's offensive and defensive military systems are based on Izzedine al-Qassam Brigades operatives and those belonging to the Hamas-controlled

internal securitys forces. There are other terrorist organizations operating in the Gaza Strip with a total of an estimated **3,000–4,000 operatives.** Most of the other organizations work in close collaboration with Hamas, which Hamas considers important. Especially conspicuous is the operation collaboration between Hamas and the Popular Resistance Committees and the Army of Islam.

25. Hamas exploits its control of the Gaza Strip and its military strength to control the other terrorist organizations, primarily by supporting them. There are two main reasons: **routinely**, it enables Hamas to camouflage its involvement in attacks against Israel and reduce harm to its own operatives; beyond routine situations, **during an escalation** it can integrate them as additional manpower to support its fighting against the IDF. In emergencies Hamas seeks to subordinate them to its authority and to use a **joint war room** to command them.[4]

26. The smaller Palestinian terrorist organizations operating in the Gaza Strip are the following:

The Palestinian Islamic Jihad

27. The second most important terrorist organization operating in the Gaza Strip. It has **1,000 operatives,** including a hard core of several dozen. Most of its activities center around Gaza City and Rafah, but it is active throughout the Gaza Strip.

28. The PIJ favors terrorism as the sole means of achieving its goals (the destruction of the State of Israel). Unlike Hamas, **it does not have the governmental responsibilities,** and under routine circumstances is the most active terrorist organization attacking Israel. Its leadership is based in **Syria.** Its activities are directed and financed by **Iran,** and it is inspired by **Hezbollah.** Its civilian infrastructure *(da'wah)* is limited, and mostly supports its terrorist activities.

29. Unlike Hamas, the PIJ focuses on carrying out routine attacks against Israel, paying relatively little attention to a military buildup for defending the Gaza Strip. Its routine activities include firing rockets and mortar shells and carrying out attacks both along the Israel-Gaza border and penetrating into Israeli territory. Its operational capabilities are relatively high and it has been responsible for a substantial number of the routine attacks originating in the Gaza Strip, especially rocket launches at civilian Israeli targets.

---

[4] From an interview with Abu Obeida, Izzedine al-Qassam Brigades spokesman, about Hamas defense plans in the case of a possible Israeli invasion (Al-Hayat, December 27, 2007).

30. With regard to its military buildup, it focuses on **improving its technological rocket launching capabilities,** particularly increased range. Its goal is to fire its rockets as deeply as possible within Israel territory, or to move its squads deeper into the Gaza Strip to hinder the IDF in its attacks on its rocket launching squads.

The Popular Resistance Committees

31. The **PRC** have **several hundred operatives** with a hard core of a few dozen. The organization has two large factions and several smaller ones. Its military-terrorist wing is the **Salah al-Din Brigades,** which has high operational capabilities and a large number of various weapons.

32. The PRC's attacks include firing rockets and mortar shells, attacks near the border fence and attempted mass-casualty attacks and abductions on the Israeli side of the border (for example, the abduction of Gilad Shalit). Sometimes Hamas subcontracts the PRC for its own attacks and moreover, many of the PRC's networks actually serve as Hamas proxies. The organization manufactures its own weapons, although on a smaller scale than Hamas and the PIJ.

Fatah/Al-Aqsa Martyrs Brigades Groups

33. Even though Hamas took over the Gaza Strip, a few Fatah groups, **with a total membership of several hundred operatives,** continue their activity with Hamas approval. Most of the groups' activities take place in the northern Gaza Strip. Their activities are supported by other terrorist organizations (usually Hamas and the PIJ) both operationally and financially.

34. The groups operate according to local and personal interest, have many commanders and in effect **do not function as an organization with a regular, hierarchical structure.** Their operatives have various types of weapons including light arms, anti-tank weapons and homemade rockets. Al-Aqsa Martyrs Brigades operatives routinely launch rockets, plant IEDs, attempt to infiltrate into Israel, sometimes in collaboration with other organizations.

The Army of Islam

35. The Army of Islam was established in 2006 after its operatives split from the PRC. It is **headed by Mumtaz Dughmush.** Publicly, its ideology is similar to that of the global jihad. In practice, however, it retains its Palestinian character and focuses on familiar forms of terrorist activities against Israel. The organization first came to public attention when it collaborated with Hamas and the PRC in the abduction of Gilad Shalit in June 2006.

36. Most of its operatives come from the **Dughmush clan,** a large clan in the Gaza Strip affiliated with Fatah and many of its members are involved

in criminal activities such as drug dealing, auto theft and extortion. Over the years the organization's operatives carried out a number of internal Palestinian attacks including the murder of Mussa Arafat, IED attacks and abducting foreign nationals inside the Gaza Strip. Since the Hamas putsch the organization has returned to attacking Israel, apparently as part of its integration into the new internal Gaza Strip order and because it is in Hamas's interest to prevent internal anarchy.

Part 3
The Physical Infrastructure of the Gaza Strip

Basic Geographic and Demographic Data

1. The area of the Gaza Strip is **365 square kilometers** and it is one of the most densely populated areas on earth. Its population is **1,400,000,** 65.5% of whom are refugees. Some 960,000 residents (73%) live in large urban settlements. Natural population increase is 3.8% annually, with an average of six children per married woman. Children under 15 make up 48.8% of the population. Unemployment stands at 54%, and between 60% and 70% of the population live below the poverty line. Most of the labor force is employed in the services (60%), industry (25%) and agriculture (10%).

2. The economic conditions of the Gaza Strip residents are harsh, especially since the Palestinian terrorist campaign began (the "second intifada," which began in September 2000). Their difficulties were exacerbated following the isolation of the Gaza Strip and the economic and political boycotts imposed by the international community on the Hamas government and the radical Islamic entity created in the Gaza Strip. As a result, a considerable number of Gaza inhabitants are dependent on external aid and support from Islamic funds and foundations abroad, international aid organizations and the financial aid provided by Iran to the Hamas government. The aid is delivered to the Gaza Strip through the border crossings with Israel and the Rafah Crossing into Egypt, which are the Gazans' lifelines.

3. Hamas's military wing is deployed throughout the Strip. **Their deployment and significance for Hamas and the other terrorist organizations is as follows:**

i) **The Gaza City sector,** the Gaza Strip's "capital," is the nerve center. It is a densely populated area with 450,000 residents, and the location of government facilities and Hamas's military center. **The heads of Hamas are based in Gaza City and many operational, organizational and government centers are located there.**

ii) **The northern sector** is mostly agricultural. The northeastern outskirts of Gaza City, mainly the areas of Beit Hanoun, Beit Lahia and Al-Atatra **serve as the main launching sites for rocket attacks against Sderot,**

Ashqelon and western Negev population centers. The region of **Jabaliya** is the terrorist organizations' nerve center in the northern Gaza Strip and provides the sector of the northern Gaza Strip with depth for the regions from which rockets are launched.

iii) **The central camps sector** has a population of 200,000 and is Gaza City's back yard. There are four large refugee camps, the city of Dir al-Balah and a number of small agricultural settlements. The sector serves are the logistic rear for Gaza City as well as the local operational infrastructure which is supposed to protect the sector and carry out attacks.

iv) The southern sector has a population of 250,000 and has three subdivisions: the Khan Yunis region, the Rafah region and along the coast, the region of Mawasi and the ruins of the former Israeli settlements of Gush Katif. **The southern region of the Gaza Strip serves as the almost exclusive connecting route to the outside and along it pass weapons, money and terrorist operatives.** From this region terrorist operatives leave the Gaza Strip to infiltrate into Israel through the Israeli-Egyptian border in the Sinai or for training in Syria and Iran.

Underground Network

"Our defense plan is based, to a great extent, on rockets which have not yet been used and on a network of ditches and tunnels dug under a large area of the [Gaza] Strip. The [Israeli] army will be surprised when it sees fighters coming up out of the ground and engaging it with unexpected equipment and weapons . . . "[5]

4. **One of the main components of Hamas's military buildup** is a **vast underground network** which includes a network of tunnels dug under various regions of the Gaza Strip for attack and defense. The network is intended to create a threat to IDF forces operating in the Gaza Strip, to neutralize some of the IDF's capability to damage the Hamas infrastructure and to give Hamas's military wing an operational breathing space during prolonged, extensive fighting.

5. Hezbollah's underground fortification system in south Lebanon inspired Hamas and the other terrorist organizations, and they adapted Hezbollah's experience to the Gaza Strip's unique physical conditions. Within the underground network is a well-developed system of tunnels which have been used by Hamas and other terrorist organizations for a variety of purposes:

i) **The tunnels are the terrorist organizations' main conduit for smuggling weapons into the Gaza Strip.** In the Rafah region and along the Philadelphi route there is a vast network of tunnels through which pass terrorist operatives, weapons, goods and equipment from Egypt into

[5] Interview with Abu Obeida, Izzedine al-Qassam Brigades spokesman (Al-Hayat, December 17, 2007).

and out of the Gaza Strip. They became more important when the Rafah Crossing into Egypt and the crossings into Israel were closed after the Hamas military takeover of the Gaza Strip.

ii) **There are tunnels which have been designated for terrorist attacks against IDF posts and villages near the border fence.** The tunnels provide the element of surprise and enable the terrorists to penetrate into Israel territory and then to return safely to the Gaza Strip. Such an attack was carried out on June 25, 2006, against an IDF post near the Sufa Crossing, during which two IDF soldiers were killed and Gilad Shalit was abducted. In August 2007 the IDF exposed a tunnel shaft inside a greenhouse growing tomatoes about 700 meters from the northern Gaza Strip border fence. A generator sunk into the ground was also uncovered, as was equipment used to dig tunnels.[6]

iii) **There are tunnels dug as bait for IDF forces operating in the Gaza Strip.** They are dug fairly obviously with the intention of having Israeli security forces find them during actions in the Gaza Strip. As the soldiers investigate and search the area they are attacked with IEDs and shot at. Such an attack was carried out along the main north-south route of the Gaza Strip on September 12, 2006, when terrorists shot light arms at IDF forces, killing one soldier. **Camouflaged IEDs** were found in the region of the tunnel and were to have been detonated when the soldiers uncovered the tunnel.

iv) **There are tunnels dug as safe passages for terrorist operatives in battle zones.** They are dug between buildings and have a variety of purposes: escape, concealment, hiding weapons and surprising IDF forces.

v) **There are many camouflaged concrete firing positions.**

Part 4
Upgrading Weapons Possessed by Hamas and other Terrorist Organizations

Sources of Weapons

1. As part of its military buildup project, Hamas is making an effort supplement its **independently-produced weapons and ammunition with standard equipment.** Hamas grants great importance to **artillery** (rockets and mortars), **anti-tank weapons and IEDs** for use against the IDF's infantry

[6] For further information see our August 19, 2007 Bulletin entitled "An IDF activity in the northern Gaza Strip exposed a tunnel shaft hidden in a hothouse, apparently dug to carry out a terrorist attack in Israel" at http://www.terrorism-info.org.il/malam_multimedia/English/eng_n/html/ct_160807e.htm.

and armored combat vehicles (since those types of weapons proved themselves in Hezbollah's fighting against the IDF on the Lebanese scene).

2. The weapons and ammunition smuggled into the Gaza Strip are usually obtained from three major sources:

i. **Iran and Syria, either directly or through Hezbollah:** They are smuggled to Sinai and from there to the Gaza Strip through the extensive network of tunnels. The breach of the border fence between the Gaza Strip and Egypt allowed Hamas and other terrorist organizations in the Gaza Strip to smuggle considerable amounts of weapons, including artillery rockets and anti-tank weapons.

ii. **Arms dealers:** They are smuggled to Sinai (or purchased there) and are then smuggled into the Gaza Strip through the network of tunnels.

iii. **Independent production:** These weapons, which include improved Qassam artillery rockets and other types of rockets, are manufactured in lathe shops and workshops in the Gaza Strip. The raw materials are smuggled into the Gaza Strip from Egypt and Israel, and include chemicals, metal parts and other substances used for the production of weapons and ammunition.

3. **Exceptionally, Hamas obtained large quantities of weapons after it took over the security services of the Palestinian Authority** in June 2007. Some of the weapons were advanced items which Hamas had not possessed before (it would have taken Hamas months or even years to smuggle them through the tunnels). The weapons seized by Hamas include the following:

i. **Several dozens of long-range 122mm rockets (Grad):** Some of them may have been fired at Ashkelon during the round of escalation that started in late February 2008.

ii. **Anti-tank weapons:** Dozens of anti-tank missiles (including Sagger missiles) and thousands of RPG rockets.

iii. **Anti-aircraft weapons:** Anti-aircraft missiles and a few dozens of various anti-aircraft machineguns.

iv. **Machine guns:** Following the putsch in the Gaza Strip, Hamas seized a large quantity of machine guns. Consequently, its military wing began to introduce them as standard weapons for its squads, and as the main weapons for designated units (such as aerial defense and firing at Israeli Navy vessels from the beach).

v. **Small arms:** Tens of thousands of rifles.

vi. **Ammunition:** Millions of bullets.

vii. **Explosives:** Dozens of tons of explosives.

viii. **Patrol ships, inflatable rubber dinghies and diving equipment** which belonged to the Palestinian naval police. The equipment is the basis for the coast guard unit established by Hamas, but could also be used for naval terrorist attacks.

ix. **Intelligence:** Various types of listening equipment.

4. **The implications of Hamas's equipping itself with advanced weapons as part of its military buildup:**

i. **Artillery rockets and mortar shells:** The range of Hamas's independently-produced rockets is over 12 km (7 ½ miles). The standard rockets and mortars smuggled into the Gaza Strip **extend the threat to Israel's civilian population to a range of about 20 km (12 ½ miles)** (Ashkelon, Netivot) and increase the threat to IDF forces operating near and inside the Gaza Strip.

ii. **Anti-tank weapons:** Advanced standard anti-tank systems have been smuggled into the Gaza Strip. Hamas is also making efforts to improve the quality of its independently-produced anti-tank rockets to increase their range, armor piercing capabilities and precision. **That improves Hamas's ability to hit IDF forces from the outskirts of urban territory and to wage anti-tank warfare at night.**

iii. **IEDs:** Hamas is making efforts to increase the armor piercing capabilities of its IEDs, **which would improve its ability to inflict multiple casualties on IDF forces and to penetrate IDF armored combat vehicles (ACVs).**

iv. **Anti-aircraft weapons:** The presence of advanced anti-aircraft weapons in the Gaza Strip **might jeopardize Israeli aircraft** operating in the Gaza Strip region.

v. **Night-vision equipment:** Advanced night-vision equipment considerably improves the ability of Hamas and the other terrorist organizations to combat IDF forces at night.

5. Some of the weapons held by Hamas are the following:.

Rockets and Mortars

6. For Hamas and the other terrorist organizations, firing rockets and mortar shells is an asymmetrical, simple, readily available and cheap solution to Israel's military superiority. While it does have problems and shortcomings, they believe that **it allows them to continually disrupt the life of the civilian population within the rockets' range over prolonged periods of time.** It would destabilize social structure, bypass the security buffer zone built by Israel along the Gaza Strip, and create a kind of balance of terror

that would make it difficult for Israel to carry out counter-terrorism activities. The rockets are launched from densely-populated areas, sometimes near residential buildings and in some cases from rooftops and schoolyards, and Palestinian civilians are used as human shields.

7. In Hamas's view, rockets and mortars will also be important if the IDF enters the Gaza Strip and engages Hamas in a limited or extended confrontation. In such a case, Hamas would seek to **preserve its ability to fire at Israel** (mainly at urban centers such as Ashkelon and Sderot) from launching sites deep within the Gaza Strip. **That strategic concept was inspired by Hezbollah's tactics in Lebanon,** which Hamas considers to have been successful in the last confrontation with Israel. In copying Hezbollah's rocket launching capabilities, Hamas and the other terrorist organizations are supported by **Iran and Syria,** which provide them with know-how, training and standard rockets.

8. **Hamas's rocket supply is based on several hundred** independently-produced **Qassam rockets,** with diameters ranging from 90 mm to 115 mm **and ranges of 9–13 km (6–8 miles).** The Hamas military wing has several **independently-produced** longer-range rockets which can reach **19 km** (almost 12 miles). Hamas also possesses dozens of standard long-range Grad rockets (122mm), **with a range of up to 20.4 km (12 2/3 miles),** smuggled into the Gaza Strip or confiscated from the Palestinian Authority security services following the Hamas takeover of the Gaza Strip. The breach of Rafah Crossing in January 2008 increased the number of standard rockets, **and perhaps even a number of rockets for ranges longer than 20.4 km.**

9. In addition, **Hamas possesses hundreds of mortar shells, both independently-produced and standard, which were smuggled into the Gaza Strip.** Hamas is responsible for most of the "routine" mortar fire, as opposed to Qassam rockets, which it only launches during escalations. The mortar shelling is aimed at villages and outposts situated near the border fence as well as IDF forces operating inside the Gaza Strip.

10. As part of its military buildup, Hamas is working to **improve its artillery capabilities.** Some of the improvements introduced during the past year **can already be seen on the ground** and were brought into play in the latest rounds of escalation:

i. **Improved range:** As early as the May 2007 escalation it was clear that rocket range had increased. In the late February 2008 escalation, 122mm Grad rockets hit **northern Ashkelon** (Hamas threatened to increase the range to include the city of **Ashdod).**

ii. **Precision:** Precision **has been improved** through the use of technical upgrades and as a result of the technical experience acquired by the rocket and mortar operators.

iii. **Increased use of hidden launch sites** (another tactic learned from Hezbollah): Launch sites are hidden in vegetation or between houses. In the February escalation, subterranean launchers were found in the northern Gaza Strip for the first time, usually activated by a delay system.

11. **The assistance provided by Iran to Hamas** and other Palestinian terrorist organizations allows them to improve their military capabilities, both by **arming themselves with standard rockets and standard mortar shells smuggled into the Gaza Strip,** and to receive the technological assistance necessary to create improved rockets with longer ranges. That was recently reflected in the terrorist organizations' use of **Iranian-made mortar shells:**

i. On February 24, **a standard 120mm mortar shell** was fired from the Gaza Strip. Examination of the remains showed that it was probably an **Iranian-made** mortar shell (a copy of one produced by Israel Military Industries in the 1970s). **The mortar shell is equipped with an auxiliary engine which increases its range from six to ten kilometers (almost 4 to 6 ¼ miles).**

ii. On February 29, a mortar shell landed **near Sufa, an IDF outpost** in the southern Gaza Strip. Examination of the remains showed that it was a **standard 120mm HE Iranian mortar shell** manufactured in 2006. Its warhead is **more destructive** than that of an improvised rocket of the same weight.

12. During the course of the latest escalation (late February–early March 2008), a significant number of standard 122 mm rockets (at least 18) were fired by Hamas on Ashkelon. **The difference** between them and the Grad rockets used till then is that their engine is made up of four 50cm sections. That feature is highly unusual and does not exist in rockets produced by countries which manufacture the same models. The technological effort put into the new development was designed, in our assessment, to make it easier for the terrorist organizations to smuggle the rockets into the Gaza Strip by dismantling the sections. There are several Middle Eastern countries producing such rockets, including **Iran,** Syria, and Egypt. The considerable assistance provided by Iran to terrorist organizations, including smuggling weapons and ammunition to the Gaza Strip, would lead to the conclusion that Iran was responsible for their manufacture.

13. **The Palestinian Islamic Jihad** also attempts to improve its rocket-launching capabilities. In the latest round of escalation, the PIJ launched an independently-produced 175 mm rocket with a longer range for the first time. **It is a step up in the threat posed by independently-produced rockets and increases their destructive ability**.

14. Launching tactics: The rockets are usually launched from **open sites or urban areas** (such as courtyards, alleys, ruined houses). Sometimes, **Palestinian civilians are used as human shields to allow the perpetrators greater chances of survival.** Thus most rockets are launched near fast access and escape routes.

15. The terrorist organizations' **preferred launch sites** are in the **northern Gaza Strip.** Those areas are in close geographical proximity to major population centers in the western Negev, mainly the cities of Sderot (the terrorist organizations' preferred target) and Ashkelon (which was intensively shelled during the last escalation). Increasing the rockets' range means that it will be possible to launch them from **deep inside the Gaza Strip,** from densely populated areas, to make it difficult for the IDF to carry out counterterrorist activities.

Anti-Tank Weapons

16. In the last several years there has been an increase in the significance ascribed by Hamas and other terrorist organizations to anti-tank weapons in fighting the IDF. That is also the result of the successful use made by Hezbollah of advanced anti-tank missiles against IDF forces in the second Lebanon war.

17. The second Lebanon war accelerated Hamas's stockpiling of advanced anti-tank weapons. There are many hundred to several thousand independently-produced **Al-Yassin** rockets (a reconstruction of the PG-2 rocket). The Hamas's arsenal also includes hundreds of **PG-2 and PG-7** anti-tank rocket launchers and several dozen advanced anti-tank missiles of various types, including **Konkurs** (AF-5) and **Saggers**. Hamas and the other terrorist organizations are trying to **increase their arsenal of anti-tank weapons.**

RPG-7 Anti-Tank Rocket Launcher Manufactured by Russia and other Countries, Including Egypt

Technical specifications:

a. **Launcher length:** 950 mm

b. **Launcher diameter:** 40 mm

c. **Launcher weight:** 6 kg (13.2 lbs)

d. **Warhead:** hollow charge (85 mm in diameter)

e. **Effective range:** stationary target 350 m; moving target 300 m

f. **Maximum range:** 800–900 m

g. **Armor piercing capability:** 300 mm of stee

Russian-made Sagger missile[7]

Technical specifications:

a. **Warhead diameter:** 125 mm

b. **Missile length:** 86.4 cm

c. **Armor piercing capability:** 450 mm of armored steel

d. **Minimum range:** 500 m

e. **Maximum range:** 3,000 m

Russian-made Konkurs missile

Technical specifications:

a. **Armor piercing capability:** 600 mm of steel; 800 mm after reactive plating[8]

b. **Maximum day range:** 4,000 m

c. **Maximum night range:** 2,500 m

18. In our assessment, when the border between the Gaza Strip and Egypt was breached, more weapons and ammunition were smuggled into the Gaza Strip, some of which might be more advanced than those currently in the Gaza Strip, including missiles and rockets with Tandem warheads.[9] Thanks to their greater range (from hundreds of meters to several kilometers), armor piercing capabilities, precision and destructive effect, the advanced anti-tank missiles pose a greater threat to the IDF's ACVs and infantry, and buildings in civilian areas or on IDF bases.

Explosives and IEDs

19. Since the Hamas putsch in the Gaza Strip, it has smuggled significant amounts of high quality explosives and raw materials for manufacturing explosives into the Gaza Strip. According to a report issued by the Israel Security Agency, between the takeover of the Gaza Strip in June 2007 and early 2008, Hamas smuggled in **at least 80 tons of explosives,** more than half the amount of explosives smuggled to the Gaza Strip since the disengagement.[10] That has resulted in the improvement of the performance of

---

[7] At the display of seized materials at the Intelligence and Terrorism Information Center there is one of the Sagger missiles seized on board the Karine-A. The Iranians scratched off the Iranian army emblem which was embedded in the missile.

[8] **Reactive plating** is a technology developed after 1967. It is an armor which reacts to an impact in such a way as to reduce damage to the vehicle fitted with the plating. Usually, reactive plating contains units of propellant explosives installed on the outside of the vehicle and explode on impact, making anti-tank weapons less effective.

[9] Two-stage hollow warhead.

[10] From a report published by the Israel Security Agency: "Summary of 2007—Data and Trends in Palestinian Terrorism."

IEDs as well as the artillery and anti-tank rocket warheads in the possession of Hamas and the other terrorist organizations.

20. Hamas also tries to imitate Hezbollah in its use of **IEDs: roadside charges and powerful underbelly charges.** Those IEDs are placed near or under roads to disrupt the IDF's combat maneuvers and take a heavy toll in human lives and weapons. Such IEDs can also be expected to be hidden in houses or other locations where the IDF is likely to carry out its activities. A prominent example was the explosion of a booby trapped house during activities conducted by the IDF in Beit Lahiya (August 1, 2007).

21. Hamas has in its possession a variety of charges, explosives, and detonation systems for use in a future confrontation:

i. **IEDs:** Hamas has a series of IEDs, including **fragmentation charges, shaped charges, and underbelly charges.** Those IEDs are designed to be used against IDF's exposed infantry and ACVs. They will be placed at the sides of roads, outside and inside cities. Hamas is independently developing shaped charges called **Shawaz** (Arabic for "flame"), with higher armor piercing capabilities than the charges produced by other Palestinian terrorist organizations. That is both the result of improved production quality and the use of more energetic explosives, based on know-how provided by Iran and Hezbollah.

ii. **Detonation system:** to activate the IEDs, Hamas makes use of various systems, some controlled by the operator (wireless or wired detonation systems) and some triggered by the victim.

iii. **Target-designated explosives:** Alongside the usual IEDs possessed by Hamas, there are also target-designated explosives for special tasks, such as a thrown charge with a grenade mechanism (which Hamas used in the abduction of IDF soldier Gilad Shalit). Other IEDs Hamas is likely to use are explosive break-in devices, such as a Bangalore torpedo, to overcome the border fence or the fence surrounding an IDF outpost or a population center.

22. Hamas (and the other terrorist organizations) now have **hundreds of anti-ACV charges** (plate, hollow, and underbelly) and **anti-infantry charges** (plate and peripheral fragmentation charge, Claymore). Shaped charges (Shawaz) have also been developed, but have yet to be implemented on a large scale.

Other Weapons, Ammunition and Military Equipment

23. Following the Hamas takeover of the Palestinian security services, the rifle stockpile of the military wing increased **from thousands to tens of thousands** (including millions of bullets). Hamas now has sufficient

amounts of small arms to increase the number of Hamas operatives in its military and security apparatuses.

24. Hamas and the other terrorist organizations have several units of **SA-7 shoulder missiles,** which have not been used so far (Hamas's entire air defense has so far consisted of firing machineguns and small arms at aircraft). There are also **dozens of** standard and improvised **sniper rifles, heavy machine guns also used for anti-aircraft fire, recoilless guns, binoculars and some night vision equipment**.

Part 5
Systems for Manufacturing, Developing and Smuggling Weapons

Self-Manufacture Systems

1. Hamas has in its disposal **an infrastructure for independent weapons and ammunition manufacture,** as well as for storage and delivery to combatants. The infrastructure includes several dozen operatives organized into professional work groups. Several dozen production sites are based in the Gaza Strip inside densely populated civilian areas. Weapons and ammunition are manufactured for offensive and defensive needs, and for carrying out terrorist attacks.

2. Over the past year Hamas operatives continued their efforts to independently produce a considerable portion of the weapons and ammunition they require for their terrorist activities, to reduce their dependence on smuggling. Hamas and other terrorist organizations have independent production capabilities.

3. Since it is situated in the heart of civilian areas, the production facilities expose the residents to risks due to attacks by Israel and to "work accidents." Thus, for example, on December 29, 2007, two "engineers" engaged in the manufacture of weapons were killed when a powerful IED exploded inside a residential building in the Gaza City neighborhood of Zaytoun. The explosion caused injuries to civilians and considerable damage to the building.

4. Key among the weapons produced in the Gaza Strip are:

i. **Anti-tank weapons,** including Hamas's manufacture of **Al-Yassin-type** anti-tank rockets (and launchers), a reproduction of the Russian **PG-2** anti-tank rockets.

ii. **Various IEDs, some of which may contain standard explosives:**

1) **Hezbollah's use of powerful IEDs in the second Lebanon war,** such as the incident in which IDF soldiers Eldad Regev and Ehud Goldwasser were abducted and a tank was destroyed, is an example

that Hamas seeks to follow. Notable in this context are shaped charges independently produced by Hamas (called **Shawaz),** with higher armor piercing capabilities than IEDs used by other Palestinian terrorist organizations. That is a result both of improvements in the quality of IEDs and of using more powerful explosives based on technological know-how provided by Iran and/or Hezbollah.

2) In the last months of 2006 such devices were exposed and operated on four occasions: two IEDs were found as part of an elaborate system uncovered on September 12, 2006 near the main road of the Gaza Strip; during Operation Autumn Clouds (October 31-November 26, 2006) four such IEDs were used against IDF forces in the town of Beit Hanoun. Hamas claimed responsibility for the incidents.

iii. **Producing artillery rockets for various ranges and manufacturing mortars and mortar shells:**[11]

1) As the terrorist organizations' spearhead, Hamas **has capabilities for producing a considerable variety of Qassam-class rockets for ranges of up to 13 km** and of improved rockets **for ranges of up to 19 km. In our assessment Hamas currently has several hundred rockets.**

2) Hamas's manufacturing facilities **constantly strive to improve rocket range** and the shelf life of independently produced rockets.

3) **The Palestinian Islamic Jihad** also independently produces rockets **(Al-Quds)** with characteristics similar to those of Hamas.

Weapons Smuggling Systems

5. Hamas and the other terrorist organizations obtain weapons and ammunition from various sources, some from Iran and Lebanon, and some from other countries, such as Sudan. In addition, the terrorist organizations acquire weapons and ammunition from Bedouins in the Sinai desert and from arms dealers operating outside the Gaza Strip. The weapons and the raw materials needed for independent manufacture are transported to the Gaza Strip by a network of smugglers from the Egyptian border, a lifeline for Hamas and the other terrorist organizations.

6. **Since the IDF's withdrawal from the Gaza Strip as part of the Israeli disengagement (September 2005), there has been a dramatic increase in weapons smuggling from Egypt into the Gaza Strip through the Philadelphi route.** The IDF forces operating along the Egyptian border were first replaced by Palestinian security forces belonging to Fatah. Now,

[11] For further information see our December 19, 2007 Bulletin entitled "Rocket threat from the Gaza Strip, 2000–2007" at http://www.terrorism-info.org.il/malam_multimedia/English/eng_n/html/rocket_threat_e.htm.

following the Hamas putsch of the Gaza Strip, its members patrol the border to facilitate weapons smuggling. The presence of Hamas forces and the ineffectiveness of the Egyptian security forces have left the border between the Gaza Strip and Egypt **wide open**, making it possible to carry out extensive smuggle activities with relative ease.

7. The **main** method of smuggling used by the terrorist organizations is the **network of tunnels** dug from Rafah to Sinai in the Rafah region and along Philadelphi road. The smuggling takes place through **scores of subterranean tunnels** connecting the Gaza Strip to Egypt. The extent of the tunnel network was demonstrated during IDF's activity in the Kerem Shalom region (October 30, 2007), in which eight tunnel entrances were located and destroyed.

8. The tunnels are used to smuggle weapons, military equipment, raw materials for independent weapons and ammunition manufacture and even funds (tens of millions of dollars).[12] Anti-tank missiles, standard 122 mm Grad rockets, dozens of tons of standard explosives, mines, anti-tank launchers, rifles and bullets have been smuggled into the Gaza Strip. In addition, the tunnels are used to smuggle terrorists from the Gaza Strip into Israel through the Israeli-Egyptian border.[13] The breach of the border fence at Rafah (January 22–February 3) reduced dependence on the tunnel network for a short time and allowed a massive influx vehicles laden with weapons and ammunition into the Gaza Strip.

9. Another smuggling method is the use of border crossings between Israel and the Gaza Strip, under cover of commercial or humanitarian equipment. That results in the absurd situation in which much of the raw materials used in the manufacture of the rockets and explosives used to attack Israelis originate in Israel (for example, **potassium nitrate** and sugar are the two basic substances used to create propellants for IEDs and rockets).[14] The use of potassium nitrate is therefore forbidden in Judea, Samaria, and the Gaza Strip; accordingly, the terrorist organizations attempt to smuggle it in by various ways and means.[15]

---

[12] Hamas is noted for its use of tunnels for smuggling funds. For example, in 2007, the military wing of Hamas received a significant portion of its budget, estimated at **tens of millions of dollars,** through the tunnels. The funds helped Hamas's military buildup in the Gaza Strip ("Summary of 2007: Information and Trends in Palestinian Terrorism," a report issued by the Israel Security Agency).

[13] For example, on July 3, 2007, Israeli security forces prevented a suicide bombing attack meant to be carried out in Beersheba when they detained a suicide bomber armed with an explosive belt. During interrogation the terrorist admitted that he had infiltrated Israeli territory from Sinai and the Gaza Strip. He had been instructed to locate a crowded place and carry out the attack there.

[14] In the past year, the Israeli security forces carried out special activities to prevent the transport of substances used as raw materials for the production of explosives into Judea, Samaria, and the Gaza Strip. Seized in raids carried out in the past year on five factories in Judea and Samaria were substances that are illegal to transport into Palestinian territory.

[15] For example, Egyptian security forces recently arrested in Rafah Mehdi Salim Abu Freij, residing near the border. Found in his house were over a half a ton of explosives and 1.2 tons of potassium. According to the detainee, those substances had been smuggled into the Gaza Strip through tunnels (Jerusalem Post, December 26, 2007).

10. The terrorist organizations operating in the Gaza Strip take advantage of the fact that Israel grants entry permits to Gaza Strip residents out of special humanitarian concerns (for example, life-saving treatments at hospitals). This is done in several ways, mainly by purchasing a fake medical authorization to undergo medical treatment in hospitals in Israel, Judea and Samaria, or elsewhere in the world. Israeli security forces are aware of several doctors and administrative workers in Gaza Strip hospitals who issue authorizations in exchange for bribe.[16]

11. Most of the weapons smuggling into the Gaza Strip is done by **independent smugglers and traders driven by financial motives.** At times, there is no particular buyer before the smuggling, and the smuggled goods are sold on the open market to the highest bidder. Some of the weapons smuggling activity is carried out on demand for a particular organization (mostly Hamas). **Following the Hamas takeover of the Gaza Strip, Hamas has tightened its control over the weapons smuggling system from Sinai into the Gaza Strip.**

12. The **funds** necessary for the acquisition of weapons (and the military buildup process in general) are introduced by Hamas into the Gaza Strip in covert ways, mostly through money changers and traders in the Arab world. Terrorist organizations also make extensive use of the tunnels to smuggle large sums of money, up to tens of millions of dollars on each run.

Part 6
Training in the Gaza Strip and Abroad (Iran, Syria and Lebanon)

1. Hamas's military buildup also includes training and qualification to increase the professional skills of operatives from all levels and in all occupations. Hamas has a core of several hundred highly-trained operatives who have undergone basic and advanced military training, specializing in such areas as anti-tank weapons, small arms, machineguns, sabotage, etc. Those operatives have acquired fighting skills that allow them to engage in personal combat, squad combat and possibly in larger-scale battles as well.

2. Operatives belonging to the Hamas military wing undergo intensive, systematic training **in the Gaza Strip,** which includes **elementary training** (fitness, rifle shooting and field training) an advanced **professional training** in sniping, anti-tank warfare, intelligence and artillery. Elementary training is held **in the Gaza Strip** and taught by local instructors (some of whom were trained abroad). The advanced professional training is given

[16] From the ISA's "Summary of 2007: Information and Trends in Palestinian Terrorism." Two potential female suicide bombers were detained at the Erez Crossing in May 2007. They had been given an authentic entry permit to Israel, based on false medical information. The two were planning to carry out a double suicide bombing attack in Tel-Aviv and Netanya.

abroad: in Iran, Syria, and Lebanon (through Hezbollah). At the same time, **operatives of the internal security services** (the Executive Force, the police, etc.) also undergo basic and advanced training in the Gaza Strip and elsewhere (Iran and Syria), preparing them to serve in Hamas's military wing in an emergency.

3. Following the Hamas putsch in the Gaza Strip, as part of the acceleration of its military buildup, Hamas operatives were sent to training courses in Iran and Syria. The operatives were smuggled back into the Gaza Strip and transferred the know-how and skills they had acquired to operatives belonging to the Hamas's operative wing and internal security services.

In 2007, Hamas undertook the most extensive and significant training effort in the history of its military wing in order to improve its operative capabilities.

4. On March 9, 2008, the British Sunday Times published an interview by reporter Marie Colvin with a senior Izzedine al-Qassam Brigades operative in the Gaza Strip, who did not identify himself by name (even though his description appears in the article). The interviewee shed light on the training undergone by Hamas operatives outside of the Gaza Strip:[17]

i. **Hundreds of Hamas terrorist operatives have trained and are training in Iran:** The Iranian Revolutionary Guards have been training them in Tehran for more than two years, ever since Israel withdrew from the Gaza Strip in August 2005 (i.e., since the disengagement). **So far 150 have finished their training. An additional 150 are currently there,** improving their fighting skills. Some of them will return as fighters and others, who are not fit to fight, will join Hamas's "research unit."

ii. **The route to Iran:** Hamas operatives leave the Gaza Strip and enter Egypt, from there they fly to Syria and from there to Tehran. Entering and leaving Tehran they are permitted not to have [their passports] stamped, for security reasons.[18]

iii. **Length and location of training:** Hamas operatives train for periods lasting **between 45 days and six months.** The training takes place at a closed military base under difficult conditions and is supervised by Revolutionary Guards. The operatives are allowed off base only once a week, and even then only in a group and accompanied by Iranian security personnel.

17 For further information see our March 17 Bulletin entitled "Senior Hamas operative figure tells London Sunday Times' Gaza Strip correspondent about Iranian and Syria military aid" at http://www.terrorism-info.org.il/malam_multimedia/English/eng_n/html/hamas_160308e.htm.

18 That was also the case in the past with Hezbollah operatives who left for training in Iran. For example, Hussein Ali Suleiman, a Hezbollah terrorist operative captured in the second Lebanon war, said that he had trained in Iran with a group of 40–50 Hezbollah operatives from Lebanon. He said that the men in his group avoided having their passports stamped in Syria and Iran to hide the fact that they had gone to Iran for training.

iv. **Training subjects:** Hamas operatives undergo training in **tactical warfare and weapons operation** and return to the Gaza Strip with the skills they acquired in advanced technology, rocket launching, detonating explosive charges, sniping and other military tactics, **similar to those used by Hezbollah.**

v. **So far seven groups of Hamas operatives have been sent to Iran.** The best students in each group remain in Iran for longer periods, participate in advanced courses and return to the Gaza Strip to serve as **instructors.**

vi. **Training in Syria:** Hamas operatives from the Gaza Strip are also sent to **Syria** for basic training. So far **600 Hamas terrorist operatives** have been trained in Syria by instructors who learned their techniques in Iran. **There are currently 62 terrorist operatives training in Syria.**

Part 7
The Lessons Hamas Learned from the Most Recent Round of Escalation

1. The latest round of escalation in the Gaza Strip (February 27–March 4) was the most intense confrontation between Hamas and Israel since the movement took over the Gaza Strip in June 2007.

2. Between February 28 and March 3, 2008, **207 rockets landed in Israeli territory,** most of them launched by Hamas. The preferred target was (as usual) the city of **Sderot** (which was hit by some 100 rockets); **however, it was the first time that Ashkelon and its immediate vicinity was also intensively targeted** (Hamas fired 18 standard 122 mm Grad rockets). The daily average was about 30 rockets. Hamas also fired standard 120 mm mortars.

3. The large number of rockets Hamas launched in several days indicates **that it possesses a significant rocket arsenal.** Of particular note is the **relatively large arsenal of standard 122 mm Grad rockets,** which for the first time allowed Hamas **to continuously and systematically fire on the city of Ashkelon** (120,000 residents).

4. However, Hamas was surprised by Israel's reaction, mainly by the ground operation in the northern Gaza Strip ("Hot Winter") in which some 70 terrorist operatives and the terrorist infrastructure were hit. Accordingly, Hamas and the other terrorist organizations were unable to carry out mass casualty attacks against the IDF. In addition, the IDF struck major locations, disrupting the production and transportation activities and resulted in the loss of operatives and infrastructure.

5. **Politically,** Hamas was able to emphasize its ability to dictate the internal Palestinian and Israeli-Palestinian agendas, particularly in view of Abu

Mazen's statement that the political negotiations with Israel had been put on hold. Of particular note was Hamas's success (joined by Abu Mazen's Palestinian Authority) in the **battle for hearts and minds:** Hamas and the Palestinian Authority waged a media campaign which emphasized the casualties caused to civilians, mainly children, while totally ignoring the rocket fire on Israel and the fact that most of those killed (about 130) were terrorist operatives.

6. The campaign made extensive use of terms like "holocaust" and "massacre," comparing the Holocaust of the Jewish people to the "holocaust" of the Palestinians in Gaza. The campaign did not obtain significant media attention in the West, but it had considerable influence among the Palestinians and in the Arab and Muslim world (one of the causes was the massive support given to the Palestinian campaign by the popular Al-Jazeera TV channel). The campaign's success again demonstrated to Hamas the importance of **developing its media capabilities** (to which the movement allocates considerable resources) **and has again shown that the battle for hearts and minds could play a significant role in any future confrontation in the Gaza Strip**.

7. In the latest escalation, Hamas made **extensive use of the civilian population as human shields,**[19] usually receiving the population's support. That was reflected by fighting in densely-populated urban areas, with Hamas operatives dressed in civilian clothes to blend into the population. In some cases, civilians helped Hamas by gathering in sites where IDF attacks were expected, in order to serve as human shields.

8. **Summary:** Hamas could learn both positive and negative lessons from the last round of escalation. On the positive side, it succeeded in consistently and systematically launching rockets at Israel, extending the rockets' range to Ashkelon, and it had victories in the battle for hearts and minds. On the negative side, the escalation demonstrated the existence of preparedness gaps in Hamas's combat system and the toll taken by a large-scale confrontation with Israel.[20] **The calm that has settled on the Gaza Strip will allow Hamas to continue its military buildup** while repairing the damage and overcoming the weak spots which became apparent during the latest round of escalation.

---

[19] For further information see our March 6 Bulletin entitled "During the last round of escalation in the Gaza Strip the terrorist organizations again made extensive use of Palestinian civilians as human shields" at http://www.terrorism-info.org.il/malam_multimedia/English/eng_n/html/human_s_e.htm.

[20] Izz al-Din al-Qassam Brigades spokesman Abu Obeida gave an interview several months before the escalation, saying that upon entering the Gaza Strip, the IDF would encounter trained warriors and new combat tactics, guided and coordinated by a joint operations room. "The Israeli army will not be able to tell where its tanks were hit from and where rockets were launched at its soldiers from," he said (Al-Hayat, December 17, 2007). **In retrospect, it seems that his statement was rather exaggerated.**

DOCUMENT NO. 4

HOW NOT TO MAKE PEACE: "CONFLICT SYNDROME" AND THE DEMISE OF THE OSLO ACCORDS

United States Institute of Peace (USIP) Report
Peaceworks No. 57

March 2006

Robert L. Rothstein

Summary

The failure of the Oslo Accords has been attributed to a variety of factors, including deficiencies in the accords themselves, failures of implementation, and the play of domestic politics. These are all critical factors that describe *what* happened, but they do not explain *why* each side behaved as it did—that is, why each side made choices that would only increase the likelihood of the accords' failure. To understand why each side behaved as it did, we must first understand the "conflict syndrome" that affected the negotiating and decision-making process—a syndrome that is, to varying degrees, present in many protracted conflicts. While the conflict syndrome is never the sole cause of failure in any given peace process and does not affect every conflict in the same way, the significant role it often plays in perpetuating conflict is frequently ignored or undervalued.

Conflict syndrome consists of a set of attitudes, assumptions, and beliefs that become embedded over decades of bitter conflict and are difficult to unlearn even if some kind of peace agreement—or exploratory truce—has been signed. The individual elements of the syndrome are familiar, but, taken as a whole, they exert a powerful influence on most peace processes and inform the choices each side makes. Thus, distrusting the opposite side's motives by default, cheating for fear of being cheated, making only tentative concessions that can easily be revoked, and asking the other side to prove its good faith by making large initial concessions, among other things, generate a peace process that can easily become a "race to the bottom."

This implies that the stop-and-go, on-and-off, crisis-driven peace processes in the Middle East and elsewhere should not be taken as aberrations: they are the norm that should be anticipated and planned for.

This argument has clear policy implications. Premature ceremonies on the White House lawn and inflated rhetoric that raises expectations too hastily need to be avoided. The search for quick solutions and "last negotiations" is likely to lead to a return of bitter discord. To solve the Middle East conflict, a carefully calibrated peace process—described herein as "gradually accelerating incrementalism"—is needed. Architects of such a process must recognize that elements of the conflict syndrome still persist in the Middle East and will for years to come, that high-risk/high-gain negotiating strategies in such a context are bound to fail, and that demands for stricter compliance with commitments can and should increase as the process begins to provide both sides with tangible evidence that it can produce mutual benefits and is worth preserving.

Acknowledgments

I would like to thank John Crist of the United States Institute of Peace for his support and advice throughout the process of editing a much longer manuscript into a shorter form. I would also like to thank Kurt Volkan, my editor.

1. Introduction

Many Israeli and Palestinian politicians and intellectuals came to recognize certain basic facts in the decade before the signing of the Oslo Accords: neither side could defeat the other, at least at an acceptable cost; the overall costs of the conflict to both sides were staggering; parts of both communities were beginning to exhibit "battle fatigue" and a strong desire to live a "normal" life; and the general outlines of a painful but bearable compromise solution—some details aside—had been apparent for many years, indeed perhaps from the partition formula of 1947. Although extremists on both sides totally rejected any compromise, majority support had been growing for some kind of mutually bearable settlement. Put differently, "rational actors" should have seen a clear interest in compromise and the marginalization of extremists. Why then did the Oslo peace process disintegrate so rapidly, and why did a conflict that had moved beyond its earlier existentialist phase return to it so savagely—and perhaps irredeemably?

The conventional explanations for Oslo's failure, some of which will be discussed below, are better at elucidating what happened during the process rather than why the accords collapsed. One could also argue that such explanations represent partial narratives of Oslo's fate rather than the whole story. To get at the roots of the Israeli-Palestinian conflict one needs to look at more than the details of any failure to agree on Jerusalem, refugees, or borders—and the Palestinians' inability or unwillingness to stop terrorism. One must also examine the tacit and unstated assumptions about the nature of the conflict itself that became embedded over time and seemed to mandate policy responses virtually guaranteed to undermine an already fragile peace process. In short, these assumptions generated patterns of behavior that deepened the conflict and produced a kind of Gresham's Law of protracted conflict: extremists drove out moderates. In such a context, one "easy" explanation for the failure of the peace process—specifically, that one needed Nelson Mandela and FW de Klerk but got Yasser Arafat and Benjamin Netanyahu—misses the deeper point that even strong and wise leaders might have chosen badly or felt compelled to make the same kinds of mistakes attributed to their weaker brethren. However, I am *not* arguing that a conflict's unstated assumptions totally determine outcomes: there are factors that can diminish or overcome such assumptions, as appeared to happen in South Africa in the early 1990s, but these factors are not always present or sufficiently powerful.

The unstated assumptions of a conflict affect the judgment of each side and are likely to affect how difficult questions that hover over any negotiating process are answered: Can the other side ever be trusted? Is real peace possible? Will any agreement offer more than a temporary truce in a continuing existential conflict? Can the ancient attitudes and beliefs that have sustained and deepened the conflict ever be transformed, especially after a seemingly endless exchange of atrocities? And will the leader(s) of the other side be able or willing to expend the necessary domestic political capital on developing enough support for an agreement that involves significant concessions? In any case of protracted conflict, these questions will have no ready answers, but the embedded assumptions of the conflict will heavily affect how these questions are interpreted, evaluated, and answered. Certain risk-reduction techniques and third-party guarantees may mitigate against negative answers to these questions—negative answers are likely in the early stages of any peace process—but such techniques and guarantees are themselves imperfect. Indeed, they may slow a process down at the point where it most needs to provide evidence that the peace is worth preserving.

The tendency to answer such questions negatively while undergoing a peace process helps to explain why apparently sensible compromises are often rejected and why the possibility of a compromise peace is often seen as a third-best option to some future outright victory or a familiar but bearable status quo, especially among elites living in relatively comfortable exile. In effect, war can become "domesticated"—that is, people learn to live with it. This normalization is facilitated—as the Sudanese case illustrates—by "the insulation of the country's elites . . . from the cruel havoc . . .

wreaked on millions of ordinary people."[1] Additionally, in some cases, certain constituencies may benefit more from the continuation of the conflict than from its resolution.[2]

Although the Oslo peace process was a failure, it did have a number of (potentially) redeeming features that can be built on by future peacemakers. In particular, certain leaders and segments of the public on both sides recognized that there was a preferable alternative to a bitter—and deteriorating—stalemate, that the historical problem of two people claiming a single territory could only be resolved through the equitable division of territory, and that working out the terms of this division and establishing new rules for peaceful coexistence were the central tasks of the peace process. While such progression fell well short of "breaking the genetic code" of the conflict, to borrow the words of Moshe Ma'oz, Oslo did lay down footprints for later negotiators to follow—even if they insist that Oslo's only useful lessons are about what not to do.[3] Either way, the Oslo experience will have shaped perceptions of what can and should be done in the future—and many of the tacit and explicit agreements reached during the Oslo years will affect the substance and atmosphere of any future negotiation. The Oslo peace process may have suffered an ignominious death but the lessons of that demise are still relevant—if frequently ignored.

2. Oslo's Demise: The Search for Understanding

Three general factors are frequently cited as having been primarily responsible for Oslo's demise.[4] The first concerns deficiencies in Oslo's terms. For example, Henry Siegman has argued that Oslo—and the current "road map"—suffered from a failure to spell out in detail what the Palestinians would get at the end of the process if they implemented their own promises effectively, thus reducing their incentive to comply in the earlier stages.[5] By implication, therefore, the negotiators missed a unique opportunity to

[1] William Finnegan, "The Invisible War," *New Yorker*, January 25, 1999, 66.

[2] See Finnegan, "The Invisible War," 70; for Sri Lanka see Robert L. Rothstein, *The Sri Lankan Peace Process: Lessons from the Middle East and Northern Ireland* (Colombo: International Centre for Ethnic Studies, 2002), 22–3.

[3] For Moshe Ma'oz's comment, see his "The Oslo Peace Process: From Breakthrough to Breakdown," in *The Israeli-Palestinian Peace Process*, ed. Robert L. Rothstein, Moshe Ma'oz, and Khalil Shikaki (Sussex, UK: Sussex Academic Press, 2002), 146.

[4] The Oslo peace process did not, of course, occur in a vacuum. It was preceded by many negotiations, large and small, official and unofficial, and it has been followed by many more such efforts. My concentration on Oslo is thus not intended to deny the importance of these other initiatives.

[5] Henry Siegman, "A 'Map' without a Destination," *International Herald Tribune*, October 9, 2002.

reach a much stronger agreement that would have generated greater willingness on both sides to comply with its terms.

However, specifying details about core issues from the start would have destroyed the peace process before it even began and would have generated immense domestic opposition on both sides. Oslo was not a peace *settlement* but rather an exploratory truce that seemed to offer some hope of gradually changing the psychological environment of the conflict and opening, if tentatively, a new set of opportunities to move forward on substantive issues. However, such opportunities were easily missed or misinterpreted by weak leaders, particularly because they were forced to make decisions in a dangerous and uncertain environment. In this sense, Oslo was not intrinsically a "bad" peace doomed to fail or a "good" peace that guaranteed each side would attain enough of its central goals to make implementation increasingly likely. Rather, it was an imperfect product of its times, the most that could be gotten at that particular stage of a bitter protracted conflict.

The second factor that led to Oslo's demise involved escalating and reciprocal failures of implementation. With inevitable uncertainties about the shape of a final agreement and pervasive distrust, neither side was willing to take great risks for peace and each side demanded that the other prove its good faith before making major concessions of its own. This was a recipe for disaster, not least because neither side made plans to deal with the inevitable failures to implement. Stricter compliance mechanisms might have helped, but they were not included in the accords, perhaps because the negotiators were so enthused about what they had accomplished that they ignored how problematic implementation was likely to be. Both sets of negotiators may have also believed that Arafat would never accept strong commitments on compliance. While failures to implement surely contributed to Oslo's rapid decline, this explanation does not account for why such failures became endemic to the process and sheds little light on the underlying cause.

The third—and perhaps the most important and widely cited—factor that contributed to Oslo's failure involved the impact of domestic politics on the process. While leaders are central to the negotiation process and make key decisions, public support is critical for deepening and sustaining any agreement. But what leaders and their associates expect or get from an agreement may be very different from what the public expects or gets. In the case of Oslo, the public did not see any immediate, substantial, or widespread benefits from the agreement and, therefore, was reluctant to bestow legitimacy on it. Each side also tended to see the other as being more unitary and monolithic than it actually was and thus did not seek potential allies on the other side, missing certain opportunities. As a result, sharp and escalating internal conflicts and declining popular support for the peace process made its collapse practically inevitable.

Central to each of the above factors is the decision-making style of the leaders themselves. Leaders weakened by a failure to produce substantive gains, to bring the conflict to a successful conclusion, and to deal with threats—real or imagined—of revolt by coalition partners, see deep risks in every decision they make. As a result, they often adopt a decision-making style that I call "negative satisficing."[6] Specifically, weak or weakened leaders begin to make last-minute decisions, fudged as much as possible, that offend the least number of actors who have the power to do them harm. Therefore, in negotiating a risky peace with an enemy that cannot be trusted, leaders often decide by deciding as little as possible. Indeed, from the perspective of Israel and the United States, Oslo failed largely because Arafat was incapable of or unwilling to make peace, perhaps because he could not deal with the prospect of having his rhetoric of ultimate triumph thrown back into his face. If true, his death should open new possibilities of reviving the peace process—and there are tentative signs that it has done so. But one must not jump too quickly to the conclusion that the major obstacle to peace has now been eliminated or, conversely, that nothing much has really changed. To understand some of the complexities of the current situation, one must first understand Arafat's vices and virtues as a leader.

Arafat: The Enigmas of Leaders

Neither Arafat's limitations as a leader nor the weaknesses of Palestinian institutions were the sole domestic problems impeding implementation of the accords. The weak coalition governments of Israel also made progress difficult, focusing the leaders' attention on internal negotiations to stay in power and generating doubts in the Palestinian community about the credibility of Israeli promises. These doubts only grew when Likud leaders asserted that they would not be bound by Oslo's principles should they return to power. In addition, Israeli society was split almost evenly between factions opposing and supporting the peace process, especially after violence surged during the Peres-Netanyahu election campaign. This made it very difficult for any leader to assemble a strong constituency for peace. However, I choose to focus on Arafat's role in the failure of Oslo because he was in power throughout the process and because he alone could decide whether to support or undermine Oslo's principles. Further, his decision to support the use of violence, his refusal to oppose Palestinian terrorist groups in a serious manner, and his illegal importation of arms directly threatened the process and destroyed the peace movement in Israel.

[6] Herbert Simon's well-known notion of "satisficing" implies choosing the first good enough option, but my adaptation of his idea rests on a strategy of avoidance and of choosing the least harmful option. See Herbert Simon, *Models of Bounded Rationality* (Cambridge: MIT Press, 1982), 35–64.

Arafat's leadership has been severely criticized not only by Israel and American sources but also by some leading Palestinian and Arab sources.[7] Dennis Ross, the former U.S. Middle East negotiator, has been particularly unflattering, as has been Bill Clinton.[8] The picture that emerges is of a leader firmly looking backward, unable or unwilling to make decisions that might generate internal dissent, and unable to adapt or learn in response to new opportunities. Why then did he accept the Oslo Accords, which did not guarantee the achievement of any Palestinian goals, but refuse to accept the flawed but much more promising Clinton-Barak offers at and after Camp David? Presumably he accepted Oslo because it provided him with real resources, such as foreign aid, international recognition as *the* leader of the Palestinians, and access to the White House, and gave him some breathing room at a moment when his power and standing were being challenged, without requiring the relinquishment of any central goals. Conversely, he rejected the Clinton-Barak offers—which included potentially significant concessions by Israel—because accepting them would have required a much more open sacrifice of some critical goals and would have generated much more domestic opposition among Palestinians. In short, Oslo's low-risk/low-gain strategy was more acceptable than Camp David's high-risk/high-gain strategy to a risk-averse, suspicious, and reluctant decision maker. To be fair, Arafat never had a strong hand to play and was never in complete control of all the Palestinian groups. Thus, while some of his actions may have appeared irrational to external observers, they may in fact have been rational and prudent in the context of his desire to remain in power and to avoid overt challenges to Palestinian unity.

A more malign interpretation of Arafat's behavior argues that he was never serious about the peace process and lied about his intentions from the day the accords were signed. Such motives are suggested in the comments of one experienced Palestinian journalist, who noted, "Arafat always described the Oslo process as the rape of the PLO. . . . He always presented the agreements . . . to his people as at best a short-term truce."[9] This interpretation also seems to explain some decisions by Arafat—and the Palestinian Authority—that otherwise seem perverse. These include his continued rhetoric to his people that the "jihad continues"; his refusal to stop his

[7] Some of the most negative views have been summarized in Dilip Hiro, *Sharing the Promised Land—An Interwoven Tale of Israelis and Palestinians* (London: Hodder and Stoughton, 1996), 485. Negative views by the Saudi ambassador to the United States are quoted in Elsa Walsh, "The Prince," *New Yorker*, March 24, 2003, 58. Negative criticism within the Palestinian community is cited in Steven Erlanger, "Arafat Outfoxes His Political Foes—Again," *International Herald Tribune*, August 17, 2004.

[8] See Dennis Ross, *The Missing Peace: The Inside Story of the Fight for Middle East Peace* (New York: Farrar, Straus and Giroux, 2004), 338, 699, and 776; and Bill Clinton, *My Life* (London: Hutchinson, 2004), 943.

[9] Quoted in David Horowitz, *Still Life with Bombers: Israel in the Age of Terrorism* (New York: Alfred A. Knopf, 2004), 116–17. The Palestinian journalist also notes that when Arafat saw that Israel had been forced out of Lebanon by twenty deaths a year, he decided he could do better than Oslo by launching a new and more violent intifada and by happily calling for a million "martyrs."

media from spewing out anti-Semitic propaganda, to change school textbooks that did not recognize Israel's right to exist, and to confront any of the Palestinian terrorist organizations; his indifference toward the inept performance of the authority under his control; his illegal creation of multiple security forces as a nascent army; and his illegal importation of vast amounts of arms. Such actions are not designed to build a constituency for peace or to convince the enemy that a real commitment to peace has been made.

There is a revisionist school that justifies Arafat's failure to accept Clinton's "final" offer in January 2001 and that instead blames Ross, Clinton, and Ehud Barak for not offering more and for being vague on details.[10] However, such criticisms seem tendentious and insufficiently contextual. For example, proponents of this school ignore Arafat's pattern of behavior after Oslo, they ignore the fact that *no* agreement at that time was going to be anything but imperfect, and they seem so concerned to point out its flaws that they forget that what *was* on the table offered the Palestinians far more than any previous—or subsequent—offer. Further, accepting the agreement would have kept the negotiating process alive and potentially made it even more productive. Did resorting to a brutal and immoral strategy of indiscriminate terrorism produce more for the Palestinian people? What better alternative do the revisionist critics have in mind, particularly given the constraints set by Oslo's failure and the declining domestic support for the peace process in both camps? Because the revisionist critics do not provide meaningful answers to these questions—or offer a superior and politically feasible alternative to what was offered at Camp David—their indictment is not convincing.

However, the very image of Arafat with a clear strategy of manipulating Oslo to prepare for the resumption of conflict is not entirely persuasive and does not fit very well with his image as a cautious, reactive, and indecisive leader whose vision was entirely tactical and who decided most things by not deciding. He was also never a dictator who could impose his views by fiat, and he seemed to value unity, even superficial unity, over what seemed likely to be the small gains of the peace process. Yet, despite the limitations of his power and his own limitations as a leader, he can be fairly blamed for a number of things: he failed to anticipate the consequences of his actions and inaction; he deliberately launched a vicious terrorist campaign that hurt Israelis but hurt his own people far more; he played into the hands of the Israeli right-wing; he largely destroyed the Israeli peace movement; and he did not understand that he needed to stabilize and to deepen the peace process before trying to take advantage of it.

[10] See, for example, Jerome Slater, "The Missing Pieces in *The Missing Peace*," *Tikkun* 20, no. 3 (2005): 22–25 and 58–61.

As a result, this combination of weak leadership, a flawed peace agreement, and pervasive distrust generated a race to the bottom of the peace process: prudent actions to lower risks and delay commitments on crucial issues created a downward cycle that neither could nor would be arrested. It is important to understand, however, that even stronger and wiser leaders may have become trapped in this cycle because both sides suffered from what I call "conflict syndrome." Specifically, deeply embedded beliefs, assumptions, and attitudes affected how policy was set and how decisions were made. This syndrome is likely to continue to affect the post-Arafat negotiating process, although *perhaps* with less power. It is also important to remember that, despite Arafat's deficiencies as a leader, he had two very important characteristics that may be sorely missed in the near term: he managed to keep a fractious Palestinian community more or less unified, and he and only he had the standing to impose a compromise agreement on his community—if, a big if, he had the will to do so.

3. The Intrinsic Nature of Peacemaking in Protracted Conflicts

Expectations about what peace or a peace process will bring are crucial to its survival. Therefore, incorrect and inflated—or deflated—expectations about what Oslo would produce are a major reason why it failed. At least some of the errors of the past decade could have been avoided and some of the individuals or groups on both sides intent on destroying the peace could have been thwarted if both sides had more clearly understood what to expect from Oslo and what kind of policies they needed to pursue to give Oslo a better chance of becoming a step toward peace, not a step backward. In effect, while the complexity of the issues on the negotiating table, the limitations of the accords themselves, and domestic political constraints all contributed to Oslo's failure, how each side thought about and conceptualized the peace process and what they expected from it may have been the determining factor in its demise.

Although Arafat may have been an incompetent leader blundering from one disaster to another, and Netanyahu and Ariel Sharon may have been deliberately trying to undermine a peace process they did not believe in, the cognitive framework that they each took for granted made it very difficult for them to make better decisions and stronger commitments to the peace process. Such an argument also provides a different perspective on the controversial issue of why Arafat turned down Clinton's final offer in January 2001. Specifically, Arafat may not have turned down the offer *solely* because of the ostensible inadequacies of its terms but also—if not largely—because of the attitudes, assumptions, and beliefs that he had developed over decades of bitter conflict. These beliefs, in turn, predisposed him to see only traps, deceit, risks, and losses. Please note that this is not a deterministic theory: there are too many factors in play and too many uncertainties to allow for precise predictions.[11] However, the concept of conflict syndrome offers insight into how such peace processes are likely to evolve and what ought to be done to help a fragile peace survive and deepen.

This syndrome—or cognitive framework—not only leads to actions and policies that intensify conflict but also makes the halting or reversing of a downward cycle of violence exceptionally difficult once begun. In the abstract, one might reasonably conclude that such a downward cycle ought not to occur. After all, in the case of the Israeli-Palestinian conflict, the political, economic, and psychological costs have been monumental and obvious to both sides, and the desire on both sides to live a normal life is pervasive. Further, compromise is not unthinkable to shifting majorities on either side: the outlines of a two-state solution are well known and various official and unofficial negotiations have gotten close to reaching bearable compromises on even the most controversial issues. Why then do we now seem even further from agreement? John Darby has asked and answered the same question in regard to Northern Ireland: "So why has the crisis in Northern Ireland not been resolved, either with a compromise settlement or genocidal carnage? The answer is simple. There has been no resolution because the violence has not been intolerable. By whatever calculus communities compute their interests, the price of compromise is still thought to be greater than the cost of violence."[12]

My answer, however, is quite different. Nothing in the process of trying to end a bitter, protracted conflict is quite that simple or quite that amenable to rational calculation of costs and benefits—if such are indeed "computable" by weakened leaders in a complex environment of choice. Even if the costs of violence exceed the costs of compromise in the minds of the leadership and some followers—perhaps even among a majority—stable peace may still be unachievable. There are a variety of reasons for this: those who lose from peace will resist it; leaders may be primarily concerned with staying in power and thus reluctant to risk internal dissent; peace may not resolve or significantly diminish some of the underlying problems that drive the conflict; and—as just noted—mind-sets ingrained after decades of conflict may still persist even after a nominal peace has been negotiated.

All conflicts are to some extent socially constructed. Therefore, more is at stake than resolving a clash of interests or even enlarging the joint benefits of peace: each side needs to alter the way it thinks about the conflict and its

[11] This concept is in the realm of pretheory, that is, of plausible hypotheses that might someday make a contribution to theory.

[12] Quoted without attribution at the beginning of Paul Arthur, "The Anglo-Irish Peace Process: Obstacles to Peace," in Robert Rothstein, *After the Peace—Resistance and Reconciliation* (Boulder, CO: Lynne Rienner, 1999), 65.

future relationship with the opposing side. I will examine certain aspects of this conflict syndrome, but it should be noted that the following discussion is somewhat stylized. The below elements apply to the Israeli-Palestinian case very well most of the time for most of the participants, while they apply to other cases more or less well—and yet others only loosely.

Primary Aspects of Conflict Syndrome

Oslo was really an exploratory truce that would have led to stable peace only if the leaders had understood the nature of the task they confronted, worked to develop public and cognitive legitimacy for an agreement that was largely procedural and incremental, and managed to contain and marginalize extremists. Oslo, like the Dayton Agreement on Bosnia or the Good Friday Agreement on Northern Ireland, largely left all the central issues unresolved. In such agreements, risks and uncertainties are so high that one cannot expect either side to make a full commitment to them: initial offers are likely to be hedged and minimal; doubts about the other's willingness or ability to offer more or to implement commitments are generally great; each side has reasonable fears about the other side's ability to get a substantive agreement through domestic political processes; and both sides are ultimately unhappy about the terms of any agreement and constantly seek to push its limits, renegotiate its terms, and get the other to move first. The parties to the conflict, in effect, seek to use the peace process for their own ends; actually achieving real peace may not rank very high on their list of priorities. Further, the agreements themselves may be open-ended and masterpieces of ambiguity and imprecision. This may be necessary to get the parties to sign an initial agreement, but ultimately this lack of clarity and precision may make it difficult to deepen and legitimize the peace process. Moreover, such agreements may also lack a self-correcting mechanism that can restore equilibrium and arrest a cycle of retaliation and revenge. These problems are compounded by the fact that such negotiations are obviously intensely political for both sides and directly affect the fate of the current leadership and real or potential opponents.

Most protracted conflicts reach a stage where both sides believe no solution is possible. For example, a U.S. official speaking at the height of the Bosnian conflict noted, "I don't think there is a solution to it. It's becoming clear that the Bosnian war simply has to be managed. We have to try to keep the violence at a tolerable level. This approach does not come easy because we, as Americans, are used to solving problems. But this one is insoluble."[13] Political scientists have made similar claims with regard to other conflicts. Sumit Ganguly has said of the conflict in Kashmir that it has seemed "impervious to resolution," and Richard Rose made the same point

[13] Quoted in *New York Times*, April 16, 1995.

about Northern Ireland some years ago.[14] Additionally, Bernard Crick proclaimed in 1989 that the conflicts in South Africa, the Middle East, and Northern Ireland were equally insoluble because no internal solution could satisfy the announced principles of either side and because an externally imposed or enforced solution would only strengthen the desperation of extremist groups.[15] More recently, some have so despaired of a solution to the Israeli-Palestinian conflict that they have advocated an externally imposed solution or argued that the conflict can only be "managed" and not resolved.[16] After so many failed attempts at resolution, these views are hardly surprising, but they also tend to affect the pattern of expectations around any tentative peace agreement. How can any agreement that resolves so little and requires the cooperation of an untrustworthy enemy overcome the anticipation of failure?

The absence of empathy is an additional element of the conflict syndrome that is often ignored or undervalued. Defined as a demonstration of an accurate and nonjudgmental understanding of the other's needs, interests, and perspectives, empathy is a learned characteristic;[17] it is virtually impossible to learn it in an environment of hatred and bitterness, where each side seeks to inflict pain on the "devilish" other. There is rarely an effort to try to see the world through the eyes of the other or to try to show the other that you understand what he is saying even if you do not agree with it. An expression of empathy—particularly if it is perceived as credible and sincere by the other—is valuable because empathy is the basis of most moral judgments: it may begin the process of diminishing distrust, and it may begin a useful process of communication, as distinct from an exchange of rhetorical barrages. In its absence, therefore, demonization of the other persists, distrust deepens, and exchanges are superficial and sometimes

---

[14] Sumit Ganguly, *The Crisis in Kashmir: Portents of War, Hopes of Peace* (Cambridge: Cambridge University Press, 1997), 2. Rose is quoted in John McGarry and Brendan O'Leary, *Explaining Northern Ireland: Broken Images* (Oxford: Blackwell, 1995), 354.

[15] Quoted in Adrian Guelke, "'Comparatively Peaceful': South Africa, the Middle East and Northern Ireland," in *A Farewell to Arms? From 'Long War' to Long Peace in Northern Ireland*, ed. Michael Cox, Adrian Guelke, and Fiona Stephen (Manchester, UK: Manchester University Press, 2000), 226. Ironically, within a few short years after Crick's negative forecast, a successful peace process was under way in South Africa, progress toward peace accelerated in Northern Ireland, and the Oslo Accords were negotiated—so, difficult yes, but "insoluble" maybe not.

[16] Shlomo Ben-Ami, foreign minister under Barak, argues for an externally imposed settlement in "Bush's Mideast Opportunity," *New York Times*, April 5, 2002. Another argument for an imposed solution in a big bang negotiation is Hussein Agha and Robert Malley, "The Last Negotiation: How to End the Middle East Peace Process," *Foreign Affairs* 81, no. 3 (May/June 2002): 10–18. The title of this piece is absurd for there will be no "last" negotiation in the Middle East, big bang or not, and the "end" might be considerably different from the authors' pious hopes for an imposed settlement. See the comments by Tom Segev on management as the only remaining option in Roger Cohen, "Israel's Wall, a Victory for the Logic of War," *International Herald Tribune*, July 14, 2004.

[17] There is a useful discussion of empathy in Robert Mnookin, Scott R. Peppet, and Adam S. Tulamello, *Beyond Winning: Negotiating to Create Value in Deals and Disputes* (Cambridge: Belknap Press of Harvard University, 2000), 46–7. For other illustrations of the absence of empathy, see Cohen, "Israel's Wall," 2, and Arthur, "The Anglo-Irish Peace Process," 75–84.

cynical or hypocritical—consider Arafat's expression of disapproval of terrorist actions that he himself had condoned or ordered. As a result, discussions about bringing an end to the violence usually revolve around its tactical costs—often concerns such as "it is losing us support" are voiced—and not about the moral evil of deliberately murdering innocent citizens of the other. This also has a practical consequence: one side always fears that the other will return to violence if it does not get its way, which implicitly implies that peace itself is only a tactic.

A related element of the syndrome is the sense of humiliation, loss of pride, and loss of face—especially among the weaker side—that deepens and sustains the desire for revenge and for recapturing past glories.[18] This, and the tendency of each side to construct biased and one-sided historical narratives that are taken on faith and are sometimes impervious to rational argument, leads to the embedding of distrust into the warp and woof of the conflict itself. Attempts by revisionist historians—usually only on the more powerful side—to construct a less tendentious and less emotional story also contribute to suspicion and doubt between the sides. The dangers of this are exacerbated by the tendency of each side to parse the other's rhetoric literally and to ignore the need to situate it contextually in terms of domestic or other needs and pressures.

One general implication of this argument is that reluctant and tentative commitment to a low-risk/low-gain strategy is intrinsic to the endgame of protracted conflict. Perhaps even the notion of an endgame is misleading because the game will go on for many years and notions of a "last" negotiation are dangerously naive. Generosity will be limited, demands to dot every "i" and cross every "t" will be pervasive, fighting over every inch of territory or every symbolic concession will be nasty, and leaders will be under pressure to display toughness and to rationalize why they say one thing to one audience and something else to another. Fearing failure, leaders will also try to protect against risk to themselves and to the peace process, in that order. Moreover, as demands increase because of rising costs—and perhaps premature euphoria—and if or as these demands are not met, attitudes will more likely be shaped by unattained aspirations than by whatever real, positive achievements may have been registered: the glass will thus always seems half-empty and progress, if it has been achieved, will be undervalued. Such a peace process is in trouble from the start. Merely keeping it alive will require strong leadership, substantial external support, the absence of negative shocks, such as the assassination of a leader, and a good bit of luck. In effect, the peace process will itself

[18] Avishai Margalit, *The Ethics of Memory* (Cambridge: Harvard University Press, 2002), 120 and 130, stresses the extent to which humiliation lasts longer than physical pain because the wounds of the former last much longer and because it "becomes constitutive of our sense of who we are."

be little more than conflict by other means and will persist only as long as its immediate benefits exceed its costs and no important sacrifices have to be made.

In such an environment, leaders will fear appearing weak or losing face, especially those who have themselves been weakened and are confronting challenges from domestic opponents. These fears will make it difficult—if not impossible—for a leader to back down or to compromise, thus thrusting the need to do so on the other side. Fear here will not be a spur to innovative thinking but, rather, a spur to rigidity, conspiratorial thinking, and perhaps even excessive personalization of the conflict. Max Frankel, in a recent book on the Cuban missile crisis, notes, "For the roots of crises, look to powerful men feeling vulnerable and underestimated. Their dread of weakness, even imagined frailty, begets belligerence."[19] Frankel later illustrates this point by describing President John F. Kennedy's reaction to Soviet leader Nikita Krushchev in the lead up to the crisis, in which he reportedly said, "[Krushchev] can't do that to me"—that is, place Soviet missiles in Cuba.[20] Such fear-based belligerence may have had something to do with the IRA's long-standing refusal to disarm, and it may have been *part of* the reason Arafat never made a serious effort to control various terrorist groups. These attitudes are not exclusively limited to the weaker side—both sides can be fearful and insecure—but they are presumably more prevalent in the side that is or sees itself as weaker and thus more vulnerable.

Therefore, the stop-and-go, off-and-on, crisis-driven negotiating process that developed after Oslo—and other such agreements, mutatis mutandis—was not simply the result of flawed leadership, bad draftsmanship, and unpredictable political events. Rather, this kind of erratic and unstable peace process was unavoidable: one should not be surprised that leaders will not take risks—why should they?—and that they act with mental reservations and a readiness to pull back quickly. Architects of future agreements must *anticipate and prepare for* a process that loses momentum, that is dominated by last-minute decisions on the edge of an abyss, and that staggers inconsistently from one crisis to another. They must also understand that reciprocal fears of cheating will be widespread, that cheating before being cheated will be the (apparently) prudent default strategy on both sides, and that the race downward will be far more likely to accelerate than decelerate.

---

[19] Quoted in a review by Ben Macintyre, "Eyeball to Eyeball," *New York Times Book Review*, November 28, 2004, 9.

[20] Ibid. Historian Peter Galison's description of the Cold War's "ontology of the enemy," in which each side saw the other as a "cold-blooded, machinelike opponent" who wanted only to win and whose every move reflected that goal, recalls my ideas on conflict syndrome. Cited in Louis Menand, "Fat Man," *New Yorker*, June 27, 2005, 97.

As noted earlier, policymaking in this context is likely to become a form of "deciding by not deciding" or, more generally, of "negative satisficing." The primary focus may well be on containing domestic opposition and pacifying external supporters rather than on making peace with the enemy—which may in some ways be less of a threat to the leader. Leaps of faith into a brave new world are likely to seem bearable only to strong leaders very sure of their domestic base—and external critics and analysts who value peace above all other virtues and who do not have to run the risks of betting on the wrong horse. Moreover, as conditions deteriorate and human and material losses mount, both sides may return to an existential phase of the conflict and begin to inflict pain and retribution on the other no matter the damage to the prospects for peace. Issues that could or should be treated dispassionately will be treated as symbolic, make-or-break demands—such as the right of return. Additionally, the process will be fueled by the leaders' absence of empathy for the other and their need to manipulate issues to rationalize their own failures.

Other Aspects of Conflict Syndrome

In situations where conflict syndrome is firmly rooted, traditional bargaining strategies are unlikely to work well because of the difficulties of working out pragmatic trade-offs on emotionally fraught symbolic issues. An intensely competitive form of distributional bargaining is likely to develop, meaning asymmetrical benefits in favor of the weaker side in the early stages of the process may be very difficult to negotiate. Additionally, fear of being duped will hinder the needed cooperation for a successful peace process, and so too will the presence of a perverse form of reciprocity: returning good for good will be inhibited by doubts about the "good," leading the exchange of bad for bad to become the norm. With an anticipation of failure, the ability to encourage cooperation through repeated games may also well be lost. Thus, interest in long-term cooperation between the two sides will be limited, particularly without reliable information about the other's intentions and actions.

Another factor that may inhibit both cooperation and the implementation of an agreement is that there may be a large gap between the intentions of the negotiators and the intentions of the people on the ground who have to carry out agreed policies in daily encounters with the citizens or officials of the other side. Specifically, the people who interact at this level, such as border guards, employers, and security personnel, may be reluctant to cooperate or change familiar patterns of interaction. The result is not only a failure to cooperate effectively but also an increase in hostility.

Traditional negotiating strategies will also be problematic because negotiating away ingrained patterns of thought and action is almost impossible, although some paths may be established at this stage that begin the process of "unlearning" what has "stood to reason" for so long. In addition, some of the standard negotiating lessons that have been extrapolated from other arenas—for example, environmental or trade negotiations—are not easily applicable in the context of bitter and protracted violent conflicts. Commonsensical notions that treaties must be self-enforcing—that is, each party must see a clear interest in implementing it—and must contain incentives to alter self-interested patterns of behavior do not work well in protracted conflicts: agreements such as Oslo are not self-enforcing because each side assumes the other will cheat and therefore decides it must cheat first. As a result, incentives to comply are weaker than incentives to fake compliance.

This model of protracted conflict reflects not only the social-psychological notion of entrapment but also cognitive notions about how to conceptualize protracted conflicts and policy notions about what can or cannot be done at any stage of a peace process. The entrapment model argues that decision makers sometimes pursue bad courses of action to justify or rationalize costly prior commitments that have not produced promised results.[21] Thus, they may become overinvested in counterproductive initiatives to deflect charges that sacrifices have been in vain. This model helps to explain why demands increase and tactics harden as costs go up and the need for compromise becomes ever more apparent, particularly to those outside the inner circle of decision makers, who suffer from "incestuous amplification." Fear of losing face and admitting fundamental errors of judgment are also crucial in entrapment, which means that the rationalization of past mistakes often plays a larger role in decision making than rational analysis. Getting out of such a psychological—and political—trap is obviously difficult, especially with weak leaders, since taking a longer-term perspective on current policy decisions or changing cognitive patterns of thinking is likely possible only if the leader can be shown clear benefits to and few risks for himself.

However, the entrapment model does not fully explain all aspects of the perpetuation of a conflict, since other domestic and external factors may be important, and the other side's tactics may compel policy responses that deepen the conflict and make talk of an exit strategy an exercise in futility. For example, the "long-war" strategy of attrition adopted by many rebel organizations, in which they demonstrate a greater willingness to accept casualties and losses than their more dominant opponents, may force a government into policy responses that simply dig a deeper hole for each side. A sustained terrorist assault, as with the Palestinians during the al-Aqsa intifada, may also achieve the same end. Still, the entrapment model

[21] There is an excellent discussion of entrapment in Joel Brockner and Jeffrey Z. Rubin, *Entrapment in Escalating Conflict: A Social-Psychological Analysis* (New York: Springer-Verlag, 1985).

does provide a useful starting point for understanding why leaders choose courses of action that seem guaranteed to make a bad situation worse. Consider briefly Arafat's support of a terrorist strategy that made peace less and less likely and Netanyahu's and Sharon's continued support for settlement activity that isolates Israel, encourages terrorism, sharply divides Israel itself, and helps to foster anti-Semitism in Europe and the Muslim world.

Although this model of protracted conflict does anticipate bad faith, it also attempts to explain why some of the familiar techniques to reduce the risks of cheating are likely to work badly or fail to produce intended effects. The mere act of signing a peace agreement will not change the attitudes and beliefs that have sustained a conflict. Thus, after a fragile exploratory truce has been negotiated, new policies and patterns of thought will be needed to deepen the peace. Making commitments that are binding, credible, and irreversible—or at least seem so to the other side—will also be necessary. However, in some cases, simple and self-committing gestures, such as Egyptian president Anwar Sadat's visit to Jerusalem, might even be rejected outright by the other side out of distrust.

When the negotiating process appears to have reached a dead end and the parties seem incapable of negotiating seriously with each other, there is inevitably a demand for third-party intervention, especially from the United States. Such intervention may indeed be useful or even necessary—as in Northern Ireland and Bosnia—since, as a vast literature has made clear, the third party may perform a variety of services that facilitate successful negotiations. However, caution is needed before advocating mediation or other forms of external intervention. At times, mediators may have interests of their own that could complicate the negotiating process, or they may not fully commit to the process, causing damage to it by abandoning it in a sensitive moment. Additionally, adaptive learning between the parties may be short-circuited and neither side may feel much ownership of a peace process that is at least partially imposed.

Perhaps an even bigger problem with third-party intervention is illustrated by this comment about Iraq by a UN official: "Iraq needs to be liberated—liberated from big plans. Every time people mentioned it in the last few years, it was to connect it to big ideas—the war against WMDs, solving the Arab-Israeli conflict, the war against terrorism, a model of democracy. That's why all these mistakes are made. They're made because Iraq is always, in someone's mind, the first step to something else."[22] Similarly, Richard Bourke has said of the Good Friday Agreement that it was regularly represented as a stepping-stone "along the road to something better."[23]

[22] Quoted in George Packer, "Letter from Baghdad: War after the War," *New Yorker*, Nov. 24, 2003, 85.
[23] Richard Bourke, *Peace in Ireland: The War of Ideas* (London: Pimlico, 2003), 307.

Put simply, third parties may feel the need to view the resolution of a given conflict as a "first step" to justify a costly intervention or to pursue a deeply held ideological fantasy, but such attitudes may also mean that the particularity or density of a conflict may be ignored or misunderstood. As a result, sometimes parties to a conflict are better off trying to resolve it themselves. For example, successful peace negotiations in South Africa were carried out directly by the two sides with very little external intervention.

The Limits of Conflict Resolution

There is a curious theme in some of the literature on resolving protracted conflicts. For example, Bourke "calls into question the usefulness of the instruments we have devised for ending conflicts. . . . [These tools] encounter the unpredictable disposition of passion and interest, of dissidence and vanity . . . [and thus] cannot consequently be rationalized into a technique."[24] Similar complaints have been made in both Sri Lanka and the Middle East about the usefulness of all the apparently commonsensical advice about, and approaches to, conflict resolution proffered by most would-be peacemakers. This raises an interesting question about why much of this material, which can appear perfectly reasonable on an analytic level, does not seem to work as well as anticipated in the "real" world of protracted conflict. One might argue that the literature often focuses on the wrong issues to begin with: it is not the clash of interests or the political constraints on leadership *by themselves* that explain success or failure. Such notions as the management of expectations, empathy, fear, distrust, and the equality of esteem also need to be taken into account. These abstractions, of course, are not on the negotiating table, at least not in any direct fashion. Often within the literature there is also an asymmetry between the search for usable generalizations across a large number of cases—a normal academic concern—and the need to account for the unique context and peculiarities of each particular case. There may also be a tacit or implicit notion among some students of conflict resolution that all right-thinking people would naturally prefer peace to war and compromise to the continued pursuit of likely unattainable goals. But the fighters have many goals and peace may not be the highest of such goals. The fighters may also work with different time horizons and different evaluations of costs and benefits, all of which make rational, interest-based analysis inherently problematic. Put differently, the clash of interests is real and consequential but conflicts are sustained and deepened over long periods because they are also socially—and psychologically—constructed. It is this dimension of conflict that must be dealt with if there is to be a serious hope of success in conflict amelioration, let alone resolution.

---

[24] Ibid., 18.

Finally, the set of assumptions, attitudes, and beliefs that characterize the syndrome tends to generate a conflict analogous to a breeder nuclear reactor that creates its own fuel. Once begun, such conflicts create their own internal momentum as "grievance and counter-grievance make compromise more difficult and violence more cyclically intense."[25] The fire is hard to extinguish—to shift the metaphor—just as many underground coal mine fires are hard to extinguish, because it fuels itself through embedded, deeply felt, learned, and relearned "lessons of our history." A fragile peace agreement will hardly even begin to challenge these lessons, even though they pose a mortal threat to the survival of any agreement.

All Is Not Lost: Some Negotiating Successes

While Oslo made the Israeli-Palestinian conflict worse and peace less likely, peace processes in protracted conflicts are not doomed to failure. In fact, a few protracted conflicts have been successfully resolved and others have at least been diminished in effect for some period of time. In South Africa, for example, the two parties negotiated a reasonable compromise peace to a seemingly intractable conflict that granted the black community majority rule and the white community continued economic power and some temporary political power. The settlement was far from perfect and its implementation has been flawed, but it has persisted and remains better than the alternative of continued conflict. Why did this peace process succeed, almost to the consternation of many experts? One answer is that the negotiators created a "peace culture" based on tolerance and jointly agreed-upon codes of conduct. More important, de Klerk and Mandela were in control of their domestic constituencies and committed to the notion of a compromise peace. In addition, a bottom-up revolt by the black population—along with the pressure of international sanctions—finally convinced the white community that continued resistance would eventually prove too costly and ultimately futile. A strong civil society had also developed over the years and it too became committed to the notion that peace was in everyone's interest.[26] Unfortunately, in the Middle East, Arafat was not committed to the notion of a compromise peace, leadership on both sides was weak, and Arafat worked to undermine the civil society that had begun to develop in the West Bank and Gaza after the first intifada.[27]

---

[25] Richard English, *Armed Struggle: The History of the IRA* (London: Pan, 2003), 359. Michael Doran has noted that "In the Middle East, as in the Balkans and Ireland, suppressed religious and ethnic groups have a kind of film playing in their minds of their own oppression. In moments of political disruption, they are ready to add another scene to the pre-existing narrative." Quoted in Robert F. Worth, "In Iraq, a Tug of War over the Truth," *New York Times*, April 24, 2005.

[26] I draw here on Patti Waldmeir, *Anatomy of a Miracle* (New York: W. W. Norton and Company, 1997).

[27] For a critical analysis of the failure of Arafat's leadership of the Palestinian Authority after Oslo, see Glen E. Robinson, *Building a Palestinian State: The Incomplete Revolution* (Bloomington: Indiana University Press, 1997).

The Northern Ireland case also provides an interesting comparison to Arafat's refusal to accept the less-than-perfect but still unprecedented Clinton-Barak offers. The Good Friday negotiations in 1998 presented the IRA and Sinn Fein with a final offer that gave them far less than they had sought and indeed less than they had already rejected in the Sunningdale Agreement of 1974. Why then did they accept it? While the end of the Cold War and Clinton's active involvement played an important role in their decision, as did the realization within the IRA and Sinn Fein that a military stalemate existed, that they could make real gains from peace, and that demography was on their side,[28] these factors do not fully account for their acceptance of the agreement. What seems to me to be the dominant factor in the decision is that the IRA and Sinn Fein leadership, especially Gerry Adams, learned from the past and was able to adjust and adapt to new conditions and new opportunities—that is, even though the IRA lived by the gun for decades, Adams realized that you do not have to die by the gun if you prepare the way for change and are willing to take some internal risks for peace when an opportunity arises.

The peace process in Northern Ireland has since floundered, although even in its current uncertain state conditions on the ground for both communities are vastly better than they are in the Middle East. The Northern Ireland case illustrates, at least tentatively, that some of the worst effects of the conflict syndrome can be diminished by intelligent leadership, strong external support, and some willingness to learn from the mistakes of the past. It is very encouraging, for example, that the IRA acceptance of monitored disarmament in early October 2005 was followed a few weeks later by an announcement that two Protestant militias had agreed to end a violent feud and that one of the militias had ordered its gunmen to stand down—a potential move toward "taking the gun out of politics" both within and between the two sides. Caution is still imperative because of rampant criminality on both sides and because of continued suspicions and resistance by Protestant hard-liners, but progress toward peace, however fitfully, has clearly taken a step forward.

Conflict Syndrome and Doubts about Negotiations

Taken individually, the hallmarks of conflict syndrome are not unknown in conflict resolution literature: they have appeared and will continue to appear in discussions of protracted conflict. Rather than being seen as discrete elements of a conflict, however, they must be taken as a whole, as a powerful syndrome that influences how each side sees itself and the other, what each side takes for granted about appropriate rules of behavior and normative standards, what attitudes and assumptions are embedded in the

[28] For an insightful discussion of these issues, see English, *Armed Struggle*, 307–15.

peace process, and what policies seem sensible or prudent. Thus, the syndrome affects not only long-term conflict resolution initiatives but also the very warp and woof of the negotiating process—if there is one—and the pattern of regular interaction. Most critically, the syndrome generates a peace process built on the anticipation of failure and an unwillingness to take large risks for peace, particularly if peace is perceived as merely a transitory stage, before the resumption of conflict, that is unlikely to produce large gains.

Dennis Ross has stressed that the failure to transform attitudes was one of the most important factors in Oslo's failure. He notes, "In the absence of transformed attitudes, mythologies were perpetuated, not challenged. Leveling with publics about compromise was avoided. The climate so necessary for rationalizing or explaining hard concessions was not created."[29] This argument is fully justified, but the argument herein goes well beyond the need to transform attitudes, as crucial as that surely is. Conflict syndrome also includes tacit and explicit assumptions about the nature of the conflict and patterns of belief about anticipated and appropriate behavior. As Ross's words suggest, we must understand in greater analytical depth the consequences of the syndrome so that its effects can be contained and confronted—especially, as the next section will make clear, in the early stages of a peace process.

This argument also implies that the management of expectations—a critical task for leaders—will be exceptionally difficult. Expectations affect how information is processed, what information is sought, and how parties interact. Negative expectations grow in intensity as conflicts deepen and reciprocal atrocities and rising costs begin to influence all calculations. This suggests that weak leaders may feel compelled to promise too much too quickly to overcome domestic resistance and to generate a constituency for peace, which means that disappointment and despair will rapidly undermine the peace process, especially one that is top-down and elite-driven. Conversely, if a leader deliberately keeps expectations low—both his own and the public's—there will be little change in patterns of behavior and a quick return to "conflict as usual." And the absence of empathy and each side's focus on its own victimization strongly increases the likelihood of missed signals and misperceptions.

Further, there is a kind of metaphysical doubt that shadows negotiations to end protracted conflicts, doubt that emerges from the syndrome's attitudes and assumptions. For example, if your experience with the other—and experience is the primary source of trust or distrust—is that the other has lied and not fulfilled commitments in the past, that the other has used

[29] Ross, *The Missing Peace*, 764.

earlier cease-fires to regroup and to prepare for the resumption of conflict, that the other consumes concessions as a preface to making new demands, and that the other often acts in bad faith, you may have legitimate fears and suspicions that the other will continue to act in such a manner. Such a dynamic has been at work not only in the Israeli-Palestinian negotiating process but also in negotiations between enemy groups all over the world. For example, just as Israelis were wary of Arafat's commitment to peace—and the Palestinians question the real motives of Israeli leaders—so too have Protestants doubted the IRA's true intentions and Tamils distrusted the Sinhalese.

Why then join the negotiating process at all? If one gains benefits from a peace process but not from a compromise peace, or if one feels strong pressures from crucial allies or domestic proponents of peace, why not replace doubt and ambivalence about the possibilities for peace with outright cynicism, opportunism, and manipulation to gain tactical leverage? There is no single overarching answer to these questions: perhaps every leader or leadership group answers them according to some complex, shifting, and uncertain evaluation of the costs and benefits of either taking some real risks for peace—or, more likely, not taking them. Pressure and promises of support from needed domestic and external allies and bottom-up pressure from the grassroots who suffer from battle fatigue and who desire to lead a normal life are also a part of this complex calculus. Domestic pressure has seemed to have had positive effects—at least indirectly—in the resolution of conflict in Northern Ireland and the Basque country, but not in the Middle East, where conditions are so desperate that hopes for peace have seemed a mirage.

Perhaps more critically, the leader may feel that the status quo is bad and likely to get worse and that it is better to run the risk of generating domestic dissent now rather than later or of dealing with the current leader of the opposition rather than with potentially more radical successors. Other factors may also diminish doubts among leaders about signing and implementing a risky agreement. For example, some failures to implement are to be expected at the start of any peace process because the terms of any initial agreement are likely to be ambiguous and each side will try to take advantage of these ambiguities. In turn, awareness among leaders that this is likely to happen will allay some fears and moderate against overreactions to certain instances of noncompliance by the opposing side. Therefore, nondecisive failures to implement should be noted but not stressed early in the post-agreement period. Additionally, as *nonimplementation* can cause a leader to lose a reputation—or not gain one—for trustworthiness, aware leaders may be less inclined to grossly violate an agreement, particularly for fear that his or her tarnished reputation may adversely affect any future negotiations. And, as there are a variety of techniques available to decrease vulnerability against the dangers of non-compliance, leaders may sign a preliminary agreement as a way to test the intentions of the other.

In short, even a peace process that one or both sides think is doomed to fail may generate a degree of political, economic, and psychic investment that might slowly accumulate into genuine support for peace. For example, even presumably untrustworthy leaders may come to enjoy a new status as a peacemaker, resource recipient, and legitimized spokesman for the cause. Or new leaders may emerge who protest the loss of earlier opportunities—as happened with the growth of internal opposition to Arafat among some young leaders. However, much will depend on the propensities of the leaders, the degree of risk they are willing to take, their judgment about the strength of the opposition, their assumptions about the future, and—above all—their alternatives to risking peace. Clearly, it is unlikely that any but the strongest leader will fully commit to a fragile and imperfect peace without fearful mental reservations. Israel's peacemakers at Oslo may seem to refute this point because they were so optimistic about what they had achieved, but that very optimism, if not naivete, may have contributed to—but not caused—the ensuing disaster.

The Oslo Accords: Why They Failed

The belief that the Oslo Accords were a major step toward the final resolution of the Israeli-Palestinian conflict is now a "shattered dream."[30] Despite repeated official efforts to restart the peace process, despite apparently endless unofficial and semiofficial efforts by notables on both sides to work out the terms of a final agreement, despite the fact that the rough outlines of a compromise settlement that seems preferable to the status quo have been obvious for many years, despite the staggering and mounting costs of the conflict, and despite the widespread awareness that the conflict could get worse and make any settlement impossible, finding a path out of the swamp of despair and bitterness has proven too difficult for even the most dedicated of peacemakers, let alone the ambivalent and fearful peacemakers of the region itself. Indeed, the notion that the conflict has no solution is widely prevalent once again and self-styled realists insist that conflict management is the only prudent alternative. Oslo, with all its imperfections, deserved a better fate.

Why did this happen? Difficulties, delays, setbacks, misunderstandings, reluctant and tentative efforts to stumble forward, and other problems were inevitable. Agreements that resolve bitter, protracted conflicts are rarely going to offer an elegant progression into a brave new world of peace

[30] The quoted phrase is from Charles Enderlin, *Shattered Dreams: The Failure of the Peace Process in the Middle East, 1995–2002* (New York: The Other Press, 2003), 235.

and reconciliation—or normalization, as the Israelis always hoped. But total failure and a peace process that made a return to an even more destructive conflict ever more likely were not inevitable. That level of failure is not attributable to a single cause. To fully understand why Oslo failed, we need to understand how the leaders and public alike came to conceptualize what to expect from the peace process, how the other was likely to behave, and how they themselves had to behave to protect their interests and advance their cause. From this perspective, what seemed to be a rational and sensible compromise in the eyes of outside analysts—and peacemakers—could also seem to be a high-risk venture into dangerous and uncharted territory to the parties involved. The status quo may have been bad, but it was rarely unbearably bad for leaders in safe exile, for those who benefited from the conflict, or indeed for ordinary citizens who adjusted to living within its constraints—even those set by an apparently endless stream of suicide bombers. Moreover, the dangers of the status quo were known and usually manageable.

While conflict syndrome was decidedly *not* the only factor that made progress toward stable peace so difficult, it did compound the negative effects of the other more widely cited factors for Oslo's failure. Although the costs of the conflict have been staggering and the outlines of a mutually beneficial—if also painful—agreement are apparent, the psychological and political constraints of the syndrome generated largely negative dynamics, creating and then exacerbating patterns of behavior that accelerated the race to the bottom. However, stronger and wiser leadership on both sides could have at least slowed the deterioration of the process and—with cooperation between them—perhaps even gradually reversed the downward trend, thereby strengthening the peace. But, as fate would have it, the failure of leadership made the constraints of the conflict syndrome even worse, leading the process to end in a disastrous fashion.

4. Resurrecting the Peace Process: Uncertainty and Hope

Despite the apparently mortal wounds that have been inflicted on the Oslo peace process, there are a number of astute and experienced analysts who insist that the peace process can be resurrected and that a mutually acceptable compromise peace is still within reach. These analysts tend to believe that the major obstacle to peace is the continued Israeli occupation of the West Bank and the continued and badly disguised efforts to increase the size of key settlement blocs. They also believe that Arafat's successors and the Palestinian people will accept the two-state solution as definitive. The evidence for this is fourfold: (1) polls seem to show that roughly 70 percent of the Palestinian people now support a two-state solution and believe that they can live in peace with Israel after their own state has been established;

(2) various unofficial negotiations have been successful in reaching agreement on even the most controversial issues on the negotiating agenda, such as the right of return; (3) a new leadership is gradually emerging within the Palestinian community that may ultimately replace the dispiriting and corrupt leadership of the past, although there are obvious conflicts over who can or will lead and in what direction; and (4) battle fatigue and a desperate desire to lead a normal life have begun to affect both communities, which may generate more support for at least thinking about the unthinkable—a compromise peace that will require some sacrifice of sacred goals on both sides.[31] Some analysts also argue that even for Israelis who distrust the peace process, the idea of hunkering down behind the so-called security wall, which separates Israelis and Palestinians and encompasses many West Bank settlements, might seem less prudent than taking a risk on peace, especially given the new dangers of catastrophic terrorism and virulent Islamic fanaticism.

There are, however, some reasons for doubt and skepticism about reaching a compromise peace in the near term. For example, there are contrary polling numbers that suggest that a majority of Palestinians now want not only the land Israel captured after the 1967 war, but all of mandatory Palestine—that is, they want the destruction of Israel as soon as possible. In effect, in a familiar dialectic, the grievous losses the Palestinian people and the Palestinian Authority have suffered in the ongoing intifada seem to have increased demands for greater compensation and diminished any willingness to compromise for peace. The Palestinian community has also expressed massive support for the continuation of terrorism despite the fact that it has made most Israelis less willing to compromise and has generated widespread support for the construction of the aforementioned security wall, which in some areas intrudes beyond the 1967 boundaries into Palestinian territory, making compromise even more difficult. The wall may even generate sharp internal conflict in Israel if it fails to protect most settlements.[32]

Equally troubling, even some Palestinians who are within the peace camp have clearly indicated that they will not recognize Israel's right to exist as a legitimate Middle Eastern state, a denial that suggests any peace will only be regarded as a temporary stage in a continuing conflict. For example, moderates such as the late Faisal Husseini have occasionally made statements suggesting that the ultimate aim of the Palestinian movement is the destruction of Israel. Further, Hamas and other terrorist groups have consistently indicated that they will oppose any peace with Israel; their

[31] For various comments supporting these views, see Glen E. Robinson, "Being Yasir Arafat: A Portrait of Palestine's President," *Foreign Affairs* 82, no. 6 (Nov./Dec. 2003): 138; Avi Shlaim, *The Iron Wall—Israel and the Arab World* (London: Penguin Books, 2000), 517ff.; Baruch Kimerling and Joel S. Migdal, *The Palestinian People* (Cambridge: Harvard University Press, 2003), 317ff.; and Agha and Malley, "The Last Negotiation."

[32] For this polling data, see Horowitz, *Still Life with Bombers*, 99–100.

ability to undermine or even destroy a fragile peace process by continued atrocities that generate increasingly harsh retaliation by Israel is already evident. It is far from clear whether a renewed peace process would be able to withstand such actions and reactions. In addition, the new scale and magnitude of the terrorist threat, coming not only from the terrorists' willingness and potential ability to use weapons of mass destruction, but also from the increasing radicalization of parts of the Muslim world, suggest that Israel may have to employ policy responses that further alienate Palestinians and its neighbors.

A continued domestication or normalization of the conflict among Israelis and Palestinians also makes it less likely that a comprehensive peace will be possible in the near term. People adjust to the war, internalize its costs, and learn to live with it—as Israelis have learned to live with suicide bombers and Palestinians with socioeconomic deprivation, if with real costs in both cases. Pressures on the leadership to "do something" or to take risks for peace will diminish and, indeed, as the entrapment model implies, the pressure to increase the level of violence may escalate, if only to rationalize past expenditures in lives and resources. This means that the stalemate between the two sides will be hard to break and that keeping it from being a race to the bottom will be difficult, precisely because the stalemate is not unbearable. The closer the stalemate comes to being unbearable, however, the likelier it will be to generate demands for revenge and retaliation—no matter the costs. The creation of a security wall might help Israel to lower the threat of terrorism and thus to continue living with a nasty but bearable status quo, but other means of terrorism, pressure from abroad, and continuing economic decline may soon force Israel to recalculate its interests—and, one hopes, resume a peace process with new leaders on both sides.

However, even if a new agreement were to be negotiated that avoided some of the mistakes of the Oslo process—for example, by making much clearer what the Palestinians would get *from* the peace—and even if external powers promised massive and continuing amounts of aid and support, the Palestinian state that emerged *might* not be viable: providing jobs and other basic human needs for the citizens of the West Bank and Gaza, as well as those who return from the refugee camps, will be a massive undertaking. It will be especially difficult because the educational system has been hampered for some time by a lack of resources, a loss of schooling time, and an environment hardly conducive to the educational process. This may, of course, only be a transitional problem, given the talents of the Palestinian community, but it does imply the existence for some time of a cadre of young people still prone to destabilizing violence. If the new state begins to perform as badly as Arafat's Palestinian Authority, discontent will be quickly generated and the likely outcome could be a renewed demand to capture the land "between the Jordan and the sea." While these negative considerations may be as unstable or ephemeral as the positive considerations suggested by the peace camp, they should not be ignored in the wave of euphoria that will inevitably be generated by a new agreement, even one that seems to resolve the most contentious issues.

Still, however the pluses and minuses of these contrary views are calculated, even a tenuous agreement that might make matters worse in the short or medium term is a better gamble than persisting with the disastrously failed policies of the past. Such an initiative might break a futile stalemate that benefits neither side and might begin to break down the idea that the only solution is no solution until one side is strong enough to win. Put differently, the disasters and frustrations of the years since Oslo was negotiated have obviously made peace vastly more difficult to achieve, and this may not be a "ripe moment"—whatever that over-used phrase is taken to mean—to seek to restart the negotiating process. But peace desperately needs to be sought now not because it is a good alternative but because it is a better alternative than any other possibility—a perspective that recalls Churchill's famous quip about democracy. Despite the pessimistic arguments just cited, nothing is written in stone, neither the arguments of the optimists nor those of the pessimists: leaders change, the views of allies evolve, some beneficial learning may go on even where it is not immediately apparent, and surprises and shocks that alter cognitive and political universes are always possible, if not probable. Even where conflict resolution remains a distant dream, conflict amelioration is always a possibility. Still, a note of caution is needed: a "bad" peace could raise expectations too high, could increase support for extremists if it failed, and could generate a moral hazard as the parties turn to other agendas. Awareness of these dangers may help to avert them—and help to focus attention on the need to deepen the peace process.

The Role of Third Parties

The episodic and inconsistent involvement of third parties in the Oslo peace process—bar the important but largely procedural involvement of the Norwegians—does not seem to have been a major or decisive factor in its demise. Even powerful third parties such as the United States cannot compel ambivalent and distrustful enemies to implement an agreement that is domestically divisive for both and that is inherently unclear about its final destination. But the situation has become so desperate and the belief that the Israelis and the Palestinians can themselves negotiate a way out of the conflict has sunk so low that some analysts have advocated leaping over the difficulties by imposing a solution from the "outside-in."[33]

[33] See Agha and Malley, "The Last Negotiation," 18. They also argue, or rather assert, that the deal itself will create trust where none existed, a dangerous assumption with no evidence to support it.

However, third-party interventions generally tend to come too late and to be of limited value for a number of reasons: early warnings about the need for intervention are ambiguous; rallying domestic support for interventions that are costly and not clearly related to an immediate national interest is difficult; the need to intervene may clash with other interests; and the parties themselves may resent and resist unwanted interventions. As a result, "big bang" negotiations do not always end happily, especially when strong minorities bitterly oppose necessary concessions. The Dayton Agreement, for example, is still very tenuous; the conflict could quickly reignite if the peacekeeping forces were removed. There may also be a kind of moral hazard in assuming that only external intervention can resolve a conflict. It relieves the participants of the obligation to take some risks for peace or to explore ways out of the disaster that their own policies have created—letting the "big guy" do it is too easy an option. Further, the failure of incremental peacemaking in the past hardly means that an imposed "big bang" negotiation will produce better results. In fact, given the persistence of old patterns of thought and behavior, a diktat could disintegrate even more rapidly than a slow, step-by-step peace process.

However, not all external interventions or cases of imposed peace are necessarily bad. There is some contrary evidence to suggest that external involvement can be useful in determining which demands should be compromised and which demands need not. Additionally, a third party (or parties) can provide useful political cover and substantial resource transfers at a critical point in the peace process. Nevertheless, external salvation is not a panacea and has not always been useful. As the economists are wont to say, it all depends. This is a universe of fuzzy logic and multidimensional patterns of causation—no single solution is likely to be uniformly adequate.

One final illustration from the peace process in Northern Ireland may be indicative of this point. The editors of *A Farewell to Arms?* note that Good Friday did not occur because of harmony or because each side saw discussion and compromise as better than violence and intransigence. Rather, they note,

> It would be comforting to report that there had been a meeting of minds; that peace was the natural result of a rapid growth of that most valuable piece of scarce political real estate—the middle ground. . . . But it did not happen like that. . . . There was no Road to Damascus conversion to the other side's point of view, no sudden outbreak of moderation, but a long and very painful, and as yet incomplete recognition that the old means of achieving desired ends would not work or were no longer acceptable to those upon whom the opposing camps depended for support.[34]

[34] Cox, Guelke, and Stephen, "Introduction," in *A Farewell to Arms?*, 1.

The peace process was therefore bound to be lengthy because many felt it was either an illusion or a mere interlude in the conflict; in effect, it engendered as much hostility as enthusiasm on both sides. Once again, premature euphoria was likely to generate rapid disillusionment rather than rapid progress.

Setting Expectations

Establishing modest expectations for any new peace initiative, especially in its early stages, is a useful and perhaps necessary preface to efforts to break through the wall of suspicion, distrust, unresolved grievances, and an unfortunate but inevitable desire for revenge for earlier atrocities. But doing so does not answer the question of how to get out of the current stalemate. Many have argued that we should emphasize shared future interests in peace and common problems, that we should seek linkages and trade-offs to make painful concessions more bearable, that we should seek like-minded allies in the enemy camp, that we should seek to enhance credibility by taking actions costly to ourselves (such as Sadat's visit to Jerusalem), that we should seek to put ourselves empathetically in the shoes of the other, or that we should extend each decision maker's time perspective so that the long-run benefits of peace become more relevant and consequential. From the same rationalist perspective, each side might also benefit from asking itself why it is participating in the peace process: if the answer is to seek a genuine peace, the appropriate policies and trade-offs are likely to be considerably different than if the answer is only to take advantage of a truce.

Unfortunately, while these are sensible and prudent suggestions, they are likely to be ignored or misused by would-be peacemakers who take the other's duplicity and hypocrisy for granted and are primarily driven by nonrational and subjective concerns. This implies that a successful Israeli-Palestinian peace process cannot focus only on resolving crucial issues through the usual trade-offs, reciprocal concessions, and adaptive learning. Initiatives that diminish prevailing patterns of thought and action and unstated fears and resentments must also be built into the peace process from the start, no matter how difficult or uncomfortable this may be for diplomats and negotiators.

5. A Way Forward? Outlines of a Strategy

It is not my intention here to attempt to lay out a fully articulated strategy to revive and sustain the peace process that began at Oslo. Nevertheless, a brief comment on a possible way forward does seem appropriate, especially one that reflects—and reflects upon—the central argument of this paper. I will begin by reemphasizing a few background points that a new peace strategy needs to keep clearly in mind. I should perhaps also note that the appropriate mind-set for this venture recalls a famous formula by Samuel Beckett: try again, fail again, fail better. Perhaps we might also add "try better" to Beckett's list.

One critical point that emerges from my argument is that there is inevitably a bad fit between the constraints set by the conflict syndrome, especially ambivalent and inconsistent commitments to implementing principles that require substantial concessions, and the measures that need to be taken to increase the public legitimacy of the peace by proving to a suspicious and disheartened populace that peace is worth preserving. As a legion of conflict resolution analysts have argued for many years, the dispute needs to be transformed or redefined to break the stalemate that emerges from the reciprocal reiteration of grievances, the reciprocal exchange of atrocities, and the reciprocal and escalating failure to implement agreements.

How to do that, however, is rarely made very clear and most of the emphasis in the literature is on long-run changes. In contrast, immediate, salient, and felt changes in assumptions about the benefits that peace can or will produce are needed. Practically no peace process could withstand the endemic and escalating failures of the Oslo peace process, but neither could it withstand asking the leaders on both sides to take actions that directly threaten their power or place. One way to try to diminish the effects of this dilemma, which has no simple solution, is to make external support contingent on *initially private* leadership guarantees that actions which aggravate red flag issues will be avoided—such as continued support for terrorism and continued settlement activity. Serious failures to follow through on these guarantees should be immediately denounced and the peace process should be suspended until there are renewed guarantees of performance. Such onerous conditions may seem excessive in light of the constraints of conflict syndrome, but the peace will fail anyway without a real commitment to avoid actions that guarantee failure. The Middle East cannot afford another venture into peace as a charade or as an exercise in rhetorical gamesmanship. A window of opportunity for serious negotiations will only occur when leaders on both sides have come to recognize that a fragile peace will survive—and, one hopes, prosper—only if and when they are willing to make serious—if initially private—commitments about new patterns of behavior. Without such commitments, the peace process will flounder and will not to be saved by cynical allusions to the need for a "peace of the brave."

In theory, a transformative process would focus on changing public attitudes, the definition of central issues, the rules by which the two sides carry on their conflict (for example, through a cease-fire or a tacit agreement to end the use of violence for some period of time), and the underlying structures that have deepened the conflict over time, such as economic inequality, social separation, and inequities in treatment. Given the necessity of building a constituency for peace and legitimizing a top-down peace process, the initial emphasis must be on changing societal structures because they have the most immediate impact on the lives of ordinary people. Given the limited resources of the government and the massive needs of the Palestinian people, such an initial effort would obviously require significant support from the international community. This happened with the Oslo agreement, but the United States and the international aid agencies yielded much too easily to Arafat's demands for control over these resources. As a result, they were wasted on security-force salaries, an inefficient bureaucracy, and the illegal purchase of arms, and were otherwise lost through corruption. A new aid effort must be designed that maintains the usual standards of transparency and accountability and that does not yield to extortion—that is, give-me-the-money-or-there-will-be-chaos demands. Because Arafat received substantial sums without sufficient oversight, the Palestinian people did not benefit. They saw a disastrous decline in living standards—and chaos still ruled.

The initial policy focus thus must be on trying to drain the swamp before seeking to build on its very shaky foundations. Decades of failed efforts at development in the Middle East and elsewhere provide abundant proof that this task will never be fully or quickly accomplished. Nevertheless, there are useful things that can be done quickly and effectively, especially in meeting basic human needs and providing evidence to the long-suffering Palestinian people that their governing institutions will not be misused for personal gain and that these institutions will seek to meet public needs and to improve their performance. These tasks are exceptionally difficult, especially in the early stages of a peace process, but substantial empirical evidence suggests that initial public expectations are usually modest and realistic—in effect, a new governing authority has a honeymoon period to prove that it is something more than an old autocracy in a new disguise. However, while the structural elements of the conflict bear a large share of the responsibility for deepening and sustaining it, they are least amenable to quick solutions, which may be one reason why they are often ignored or underemphasized in the peace process. Thus, getting quick results will be dependent on external support that is both generous and carefully planned. And, through this support, the problems created by the need for quick and tangible results and the ambivalence of the parties about trusting the peace process will be diminished: the initially strong commitments will come from external parties and the benefits will be (relatively) quickly felt on the ground.

Since negotiations tend to begin because of leadership judgments about future developments, changes in the pattern of expectations are crucial. These changes reflect new interpretations of what the peace process can produce and what needs to be done at what point to improve the chances that the peace will begin to be perceived as intrinsically valuable and not merely as a new stage in the conflict. Success at this stage will be closely linked to the success of the initial aid effort. But attitudes, beliefs, and behaviors must also be changed. Unsurprisingly, new patterns of thought have been slow in coming and have been largely confined to tactical shifts about how to pursue traditional goals. But recent leadership changes, generational shifts, pressure from external allies, and shocks that precipitate the rethinking of conventional wisdom—for example, judgments about the utility of terrorism after 9/11—may be accelerating new patterns of thought. Paul Pillar, a career CIA officer, has noted recently that "major policy changes tend to come only from actual disasters."[35] As Oslo clearly qualifies as one, it should generate new patterns of thought, although they are—as yet—very hard to detect. Of course, there is no guarantee that new patterns will be entirely beneficial, but it seems unlikely that they will produce results that are more dysfunctional than existing patterns of thought. Seeking to manage expectations more effectively, or at least being aware of how important they can be, may help—if nothing else—to avert rapid oscillation between premature euphoria and deep despair and cynicism.

An effective multidimensional peace process that will continue for years—or decades if genuine reconciliation is the goal—cannot be built on the fly. One consistent failure, as I have already emphasized, not only in the Oslo process but also in a number of other peace processes, has been the lack of planning in the steps needed to build support for a very fragile peace, to maintain its momentum, to deal with the inevitable misunderstandings, setbacks, and failures, and to create institutions to facilitate cooperation and communication. Failure to do so usually reflects the persistence of old patterns of thought and the belief that the peace is only transitory. Why plan for a post-peace period when the conflict will resume? Even if planning has been undertaken, it will not accomplish much if leaders are indifferent or blinded by ideology or ignorance. But this sort of planning could become very valuable for leaders who do want to drive the peace process forward in a very inhospitable environment.

Gradually Accelerating Incrementalism

In effect, one needs a peace strategy for the Middle East that takes into account the contextual constraints of peacemaking in a protracted conflict, that is heavily aware of the need for very salient improvements on the ground as quickly as possible, that plans and prepares for inevitable failures and setbacks, and that is increasingly demanding in terms of implementation and compliance as the peace process begins to prove its worth.

[35] Paul R. Pillar, "A Scapegoat Is Not a Solution," *New York Times*, June 4, 2004.

This is a peace process that is initially modest, flexible, and front-loaded, but ultimately ambitious, sustained, and committed. Such a peace process, which I call "gradually accelerating incrementalism," differs from traditional incrementalism by establishing as early as possible—perhaps tacitly among leaders at the start—a mutually agreed-upon set of shared goals to be achieved in defined stages of the process. It would begin with a major effort by the international community—and Israel as the stronger party—to improve standards of living and quality of life for the Palestinian people and would focus on meeting basic human needs, such as health, sanitation, clean water, housing, and education. Commitments on implementation of proposals can be loose and permissive at this stage, but commitments not to violate tacit agreements on certain red flag issues must be firm—or the slide downward could accelerate once again. However, the leaders should not be asked at this stage to sacrifice central goals or to take actions that commit too early or preclude a quick retreat if such seems necessary. After all, the leaders may decide to explore a peace process, but this does not mean they want to do so at the risk of losing power or status.

Additionally, since there is a very strong need to begin strengthening the public legitimacy of peace as quickly as possible, efforts to contain or diminish corruption must commence immediately. Failure to do so was one of the major reasons why support for Oslo rapidly deteriorated in the Palestinian community: it was impossible to believe that a regime that was corrupt, brutal, and incompetent would produce major public benefits or deepen a fragile peace process. In the next stage, after some initial progress, there needs to be relatively flexible commitments to implement more of the principles and provisions of the peace agreement, but with both sides aware that support for the peace will still be tentative and that extremists will be increasingly desperate to destroy the peace process. This bears at least a rough resemblance to the difficulties that some Eastern European and developing countries faced in moving from discredited authoritarian regimes to relatively more democratic regimes amid resistance by the old guard and a disintegrating economy. The "politics of accommodation" that prevailed in many of these cases, in which some painful compromises were accepted to avoid a descent into civil war, may also be relevant in the present Israeli-Palestinian context. This is also a period in which cheating may be disproportionately dangerous because it confirms the other's worst fears and accelerates reciprocal defections from commitments. One hopes, however, that success in the first phase will diminish such dangers and that careful monitoring without harsh sanctions will reduce incentives to cheat. Once progress has been achieved on these fronts, the process must turn to resolving the central issues of the conflict and to making increasingly firm commitments about implementation and deadlines. An independent and presumably unbiased panel should be tasked with monitoring these commitments and any violations of them should lead to serious sanctions. Since the concessions and compromises at this stage are more burdensome and dangerous to both sides, the threat of coercive and punishing sanctions for noncompliance may increase incentives to comply and to fulfill painful obligations.

Such a process would resemble the economic concept of a "cascade of information," except that the cascade here is of small steps that accumulate into a sustained progression toward an agreed vision of peace. Any and all measures can be used in this pursuit, but it should be emphasized that changes in the rhetoric of mutual invective are imperative immediately—a point Arafat ignored, to his detriment. Such changes should be accompanied by an attempt to begin to alter educational practices aimed at vilifying and denying the legitimacy of the other. These are more than atmospherics because they provide crucial information about how serious one or both parties are about the peace process. Failure to pay attention to these issues during the Oslo years, whether deliberately or because of a lack of awareness of their importance, was crucial, not least because it generated or exacerbated Israeli fears that the Palestinians and larger Arab world would never accept Israel as a legitimate Middle Eastern state. (Similar educational failures have occurred in Sri Lanka and Northern Ireland.) As a result, the legitimacy of the peace process was always under threat and the fear that it was merely an interlude in the conflict affected attitudes and behaviors on both sides.

In beginning a new process, one might also think about reviving the old Cold War idea of GRIT—that is, graduated, unilateral, and reciprocal reductions in tension.[36] Such initiatives are designed to break a stalemate in which each side resists movement for fear of seeming weak. Given persistent mistrust, initial steps may require third-party support or strong leadership from the more powerful side in the conflict. However, this perfectly reasonable image of reciprocal and unilateral concessions will not work well if one or both sides see concessions as a sign of weakness and if one or both leaders feel too weak to respond appropriately. And it will not work if one or both leaders are using the peace process only to prepare for renewed conflict or as a means of deflecting domestic discontent. If careful draftsmanship can allay some fears about conceding too much too soon, so too can an agreement not to press for too quick a resolution of the most difficult issues—or not to surrender any demands until there is a final agreement.

Finally, the obviously severe problems of generating and sustaining cooperation in these circumstances can be diminished not only by a variety of familiar techniques, such as side payments, recognition that the parties are

[36] For a successful illustration in a similar context, see Ed Moloney, *A Secret History of the IRA* (London: Allan Lane, 2002), 352ff.

in a continuing game, and hedging strategies to reduce risk, but also by joint recognition of the need to focus on "diffuse reciprocity."[37] In such circumstances, the parties choose to cooperate because they hope to benefit over many years and many issues but not necessarily in every year or on every issue. It should be emphasized that the notion of diffuse reciprocity is likely to work best and to produce more joint benefits if the stronger party accepts the need to act first and to expect less in the initial period after a negotiation. Israeli governments, especially the right-wing administrations of Netanyahu and Sharon, failed miserably in this regard, raising justified suspicions about their commitment to the peace process. Northern Ireland offers a more positive illustration of the potential benefits of reciprocated unilateral actions: as noted, shortly after the IRA accepted the need to disarm, one of the main Protestant militias announced that it had ordered its gunmen to stand down. This may illustrate that leaders in Northern Ireland are more aware than those in Israel that domestic politics is not the only game in town: one also needs to respond to the actions of the other without perceiving them only as traps.

6. Alternative Roads to Peace

The approach to peace that I have outlined here stands in sharp contrast to two recent contributions to the debate over the direction future Israeli-Palestinian peace initiatives might take. The first is reflected in an unofficial agreement negotiated by a group of Israeli and Palestinian political figures and intellectuals in Geneva, Switzerland, that was presented to the public in October 2003. The participants managed to reach agreement on many of the conflict's central issues, if with some ambiguity in places, but this effort ultimately disappeared as rapidly as so many prior attempts to break through the stalemate. One reason why it floundered is that none of the subjective elements of conflict syndrome were discussed, perhaps because addressing them requires a long-term peacemaking strategy—and not merely a peace of grand gestures. An even stronger reason for its failure was that this initiative got too far ahead of where the publics were—as yet—willing to go. Many on both sides stated that the other side could not be trusted to implement commitments. As I argue, the respective publics need to see the benefits of peace and to be *reeducated* in new beliefs and attitudes before any such agreement can survive and prosper. One might presume that the negotiators of this agreement, many of whom were involved in negotiating Oslo, would have painfully learned this lesson during the Oslo years, but apparently they had not. Moreover, if such an agreement were to begin to earn public support, it would require leaders

[37] I am not sure who devised this term, but I think I first saw it some years ago in several works on regime theory.

committed to peace, to containing their own extremists, and to speaking the truth to their own people about the need to accept painful compromises and to alter ancient beliefs. One doubts that the current leadership on either side is willing or able to rise to such tasks.

Sharon has his own version of what he calls a "long-term interim agreement," or standstill agreement, with the Palestinians. This involves unilateral withdrawal from the Gaza Strip, a limited Palestinian state in parts of the West Bank and all of Gaza, completion of the security wall between Israel and the Palestinian territories, and discussion of the central issues, such as Jerusalem and the right of return, only on some distant date.[38] This is a peace policy virtually guaranteed to sustain and deepen the conflict, especially if it goes hand in hand with an effort to expand the main settlement blocs in the West Bank, and is a testament to the unwillingness of the right wing in Israel to give up its hopes and delusions about the retention of territory. Israel is powerful, but its position is also precarious: its ability to contain the escalating threat of catastrophic terrorism may not go on for long, and its tendency to ignore the opinion of rising numbers of people—not all of whom can be dismissed as anti-Semites—who believe that Israel's policies are generating support for Islamic terrorism in their own countries may become increasingly costly. In Europe, for example, the media, intellectuals, and academics, especially those on the Left, continue to turn against Israel. In fact, many of them justify or rationalize violence against Israel while denouncing any Israeli retaliation as excessive or unjustified. As a result, Israel risks becoming even more of an international pariah with few friends. The attendant dangers and discomforts of being in such a state will surely rise.[39]

After Arafat—Possibilities and Constraints

Arafat's death may create new opportunities for negotiation and new dangers for both Israelis and Palestinians. However, it does not change the analytical argument about why Oslo failed and what share of the responsibility for that failure should be attributed to Arafat himself. Nor does it change the underlying theoretical argument about the impact of conflict syndrome on how the conflict continues to deepen or why it is so difficult

[38] Sharon's views are discussed in James Bennet, "Shaper of Modern Israel: Sharon the Warrior," *International Herald Tribune*, August 16, 2004.

[39] One does not mean to deny that some Israeli actions and some of its policies have been unacceptable violations of international norms, such as the targeted assassinations of terrorist leaders, but the failure of the Palestinian Authority to act must also share some of the blame. While Israel should be bound by the various Geneva Conventions, it does have the legal and moral right to maintain order and to act in self-defense. The dilemmas that all countries now face in dealing with sustained terrorist assaults or in averting them are apparent, in terms of civil rights and in the unfortunate likelihood that casualties may be inflicted on civilians in the course of preventive or retaliatory actions. But Israel has faced the severest terrorist threat, and it is ironic to see some of its critics (for example, the Labor Party in the United Kingdom) chastising it for certain actions and policies that they now advocate against real or potential terrorists in their own countries.

to resolve the conflict despite its ever-mounting costs and the fact that shifting majorities on both sides seem willing to risk peace. What his death does change is short-run calculations about what *may* become possible and what needs to be done on both sides to grasp new opportunities—which may arise not merely from his passing but also from the Bush administration's willingness to expend some political capital on the Middle East peace process.

Although Arafat is gone, the beliefs, attitudes, and assumptions on both sides that undermined the implementation of Oslo are still powerfully present and cannot be quickly altered. In addition, terrorist groups, both secular and religious, remain committed to Israel's destruction. The fact that they are seeking and may acquire more deadly arms raises the stakes considerably. However, there have been some tentative signs of moderation from Hamas. Whether such signs are related to its hope to benefit from the electoral process or are simply a tactical lull related to the threat of Israeli retaliation is unclear. Much will depend obviously on whether an effective peace process can be initiated, on how well a new Palestinian Authority performs, and on how effective it is in marginalizing extremists by altering the beliefs and behaviors that have made groups such as Hamas popular.

An upsurge in optimism over the possibility of a resumption of negotiations also reflects the obvious fact that Arafat's death removes at least part of the excuse that Israel and the United States had for largely ignoring the peace process or whatever was left of it—specifically, that Arafat had repeatedly failed to honor commitments or to do anything to stop terror. Unfortunately, as many commentators have been quick to note, his death does not remove the more general reason for Israel's refusal to negotiate: the absence, as yet, of a reliable partner who is able and willing to stop or at least limit the violence and who is willing to accept a two-state solution (on mutually agreed terms) as final. There are a variety of reasons to doubt that any such leader either can or will emerge any time soon. Arafat's success in putting the Palestinian cause on the international agenda is unquestioned, but, in retrospect, his record will be tarnished not only by what he did not do but also by his refusal to share power, to allow other leaders to emerge, and to prepare for an orderly succession.

The election of Mahmoud Abbas is potentially encouraging, but Abbas also lacks the power and perhaps the will to contain the extremists. Further, he probably lacks the status needed to make necessary concessions on symbolic issues that Arafat long manipulated to retain popular support, such as the right of return. Abbas's desire to incorporate extremist groups into the political process, rather than to attempt to crush them militarily, is undoubtedly a reflection of his own desire to avoid civil war and the general weakness and unreliability of his security forces. But neither Israel nor the United States have seemed willing to give him the time and support needed to strengthen his hold on power. They also have failed to understand that making demands that are too risky for him to address will only lead to inconsistent policy responses that could potentially generate instability and perhaps chaos.

Moreover, Arafat maintained power by buying off dissent and avoiding decisions that would likely generate significant dissent. Now, with different groups wanting different things—not all of which are compatible—and with a strong likelihood of weak leadership emerging from the struggle to take over, the willingness of any leader to take large risks for a compromise peace is likely to be sharply constrained. This will be especially so if personal ambition trumps group needs and if Arafat's "old-boy network," desperately afraid of losing economic benefits, tries to retain power. In the worst of circumstances, internal violence could erupt until one strong leader emerges. Unless the Palestinians can remain united without Arafat's dominant presence, the short-run prospects for peace may actually deteriorate.

Much will also depend, of course, on the willingness of the Sharon government to make a more generous offer than anything it has been willing to put on the table in the past. The new Palestinian leadership will be in desperate need of substantive concessions from Israel—for example, on the release of prisoners, the turning over of tax resources, and the pulling of some troops from Palestinian areas—but it is far from clear that Sharon will be willing to offer more than cosmetic gestures or that the Israeli public—badly scarred by the terrorism of the Oslo years—will accept offering any more concessions until the Palestinians prove they are serious about peace. Needless to say, the Palestinians are unlikely to do so unless they receive significant benefits quickly. Nor is it clear that the Bush administration's brave words about its willingness to expend political capital on the Middle East peace process will survive the inevitable disappointments and frustrations of peacemaking or even protests from domestic supporters of Sharon's hard-line policies, such as Christian fundamentalist groups and some conservative Jewish organizations. Yet Sharon's successful withdrawal from Gaza and the less-than-feared reaction of the settlers might suggest that the old warrior wants to leave a mark as a peacemaker. It might further suggest that—if he can remain in power and maintain majority support in the Israeli electorate—he *might* risk even more in the future by ordering major withdrawals from the West Bank and a major confrontation with the settlers and their supporters.[40]

The severe dilemmas confronting weak leaders in a complex and dangerous environment are major obstacles that impede progress toward an effective peace process. The greatest dangers to such leaders may reflect two

[40] This paper was in press when Sharon suffered an incapacitating stroke, making revisions impossible. Since my argument is not about the short-term policies of any one leader but about the long-term effects of the conflict syndrome, the costs of not being able to revise the paper are bearable.

linked factors: the failure to think contextually about the constraints of working within an environment created by decades of bitter conflict and pervasive distrust, and the consequent failure to abandon tactics and strategies that have failed so miserably in the past. Instead, failure is too easily attributed to the duplicity and bad faith of the other and change in "normal" patterns of interaction is resisted as being too risky. As a result, the guilt for past failures is shared. Thus, Israelis continue to make demands on the Palestinians that they know cannot or will not be fulfilled, such as confronting terrorist groups directly and forcefully. The dangers of doing so are simply too great for a weak Abbas regime that is unwilling to risk civil war and fearful of delegitimizing the electoral process before it can prove its worth. However, such demands are obviously understandable from an Israeli domestic perspective: forestalling terrorist actions by groups dedicated to Israel's destruction is a prime purpose of the peace process. But asking for too much too soon merely indicates that Israeli policy has not adjusted to the singular needs of a very fragile peace process.

By the same token, the Palestinians continue to use the rhetoric of the Arafat years, continue to extol the heroism of the "martyrs," and continue to demand large concessions from the Israelis before there is sufficient evidence that the peace process can and will provide *mutual* benefits. Israel needs to act more generously and more quickly than it has yet done, but it is not sensible for the Palestinians to ignore the profound political and psychological damage created by repeated terrorist atrocities or Israel's own domestic constraints. In short, peace requires more than Arafat's departure. Both sides need to understand the complex and critical linkages and feedback between their own beliefs, needs, and actions, and the beliefs, needs, and actions of the other.

Conclusion: Short-Run Pessimism, Long-Run Hope

Only the very brave or the very foolish are willing to offer confident predictions about short-term prospects in the Middle East. Developments are still mostly driven by largely unpredictable events within the conflict itself, the region, and even the wider world. Such events could thrust the Israeli-Palestinian peace process to the top of the international agenda or onto the back burner—or some uncomfortable place between these extremes. The only certainty is that the problem itself will not disappear and will fester without sustained effort. Short-term forecasting is also bound to be unreliable because of one ancient social science axiom that continues to operate: every darn thing is related to every other darn thing. Multiple linkages and complex patterns of feedback guarantee high levels of risk and uncertainty. These considerations come together to suggest that short-term pessimism about a rapid breakthrough to peace in the post-Arafat years is probably justified. The transition to a new era in the relationship between Israelis and Palestinians is likely to be rough and perhaps even traumatic if the Palestinians do not quickly resolve their domestic conflicts and the Israelis try to hang on to too much land in the West Bank. Nevertheless, longer-term prospects for peace are brighter because certain factors are pushing both sides—suspiciously and reluctantly—toward "thinking about the unthinkable." This presupposes, of course, a carefully planned peace process that receives generous and sustained external support and much wiser internal leadership. The fact that much has not changed after Arafat's death, and some things have indeed gotten worse, should not be used as a rationalization for doing nothing or arguing that failure is inevitable. Improvements that can slowly accumulate into significant change are always possible and small steps consistently implemented can produce large effects.

The need to institutionalize the peace process may be the least understood factor in successful peacemaking. The Israelis and Palestinians did create, especially after the Madrid Conference of 1991, a number of functional committees to discuss a variety of specific issues. Unfortunately, they never achieved much because of turmoil in the political and security arenas. Something quite different is needed here—specifically, a high-level, well-staffed, and tripartite committee that is asked to try to avert or at least to diminish the effects of the inevitable crises, shocks, and misunderstandings that are likely to occur. Such an institution with a five-or seven-year mandate would not be a panacea, but it would offer a degree of hope that some of the worst crises can be contained, that some of the least anticipated surprises can be anticipated, and that the most destabilizing misunderstandings can be clarified. The habits of cooperation that this committee establishes could prove useful, as could the possibility of public exposure for cheating, but perhaps the most important *potential* benefit is that such an institution might forestall or certainly delay another race to the bottom.

Such an approach offers no quick solutions or guarantees of progress. It may also seem too slow and too modest for a conflict that always seems on the verge of an explosion. But all the grandiose efforts to impose solutions, to compel the parties to leap into the unknown, and to capitalize on the seemingly unending initiatives of various officials, former officials, and notable leaders to negotiate a stable peace have floundered. This is not surprising given the failure of such efforts to deal with or understand the Israeli-Palestinian conflict syndrome. Perhaps, then, gradually accelerating incrementalism, which does recognize how far the peace process has to travel and does take account of the range of obstacles to progress, may offer some hope of arresting and ultimately breaking out of an apparently unstoppable race to the bottom. A focus on sustained conflict amelioration is obviously less heroic—no Nobel Peace Prizes, no ceremonies on the White House lawn—than a focus on conflict resolution, but it may provide the best long-run hope for peace.

About the Author

Robert L. Rothstein is the Harvey Picker Distinguished Professor of International Relations (Emeritus) at Colgate University. He has written or edited nine books and some eighty articles and has been a past fellow of the United States Institute of Peace, the Woodrow Wilson International Center for Scholars, the Rockefeller Foundation, and the Carnegie Foundation. He has also received several research grants from the U.S. Department of State and the United Nations. His most recent book, jointly edited with Moshe Ma'oz and Khalil Shikaki, is *The Israeli-Palestinian Peace Process: The Lessons of Failure.*

About the Institute

The United States Institute of Peace is an independent, nonpartisan federal institution created by Congress to promote the prevention, management, and peaceful resolution of international conflicts. Established in 1984, the Institute meets its congressional mandate through an array of programs, including research grants, fellowships, professional training, education programs from high school through graduate school, conferences and workshops, library services, and publications. The Institute's Board of Directors is appointed by the President of the United States and confirmed by the Senate.

Other Titles in the Peaceworks Series

- *Chaplains as Liaisons with Religious Leaders: Lessons from Iraq and Afghanistan,* by George Adams (No. 56, February 2006)
- *Religious Contributions to Peacemaking: When Religion Brings Peace, Not War,* edited by David R. Smock (No. 55, January 2006)
- *Dismantling the DPRK's Nuclear Weapons Program: A Practicable, Verifiable Plan of Action,* by David Albright and Corey Hinderstein (No. 54, January 2006)
- *Downward Spiral: HIV/AIDS, State Capacity, and Political Conflict in Zimbabwe,* by Andrew T. Price-Smith and John L. Daly (No. 53, July 2004)
- *Biosecurity: Limiting Terrorist Access to Deadly Pathogens,* by Jonathan B. Tucker (No. 52, November 2003)
- *Healing the Holy Land: Interreligious Peacebuilding in Israel/Palestine,* by Yehezkel Landau (No. 51, August 2003)
- *Boundary Disputes in Latin America,* by Jorge I. Domínguez with David Mares, Manuel Orozco, David Scott Palmer, Francisco Rojas Aravena, and Andrés Serbin (No. 50, August 2003)
- *The Road Ahead: Lessons in Nation Building from Japan, Germany, and Afghanistan for Postwar Iraq,* by Ray Salvatore Jennings (No. 49, May 2003)

- *The Palestinian Reform Agenda,* by Nathan Brown (No. 48, December 2002)
- *The Israeli Military and Israel's Palestinian Policy: From Oslo to the Al Aqsa Intifada,* by Yoram Peri (No. 47, November 2002)
- *The Chaplain's Evolving Role in Peace and Humanitarian Relief Operations,* by Captain Paul McLaughlin (No. 46, September 2002)
- *The Ethics of Armed Humanitarian Intervention,* by C. A. J. Coady (No. 45, July 2002)
- *Democratic Values, Political Structures, and Alternative Politics in Greater China,* by David Zweig (No. 44, June 2002)
- *Training for Peace and Humanitarian Relief Operations: Advancing Best Practices,* by Robert M. Schoenhaus (No. 43, April 2002)
- *The Role of International Financial Institutions in International Humanitarian Law,* by Laurie R. Blank (No. 42, January 2002)
- *Controlling Weapons of Mass Destruction: Findings from USIP-Sponsored Projects,* edited by Deepa M. Ollapally (No. 41, September 2001)
- *Passing the Baton: Challenges of Statecraft for the New Administration,* with remarks by Samuel R. Berger and Condoleezza Rice (No. 40, May 2001)
- *From Revolutionary Internationalism to Conservative Nationalism: The Chinese Military's Discourse on National Security and Identity in the Post-Mao Era,* by Nan Li (No. 39, May 2001)
- *El Salvador: Implementation of the Peace Accords,* edited by Margarita S. Studemeister (No. 38, January 2001)
- *The News Media and Peace Processes: The Middle East and Northern Ireland,* by Gadi Wolfsfeld (No. 37, January 2001)
- *Conflict Management Training: Advancing Best Practices,* by Robert M. Schoenhaus (No. 36, January 2001)

Of Related Interest

Several other recent publications from the United States Institute of Peace address issues of direct relevance to the Middle East peace process.

Recent Institute reports include:

- *The Future of the Israeli-Palestinian Conflict: Critical Trends Affecting Israel,* by Yossi Alpher (Special Report, September 2005)
- *Healing the Holy Land: Interreligious Peacebuilding in Israel/Palestine,* by Yehezkel Landau (Peaceworks, August 2003)

- *The Israeli Military and Israel's Palestinian Policy: From Oslo to the Al Aqsa Intifada, by* Yoram Peri (Peaceworks, November 2002)

To obtain an Institute report (available free of charge), write United States Institute of Peace, 1200 17th Street NW, Suite 200, Washington, DC 20036–3011; call 202-429-3832; fax 202-429-6063; or e-mail: usip_requests@usip.org.

DOCUMENT NO. 5

THE COVENANT OF THE ISLAMIC RESISTANCE MOVEMENT (HAMAS)

August 18, 1988

In The Name of the Most Merciful Allah

"Ye are the best nation that hath been raised up unto mankind: ye command that which is just, and ye forbid that which is unjust, and ye believe in Allah. And if they who have received the scriptures had believed, it had surely been the better for them: there are believers among them, but the greater part of them are transgressors. They shall not hurt you, unless with a slight hurt; and if they fight against you, they shall turn their backs to you, and they shall not be helped. They are smitten with vileness wheresoever they are found; unless they obtain security by entering into a treaty with Allah, and a treaty with men; and they draw on themselves indignation from Allah, and they are afflicted with poverty. This they suffer, because they disbelieved the signs of Allah, and slew the prophets unjustly; this, because they were rebellious, and transgressed." (Al-Imran - verses 109-111).

Israel will exist and will continue to exist until Islam will obliterate it, just as it obliterated others before it" (The Martyr, Imam Hassan al-Banna, of blessed memory).

"The Islamic world is on fire. Each of us should pour some water, no matter how little, to extinguish whatever one can without waiting for the others." (Sheikh Amjad al-Zahawi, of blessed memory).

In The Name of the Most Merciful Allah

Introduction

Praise be unto Allah, to whom we resort for help, and whose forgiveness, guidance and support we seek; Allah bless the Prophet and grant him salvation, his companions and supporters, and to those who carried out his message and adopted his laws – everlasting prayers and salvation as long as the earth and heaven will last. Hereafter:

O People

Out of the midst of troubles and the sea of suffering, out of the palpitations of faithful hearts and cleansed arms; out of the sense of duty, and in response to Allah's command, the call has gone out rallying people together and making them follow the ways of Allah, leading them to have determined will in order to fulfill their role in life, to overcome all obstacles, and surmount the difficulties on the way. Constant preparation has continued and so has the readiness to sacrifice life and all that is precious for the sake of Allah.

Thus it was that the nucleus (of the movement) was formed and started to pave its way through the tempestuous sea of hopes and expectations, of wishes and yearnings, of troubles and obstacles, of pain and challenges, both inside and outside.

When the idea was ripe, the seed grew and the plant struck root in the soil of reality, away from passing emotions, and hateful haste. The Islamic Resistance Movement emerged to carry out its role through striving for the sake of its Creator, its arms intertwined with those of all the fighters for the liberation of Palestine. The spirits of its fighters meet with the spirits of all the fighters who have sacrificed their lives on the soil of Palestine, ever since it was conquered by the companions of the Prophet, Allah bless him and grant him salvation, and until this day.

This Covenant of the Islamic Resistance Movement (HAMAS), clarifies its picture, reveals its identity, outlines its stand, explains its aims, speaks about its hopes, and calls for its support, adoption and joining its ranks. Our struggle against the Jews is very great and very serious. It needs all sincere efforts. It is a step that inevitably should be followed by other steps. The Movement is but one squadron that should be supported by more and more squadrons from this vast Arab and Islamic world, until the enemy is vanquished and Allah's victory is realised.

Thus we see them coming on the horizon "and you shall learn about it hereafter" "Allah hath written, Verily I will prevail, and my apostles: for Allah is strong and mighty." (The Dispute - verse 21).

"Say to them, This is my way: I invite you to Allah, by an evident demonstration; both I and he who followeth me; and, praise be unto Allah! I am not an idolator." (Joseph - verse 107).

Hamas (means) ***strength and bravery*** **-(according to) Al-Mua'jam al-Wasit: c1.**

Definition of the Movement

Ideological Starting-Points

Article One

The Islamic Resistance Movement: The Movement's programme is Islam. From it, it draws its ideas, ways of thinking and understanding of the universe, life and man. It resorts to it for judgement in all its conduct, and it is inspired by it for guidance of its steps.

The Islamic Resistance Movement's Relation 7 the Moslem Brotherhood Group

Article Two

The Islamic Resistance Movement is one of the wings of Moslem Brotherhood in Palestine. Moslem Brotherhood Movement is a universal organization which constitutes the largest Islamic movement in modern times. It is characterised by its deep understanding, accurate comprehension and its complete embrace of all Islamic concepts of all aspects of life, culture, creed, politics, economics, education, society, justice and judgement, the spreading of Islam, education, art, information, science of the occult and conversion to Islam.

Structure and Formation

Article Three

The basic structure of the Islamic Resistance Movement consists of Moslems who have given their allegiance to Allah whom they truly worship,—"I have created the jinn and humans only for the purpose of worshipping"—who know their duty towards themselves, their families and country. In all that, they fear Allah and raise the banner of Jihad in the face of the oppressors, so that they would rid the land and the people of their uncleanliness, vileness and evils.

"But we will oppose truth to vanity, and it shall confound the same; and behold, it shall vanish away." (Prophets - verse 18).

Article Four

The Islamic Resistance Movement welcomes every Moslem who embraces its faith, ideology, follows its programme, keeps its secrets, and wants to belong to its ranks and carry out the duty. Allah will certainly reward such one.

Time and Place Extent of the Islamic Resistance Movement

Article Five

Time extent of the Islamic Resistance Movement: By adopting Islam as its way of life, the Movement goes back to the time of the birth of the Islamic message, of the righteous ancestor, for Allah is its target, the Prophet is its example and the Koran is its constitution. Its extent in place is anywhere that there are Moslems who embrace Islam as their way of life everywhere in the globe. This being so, it extends to the depth of the earth and reaches out to the heaven.

"Dost thou not see how Allah putteth forth a parable; representing a good word, as a good tree, whose root is firmly fixed in the earth, and whose branches reach unto heaven; which bringeth forth its fruit in all seasons, by the will of its Lord? Allah propoundeth parables unto men, that they may be instructed." (Abraham - verses 24-25).

Characteristics and Independence

Article Six

The Islamic Resistance Movement is a distinguished Palestinian movement, whose allegiance is to Allah, and whose way of life is Islam. It strives to raise the banner of Allah over every inch of Palestine, for under the wing of Islam followers of all religions can coexist in security and safety where their lives, possessions and rights are concerned. In the absence of Islam, strife will be rife, oppression spreads, evil prevails and schisms and wars will break out.

How excellent was the Moslem poet, Mohamed Ikbal, when he wrote:

> "If faith is lost, there is no security and there is no life for him who does not adhere to religion. He who accepts life without religion, has taken annihilation as his companion for life."

The Universality of the Islamic Resistance Movement

Article Seven

As a result of the fact that those Moslems who adhere to the ways of the Islamic Resistance Movement spread all over the world, rally support for it and its stands, strive towards enhancing its struggle, the Movement is a universal one. It is well-equipped for that because of the clarity of its ideology, the nobility of its aim and the loftiness of its objectives.

On this basis, the Movement should be viewed and evaluated, and its role be recognised. He who denies its right, evades supporting it and turns a blind eye to facts, whether intentionally or unintentionally, would awaken to see that events have overtaken him and with no logic to justify his attitude. One should certainly learn from past examples.

The injustice of next-of-kin is harder to bear than the smite of the Indian sword.

"We have also sent down unto thee the book of the Koran with truth, confirming that scripture which was revealed before it; and preserving the same safe from corruption. Judge therefore between them according to that which Allah hath revealed; and follow not their desires, by swerving from the truth which hath come unto thee. Unto every of you have we given a law, and an open path; and if Allah had pleased, he had surely made you one people; but he hath thought it fit to give you different laws, that he might try you in that which he hath given you respectively. Therefore strive to excel each other in good works; unto Allah shall ye all return, and then will he declare unto you that concerning which ye have disagreed." (The Table, verse 48).

The Islamic Resistance Movement is one of the links in the chain of the struggle against the Zionist invaders. It goes back to 1939, to the emergence of the martyr Izz al-Din al Kissam and his brethren the fighters, members of Moslem Brotherhood. It goes on to reach out and become one with another chain that includes the struggle of the Palestinians and Moslem Brotherhood in the 1948 war and the Jihad operations of the Moslem Brotherhood in 1968 and after.

Moreover, if the links have been distant from each other and if obstacles, placed by those who are the lackeys of Zionism in the way of the fighters obstructed the continuation of the struggle, the Islamic Resistance Movement aspires to the realisation of Allah's promise, no matter how long that should take. The Prophet, Allah bless him and grant him salvation, has said:

> "The Day of Judgement will not come about until Moslems fight the Jews (killing the Jews), when the Jew will hide behind stones and trees. The stones and trees will say O Moslems, O Abdulla, there is a Jew behind me, come and kill him. Only the Gharkad tree, (evidently a certain kind of tree) would not do that because it is one of the trees of the Jews." (related by al-Bukhari and Moslem).

The Slogan of the Islamic Resistance Movement

Article Eight

Allah is its target, the Prophet is its model, the Koran its constitution: Jihad is its path and death for the sake of Allah is the loftiest of its wishes.

Objectives

Incentives and Objectives

Article Nine

The Islamic Resistance Movement found itself at a time when Islam has disappeared from life. Thus rules shook, concepts were upset, values changed and evil people took control, oppression and darkness prevailed, cowards became like tigers: homelands were usurped, people were scattered and were caused to wander all over the world, the state of justice disappeared and the state of falsehood replaced it. Nothing remained in its right place. Thus, when Islam is absent from the arena, everything changes. From this state of affairs the incentives are drawn.

As for the objectives: They are the fighting against the false, defeating it and vanquishing it so that justice could prevail, homelands be retrieved and from its mosques would the voice of the mu'azen emerge declaring the establishment of the state of Islam, so that people and things would return each to their right places and Allah is our helper.

". . . and if Allah had not prevented men, the one by the other, verily the earth had been corrupted: but Allah is beneficient towards his creatures." (The Cow - verse 251).

Article Ten

As the Islamic Resistance Movement paves its way, it will back the oppressed and support the wronged with all its might. It will spare no effort to bring about justice and defeat injustice, in word and deed, in this place and everywhere it can reach and have influence therein.

Strategies and Methods

Strategies of the Islamic Resistance Movement: Palestine Is Islamic Waqf

Article Eleven

The Islamic Resistance Movement believes that the land of Palestine is an Islamic Waqf consecrated for future Moslem generations until Judgement Day. It, or any part of it, should not be squandered: it, or any part of it, should not be given up. Neither a single Arab country nor all Arab countries, neither any king or president, nor all the kings and presidents, neither any organization nor all of them, be they Palestinian or Arab, possess the right to do that. Palestine is an Islamic Waqf land consecrated for Moslem generations until Judgement Day. This being so, who could claim to have the right to represent Moslem generations till Judgement Day?

This is the law governing the land of Palestine in the Islamic Sharia (law) and the same goes for any land the Moslems have conquered by force, because during the times of (Islamic) conquests, the Moslems consecrated these lands to Moslem generations till the Day of Judgement.

It happened like this: When the leaders of the Islamic armies conquered Syria and Iraq, they sent to the Caliph of the Moslems, Umar bin-el-Khatab, asking for his advice concerning the conquered land—whether they should divide it among the soldiers, or leave it for its owners, or what? After consultations and discussions between the Caliph of the Moslems, Omar bin-el-Khatab and companions of the Prophet, Allah bless him and grant him salvation, it was decided that the land should be left with its owners who could benefit by its fruit. As for the real ownership of the land and the land itself, it should be consecrated for Moslem generations till Judgement Day. Those who are on the land, are there only to benefit from its fruit. This Waqf remains as long as earth and heaven remain. Any procedure in contradiction to Islamic Sharia, where Palestine is concerned, is null and void.

"Verily, this is a certain truth. Wherefore praise the name of thy Lord, the great Allah." (The Inevitable - verse 95).

Homeland and Nationalism from the Point of View of the Islamic Resistance Movement in Palestine

Article Twelve

Nationalism, from the point of view of the Islamic Resistance Movement, is part of the religious creed. Nothing in nationalism is more significant or deeper than in the case when an enemy should tread Moslem land. Resisting and quelling the enemy become the individual duty of every Moslem, male or female. A woman can go out to fight the enemy without her husband's permission, and so does the slave: without his master's permission.

Nothing of the sort is to be found in any other regime. This is an undisputed fact. If other nationalist movements are connected with materialistic, human or regional causes, nationalism of the Islamic Resistance Movement has all these elements as well as the more important elements that give it soul and life. It is connected to the source of spirit and the granter of life, hoisting in the sky of the homeland the heavenly banner that joins earth and heaven with a strong bond.

If Moses comes and throws his staff, both witch and magic are annulled.

"Now is the right direction manifestly distinguished from deceit: whoever therefore shall deny Tagut, and believe in Allah, he shall surely take hold with a strong handle, which shall not be broken; Allah is he who heareth and seeth." (The Cow - Verse 256).

Peaceful Solutions, Initiatives and International Conferences

Article Thirteen

Initiatives, and so-called peaceful solutions and international conferences, are in contradiction to the principles of the Islamic Resistance Movement. Abusing any part of Palestine is abuse directed against part of religion. Nationalism of the Islamic Resistance Movement is part of its religion. Its members have been fed on that. For the sake of hoisting the banner of Allah over their homeland they fight. "Allah will be prominent, but most people do not know."

Now and then the call goes out for the convening of an international conference to look for ways of solving the (Palestinian) question. Some accept, others reject the idea, for this or other reason, with one stipulation or more for consent to convening the conference and participating in it. Knowing the parties constituting the conference, their past and present attitudes towards Moslem problems, the Islamic Resistance Movement does not consider these conferences capable of realising the demands, restoring the rights or doing justice to the oppressed. These conferences are only ways of setting the infidels in the land of the Moslems as arbitrators. When did the infidels do justice to the believers?

"But the Jews will not be pleased with thee, neither the Christians, until thou follow their religion; say, The direction of Allah is the true direction. And verily if thou follow their desires, after the knowledge which hath been given thee, thou shalt find no patron or protector against Allah." (The Cow - verse 120).

There is no solution for the Palestinian question except through Jihad. Initiatives, proposals and international conferences are all a waste of time and vain endeavors. The Palestinian people know better than to consent to having their future, rights and fate toyed with. As in said in the honourable Hadith:

> "The people of Syria are Allah's lash in His land. He wreaks His vengeance through them against whomsoever He wishes among His slaves It is unthinkable that those who are double-faced among them should prosper over the faithful. They will certainly die out of grief and desperation."

The Three Circles

Article Fourteen

The question of the liberation of Palestine is bound to three circles: the Palestinian circle, the Arab circle and the Islamic circle. Each of these circles has its role in the struggle against Zionism. Each has its duties, and it is a horrible mistake and a sign of deep ignorance to overlook any of these circles. Palestine is an Islamic land which has the first of the two kiblahs (direction to which Moslems turn in praying), the third of the holy (Islamic) sanctuaries, and the point of departure for Mohamed's midnight journey to the seven heavens (i.e. Jerusalem).

"Praise be unto him who transported his servant by night, from the sacred temple of Mecca to the farther temple of Jerusalem, the circuit of which we have blessed, that we might show him some of our signs; for Allah is he who heareth, and seeth." (The Night-Journey - verse 1).

Since this is the case, liberation of Palestine is then an individual duty for very Moslem wherever he may be. On this basis, the problem should be viewed. This should be realised by every Moslem.

The day the problem is dealt with on this basis, when the three circles mobilize their capabilities, the present state of affairs will change and the day of liberation will come nearer.

"Verily ye are stronger than they, by reason of the terror cast into their breasts from Allah. This, because they are not people of prudence." (The Emigration - verse 13).

The Jihad for the Liberation of Palestine is an Individual Duty

Article Fifteen

The day that enemies usurp part of Moslem land, Jihad becomes the individual duty of every Moslem. In face of the Jews' usurpation of Palestine, it is compulsory that the banner of Jihad be raised. To do this requires the diffusion of Islamic consciousness among the masses, both on the regional, Arab and Islamic levels. It is necessary to instill the spirit of Jihad in the heart of the nation so that they would confront the enemies and join the ranks of the fighters.

It is necessary that scientists, educators and teachers, information and media people, as well as the educated masses, especially the youth and sheikhs of the Islamic movements, should take part in the operation of awakening (the masses). It is important that basic changes be made in the school curriculum, to cleanse it of the traces of ideological invasion that affected it as a result of the orientalists and missionaries who infiltrated the region following the defeat of the Crusaders at the hands of Salah el-Din (Saladin). The Crusaders realised that it was impossible to defeat the Moslems without first having ideological invasion pave the way by upsetting their thoughts, disfiguring their heritage and violating their ideals. Only then could they invade with soldiers. This, in its turn, paved the way for the imperialistic invasion that made Allenby declare on entering Jerusalem: "Only now have the Crusades ended." General Guru stood at Salah el-Din's grave and said: "We have returned, O Salah el-Din."

Imperialism has helped towards the strengthening of ideological invasion, deepening, and still does, its roots. All this has paved the way towards the loss of Palestine.

It is necessary to instill in the minds of the Moslem generations that the Palestinian problem is a religious problem, and should be dealt with on this basis. Palestine contains Islamic holy sites. In it there is al-Aqsa Mosque which is bound to the great Mosque in Mecca in an inseparable bond as long as heaven and earth speak of Isra` (Mohammed's midnight journey to the seven heavens) and Mi'raj (Mohammed's ascension to the seven heavens from Jerusalem).

"The bond of one day for the sake of Allah is better than the world and whatever there is on it. The place of one's whip in Paradise is far better than the world and whatever there is on it. A worshipper's going and coming in the service of Allah is better than the world and whatever there is on it." (As related by al-Bukhari, Moslem, al-Tarmdhi and Ibn Maja).

"I swear by the holder of Mohammed's soul that I would like to invade and be killed for the sake of Allah, then invade and be killed, and then invade again and be killed." (As related by al-Bukhari and Moslem).

The Education of the Generations

Article Sixteen

It is necessary to follow Islamic orientation in educating the Islamic generations in our region by teaching the religious duties, comprehensive study of the Koran, the study of the Prophet's Sunna (his sayings and doings), and learning about Islamic history and heritage from their authentic sources. This should be done by specialised and learned people, using a curriculum that would healthily form the thoughts and faith of the Moslem student. Side by side with this, a comprehensive study of the enemy, his human and financial capabilities, learning about his points of weakness and strength, and getting to know the forces supporting and helping him, should also be included. Also, it is important to be acquainted with the current events, to follow what is new and to study the analysis and commentaries made of these events. Planning for the present and future, studying every trend appearing, is a must so that the fighting Moslem would live knowing his aim, objective and his way in the midst of what is going on around him.

"O my son, verily every matter, whether good or bad, though it be the weight of a grain of mustard-seed, and be hidden in a rock, or in the heavens, or in the earth, Allah will bring the same to light; for Allah is clear-sighted and knowing. O my son, be constant at prayer, and command that which is just, and forbid that which is evil: and be patient under the afflictions which shall befall thee; for this is a duty absolutely incumbent on all men. Distort not thy face out of contempt to men, neither walk in the earth with insolence; for Allah loveth no arrogant, vain-glorious person." (Lokman - verses 16–18).

The Role of the Moslem Woman

Article Seventeen

The Moslem woman has a role no less important than that of the moslem man in the battle of liberation. She is the maker of men. Her role in guiding and educating the new generations is great. The enemies have realised the importance of her role. They consider that if they are able to direct and bring her up they way they wish, far from Islam, they would have won the battle. That is why you find them giving these attempts constant attention through information campaigns, films, and the school curriculum, using for that purpose their lackeys who are infiltrated through Zionist organizations under various names and shapes, such as Freemasons, Rotary Clubs, espionage groups and others, which are all nothing more than cells of subversion and saboteurs. These organizations have ample resources that enable them to play their role in societies for the purpose of achieving the Zionist targets and to deepen the concepts that would serve the enemy. These organizations operate in the absence of Islam and its estrangement among its people. The Islamic peoples should perform their role in confronting the conspiracies of these saboteurs. The day Islam is in control of guiding the affairs of life, these organizations, hostile to humanity and Islam, will be obliterated.

Article Eighteen

Woman in the home of the fighting family, whether she is a mother or a sister, plays the most important role in looking after the family, rearing the children and embuing them with moral values and thoughts derived from Islam. She has to teach them to perform the religious duties in preparation for the role of fighting awaiting them. That is why it is necessary to pay great attention to schools and the curriculum followed in educating Moslem girls, so that they would grow up to be good mothers, aware of their role in the battle of liberation.

She has to be of sufficient knowledge and understanding where the performance of housekeeping matters are concerned, because economy and avoidance of waste of the family budget, is one of the requirements for the ability to continue moving forward in the difficult conditions surrounding us. She should put before her eyes the fact that the money available to her is just like blood which should never flow except through the veins so that both children and grown-ups could continue to live.

"Verily, the Moslems of either sex, and the true believers of either sex, and the devout men, and the devout women, and the men of veracity, and the women of veracity, and the patient men, and the patient women, and the humble men, and the humble women, and the alms-givers of either sex who remember Allah frequently; for them hath Allah prepared forgiveness and a great reward." (The Confederates - verse 25).

The Role of Islamic Art in the Battle of Liberation

Article Nineteen

Art has regulations and measures by which it can be determined whether it is Islamic or pre-Islamic (Jahili) art. The issues of Islamic liberation are in need of Islamic art that would take the spirit high, without raising one side of human nature above the other, but rather raise all of them harmoniously an in equilibrium.

Man is a unique and wonderful creature, made out of a handful of clay and a breath from Allah. Islamic art addresses man on this basis, while pre-Islamic art addresses the body giving preference to the clay component in it.

The book, the article, the bulletin, the sermon, the thesis, the popular poem, the poetic ode, the song, the play and others, contain the characteristics of Islamic art, then these are among the requirements of ideological mobilization, renewed food for the journey and recreation for the soul. The road is long and suffering is plenty. The soul will be bored, but Islamic art renews the energies, resurrects the movement, arousing in them lofty meanings and proper conduct. "Nothing can improve the self if it is in retreat except shifting from one mood to another."

All this is utterly serious and no jest, for those who are fighters do not jest.

Social Mutual Responsibility

Article Twenty

Moslem society is a mutually responsible society. The Prophet, prayers and greetings be unto him, said: "Blessed are the generous, whether they were in town or on a journey, who have collected all that they had and shared it equally among themselves."

The Islamic spirit is what should prevail in every Moslem society. The society that confronts a vicious enemy which acts in a way similar to Nazism, making no differentiation between man and woman, between children and old people—such a society is entitled to this Islamic spirit. Our enemy relies on the methods of collective punishment. He has deprived people of their homeland and properties, pursued them in their places of exile and gathering, breaking bones, shooting at women, children and old people, with or without a reason. The enemy has opened detention camps where thousands and thousands of people are thrown and kept under sub-human conditions. Added to this, are the demolition of houses, rendering children orphans, meting cruel sentences against thousands of young people, and causing them to spend the best years of their lives in the dungeons of prisons.

In their Nazi treatment, the Jews made no exception for women or children. Their policy of striking fear in the heart is meant for all. They attack people where their breadwinning is concerned, extorting their money and threatening their honour. They deal with people as if they were the worst war criminals. Deportation from the homeland is a kind of murder.

To counter these deeds, it is necessary that social mutual responsibility should prevail among the people. The enemy should be faced by the people as a single body which if one member of it should complain, the rest of the body would respond by feeling the same pains.

Article Twenty-One

Mutual social responsibility means extending assistance, financial or moral, to all those who are in need and joining in the execution of some of the work. Members of the Islamic Resistance Movement should consider the interests of the masses as their own personal interests. They must spare no effort in achieving and preserving them. They must prevent any foul play with the future of the upcoming generations and anything that could cause loss to society. The masses are part of them and they are part of the masses. Their strength is theirs, and their future is theirs. Members of the Islamic Resistance Movement should share the people's joy and grief, adopt the demands of the public and whatever means by which they could be realised. The day that such a spirit prevails, brotherliness would deepen, cooperation, sympathy and unity will be enhanced and the ranks will be solidified to confront the enemies.

Supportive Forces Behind the Enemy:

Article Twenty-Two

For a long time, the enemies have been planning, skillfully and with precision, for the achievement of what they have attained. They took into consideration the causes affecting the current of events. They strived to amass great and substantive material wealth which they devoted to the realisation of their dream. With their money, they took control of the world media, news agencies, the press, publishing houses, broadcasting stations, and others. With their money they stirred revolutions in various parts of the world with the purpose of achieving their interests and reaping the fruit therein. They were behind the French Revolution, the Communist revolution and most of the revolutions we heard and hear about, here and there. With their money they formed secret societies, such as Freemasons, Rotary Clubs, the Lions and others in different parts of the world for the purpose of sabotaging societies and achieving Zionist interests. With their money they were able to control imperialistic countries and instigate them to colonize many countries in order to enable them to exploit their resources and spread corruption there.

You may speak as much as you want about regional and world wars. They were behind World War I, when they were able to destroy the Islamic Caliphate, making financial gains and controlling resources. They obtained the Balfour Declaration, formed the League of Nations through which they could rule the world. They were behind World War II, through which they made huge financial gains by trading in armaments, and paved the way for the establishment of their state. It was they who instigated the replacement of the League of Nations with the United Nations and the Security Council to enable them to rule the world through them. There is no war going on anywhere, without having their finger in it.

"So often as they shall kindle a fire for war, Allah shall extinguish it; and they shall set their minds to act corruptly in the earth, but Allah loveth not the corrupt doers." (The Table - verse 64).

The imperialistic forces in the Capitalist West and Communist East, support the enemy with all their might, in money and in men. These forces take turns in doing that. The day Islam appears, the forces of infidelity would unite to challenge it, for the infidels are of one nation.

"O true believers, contract not an intimate friendship with any besides yourselves: they will not fail to corrupt you. They wish for that which may cause you to perish: their hatred hath already appeared from out of their mouths; but what their breasts conceal is yet more inveterate. We have already shown you signs of their ill will towards you, if ye understand." (The Family of Imran - verse 118).

It is not in vain that the verse is ended with Allah's words "if ye understand."

Our Attitudes Towards

A. Islamic Movements

Article Twenty-Three

The Islamic Resistance Movement views other Islamic movements with respect and appreciation. If it were at variance with them on one point or opinion, it is in agreement with them on other points and understandings.

It considers these movements, if they reveal good intentions and dedication to Allah, that they fall into the category of those who are trying hard since they act within the Islamic circle. Each active person has his share.

The Islamic Resistance Movement considers all these movements as a fund for itself. It prays to Allah for guidance and directions for all and it spares no effort to keep the banner of unity raised, ever striving for its realisation in accordance with the Koran and the Prophet's directives.

"And cleave all of you unto the covenant of Allah, and depart not from it, and remember the favour of Allah towards you: since ye were enemies, and he reconciled your hearts, and ye became companions and brethren by his favour: and ye were on the brink of a pit of fire, and he delivered you thence. Allah declareth unto you his signs, that ye may be directed." (The Family of Imran - Verse 102).

Article Twenty-Four

The Islamic Resistance Movement does not allow slandering or speaking ill of individuals or groups, for the believer does not indulge in such malpractices. It is necessary to differentiate between this behaviour and the stands taken by certain individuals and groups. Whenever those stands are erroneous, the Islamic Resistance Movement preserves the right to expound the error and to warn against it. It will strive to show the right path and to judge the case in question with objectivity. Wise conduct is indeed the target of the believer who follows it wherever he discerns it.

"Allah loveth not the speaking ill of anyone in public, unless he who is injured call for assistance; and Allah heareth and knoweth: whether ye publish a good action, or conceal it, or forgive evil, verily Allah is gracious and powerful." (Women - verses 147-148).

B. Nationalist Movements in the Palestinian Arena

Article Twenty-Five

The Islamic Resistance Movement respects these movements and appreciates their circumstances and the conditions surrounding and affecting them. It encourages them as long as they do not give their allegiance to the Communist East or the Crusading West. It confirms to all those who are integrated in it, or sympathetic towards it, that the Islamic Resistance Movement is a fighting movement that has a moral and enlightened look of life and the way it should cooperate with the other (movements). It detests opportunism and desires only the good of people, individuals and groups alike. It does not seek material gains, personal fame, nor does it look for a reward from others. It works with its own resources and whatever is at its disposal "and prepare for them whatever force you can", for the fulfilment of the duty, and the earning of Allah's favour. It has no other desire than that.

The Movement assures all the nationalist trends operating in the Palestinian arena for the liberation of Palestine, that it is there for their support and assistance. It will never be more than that, both in words and deeds, now and in the future. It is there to bring together and not to divide, to preserve and not to squander, to unify and not to throw asunder. It evaluates every good word, sincere effort and good offices. It closes the door in the face of side disagreements and does not lend an ear to rumours and slanders, while at the same time fully realising the right for self-defence.

Anything contrary or contradictory to these trends, is a lie disseminated by enemies or their lackeys for the purpose of sowing confusion, disrupting the ranks and occupy them with side issues.

"O true believers, if a wicked man come unto you with a tale, inquire strictly into the truth thereof; lest ye hurt people through ignorance, and afterwards repent of what ye have done." (The Inner Apartments - verse 6).

Article Twenty-Six

In viewing the Palestinian nationalist movements that give allegiance neither to the East nor the West, in this positive way, the Islamic Resistance Movement does not refrain from discussing new situations on the regional or international levels where the Palestinian question is concerned. It does that in such an objective manner revealing the extent of how much it is in harmony or contradiction with the national interests in the light of the Islamic point of view.

C. The Palestinian Liberation Organization

Article Twenty-Seven

The Palestinian Liberation Organization is the closest to the heart of the Islamic Resistance Movement. It contains the father and the brother, the next of kin and the friend. The Moslem does not estrange himself from his father, brother, next of kin or friend. Our homeland is one, our situation is one, our fate is one and the enemy is a joint enemy to all of us.

Because of the situations surrounding the formation of the Organization, of the ideological confusion prevailing in the Arab world as a result of the ideological invasion under whose influence the Arab world has fallen since the defeat of the Crusaders and which was, and still is, intensified through orientalists, missionaries and imperialists, the Organization adopted the idea of the secular state. And that it how we view it.

Secularism completely contradicts religious ideology. Attitudes, conduct and decisions stem from ideologies.

That is why, with all our appreciation for The Palestinian Liberation Organization—and what it can develop into—and without belittling its role in the Arab-Israeli conflict, we are unable to exchange the present or future Islamic Palestine with the secular idea. The Islamic nature of Palestine is part of our religion and whoever takes his religion lightly is a loser.

"Who will be adverse to the religion of Abraham, but he whose mind is infatuated? (The Cow - verse 130).

The day The Palestinian Liberation Organization adopts Islam as its way of life, we will become its soldiers, and fuel for its fire that will burn the enemies.

Until such a day, and we pray to Allah that it will be soon, the Islamic Resistance Movement's stand towards the PLO is that of the son towards his father, the brother towards his brother, and the relative to relative, suffers his pain and supports him in confronting the enemies, wishing him to be wise and well-guided.

"Stand by your brother, for he who is brotherless is like the fighter who goes to battle without arms. One's cousin is the wing one flies with - could the bird fly without wings?"

D. Arab and Islamic Countries

Article Twenty-Eight

The Zionist invasion is a vicious invasion. It does not refrain from resorting to all methods, using all evil and contemptible ways to achieve its end. It relies greatly in its infiltration and espionage operations on the secret organizations it gave rise to, such as the Freemasons, The Rotary and Lions clubs, and other sabotage groups. All these organizations, whether secret or open, work in the interest of Zionism and according to its instructions. They aim at undermining societies, destroying values, corrupting consciences, deteriorating character and annihilating Islam. It is behind the drug trade and alcoholism in all its kinds so as to facilitate its control and expansion.

Arab countries surrounding Israel are asked to open their borders before the fighters from among the Arab and Islamic nations so that they could consolidate their efforts with those of their Moslem brethren in Palestine.

As for the other Arab and Islamic countries, they are asked to facilitate the movement of the fighters from and to it, and this is the least thing they could do.

We should not forget to remind every Moslem that when the Jews conquered the Holy City in 1967, they stood on the threshold of the Aqsa Mosque and proclaimed that "Mohammed is dead, and his descendants are all women."

Israel, Judaism and Jews challenge Islam and the Moslem people. "May the cowards never sleep."

E. Nationalist and Religious Groupings, Institutions, Intellectuals, The Arab and Islamic World

The Islamic Resistance Movement hopes that all these groupings will side with it in all spheres, would support it, adopt its stand and solidify its activities and moves, work towards rallying support for it so that the Islamic people will be a base and a stay for it, supplying it with strategic depth an all human material and informative spheres, in time and in place. This should be done through the convening of solidarity conferences, the issuing of explanatory bulletins, favourable articles and booklets, enlightening the masses regarding the Palestinian issue, clarifying what confronts it and the conspiracies woven around it. They should mobilize the Islamic nations, ideologically, educationally and culturally, so that these peoples would be equipped to perform their role in the decisive battle of liberation, just as they did when they vanquished the Crusaders and the Tatars and saved human civilization. Indeed, that is not difficult for Allah.

"Allah hath written, Verily I will prevail, and my apostles: for Allah is strong and mighty." (The Dispute - verse 21).

Article Thirty

Writers, intellectuals, media people, orators, educators and teachers, and all the various sectors in the Arab and Islamic world—all of them are called upon to perform their role, and to fulfill their duty, because of the ferocity of the Zionist offensive and the Zionist influence in many countries exercised through financial and media control, as well as the consequences that all this lead to in the greater part of the world.

Jihad is not confined to the carrying of arms and the confrontation of the enemy. The effective word, the good article, the useful book, support and solidarity—together with the presence of sincere purpose for the hoisting of Allah's banner higher and higher—all these are elements of the Jihad for Allah's sake.

"Whosoever mobilises a fighter for the sake of Allah is himself a fighter. Whosoever supports the relatives of a fighter, he himself is a fighter." (related by al-Bukhari, Moslem, Abu-Dawood and al-Tarmadhi).

F. Followers of Other Religions: The Islamic Resistance Movement Is A Humanistic Movement

Article Thirty-One

The Islamic Resistance Movement is a humanistic movement. It takes care of human rights and is guided by Islamic tolerance when dealing with the followers of other religions. It does not antagonize anyone of them except if it is antagonized by it or stands in its way to hamper its moves and waste its efforts.

Under the wing of Islam, it is possible for the followers of the three religions—Islam, Christianity and Judaism—to coexist in peace and quiet with each other. Peace and quiet would not be possible except under the wing of Islam. Past and present history are the best witness to that.

It is the duty of the followers of other religions to stop disputing the sovereignty of Islam in this region, because the day these followers should take over there will be nothing but carnage, displacement and terror. Everyone of them is at variance with his fellow-religionists, not to speak about followers of other religionists. Past and present history are full of examples to prove this fact.

"They will not fight against you in a body, except in fenced towns, or from behind walls. Their strength in war among themselves is great: thou thinkest them to be united; but their hearts are divided. This, because they are people who do not understand." (The Emigration - verse 14).

Islam confers upon everyone his legitimate rights. Islam prevents the incursion on other people's rights. The Zionist Nazi activities against our people will not last for long. "For the state of injustice lasts but one day, while the state of justice lasts till Doomsday."

"As to those who have not borne arms against you on account of religion, nor turned you out of your dwellings, Allah forbiddeth you not to deal kindly with them, and to behave justly towards them; for Allah loveth those who act justly." (The Tried - verse 8).

The Attempt to Isolate the Palestinian People

Article Thirty-Two

World Zionism, together with imperialistic powers, try through a studied plan and an intelligent strategy to remove one Arab state after another from the circle of struggle against Zionism, in order to have it finally face the Palestinian people only. Egypt was, to a great extent, removed from the circle of the struggle, through the treacherous Camp David Agreement. They are trying to draw other Arab countries into similar agreements and to bring them outside the circle of struggle.

The Islamic Resistance Movement calls on Arab and Islamic nations to take up the line of serious and persevering action to prevent the success of this horrendous plan, to warn the people of the danger emanating from leaving the circle of struggle against Zionism. Today it is Palestine, tomorrow it will be one country or another. The Zionist plan is limitless. After Palestine, the Zionists aspire to expand from the Nile to the Euphrates. When they will have digested the region they overtook, they will aspire to further expansion, and so on. Their plan is embodied in the "Protocols of the Elders of Zion", and their present conduct is the best proof of what we are saying.

Leaving the circle of struggle with Zionism is high treason, and cursed be he who does that. "for whoso shall turn his back unto them on that day, unless he turneth aside to fight, or retreateth to another party of the faithful, shall draw on himself the indignation of Allah, and his abode shall be hell; an ill journey shall it be thither." (The Spoils - verse 16). There is no way out except by concentrating all powers and energies to face this Nazi, vicious Tatar invasion. The alternative is loss of one's country, the dispersion of citizens, the spread of vice on earth and the destruction of religious values. Let every person know that he is responsible before Allah, for "the doer of the slightest good deed is rewarded in like, and the does of the slightest evil deed is also rewarded in like."

The Islamic Resistance Movement consider itself to be the spearhead of the circle of struggle with world Zionism and a step on the road. The Movement adds its efforts to the efforts of all those who are active in the Palestinian arena. Arab and Islamic Peoples should augment by further steps on their part; Islamic groupings all over the Arab world should also do the same, since all of these are the best-equipped for the future role in the fight with the warmongering Jews.

". . . and we have put enmity and hatred between them, until the day of resurrection. So often as they shall kindle a fire of war, Allah shall extinguish it; and they shall set their minds to act corruptly in the earth, but Allah loveth not the corrupt doers." (The Table - verse 64).

Article Thirty-Three

The Islamic Resistance Movement, being based on the common coordinated and interdependent conceptions of the laws of the universe, and flowing in the stream of destiny in confronting and fighting the enemies in defence of the Moslems and Islamic civilization and sacred sites, the first among which is the Aqsa Mosque, urges the Arab and Islamic peoples, their governments, popular and official groupings, to fear Allah where their view of the Islamic Resistance Movement and their dealings with it are concerned. They should back and support it, as Allah wants them to, extending to it more and more funds till Allah's purpose is achieved when ranks will close up, fighters join other fighters and masses everywhere in the Islamic world will come forward in response to the call of duty while loudly proclaiming: Hail to Jihad. Their cry will reach the heavens and will go on being resounded until liberation is achieved, the invaders vanquished and Allah's victory comes about.

"And Allah will certainly assist him who shall be on his side: for Allah is strong and mighty." (The Pilgrimage - verse 40).

The Testimony of History

Across History in Confronting the Invaders

Article Thirty-Four

Palestine is the navel of the globe and the crossroad of the continents. Since the dawn of history, it has been the target of expansionists. The Prophet, Allah bless him and grant him salvation, had himself pointed to this fact in the noble Hadith in which he called on his honourable companion, Ma'adh ben-Jabal, saying: O Ma'ath, Allah throw open before you, when I am gone, Syria, from Al-Arish to the Euphrates. Its men, women and slaves will stay firmly there till the Day of Judgement. Whoever of you should choose one of the Syrian shores, or the Holy Land, he will be in constant struggle till the Day of Judgement."

Expansionists have more than once put their eye on Palestine which they attacked with their armies to fulfill their designs on it. Thus it was that the Crusaders came with their armies, bringing with them their creed and carrying their Cross. They were able to defeat the Moslems for a while, but the Moslems were able to retrieve the land only when they stood under the wing of their religious banner, united their word, hallowed the name of Allah and surged out fighting under the leadership of Salah ed-Din al-Ayyubi. They fought for almost twenty years and at the end the Crusaders were defeated and Palestine was liberated.

"Say unto those who believe not, Ye shall be overcome, and thrown together into hell; an unhappy couch it shall be." (The Family of Imran - verse 12).

This is the only way to liberate Palestine. There is no doubt about the testimony of history. It is one of the laws of the universe and one of the rules of existence. Nothing can overcome iron except iron. Their false futile creed can only be defeated by the righteous Islamic creed. A creed could not be fought except by a creed, and in the last analysis, victory is for the just, for justice is certainly victorious.

"Our word hath formerly been given unto our servants the apostles; that they should certainly be assisted against the infidels, and that our armies should surely be the conquerors." (Those Who Rank Themselves - verses 171-172).

Article Thirty-Five

The Islamic Resistance Movement views seriously the defeat of the Crusaders at the hands of Salah ed-Din al-Ayyubi and the rescuing of Palestine from their hands, as well as the defeat of the Tatars at Ein Galot, breaking their power at the hands of Qataz and Al-Dhaher Bivers and saving the Arab world from the Tatar onslaught which aimed at the destruction of every meaning of human civilization. The Movement draws lessons and examples from all this. The present Zionist onslaught has also been preceded by Crusading raids from the West and other Tatar raids from the East. Just as the Moslems faced those raids and planned fighting and defeating them, they should be able to confront the Zionist invasion and defeat it. This is indeed no problem for the Almighty Allah, provided that the intentions are pure, the determination is true and that Moslems have benefited from past experiences, rid themselves of the effects of ideological invasion and followed the customs of their ancestors.

The Islamic Resistance Movement is Composed of Soldiers

Article Thirty-Six

While paving its way, the Islamic Resistance Movement, emphasizes time and again to all the sons of our people, to the Arab and Islamic nations, that it does not seek personal fame, material gain, or social prominence. It does not aim to compete against any one from among our people, or take his place. Nothing of the sort at all. It will not act against any of the sons of Moslems or those who are peaceful towards it from among non-Moslems, be they here or anywhere else. It will only serve as a support for all groupings and organizations operating against the Zionist enemy and its lackeys.

The Islamic Resistance Movement adopts Islam as its way of life. Islam is its creed and religion. Whoever takes Islam as his way of life, be it an organization, a grouping, a country or any other body, the Islamic Resistance Movement considers itself as their soldiers and nothing more.

We ask Allah to show us the right course, to make us an example to others and to judge between us and our people with truth. "O Lord, do thou judge between us and our nation with truth; for thou art the best judge." (Al Araf - Verse 89).

The last of our prayers will be praise to Allah, the Master of the Universe.

DOCUMENT NO. 6

FATAH AND HAMAS: THE NEW PALESTINIAN FACTIONAL REALITY

CRS Report
RS22395

March 3, 2006

Aaron D. Pina
Analyst in Middle Eastern Affairs
Foreign Affairs, Defense, and Trade Division

Summary

For the first time in its history, the Palestinian parliament is set to be led by Hamas, which the United States and European Union have designated a foreign terrorist organization. Although some lauded the generally free and fair election in January 2006, others criticized the outcome and accused Hamas of "hijacking" democracy. This report provides an overview of the new political realities in the West Bank and Gaza after the election, the challenges Fatah and Hamas face, and possible implications for U.S. policy. This report will be updated as warranted. For more information on the Palestinians, see CRS Report RL33269, *Palestinian Elections*, by Aaron D. Pina, CRS Issue Brief IB91137 *The Middle East Peace Talks*, by Carol Migdalovitz, and CRS Report RS22370, *U.S. Assistance to the Palestinians*, by Jeremy M. Sharp.

Background

On January 25, 2006, Palestinians voted in parliamentary elections and Hamas emerged as the clear winner, with 74 out of 132 parliamentary seats. Fatah, the dominant party in the Palestine Liberation Organization (PLO), won 45 seats, and 13 seats went to other minor parties. Since then, several governments, including the United States, have cautioned that unless

Hamas disavows terrorism, recognizes Israel, and accepts all previous Israeli-Palestinian agreements, diplomatic and economic relations with the Palestinian Authority may be circumscribed or ended altogether.

Hamas[1]

During the 1970s and 1980s, Palestinians experienced a rise in political Islam, embodied in Hamas, founded in 1987 by the late Sheik Ahmad Yasin. Hamas couches the Palestinian national struggle in religious terms and is a Palestinian offshoot of the parent Muslim Brotherhood, an Islamist group founded in Egypt in 1928 by Hassan al-Banna. During the late 1980s, Israel lent tacit support to Hamas in an effort to check the growing authority of a secular and nationalist PLO. Over the past three decades, Hamas has risen to prominence, in part due to a well-organized network that provides Palestinians with social services and charity, and augments civil society.

Leadership and Structure. Hamas appears to include political and military wings, but distinctions between the two are not fully clear. Hamas' leadership structure is more difficult to discern. Various sources describe the leaders as follows:

- **Khaled Mishal:** Mishal was born in the West Bank in 1956 and studied physics at Kuwait University, where he led the Islamic Palestinian student movement. Mishal is considered the leader of Hamas and resides in Damascus, Syria, where he has lived in exile since the early 1990s.
- **Ismail Haniya:** Haniya, who is in his forties, graduated from Gaza's Islamic University with a degree in Arabic literature. He was also the dean of the university. Along with many Hamas figures, Haniya was expelled to Lebanon in the early 1990s. Though considered a Hamas moderate, some believe Haniya's moderation to be a political tactic. Haniya has been designated the new Palestinian Prime Minister and has until mid-March to form a government.
- **Musa Abu-Marzuq:** Born in Gaza in 1951, Marzuq received a doctorate in industrial engineering in the United States. He serves as Hamas' deputy political leader, and is based in Syria. He lived in the United States and Jordan for many years and was expelled from both countries. In 2004, a U.S. court indicted him in absentia for coordinating and financing Hamas activities.
- **Mahmoud al-Zahar:** Born in Gaza, Zahar, studied medicine in Cairo and is a founding member of Hamas. Referred to as a "hardliner," Zahar is to lead the Hamas faction in parliament.

[1] Hamas is an acronym for *Harakat al-Muqawamah al-Islamiyyah* (the Islamic Resistance Movement). Hamas also means "zeal" in Arabic.

- **Aziz Dweik:** Dweik, an academic by profession, was born in 1948 and has a doctorate from the University of Pennsylvania. Dweik was deported to Lebanon in 1992 and served as spokesperson of the deportees. Dweik is slated to become Speaker of parliament.
- **Sheik Hassan Yousef:** Yousef, in his fifties, has been the head of Hamas in the West Bank since 2001, and is currently in an Israeli prison. Considered by many experts to be pragmatic, Yousef's participation in parliament, should he be released, may promote moderation within Hamas.
- **Sheik Muhammed Abu Tayr:** Tayr, from Jerusalem, is in his fifties and garnered the second-most votes on Hamas' national candidates list. Tayr spent 25 years in prison, is a former member of Fatah, and generally keeps a lower profile than other Hamas leaders. Though multiple reports claim Tayr supports *sharia* (Islamic law) influenced legislation, he does not appear to want to impose Islamic law.
- **Mohamed Deif:** Deif, 40 years old, is from Gaza. Since 2002, he has been the Gaza commander of the military wing of Hamas. According to some, Deif's mentor was Yahya Ayyash, a renowned Hamas bomb maker and head of the Qassam brigades until his assassination in late 1995. Deif's exact whereabouts are unknown.

Hamas' Challenges. Hamas has never entered the political realm, and in the view of many, may have to be more accommodating politically if it wants to retain governing authority.

Forming the Next Government. The new Palestinian parliament was sworn in on February 18, and Hamas is expected to form a government within five weeks. Some within Hamas appear to support forming a government of non-political technocrats, which might forestall recognizing Israel or losing much needed foreign aid. Israeli leaders, however, have said a government influenced by Hamas or containing Hamas representatives would be unacceptable, and the United States along with others in the international community have a similar view.

Foreign Aid. Israel and the United States are moving to restrict aid to the Palestinians unless Hamas renounces terrorism, recognizes Israel, and accepts all Israeli-Palestinian agreements. Though some within Israel and the United States have discussed the possibility of continuing humanitarian assistance, the aid dilemma may push Hamas toward Iran. In the late 1980s, 10% of all Hamas funding came Iran, and the government of Iran recently pledged to transfer $250 million to the PA if Israel and the United States cut off funding. The Arab League is to meet in March to possibly finalize an aid package to the Palestinians. Saudi Arabia has pledged $20 million and Qatar has pledged $13 million to the PA. Saudi Arabia also plans to provide the PA with $1.2 billion in financial assistance over the next two years. On February 27, the EU announced that it would release

$142 million in aid to the Palestinians. The aid will pay energy bills ($47 million) and support the United Nations Refugee Works Agency ($75 million). The EU also decided to unblock over $20 million to pay salaries; this is the only part of the new aid package to be paid directly to the PA. The move comes in the wake of the Israeli cabinet's decision to withhold monthly tax payments to the Palestinians and the U.S. demand that the PA return $50 million in aid to prevent it from falling into Hamas' hands.

Relations with Israel and the International Community. So far, Russia (with French support) and Turkey appear to have been the only major states to engage Hamas publicly. Turkish officials met with a Hamas delegation on February 17, and Russia plans to host a Hamas delegation in early March. After initially freezing monthly customs and tax revenues owed to the PA (more than $50 million per month), the Israeli government released $55 million to the PA. On February 19, after the Hamas-led parliament was seated, the Israeli cabinet decided to suspend similar transfers to the PA in the future. Israeli Foreign Minister Tzipi Livni stated that Israel may transfer funds to the PA for humanitarian purposes only. There are also some reports that suggest Hamas officials may seek aid from Brazil, Argentina, Venezuela, Bolivia, and Iran. On February 21, Secretary of State Rice met with Egyptian officials to advance U.S. efforts to isolate Hamas economically. At a joint press conference, Egyptian Foreign Minister Ahmed Aboul Gheit stated his belief that Hamas will evolve and that Egypt and the United States should not prejudge the issue.

Fatah and the Palestinian Liberation Organization

In 1964, in partial response to the wider trend of militant radicalism, the Arab League founded the PLO. Fatah subsequently became dominant in the PLO and between 1968–2006 the organization monopolized nearly all aspects of factional politics in the West Bank and Gaza Strip.

Leadership and Structure. President Mahmoud Abbas is the Chairman of the PLO and the head of Fatah. The leading political body within Fatah is the Central Committee, elected by the general membership. Fatah's Revolutionary Council parallels the Central Committee as a decision-making body and includes armed resistance as an option. Additionally, three militia-type organizations have developed from Fatah: the al-Aqsa Martyrs Brigades, a designated foreign terrorist organization that emerged during the *intifada* that began in September 2000, and takes a violent approach to force Israel to end its occupation; Force 17, a personal security force for PLO leaders that was involved in attacks on Israeli targets in the early 1980s; and the *Tanzim* (or organization) militia, which is considered to be an armed offshoot of Fatah. The leaders are often described as follows:

- **Mahmoud Abbas:** Abbas (a.k.a. Abu Mazen) was sworn in as President of the PA on January 15, 2005. Prior to that, Abbas served as Prime

Minister in 2003. A founding member of Fatah, Abbas also holds a doctorate from the Oriental University in Moscow.

- **Ahmed Qurei:** Qurei first joined Fatah in 1968 and headed the PLO's financial portfolio. He founded the Palestinian Economic Council for Development and Construction. He also served as Prime Minister between 2003–2005.
- **Mohammed Dahlan:** Dahlan, a longtime Fatah member and founder of the Fatah Youth Association in 1981, was jailed in Israel for political activism between 1983–1988. He participated in Israeli-Palestinian negotiations and is considered a major political figure in Gaza. He is the former Minister of the Interior and now heads the Third Way Party.
- **Nabil Shaath**: Shaath, the Palestinian foreign minister, has been a member of the Fatah Central Committee since 1971, and headed the PLO's first delegation to the United Nations in 1974. He was chief negotiator from 1993 to 1995, and participated in peace talks conducted at Camp David in 2000 and Taba in 2001.
- **Marwan Barghouti:** Barghouti is a militant political figure currently serving consecutive life sentences in Israel for murder. He is the leader of the *Tanzim*. Though currently jailed, Barghouti won a parliamentary seat in the election, and many see him as an opponent to Israeli-Palestinian peace agreements.

Fatah's Challenges. Fatah is out of power for the first time in its history and, some say, may have to alter its political outlook in order to regain popularity.

New Political Role. In addition to corruption, many claim that ongoing power struggles between "old guard" Fatah stalwarts and "young guard" members contributed to political fissures within the party, which Hamas exploited in the parliamentary elections. The inability of Fatah leaders to contain old-guard/new-guard tensions have reportedly increased internal political dysfunction. As a result of poor party discipline, multiple party lists, and limited technical preparation for the parliamentary vote, Fatah gained only 45 parliamentary seats (out of 132). Fatah did, however, capture 42% of the popular vote.

Fatah faces a need to re-evaluate its political agenda, tackle corruption, and rebuild the allegiance of its constituents, who launched mass demonstrations immediately following the elections and called for the resignation of Fatah's central committee. For Fatah to compete effectively, it will most likely need to cultivate effective internal methods of conflict resolution, consensus building, and reconcile intra-party rivalry.

President vs. Parliament. Many observers fear that unless a national unity coalition government is formed, the PA may be hampered by infighting, rivalry, and political deadlock or even civil war. A situation whereby the President does not belong to the ruling parliamentary bloc is foreign to Palestinian politics and some contend that President Abbas will have great difficulty implementing his goal of a negotiated settlement to the Israeli-Palestinian conflict. Other experts point to Abbas' own declarations that suggest he may resign if his political vision of a negotiated settlement to the Israel-Palestinian conflict is not followed. Still others contend that if Hamas resists President Abbas or refuses to dissociate itself from violence, Abbas may dissolve the parliament and call for new elections.

Peace Process. Most experts agree that as long as a Hamas-led Palestinian government remains hostile toward Israel, the peace process is likely to remain moribund, and Israel may quicken the pace of unilateral withdrawal. President Abbas may try to continue the peace process through the PLO, which is signatory to all Israeli-Palestinian agreements. Yet it is unclear how Hamas would react to political actions that parallel its own. Some Hamas officials have also intimated that they may join the PLO.

Outlook

The full implications of Hamas' victory in the January 2006 parliamentary elections are not yet clear. The most significant question may be whether Hamas' participation in government, and the responsibility that accompanies elected office will moderate its militancy. As for Fatah, although it accepted the outcome of the parliamentary elections, its political future is uncertain. While recent reports suggest that Fatah may have agreed in principle to join Hamas in a national coalition government, Fatah hardliners may decide to undermine the government from within or leave the coalition government in protest. The future of the PLO is also undecided. As signatory to all peace agreements with Israel, the PLO has the authority to continue negotiations. Hamas is not a member of the PLO. As head of the PLO, President Abbas may elect to conduct future negotiations via the PLO's good offices although his defacto political authority to do so is questionable. Yet there are growing signs that Hamas may wish to join the PLO in a move designed to possibly re-shape the organization and bring it within Hamas' sphere of influence.

There is little doubt that the Hamas electoral victory complicates U.S. policy toward the Palestinians and its wider strategy of democracy promotion in the Middle East. Following the election, President Bush stated that the results had "given a wake-up call to the leadership," adding that "a party that articulates the destruction of Israel is a party with which we will not deal."[2] Many in Congress appear to support isolating Hamas economically

[2] White House Press Conference, January 26, 2006.

unless it recognizes Israel and disavows violence, while others are concerned that any funding void will be filled by Saudi Arabia, or possibly Iran. Still other experts contend that if the Palestinian economic crisis deepens, Hamas may be able to exploit decreases in U.S. aid to deflect any possible criticism that the new government is unable to improve Palestinian lives, and lay the blame on U.S. policy.

Recent Legislation

H.R. 4668 (introduced in the House International Relations Committee on January 31, 2006) resolves that the President would have to certify, among other conditions, that the PA is not controlled by a designated foreign terrorist organization (FTO).

H.R. 4681 (referred to the House Committee on International Relations, and in addition to the Committees on the Judiciary, and Financial Services, for a period to be subsequently determined by the Speaker) requires that the President certify that no element of the PA is controlled by a FTO and no member of an FTO serves in a ministry, agency, or instrumentality of the PA.

S. 2237 the Palestinian Compliance Act of 2006 (introduced in the Senate Foreign Relations Committee on February 1, 2006) includes a requirement that the President's waiver authority (Section 550 (b) of P.L. 109-102, the FY2006 Foreign Operations Appropriations Act) may only be used if the PA renounces terrorism and recognizes Israel's right to exist and takes appropriate steps to amend the Hamas Covenant to delete statements that are hostile to Israel and that support violence.

S.Con.Res. 79 (passed the Senate on February 1, 2006, and referred to the House International Relations Committee on February 7, 2006) resolves that it is the sense of Congress that no U.S. assistance should be provided directly to the PA if any representative political party holding a majority of parliamentary seats within the PA maintains a position calling for the destruction of Israel.

H.Con.Res 228 (referred to the House Committee on International Relations on February 8, 2006) urges members of the Organization of American States to designate Hezbollah, Hamas, Palestinian Islamic Jihad, al-Qaeda and its constituent entities, and other such groups as terrorist organizations if they have not already done so.

DOCUMENT NO. 7

A HAMAS GOVERNMENT: ISOLATE OR ENGAGE?

United States Institute of Peace (USIP) Briefing

March 2006

Shlomo Brom

The landslide victory of the Palestinian Islamist movement Hamas in the January 25 Palestinian legislative elections has been met with concern and alarm by Israel, the United States, and others in the international community. This concern is rooted in Hamas' history as an organization that sponsors terrorism and that is ideologically committed to the destruction of Israel. For many observers in Israel and throughout the international community, Hamas' victory signaled the end of Israeli-Palestinian peacemaking.

This paper reviews the position of the major stakeholders in the conflict and assesses the advantages and risks of the two strategies that have crystallized since the election: isolate and undermine a Hamas government, or engage with it in a cautious, selective, and conditional manner. This paper argues that a policy of engagement, if properly executed, could encourage fundamental changes in Hamas' policies and, eventually, its ideology. Moreover, this approach is preferable to the "isolate and undermine" option because it will be easier to move from a policy of engagement to one of confrontation if it becomes clear that engagement has failed to induce changes in Hamas' policies and actions. A movement in the opposite direction may not be possible.

Where the Parties Stand

- The "Quartet" (the United States, the EU, Russia, and the UN) has demanded that Hamasrecognize Israel's right to exist, forswear violence, and accept previous Israeli-Palestinian agreements—or face isolation and sharp reductions in foreign aid. The United States has already stopped aid to the Palestinian Authority (P.A.) and has even suggested it will rescind some earlier assistance packages.

- Israel has put forward its own preconditions for any dialogue with Hamas, demands that go beyond the Quartet's. Israeli leaders have said that terrorist infrastructure must be dismantled, and Hamas must repudiate and revise those parts of its covenant that deny Israel's right to exist. Until these conditions are met, Israel is prepared to cut off relations with the Palestinian Authority by severing economic ties, suspending the transfer of taxes and customs collected on behalf of the P.A., barring the entry of Palestinian workers into Israel, and preventing construction of a seaport and airport in Gaza. Israel has already suspended revenue transfers and intends to implement additional steps following the formation of the Hamas government. These steps will undoubtedly lead to a major financial crisis for Palestinians, if not to a collapse, since Israel's leverage far exceeds that of Western donors.
- Recent public pronouncements from Hamas are mixed. So far, Hamas has refused to recognize Israel; suggested that they will selectively adhere to previous Israeli-Palestinian agreements ("to the extent that they serve Palestinian national interests"); and indicated that they are only willing to enter into a long-term ceasefire (*hudna*) if Israel withdraws to the 1967 borders. At the conclusion of a recent visit to Moscow, Hamas leaders publicly asserted that the party will remain inflexible and uncompromising, though statements by some Hamas officials in the territories suggest the possibility of pragmatism.

Policy Options

There are two basic policy options, with variations, for Israel, the United States, and other members of the international community. The first is based on the assumption that a radical Islamist organization such as Hamas, with its deep ideological roots, is incapable of changing. It therefore asserts that there is only one rational response: to isolate the Hamas government, undermine it, bring about its downfall, and then wait for a new reality to emerge that will be more amenable to peace and stability.

There are several problems with this strategy. First, if there is any potential for Hamas to change, implementation of this policy forecloses such a possibility. Second, it is more likely to result in anarchy and chaos and possibly a resumption of full-scale violent conflict with Israel. Engineering the collapse of a Hamas government is unlikely to result in greater stability. Furthermore, Hamas will have little interest in keeping even to the limited ceasefire (*tahdi'a*) it has committed itself to if outside actors are undermining their elected government.

Third, the failures of the Hamas government and the hardships suffered by the Palestinian population will, most probably, not be attributed to Hamas. Instead, Israel and the West will be blamed, and the rift with the Palestinians and the Islamic world will only widen. Fourth, it will be difficult to convince the international community and the major aid providers to maintain such an approach as conditions in the Palestinian territories deteriorate. In fact, such a policy will probably enhance attempts by Iran to expand its role.

That said, the main advantages of this policy option are its simplicity and its moral clarity. It expresses a clear, unequivocal stance against terrorism and against the objectionable positions in Hamas' covenant. Supporters of the "isolate and undermine" approach sometimes argue that it would deter others in the region from making similar policy choices, if given the opportunity at the ballot box. But this is a dubious proposition.

The second approach gives Hamas the opportunity to change without foreclosing on the option of isolating it if it refuses. There are a few reasons to hope that Hamas is capable of change. First, it is not al-Qaeda. Although it is a radical Islamist movement, it is rooted in a national program, not a pan-Islamic cause. Hamas was elected primarily on its promises to provide effective, honest governance. This program depends on wider public support than Hamas currently enjoys, given that only 45percent of voters chose Hamas in the January election. Moreover, many Hamas voters cast a protest vote against Fatah and what the public perceived as a corrupt ruling elite. The vote was not an endorsement of Hamas' platform vis-à-vis Israel. Hamas knows the vast majority of the Palestinian public want quiet, law and order, security, good governance, and basic services. It will be up to Hamasto deliver on these expectations.[1]

The organization that Hamas will lead, the Palestinian Authority, is a unique governing body. First, it is completely and utterly dependent on the good will of external actors. Its budget depends on taxes and customs collected by Israel and on foreign aid from the outside world. The P.A. is composed of two disconnected territorial units, the West Bank and Gaza, and passage between them is dependent on another state. Its imports and exports are almost completely dependent on Israel, its biggest market and its main outlet to the international market.

The behavior of Hamas leaders since the election indicates they are aware of their dependence and have a sober assessment of its implications. This may be why Hamas was initially interested in a coalition government with Fatah headed by a non-Hamas figure. Its own campaign promises, combined with the public's expectations—not to mention the inherent constraints of the P.A.—may be leading Hamas to acquiesce to more moderate and pragmatic policies.

[1] See Khalil Shikaki, "Willing to Compromise: Palestinian Public Opinion and the Peace Process," United States Institute of Peace, Special Report #158, January 2006.

In order to succeed, this alternative approach will have to differentiate between what realistically can be expected from Hamas now and what can be expected at later stages. It should be made absolutely clear to Hamas that recognition of Israel is a necessary end following the process of engagement, but it should not be presented as an ultimatum that requires immediate acceptance. Hamas should be presented with a plan that delineates each stage of the process, describes milestones within each stage, and outlines sanctions and rewards if it stays the course with the Quartet's Road Map peace plan. In the first stage, what is important is:

a) Action by a Hamas government to strengthen the ceasefire and prevent other armed groups (e.g., Islamic Jihad, al Aqsa Martyrs Brigade, Popular Resistance Committees) from acting violently against Israel;

b) Maintaining existing agreements with Israel without exceptions and reservations; and

c) Avoiding steps that would undermine Palestinian democracy and human rights.

These demands are within Hamas' capacity to fulfill. At later stages, other key steps would include dismantling militias, including their own, and making the necessary ideological changes, including the recognition of Israel.

It must be recognized that this approach carries significant risks. First, it demands a common, coordinated, and nuanced policy on the part of the external actors, which will be difficult to achieve. Second, if not properly executed, this policy could lead Hamas to believe it can play outsiders against each other, escape meaningful change, and eventually bypass the tougher policy goals such as dismantling the militias and making ideological concessions. Third, there is a concern that Hamas could play a double game and use any pause to re-arm and build up its terrorist infrastructure. Fourth, less committed members of the international community could waver on maintaining the system of milestones, sanctions, and rewards. Finally, there is a risk that such an approach might encourage other societies in the region to support similar radical movements.

Some of these risks should not be exaggerated; others are misplaced. To some extent, Israel's withdrawal from Gaza already enabled Hamas to reorganize and rebuild while they adhered to the *tahdi'a*. But any build-up by Hamas can be countered by the continued control of external boundaries by other parties, Israeli security control over the West Bank, and the continuation of Israel's separation barrier/fence.

The main advantage of the engagement approach is that it provides a framework to test the new Palestinian leadership, while at the same time denying it excuses for failure to change its ways. Should Hamas fail because of outside pressure, which remains a likely outcome, it will be more difficult to attribute its failure to its obduracy. They will shift blame to outside parties. Furthermore, this approach could widen the Palestinian consensus for a two-state solution without compromising support for Palestinian democracy. It could also create a relatively stable and secure situation on the ground. Past experience shows that cautious, selective, and conditional engagement, when combined with the right mix of pressure, can be productive, particularly in terms of alliance management. Should engagement fail, it will be easier to build a coalition that supports confrontation. The present case of Iran is instructive.

A period of conditional engagement not only deals with the risks presented by the new situation, but also exploits possible opportunities. Moreover, the engagement approach—if properly designed—is consistent with the Quartet statement of January 30 and the conditions placed on Hamas, there by creating a pathway for the parties to return to the Road Map. Finally, should a Hamas government be destined to fail, as many believe it is, allowing it to collapse under its own weight is far preferable to being seen as responsible for its demise.

About the Author

This USIPeace Briefing was written by General Shlomo Brom, guest scholar in the Center for Conflict Analysis and Prevention at the United States Institute of Peace and contributor to USIP's Project on Arab-Israeli Futures. General Brom served for thirty years in the Israel Defense Forces, holding a variety of high-level positions in military intelligence and strategic planning. He served most recently as deputy national security advisor for strategic planning, and has many years of experience as a negotiator with Syria and the Palestinians. Brom has also served as a senior scholar at the Jaffee Center for Strategic Studies at Tel Aviv University. The views expressed here are not those of USIP, which does not advocate specific policies.

About the Center for Conflict Analysis and Prevention

The purpose of USIP's Center for Conflict Analysis and Prevention (CCAP) is to initiate and support programs aimed at forestalling serious outbreaks of violence in key areas of the world. Established in 2005, the Center is directed by Dr. Paul Stares and staffed by a team of regional and functional experts.

About the United States Institute of Peace

The United States Institute of Peace is an independent, nonpartisan, national institution established and funded by Congress to help prevent, manage, and resolve international conflicts by empowering others with knowledge, skills, and resources, as well as by direct involvement in peace building efforts around the world.

DOCUMENT NO. 8

THE BORDER FENCE BETWEEN THE GAZA STRIP AND EGYPT BREACHED

Intelligence and Terrorism Information Center at the Israel Intelligence Heritage & Commemoration Center (IICC) Report

January 29, 2008

With the border fence between the Gaza Strip and Egypt breached, Hamas and other terrorist organizations can freely smuggle operatives and weapons into the Gaza Strip and dispatch terrorists to Israel through Sinai. The Egyptians are looking for a solution but Hamas does not intend to give up its achievement.[1]

Overview

1. Breaching the border fence between the Gaza Strip and Egypt and the flow of hundreds of thousands of Gazans into Egyptian Rafah are, in our assessment, **a well-planned Hamas move** which is liable to have far-reaching implications for the status of the radical Islamic terrorist entity which was created in the Gaza Strip when Hamas took over in June 2006.

2. In our assessment Hamas's main objectives were the following:

   1) **Removing or seriously easing Israel's pressure on the Gaza Strip which followed the closing of the crossings into Israel and Egypt.**

Editor's note: The original version of this document included some color images that could not be adequately reproduced in this publication. Where necessary, captions and/or headings specifically relating to any omitted images have also been left out of the version reprinted herein. The main text of the document has not been affected by these omissions.

[1] Follow-up of our January 23 Bulletin "Crowds of Gazans streamed into Egypt after the border fence was breached" at http://www.terrorism-info.org.il/malam_multimedia/English/eng_n/html/gaza_230108e.htm and http://www.terrorism-info.org.il/malam_multimedia/English/eng_n/pdf/gaza_230108e.pdf.

2) As a result **freedom of action** for Hamas and the other terrorist organizations to fire rockets and carry out terrorist attacks from other areas in the Gaza Strip has increased.

3) Accelerating Hamas's **military buildup** by establishing a border regime which will enable **the easy and unobstructed passage of operatives and weapons into the Gaza Strip,** including advanced weapons such as standard rockets and anti-aircraft guns, etc.

4) **To display Hamas's strength to Egypt** (and the rest of the Arab world) and to motivate the Egyptians to support it in its **confrontation** of Abu Mazen's **Palestinian Authority**.

3. As in the past, Egypt avoided confronting the Hamas challenge and ensuing dilemmas. **On the ground,** the Egypt security forces allowed the flow of Gazans into Egyptian Rafah without using excessive force. **Politically,** Egypt is trying to mediate between Hamas and Abu Mazen to find an internal Palestinian solution which will lead to the reopening of the Rafah Crossing on a basis different from the Crossings Agreement of 2005. **In our assessment, any solution reached will mean Hamas control of the crossing into Egypt, the Gaza Strip's "oxygen tube."**

4. As far as Israel is concerned, the situation created is a **clear and present security threat.** A breached border fence and the possibility of a reopened Rafah Crossing under Hamas control enable the terrorist organizations to keep up **a steady stream of weapons and operatives** into the Gaza Strip **(including global jihad operatives,** who have easy access to weapons and supporters in the Sinai Peninsula). In addition, it will be relatively easy for the terrorist organizations to dispatch squads into Israel through the wide-open Israel-Egyptian border from the Gaza Strip to Eilat.

5. The situation on the ground since the fence was breached until noon of January 28 is as follows:

The Main Developments Along the Gazan-Egyptian Border

6. **For the sixth consecutive day,** there has been a steady flow of Gazans in and out of Egyptian Rafah, although it has slowed somewhat due to the weather. Gazans continue to cross into Egyptian territory to buy basic foodstuffs and various types of fuel. It has been estimated that hundreds of thousands have passed through the breaches. As they were widened vehicles began crossing at three main locations. Scores of trucks have entered carrying basic commodities and fuel from Egypt. The Gazans have emptied most of the shelves in the stores in Egyptian Rafah and El-Arish.

7. At first the Egyptian security forces tried to control the breaches and stop the flow of Gazans, but Hamas operatives breached the fence in additional locations with bulldozers. The security forces showed relative restraint,

did not use much force to block the crossing and did not fire on the Palestinians. Nevertheless, there were several violent confrontations when they tried to disperse the crowd using night-sticks, water cannons and dogs; the Gazans threw rocks at the Egyptian forces Al-Aqsa TV, January 25).

8. Egypt announced that there were 30–40 wounded security force members and border guards, among them two senior officers. The Egyptian foreign minister said that he was worried by the Palestinian provocations and that it had to be made clear to them that it was absolutely out of the question that Egypt's desire to host them and make their lives easier threaten the lives of the Egyptian security forces (Middle East News Agency, January 26). At the same time, Egyptian authorities appealed to the Hamas leadership to take action to stop the provocations (Al-Hayat, January 26).

9. **On January 26 Egyptian president Hosni Mubarak said that the border would remain open** in the coming days and that Egypt would continue to allow Palestinians to cross to buy the basic items them needed (Middle East News Agency, January 26). However, **Egypt demanded that the Palestinians go no further than Egyptian Rafah and said they would not be permitted to enter Sinai toward El-Arish.** On the ground the reinforced Egyptian security forces managed to block the entrance to El-Arish and used force to close stores in the city, although Rafah and the border crossings remained open.

10. On the afternoon of January 28, after six days of uninterrupted Palestinian movement in and out of the Gaza Strip, the Egyptian security forces, in collaboration with armed Hamas operatives, began closing the breaches to stop the stream of cars crossing the border. The feeling in the Gaza Strip is that the mass movement of Palestinians into Egypt will stop by the weekend (Ali Waked, Ynet, January 28).

Arms and Weapons Smuggling

11. The collapse of the border fence enabled the Palestinian terrorist organizations to freely smuggle weapons and terrorist operatives into the Gaza Strip, including advanced weapons, and no longer need the extensive network of tunnels constructed under the Philadelphi route. In addition, breaking through the crossing provided a clear avenue for terrorist operatives who are liable to leave for the Sinai peninsula, cross the wide-open border between Egypt and Israel and carry out terrorist attacks within Israeli territory.

12. According to the first media reports, during the past few days the terrorist organizations smuggled weapons and military equipment into and from the Gaza Strip. The Israeli daily newspaper Yediot Aharonot quoted sources within Hamas who said that during the last three days large

quantities of assault rifles, machine guns and ammunition were smuggled into the Gaza Strip of the sort used in the past to attack IDF helicopters (Yediot Aharonot, January 27). The Egyptian authorities recently detained dozens of Palestinians armed with assault rifles and pistols who crossed the border into Egyptian Rafah (Haaretz daily newspaper, January 28). Egyptian sources revealed that their security forces had detained Palestinians in a number of districts who had explosives and latest generation cellular phones in their possession, capable of eavesdropping on the Egyptian security forces' communications networks (Al-Sharq al-Awsat, January 27).

13. The radical Islamic nature of the Gaza Strip, the freedom of action of the terrorist organizations and the relative ease in entering and leaving are liable, in our estimation, to encourage global jihad groups to enter. For example, **Abu Abd al-Rahman al-Ansari,** responsible for information coming from an organization called Fatah al-Islam in the Land of Ribat,[2] issued a call to jihad fighters around the world to exploit the breached Rafah Crossing to go to the Gaza Strip (a global jihad forum called Al-Hesbah, January 24).

Reactions

Egypt

14. Caught between Hamas's defiance and the Islamic opposition's identification with Hamas, Egypt has avoided trying to resolve the crisis by employing military force against the Palestinians. Its activity has focused on diplomacy in an attempt to promote a political solution based on an agreement between Hamas and Abu Mazen:

1) **Egyptian president Hosni Mubarak has called for a renewal of the Fatah-Hamas dialogue and expressed willingness to host the talks in Egypt.** He said that the break through the crossing and the flow of Palestinians were the direct result of Israel's blockade and collective punishment of the Gaza Strip. He also said that Egypt was prepared to act immediately to mediate between the Palestinians but was not a side in internal Palestinian conflicts and was not prepared to get involved in them (Middle East News Agency, January 25).

2) **The Egyptian foreign minister** said that Egypt was interested in restoring former arrangements and agreements regarding the operation

[2] A terrorist organization which is a branch of the global jihad. Its center of power was in the Nahr al-Bared refugee camp in north Lebanon, where it was suppressed by the Lebanese army in September 2007. It recently began claiming responsibility for attacks in the Gaza Strip. **The Land of Ribat** ("frontier" in Arabic) is a nickname for the territory called **Palestine** which includes the Temple Mount, one of three places holy to Islam. Since the territory is controlled by Israel, it is considered a kind of garrison whose role is to take part in the future jihad for the liberation of the Islamic holy places.

of the border crossings and had invited the two rival Palestinian leaderships to arrive in Cairo separately to discuss the issue. However, he made it clear that Egypt would call upon Fatah and Hamas to deliberate only after a suitable arrangement had been formulated and that Hamas would agree to sign it (Middle East News Agency, January 26). At this point it would seem that Hamas and Fatah delegations will meet separately with members of the Egyptian administration and that a tripartite meeting will not take place (BBC Radio, January 27).

15. **Expressions of identification with the Palestinians in the Gaza Strip continued throughout Egypt, coming particularly from the Muslim Brotherhood opposition:**

1) About 1,500 Egyptians recently held a demonstration at the Cairo Book Fair. They gathered in answer to a call sent out by the Muslim Brotherhood after the Friday prayer and were surrounded by hundreds of security police (Agence France Presse, January 25).

2) Many convoys of humanitarian aid which left from various locations in Egypt drove to Rafah to relieve the blockade in the Gaza Strip. They were not permitted to enter northern Sinai, forcing most of them to return. The largest convoy was sent by the Arab Doctors'Association and included food and drugs worth $1 million (Muslim Brotherhood Website, January 25).

16. On January 27, official Egypt television's morning program broadcast live from Egyptian Rafah, Palestinian Rafah and El-Arish. In addition to its regular programming, in an exceptional move a number of anti-Israeli incitement songs were broadcast and pictures were shown "testifying" to the so-called "slaughter" of the Palestinian people (Egyptian TV, January 27).

The Hamas Movement

17. Hamas is playing a double game with Egypt: **on the one hand,** it was behind the collapse of the fence, sent Gazans to confront the Egyptian security forces, absolutely refuses to return to the status quo ante and is not prepared to accept any solution which will not ensure it control over the Rafah Crossing. **On the other,** Hamas spokesmen publicly praise Egypt, state that breaching the fence was not aimed against it, apologize for the confrontations between the Gazans and the Egyptian security forces and even express willingness to reach an arrangement regarding Palestinian-Egyptian management of the Rafah Crossing **(an arrangement which would ensure Hamas control of entrance into and exit from the Gaza Strip).**[3]

[3] Ismail Haniya's government exploited the crisis and announced that the Crossings Agreement of August 2005 was obsolete. He claimed that it had been limited to one year and that it could not be renewed after having once been extended (Palestine-info Website, January 27). It is doubtful whether

18. **Khaled Mashal,** head of Hamas's political bureau in Damascus, said that the movement was going to send a delegation to Egypt to discuss the Rafah Crossing. He congratulated the Egyptians on their handling of the situation and said that breaking through the crossing had not been aimed against the Egyptians. He called upon Egypt to **reach an agreement with the Palestinians for Palestinian-Egyptian management of the Rafah Crossing** which would replace the previous agreement. On January 27 he also communicated with the Arab foreign ministers who had met in Cairo and demanded that they support the Egyptian position, which was to open the border to the residents of the Gaza Strip (Palestine-info Website, January 27).

19. **Ahmed Yussuf,** Ismail Haniya's political advisor, said that the Hamas delegation which would go to Cairo would discuss a final solution for managing the Rafah Crossing. He said that Hamas was interested in joint Palestinian-Egyptian control **without** Israel and the European Union, as required by the Crossings Agreement of August 2005 (Ma'an News Agency, January 28).

The Palestinian Authority

20. **Abu Mazen and the PA** are in favor of turning control of the Rafah Crossing and the crossings between the Gaza Strip and Israel over to **the PA's security services.** At the same time, they oppose giving Hamas control, which would aid Hamas's buildup and strengthen its control of the Gaza Strip. Abu Mazen is expected to leave for Cairo on January 30 to discuss the issue of the crossings with President Hosni Mubarak. In our assessment, the presence of Abu Mazen's security services at the Rafah Crossing (or the crossings into Israel) would **not have practical importance** both because of the absence of territorial continuity between the Gaza Strip and the West Bank and because of Hamas's military control of the Gaza Strip.

21. In view of the collapse of the border fence contacts are being made between the PA and Egypt: PA prime minister Salam Fayyad went to Egypt and spoke with Omar Suleiman, head of Egyptian intelligence and with foreign minister Ahmad Abu al-Gheit. Senior figures in the PA said the following:

1) **Nimr Hamad,** Abu Mazen's political advisor, said that the suggestion to turn the crossings over to the PA had been made at the Paris conference and again after the recent incidents. He said that Israel's ideas for solving the problem are an attempt to place responsibility on Egypt for

---

the announcement carries political-legal meaning since Hamas and Ismail Haniya's government are not party to the Crossings Agreement, but it definitely has **practical importance** because Hamas is in control of the Palestinian side of the Rafah Crossing.

the Gaza Strip or to found a Hamas-controlled emirate there (Al-Sharq Al-Awsat, January 26).

2) **Yasser Abed Rabbo,** secretary of the PLO's executive committee, said that if the situation continued it would play into Israel's hands because it would separate the West Bank from the Gaza Strip. In his opinion, the only solution would be to turn over control of all the crossings to the PA (Al-Hayat, January 26).

3) **Riyadh al-Maliki,** foreign minister in Salam Fayyad's government, said that the Egyptians had agreed to resolve the crisis **by implementing the Crossings Agreement and renewing the control of the Presidential Guard over the Rafah Crossing** (Reuter's, January 27).

Israel

22. The IDF is following the developments and continues to reinforce the border with Egypt, which is 300 kilometers (more than 185 miles) long. Following warnings, Route 10 along the Israeli-Egyptian border was closed. In addition, tourists and day trippers were forbidden to visit 20 tourist sites along the border (Haaretz, January 27). All Israeli tourists vacationing in the Sinai peninsula were requested to leave the area by the Israeli Counter-Terrorism Bureau.

23. Israeli security sources regard the breach of the crossing as a strategic problem with far-reaching implications. The collapse of the fence created a new security situation on the ground by making it much easier to smuggle large quantities of weapons which may upset the on-going balance with Hamas (such as anti-aircraft and anti-tank missiles). It can also be expected that squads of terrorists will leave the Gaza Strip for Sinai to infiltrate into Israel through the wide-open Israeli-Egyptian border to carry out terrorist attacks in Israeli territory (Yediot Aharonot, January 27).

24. Deliberations were held in the prime minister's office about the strategic implications of the crisis and the decision reached was to dialogue with the Egyptians to resolve rather than to confront the crisis (Yediot Aharonot, January 27). **Israel's demand is that Egypt restore the status quo ante to the Rafah region.** Under instructions from the minister of defense, head of Israel's political security staff General (Ret.) Amos Gilad spoke with Egyptian officials over the weekend and demanded that they stop the unmonitored movement of Palestinians from the Gaza Strip to Egypt. He stressed the security threat to Egypt resulting from the open border (Haaretz, January 27).

DOCUMENT NO. 9

ISRAELIS, PALESTINIANS URGED TO 'STEP BACK FROM THE BRINK', AVERT FULL-SCALE CONFLICT, AS SECURITY COUNCIL DEBATES EVENTS IN GAZA

UN Security Council
SC/8768

June 30, 2006

Transcript from the Security Council's 5481st Meeting (PM):

Palestine Observer Says Israeli Military Aggression Premeditated; Israel Tells Council Worst Fears Realized—Gaza Now Terror Base

As the Security Council met this afternoon to consider the growing crisis between the Israelis and Palestinians, both parties were urged to "step back from the brink", and give dialogue a chance, in order to avert a full-scale confrontation that would only lock them in deeper and deadlier conflict.

"The slightest turn of events could easily set off another full-scale conflict between Israelis and Palestinians, bringing greater dangers to civilians, and with serious regional repercussions," Assistant-Secretary-General for Political Affairs Angela Kane told the Council, at the outset of its meeting on the situation in the Middle East, including the Palestinian question.

Recalling the events of recent days, beginning with the Palestinian militant attack that had led to the abduction of a member of the Israeli Defense Forces and the subsequent Israeli military incursions into Gaza, she urged all parties to exercise restraint and act with wisdom, and in conformity with international law.

Nothing justified the holding of hostages, she said. Corporal Gilad Shalit must be released and the Palestinian Authority must act to stop indiscriminate rocket attacks against Israel. Meanwhile, Palestinian civilians should not pay the price of those actions, and Israel must cease the destruction of civilian infrastructure, ensure the protection of civilians and allow humanitarian assistance to get through.

The Permanent Observer of Palestine believed Israel's recent military aggression was premeditated and planned, using the soldier's capture as the pretext for launching operations into Gaza. Hundreds of Palestinians had fled their homes to stay safe from Israel's military onslaught. Sealed border crossings and the deprivation of electricity and water, had intensified the dire conditions in hospitals and elsewhere in the community, leading the International Red Cross to call on Israel to allow the delivery of urgent medical supplies to Palestinian civilians.

Yet, he went on to say, despite the Israeli onslaught and "State terror", the Palestinian leadership continued to choose the diplomatic option. Under President Mahmoud Abbas' leadership, it was working to resolve the issue of the Israeli soldier taken prisoner, to make sure he was being treated according to the rules of international humanitarian law and to secure his release unharmed. It was the duty of the Council, he added, to address the crisis. A failure to do so would only serve to bolster the occupying Power's impunity.

Israel, stated its representative, could not tolerate a situation, in which its citizens were being held hostage by members of a terrorist group such as Hamas. Sadly, Israel's worst fears about a terrorist organization taking over the Palestinian Authority had now been realized, and the world was witnessing the true colours of Hamas. He urged the international community to continue applying all possible political pressure on the Palestinian Authority and on the Hamas terrorist organization, including its members and sponsors in Damascus, so as to ensure the immediate and safe release of the Israeli soldier, Gilad Shalit, and to finally bring to an end the use of Palestinian territory as a base for terrorist operations.

He said Israel had withdrawn from the Gaza Strip last August, with the hope of creating a window of opportunity and re-energizing the peace process. Instead, the response had been an actualisation of Israel's worry—an increase in terrorist attacks. Gaza was now a terror base, actively supported by the elected Hamas Government. The aggressive terrorist provocations of the past week and those of recent months had persisted, only because they were supported by the official Palestinian Government, a terrorist regime with a sworn intent to deny Israelis their most fundamental human rights. But Hamas was not alone in its campaign of terror. The dangerous realities in the Middle East were further inflamed by the active and direct collaboration between Syria, Iran, Hizbollah and Palestinian terror groups, comprising an "axis of terror".

During the discussion that followed, with nearly 40 speakers, representatives called for the immediate and unconditional release of Gilad Shalit and urged Israel to exercise the utmost restraint in the current crisis. The detention of elected members of the Palestinian Government and legislature was of particular concern to several delegations, as was the protection of civilians, both Palestinian and Israeli. They called for a resumption of the peace process, warning that further escalation could jeopardize the stability of the entire region.

Also making statements today were the representatives of Qatar, France, Congo, United States, Russian Federation, Slovakia, United Kingdom, Japan, United Republic of Tanzania, Ghana, Greece, China, Argentina, Peru, Denmark, Algeria, Iran, Egypt, Austria (on behalf of the European Union), Malaysia (on behalf of the Non-Aligned Movement), Jordan, Yemen, Syria, Cuba, Libya, Indonesia, South Africa, Lebanon, Norway, Morocco, Zimbabwe (on behalf of the African Group), Pakistan and Saudi Arabia.

The meeting, which began at 3:25 p.m., ended at 6:55 p.m.

Background

The Security Council met this afternoon, at the requests of Qatar and the Arab League, to consider the situation in the Middle East, including the Palestinian question. Those requests are contained in documents S/2006/458 and S/2006/462.

Also before the Council are *identical letters dated 28 June 2006 from the Chargé d'affaires a.i. of the Permanent Observer Mission of Palestine to the United Nations, addressed to the Secretary-General and the President of the Security Council* (document A/ES/-10/341-S/2006/443). It states that Israel, the occupying Power, had launched a major air and ground military assault on the Gaza Strip on 28 June, threatening the lives of the defenceless Palestinian civilian population in the area, and causing the further deterioration and destabilization of the grave situation on the ground. After deploying thousands of troops in recent days along the southern border of the Gaza Strip, following the capture of an Israeli soldier on 25 June from a military outpost of the occupying forces on the Gaza border, the occupying Power has begun firing missiles and launching artillery at Gaza.

These attacks are deepening the humanitarian suffering of the Palestinian people and causing extensive physical and environmental destruction on the ground, with far-reaching detrimental consequences for the population, the letter states. It should be highlighted that, even prior to the capture of the soldier of the occupying forces, Israeli officials had been issuing a series of threats regarding the intention to launch a major invasion of the Gaza Strip.

The international community must exert urgent efforts to bring the Israeli military invasion of Gaza to a halt and halt the collective punishment and crimes being committed against the Palestinian people by the occupying Power with sheer impunity, it states. The Council should take the necessary measures and condemn the aggression, as well as demand that Israel, the occupying Power, cease its attacks, withdraw its occupying forces and abide by its obligations under international law, including humanitarian and human rights law, in all of its actions vis-à-vis the Palestinian civilian population under its occupation.

In addition, the Council had before it *identical letters dated 26 June 2006 from the Chargé d'affaires a.i. of the Permanent Mission of Israel to the United Nations, addressed to the Secretary-General and the President of the Security Council* (document A/60/905-S/2006/436), drawing the attention of the Council to a violent attack perpetrated by Palestinian terrorist organizations against Israel on 25 June, which resulted in the death of two Israeli soldiers, the wounding of three others and the kidnapping of Corporal Gilad Shalit. Hamas, the Popular Resistance Committees and Jish al-Islam ("the Army of Islam") took responsibility for the attack.

Israel views the Hamas-led Palestinian Government as specifically responsible for this attack, and the Palestinian Authority Chairman Mahmoud Abbas responsible for the welfare of Corporal Gilad Shalit.

Israel has fully disengaged from the Gaza Strip, with the hope of opening a window of opportunity to peace. Nevertheless, Gaza has increasingly turned into a terror base, actively supported by the Hamas Government. This terrorist attack emphasizes, once again, that the takeover of the Palestinian Authority by a terrorist organization is not an internal political matter. It is an event of major significance that affects the stability of the entire region. Moreover, this attack was supported by Khaled Mashaal, a Hamas leader who is currently operating from Damascus with the support of the Syrian regime.

Israel calls on the international community to maintain a firm stand against the Hamas terrorist organization, and deny it any form of legitimacy, until it fully meets the three conditions set out by the international community: to recognize Israel, renounce violence and terror, and abide by prior international agreements. The main concern should focus now on the well-being and safe release of Corporal Gilad Shalit. Israel expects the international community to voice strong condemnation of this violent attack and call for Corporal Shalit's immediate return.

Statements

ANGELA KANE, Assistant-Secretary-General for Political Affairs, said that, at approximately 5 a.m. on 25 June, eight Palestinian militants had left the southern Gaza Strip via a tunnel and infiltrated an Israel Defense Force base near the Kerem Shalom Kibbutz. They had fired several anti-tank rockets into the Israel Defense Forces base, leading to a gun battle. Coporal Gilad Shalit, an Israel Defense Forces soldier also holding French nationality, had been taken hostage and was currently being held hostage by militants in Gaza. Two Israel Defense Force soldiers had been killed and a further three wounded. Two Palestinian militants had been killed in the operation.

She said a statement had been issued by three Palestinian militant groups, confirming that they had conducted the operation. They had subsequently stated that he would not be released, nor information on his health provided, unless Israel released all Palestinian female and underage detainees. The Palestinian Authority spokesman had called upon them to guarantee his safety and President Abbas had called for his release, as well as met with Prime Minister Ismail Haniyeh and contacted counterparts.

Israel's Prime Minister Ehud Olmert had ruled out negotiations over any exchange of prisoners, and the Israeli Cabinet had agreed that the Palestinian Authority would bear full responsibility for any harm to Corporal Shalit, she said. The Prime Minister had approved recommendations to prepare and deploy Israeli forces for urgent military action.

Meanwhile, she said, international efforts to secure the release of the soldier had been undertaken by Egypt, and reportedly France and Jordan. The Secretary-General had been in frequent touch with Prime Minister Olmert, President Abbas and President Assad in Syria, as well as consulted individually with his Quartet partners.

Israel had begun operations to obtain the release of Corporal Shalit, just after midnight on 28 June. The Israel Defense Forces had struck Gaza's only power station from the air, and ground forces had moved into the Gaza Strip. Israeli tanks and armoured personnel carriers had moved into the airport. Israeli military aircraft had broke the sound barrier over Gaza, causing sonic booms and, on the same day, four Israeli Air Force Fighter jets had flown over Syrian territory, breaking the sound barrier over the presidential villa in Lattakia.

A further air strike had taken place in the afternoon of 28 June, she continued, on a largely disused training camp in the south of the Gaza Strip. Another Israeli incursion into Gaza had taken place in the early morning of 29 June. The Israeli air force had shelled an open area in the compound of the Islamic University in Gaza, and Israeli tanks had entered northern Gaza. In the afternoon of 29 June, the Israeli air force had attacked a car in the Gaza Strip, though its occupants had escaped.

On 25 June, an 18-year-old Israeli from the West Bank settlement of Itamar had been abducted by Palestinian militants as he was hitchhiking, and his body had been found in Ramallah on the morning of 29 June. The Palestinian Popular Resistance Committee had claimed responsibility for the acts.

She said, on 29 June, an Israel Defense Forces spokesman had said that the ongoing operation was aimed at halting rocket attacks on Israel from northern Gaza, in addition to securing release for the missing soldier. Between 25 and 30 June, Palestinian militants had reportedly fired 17 rockets from the Gaza Strip into Israel, including 11 on 29 June. There had been no reported casualties.

Also, on the night of 29 June, Israeli forces had undertaken a large-scale arrest raid, detaining 64 Palestinian Authority officials and 23 suspected militants. The Israeli Attorney General had said those arrested would be charged under anti-terrorism legislation.

She said violence had continued on the night of 29 June, including 30 air strikes. The air attack on the power station on Wednesday had destroyed six transformers and the switchyard, resulting in 40 per cent of Gaza residents living without power. Water pipes had also been damaged, so that 130,000 people were now without water. There were sufficient food supplies to last two or three weeks more. Supplies of food and medicine would decrease to critical levels, however, because crossing points between the Gaza Strip and Israel had been closed since the beginning of the Israel Defense Forces operation. Private pipelines bringing fuel from Israel to the Gaza Strip had not been functioning for the past five days, meaning supplies would run out as early as Sunday, 2 July.

Nothing justified the holding of hostages, she said. Corporal Shalit must be released, and the Palestinian Authority must act to stop indiscriminate rocket attacks. Meanwhile, Palestinian civilians should not pay the price of those actions, and Israel must cease the destruction of civilian infrastructure, ensure the protection of civilians and allow humanitarian assistance to get through. She urged all concerned parties to step back from the brink and give dialogue a chance, to avert full-scale confrontation.

RIYAD MANSOUR, Permanent Observer of *Palestine*, said the Palestinian civilian population being held captive under Israel's belligerent military occupation exemplified the sentiments expressed by the Under-Secretary-General for Humanitarian Affairs to the Security Council two days prior, in which he had said: "There are too many times when we still do not come to the defence of the civilian populations in need. The world is a safer place for most of us, but it is still a death trap for too many defenceless civilians, men, women and children."

Indeed, he continued, the list of violations and breaches of international law that had been and were being committed by Israel against the Palestinian people were endless, and the list of pretexts used to continue those violations and crimes just as endless. Those included having "no partner for peace", so called security concerns, and now the capture of a soldier. Yet, those pretexts rang hollow when the situation was examined in the context of a long history of Israel's brutalization, humiliation and de-humanization of the Palestinian people, for the purpose of acquiring land through a settlement campaign and construction of the wall.

The recent military aggression had been premeditated and planned, he continued. Prior to the capture of the Israeli soldier on 25 June, Israel had issued threats and declarations about an intention to launch a major invasion of the Gaza Strip, and had mobilized troops. It had then used the soldier's capture as the pretext for launching the invasion. Then, on 28 June, after amassing thousands of troops along the southern border of the Gaza Strip, Israel had launched an air and ground military assault by warplanes and tank artillery bombardment. Hundreds of Palestinians had fled their homes, particularly from Rafah, to stay safe from Israel's military onslaught, which was expected to expand, as Israel had deployed thousands more troops along the northern border of Gaza, threatening to invade Palestinian towns and refugee camps in the north. Sealed border crossings and the deprivation of electricity and water had intensified the dire conditions in hospitals and elsewhere in the community, leading the International Red Cross to call upon Israel—in accordance with international law—to allow the delivery of urgent medical supplies to Palestinian civilians.

He said, following the launch of the invasion on Wednesday, Israel had expanded their aggression into the West Bank, carrying out kidnappings and detentions of at least 64 Palestinians, the majority of them high-ranking, democratically-elected officials, including eight Cabinet ministers of the Palestinian Authority, 24 members of the Palestinian Legislative Council and several mayors. Those officials were being held, along with 9,000 other Palestinians, in Israeli jails in violation of the Fourth Geneva Convention. Further, the targeting of senior Palestinian officials was a clear indication that everything was being done for political objectives intended to sabotage recent agreements among Palestinian parties for reconciliation, to hamper the functioning of the Palestinian Authority and to cause the complete collapse of the Authority as a whole.

Yet, he went on to say, despite the Israeli onslaught and "State terror", the Palestinian leadership had continued to choose the diplomatic option. Under President Mahmoud Abbas' leadership, it was working to resolve the issue of the Israeli soldier taken prisoner and making sure he was being treated according to the rules of international humanitarian law, and to secure his release unharmed. Such efforts had been exerted simultaneously with efforts to secure agreement among all Palestinian parties for national unity and to promote calm. Israel should reciprocate such efforts by abandoning military options.

He said it was the duty of the Security Council to address the crisis situation in the Occupied Palestinian Territory. It should begin by condemning Israeli aggression and call for the immediate cessation of hostilities, compliance with international law, the withdrawal of Israeli occupying forces from within the Gaza Strip and the release of Palestinian officials being detained. A failure to do so would only serve to bolster the occupying Power's impunity. It was not too late for the Security Council to asserts its rightful role and use its authority to bring an end to the breaches being committed and salvage the prospects for reaching peace on the basis on international law, United Nations resolutions, the Quartet Road Map and the Arab Peace Initiative.

DANIEL CARMON (*Israel*) shared with the Council the facts concerning the latest developments on the ground. He recalled that, during the attack of 25 June, Palestinian terrorists had killed two Israeli soldiers, kidnapped one soldier—Corporal Gilad Shalit—and wounded three other soldiers. The terrorist organizations Hamas, the Popular Resistance Committees (PRC) and Jish al-Islam ("the army of Islam") had taken responsibility for the attack. Gilad Shalit was currently being held hostage and his whereabouts were not known. On that same day, the Popular Resistance Committees had kidnapped and, subsequently, murdered an 18-year-old Israeli civilian. Those Palestinian terrorist attacks had been launched after long weeks of Israeli restraint in the face of numerous attempted kidnappings and unceasing Qassam rocket attacks from the Gaza Strip that had targeted civilians, schools and homes, traumatized children and paralysed the city of Sderot.

He said Israel had withdrawn from the Gaza Strip last August, with the hope of creating a window of opportunity and re-energizing the peace process. Instead, the response had been an actualisation of Israel's worry—an increase in terrorist attacks. Gaza was now a terror base, actively supported by the elected Hamas Government. One particular form of continuous Palestinian terror had been the barrage of Qassam rockets launched into Israeli territory from the Gaza Strip. Since last October, more than 600 Qassam rockets had fallen onto Israeli cities and territory, and, in just this past week, more than 50 rockets had been launched from Gaza. The clear target of those attacks was men, women and children—Israeli civilians.

The aggressive terrorist provocations of the past week and those of recent months had persisted, only because they were supported by the official Palestinian Government, a terrorist regime with a sworn intent to deny Israelis their most fundamental human rights. Hamas had declared this month that it was renouncing its ceasefire. But Hamas was not alone in its campaign of terror. The dangerous realities in the Middle East were further inflamed by the active and direct collaboration between Syria, Iran, Hizbollah and Palestinian terror groups, comprising an "axis of terror".

The first and foremost obligation of every State was to protect its citizens, he said. From the moment the initial reports of Gilad's kidnapping had been received, Israel had spared no effort in exploring and exhausting all diplomatic channels and had, in particular, given Chairman Abbas every opportunity to secure his safe release, which could be seen as a test of his leadership. Even in Damascus, where Khaled Mashaal, a leader of Hamas, kept his headquarters and liaised with the Assad regime, many important communications had been received, in order to influence Corporal Shalit's safe return. Indeed, many leaders in the region agreed that Mashaal was the key to resolving the humanitarian crisis. Nevertheless, so far, the diplomatic efforts had been fruitless.

Israel, like any other responsible Government, could not tolerate a situation, in which its citizens were being held hostage by members of a terrorist group such as Hamas, he stated. Israel did not disengage from the Gaza Strip, in order to return to it. As it now stood, the Israeli army's presence was limited to a very small area in southern Gaza, with the sole aim of preventing Corporal Shalit from being smuggled outside the Gaza Strip. The military operation now taking place was thus specific in nature and limited in scope. Its objective was not punishment or retaliation, and Israel was taking every effort to minimize any harm to Palestinian civilians. In fact, just an hour ago, the Israeli Defence Minister had declared that Israel was immediately planning to take steps to ease the humanitarian situation on the ground in Gaza.

In light of the escalation of Palestinian terrorism, Israel had decided to intensify its efforts to arrest those operatives responsible for terrorist attacks, so they could be tried and brought to justice. Israel would not accept allowing terrorists to hide behind "political" titles. Sadly, Israel's worst fears about a terrorist organization taking over the Palestinian Authority had now been realized, and the world was witnessing the true colours of Hamas. He urged the international community to continue applying all possible political pressure on the Palestinian Authority and on the Hamas terrorist organization, including its members and sponsors in Damascus, so as to ensure the immediate and safe release of Gilad Shalit, and to finally bring to an end the use of Palestinian territory as a base for terrorist operations.

NASSIR ABDULAZIZ AL-NASSER (*Qatar*) said that, during the past two days, Israel had conducted military activities, including air bombardments and use of ground forces, to destroy infrastructure, bridges, universities and power stations. The total closure of the Gaza Strip from all sides—air, land and sea—had caused the isolation of 1.5 million Palestinians from the outside world, not only restricting their movements, but also causing their economic strangulation. For instance, they would soon face food shortages and international relief agencies were prevented from delivering humanitarian assistance.

He said the Israeli air force had broken the sound barrier, causing sonic booms to intimidate the population. Israel had also detained 64 members of the Palestinian Government, or one third of the entire Government, which was an act disproportionate to its declared objective. Indeed, such acts served as collective punishment of the Palestinian people, which was banned by the Geneva Convention. Furthermore, the escalation in Israeli Government policy was irresponsible, and constituted violations of the Fourth Geneva Convention and international human rights laws. It served to abort the Road Map and dealt a blow to any chance to realize peace in the Middle East. Flying in the air space of a neighbouring Arab State only served to exacerbate the situation.

The Security Council had a responsibility to act to end those violations, he said. In recent weeks, it had met to discuss the strengthening of the rule of law, preserving international peace and security, and ensuring the protection of civilians during times of armed conflict. Members had listened, and affirmed their support for, all those important issues. How it would deal with the presence of one country that was ignoring those initiatives, was a test of the credibility of the Security Council regarding its commitments. If no firm action was taken, it might erode its authority.

JEAN-MARC DE LA SABLIÈRE (*France*) said he was extremely concerned by the developments in the Middle East. While he recognized Israel's right to self-defence, he called for the greatest restraint in the military operations under way, particularly regarding the protection of Palestinian civilians. He called for the speediest end to the Israeli incursions into Gaza. It was essential that the Palestinian Authority take all necessary measures to halt the firing of missiles. He condemned the killing of the Israeli settler and the kidnapping of the soldier in the West Bank. Hamas must adhere to the three principles laid down by the international community. It was also essential to protect the Palestinian Authority as an institution, and to guarantee the possibility for future dialogue and negotiations. The arrest of Palestinian political leaders was a direct threat to the existence of Palestinian institutions, and he called for their release. It was essential, he added, for all parties to take measure towards the de-escalation of the crisis.

BASILE IKOUEBE (*Congo*) said the spark that had set off the conflagration had been the abduction of an Israeli soldier, by means of a commando operation against an Israeli military unit. It had disrupted the relaxed atmosphere that recently prevailed—spurred on by positive developments such as progress in the reconciliation between Hamas and Fatah, for example, which had hinted at a de facto recognition of Israel among them. During that time too, assistance had increasingly been given to the Palestinian Authority by its international partners. Most importantly, there had been talk by President Abbas and Prime Minister Olmert of a resuming the Road Map, with the support of Egypt and other international partners.

He said Congo deplored bellicose activities and attitudes that weakened the chances of peace. As such, the abduction of soldiers by Palestinian groups was not acceptable, and should not to be encouraged. Military operations of disproportionate nature by Israel, in turn, aggravated the living conditions of an already long-suffering Palestinian population, making them official victims of terrorism and should also not be encouraged. He appealed to all parties to place peace ahead of other concerns, so that the Middle East could turn on the road towards peace in the context of the Road Map. The Security Council should make a contribution to the efforts of individuals and institutions of goodwill that stood ready to help both Israel and the Palestinians to exist side by side in peace.

JOHN BOLTON (*United States*) said everyone was aware of the seriousness of the situation evolving in the Middle East, and the foremost responsibility of the Security Council should be to avoid taking steps that would exacerbate that situation. The Council should tread cautiously before issuing any remarks, much less a formal statement, and should not undermine its limited credibility by engaging in rhetoric for its own sake.

He called for the immediate and unconditional release of Corporal Shalit, which was the best way to achieve a peaceful resolution of the immediate crisis. Terrorism, in any form, was intolerable, and the international community must stand united in opposing it. The attack and hostage taking had precipitated the current crisis, and the refusal to release the hostage continued to place innocent Palestinians in harm's way. He also condemned the killing of the Israeli settler. Upon the safe release of Corporal Shalit, he hoped the parties could continue discussions on the best way forward to achieve lasting peace.

The prerequisite for ending the conflict was for Syria and Iran to end their role as State sponsors of terror, he stated. As the international community called for calm in the region, it must remain cognizant of the fact that the region would not be in the situation in was now in, if not for Syria's harbouring of terrorists. Syria should arrest Khaled Mashaal, a terrorist and member of Hamas; close down various terrorist headquarters in Damascus; stop financing terrorism; and stop cooperating with States, such as Iran, which financed terrorism. At the same time, the representatives of the Palestinian Authority must take measures to stop acts of terrorism. He called on the current leaders of Hamas and the Palestinian Authority to implement the principles set forth by the Quartet: renounce terror, recognize Israel and accept previous agreements, including the Road Map. He reiterated the need for Hamas to secure the safe release of Corporal Shalit. In addition, he called on all parties to avoid actions that could escalate the situation or harm innocent civilians, while acknowledging Israel's right to defend itself and its citizens.

VITALY CHURKIN (*Russian Federation*) said urgent action was required to further reduce activities that could destabilize peace in the region. The large-scale military action undertaken by Israel, for example, only complicated the search for a solution. To avoid a full-blown crisis, he called on the Palestinian Authority to curb the activities of extremists, including terrorist attacks on the citizens of Israel, using missiles. Also, the Israeli soldier must be released.

He said, although Israel had a right to protect its citizens, it could not do so at the price of the entire Palestinian population, through methods of collective punishment on residents of Gaza and other places in Palestine. Activities involving the violation of the Syrian border were also insupportable. Finally, Israel's arrest of members of the Palestinian Government should be condemned; those officials had received a mandate to serve their people through a democratic process, for which there was broad international agreement.

Bringing the parties back to the negotiating table was the only viable alternative to peace, he said. Any other alternative would lead to more destabilization. Regarding the worsening humanitarian situation, it was important to implement proposals of the Quartet for assisting the people of Palestine, by providing them with fuel and medicines, with the support of international donors. The Russian Federation, in turn, would use its contacts with Israel and Palestine, to try to bring the parties in line with agreements of the Quartet.

PETER BURIAN (*Slovakia*) called on all parties to exercise the utmost restraint and do everything possible to calm the situation, and prevent a further dangerous escalation that would only lead to suffering and loss of lives. In that regard, he strongly condemned the recent killing of the kidnapped Israeli civilian. Also, he urged the Palestinian Authority to undertake all necessary measures and make all efforts to find and release the kidnapped Israeli soldier and prevent further military and terrorist attacks on Israel, notably the launching of rockets against the Israeli population centres. Although he believed Israel had the right of self-defence against terrorism and its perpetrators, and understood its anxiety over the well-being of the kidnapped soldier, he stressed that Israel's measures and responses must be proportionate, and everything possible must be done to avoid loss of innocent lives, destruction of infrastructure and further deterioration of the humanitarian situation. He also called on Israel to exercise the utmost restraint regarding flights over Syrian territory.

He stressed that there was no military solution to the Israeli-Palestinian dispute. The only way to achieve a comprehensive and lasting settlement to the conflict was through the peaceful negotiations leading to a two-State solution, in accordance with the Road Map. In spite of the latest wave of violence, he believed there was still a window of opportunity for the

Palestinian and Israeli Governments to put the peace process on the right track. That window of opportunity must be seized through concrete and immediate action, leading from mutual recognition of the right to exist, to the mutual peaceful coexistence of two viable States.

EMYR JONES PARRY (*United Kingdom*), aligning himself with the European Union, expressed concerned over the situation in Gaza, and urged both sides to show restraint. He called for the release of Corporal Shalit, and condemned the murder of the other soldiers captured during the same operation. Israel, in turn, should seek to avoid civilian casualties in its acts, as well as committing actions that added to the suffering of the Palestinian people. The detention of elected members of the Palestinian Government raised particular concerns, and those officials should be accorded their full legal rights. Political solutions should be favoured over violence; diplomatic solutions should be sought in cases of conflict. As such, the parties in question should strive to find their way back to the negotiation table.

He said he shared the concerns expressed by others regarding the deteriorating humanitarian situation in the Palestinian Territory, and hoped Israel would ease the situation by restoring electricity and water, as well as allowing access to affected areas by humanitarian organizations. The United Kingdom recognized the need to help provide for the basic needs of the Palestinian people. While the United Kingdom was not in the business of punishing people for the way they voted, it, nevertheless, did not want provide funds to a Government that did not support the Quartet principles. Under the temporary international mechanism endorsed by the Quartet, the European Commission had established teams, on the ground, to deliver allowances to frontline workers by mid-July, which was currently helping to pay for some utility bills, health supplies and social security for the poorest Palestinians.

A return to negotiations was the best way to ensure lasting peace, he added. The Security Council had a responsibility to encourage such negotiations and to help give them best chances of success. He reminded members that those goals could not be achieved, so long as one party refused to accept the right of the other to exist.

SHINICHI KITAOKA (*Japan*) said all parties must avoid measures that would escalate the situation. He called on the Palestinian Authority to bring violence by Palestinian extremist groups to an end, including rocket attacks, and to secure the immediate release of the Israeli soldier taken hostage. In that regard, the special envoy of the Government of Japan had appealed to President Abbas to resolve that matter. He called on Israel to exercise maximum restraint, and to avoid actions that caused casualties among Palestinian civilians and destroyed Palestinian infrastructure, thereby impacting on the daily lives of Palestinians. The detention of elected Palestinian officials was a cause for concern.

He was deeply concerned over the negative impact that the deteriorating situation would have on future efforts for peace. He strongly hoped the situation would calm down and an environment would prevail that was conducive to negotiations for peace. He welcomed the pledges of Prime Minister Olmert and President Abbas last week to undertake negotiations. He expected Israel to refrain from taking any unilateral actions that might prejudge the final status negotiations.

He also expressed his concern over the humanitarian situation in the Occupied Palestinian Territory. The international community, including Israel, must continue to provide humanitarian assistance. One year ago, Prime Minister Koizumi had announced an assistance package of $100 million for the well-being of the Palestinian people. To date, 80 per cent of that amount had been disbursed. As one of the major donors to the Palestinians, Japan would address the human situation in an appropriate manner. It had been announced last Wednesday that Prime Minister Koizumi would be visiting the region just prior to the "Group of Eight" Summit, if the circumstances permitted.

BEGUM K. TAT (*United Republic of Tanzania*) said that the Israeli incursion into Gaza was aimed at persuading the Palestinian side to free the abducted soldier. However, rather than engaging in such broad military action, dialogue should have been given a chance. Indeed, such action had hurt the civilian population of Palestine disproportionately, and would likely lead to a humanitarian disaster. She called for immediate cessation of such activities, and called for dialogue to replace military actions.

She said her country supported the attempts of President Hosni Mubarak in pursuing a peaceful solution to the conflict, and urged both sides to exercise maximum restraint. Indeed, the use of force would only aggravate tensions. As a start, the Hamas-led Government should work to release the abducted soldier. For its part, Israel should realize that military pressure only results in counter-violence from the Palestinian side. Israel should avoid acts that could strengthen the resolve of the military wing of Hamas and other groups to continue fighting. It should consider releasing the 64 Government officials, as that would help to release a great deal of tension. The international community should also play its part, by taking actions to avert further crises.

L. K. CHRISTIAN (*Ghana*) said that hopes for peace in the Middle East had been kindled last week at the news of an initial meeting in Jordan between the Israeli Prime Minister and the Palestinian Authority President. However, the events occurring in Gaza since the abduction on 25 June had plunged members, once more, into despair. To address the situation, Ghana called on the Palestinian Authority to do all it could to secure the release of the Israeli soldier. For its part, Israel should cease military operations, withdraw its forces from Gaza and release detained Palestinian officials.

Further, he reiterated the condemnation of all acts of violence and called on the Palestinian Authority to act decisively against rocket attacks on Israel, while Israel must desist from launching future military attacks into the Occupied Palestinian Territory. The consequences of Israeli military operations on the Palestinian people, who already found life unbearable because of economic pressure, were grave—air strikes had affected power supplies, there was an acute lack of fuel and the water system could also be affected. The economic and institutional collapse of the Occupied Palestinian Territory must be avoided at all costs.

Israel and the Hamas Government should move from the brink of full-scale hostilities and seek peace, while the international community must actively search for a solution to the crisis. That meant renewing its commitment to the objectives of the right of Israelis to their own State within well-defined and secure boundaries, and the equal rights of Palestinians to their own independent State that guaranteed freedom of movement for its citizens.

ALEXANDRA PAPADOPOULOU (*Greece*) deeply deplored the killing of the abducted Israeli settler, confirmed only yesterday, and the continued holding of an Israeli soldier as hostage. She equally deplored the increasing number of victims among the civilian population in Gaza and the West Bank, and the exacerbation of the humanitarian crisis. The suffering of the Palestinian civilian population had reached new alarming levels. She called on Israel to exercise the utmost restraint in dealing with the current crisis.

In taking measures to defend itself, Israel must respect its obligations under international law, she said, repeating her call to Israel for proportionate use of force. She was also concerned over the detention of elected members of the Palestinian Government and legislature, and the way that was carried out by the Israeli army. In addition, she continued to believe that it was imperative that the Palestinian Government take effective and immediate action to improve security and to prevent terrorist attacks against Israel. She called for the immediate release of the abducted Israeli soldier. In the midst of the current dire situation, she welcomed Prime Minister Olmert's and President Abbas' pledge to negotiate, and commended the efforts of the latter to unite all Palestinian political forces to work towards achieving the widest possible consensus in support of the objectives of the Road Map.

LI KEXIN (*China*) said his country advocated the peaceful settlement of the Israeli-Palestinian conflict. Towards that end, immediate action must be taken to end the vicious cycle of "violence for violence". Certainly, every Government had the right to protect its citizens, but it must be done within the bounds of international law. Current Israeli action had taken place at the expense of innocent Palestinian civilians, including the detention of democratically-elected Government officials, and it should put an end to such activities.

He said recent military activities had resulted in many civilian casualties. An appeal was made to Israel to respect international humanitarian law and avoid actions that could worsen the situations. He called for the international community to work together to facilitate assistance to the affected community. Indeed, the rapid deterioration of the peace process served as a reminder that hard work in the area must continue, and that both parties must be persuaded to resume their dialogue at an early date. Practical action must also be taken by the Security Council, because it had the responsibility to uphold peace and security in the world.

CESAR MAYORAL (*Argentina*) noted that the situation in the Middle East was deteriorating in an alarming manner. The events of past days had the potential to destabilize the entire region. He appealed to Israel and the Palestinian Authority to take emergency measures to de-escalate the situation, in order to avoid any large-scale confrontation. The abduction of the Israeli soldier was an unacceptable "provocative act". He appealed to Hamas to set him free and to hand him over to Israel in good health. He condemned the abduction and killing of the Israeli civilian. Those responsible for the death of civilians should be brought to justice. In addition, he reiterated that the Palestinian Authority must take every measure it could to put an end to Qassam rocket attacks fired from Gaza towards Israel. The conditions set out by the Quartet remained in force, and must be complied with by Hamas.

Likewise, he said, the Israeli Government also had responsibilities and obligations. He was concerned by the military operations and other Israeli activities that had affected Palestinian civilians. The "reoccupation" of the Gaza Strip could only fuel tensions. There could not be a military solution to the conflict. Israel must take a series of emergency measures to put an end to military operations in the populated areas of Gaza. Similarly, all Israeli practices in contravention of international law must cease, particularly those that violated the Geneva Conventions. The detention of elected Palestinian officials was an additional cause of concern. He called on Israel to reconsider that decision, as it might have negative repercussions for the Government and people of Israel.

He shared the concern of the international community over the humanitarian situation in the Gaza Strip. Measures must be taken to restore the provision of basic services in the Palestinian areas. At the regional level, it was indispensable to put an end to all acts of provocation. All countries in the region must contribute to resolving the current crisis, as any confrontation could have repercussions for the entire region. He hoped the Council would remain cohesive and send a clear message to all parties, emphasizing that the only solution to the Middle East conflict was negotiations in good faith based on Council resolutions, earlier agreements and the principle of land for peace.

OSWALDO DE RIVERO (*Peru*) condemned what he called the unnecessary and provocative actions of Hamas, as it had tunnelled to a military post in Israel, murdered three soldiers and kidnapped one. He also condemned the kidnapping and killing of another Israeli citizen in the West Bank. At the same time, Israel must halt its attack upon the infrastructure of Palestinian cities, which was worsening the situation for the civilians there. He also expressed concern regarding the detention of elected officials of the Palestinian Authority.

He said it was urgent for the Quartet to act resolutely to bring about a permanent ceasefire and to ensure that the Palestinian Authority hand over the abducted Israeli soldier. He exhorted both sides to put an end to all violence, and the Security Council, should, in turn, impress upon the current Hamas-led Government to recognize Israel and abide by the obligations previously agreed to by the Palestinian Authority.

Council President ELLEN MARGRETHE LØJ (*Denmark*), speaking in her national capacity, said she was deeply concerned about the current deterioration of the security situation in the Middle East. In particular, she was concerned by the situation on the border between the Gaza Strip and Israel, following the attack by militant Palestinians, the abduction of Corporal Gilad Shalit, as well as the killing of a young Israeli settler. She called for the immediate and unconditional release of Corporal Shalit, and urged the Palestinian leadership to undertake all necessary efforts in that regard. She also called on Israel to exercise the utmost restraint in the current crisis. The detention of elected members of the Palestinian government and legislature gave rise to particular concern.

All parties must do their utmost to avoid further escalation, she said. They should not let themselves be provoked further. Additional violence would only serve to promote the agendas of extremists. Hopes for a resumption of a political dialogue after the recent positive signals, including the meeting between Prime Minister Olmert and President Abbas, must not be dashed. She called for an early engagement between the Israeli Prime Minister and the President of the Palestinian Authority, and reiterated her expectation from both parties to respect existing agreements and obligations, including the Road Map. She also called on all parties to protect all civilians, and not add to their suffering. She urged them to resume their full responsibility to restore security, allowing for the resumption of the peace process and the return to the Road Map.

Mr. YOUSFI (*Algeria*) said that Israel had the habit of using all its military might to target innocent people living in the Palestinian Occupied Territory. He said he feared the recent Israeli act of detaining members of the Palestinian Government and legislature would set a dangerous precedent. Attacks on infrastructure had served to further complicate the life of 1.5 million citizens already suffering under a long history of collective punishment, and would lead to a new cycle of violence. Further, Israel had violated Syrian air space and sovereignty, threatening the security of the entire region. He condemned all those acts.

He said Israel's recent aggression was an addition to a long list of aggressions against the Palestinian people that it had been committing for decades. Indeed, it was difficult to count the total number of illegal practices by Israel, since it had been contravening various international law, as well as General Assembly and Security Council resolutions, since 1967. He said he believed the true reason for the recent aggression was to destroy recent diplomatic efforts, and was an example of State terrorism. Hence, he called on the international community to work at all levels to stop upholding double standards, and to compel Israel to withdraw from Gaza. The Council was also called upon to provide international protection to the Palestinian people, in line with the Geneva Convention, as well as to hold Israel fully responsible for the safety of detainees and others being held in Israeli prisons. He also called for the immediate release of the Palestinian Government officials.

It was well known, he said, that the continued Israeli occupation of Palestine was the root cause of the problem. Indeed, peace could not be realized without the total withdrawal of Israel forces to 1967 borders.

S.A. ARAGHCHI (*Iran*) said the international community was, once again, witnessing yet another military invasion by the Zionist army against the innocent Palestinian people, which was in flagrant defiance of the most basic principles of international law. Warplanes, tanks and thousands of troops invading the Gaza Strip had targeted civilians. The aggressors were depriving the civilians from basic necessities. With the Palestinian economy already strangulated under an unjust embargo, the Palestinians remained under siege, and new aggression threatened to inflict further suffering on civilians.

He said there should be no doubt the new round of aggression pursued more important political and strategic objectives, which included the undermining of the democratically-elected Palestinian Government. After more than 50 years, the occupying forces still hoped to force the Palestinian people into submission. They failed to understand that only the restoration of justice could remedy the grievances. They also failed to understand that the oppression they imposed upon a whole people was one of the root causes of many global problems. Iran was very concerned over the implications of the new aggression for the whole region. The new aggressive posture stood to create more instability and threatened to further destabilize the region. It was imperative that the international community get effectively involved. The Security Council had an important role to play, and should act.

MAGED ABDELAZIZ (*Egypt*) said the military escalation by Israeli forces over recent days threatened to widen the scope of violence and counter-violence, and negatively affected the chance for both Israelis and Palestinians to live in peace and security. Israel, over the last few days, had launched a number of consecutive military attacks on the Palestinian people, which had led to many civilian victims, particularly children. The attacks had now reached full-scale operations, with Israel targeting infrastructure and detaining many Palestinian officials. Those attacks were another flagrant violation by Israel of international law. That required the Council to take all necessary measures to ensure international protection for the Palestinians, and Israel to bear full responsibility as the occupying Power.

The present situation clearly required the Council to assume its responsibilities in the maintenance of international peace and security, he said. A number of concrete and immediate measures should be taken to diffuse the situation. First, both the Israelis and the Palestinians should take mutual steps to calm the situation and return to the status quo prior to the initiation of the military operations. The second step was the immediate Israeli withdrawal from the territories it had stormed in Gaza, the full cessation of all military operations there, and the release of the Palestinian officials it had detained. Third, the Palestinian Authority should commit itself to exert maximum efforts in ensuring the immediate release of the kidnapped Israeli soldier, and in ensuring the halt to rocket attacks on Israel, in return for a halt to all Israeli military operations and withdrawal of its forces outside the Gaza Strip. Fourth, the Quartet should immediately initiate measures to build confidence between both parties, in preparation for starting final status negotiations.

GERHARD PFANZELTER (*Austria*), speaking on behalf of the European Union, called on Israel and the Palestinians to abstain from any actions that were in violation of international law. The European Union called for the immediate and unconditional release of the kidnapped Israeli soldier, and it condemned the murder of the Israeli victim of a kidnapping in the West Bank. It also called on Palestinian leadership to bring an end to violence and terrorist activities, and expressed its concern about the detention of elected members of the Palestinian Government and legislature. Reminding all parties of their responsibility to protect civilian lives, he said ongoing military operations should be in accordance with international law. The European Union called on Israel to exercise the utmost restraint, and it regretted the destruction of essential infrastructure, which contributed to the deterioration of the humanitarian situation in Gaza.

He said the European Union called upon all parties in the region to make every effort possible to resolve the current situation by peaceful means. Only a negotiated two-State solution could bring peace and security to the region, and a return to the peace process and the implementation of the

Road Map was imperative. On 15 July, the European Union's Heads of State and Government had endorsed the proposed temporary international mechanism to channel assistance directly to the Palestinian people. In order to achieve an immediate impact, the mechanism would focus on essential supplies and running costs for social services and health. Other donors, including Arab States, were invited to provide funding. The Union stood ready to contribute a substantial amount to the international mechanism.

RADZI RAHMAN (*Malaysia*), speaking on behalf of the Non-Aligned Movement, condemned the kidnapping and detention by Israel of Palestinian Cabinet ministers, members of the Legislative Council and officials. He further condemned the kidnapping and detention by Palestinian militants of an Israeli soldier, and also condemned the killings, including extrajudicial killings, and injuring of all civilians, as a result of recent events. He also condemned the use of force by Israel against the Palestinians, and acts of violence and terrorism carried out by Palestinian militants against Israeli civilians.

He urged Israel to respect its obligations under the Geneva Convention relating to the protection of civilian person in time of war, and said that both sides must ensure that kidnapping and counter-kidnapping be checked. For its part, the Security Council must bear its responsibility of maintaining international peace and security, by demanding that both sides release all recently kidnapped and detained individuals, and by compelling Israel to cease its campaign of aggression in the Gaza Strip, to uphold its obligations under international law, and to cease its military attacks against Palestinian civilians and destroying civilian property and infrastructure. The Council should also assist President Abbas and the Palestinian Authority to prevail upon groups in its territories to halt rocket attacks against Israel and its civilians.

He said it was incumbent upon both Israel and Palestine, with the assistance of the international community, to create the conditions necessary to resume negotiations. The Council must not be reluctant to invoke its authority and power on the question of the Israeli-Palestinian conflict.

BASHEER ZOUBI (*Jordan*) condemned Israel's campaigns against civilians, as well as any form of collective punishment imposed on civilians in the Gaza Strip. He condemned the killing of civilians anywhere. He hoped that both parties would display a high degree of restraint. What the Israeli forces of occupation had done in Gaza did nothing but weaken the prospects for peace. He hoped the Council would send a clear, strong message about that unproductive attitude, which should end. Efforts should focus on de-escalating tensions. Any failure to send that message would facilitate a further deterioration of the situation. The international community had the paramount responsibility in the implementation of the Road Map.

He called on both parties to respect all the agreements they had signed, end any activities aimed at escalation and focus on the political process. He welcomed the efforts of President Abbas to reactivate the political process, and welcomed the positive measures taken by both sides. He called on Israel to put an end to all practices that violated the rights of the Palestinian people. The settlement of the Israeli-Palestinian conflict was based on an end to Israeli occupation and a solution to the problem of Palestinian refugees.

ABDULLAH ALSAIDI (*Yemen*) aligning himself with the Arab Group and the Non-Aligned Movement, said it was time to end "the arrogance of Israeli might". It was not the first time that Israeli forces had practiced State violence against a defenceless people, he said. With its recent operations, Israel had taken its activities to new heights, by destroying Palestinian infrastructure, kidnapping Palestinian officials and sending warplanes to violate Syrian air space, to prompt the region into war. His country steadfastly condemned those acts.

The Israeli act of aggression came on the heels of Palestinian domestic reconciliation, he said. In fact, Israel's military movements and threats had begun prior to the detention of the Israeli soldier, who was presently being used as a pretext for launching the eventual attack. Such actions showed that Israel was not truly sincere in seeking peace, but was intent on usurping more Palestinian territories and settling colonists on those lands. Yet, the Security Council was paralysed to act against it—Israel seemed protected from any punishment and no one seemed to question any acts committed by it that ran counter to international laws.

He said that, to create conditions for peace, the international community was required to exert pressure on Israel to respect international instruments. Their crimes tended to generate hatred and incite violence in the region. A defenceless people, subject to regular tensions, would naturally feel frustrated, he added, leading to hatred and terror. Therefore, the international community must put an end to such acts of aggression, hold Israel accountable for its actions and help the parties implement agreements of the final status negotiations.

MILAD ATIEH (*Syria*) said that the Council was meeting as the situation in the Middle East was deteriorating from bad to worse, as a result of arrogant Israeli practices that constituted a real threat to international peace and security. Israel, which had never cared for international legitimacy, was trying to drag the entire region into confrontation. The flights of Israeli war planes over Syrian shores were a blatant violation of the sovereignty of a Member State and of international law. In addition, Israeli aggression against the Palestinians was a war crime, for which it should be held accountable. Those acts of aggression were unjustifiable and reflected the internal failures of Israel, which was trying to avoid a just, lasting and comprehensive peace. The events of the last few hours had proved that Israel had never been sincere in its withdrawal from the Gaza Strip. The destruction of Palestinian infrastructure was a violation of international humanitarian law and the Fourth Geneva Convention.

Israel did not hesitate to make charges against others to cover up the war crimes it was daily perpetuating against an unarmed Palestinian population, he said. He was concerned by the past experience of the Council, due to its repeated failure to fulfil its responsibility regarding the maintenance of international peace and security vis-à-vis the Middle East. Why did the situation in the Middle East continue to deteriorate? The answer was in the continuation of the Israeli occupation and the blocking of the Council assuming its mandate, as well as the lack of seriousness in finding a lasting solution to the Israeli-Palestinian conflict. He hoped the Council could assume its responsibility this time, regarding the humanitarian situation of the Palestinians.

He said the United States Ambassador had attacked Syria, in an unacceptable manner, with baseless allegations. The Ambassador had made himself the defender of Israel in its aggression towards the Palestinians. That the United States provided cover to Israel, in the Council, in its pursuit of destructive policies, would never serve the cause of peace in the region and would only lead to more tension there. The allegations by Israel against Syria and others for supporting terrorism was a cause for irony. Israel wanted to cover up the war crimes and terrorism that its Government was pursuing daily against the Palestinians. What Israel was doing through its destructive military operations during the past few days was more evidence of State terrorism. Israel must be held accountable for its actions, in connection with international law.

Mr. BENITEZ VERSON (*Cuba*) said that saving the kidnapped Israeli soldier had been used a pretext to launch a military attack against the Gaza Strip. It had been disruptive to the peace process, especially since it had taken place shortly after parties were seeking reconciliation. He also rejected the incursion into Syrian airspace by Israel.

As in the past, Israel had acted with arrogance and impunity, supported by the United States permanent veto in the Security Council, he said. He voiced a vigorous condemnation of current attacks, and demanded the immediate and unconditional withdrawal of troops, the return of refugees to their lands and the return of territorial boundaries to those of 1967. Those were the only ways to achieve lasting peace, he added.

Also, the new escalation of military action had aggravated the humanitarian situation, he said. For that reason, the Security Council could not afford to remain silent. He urged members to consider living up to the Council's commitment to the inalienable rights of the Palestinian people and the establishing a sovereign State of Palestine, sooner rather than later.

AHMED OWN (*Libya*) said that the serious developments resulting from the barbaric and continuing Israeli aggression in the Gaza Strip, the targeting of innocent civilians and infrastructure, and the detention of several Palestinian officials, were all violations of international law, particularly the Fourth Geneva Convention. The international community should bear the moral and legal responsibility to stand up to that cowardly action. It should condemn the Israeli military campaign against unarmed Palestinians and consider that aggression a crime. The international community, including the Council, should not be fooled by the claims made by Israeli occupation forces, which had justified their aggression as a response to the kidnapping of the Israeli soldier and as self-defence. Its military operations had been planned for weeks, in order to detain Hamas leaders.

He said self-defence could not take place in occupied territory. The deterioration and increasing complexity of the situation was the result of the continued Israeli occupation of Palestinian territory. He requested the Council to ensure adequate international protection for the Palestinian people and the implementation of the Fourth Geneva Convention; to consider Israel responsible for the safety of all detainees and prisoners, as well as for their immediate release; to condemn the Israeli aggression and to put an end to it, as well as to put an end to any violation of Syrian air space; and to call for international assistance for the Palestinian people and to ensure it reached them as soon as possible.

REZLAN ISHAR JENIE (*Indonesia*) said his delegation was very concerned about the increasingly dangerous situation in the Middle East. Israel had mounted a major and indiscriminate offensive in Gaza. It had captured eight Cabinet ministers and dozens of Hamas officials. Furthermore, the Israeli air force had hit more than 30 targets in Gaza. The power supply had almost completely disappeared in northern Gaza, following the disabling of two of the remaining electrical relay stations in the blasts. The Territory was on the edge of a humanitarian crisis. If the objective was truly to see to the return of a captured soldier, this was unwarranted aggression and a grave violation of international law. The standoff between the Palestinian leadership and the Israelis was threatening to explode, and it was appropriate that the Security Council was meeting to reflect on the issues.

Indonesia condemned that show of military force. It called upon the Security Council to act urgently to have Israel pull out of Gaza without delay and without preconditions. Both sides should be urged to resolve, by peaceful means, the issue of the kidnapped soldier, as well as the release of all recently kidnapped and detained Palestinians. The longer the current stalemate went on, the worse the humanitarian situation in the Palestinian Territory.

Indonesia called on Israel to resist the temptation to escalate the crisis. There could be no military resolution of the conflict.

DUMISANI S. KUMALO (*South Africa*) condemned the Israeli Government's policy of collective punishment, as a direct violation of international law. Israel's bombing campaign, which had continued unabated, had resulted in the destruction of strategic bridges and access roads, as well as Gaza's only power plant. Gaza's medical facilities were in a dire state. The loss of Gaza's only power plant had resulted in a lack of electricity and water for those critical facilities, which could only exacerbate the humanitarian crisis. Although Israel had legitimate security concerns, they should not be addressed at the expense of international law and the human rights of the Palestinian people.

The South African Government called for caution with regard to the situation in the Occupied Palestinian Territory, he said. The unlawful arrest of Palestinian Cabinet members was illegal and unacceptable, and they should be released immediately.

He also called on the Israeli Government to stop its military offensive and take all necessary measures to ensure that the situation was not further exacerbated. Peace could only be achieved through a negotiated settlement, based on a two-State solution that provided for a sovereign Palestinian State and guaranteed the right of Israel to live within secure borders. The military intervention and arrests of senior Palestinian leaders had come hours after the historic Palestinian acceptance of a plan from leaders of all Palestinian factions incarcerated in Israeli prisons. That had been a major step forward and opened up real possibilities for ending violence. Given that reality, how could anyone justify the invasion, arrests and massive destruction of Palestinian infrastructure? "Sadly, we have entered a very dangerous period, which will threaten the stability of the region and international peace and security," he said.

Ms. ZIADE (*Lebanon*) said there was a need to promptly take several steps. First, the Council should take decisive steps to achieve a ceasefire and restore security in the Occupied Territory, as well as ensure international protection in line with the Fourth Geneva Convention. Second, the Quartet must shoulder its responsibilities and facilitate the establishment of a machinery to channel assistance to the Palestinians. Third, steps were needed to allow the Palestinian Authority to move immediately to restore the security situation and to allow the Palestinians and the Israelis to return to the negotiation table.

The actions taken by Israel were flagrant violations of the human rights and safety and security of the Palestinian people, she continued. They were also a challenge to peace. Israel's aggression was not confined to the Palestinian territories. It had used its military forces along the "Blue Line", under the pretext of self-defence. It had also violated the air space of Syria and the air space and territorial waters of Lebanon. It continued to carry out acts of aggression against States that had expressed their wish for lasting peace. Lebanon, while condemning Israeli aggression, joined the call for a ceasefire, a return to calm and negotiations, and the release of all prisoners.

JOHAN L. LØVALD *(Norway)* expressed concern over the dramatic situation unfolding in and around Gaza, and said all parties must exercise the utmost restraint to prevent it from getting out of control. The abduction of the Israeli soldier and the killing of the young Israeli settler were unacceptable and deplorable acts, as they could only aggravate the already precarious situation of Palestinian civilians. Norway also deplored the arrest of lawfully elected Palestinian politicians, saying they needed to be released immediately.

He said his country had also repeatedly condemned rocket attacks from Gaza into Israel. Meanwhile, Israeli military operations in the densely populated areas had endangered lives and caused suffering to the civilian population of Gaza. He called on Israel to withdraw its forces. He expressed further concern for the humanitarian situation in Gaza, caused by Israeli attacks on vital infrastructure, saying such collective punishment was unacceptable.

According to international law, he added, any use of violence should be proportionate, while countermeasures against the civilian population were unacceptable under international law. Israel must help restore water and energy supplies to Gaza, desist from any action that might damage vital infrastructure and show consideration for the Palestinian civilian population. Palestinian leaders must make every effort to release the kidnapped Israeli soldier and bring to justice those responsible for the murder of the Israeli settler.

Mr. SAHEL (*Morocco*) said he was following with grave concern developments in the Occupied Palestinian Territory, in the face of the wave of destruction that had been unleashed. He deplored the escalation, the violence and the campaign carried out by the occupation forces and called for the immediate cessation of Israeli military operations. He also called for the release of all Palestinian officials detained by Israel.

He fully rejected the approach adopted by Israel in dealing with the crisis, he said, adding that there was no alternative to dialogue. He also reiterated the need to enable the President and members of the Palestinian Government to move freely within the Palestinian territories. Israeli provocations and violations of Syrian air space constituted a threat to international stability. He called on the Council to take tangible measures to put an end to Israeli aggression against the Palestinians. He continued to be hopeful about the possibility of arriving at an end to violence in the region, and was convinced that negotiations were the best way to achieve lasting peace.

B. G. CHIDYAUSIKU (*Zimbabwe*), speaking on behalf of the African Group, joined others in expressing his deep concern over the escalating tensions in the Middle East, which had seen Israeli military invasions of the Gaza Strip and the resultant wanton destruction of Government buildings, roads, bridges and power stations; the illegal arrest of elected representatives; and threats to the lives of defenceless Palestinian civilians, including women and children. In his view, those unfortunate developments were the result of the lack of progress in addressing the major issues and in following up on core positions regarding the question of Palestine. He condemned the ongoing excessive use of military might by Israel, which was disproportionate to the issues at hand, and demanded that Israel immediately cease all violations of international law, including international humanitarian and human rights law. He called on the Council to take urgent measures to bring the ongoing Israeli military invasion to an immediate halt, in order to advance the peace process in the region.

AIZAZ AHMAD CHAUDHRY (*Pakistan*) said that, since the last public meeting of the Council on the Middle East, definitive changes had taken place in the region. The massive operation by the Israeli army, however, had undermined the atmosphere of hope for peace following the elections in Palestine. He regretted the Israeli incursion into Gaza, including the destruction of Palestinian infrastructure, saying the increased hostilities would further impede international efforts to jumpstart negotiations.

He said the current challenge facing the international community was finding ways to halt the massive human suffering resulting from Israel's military operations; how to encourage the resumption of negotiations on the Middle East peace process; and how to prevent acts by Israel that could unilaterally make a negotiated settlement based on the principle of "land for peace" impossible. Here, the United Nations, including the Security Council and the Secretary-General, must play a more central role in calling upon the two Governments to heed the call of their people for peace.

Regarding the situation on the ground, there should be an immediate cessation of hostilities, he said. Also, efforts should be made to resolve the humanitarian crisis in Palestinian areas. In the medium term, Israel should stop its construction of the wall and halt attempts to change the demographics in certain areas. The two parties must deepen their dialogue towards final status issues. The implementation of the Road Map was the best hope of settling the Israel-Palestine dispute, and it was the collective obligation of the international community to help facilitate its implementation.

Mr. GAHRAH (*Saudi Arabia*) said that, once again, Israel was reasserting its aggressive nature. Its aggression against the Palestinians in Gaza was a form of terrorism that was unjustified and that was clear in its aims and objectives. The Palestinian resistance had suffered many victims, including members of a family on the beach in Gaza. Five people in one family had been killed by Israeli artillery from the land and the sea. An international investigation commission had not been dispatched, nor had that act been condemned. Israel continued to isolate the Palestinians, prevented the delivery of their wages, and carried out assassinations.

The Palestinians were only exercising legitimate resistance, he stated. Israeli aggression in Gaza was a flagrant violation of international law and agreements reached. The kidnapping of Palestinian ministers and representatives was a terrible crime and a violation of international law. Israeli terrorism in Gaza was not due to the capture of an Israeli soldier, but rather part of Israel's plans to destroy the legitimately elected Palestinian Government. The aim of Israeli aggression was to prevent Palestinians from reaching agreement among themselves, and then to claim there was no partner for peace.

The Israeli Government, he said, would not have continued its aggression, if not for the failure of the Council to uphold its responsibilities, and its failure to have its resolutions implemented. The Israeli Government was able to disregard international resolutions, because it believed it could get away with its acts under the pretext of self-defence. He appealed to the international community, the Council and the Quartet to put an immediate end to Israel's aggression against Gaza, and to ensure that it released prisoners and implemented all agreements reached.

DOCUMENT NO. 10

TERROR IN GAZA: ELEVEN MONTHS SINCE THE HAMAS TAKEOVER

Israel Ministry of Foreign Affairs

May 15, 2008

June 2007–May 2008

Since the Hamas takeover of the Gaza Strip in mid-June 2007 through the middle of May 2008, a total of 1396 rockets and 1553 mortar bombs hit Israel.

Summary of Main Events Emanating from the Gaza Strip Since June 2007

I. Rocket and Mortar Fire at Targets in Israel

14 May: A *Grad rocket struck the third floor of a crowded shopping mall* in Ashkelon, crashing down on a children's health clinic on the floor below and causing extensive damage to the building. Four people were seriously injured, including a two-year-old girl and her mother who were at the clinic, two were moderately injured and many people suffered post-traumatic stress reactions. In all, 100 people were evacuated for treatment to Barzilai Medical Center. The Iranian-made rocket was launched from Dugit, a former Jewish fishing village in the northern Gaza Strip that was evacuated and destroyed in August 2005.

In the evening, rockets hit a synagogue and a kindergarten in Sderot; several people were treated for shock.

Editor's note: The original version of this document included some color images that could not be adequately reproduced in this publication. Where necessary, captions and/or headings specifically relating to any omitted images have also been left out of the version reprinted herein. The main text of the document has not been affected by these omissions.

12 May: *Shuli Katz*, 69, from Kibbutz Gevaram, was killed when a Kassam rocket fell a few meters from where she was standing in Moshav Yesha, 15 km (9 miles) east of the Gaza Strip.

In the morning, two Kassam rockets hit Ashkelon, one falling near a school. Damage was done to several buildings. Two mortar bombs also struck Israel, launched from the Gaza Strip.

11 May: Three rockets and three mortar bombs landed in Israeli territory. A rocket narrowly missed a busload of students in the parking lot of Sapir College in Sderot. A car was damaged. Earlier this year, student Roni Yichye was killed by a Hamas-fired rocket in the same parking lot.

9–10 May: Twenty-six rockets and ten mortar bombs struck Israel over the weekend. Two struck the Tnuvele dairy factory. One of the Kassams exploded close to an apartment building, causing serious damage to the structure and several nearby buildings. The attack also caused a dangerous gas leak. Miraculously, no one was physically injured although a number of people suffered emotional trauma.

In another miracle earlier in the day, a Kassam rocket scored a direct hit on a house while family members were inside and, although the home was damaged, no one was physically injured.

A Kassam also slammed into the courtyard of Sapir College on the outskirts of the city and damaged a building. Another rocket exploded next to a yeshiva in Sderot. There, too, the building was damaged but no one was hurt.

In all, five people were injured in the attacks over the weekend.

9 May: *Jimmy Kedoshim*, a member of Kibbutz Kfar Aza for 30 years, was killed by a direct mortar bomb hit while working in his garden.

A second mortar shell exploded next to the kibbutz community hall. Three other people were wounded, including an IDF soldier who sustained moderate injuries. Two other people were lightly wounded and several more people suffered severe emotional shock.

6–7 May: In the past 24 hours, three Kassam rockets and two mortar bombs were launched from the Gaza Strip.

5 May: In the past 24 hours, there were two intensive barrages of Kassam rocket attacks aimed at Sderot and the western Negev communities. Two rockets landed in Sderot, hitting a cemetery and damaging headstones while one hit a supermarket, causing structural damage. There were five shock victims. Today, 5 May, three rockets fell in Sderot; one hit a potato chip factory and one landed in an agricultural field near Sapir College. Civilian workers were shot at in the southern Gaza Strip; no injuries or damage reported.

1–2 May: Agricultural workers were fired upon near the fence in the southern Gaza Strip. In addition, rockets or mortar bombs fell on Sapir College, a private home, a grocery store, a playing field, and near the Sderot cemetery (IDF Spokesperson).

29 April: A Kassam rocket scored a direct hit on a house in Sderot; another Kassam damaged a clinic in Kissufim.

28 April: Two rockets landed in Sderot, one next to a school, one a direct hit on a house (no injuries, except for trauma and emotional shock). Two rockets fell in the Ashkelon area, more on kibbutzim in Eshkol Regional Council, with damage to buildings. Mortar bombs struck fields around the Kerem Shalom crossing.

25 April: ***Two security guards were shot to death*** by a terrorist at the Nitzanei Shalom industrial park in central Israel, not far from Tulkarm (east of Netanya).

21 April: Rockets were fired at Sderot and Ashkelon.

19–20 April: Seven Kassam rockets and dozens of mortar bombs were fired at Israel over the weekend.

14 April: Two Kassams and one mortar bomb fell northwest of Sderot. On **12–13 April**, a mortar bomb hit near Nir Oz. On **11 April**, terrorists fired a machine gun at an agricultural worker in the fields of Kibbutz Nir Oz, damaging the bullet-proof glass enclosing the cabin of his tractor. Attacks on agricultural workers in the northwestern Negev have been increasing, causing many workers to wear bullet-proof vests while working in the fields.

9 April: *Two civilians employed at the Nahal Oz fuel depot were murdered* in a terrorist attack. The terrorists first launched a barrage of 24 mortar bombs at the nearby communities of Nachal Oz and Alumim as a distraction, and four of them infiltrated near the Karni crossing, shot at the unarmed workers and fled back to the Gaza Strip when the IDF responded. The terrorists attacked despite the fact that the Nahal Oz depot is the only source of fuel supply for the Gaza Strip.

Attacks on Gaza Belt communities continued on Wednesday following the Nachal Oz attack, with Kassam rockets and mortar bombs; no injuries were reported.

8 April: Terrorists in the Gaza Strip fired 32 mortar bombs and three Kassam rockets at Israeli territory during the day. Two more rockets were fired at Ashkelon at night. No injuries or damage was reported.

6 April: Two Grad missiles were fired at the coastal city of Ashkelon.

4 April: A civilian was wounded by Palestinian fire near Nir Am and taken to Barzilai hospital (IDF).

28 March: Two Kassam rockets struck the Negev: one hit a kindergarten in a kibbutz in the Shaar Hanegev region. The teacher and the children managed to reach a protected room and no one was injured.

26 March: A barrage of 22 rockets landed in the western Negev. Three people were wounded from shrapnel, one a Sudanese refugee. One of the rockets caused heavy damage to a house and nearby buildings in a kibbutz south of Sderot.

An Israeli farmer was wounded when terrorists in Gaza fired at Kibbutz Ein HaShlosha (where, on 15 January this year, a volunteer from Ecuador was murdered in the fields in a similar attack).

20 March: A rocket hit Kibbutz Nir-Am, breaking windows.

13 March: A Kassam rocket caused damage to a soccer field and a shed.

12 March: Rockets damaged buildings in Sderot.

11 March: A rocket hit an industrial park south of Ashkelon.

6 March: A direct rocket hit on a house in Sderot seriously wounded a grandfather watching his two granddaughters. Three others were lightly wounded.

4 March: A rocket destroyed a house in Sderot in the early morning; no one was home. The Kassam attack was launched from the northern Gaza town of Beit Hanoun, located less than a mile away from Sderot.

3 March: A seven-story apartment building in Ashkelon sustained a direct hit by a Grad missile. Three other buildings in the area were damaged by the blast. A number of Kassam rocket barrages hit elsewhere in the western Negev. All victims were taken to Ashkelon's Barzilai Medical Center (32 treated for trauma and four for light injuries). One little girl was injured by flying shrapnel.

A second Grad missile slammed into a playground, narrowly missing a nursery for toddlers under age 3. The nursery teacher told Voice of Israel radio that the children were in the middle of eating breakfast when she heard the Color Red incoming rocket alert siren (which gives residents a 15-second warning). The children's teachers managed to take them to a bomb shelter. No one was injured, but they had to calm down the hysterical toddlers.

An especially **sharp escalation** of rocket attacks occurred **between 27 February and 2 March**, with 182 rockets striking Israel. in addition to Kassam rockets, longer-range **GRAD missiles** were launched on Ashkelon, Netivot and the whole area (19 in this 5-day period).

Ashkelon, with over 107,000 residents, is more densely built than Sderot. Therefore, rockets are likely to cause more damage there. Over 26,000 children go to school in Ashkelon.

2 March: 25 rockets; a Grad-type katyusha hit Netivot, near the grave of a holy man. Three Grads were fired at Ashkelon; two hit the city center, one hit a house. 5 people were lightly wounded, 15 treated for anxiety.

1 March: 22 wounded; property damage.

29 Feb (or 28): Three-year-old Arab girl was killed when a rocket launched by Hamas terrorists fell short and struck near where she was standing outside her house in Bein Hanoun.

28 Feb: 20 rockets; 5 long-range rockets on Ashkelon; one hit Barzilai Hospital's helipad and two landed near the power station. Barzilai Hospital serves the entire region, including the Arab population; the power station supplies electricity to the region, including to parts of the Gaza Strip.

27 Feb: 48 rockets struck Israel. One hit Sapir College and **killed student** *Roni Yihye*, married and father of 4. He was the 14th victim of a rocket since the attacks began in 2004. Damage was caused to Sderot industrial zone.

25 Feb: One-year-old baby injured; 10-year-old boy seriously injured—doctors were able to save his arm with surgery.

17 Feb: A rocket hit the yard of a house in Sderot, sending five people into shock and damaging the building.

9 February: Eight-year-old Osher Twito and his brother Rami, 19, were seriously wounded when a Kassam rocket fired by terrorists in the northern Gaza Strip exploded as they were walking on a street in Sderot on Saturday evening. **Doctors were forced to amputate one of Osher's legs** but succeeded in saving the second. (update March 26, *Haaretz* website [http://www.haaretz.com/hasen/spages/965269.html])

8 February: Hamas claimed responsibility for the rockets that targeted the power station in Ashqelon, which provides the Gaza Strip with most of its electricity (*Al-Qassam website*, Feb. 8).

7 February: The Associated Press, reporting a claim that Israel targeted a Gaza agricultural school, exposed the fact that rockets were being fired from inside the school, using it as a shield. Associated Press Television News footage showed the school to be a series of huts in a rural area. A rocket-launching device was spotted between some olive trees, indicating militants had used the school for cover to launch attacks.

Seventeen rockets and three mortar bombs hit the western Negev, one setting fire to a garage adjacent to a private home. Hamas's armed wing, Izzadin Kassam, claimed responsibility for firing the rockets that hit Sderot.

6 February: A rocket landed in a playground in Kibbutz Beeri, wounding two girls, age two and age 12 years.

5 February: One of the rockets fired at Sderot scored a direct hit on a private house. A 14-year-old girl was wounded by shrapnel. One rocket hit a power line in Sderot, knocking out electricity in parts of the city for two hours.

Terrorists fired at Jewish farmers of Kibbutz Nir Oz, just east of Khan Yunis and over the border. No one was hurt, but damage was caused to a tractor.

15–28 January: There were **170 identified rocket hits** (150 of them in the four-day period 15–18 January; Hamas claimed responsibility for most) and 83 mortar bomb hits.

15 January 2008: Twenty-eight rockets hit the western Negev. One scored a direct hit on a home, wounding five people, including Lior Ben-Shimol, age 5, from Sderot, and a 19-year-old boy who was lightly injured from shrapnel. One of the rockets that fell in Sderot hit a high-tension power line, causing a black-out for several hours.

A 20-year-old Ecuadorian citizen, **Carlos Chavez, was shot and murdered** by a Palestinian sniper near the security fence, while working as a volunteer on a potato farm near Kibbutz Ein Hashlosha in the northwestern Negev.

13 January: Eight mortar bombs were fired at Israeli, including one that exploded in Netiv HaAsarah, just north of Gaza, causing damage to a building. On **10 January**, a rocket hit close to the dining hall in Kibbutz Yad Mordechai, north of the Gaza Strip.

9 January: Palestinian Authority terrorists in Gaza launched a barrage of mortar bombs and Kassam rocket fire at Israeli communities in the western Negev, coinciding with the arrival of US President George W. Bush for a three-day visit. One of the missiles slammed into a house, landing in a young child's bedroom. Miraculously, the three-week-old baby had been taken by his mother to the shelter as soon as the Color Red alert siren sounded.

3–4 Jan. 2008: An Iranian-supplied Katyusha rocket fired from Gaza towards the Israeli port city of Ashkelon landed further north than any rocket since the rocket fire began seven years ago—16.5 kilometers (10 miles). No one was hurt in the attack, though the missile landed only some 50 meters (55 yards) from a residential neighborhood.

The Katyusha fired at Ashkelon, a Grad model 122 millimeters (nearly 5 inches) in diameter, was the fifth such rocket fired towards Ashkelon. The Katyusha rocket has a range of 20 kilometers (12.4 miles); its use could bring 1/4 million Israelis within rocket range (International Herald Tribune).

A Kassam rocket fired from Gaza landed in the yard of a residential home in Sderot. A woman who had been hanging laundry ran for cover when she heard the Color Red early warning alarm, and the rocket fell just several feet from the laundry lines. The woman, and several other Sderot residents, were evacuated to a hospital and treated for shock.

On **31 December**, a barrage of 14 mortar bombs and one Kassam landed in open areas in the northern and southern Negev. No damage or injuries were sustained.

On **25 December**, an exceptionally large barrage of rockets was launched, with 23 identified hits. Rockets were fired at at Kerem Shalom and Sufa crossings and towards Ashkelon. In addition, rockets were fired toward Sderot in the morning while children were on their way to school.

On **23 December**, a rocket landed in the courtyard of a Carlsberg beer factory in Ashkelon, a port city with 120,000 residents.

On **20 December**, a Kassam rocket struck 40 meters from a Sderot school. Eighteen people were treated for shock, including ten children.

On **16 December**, a Kassam rocket landed near a house in Kibbutz Zikim, causing damage to the house and wounding a two-year-old baby in the face.

In the **183 days** from the middle of June until the middle of December, **428 rockets and 590 mortar bombs** were fired from the Gaza Strip at Israeli civilians and soldiers. The IDF reported that, since June, a **rocket is launched at Israel every three hours**.

A barrage of rockets was launched between December 12 and 14 (peaking with **26 identified rocket hits on December 12**), most of them in and around Sderot. On **December 13** a direct rocket hit destroyed a private residence, critically injuring a woman living there. The Palestinian Islamic Jihad claimed responsibility for most of the rocket launches; the rest were claimed by Fatah-Al-Aqsa Martyrs Brigade and the Popular Resistance Committees.

Mortar fire also continued, for a total of 68 bombs in the first half of December, compared to 100 during the entire month of November (78 of them were fired in the second half of November, presumably because of the Annapolis conference). In the past few months, the number of mortar bombs has increased dramatically (from one in March, to an average of 105 a month since August).

On **November 27–28** (during the Annapolis meeting) five rockets and 12 mortar bombs were fired at Israeli communities.

On **November 16–17**, a number of rockets were fired at Sderot, causing great damage to a factory and several vehicles. On **November 22**, following warnings that terrorists were trying to infiltrate into Israeli territory through tunnels, the gates of the communities bordering the Gaza Strip were closed and the residents were confined to their homes, while IDF helicopters scanned the area from the air. Six mortar bombs landed in the farming community of Netiv Haasarah, just north of the Gaza Strip and rockets and mortar bombs (at least 20 that day) fell on other Negev communities.

November 11: Terrorists from the Palestinian Islamic Jihad in Gaza fired three Kassam rockets at Israel, scoring a direct hit on a cowshed in Kibbutz Zikim. Six cows were killed and four others were injured, and damage was caused to the structures.

November 6: a Kassam rocket hit a residential home in Sderot, sending four residents to the Shock Treatment Center for treatment. Another rocket hit the city at the same time, without incident.

On **November 1**: A volley of rockets was fired at Sderot and the western Negev settlements, with at least nine identified hits in Israeli territory.

On Monday, **October 29th**, at approximately 9 am, a cell of terrorists fired three mortar bombs at Israeli territory. The bombs were launched from the courtyard of an elementary school for boys in Beit Hanoun, in northern Gaza.

The ***use of an elementary school as a shield for terrorist activity*** is a blatant violation of international humanitarian law, which absolutely prohibits the location of military facilities—which in times of conflict become legitimate military targets—in the vicinity of the civilian population. Additionally, humanitarian law (Article 51 (7) of Protocol 1) prohibits belligerents from using civilians to shield military objectives or operations from attack.

The use of civilians as human shields in direct violation of international laws is routine among the Palestinian terrorist organizations, especially in the Gaza Strip. It has many variations: rocket and mortar fire at Israel from populated areas; conducting exchanges of fire with the IDF from civilian dwellings and public institutions; installing terrorist facilities in densely populated areas; and enlisting Palestinian civilians, including women and children, where there is fighting going on and encouraging them to serve as human shields.

This violation of international humanitarian law, which was caught on film, is yet another example of the Palestinian use of children and their schools as shields for their terrorist activity. In the film, the terrorists can be seen loading the mortar, and then running for cover into the school as the projectile is launched.

On **October 25**, a rocket landed adjacent to a kindergarten; three people were treated for shock.

On **October 23**, a rocket hit a private residence in Sderot and caused extensive property damage.

October 7: A Grad missile, launched from the Gaza Strip, landed near the southern Israeli town of Netivot, about 15 km inside Israeli territory. This was the first time since 16 July 2006 that a rocket was fired on Netivot. The 122 mm Grad heavy artillery rocket, apparently produced in the former Soviet Union and smuggled into Gaza from Egypt, is an improved version of the infamous Katyusha rocket recently used by the Hizbullah to bombard northern Israel from Lebanese territory. The use of this weapon marks a significant escalation in the Palestinian campaign of terror against Israeli civilians, both in the range of the missile and the destructive force of the missile's warhead.

September 26: On the eve of the Sukkot holiday a particularly high number of rocket and mortar attacks was recorded: nine rockets and 22 mortar bombs.

September 11: A Palestinian rocket launched from the region of Beit Lahiya in the northern Gaza Strip exploded in an Israeli army base, wounding 69 recent recruits undergoing basic training, one critically, four seriously, and the rest moderately or lightly.

September 3: An exceptional number of Kassam rockets were launched at Sderot on the second day of school. The Palestinian Islamic Jihad claimed responsibility for the rocket fire, exulting that it was a "gift" to the children of Israel for the opening of the school year. A total of nine rockets fell on the town between 6 am and 1 pm, two of them at 7:50 in the morning, when thousands of children and babies with their parents were on their way to schools and day-care centers. Shortly afterwards, a rocket landed next to a kindergarten, causing damage to the building and sending 12 children to the hospital to be treated for shock.

August 28: A rocket hit a bedroom in Sderot, moderately wounding a resident standing nearby. Several people were treated for shock.

On **August 25**, a car went up in flames as a result of rocket fire.

There was a direct hit on a house in Sderot on **August 24**.

August 21: Kassam rockets hit a factory in Sderot's industrial area, causing extensive damage. Three Kassam rockets struck the western Negev, one hitting a kindergarten in Sderot. Luckily, the children were not present at the time, due to the summer vacation, and no injuries were reported.

On **July 26 and 27**, rockets and mortar bombs landed in the western Negev, causing a fire, considerable property damage and slightly wounding a woman in Sderot.

July 23: There was a direct rocket hit on a house in Kibbutz Carmia. An eight-month-old baby girl was slightly wounded and her mother and grandmother had to be treated for shock; considerable damage was done to the building.

On **July 22**, a rocket hit the Sapir College near Sderot, slightly wounding an Israeli woman.

II. Terrorist Attacks on the IDF and Israeli Counter-Terrorist Operations

The IDF is constantly on the lookout for rocket-launching squads as well as rocket-manufacturing and storage facilities and continues to attack them from the air and from the ground in order to destroy, or at least damage, the terrorists' capabilities. If it were not for the success of IDF efforts in interdicting many terrorist attacks, there would be many more civilian casualties on the Israeli side.

The fact that rockets are launched from populated areas—even areas normally immune from counterattack, such as schoolyards—and the practice of using civilians as human shields account for civilian casualties on the Palestinian side and are the responsibility of Hamas, which could remove its operatives from populated areas if it was interested in doing so.

Some of the significant events:

14 May: Following the attack on the Ashkelon mall, IAF conducted two air strikes Wednesday night against targets in Gaza City. Two terrorists were killed and four wounded.

Earlier in the day, four terrorists were killed and 14 wounded in IDF operations in Jabalya (northern Gaza Strip) and Khan Yunis (southern Gaza Strip) (*INN.com* 15/5/08).

Late Tuesday or early Wednesday (**13–14 May**), in the course of IDF counterterrorist operations, mortar bombs were fired at IDF forces and the commander was lightly wounded (IDF Spokesperson).

12–13 May: The IDF attacked a Kassam rocket-launching cell minutes after it had launched rockets towards Israel and was preparing to launch more.

10 May: In response to the continuous launching of rockets and mortar shells at Israeli communities in the western Negev (in particular, an attack on Kibbutz Kfar Aza Friday evening, 9 May, in which a civilian was killed by mortar fire), IAF attacked two Hamas posts in the Rafah area on Friday night (9–10 May) and killed 5 Hamas terror operatives.

Saturday morning (10 May), the IAF attacked a terrorist cell near the security barrier in a separate strike.

6–7 May: The IDF attacked a cell of armed terrorists in the southern Gaza Strip.

1 May: In a joint IDF and ISA operation in Rafah, the Israeli air force targeted and killed Nafez Manzur, a Hamas terror operative. Manzur was involved in the attack in which Gilad Shalit was captured and two IDF soldiers were killed, in the infiltration attack in Kerem Shalom in July 2006. He was also involved in the suicide bombing attack in Kerem Shalom crossing on Passover this year and in firing rockets at Israeli communities and posts in the western Negev (*IDF Spokesperson*, 1.5.2008).

A workshop for manufacturing arms in the southern Gaza Strip was attacked by IDF forces.

28 April: Several terrorists, as well as a mother and four children, were killed in **Beit Hanun** during IDF counterterrorist operations in northern Gaza.

The inquiry group appointed by the GOC Southern Command, Major General Yoav Galant, to investigate the circumstances of the incident in Beit Hanoun brought the following to light:

During IDF operations to locate and arrest wanted terrorists in Beit Hanun on the morning of 28 April, complex fighting occurred in which armed gunmen fired mortar shells, anti-tank missiles, light weapons and explosive devices at IDF forces from within densely populated areas. Three IDF soldiers were lightly wounded during the fighting.

Four gunmen firing at the soldiers were spotted carrying back packs loaded with ammunition. One gunmen carrying one of the back packs was targeted and hit from the air. As a result a strong secondary explosion occurred. Immediately after the explosion the second gunmen was targeted and hit, causing an even bigger explosion.

Conclusions of the IDF investigation:

The attacks against the gunmen were accurate and the gunmen were hit.

The secondary explosions triggered by the weaponry and ammunition carried by the gunmen were bigger than the ones caused by the ammunition used by the IDF.

The possibility that the family was hit by other IDF fire was eliminated since this was the only incident recorded that day in which attacks were carried out in the area.

The professional opinion of the IDF states that the family was hit during the explosion of the second missile that ignited the secondary explosions.

It should be emphasized that the armed gunmen were operating near the family's house, therefore endangering their lives.

The IDF wises to express sorrow for any harm to unassociated civilians caused due to terrorist organizations operating from populated centers, using them as human shields (IDF Spokesperson, 2 May 2008).

27 April: IDF forces located and captured two Palestinian Authority terrorists who slipped through the security barrier north of the Kissufim Crossing Saturday night.

26 April: IDF soldiers captured a wanted local Hamas kingpin in the northern Gaza town of Beit Lahiye. According to local sources, terrorists around the home of Hassan Marouf opened fire at the troops when they came to arrest him.

21 April: IAF and IDF forces killed three terrorists in two different strikes. Large quantities of weapons, including anti-tank missiles, were found in their possession.

19–21 April: Following rocket and mortar bomb attacks, the IAF struck at a terrorist cell in Rafiah on the southern Gaza border, at squads in the northern Gaza neighborhood of Jabalya and at other targets, killing a total of eight terrorists over the weekend.

19 April, the eve of the Passover festival: A broad-scale combined attack was prevented. Under the cover of early-morning fog, as well as gun and mortar bomb fire directed at Kibbutz Kerem Shalom and nearby soldiers, an armored personnel carrier broke through the gate at the Kerem Shalom Crossing. Terrorists drove two vehicles disguised as IDF jeeps and loaded with explosives through the break. One blew up close to the guard tower and the second near a group of IDF soldiers. Thirteen soldiers were wounded by flying shrapnel; four terrorists were killed.

This was the fifth such attack in 10 days on crossing points into Gaza through which humanitarian supplies for the PA population are delivered.

16 April: ***Three IDF soldiers were killed*** this morning in a confrontation with armed Palestinian gunmen identified approaching the security fence south of Nahal Oz, between the fuel terminal and Kibbutz Beeri. Two soldiers were moderately wounded and another soldier was lightly wounded during the incident. The wounded soldiers were evacuated to a hospital for medical treatment.

During a separate anti-terrorist operation near the security fence in the northern Gaza Strip, Palestinian gunmen opened fire at IDF forces from within a mosque used for storing explosives and explosive devices. The use of mosques for terrorist activity demonstrates how terrorist organizations use holy sites and civilian centers to carry out attacks, exploiting the uninvolved Palestinian population.

During the operation, a number of mortar shells and anti-tank missiles were fired at IDF forces. One soldier was moderately wounded. IDF forces identified hitting 10 armed gunmen during exchanges of fire that included a number of aerial attacks.

14 April: An IAF strike killed the commander of the DFLP's military wing in northern Gaza. He was involved in infiltration plans and rocket attacks against Israel.

9 April: One IDF soldier, ***Sgt. Sayef Bisan*, 21, was killed** and two lightly wounded in a defensive operation against the terror infrastructure in southern Gaza.

Later, in response to the *murderous attack on the civilian-run Nachal Oz fuel depot,* IDF forces comprised of air and ground forces, including at least one tank unit, shelled terrorist targets in northern Gaza. Two of the terrorists were killed. The other two terrorists were killed shortly afterwards in another IAF strike. A total of nine Gaza Arabs were killed in the attack on Nachal Oz and the two IAF strikes that followed. At least six of those killed were armed terrorists who were directly involved in the attack.

8 April: During an IDF operation against terrorists near the border fence between Israel and the northern Gaza Strip, terrorists opened fire on the IDF force. The IDF soldiers returned fire, killing three gunmen. Rocket-propelled grenades and AK-47 rifles were found on the two terrorists.

A **tunnel** shaft, approximately 3.5 meters deep, in a house located 700 meters from the security fence, was discovered in the morning in a joint IDF and ISA operation against the terrorist infrastructure in the northern Gaza strip. The tunnel was apparently dug in order to carry out a terror attack within Israel. In another incident, the force fired towards armed gunmen who approached them. During the operation, 30 mortar shells were fired at the soldiers.

4 April: Four terrorists were killed Sunday afternoon in fierce fighting with IDF troops in central Gaza.

A similar fierce battle took place near the city of Khan Yunis. Terrorists used anti-tank missiles and mortar shells in a clash with IDF soldiers. Six terrorists were killed in the fighting; there were no casualties among Israeli troops. Sources linked to the ruling Arab Hamas party in Gaza announced that an Arab farmer had been killed in an IDF attack. However, local Arabs told the Associated Press that the man had actually been killed by a terrorist rocket that fell short of its target.

29 March: Israeli Air Force pilots struck a rocket-launching cell near the town of Jabaliya in northern Gaza. IDF sources confirmed that the air strike targeted a terror cell responsible for firing rockets and mortars at Jewish communities in southern Israel.

28 March: Two terrorists killed: a Hamas gunman was killed and another wounded during a firefight with soldiers near Kissufim in central Gaza Strip. And in northern Gaza near the Jewish town of Netiv HaAsarah, located barely 100 meters from the security barrier with Gaza, an armed

Palestinian was killed after he approached the security fence and threw a grenade at soldiers there.

27 March: Two terrorists were killed while making Kassam rockets (a "work accident").

24-18-15-13 March: Terrorists placed IEDs along the border; some exploded and others were detonated in monitored explosions. No one was hurt in any of the incidents. The IAF carried out aerial attacks against armed rocket squads.

14 March: An IDF helicopter was slightly damaged by machine gun fire from the ground. Hamas claimed responsibility.

Security forces launched a wide-scale search for a Gazan man, who had been granted humanitarian passage through Israel for medical treatment in Egypt, after he evaded security forces at the Erez Crossing. It was feared that he intended to carry out a terrorist attack inside Israel. He was later apprehended in the northern Israeli town of Nazareth.

9 March: St.Sgt. *Liran Banai,* critically wounded on 6 March, died of his wounds.

6 March: Two soldiers were killed and two wounded by an IED detonated by remote control near their jeep while on routine patrol along the security fence near Kissufim. Later, a squad that was seen placing an IED near the same site was attacked by an IDF force and 3 terrorists were killed.

4 March: The IAF attacked two rocket-launching terrorist cells in separate strikes (retaliation for the rocket that destroyed a house in Sderot an hour earlier). Soldiers confirmed hits on both cells. The IDF said the attacks targeted terrorists who were launching rockets at Israel from areas north of Jabalya and east of Gaza City. Two terrorists were killed.

The Security Cabinet was warned Monday that the Grad rockets used to attack Ashkelon came from Iran.

Security officials added that the Air Force has bombed out the largest explosives laboratory in the Gaza region.

28 Feb.–3 Mar: In response to a sharp escalation of rocket fire from the Gaza Strip, **the IDF conducted a four-day intensive military operation that eliminated more than 100 terrorists in Gaza** between Thursday 28 February and Monday 3 March, when the ground forces withdrew. **The IDF operation targeted facilities for manufacturing and storing weapons; the neighborhoods from which most of the rockets are launched; terrorist squads on their way to launch rockets; and Hamas institutions.**

IDF Chief of Staff Gabi Ashkenazi told ministers that the IDF distributed notices in Gaza before the operation warning the civilian population in rocket-launching areas of the upcoming attacks.

General Ashkenazi told ministers: "In one incident we saw an elderly Palestinian leaving Jabaliya with a wagon, in which was hidden a Grad missile. He stopped 'as if coincidentally' next to an orchard. Two militants then arrived there, took the missile, positioned it on the launcher - and fired."

The IDF chief added that despite the operation, the IDF would continue its efforts to prevent a humanitarian crisis in Gaza and ensure a regular supply of food and medicines though the border crossings.

3 March: An Israeli missile struck a rocket launch squad near the northern Gaza town of Beit Hanoun, killing one man. A second missile struck a donkey cart loaded with rockets.

Friday night (29 Feb.): Infantry, armored and engineering corps, with air support, began operations in northern Gaza Strip—Sejaiya neighborhood in Gaza City and Jabalya refugee camp. Troops also searched for arms, including in private houses. This was a limited operation, not the major operation that was expected. **On Shabbat, 1 March, two soldiers were killed,** Staff Sergeant Eran Dan-Gur and Staff Sergeant Doron Asulin, both 20 and both of the Givati Brigade. Seven soldiers were wounded.

28 Feb: IAF made 23 air attacks on terrorist targets, mostly Hamas. One attack was on a **truck carrying 160 rockets**. Also targeted were structures that housed Hamas institutions, such as Haniya's offices and police stations.

24 Feb: In the southern Gaza Strip, IDF exposed five smuggling tunnels and detained 40 operatives suspected of terrorist activities. During the operation there were exchanges of fire with armed terrorists in the region. Near Beit Hanoun, in northern Gaza, IAF attacked rocket launchers and armed terrorists moving towards the security fence in central Gaza (IDF Spokesperson's website).

17 Feb: During an exchange of fire between armed terrorists and IDF forces in southern Gaza, an IDF soldier was critically wounded. During the action, he IAF killed a number of terrorists belonging to Hamas.

14 Feb: In a counterterrorist action near the Erez industrial zone, the IDF destroyed 20 structures that had been used for attacks against IDF forces. Terrorists fired a mortar bomb at the soldiers; there were no injuries.

9 February: The IDF retaliated for rocket attacks with a strike on a terrorist squad spotted near ready-to-fire rocket launchers in the nearby Gaza town of Beit Hanoun in northern Gaza.

6 February: The IAF conducted air strikes against a weapons storehouse and a rocket factory and, with support of IDF ground forces, attacked squads in rocket-launching areas of northern Gaza. Five Hamas operatives and an Islamic Jihad member were killed in two Israeli strikes in Jabalya and Beit Hanoun.

5 February: An IAF helicopter struck a building.that housed Hamas's Executive Force (police) in Khan Yunis, killing seven Hamas-Al Aqsa Martyrs Brigades terrorists.

22–27 January: Four terrorists killed in several incidents; two were involved in firing rockets at Israel and one in an exchange of fire near the Sufa crossing. The Israeli Air Force attacked a building in Rafah; there were two IAF attacks on vehicles carrying terrorists and possibly explosives.

15 January: Elite troops from the Golani Brigade's Egoz Unit, backed by tanks and Engineering Corps squads, swept into central Gaza in the early morning in pursuit of Kassam rocket squads and terror infrastructure the IDF feared was being built up along the border fence.

Nineteen Palestinians—including three civilians, according to hospital officials in Gaza—were killed in the ensuing gun battles and air strikes. One was Hussam Zahar, 24, son of hard-line Hamas leader Mahmoud Zahar, who is viewed as the mastermind behind the violent Hamas takeover of the Gaza Strip in June.

14 January: Israel Airports Authority security personnel on Monday discovered two tons of a chemical substance, used to manufacture explosives and rockets, in a truck that was supposedly bringing humanitarian aid into the Gaza Strip though the Kerem Shalom crossing.

9 January - The Israel Air Force targeted an Islamic Jihad terrorist cell that was firing mortar bombs from Beit Lahiyeh in northern Gaza, killing two terrorists and wounding six others, according to both Israeli and PA sources.

7 January: A man and woman, residents of the Palestinian Authority, approached an army installation adjacent to the Gaza region's Erez Crossing while holding hands and pretending to be a couple out on a walk. When the "couple" was in proximity to the IDF position, however, they both drew firearms and began shooting at soldiers. IDF forces returned fire, killing them both. Soldiers found explosives on the woman's body after the attack. No Israelis were injured in the attack.

In a second attack in the same region later in the day, terrorists opened fire on a group of Israeli journalists. The four journalists, working for various news agencies, were standing on a hill near the Erez Crossing when they came under attack. None of the journalists were hurt in the shooting, but a car they were using was hit by several bullets.

Senior IDF officers criticized the terrorist factions for their frequent attacks on Israeli-controlled crossings into Gaza, such as that at Erez. The attacks make it difficult for Israel to transfer food and medicine into Gaza, and sometimes delay the transfer of crucial aid.

6 January: Five soldiers were wounded by an anti-tank missile in the central Gaza Strip.

On **5 January**, an explosives lab was discovered in Gaza. Over the weekend, 42 rockets and 14 mortar bombs were fired at Israel.

1–3 January: The Israel Air Force bombed Gaza in retaliation for rocket attacks, including a Katyusha rocket that landed further north than any rocket ever fired from Gaza. Eight Palestinian terrorists were killed in clashes with Israeli forces; the last one was in the midst of trying to fire anti-rocket rockets when he was killed. IDF forces also fired on and hit Palestinian gunmen approaching the security fence in central Gaza.

On **29 December**, the IDF released the information that, a few weeks ago, 6 tons of potassium nitrate were discovered in a humanitarian aid truck. The chemical, used for making explosives and rocket propellants, was packed in sugar bags with EU markings. The truck was on its way to the Gaza Strip.

The Israel security forces carried out a series of counterterrorist activities in the Gaza Strip, focusing on senior terrorist operatives belonging to the Palestinian Islamic Jihad (PIJ), the organization launching most of the rockets at the western Negev towns and farming villages. The activities were successful and caused damage to the PIJ's operational infrastructure.

On **27 December**, terrorists fired an RPG at IDF forces in southern Gaza. The soldiers responded with small arms fire, killing three terrorists. There was also an air strike against a vehicle carrying explosives and terrorist operatives en route to execute an attack.

Aerial attacks against Kassam launchers and rocket-launching squads were carried out throughout the Gaza Strip.

On **20 December**, a day-long counterterrorism operation in central Gaza ended with seven Hamas and PIJ terrorists killed and three soldiers injured, one seriously. The IDF Spokesperson expressed hope that the success of the operation would prevent terrorists from approaching the Gaza security fence, which has been the site of numerous attempted attacks in recent weeks.

On **17–18 December** four aerial attacks were carried out, killing 12 terrorists, including a senior Islamic Jihad terrorist (Majed Harazin) in charge of rocket launching.

First half of December: The IDF, including the air force (IAF), carried out numerous counterterrorist activities throughout the Gaza Strip from Khan Yunis and the Sufa crossing in the south, through Dir al-Balah in the central

Gaza Strip, and near Beit Lahia in northern Gaza. Four IDF soldiers were injured and twelve Hamas terrorists were killed in various operations.

December 11 showed particularly intensive activity—in the southern Gaza Strip, terrorists fired at IDF forces and launched anti-tank missiles (two soldiers were injured); the Israeli Air Force attacked a Hamas position in the central Gaza Strip (three Hamas operatives were killed); and, in response to mortar fire on Kibbutz Nahal Oz, IDF forces attacked a terrorist squad in the northern Gaza Strip.

Second half of November: Israeli security forces continued preventing terrorist activity close to the security fence. Daily fighting continued between the IDF and terrorist squads. Many attempts were made to attack IDF forces or to infiltrate into Israel territory. Conspicuous were the attacks centering on the Erez industrial zone, during which terrorist operatives infiltrated into buildings there. During this two-week period, at least 13 terrorists engaged in terrorist activities—such as launching rockets or mortar bombs, attacking IDF soldiers or placing charges near the security fence—were killed by IDF forces.

November 11: Israeli soldiers and General Security Services (GSS) agents uncovered seven smuggling tunnels in 36 hours. The tunnels, which are used for smuggling terrorists and arms from Egypt to be used against Israel, were found in the southern city of Dahania during operations to stop rocket and mortar shell attacks from the area. The forces also discovered that the area around the tunnels had been booby-trapped. The tunnels and the explosive devices were disposed of in controlled explosions by IDF sappers.

October 30: Near Khan Yunis, the air force struck a Hamas Executive Force postion, killing four terrorist operatives.

On **October 29** an IDF force conducting a security sweep near the security fence came upon a terrorist ambush, in which First Sergeant (Res.) **Ehud Efrati was killed.** Efrati, 34, was married and the father of three. Two other IDF soldiers were slightly injured (IDF Spokesperson website, October 29).

At a briefing, Brig.Gen Moshe Tamir, IDF Commander of the Gaza division, explained the **IDF's operational goals**: "The action (on October 29th) is part of the Gaza brigade's operations to keep the Hamas terror organization away from the security fence . . . The operations are conducted 2–3 km from the fence in order to prevent the digging of tunnels, planting of explosive devices, infiltration into Israeli communities, shooting attacks against Israeli farmers on their land near [the Israeli side of] the fence, and the firing of rockets and mortal bombs at Israel . . .

"The Hamas is continuing to arm itself and improve its abilities; today it has more weaponry . . . There is no magical solution to the threat from the

Qassam rockets. By keeping the pressure on Hamas, we reduce their ability to attack Israeli civilians" (IDF Spokesperson, October 29, 2007).

October 28: The air force attacked terrorists in Sajaiya three times, killing six terrorist operatives.

On **October 26** an IDF force operating in the northern Gaza Strip came upon an armed terrorist squad. Two terrorists were killed in the ensuing firefight and two IDF soldiers were slightly wounded.

October 25: An IDF force operating in the southern Gaza Strip encountered two armed terrorists, and killed them in the ensuing clash. The terrorists had in their possession large quantities of explosives and anti-tank missiles.

On **October 22**, one terrorist operative was killed and three wounded in an air force attack in the region of Beit Hanoun in the northern Gaza Strip.

October 17: IDF forces killed an armed terrorist in the course of a counter-terrorist operation east of Khan Yunis in the southern Gaza Strip. **Sergeant Ben Koveni, 20, was killed** by terrorist fire.

During the **first half of October**, the IDF and the IAF responded to shooting, grenade and Kassam rocket attacks. Several terrorists were killed and others wounded in the operations.

September 12: A terrorist from the Gaza Strip wearing an explosive belt was apprehended shortly after infiltrating into Israel through the Egyptian border. During questioning he said that he had been sent to carry out an attack in the Israeli city of Beersheba.

September 6: An attempt by a terrorist squad to infiltrate into Israeli territory was foiled. The goal of the squad, according to the IDF Southern Brigade commander, was to kidnap soldiers at an IDF post north of Kibbutz Kissufim and to attack the kibbutz. The squad of seven terrorists, who arrived in two vehicles equipped with explosive vests, hand grenades and rocket-propelled grenades was discovered about 250 meters (about 275 yards) from the security fence in the central Gaza Strip. IDF ground forces and Israel Air Force aircraft attacked, triggering several large explosions in the vehicles, which proved to be car bombs loaded with hundreds of kilograms of explosives. Six of the terrorists were killed and one managed to escape.

In a separate incident the same day, an IDF officer was lightly wounded and four terrorists were killed during an operation against Kassam rocket launchers in the Khan Yunis area.

On **September 5**, IDF forces discovered and seized 11 rocket launchers in the northern Gaza Strip aimed at Israel and ready for firing.

August 29: The IDF struck several rocket launchers aimed at Israel in the Beit Hanoun industrial area in northern Gaza. Three Palestinians were killed in the strike. An IDF statement said, in part: "The IDF received information that the Palestinians handling the launchers were teenagers. The IDF wishes to express sorrow for the cynical use the terror organizations make of the active participation of teenagers in terror attacks."

August 28: An IDF force detained a 15-year-old Palestinian near Beit Hanoun who attempted to attack them. A body search of the youth revealed two concealed explosive devices ready for detonation.

August 25: IDF forces foiled an attempted terrorist attack on the settlement Netiv Ha'asara, north of the Gaza Strip. Two terrorists dressed in IDF uniforms and exploiting the early morning fog, managed to climb over the security fence using a rope ladder. They then shot at a soldier in a guard post of the Liaison and Coordination Administration near the Erez Crossing. While advancing towards Netiv Ha'asara, the terrorists were killed by an IDF force. Light arms, hand grenades and two explosive devices were found in their possession. Two IDF soldiers were slightly wounded in the incident.

August 21: Three Islamic Jihad terrorists were killed by IDF fire near the security fence. Weapons, including sniper rifles, were found near the bodies.

IDF ground forces fired upon two figures seen handling a rocket launcher near Beit Hanoun and discovered that two teenage boys had been killed. The IDF has evidence that children and teenagers are involved in retrieving Kassam launchers after the rockets have been fired, placing roadside bombs, and other terrorist activities.

August 20: The Israeli Air Force struck a vehicle carrying a squad of rocket-launching terrorists near the Al-Bureij refugee camp (central Gaza Strip). Six Hamas terrorist operatives were killed. In the northern Gaza Strip the IDF attacked a squad of terrorists engaged in launching rockets into the western Negev.

August 15: During counter-terrorist activities in the Beit Hanoun area, a tunnel shaft was discovered in a tomato hothouse, about 700 meters (4/10 of a mile) from the northern Gaza Strip security fence. A generator sunk into the earth and tools used to dig the tunnel were also found. The IDF detonated the tunnel. The terrorist organizations in the Gaza Strip, especially Hamas, have built a vast number of tunnels in recent years. The tunnel, of which only about 20 meters (22 yards) had been dug when it was exposed, was intended to be used to infiltrate terrorists into Israel or to set off explosives under an IDF post.

July 26: Two terrorists threw hand grenades at an IDF force near the border fence in the northern Gaza Strip. The force returned fire and killed them.

July 22: Two Hamas operatives threw a hand grenade at an IDF force near the Erez crossing. The soldiers returned fire and killed the terrorists, who had been planning to ambush the security forces operating in the area (Hamas/Izzedine al-Qassam Brigades Website, July 22, 2007).

July 12: Staff Sergeant **Arbel Raich, 21 years old, was killed** when his unit was attacked near the al-Bureij refugee camp during a counter-terrorist operation in the central Gaza Strip. Two additional soldiers were wounded. Hamas claimed responsibility for the attack and Hamas spokesman Fawzi Barhoum praised the killing (Al-Aqsa TV, July 12). In an exchange of fire between an IDF force and armed Hamas terrorists on **July 5**, a number of terrorists were killed.

June 24–27: In firefights and air strikes against Hamas and Islamic Jihad terrorists engaged in launching rockets at Negev settlements and in shooting at Israeli soldiers with light arms and anti-tank missiles, at least 13 Palestinians were killed and several wounded. Two IDF soldiers were slightly wounded in the counter-terrorist operations.

June 18–19: Near Kissufim, in the central Gaza Strip, and near the Erez Crossing in the northern Strip, terrorists tossed hand grenades and fired at IDF soldiers, who returned fire. An armed Palestinian and a civilian were killed, at least 12 others were wounded, and a soldier was wounded in the exchange of fire.

III. Statistical Data:

Monthly distribution of identified rocket hits over the past year

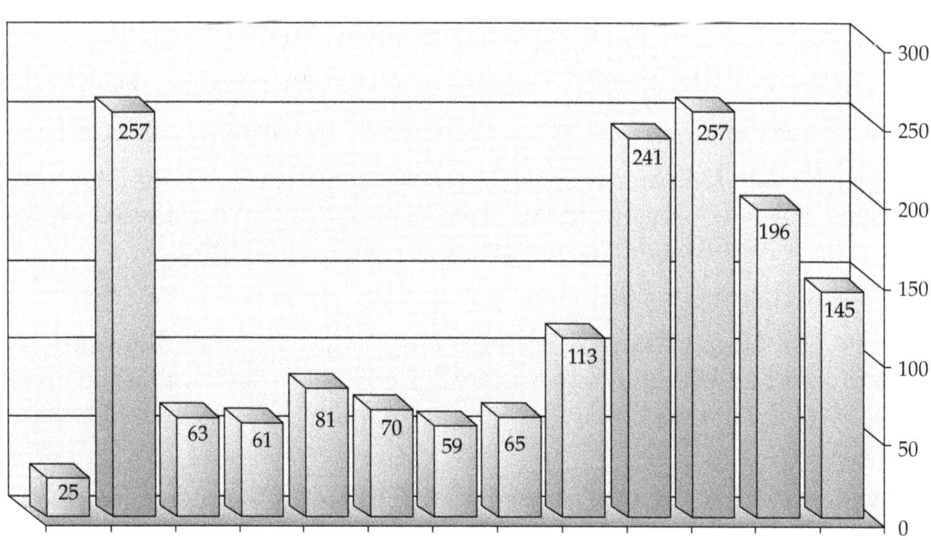

Monthly distribution of identified mortar bomb hits

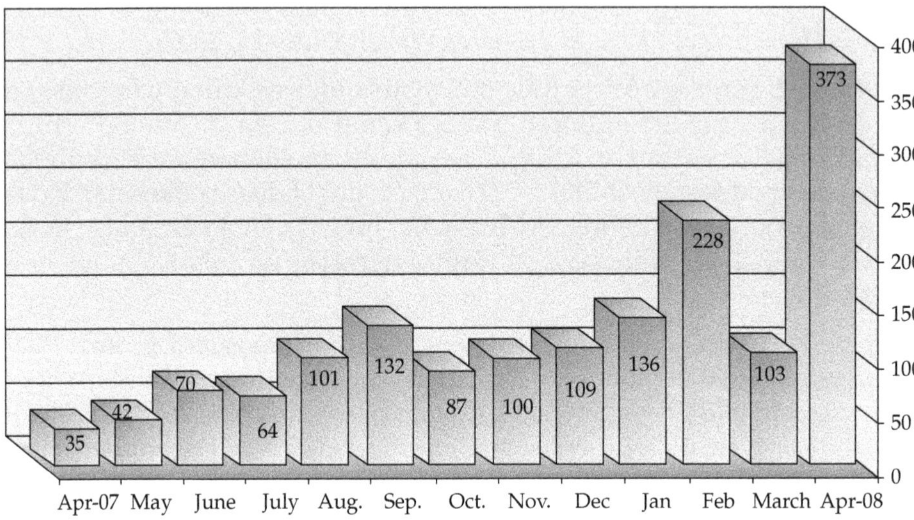

IV. Human Shields

The terrorist organizations operating in the Gaza Strip make frequent use of civilians as human shields. One such incident occurred on **April 13**, when the IAF struck several houses of senior terrorist operatives. Hamas used its website to ask Gaza Strip civilians to go to the house of the commander of the Al-Aqsa Martyrs Brigades in Gaza City, where it had been announced that the IDF was planning to blow up the house.

In several instances, Al-Aqsa TV called upon civilians to form a human shield around houses that the IDF had threatened to blow up:

- the home of Abu al-Hatal in Sajaiya or al-Sha'af neighborhood (1 March).
- the northern Gaza Strip house of shaheed Othman al-Ruziana (29 Feb.);
- the house of Ma'amoun Abu Amer in Khan Yunis (an hour later, dozens of Khan Yunis residents were reported to have gathered on the roof of Abu Amer's house—Pal-today website, 28 Feb.);
- the northern Gaza Strip house of shaheed Musab al-Jaabir (29 Feb.);

Hamas PM **Ismail Haniya** boasted that hundreds and thousands of Palestinians had left their homes in the middle of the night and gone up on the roofs of the houses that the Israeli "occupation" had threatened to blow up (Aljazeera TV, 29 Feb.).

Minister for Public Security, **Avi Dichter** (3 March): "In a state of war with a terror entity we must not shirk from hitting terrorists who try to carry out a terror attack from within an envelope of civilians. Civilians who provide a human shield for terrorists are terrorists, plain and simple."

V. Hamas' Offensive Strategy and its Military Buildup

The former Hamas foreign minister, **Mahmoud a-Zahar**, explaining **why Hamas in the past two years has favored rocket attacks over suicide bombings**, told the Sunday Telegraph's correspondent (21 August 2007), "Which do you think is more effective, martyrdom operations or rockets against Sderot? Rockets against Sderot will cause mass migration, greatly disrupt daily lives and government administration and can make a much huger impact on the government. We are using the methods that convince the Israelis that their occupation is costing them too much. We are succeeding with the rockets. We have no losses and the impact on the Israeli side is so much."

Moshe Kaplinsky, Deputy Chief of Staff, told the New York Times (28 August 2007) that Hamas was building a force similar to that of Hezbollah in south Lebanon. He said that several hundred Hamas **terrorist** operatives had been sent abroad for **military training**, most of them **to Iran**.

The Turkish daily *Sabah* reported on 10 March 2008 that Hamas operaties are undergoing training in Iran. A member of the Izzeddin el Kassam Brigades, the armed wing of the Hamas, stated that its members undergo **training in Iran and Syria**: "Hamas engineers from Gaza are being sent to Syria and Iran for training in rocket manufacturing. Until today over 400 of our engineers have returned after having undergone rocket training. **These missiles are being manufactured in workshops underneath secret houses.** 'Carriers' are carrying them to the points determined by the watchmen. If there are no helicopters or UAVs, we are firing them to towards the target."

Israel Security Agency chief **Yuval Diskin** told the government (February 3, 2008) that, during the past few days, large quantities of weapons had been smuggled into the Gaza Strip through the open fence along the Philadelphi route. He said that "no exact quantities can be indicated. Apparently standard **weapons were smuggled** in, including long-range rockets, anti-tank and anti-aircraft missiles." Also, according to Diskin, many terrorist operatives have returned from training in Iran, Syria and Egypt and are now in the Gaza Strip.

Hamas taxes the estimated 150 smuggling tunnels leading from Egypt into the Gaza Strip, charging the owners $3000 each a day. The tunnels bring in a total of $150 million annually, while the value of men, weapons and other merchandise smuggled in each year total close to a half-billion dollars. Five tunnels were blown up when their owners refused to pay the fee; the others quickly paid up, giving Hamas a monopoly on the tunnels.

The tunnels are run in a systematic manner and categorized according to the goods that pass through them—weapons, cash, Hamas military commanders who seek to return to Gaza, food, medicine, computer equipment, and dangerous drugs.

In a report for the Jerusalem Center for Public Affairs (vol. 7 no. 25, 19 December 2007), former IDF Southern Command chief Maj.Gen. (res.)Yom Tov Samia stated, "The Palestinians have brought into Gaza more than 30,000 rifles during the past two years, more than six million rounds of ammunition, more than 230 tons of explosives, and scores of anti-tank and anti-aircraft missiles."

VI. Hamas Behavior Towards their Brethren in Gaza

16 May: Unknown assailants detonated a bomb outside a Christian school in Gaza City before dawn Friday. The Zahwa Rosary School, which is run by Catholic nuns, caters mainly to Muslim students. The school had been ransacked in June 2007, along with the nuns' adjacent convent, during a week of intense fighting that ended with Hamas' seizure of power.

The bombing was the latest in a string of attacks on Christian institutions in the overwhelmingly Muslim territory. In the most serious attack, a local Christian activist was murdered in October. His killers have not been found (AP/Jerusalem Post).

On **November 12, 2007**, at a rally commemorating the third anniversary of Yasser Arafat's death attended by at least 250,000 people, Hamas security forces opened fire on the crowd. Seven Palestinians were killed and 150 wounded, some critically. Afterwards, Hamas police carried out a wave of arrests of Fatah activists throughout the Gaza Strip.

The well-organized rally, attended by hundreds of thousands of people, was evidently interpreted by Hamas as an expression of public protest against its regime.

VII. Statements by Hamas Leaders

Hamas's Continued Opposition to Negotiations

Hamas spokesmen expressed their views at a mass rally celebrating the 20th anniversary of the movement (December 15, 2007). A recurring theme in the day's speeches was that there are two tracks in the struggle to destroy the Jewish State; but that Hamas's armed attacks are more effective than Fatah's negotiations—as was proven by Israel's retreat from the Gaza Strip. Hamas prime minister Ismail **Haniyya** stressed, "The option of the resistance and jihad is the shortest way to liberate Palestine, and to restore Jerusalem and Palestinian rights. Not the path of negotiations, not the path of bargaining . . . " Haniyya said that realizing "the right of resistance" would prevent the implementation of the first stage of the Road Map.

Musheir al-Masri, member of the Palestinian Legislative Council: "the Jews have to return to where they came from, we are digging graves for them . . . We will remain firm until the liberation of Palestine, all Palestine, from the [Mediterranean] sea to the [Jordan] river . . . " (Al-Aqsa TV, December 14).

Khaled Mashal, head of Hamas' "political" bureau in Damascus: Since the movement was founded in 1987, "it restored the honor of the option of resistance" in contrast to those who believed in "the option of an arrangement and negotiations." Hamas created "new models" of heroism, sacrifice and suicide bombings . . . The lesson Hamas taught Israel and the world was that "the land [of "Palestine"] will only be liberated by the rifle . . . "

Hamas Position on *"Hudna"* and *"Tahadiya"*

(The following definitions and assessment are taken from "The Egyptian initiative for a lull in the fighting," a report by the Intelligence and Terrorism Information Center, published May 6, 2008.)

The term *hudna* [هدنة] is taken from Islamic tradition, and means an agreement or contract which entails the cessation of all fighting for a specific period of time and under conditions which have been agreed upon. A Muslim leader is permitted to announce a *hudna* during a war against infidels. **The *hudna's* objective is a temporary cease fire to improve the Muslim positions for a new round of fighting** and to improve their resources. It is a stage in *jihad* and does not express either willingness or a commitment to solve a conflict or even to preserve a truce. It is limited in time, and **the Muslim side can violate it** or extend the time limit if it serves Muslim interests. For that reason, the *hudna* is considered a tactical move integral to fighting the enemy until in due time he is overcome.

Tahadiya [تهدئة] on the other hand, is a modern, secular term that has no religious Islamic validity. It means "lull in the fighting," that is, **lowering the intensity of a confrontation** through a mutual commitment to stop the fighting, **which does not necessarily include the complete cessation of all military activities** (such as collecting intelligence, procuring arms, etc.). It can be translated "as a quiescent period in the fighting," even though the media often mistranslate it as "truce." It is less binding than a *hudna* and permits Hamas and other organizations to carry out military activities except for engaging in actual fighting.

May 2008: Egypt has been working to broker a *tahadiya* between Israel and the Palestinians. (Because it is far less binding, as explained above, Hamas prefers a *tahadiya* to a *hudna*.) Hamas is interested in the lull, which includes opening the Gaza Strip crossings on Hamas terms, as a means of strengthening and stabilizing its control of the Gaza Strip, as well as enabling it to accelerate its military buildup in preparation for a future confrontation with Israel.

According to **Khaled Mashal**, head of Hamas's political bureau in Damascus, Hamas regards the lull as "a tactic, a stage in the resistance, and nothing more" (*Al-Jazeera TV*, April 27). Senior Hamas activist **Mahmud al-Zahar** claimed that arms smuggling is in the hands of Israel and Egypt. Regarding the manufacture of weapons, he said, "that cannot be supervised," implying that the lull in fighting does not include any commitment on the part of Hamas to stop manufacturing and smuggling weapons (*Al-Aqsa TV*, April 29).

Osama Hamdan, Hamas's representative in Lebanon, said (19 May) that Israel is mistaken if it thinks a truce with Hamas would mean that the "resistance operations" would end. "The confrontation with the [Israeli] Occupation will continue despite the talk about a *tahdiya*," he said. "As far as Hamas is concerned, all options remain open" (*Jerusalem Post*, 20 May, 2008).

December 2008: In the wake of the intensive activity carried out by the Israeli security forces in the Gaza Strip and the media reports of a possible extensive IDF incursion into the Strip to stop the rocket fire on Israel, Hamas talked about implementing a potential hiatus (*hudna*) in the fighting. However, the statements are not uniform, which may indicate differences of opinion.

Prime Minister Ismail Haniyya told a reporter for Israel TV's Channel 2, "we have no problem in negotiating with Israel at least about two topics, Kassam rocket fire and targeted killing, to achieve a mutual *hudna*" (Dec. 18).

However, Ahmed Yussuf, a political advisor in the foreign ministry of Haniyya's government, said it was a question of a short-term lull and not a cease fire (hudna). "Resistance [i.e., terrorism] will remain an option. As long as the Occupation exists, the resistance will exist" (*al-Jazeera TV website*, Dec. 24).

An important figure in the PIJ (the organization responsible for most of the rocket attacks), Khaled al-Batash, said, "no one can impose a lull on the PIJ because it is a resistance movement" (*Nidaa al-Quds website*, Dec. 23).

Other Statements by Hamas and Related Organizations:

After the Hamas-perpetrated suicide bombing in Dimona (4 February), in which an Israeli woman was killed and ten civilians were wounded, senior Hamas official in the Gaza Strip Osama al-Muzeina said that if it seemed as though there were fewer suicide bombing attacks, Dimona proved that it was an illusion. Asked whether there would be more suicide attacks, he answered "all possibilities are open" (*Filastin al-An website*, 6 February). Another senior Hamas official, Yahya Musa, said that more attacks would follow the one in Dimona and that a new terrorist campaign (intifada) would break out (*Al-Aqsa TV*, 6 February).

Following the breaching and resealing of the border fence between Egypt and the Gaza Strip, Hamas threatened that, if the border with Egypt were hermetically sealed, this time its operatives would "blow up the entire border fence and not just parts of it" (*Agence France Presse*, February 1, 2008).

Khalid al-Batish, a high-ranking member of the Palestinian Islamic Jihad (PIJ), declared that his organization will not be bound by anything that may come out of the Annapolis conference and that the PIJ would continue to carry out attacks ('resistance'), even if an agreement is reached to establish a Palestinian state in the 1967 borders. In his view, "all of Palestine is occupied and not only the territories captured in 1967" (*Al-Quds al-Araby*, 3 October).

Hamas Celebrates 60th *Nakba Day*

Hamas exploits *Nakba Day* for a propaganda campaign against Israel and the Jewish people. Its television station broadcasts programs glorifying Hamas terrorist operatives, and a special effort is invested in children's programs, which are rife with hatred for Israel. The message, repeated over and over in order to brainwash the children, is: "the Palestinians will soon return to Jaffa, Acre, Lod, Ramle and Ashdod, and also to Tel al-Rabia (Tel Aviv in Arabic)" (from a children's program broadcast by *Al-Aqsa TV*, May 2, 2008).

VIII. ISA Summary of Terror 2007

In contrast to the impressive decrease in successful terrorist suicide and shooting attacks in Israel, which the IDF attributes to the security fence, quality intelligence and operational freedom of action throughout Judea and Samaria, rocket and mortar attacks continue from the Gaza Strip. In 2007, 1,263 rockets and 1,511 mortar bombs struck Israel, compared to 1,722 rockets and 55 mortar bombs in 2006. Two residents of Sderot were killed in 2007. The ISA estimates that since the Hamas takeover in the middle of June 2007, 80 tons of explosives have been smuggled into the Gaza Strip from the Sinai.

IX. Hamas-Manufactured 'Fuel Crisis'

May 10: The Palestinians shut down the power plant in the Gaza Strip, claiming there was no more diesel fuel to keep it working. On May 5, the Nahal Oz crossing, where fuel is delivered from Israel to the Gaza Strip, was closed after a mortar bomb was fired at the crossing from the Gaza Strip. On May 12 it was reopened and the fuel supply was renewed.

It is important to note that the Gaza power plant supplies only about 26% of the Gaza Strip's electricity, Israel provides about 70%, and Egypt 7%. Therefore, shutting down the power plant cannot cause a complete power outage and the authorities (Hamas) are able to direct the electricity to ensure that vital services continue.

Col. Nir Press, head of the Coordination & Liaison Administration to the Gaza Strip addressed the issue of UNRWA fuel shortages (**24 April 2008**). Excerpts from his statement: "The [fuel] deposits accumulated in the Palestinian fuel depot at Nahal Oz amount to one million liters. The Palestinians have not withdrawn any fuel during the past month, and are not supplying the fuel necessary for humanitarian and civilian requirements. In this manner, the Palestinians, led by the Hamas organization, are creating shortages, misery and disaster."

When the first fuel tanker arrived (24 April) to withdraw fuel for UNRWA, according to the transfer arrangement, tens of thousands of Palestinians blocked one of the main intersections leading to the fuel depot, preventing the tanker from reaching the depot and thus preventing the supply of fuel (*Coordination and Liaison Administration, Erez,* 24 April 2008).

"Members of Hamas in the Gaza Strip opened fire on Sunday (**27 April**) on fuel trucks that were full of fuel destined for hospitals in the territory," the Palestinian health ministry said in a statement issued in Ramallah.

Israel halted deliveries of fuel to Gaza on **April 9** after Palestinian militants attacked the Nahal Oz terminal, through which all of Gaza's fuel needs are delivered. It says it cannot deliver any more fuel as the tanks on the Palestinian side of the terminal are full because Hamas will not allow the distribution of the one million litres of petrol and diesel stored there" (AFP 27 April 2008; *http://news.yahoo.com/s/afp/20080427/wl_mideast_afp/mideast-conflictgaza*).

On **January 20**, following a massive Hamas rocket attack on Israel, most of the crossings between Israel and the Gaza Strip were temporarily closed and no merchandise or fuel was allowed into Gaza. The Erez Crossing remained open for cases of humanitarian aid.

Hamas exploited the situation to create an impression of a humanitarian crisis in the Gaza Strip.

The crossings were closed on January 20; already on January 22, they were partially reopened, with limited amounts of supplies (such as diesel and cooking fuel, milk, flour and drugs) being allowed through. Israel did not provide gasoline for cars, however, since gasoline stores were diverted by Hamas for use in its rocket-launching apparatus.

X. Egypt-Gaza Border

Another event orchestrated by Hamas with impeccable timing was the collapse of the security fence on the Egypt-Gaza border. The breaching of the fence seemed to be a spontaneous reaction to the pressure created inside Gaza by Israel's closing the border crossings (see above). In fact, work on demolishing the fence had been going on for months—long before Israel placed a blockade on Gaza. As soon as the fence was breached, hundreds of thousands of Gazans streamed into Egypt, spending millions of dollars in a week-long shopping spree.

One of Hamas's goals in breaching the fence was to force the Rafah crossing (which is controlled by Egypt) to be opened and to create a new arrangement for control of the border, effectively canceling the *Agreed Principles for Rafah Crossing November 15, 2005* achieved by Israeli and Palestinian negotiators after Israel withdrew from Gaza in August 2005. A breached border fence and the possibility of a reopened Rafah Crossing under Hamas control would enable the terrorist organizations to keep up a steady stream of *advanced weapons and Iranian-trained operatives* into the Gaza Strip, including global jihad terrorists, who have easy access to weapons and supporters in the Sinai Peninsula (*Intelligence and Terrorism Information Center, IICC,* 29 January 2008).

While Gaza is bounded on the Israeli side by a relatively secure perimeter barrier, the border between Egypt and Israel is much more open. Security officials estimate that hundreds of people, most of them African refugees, smugglers and migrant workers, manage to cross the border illegally every month.

XI. The Crossings Between Israel and the Gaza Strip

On 30 January, in its response to an appeal against restricting supplies of electricity and fuel to the Gaza Strip, the Israeli Supreme Court determined that since Israel had disengaged from the Gaza Strip it had no effective control over what occurred there. The judges also determined that Israel had no commitment "to deal with the welfare of the residents of the Gaza Strip or to allow unlimited amounts of goods and merchandise" to pass through, but only vital and humanitarian goods (*Israel Supreme Court website,* January 30). At present, fuel, gas and humanitarian goods continue to pass through the Sufa and Nahal Oz Crossings, and pedestrians with serious humanitarian needs are permitted to use the Erez crossing.

B. INTERNAL PROBLEMS WITHIN THE PALESTINIAN TERRITORIES

DOCUMENT NO. 11

HOUSE DEMOLITION IN THE PALESTINIAN TERRITORIES

Amnesty International Report
MDE 15/033/2004

May 2004

Israel and the Occupied Territories Under the Rubble: House Demolition and Destruction of Land and Property

I. Introduction

For decades Israel has pursued a policy of forced eviction[1] and demolition of homes of Palestinians living under occupation in the West Bank and Gaza Strip and the homes of Israeli Arabs in Israel. In the past three and a half years the scale of the destruction carried out by the Israeli army in the Occupied Territories has reached an unprecedented level. The victims are often amongst the poorest and most disadvantaged in both Israeli and Palestinian society. Most of the houses demolished by the Israeli army in the Occupied Territories were the homes of refugee families, who were expelled by Israeli forces or who fled in the war that followed the creation of Israel in 1948.

More than 3,000 homes, hundreds of public buildings and private commercial properties, and vast areas of agricultural land have been destroyed by the Israeli army and security forces in Israel and the Occupied Territories in the past three and a half years. Tens of thousands of men, women and children have been forcibly evicted from their homes and made homeless or have lost their source of livelihood. Thousands of other houses and

---

Editor's note: The original version of this document included some color images that could not be adequately reproduced in this publication. Where necessary, captions and/or headings specifically relating to any omitted images have also been left out of the version reprinted herein. The main text of the document has not been affected by these omissions.

[1] For the definition of forced eviction, see p 56.

properties have been damaged, many beyond repair. In addition, tens of thousands of other homes are under threat of demolition, their occupants living in fear of forced eviction and homelessness.

Forced evictions and house demolitions are usually carried out without warning, often at night, and the occupants are given little or no time to leave their homes. Sometimes they are allowed a few minutes or half an hour, too little to salvage their belongings. Often the only warning is the rumbling of the Israeli army's bulldozers and tanks and the inhabitants barely have time to flee as the bulldozers begin to tear down the walls of their homes. Thousands of families have had their homes and possessions destroyed under the blades of the Israeli army's US-made Caterpillar bulldozers. In the wake of the demolitions men, women and children return to the ruins of their homes searching for whatever can be salvaged from under the rubble: passports or other documents, children's schoolbooks, clothes, kitchenware or furniture which were not destroyed.

In most cases the justification given by the Israeli authorities for the destruction of homes, agricultural land and other properties is "military/security needs", while in other cases the justification is lack of building permits. The result is the same: families are left homeless and destitute. They must rely on relatives, friends and charity organizations for shelter and subsistence.

The destruction of Palestinian homes, agricultural land and other property in the Occupied Territories, including East Jerusalem, is inextricably linked with Israel's long-standing policy of appropriating as much as possible of the land it occupies, notably by establishing Israeli settlements. The establishment of Israeli settlements in the Occupied Territories violates international humanitarian law,[2] and the presence of these settlements has led to mass violations of human rights of the local Palestinian population.

As well as violating international humanitarian law *per se*, the implementation of Israel's settlement policy in the Occupied Territories violates fundamental human rights provisions. The seizure and appropriation of land for Israeli settlements, bypass roads and related infrastructure and the

---

[2] - Article 49 of the Fourth Geneva Convention states categorically: "... *The Occupying Power shall not deport or transfer parts of its own civilian population in the territory it occupies.*"

- Article 55 of the Hague Regulations forbids the occupying State from changing the character and nature of state property, except for security needs and for the benefit of the local population. Israel's building of settlements, roads and related infrastructure for Israeli civilians in the West Bank and Gaza does not meet these two exceptional criteria.

- The Rome Statute of the International Criminal Court, in force since 1 July 2002, includes among the war crimes within the jurisdiction of the court the: "*transfer, directly or indirectly, by the Occupying Power of parts of its own civilian population into the territory it occupies ...*" "*when committed as part of a plan or policy or a part of a large scale commission of such crimes*" (Article 8 (2) (b) (viii)).

This crime is further defined in the Elements of Crimes, a supplementary instrument to the Rome Statute adopted in September 2002.

discriminatory allocation of other vital resources, including water, have had a devastating impact on the fundamental rights of the local Palestinian population, including their rights to an adequate standard of living and to housing.

Israeli settlements in the West Bank and Gaza Strip have spread considerably in the past decade and in the same period the number of Israeli settlers has increased by more than 50%.[3] With the spread of Israeli settlements and related infrastructure throughout the Occupied Territories, in order to ensure the safety and freedom of movement of Israeli settlers in the West Bank and Gaza Strip, the Israeli army has committed increasingly frequent and grave violations of the human rights of the Palestinian population. These violations include widespread destruction of Palestinian homes, land and other properties, as a result of which thousands of Palestinians have been forcibly evicted and made homeless.

In Israel it is essentially the homes of Palestinian citizens of Israel (Israeli Arabs) which are targeted for demolition. House demolition in the Arab sector is linked to the state's policy of large-scale confiscation of land and to restrictive planning regulations. Much of the land surrounding Arab towns and villages has been confiscated and the remaining Arab owned land has been mostly zoned as green land on which it is forbidden to build. In addition, discriminatory policies in the allocation of state land have further reduced the possibilities for Israeli Arabs to obtain permits to build homes to accommodate their growing housing needs. The resulting longstanding problem of lack of building permits in the Arab sector has led many to eventually build their homes without permits and these homes are frequently demolished. Whereas government policies and planning regulations have curtailed the growth and development of Arab towns and villages, in the Jewish sector the policy has been to expand existing towns and villages and establish hundreds of new villages. Moreover, even though violations of planning and building regulations are also widespread in the Jewish sector, it is in the Arab sector that homes are frequently demolished.

This report analyses the main patterns and trends of forced eviction, house demolition and destruction of property by the Israeli army and security forces in Israel and the Occupied Territories in the light of international human rights and humanitarian law.

Amnesty International has campaigned against the practice of house demolition for years.[4] The organization's researchers have visited hundreds of

[3] At present there are more than 380,000 Israeli settlers in the Occupied Territories, which have a population of some 3,500,000 Palestinians.

[4] See for example *Israel and the Occupied Territories: Demolition and dispossession: the destruction of Palestinian homes;* December 1999 (AI Index MDE 15/59/99) and *Israel/Occupied Territories: Wanton destruction constitutes a war crime,* 13 October 2003 (AI Index: MDE 15/091/2003).

sites of homes and other properties destroyed by the Israeli army and security forces, and interviewed the inhabitants, neighbours, eyewitnesses, relief workers and others. In compiling this report the organization has drawn on information gathered in the course of its research and field work, as well as on information provided by or available from other sources. These include the Israeli authorities, bodies, agencies and mechanisms of the United Nations, international organizations working on the ground, and Israeli and Palestinian lawyers and non-governmental organizations.

The issue of forced evictions, house demolitions and destruction of properties in Israel and the Occupied Territories is only one of the many issues on which Amnesty International campaigns. The organization's main concerns include:

- extrajudicial executions and other unlawful killings of Palestinians by the Israeli army and security forces;
- deliberate killings of Israeli civilians in suicide bombings and other indiscriminate and targeted attacks by Palestinian armed groups;
- the lack of concrete measures by both Israel and the Palestinian Authority to stop and prevent killings of civilians, the lack of adequate investigations and prosecution for the majority of killings, and the impunity afforded by both sides to those who commit gross human rights violations, including war crimes and crimes against humanity;
- arbitrary detention without charge or trial for prolonged periods of individuals suspected of security-related offences and ill-treatment and/or torture of detainees by both Israel and the Palestinian Authority;
- increasingly stringent restrictions imposed by the Israeli army on the movement of Palestinians inside the Occupied Territories and the impact of these restrictions on the fundamental rights of the Palestinian population, including their right to work, to healthcare, to education and to food.

These and other concerns are addressed in numerous reports and other material issued by Amnesty International in recent years.[5]

II. Historical Background

Between the two world wars the British authorities ruled Palestine under a League of Nations mandate, which ended when the State of Israel was proclaimed on 14 May 1948. Arab protests against a UN partition plan were followed by war between Arab and Israeli armies from which Israel

[5] Amnesty International's reports, statements and other material are available on http://web.amnesty.org/library/eng-isr/index.

emerged victorious. More than 800,000 Palestinians were expelled or fled from Israel and became refugees in the Gaza Strip, West Bank or neighbouring countries. Two parts of mandate Palestine remained outside Israel: the Gaza Strip, which came under Egyptian administration; and the eastern part of Palestine, which was taken over by Jordan in 1950 and became known as the West Bank. Hostilities between Israel and Egypt, Syria and Jordan in June 1967 ended in Israel's occupation of the West Bank (including East Jerusalem, which was annexed by Israel) and the Gaza Strip. Israel also occupied Syria's Golan Heights (annexed by Israel in 1980) and the Sinai Peninsula (later returned to Egypt).

The Palestinians who remained in Israel after the establishment of the state became Israeli citizens but were placed under military rule until 1966. Many became internally displaced after they were expelled or fled from their villages. The land and properties of the Palestinians refugees and of those internally displaced by the war were confiscated. Today more than 1,000,000 Palestinian and Bedouin citizens of Israel, known as Israeli Arabs, account for some 18% of the population of Israel. Most of them live in northern Israel, in the Galilee and Triangle regions; about 100,000 live in towns known as mixed towns (such as Haifa, Ramle, Lod, Jaffa and Akko); and some 130–140,000 Bedouins live in the Negev in the south of the country. In the West Bank and Gaza Strip some 3,500,000 Palestinians, more than 1,500,000 of them refugees,[6] have lived under Israeli military occupation since 1967 and some 200,000 live in East Jerusalem with a special status as permanent residents.

Recent developments:

Between 1993 and 1995, negotiations between Israel and the Palestine Liberation Organization (PLO) led to a series of agreements, known as the Oslo Accords, between the two parties. A Palestinian Authority (PA) was established, with jurisdiction over parts of the West Bank and Gaza Strip. In 1995 Yitzhak Rabin, the Israeli Prime Minister who signed the Oslo Accords with the Palestinians, was assassinated by an Israeli right-wing activist opposed to the peace agreement with the Palestinians. After that, many of the provisions of the Oslo Accords were never implemented.

In September 2000 a Palestinian uprising (*intifada*) broke out. Since then some 2,500 Palestinians, more than 450 of them children, have been killed by the Israeli army and more than 900 Israelis, including more than 100 children, have been killed by Palestinian armed groups. Tens of thousands of Palestinians have been arrested by the Israeli army, and some 6,000 remain detained, many on charges of involvement in attacks against Israelis. The Israeli army has destroyed thousands of Palestinian homes,

[6] More than 2,500,000 other Palestinian refugees live in Jordan, Syria and Lebanon.

large areas of agricultural land and hundreds of other properties. This, and the stringent restrictions imposed by Israel on the movement of Palestinians within the Occupied Territories, have led to the virtual collapse of the Palestinian economy. Most Palestinians in the Occupied Territories live below the poverty line and depend on some form of assistance for survival. Since the outbreak of the *intifada* in 2000 the Oslo Accords have essentially become moot. The PA remains in place but its ability to function has been increasingly curtailed. The Israeli army has repeatedly bombed and raided most of the PA security services installations, prisons and other institutions, and it routinely carries out raids and incursions in Palestinian towns, refugee camps and villages which are supposed to be under the PA's jurisdiction. For the past two years Israel has confined PA President Yasser 'Arafat to his headquarters in the West Bank city of Ramallah, and does not allow Palestinian officials, legislators and civil servants to move freely in the Occupied Territories. Recently rivalries and infighting within the PA leadership, its security and political apparatus and among Palestinian political factions have increased, resulting in a further deterioration of the situation and an increasing spread of lawlessness.

Case Study: The Bashir Family

The case of the Bashir family illustrates many of the patterns of forced eviction, house demolition and destruction and expropriation of land described in this report. The family—Khalil Bashir, a school principal, his wife Souad, their six children and his elderly mother—has long been under pressure from the Israeli army to leave their home and their land, situated on the edge of the village of Deir al-Balah, in the Gaza Strip, near the Israeli settlement of Kfar Darom.

From the beginning of October 2000 onwards Israeli soldiers frequently raided the house and prohibited the family from using the upper floors and pressured them to leave the house. The family complied with the restrictions, fearing that if they left the house would be destroyed. In November 2000 Khalil Bashir's brother, who lived next door (about 150 meters to the east, further away from the Kfar Darom settlement) gave in to the Israeli army pressures and moved to temporary accommodation, so as to keep his family safe during what he thought would be a passing tension. Within days the army destroyed his house and most of the Bashirs' land around the house, uprooting the olive and date trees and the vegetable orchard.

A few days later, on 4 December 2000, the army destroyed Khalil Bashir's parents' old house, adjacent to his, and occupied the upper floor of his house. Since that date the Bashir family have been confined to the ground floor, while the top floor has been turned into an army base. The middle floor does not appear to be used by the soldiers but the family is not allowed upstairs.

The soldiers have placed their own ladder at the back of the house to access the top floor and the roof, have blocked the upstairs windows and the edges of the roof-terrace with sandbags and camouflage, and have made holes in the external walls all around the house which they use as sniper positions. Loud banging and debris thrown into the courtyard indicate that internal walls have been torn down.

Even though the Israeli army has full control of the house, from the house itself and from the watchtower a few meters away,[7] soldiers have frequently opened fire on the house from their watchtower and from the settlement. The sides of the house which face the army position and the settlement are riddled with bullets, including heavy calibre bullets and shells, and the ground floor rooms facing the army position (the kitchen and a bedroom) have sustained extensive damage from army fire. Amnesty International delegates have visited the Bashirs' house on several occasion in the past three years and inspected the damage. Three members of the Bashir family have been injured by Israeli army fire. On 13 October 2000, Khalil Bashir's 17-year-old son Yazen was shot and injured in the leg while he was getting water to put out a fire in the garden, apparently caused by a flare thrown by the army. On 28 April 2001 soldiers shot from the watchtower into Khalil Bashir's bedroom while he was lying on his bed reading, injuring him in the back of the head and neck, and causing extensive damage inside the room. On 18 February 2004 Israeli soldiers shot from the watchtower opposite the house and seriously injured Khalil Bashir's 15-year-old son Yusuf. At the time Yusuf was outside the house with his father, seeing off their visitors, two United Nations (UN) staff members and a staff member of the United Nations Association International Services (UNAIS). The three visitors had just got into their vehicle, clearly marked with the UN emblem, and were about to leave when a single shot was fired from the Israeli army watchtower, about 20 meters from where they were standing. Yusuf was hit by a bullet in the back, very close to the spine. At the time of writing he remains in hospital and it is not know if he will walk again.

Over the past three and a half years the Israeli army has progressively destroyed all the cultivated land around the Bashirs' house. By the late summer of 2001 only the garden in front of the house remained untouched, with well-tended palm trees and flowers. On the evening of 23 August 2001 the army uprooted the palm trees and the rest of the vegetation and destroyed the low wall separating the garden from the road. Four days later the army destroyed a chicken barn adjacent to the house. The destruction of the Bashirs' garden appears to have been part of a large scale operation

[7] In 1992, after the killing by a Palestinian of an Israeli settler from the Kfar Darom settlement, Israeli settlers damaged some Palestinian properties in the area and appropriated a piece of the Bashirs' land, between their house and the settlement. Shortly afterwards, the Israeli army built a watchtower on the piece of land which had been appropriated by the settlers.

carried out by the IDF in the area in retaliation for a Palestinian mortar attack against the Kfar Darom settlement earlier that day.[8]

The repeated attacks against the Bashirs' home and the destruction and damage of their houses and land serve no apparent security purpose and appear to be part of a pattern of intimidation and harassment aimed at forcing the family to leave their home.

In January 2004 the Israeli army issued a seizure order for some land belonging to Palestinians in the area around the Kfar Darom settlements (see p. 27). Part of the land being seized belongs to the Bashir family and is situated behind their house. An appeal challenging the seizure order is currently pending.

Usually houses which have been taken over by the Israeli army cannot be accessed without prior authorisation from the Israeli army but for the first three years some representatives of international organizations and foreign journalists were able to visit the Bashir family without seeking permission from the army. However, in February 2004 Israeli soldiers in the watchtower opposite the Bashirs' house told international UN staff members that they needed prior authorization from the army's command to visit the family. The family has consistently avoided receiving relatives or friends out of fear that the Israeli army may harm local visitors or accuse them of attempting to attack the soldiers stationed in the house.

Khalil Bashir and his family told Amnesty International about the difficult situation in which they live: *"I do not understand why the soldiers behave as they do, why they treat us as if we were enemies when they know that we have never caused any harm to them or to others. We have always extended our hands in peace and still do, in spite of everything. We are absolutely opposed to violence and have told the soldiers many times that so long as we are in our house we will never allow anyone to shoot from this house. The soldiers know that no attack, no act of violence has ever been committed by us or by anyone else from this house. It is for this reason that we will never leave our house, because we know that the minute we leave the house empty the army will claim that it was used by gunmen and will destroy it. That is what they did to my brother and to many others. They forced my brother to leave, and as soon as he left they destroyed his house. I do not understand this logic, what are they thinking when they do such things? One day they destroy a piece of land and the next week they destroy something else, as if it was a game, but they destroy people's lives. They are putting our family through a terrible ordeal. But in spite of everything we believe in peace, because we should*

[8] On 23 August a mortar launched by Palestinians fell on a house in the Kfar Darom settlement, smashing the roof and the ceiling of a room but causing no injuries. A statement issued the following day by the Israeli army Spokesperson's Unit makes no mention of the destruction of the Bashirs' property and of other properties in the area.

live in peace as good neighbours. This is what we have always taught our children and this is what we believe even now with the soldiers on top of us, raiding our home, shooting at us and humiliating us. We do not respond to the soldiers' provocations. We do not respond to violence with violence and we are determined not to leave our home, no matter what they do. This ordeal has been going on for years, they took some of our land, raided my house, and in the last years it got so much worse; our greatest worry is for the safety of our children."

In the past two years three of the Bashirs' oldest children have gone to study abroad. In February 2004, shortly after the Israeli army shot Yusuf Bashir, his 18-year-old sister Amira, who is now studying abroad, told Amnesty International: *"I am so worried for my brother, I don't know if he will walk again; and I am worried about my three little siblings, my parents and my grandmother and I pray that they will be safe, that nothing will happen to them. The home should be the safest place but for our family it is not; but it is our home and we should not be forced to leave it. No one should be forced out of their home and we won't leave our house. We have never harmed any Israeli or anyone else. We just want to live in our home in peace".*

III. Patterns and Impact of Property Destruction and Forced Eviction

The destruction of houses, land and other properties falls into two categories: houses built without a permit and houses, land and other properties which the Israeli army claims are destroyed for "military/security needs", including the destruction of the family homes of Palestinians suspected of carrying out attacks.

1 – Unlicensed houses: The destruction of houses in the Arab sector in Israel and in parts of the Occupied Territories on the ground that they were built without a permit. Hundreds of homes have been demolished in the Arab sector in Israel in the past few years alone, whereas such demolitions in the Jewish sector are an extremely rare occurrence, if they occur at all. Similarly, in the Occupied Territories it is invariably Palestinian homes and other properties which are destroyed while Israeli settlements, which are illegal under international law, continue to be expanded. The main reasons why many houses are built without a permit in the Arab sector in Israel and in parts of the Occupied Territories, including in East Jerusalem, is the fact that it is very difficult and often impossible for Israeli Arabs and Palestinians to obtain building permits in these areas.

2 – "Military/security needs": The vast majority of the homes, land and other properties destroyed by the Israeli army in the West Bank and Gaza Strip in recent years fall under the category, which Israel defines as destruction for "military/security needs". The scale of the destruction in this category is massive, including more than 3,000 Palestinian homes, large areas of cultivated land, hundreds of commercial properties (shops, workshops and factories) and public buildings, as well as tens of thousands of other homes and properties which have been damaged, many beyond repair. The criteria used by the Israeli army to define "military/security needs" are extremely broad. This category can be divided into four, at times overlapping, sub-categories:

A. Punitive demolitions of houses belonging to families of Palestinians who are known or suspected of involvement in suicide bombings and other attacks against Israeli civilians and soldiers have become routine. The Israeli authorities assert that these homes are destroyed as a "deterrent", in order to dissuade other Palestinians from carrying out attacks against Israelis. Usually these houses are blown up by the Israeli army, frequently resulting in neighbouring houses also being destroyed or damaged.

B. Houses, land, and other properties which the Israeli authorities claim it is necessary to destroy for "security needs", notably to build or expand roads or other infrastructure for the benefit or protection of Israeli settlers or soldiers.

C. The destruction of houses, land and other properties which the authorities contend were used or could be used by Palestinian armed groups to shoot or launch attacks against Israelis, and which Israel argues it is entitled to destroy at any time. This category, which the authorities often refer to as "preventive", may include any house or property near Israeli settlements, army positions and roads used by Israeli settlers and soldiers. When carrying out this kind of operations, the Israeli army frequently targets several homes, and on a number of occasions tens or even scores of homes have been destroyed in one single operation. Even though the Israeli authorities claim that the destruction is intended to prevent future attacks from the area, such demolitions are often also manifestly carried out in retaliation for Palestinian attacks and as a form of collective punishment on the inhabitants of a given area. In some cases the destruction also serves the purpose of removing Palestinians from areas where Israel has a particular interest in seizing control of the land, notably near Israeli settlements and army positions, along the Green Line between Israel and the Occupied Territories and along the border with Egypt, with a view to subsequently expanding Israeli settlements or building new roads or other infrastructure intended to consolidate and/or benefit Israeli settlements and/or strengthen Israel's hold on the land.

D. Properties which Israeli authorities claim were destroyed in the course of combat activities.

The majority of the homes that were demolished and damaged on grounds of "military/security-related needs" were located in the Gaza Strip and a large percentage were in refugee camps. These demolitions have targeted the poorest and most vulnerable sector of the Palestinian population in the Occupied Territories. The destruction of homes is mostly carried out at night, with no prior notification. Usually, the only warning for the inhabitants is the rumbling of armored bulldozers and tanks approaching and beginning the destruction. Their arrival is often accompanied by Israeli army gunfire in an effort to make the residents vacate their homes and discourage resistance. The occupants of the targeted houses are almost without exception given no opportunity to salvage their possessions. In some cases people have been injured and even killed by collapsing structures or while fleeing; others were beaten, ill-treated or fired upon as they tried to protest or resist the demolition.

III. 1. Impact on the Economic Situation

In addition to the demolition of thousands of homes, the extensive destruction of agricultural land will continue to have severe repercussion on the Palestinian economy for many years to come. Hundreds of thousands of olive, citrus, almond, date and other trees have been uprooted by Israeli army bulldozers, along with vegetable and other crops. Olive trees particularly take many years to grow and become productive. The trees and orchards uprooted in the past three and half years constituted a source, and in many cases the only source, of livelihood for hundreds of thousands of people. Agriculture was a major sector of the Palestinian economy, especially since most Palestinians who used to work in Israel have no longer been permitted to do so in recent years. Many had invested their savings to develop and improve their family farms with costly greenhouses and irrigation networks, only to see them destroyed by Israeli army bulldozers, often before they could harvest their crops. The land on which trees and crops stood has since been made inaccessible to Palestinian farmers and it now either lies in waste or is being used by the Israeli army. Even if Palestinians were allowed to resume farming the land which has been destroyed in recent years, it would take a long time and considerable resources for it to become productive again.

III. 2. Impact on Women

"The children look to us, their parents, for protection and security and when our home was destroyed they were traumatized by the experience and destabilized by the situation we found ourselves in, without a home. People came to destroy our home and we, their parents, could do nothing to prevent it; they lost all their belongings and we could not replace them; I was no longer able to give them what they needed most, a home and a sense of security. I tried to comfort them but didn't have the means to make them feel secure. I myself was so traumatized by what happened that I could not cope for quite a long time".

'Arabia Shawamreh, mother of seven children, whose home was demolished four times

The majority of the tens of thousands of people who have been forcibly evicted and made homeless by the destruction of their homes are women and children, mostly refugees. All those whose homes have been destroyed have been affected, individually and as families, as they are forced to make adjustments and live in conditions which often place additional strains on their family relations.

Most Palestinian women do not work outside the home and their house is the space which they feel is their own. Men spend more time outside the house for work and social activities, and children go to school and play outside, whereas for most women the running of the house is mainly their responsibility or their primary activity. Whether they work outside the house or not, women devote a significant amount of their time and energy in unremunerated and often overlooked work in the home, and are therefore particularly affected by forced eviction and the destruction of their homes. When families are made homeless by the demolition of their homes, women bear the brunt of rebuilding the home.

In most cases the families whose homes have been demolished cannot afford to pay for alternative accommodation and have therefore been forced to move in with relatives, who often do not have sufficient space to accommodate an additional family. Since women spend more time in the house it is they who are more affected by the discomfort of living in someone else's space, where they can no longer take responsibility for the administration of the family space and activities.

In addition to the practical problems, the loss of privacy and space often puts strain on the relationships between family members. Mothers often feel undermined in their role as a source of authority and emotional and material support for their children.

> *"That was the beginning of a new type of suffering. Staying in my parents' old house has robbed me of my freedom—I have to take their feelings constantly into account, and I do not want to become a burden. I also have to keep the house spotless; it is not our home so we have to be considerate. I am missing out on spending time with my husband because I'm so preoccupied with taking care of the children. I feel constantly tense, desperately needing a private place for my family; even a small room with mice would be fine for us! I want my children to be able to move around as they wish and to play freely with their toys. I want us to feel that we are still a family. I have become so depressed that I cannot eat, and this depression has had an effect on my husband and children."*
>
> Testimony of a woman whose home was demolished, to the Women's Centre for Legal Aid and Counselling (WCLAC), Ramallah, West Bank.

In its submission to the 59th session of the UN Commission on Human Rights in March 2003 the Centre on Housing Rights and Evictions (COHRE) noted that:

> *"Women suffer immensely from forced eviction. . . . Domestic violence is higher in the precarious and often stressful situation of inadequate housing, especially before and during a forced eviction."*

Women's rights organizations in the Occupied Territories agree that Palestinian women are particularly affected by forced eviction and house demolition and by the increased tensions which often develop within the affected families as a result, including an increase in domestic violence. Moreover, women whose families have been made homeless as a result of the demolition of their homes feel even less able to complain and seek redress, both because they feel that in the face of the loss of the family home their grievances are not seen as a priority and because the additional practical and financial difficulties caused by the destruction of the family home make it more difficult to find a solution to their individual problem.

IV. Destruction for "Military/Security Needs"

IV. 1. Punitive House Demolition

On 3 March 2003 Noha Maqadmeh, a mother of 10 children who was nine months pregnant, was killed in her bed in the middle of the night when her home collapsed as Israeli soldiers blew up a neighbouring house, in the al-Bureij refugee camp in the Gaza Strip. (The targeted house belonged to the family of a Palestinian who had carried out a shooting attack against Israeli soldiers three weeks earlier at the Gush Katif Junction). Noha's husband and most of her children were injured, some of them seriously. Six other nearby houses were destroyed by the blast, leaving some 90 people homeless. Noha's husband Shukri, still wearing a neck brace and in pain from the injuries he sustained when their home collapsed on the family, told Amnesty International: *"We were in bed, the children were asleep; the bedroom was the most sheltered room, at the back of the house, away from the tanks shooting in the street. There was an explosion and walls collapsed on top of us. I pulled myself from under the rubble and called for help from my neighbours, but the tanks were shooting at anyone who went outside into the street and no one could come. I was in pain, didn't know what to do. I started to dig in the rubble with my hands; first I found my two little boys and my three-year-old girl. Then my older boy and girl (17 and 16 years old) managed to get out from under the rubble and helped me to dig for my wife and the other children. Then my neighbours came in to help and one by one we found the other children but my wife remained trapped under the rubble with our youngest daughter, who is two; she was holding her when the wall fell on her. As we got to them I could hear that she was in pain, she was injured and she kept urging me to help the children, and the children were crying for their mother. We called an ambulance but it could not approach because the tanks were still outside. We wanted to carry her in a blanket to the nearby UNRWA clinic but the tanks were shooting at anyone who got out into the street. When the soldiers left my neighbours took us to hospital but she died before reaching the hospital. Maybe if the ambulance had been allowed to come, if she could have got to hospital soon, she would have been saved, I don't know. She died, the baby who was due to be born a few days later died, and now our 10 children don't have a mother anymore and we don't have a home anymore. I still can't move my neck; the children were injured and are traumatized. What can I tell them when they ask me why the Israelis did this to us? We never harmed anyone, they killed my wife and destroyed our lives."*

According to the Israeli army *"the demolition of houses of terrorists sends a message to suicide bombers and their accomplices that anyone who participates in terrorist activity will pay a price for their actions"*.[9]

The practice of destroying the homes of the families of Palestinians known or suspected of attacks against Israelis was widely used by Israel in previous decades but had been discontinued since 1997. It was resumed in 2001 and since then hundreds of houses have been destroyed for this reason in the West Bank and Gaza Strip. Israel has never used this practice against Israeli Jews convicted of serious politically motivated crimes, such as the murder of the Prime Minister or bomb attacks against Palestinians or Israeli Arabs.

Since it resumed this policy in 2001 the Israeli army has destroyed close to 500 homes of families of known or suspected Palestinian attackers. These houses are usually blown up, whereas for other types of demolitions the army generally uses armored bulldozers, except for larger and sturdier buildings. The army uses powerful explosive charges and frequently nearby houses are also destroyed or seriously damaged in the process. In the past, when the Israeli army targeted the homes of families of known or suspected Palestinian attackers it often sealed, rather than destroyed, the houses, a measure which, unlike demolition, can eventually be reversed.[10] However in the past three years the targeted houses have been systematically destroyed.[11]

The two armed Palestinians who were killed inside the building did not live there and the inhabitants of the building said they were not known to them.[12] It is not entirely clear what was the reasoning of the Israeli army behind the destruction of this building. The Israeli army announced that it had ". . . *demolished the house of Abdallah Kawasamah, and his brother, Basal Shafik Kawasmah. The two Hamas operatives planned many terrorist attacks and dispatched*

[9] This sentence is usually included in the announcements made by the Israeli army's Spokesperson about this category of house demolition. See: www.idf.il/newsite/english/main.stm.

[10] These practices became widespread during the first *intifada* (1987 to 1993). Between 1987 and 1997 the Israeli army demolished some 500 homes of families of known or suspected Palestinian attackers and sealed more than 300 others.

[11] The only exceptions have been some three apartments in the Jerusalem area, which have been sealed or filled with concrete.

[12] One of them was 'Izzeddine Misk, whose house was also destroyed the following day. See: http://www.idf.il/english/announcements/2003/september/12.stm.

> *a number of terrorists".*[13] However, according to the inhabitants of the building neither man lived in the building. The building was new and contained 26 apartments, 16 of which were inhabited (the families had moved in the previous few months) and the rest were not yet occupied. The building belonged to 'Umar Hassan al-Qawasmi and one of the tenants in the building was Jawad 'Umran al-Qawasmi, whose son Fu'ad had had his house destroyed by the Israeli army on 18 May 2003.[14] The al-Qawasmi family is a very large extended family. Most of the 15 other families who lived in the building had bought their apartments.

The Israeli authorities contend that these demolitions are not intended to punish the families of suicide bombers and others known or suspected of involvement in attacks, but rather to "deter" potential attackers, who may refrain from getting involved in attacks if they know that their families will be made homeless and will suffer because of their actions.

Amnesty International considers these punitive forced evictions and house demolitions as a flagrant form of collective punishment, a violation of a fundamental principle of international law. The Israeli authorities' claim that such demolitions are effective in dissuading potential attackers is entirely irrelevant in light of International humanitarian law, which places clear limits on the actions which an occupying power may take in the name of security, and the absolute prohibition on collective punishment is one of the most important of these rules. Collective punishment is never permissible under any circumstances.

> The al-Najmah family, whose son Shadi participated in a shooting attack in Netanya on 9 March 2002, in which two Israeli civilians were killed and 50 wounded, was punished for the act committed by their son. The family house in al-'Ayn refugee camp in Nablus was destroyed on 22 October 2002 at 2.30am. Shadi's parents and siblings, including a married brother with his wife and their child, lived in the house. The powerful explosive charge used by the Israeli soldiers to blow up the al-Najmah family house also destroyed six other nearby houses in which nine families lived. The 61 inhabitants of these houses were left homeless as a result. One of the destroyed houses belonged to Maryam Sheikh. She told Amnesty International: *"This was our home, for me, my three sons and my daughters-in-law and their children, 27 of us in all. One of my sons raised birds for a living; all the birds were killed when the army blew up the houses; he had 4,000 shekels worth of birds at the time. The army gave us no time to take out anything; just a few minutes to gather the children and get out of the house"*. The following day the Israeli army issued a statement announcing that it had destroyed the al-Najmah house, but making no mention of the fact that six neighbouring houses were also destroyed when the soldiers blew up the al-Najmah house.[15]

---

13 http://www.idf.il/english/announcements/2003/september/11z.stm
14 http://www.idf.il/english/announcements/2003/may/19.stm
15 http://www.idf.il/english/announcements/2002/october/23.stm

On 10 September 2003, the Israeli army blew up an eight-storey apartment building in the Wad Abu Kteila district of Hebron. 68 people were made homeless, 53 of them women and children.

Hana 'Ajluni, who lived in the building, told Amnesty International: *"My husband was in hospital and I was at home with my five children: Muhammad who is just two months old, Rania, 2, 'Umar, 4, Rami, 5, and Shadi, 11. At about 3 or 4am I heard shooting and sound bombs and got up in a panic. The soldiers were shouting in Arabic* 'those who want to live get out and those who stay will die'. *They kept shouting but I don't know what; I froze, didn't know what to do. Then I grabbed the children and started to leave the building; the soldiers were still shooting as we reached the front door of the building to get out. One of my neighbours, Basem, was injured in the neck. As we stood outside the front door the soldiers made all of us women take off our headscarves and all the men undress, there in the street in front of us and the children. Then they handcuffed and blindfolded all the men one by one and took us across the road and put us all (women and children) together in a room, and the men in another room. Before they took us into that house they had put all the residents of that house into one room. Basem, who was injured in the neck, was not taken to hospital until a few hours later. At about 10am they let us women and children go out but we could not return to our homes because the soldiers were still shelling the building. The men were kept until about 6pm. At about 2pm the soldiers took out the bodies of two armed men they had been chasing but we were still not allowed to go back to our homes. I kept wondering how much damage there would be to my apartment; I had no idea that I would never see my home again. At about 6pm the soldiers blew up the building but it did not collapse; the first three floors were partially destroyed but the building was still standing, but we could not go back in anymore because it was very dangerous. The following morning the soldiers put more explosives and the whole building collapsed, as you see it now. When my husband came home from hospital the following day he found that we don't have a home any more. We had been living in this building for six months only, we had bought our apartment, spent all our savings; it was a beautiful and spacious apartment with four bedrooms; it was a new building, Now we are living in a tent, with nothing . . ."*

A nine-year-old child, Tha'ir Muhammad al-Suyuri, who lived in a nearby building, was killed by shrapnel from a shell fired by an Israeli army tank during the attack. He had been standing at the kitchen window to see what was happening. Tartil Abu Hafez Ghaith, an 18-year-old student, was also standing at her kitchen window one floor above, and was seriously injured in the stomach by shrapnel from the same tank shell.

IV. 2. "Preventive" and "Security" Destruction

IV. 2.1 The West Bank

Forty-year-old Nabila al-Shu'bi, who was seven months pregnant, her three children Anas, 'Azzam and 'Abdallah, aged 4, 7 and 9, her 48-year-old husband Samir, her sisters-in-law Fatima and 'Abir (aged 57 and 38 respectively) and her 85-year-old father-in-law 'Umar, were left to die under the rubble of their home, when it was demolished by Israeli army bulldozers on 6 April 2002 in the old city of Nablus. The Israeli army kept the area under strict curfew for days, denying access to rescue workers, and it was not until a week later, on 12 April, that their bodies were found under the rubble of the house by relatives and neighbours. It is not known if they were killed by the collapsing walls or if they died later from injuries or of asphyxiation. Two other relatives survived trapped under the rubble for a week.

When the army briefly lifted the curfew on 12 April 2002 Nabila's brother-in-law, Mahmud 'Umar, started to dig in the rubble of the house with the help of his neighbours, hoping to find his relatives alive. They continued to dig after the Israeli army re-imposed the curfew after two hours, in spite of warning shots fired by Israeli soldiers in their direction. They first came across a small opening on the ground floor of where the house once stood; miraculously, in the small space that remained, 67-year-old Shamsa and her 68-year-old husband 'Abdallah were still alive. The rescuers went on digging through the night and eventually found the bodies of the other eight members of the family, all huddled in a circle in a small room.

Neighbours whose homes were demolished at the same time as the al-Shu'bi's house and who fled when the demolition began, told Amnesty International that the soldiers did not warn the residents to evacuate the houses before beginning the demolition. No comment was issued by the Israeli army about individual demolitions during these large-scale military operations.[16]

Large scale destruction of houses and other properties in the West Bank began in early 2002, when Israel launched a series of prolonged offensive operations, incursions and raids in refugee camps and towns throughout the West Bank. In every refugee camp and town they raided, Israeli soldiers left a trail of destruction. Army tanks rolled over parked cars, broke down walls and house fronts and smashed electricity poles. Extensive damage was also caused to houses, shops and other buildings by bullets and tank rounds.

The largest single demolition operation carried out by the Israeli army was in Jenin refugee camp in April 2002. The army completely destroyed the al-Hawashin quarter, an area of 400 x 500 meters, and partially destroyed two additional quarters of the refugee camp, leaving more than 800 families, totaling some 4000 persons, homeless.[17] In the course of this and other Israeli army offensives there was considerable armed resistance by Palestinians, and the Israeli authorities claimed that the army destroyed the area in the course of combat with Palestinian gunmen. However the evidence, including aerial photographs of the refugee camp, indicates that when the Israeli

[16] See Amnesty International's report *Israel and the Occupied Territories: Shielded from scrutiny: IDF violations in Jenin and Nablus,* 4 November 2002 (AI Index: MDE 15/143/2002).

[17] Information supplied to Amnesty International by UNRWA on 13 June 2002.

army carried out much of the bulldozing of houses the armed clashes between Israeli soldiers and Palestinian gunmen had already stopped and Palestinian gunmen had already been arrested or had surrendered.[18] After thorough investigation of the Israeli army operations in Jenin and Nablus. Amnesty International concluded that the extensive destruction of homes and properties by the Israeli army was not justified by military necessity and as such constituted a war crime.

Since mid-2002 Israeli army raids in refugee camps in the West Bank have been less intensive and prolonged but more frequent, and destruction of Palestinian homes and other properties by the army in the course of such operations has continued. Amnesty International considers that most of the destruction carried out in these raids has been unnecessary and/or disproportionate.

> On the morning of 5 September 2003 Israeli soldiers blew up a seven storey building in Nablus in which eight families lived, including 31 children, most of them less than 12 years old. Ibtisam, a teacher and mother of four children (three girls aged 13, 9 and 9 months and one boy aged 11) told Amnesty International: *At about 9–9.30 pm Israeli soldiers called on all of us living in the building to get out; they used a megaphone and spoke in Arabic; they said we had to leave the building immediately. We were in pajamas, the children were in bed already; me and my husband took the children from their bed and we all went downstairs as we were, we didn't even have time to get dressed. It was the same for the other neighbours; we all have children, we all scrambled to get the children from their bed and get out. It was a panic; I didn't have time to take milk or anything else for my baby; I just had time to wrap her up. We were scared, didn't know what was happening. I was still in pain from the recent back operation I have had and I tried to explain this to the soldiers but they were rude and did not allow me to sit down. They took us all to the school across the road (the Said Ibn 'Amr School), blew up the door to get it open and put us all inside, we women and children in the basement and all the men on the third floor. We were kept there all night, with no food, water, nothing; we had no idea what was happening with our husbands, we were worried; we kept trying to get the children to sleep but most cried and did not sleep. There was a lot of shooting, heavy shooting from tanks. At about 6am the soldiers allowed me and four other women who had small babies to go back into the building to get milk for the babies; we needed things to change the babies and for the other children too but the soldiers only gave us 5 minutes. The building was in a bad state, it had been fired at a lot. Before we were allowed to go in, at about 3.30am, the soldiers had sent one of the men in with a group of soldiers to inspect the place, then they sent him back to the school and later they sent him back in with another of the men; just the two of them without the soldiers, and told them to go bring the body of the armed man they had killed. They found the armed man who had been killed by the army; his head and right arm were missing, his left arm was broken and he had other injuries. He was armed. The two men took his body downstairs but left his gun upstairs*

[18] See footnote 15.

and the soldiers sent them back up to get it and made them inspect the body before they approached. Then the soldiers took the two men back to the school and we all stayed there a few hours more. Then suddenly the soldiers blew up the building, without telling us and without allowing us to go in to get anything. We were left with nothing, in our pajamas. Why did they have to blow up the place? There was no one left in the building after they killed that armed man; he didn't live in our building, we didn't know him and didn't know he had got into the building; how could we know? I stayed in my apartment, we all did, and all the more so after dark; how can we know who comes in and out of the building? It was a big building. We had saved for 14 years to buy this apartment; it was fully equipped and we had lived in it less than a year. Now we have nothing, all our furniture, clothes, documents, money, the children's school bags, our photographs, everything got buried in the rubble. The children have been traumatized by what happened, they saw their home destroyed, and every day they see the rubble of their home and don't have a home any more. Now me and the children are staying with my father and my husband moves between relatives; it is very difficult. What am I supposed to tell my children when they ask what happened and why this happened to us? We just want to live in peace and dignity, we ask for nothing else". There was no comment from the Israeli army about the destruction of this building.

IV.2.2 Farms and Agricultural Land Destroyed to Build the Fence/Wall

Since the summer of 2002 the Israeli army has been destroying large areas of Palestinian agricultural land, as well as other properties, to make way for a fence/wall which it is building in the West Bank. The fence/wall is planned to run for some 650 kilometers, most of it through the West Bank, from north to south.[19] It has an average width of 60 to 80 meters, including barbed wire, ditches, large trace paths and tank patrol lanes on each sides of the fence/wall, as well as additional buffer zones/no-go areas of varying depths. To date less than half of the route has been completed, mostly in the northern regions of the West Bank and around Jerusalem. In addition to the large areas of particularly fertile Palestinian farmland that have been destroyed, other larger areas have been cut off from the rest of the West Bank by the fence/wall. According to the Israeli authorities the fence/wall is intended to block entry into Israel to Palestinian suicide bombers and other potential attackers. However, the fence/wall is not being built *between* Israel and the Occupied Territories but mostly (close to 90%) *inside* the West Bank, turning Palestinian towns and villages into isolated enclaves, cutting off communities and families from each other, separating farmers from their land and Palestinians from their places of work, education and health

[19] In February 2004, on the eve of the International Court of Justice's hearing on the legality of the location of the fence/wall inside the West Bank, changes were made to some 15 km of the already built fence/wall in the West Bank and Israeli officials announced that further changes were being considered to the planned route in areas where the fence/wall has not yet been built. At the time of writing no confirmed information was available concerning possible changes.

care facilities and other essential services. This in order to facilitate passage between Israel and more than 50 illegal Israeli settlements located in the West Bank.[20]

"Military/security needs" cannot be invoked to justify measures that benefit unlawful civilian Israeli settlements at the expense of the occupied Palestinian population. The construction of the fence/wall inside the Occupied Territories is such a measure. Routing the fence/wall *inside* the West Bank in a manner purportedly aimed at protecting unlawful settlements and resulting in unlawful destruction and appropriation of Palestinian property and other violations of Palestinian rights is not proportionate or necessary. The fence/wall, in its present configuration, violates Israel's obligations under international humanitarian law.

> In the village of 'Izbat Salman, near Qalqilya, the Quzmar family, like their neighbours, lost most of their land when the fence/wall was built around their village. 'Abd al-Nasser Quzmar used to work in Israel but with the outbreak of the *intifada* access to Israel became impossible and his land became his only source of income, the only means for him to support his family of six. He invested all his savings in the family farm to make it more efficient and productive, built greenhouses and a sophisticated irrigation system for intensive cultivation. When Amnesty International first visited the village in October 2002, 'Abd al-Nasser Quzmar and the other villagers had just learned that the fence/wall was going to encircle their village, destroying much of their land and cutting them off from the rest of it. Marks made by the Israeli army on stones and trees indicated where the fence/wall was going to be built, tightly around the village. However the villagers were not notified in advance of its exact locations. Some only found out when the Israeli army bulldozers arrived and started to uproot trees and whatever else was on the land and others found the military orders for the seizure of their land left by the Israeli army posted on trees. The villagers' protests and court appeals were to no avail. Thousands of olive and citrus trees and vast vegetable orchards were destroyed to make way for fences, ditches and patrol lanes. Most of the remaining land belonging to 'Abd al-Nasser Quzmar and his neighbours is now on the other side of the fence/wall, and it is difficult at best and often impossible for the farmers to reach their land.

IV. 2.3 The Gaza Strip

> *"You have a very striking picture of people fleeing. But fleeing to where? If you're in Rafah, you can't go south because there is a border, you can't go west because there is an ocean, and you can't go north and you can't go east because there is nowhere to go. You can't get out of Gaza. So, if you've been a refugee many times over there is no longer anywhere to where you can flee".*

[20] For more details see Amnesty International's report *Israel and the Occupied Territories: The place of the fence/wall in international law*, 19 February 2004 (AI Index: MDE 15/016/2004).

Peter Hansen, UNRWA Commissioner-General, speaking after the large-scale destruction of refugee homes in Rafah (Gaza Strip) in October 2003.

The destruction of homes has been most extensive in the Gaza Strip, one of the most densely populated areas in the world,[21] where in the past three and half years close to 3,000 homes have been destroyed, most of them homes of refugees. According to the United Nations Relief and Works Agency (UNRWA) between October 2000 and October 2003, more than 2,150 homes were destroyed and more than 16,000 damaged. In the same period 600 homes were destroyed in the West Bank.[22] The families whose houses were demolished have been living in tents donated by humanitarian organizations, in already over-crowed relatives' homes or in rented apartments. However, the latter option is one which most victims of house demolition cannot afford, unless they receive assistance from the donor community. In his 2003 annual report to the UN Secretary-General, UNRWA's Commissioner-General, referring to the large-scale destruction by the Israeli army of Palestinian refugees' homes, stated that:

"the rhythm of shelter destruction in the Gaza Strip increased significantly"[23] and that UNRWA *"was not able to keep up with the pace of shelter destruction"*.[24]

In a three-day operation which started on 10 October 2003 the Israeli army destroyed some 130 houses and damaged scores of others in Rafah refugee camp and nearby areas, making more than 1,200 Palestinians homeless. According to UNRWA 76 refugee homes were completely destroyed, 44 were partially destroyed and 117 were damaged. Several non-refugee homes were also destroyed in the same operation near the refugee camp. Most of those left homeless were children.

Hamda Radwan, a 67-year-old refugee and several of her relatives were among those whose homes were destroyed. Hamda, a refugee, had previously lost her home in 1948, when she and her family had to flee from their homes in Jaffa during the war which followed the establishment of the state of Israel.

Suha 'Abdallah, whose house was partially destroyed in the same operation, told Amnesty International: *"There was no tunnel or anything in our home, anyone can come and see for themselves; part of the house is still standing but it is not safe anymore; the remaining walls could collapse at any moment. The soldiers know that we didn't do anything, they came to the house and my husband and my son were there and they told us to leave immediately. We had no choice. They smashed some things and took other things and destroyed part of the house; why?*

21 The Gaza Strip covers an area of 360 km^2, and is home to some 1.3 million Palestinians. Palestinians are barred from more than a third of the land in the Gaza Strip, which is used exclusively by some 6–7,000 Israeli settlers and by the Israeli army.

22 See: www.un.org/unrwa/emergency/appeals/7th-appeal.pdf.

23 Shelter is the term used by UNRWA for the homes in the refugee camps it administers.

24 Report covering the period 1 July 2002–30 June 2003. Ref: A/58/13, Supplement No. 13, dated 10 October 2003.

And now what are we to do? Destroy the rest of the house ourselves so that it does not fall on anyone".

The already poor sewage system was further damaged by the Israeli army tanks and bulldozers, along with water mains and electricity and telephone lines. The Israeli army stated that during the operation it had uncovered three tunnels used by Palestinian armed groups to smuggle weapons from Egypt to the Gaza Strip.[25] In the preceding six weeks some 50 other s more Palestinians homeless.

The area of the Gaza Strip where the largest number of homes has been destroyed is the refugee camp in Rafah, in the south of the Gaza Strip, on the Egyptian border, where close to 1,000 homes have been destroyed and hundreds of others have been partially destroyed or very seriously damaged since October 2000. The refugee camp is very densely populated, with rows of houses separated by narrow alleyways. Up to the autumn of 2000 the first rows of houses in the refugee camp stood only meters from the border, which is controlled and patrolled by the Israeli army.[26] Since then, the massive destruction progressively carried out by the Israeli army has turned to rubble several rows of houses, up to 300 meters from the border.

On 23 June 2001, at about 3am, the Israeli army threw stun bombs and used loudspeakers to call on the inhabitants of the Barahmeh district of the refugee camp, along the Egyptian border, to leave immediately. Within two hours 20 houses were destroyed. The Barhoum family lost 11 houses, in which 75 people lived.

Suhaila Ahmad Salim Barhoum, a widow, lived in one of the demolished houses with her son and daughter and her brother. She told Amnesty International: *"I woke up at the sound of the army shooting and I ran off inside the camp with the children; other times when the army shot we ran away and waited until the shooting stopped to come back. But this time the tanks came up against the houses with the bulldozers. When they left there was only rubble and dust left in the place of our houses. I had a nice house; four rooms, one for each of us, the kitchen, the bathroom and a hall. I built it four years ago. My previous house was demolished in 1982, when they established the border. Then my house was right where the border is now. After some time I got some compensation but it was not enough, and I had to wait to have enough money to build a new house. And now I won't be able to build another house again; I have nothing left, nothing for my children".*

Suhaila's aunt, 70-year-old Fadhiya Suleiman Ibrahim Barhoum, lived in a house nearby with her two sons, their wives and their 12 children. She told Amnesty International: *"They destroyed the house with all our things; I worked all my life and now I have nothing left, and my sons have nothing left and they have*

[25] http://www.idf.il/english/announcements/2003/october/16.stm.

[26] Up to 1982, during Israel's occupation of the Egyptian Sinai Peninsula, the refugee camp was spread on both side of the border. When Israel ended its occupation of the Sinai in 1982 the border was drawn in the middle of the refugee camp and the refugee homes on the border line were demolished and later rebuilt further inside the camp or elsewhere.

children; one has eight and the other has four. The house was three homes, one for me and two for my sons; there were six rooms and two bathrooms, one for each of them. We worked so much to build our house. God help us, I don't sleep at night any more. And they keep destroying more houses, every day more houses; maybe tomorrow they'll destroy this one too (her relatives' house where she is staying). *God help us; why this on top of everything else? The army also destroyed my land, over there, near the house* (pointing to the rubble of her house nearby); *all my olive trees, you can still see them, there; they uprooted all of them, didn't leave even one; they uprooted them from here, from my heart; even if I plant other olive trees, I won't live to see the olives; I'm too old, and I have no more land and no home, nothing."*

The destruction in the Rafah refugee camp has been progressive, targeting row after row of houses—contrary to claims by the Israeli authorities that only houses used by Palestinians to shoot at Israeli soldiers patrolling the border and houses used as cover for tunnels used for smuggling weapons from Egypt were destroyed. However, already from the end of 2000 Palestinians living in the refugee camp close to the border told Amnesty International that Israeli soldiers had told them that many rows of houses were going to be destroyed. Statements by Israeli army and government officials confirm that this was indeed the intention. In January 2002 Major-General Yom Tov Samiah, Commander of Israeli army Southern Command at the beginning of the *intifada*, commenting on the destruction of some 60 Palestinian homes in Rafah refugee camp by the Israeli army on 9 and 10 January 2002 told Israeli Radio:

"These houses should have been demolished and evacuated a long time ago . . . Three hundred meters of the Strip along the two sides of the border must be evacuated . . . Three hundred meters, no matter how many houses, period."[27]

Israeli officials have put forward different arguments for the demolition of these houses. Some argued that the demolitions had been made necessary because armed Palestinians attacked Israeli army troops from these houses and/or because the houses served as cover for tunnels used to smuggle weapons into the Gaza Strip from Egypt, while others indicated that the demolition was in retaliation for the killing of four Israeli soldiers at the Kerem Shalom army base in southern Israel on 9 January 2002. Major-General Doron Almog, Commander of the Southern Command, said that *"Most of our operations have focused on the Rafah area, as that is where the two Hamas terrorists came from."*[28]

The Israeli army spokesperson's office issued different statements according to which the demolished houses: *"served as cover for gunmen's fire"*, *"were suspected of serving as cover for tunnels used weapon in smuggling operations"*;

[27] Voice of Israel, 16 January 2002.
[28] Jerusalem Post, 13 January 2002, quoting Major-General Doron Almog speaking on Israeli TV Channel 2's "Meet the Press".

or were targeted *"in response to the terrorist attack that killed an IDF officer and three soldiers."*[29]

North of Rafah, the Khan Yunis refugee camp has also suffered large-scale demolition of homes at the hands of the Israeli army. The refugee camp is surrounded on three sides (north, west and south) by the Gush Katif block of Israeli settlements, inside which are several Israeli army bases. Since its establishment the settlement block, a former Israeli army base which was turned over to Israeli settlers in 1977, has continued to expand and in 2000 the perimeter fence of the settlement was only meters from the outer row of houses of the Khan Yunis refugee camp. As in the Rafah refugee camp, the Israeli army has progressively destroyed row after row of homes in the refugee camp, clearing a large area of the camp near the perimeter of the Israeli settlement. To date more than 200 homes have been destroyed and a similar number have been damaged beyond repair and rendered uninhabitable. After the destruction of Palestinian homes in the refugee camp the Israeli army has built an eight-meter concrete wall around the perimeter of the Israeli settlement, where the settlement buildings are closest to the refugee camp.

In addition to the destruction carried out in the refugee camps, the Israeli army also destroyed hundreds of non-refugee homes and other properties throughout the Gaza Strip, notably in the agriculture sector. More than 10% of Gaza's agricultural land has been destroyed in the past three and a half years. According to the UN Office for the Coordinator of Humanitarian Affairs (OCHA) more than 1,800 acres of agricultural land were destroyed and more than 226,000 trees were uprooted in the Gaza Strip in 2002 and 2003 alone.[30]

Much of the destroyed land was cultivated with olive, citrus, date and almond trees, and a variety of vegetables cultivated in greenhouses, a method used to maximize the production of the small amount of agricultural land available in the densely populated Gaza Strip. Frequently greenhouses were destroyed without allowing the farmers to dismantle them and at least salvage the frame and canvas for future use. Trees have been systematically uprooted by Israeli army bulldozers, even in cases where the farmers themselves had previously cut them down in the hope that they would be spared and could grow again.

Hundreds of wells, water storage pools and tanks, and electrical water pumps providing water for drinking, irrigation and other needs for thousands of people, have been destroyed along with tens of kilometers of irrigation networks. While destroying land and agricultural facilities Israeli

[29] http://www.idf.il/english/announcements/2002/january/10.stm and january/11.stm.
[30] Consolidated Appeal Process 2004 (CAP) on: http://ochadms.unog.ch.

bulldozers also uprooted electricity poles and cables, leaving the surrounding areas without electricity.

Another area frequently targeted by the Israeli army is around the Israeli settlement of Kfar Darom, the Kissufim/Abu Houli and Katif/al-Matahin Junctions, and along the east-west road from the Gush Katif settlement to the Kissufim crossing into Israel. Vast areas of date palms, citrus orchards and other crops have been bulldozed by the Israeli army, ostensibly to protect the roads used by Israeli settlers.

> The Abu Houli family, who lives and owns much of the land near the Kfar Darom settlement, has had nine houses (belonging to seven families), some 350 dunums of land, a food-processing factory, a plant nursery, a chicken farm (5,000 hens), three wells, and several water storage pools destroyed between October 2000 and August 2001. In all 84 members of the extended family have been affected by the destruction of their land, and 57 were made homeless. Around 10 October 2000 the Israeli army began to destroy some of the family land along the main north-south road (Salah al-Din road/Road No 4) and on 26 October they demolished the first of the family's houses. Yusuf Muhammad Abu Houli, his wife and their nine children were in their home when they suddenly realized that the house was surrounded by tanks and bulldozers. He said: "*We were stunned; all we had time for was to get the children to safety; by the time we had done that, within a few minutes the bulldozers began destroying the house and there was no time to salvage anything.*"
>
> A few days later, on 9 November, 'Abd al-Hakim 'Abedrabbo Abu Houli (Yusuf's nephew), an executive in UNRWA's administration, married with four children, had his house demolished. He told Amnesty International: "*The work of years smashed up just like that. The army came at 11pm with two tanks, one bulldozer and one jeep. They shouted at us to get out immediately or they would tear the house down over our heads. Our house was not the first to be demolished but still, you can't really be prepared for something like that; we had no idea that this was just the beginning, that within a few months we would be left with nothing; it's not just the houses, the furniture, the land, everything; it's a part of our lives which has gone. . . .*" After the destruction of his house followed the houses of five other brothers and cousins, and more of the family land.
>
> The Israeli army provided no account or explanation for the destruction of these and other properties in the area.

Between 20 and 22 November 2000 the Israeli army destroyed some 29 houses, and large areas of cultivated land in the area, making some 180 Palestinians homeless. The army made no mention of the destruction of these properties, which was seemingly carried out in retaliation for a roadside bomb attack carried out by Palestinians on the morning of 20 November against a bus carrying Israeli settlers between the Kfar Darom and Gush Katif settlements. Two Israelis were killed in the attack and nine others were injured, including five children.

Among the properties destroyed were five houses and several plots of cultivated land belonging to the 'Abidin family and located to the north-east of the Katif/al-Matahin Junction, which were all destroyed on 21 November 2000. A sixth house and 50 dunums of palm and citrus trees belonging to the same family were destroyed in the same area on 12 August 2001. Seventy-five-year-old Halima 'Abidin was living in the house, which belonged to her two sons, who were working abroad. The destruction of this house and of the land around it appears to have been in retaliation for a shooting incident which was reported earlier that day at the nearby junction.[31] Halima 'Abidin and her daughter Samiha told Amnesty International that they were in the house the whole day and that they had not seen anyone nor heard any suspicious movement near the house. Approximately two hours after the reported shooting, two Israeli army tanks and a bulldozers stationed at the nearby junction approached the 'Abidin house and destroyed it and the land around it. Two electricity poles and the connecting cables were also crushed by the tanks in the process, cutting off the electricity supply to scores of families living in the area.

In the north of the Gaza Strip since the Autumn of 2000, the Israeli army has destroyed large areas of land, as well as houses and other properties. More recently one of the reasons given by the army to justify the destruction is the increase of firing by Palestinian armed groups of *Qassam* mortar/rockets from this area across the fence into Israel.

> Between 14 May and 29 June 2003 the Israeli army conducted an incursion in Beit Hanoun in northern Gaza in retaliation for the repeated firing of mortars by Palestinians towards the southern Israeli town of Sderot. The army demolished 21 houses, home to 35 refugee families, and damaged scores of others, destroyed several factories and large areas of olive and citrus tree orchards, bulldozed other land and destroyed water, sewage and road infrastructure.
>
> On 15 May 2003, announcing the beginning of the operation the Israeli army stated: "*During the operation, IDF forces took control of key positions overlooking areas used to fire Qassam rockets at Israeli communities and demolished four structures used by terrorists who have been linked to firing Qassam rockets. In addition, IDF forces exposed wide areas of vegetation used to conceal the launch of rockets. . . . The IDF will not allow terrorist organizations to interfere with the daily routine of the residents of Israeli communities in the Gaza Strip and nearby areas*".[32]
>
> One of the properties destroyed was the tile factory of the Abu Ghaliun family, the biggest and most sophisticated tile factory in the Gaza Strip. Amnesty International delegates visited the factory and witnessed the destruction: a vast quantity of tiles had been smashed into pieces, cement bags had been

[31] It is not clear if the shots were fired by a Palestinian gunman targeting the Israeli army base at the junction or from Israeli soldiers targeting a Palestinian suspect. No injuries or casualties were reported.
[32] http://www.idf.il/english/announcements/2003/may/15.stm.

torn and their contents scattered, large and sophisticated tile-making machines had been deliberately broken, some of the walls of the factory had been demolished and a large number of citrus trees near the factory had been uprooted.

The owner of the factory, Jamil Abu Ghaliun told Amnesty International: *"The factory gave work to 600 people, including those who worked in the factory and those who laid the tiles in the housing projects. Now 600 families have lost their income as a result of the destruction of the factory. We had the best fully automated Italian machines and produced good quality tiles; we exported part of our production to Israel. I worked very hard all my life and the fruit of this hard work was destroyed for no good reason. No one ever fired mortars from anywhere near my factory; I am sure of that because the place was well guarded day and night; I always made sure of that. I have been working with the Israelis for decades; we buy material from them and sell them the tiles we produce. I would never have allowed anyone to commit any act which could jeopardize this. But the army came here, kept us all confined to our home under curfew for days and destroyed so much and left. How can such a thing help security? Has security improved? For me, for our family, this has destroyed our lives; and for so many others. What about the hundreds of families who depended on this factory for their living, to feed their children? I have never harmed any Israeli, on the contrary. The army knows that neither me nor my family have ever done anything against them; they themselves have never accused me or my children of anything, so why destroy our factory, our trees, our lives? More than US$ 5,200,000 worth of damage. You can see how deliberately, how purposefully they destroyed everything in here, crushing all the tiles, breaking all the cement bags and the machines which are so big and heavy and could not be destroyed in any other way they broke up with explosive, you can see it with your own eyes."*

IV. 2.4 Destruction of "Temporarily" Confiscated Land

On 5 February 2004 Israeli soldiers went to the outskirts of the village of al-Mutila (north-east of the West Bank) and left a plastic folder tied to a tree containing a seizure order for a piece of land on which Israeli army bulldozers had already been working for about a month, uprooting trees and crops. Even before receiving the seizure order the villagers had understood that their land was being taken and destroyed to make way for the fence/wall which Israel is building through the West Bank. The seizure order, signed by Major General Moshe Kaplinsky, Head of the Israeli army Central Command, is similar to the one shown below, and is dated 3 January 2004. According to the order 141.6 dunums of land are seized by the army until 31 December 2005. However, since the seized land is being used by the army to build a sophisticated fence/wall (equipped with electronic sensors and flanked on each side by deep trenches, trace paths, roads for army tanks patrols, and additional barbed wire fences) which is costing Israel some US$ 2 million per kilometer, few believe that the land seized for this project will ever be returned to their owners—as this would entail dismantling the costly fence/wall. Given that the work on the seized land was already well underway by the time the villagers received the seizure order, the owners of the land felt that there was no point in appealing against the seizure. In the past 20 months the land of thousands of Palestinian families in the West Bank has been "temporarily" seized in the same manner and destroyed to make way for the fence/wall.

Palestinian land seized by the Israeli army for "military/security needs" has most often been used to expand and build Israeli settlements and related infrastructure, notably roads for the settlers and most recently a fence/wall which separates Israeli settlements in the West Bank from Palestinian towns and villages.

The process began after Israel' occupation of the West Bank and Gaza Strip in 1967 and continues today. On paper the land is not confiscated but only "temporarily" seized by the Israeli army for unspecified "security" needs for a set period only. But such seizure orders can be extended indefinitely and in the overwhelming majority of cases the land "temporarily" seized by the Israeli army has never been returned to its owners. Hence, in practice land "temporarily" seized is invariably lost. For Palestinians the loss of land means the loss of livelihood, as agriculture has become one of the key means of subsistence since the Israeli labor market has been mostly closed to Palestinians.

Seizure orders are generally not delivered to the owners of the land but are left on the seized land, often stuck on trees, and often not for days or weeks after the date of coming into force of the seizure orders. In any event, most owners of seized land no longer feel that it is worth it to appeal. Few have the financial resources for the legal costs and most believe it is futile to engage in a process which invariably fails them. In the 37 years of Israeli military occupation most of the "temporary" seizures have become a permanent reality. (See chapter on land confiscation/ expropriation).

In January 2004, the Israeli army issued at least 12 "temporary" seizure orders for tracts of land near Israeli settlements in the Gaza Strip. The orders, signed by the Israeli army Commander in the Gaza Strip, Brigadier General Dan Harel, state:

In the framework of my authority as commander of the Israeli Defense Forces (IDF) in the region, in accordance with all laws and security legislation, I am of the opinion that it is requested for imperative military needs, in wake of the special security circumstances which exist in the region; I hereby declare the following: I hereby declare that the land is being seized for military needs.

The land shall be maintained by the IDF and the sole maintenance shall be handed to the land officer at the Southern Command Headquarters, via the Ministry of Defense Coordinator at the administration.

The date of entry into force of this declaration is the date of its signature and until 31 December 2005.

As is current practice, attached were maps of the plots of land being seized and a standard printed form with blank gaps which are filled in by the army commander with details such as the location of the seized land, the name of the owner, the dates etc. The form states:

Notice regarding the seizure of land for military needs

Notice is hereby given that on ___ the _____ the Commander of the IDF in the Gaza region, in wake of the special circumstances which exist in the region, and for imperative military needs, has ordered that the land marked on the appended map[33] *to the order regarding seizure of land (2004-2) (Kfar Darom security fence) (Gaza region) shall be seized for the construction of security components.*

Your are hereby given a seven-day period to submit reservations to the Commander of the IDF in the Gaza region regarding his decision. Reservations may be submitted as mentioned to the Commander of the IDF in the Gaza region, through the offices of the (IDF) Legal Advisor of the region:

Fax: ________

Name of the recipient of the notice: ___________

Statues of recipient: owner/maintainer Bloc ____ *Plot* _____

ID number: ____________

Name of the IDF Commander: ______________

Signature: _______________

*Date:*______________

The seized land is located partly between the two sections of the Israeli settlement of Kfar Darom (central Gaza Strip) and partly near its outskirts. This settlement, like others, was built on confiscated Palestinian land, some of it by means of "temporary" seizures issued decades ago. The owners of the seized land have appealed the seizure but have little hope that their appeal will be successful.

IV. 3. Israel's Justifications for the Destruction in the Occupied Territories: "Military/Security Needs"

Setting the trend

In the days that followed the outbreak of the *intifada*, the Israeli army abandoned policing and law enforcement tactics and adopted military measures generally used in armed conflict, including large-scale destruction of houses, land and other properties. This pattern quickly became entrenched and widespread and has continued to date.

In East Jerusalem and within Israel, protestors participating in demonstrations after 29 September 2000 threw stones. In the West Bank and Gaza Strip, although most of the demonstrations involved stone-throwing protests, on

33 Maps are usually on a much reduced scale, making it virtually impossible to establish the exact boundaries of the seized land; owners generally find out when the army destroys the land and/or builds roads, fences, or other structures on it.

a number of occasions firearms were used against Israeli security forces by members of the PA's security forces or others.

In responding to these demonstrations, Israeli security forces repeatedly resorted to excessive use of lethal force in circumstances in which neither the lives of the security forces nor others were in imminent danger, resulting in unlawful killings. In the first three weeks of the *intifada* more than 100 Palestinians, including 27 children, were killed by the Israeli security forces. In addition, the army destroyed homes, cultivated land and factories. Much of the initial destruction was in the area around Netzarim/Shuhada Junction, in the Gaza Strip, near the site of demonstrations. For example, on 7 and 8 October 2000 the Israeli army destroyed two four-storey buildings, known as the "twins", which were home to 39 families, large tracts of cultivated land around the junction, and a nearby metal foundry. After the demolition the Israeli army announced that it had:

". . . carried out engineering works to remove the continual threat in Netzarim junction. Among these activities—the destruction of the buildings known as the 'Twins', the destruction of the nearby building known as 'the factory' and clearing the terrain several dozens of meters around the IDF position at the junction. . . . Netzarim junction is a key position, controlling the main entry route into the Jewish settlement of Netzarim. The violence which occurred at the junction this last week, disrupted the daily life in the settlement".[34]

The Israeli army claimed that Palestinian gunmen had fired towards army positions from these properties during the demonstrations. While law enforcement officials are entitled to respond to threats to their security and the security of others, the response must be proportionate; Amnesty International believes that the destruction of these residential buildings and land in these circumstances was a disproportionate response.

The Israeli authorities contend that destruction of houses and other property is entirely justified and proportionate to their "military/security needs" to prevent or respond to attacks by armed Palestinians against Israeli settlements and Israeli army positions. They describe this kind of destruction as "preventive" or "in the course of combat activities."

The "preventive" category is extremely broad. It includes destruction of properties from which the army claims attacks were carried out or properties which were used for cover during attacks. It also includes the destruction of properties to clear the army's lines of sight in areas considered as sensitive, to create buffer zones around likely targets, and to clear areas in order to build fences or military installations. In addition, it includes destruction of property for the purpose of building roads to improve access between Israeli settlements within the Occupied Territories and between the settlements and Israel.

[34] http://www.idf.il/english/announcements/2000/october/8.stm: IDF Acts to Remove Threat in Netzarim Junction.

According to the Israeli authorities all such activities fall within the framework of "military/security needs", as they are deemed necessary to prevent attacks by Palestinians against Israeli settlements, settlers and soldiers in the Occupied Territories. According to the Israeli army:

> *"The source of authority for the Israeli Defense Forces to harm private property during times of fighting and due to military needs is part of the laws of war, which are part of the international law. Specifically it refers to regulation 23(g) of the Hague Convention of 1907 which permits destruction of property in cases in which 'such destruction [is] imperatively demanded by the necessities of war . . .'"*[35]

Although insisting that it has the right to demolish whatever will assist its military operations, the Israeli army claims it applies the principal of proportionality to ensure that operations do not have a disproportionately adverse effect on civilians. Amnesty International disputes Israel's interpretation of the permissible scope of property destruction under international law (see legal section). The circumstances surrounding the massive destruction of homes, land and other property in the Occupied Territories and its consequences for Palestinians belie the claim that the principle of proportionality enshrined in international law has been respected.

IV. 4. Definition of Legitimate Targets, Combat Activities and Proportionality

The Israeli army contends that any house or property which is used in any way by members of Palestinian armed groups is a military target which may lawfully be attacked and destroyed at any time. These demolitions are described by the Israeli army as occurring "in the course of combat activities." The decision to engage in this type of demolition is left to the discretion of the commander in the field, and therefore such actions are not subject to legal deliberation, supervision or appeal.

Within the category defined as destruction for military/security needs, in practice there appears to be little or no difference between demolitions defined as "in the course of combat activities" and those described as "preventive". For example, a house from which a Palestinian gunman has allegedly fired at Israelis and a building, which—due to its proximity to a road or settlement—could be used to target Israelis, may both be destroyed at any time. Both these categories of demolition are also often carried out as a form of collective punishment in retaliation for attacks committed by Palestinians against Israeli civilians or soldiers.

According to the Israeli army's interpretation of international humanitarian law, given the spread of Israeli settlements, settlers' roads and army

---

[35] IDF Spokesperson's response to the Israeli human rights organization B'Tselem, published in B'Tselem's report: *Policy of Destruction, House Demolition and Destruction of Agricultural Land in the Gaza Strip*, February 2002 (www.btselem.org).

positions throughout the densely populated Gaza Strip right next to Palestinian refugee camps, towns and villages, virtually every building or plot of land in the Gaza Strip could potentially be considered as a threat and hence as a military target for demolition.

This is clearly not the case. According to international humanitarian law, there are no military objectives in the Occupied Territories which Israeli forces may lawfully attack and destroy at any time. The Israeli security forces may target individuals using a property to attack soldiers or others. In such cases, however, they must use only as much force as is strictly necessary to counter any threat posed to their lives or the lives of others. Israeli forces may, in exceptional circumstances, seize or destroy Palestinian property for a legitimate military purpose—not for the expansion of illegal settlements or settlement infrastructure, nor in retaliation for attacks committed by Palestinians against Israelis. Palestinians affected must have a meaningful right to legally challenge any seizure or destruction order.

In the past three and a half years Israel has failed to uphold such principles by carrying out extensive destruction and eviction without adequate legal safeguards, violating the rights of tens of thousands of Palestinians to adequate housing and a decent standard of living.

IV. 5. Claims that Property had been Used for Attacks

Israel's most common assertion to justify the destruction of houses, land and other properties is that only properties which have proven to be a threat have been destroyed. The Israeli army's announcements frequently claim that the destroyed properties have been used to carry out attacks. Often Palestinians do not deny that attacks or armed confrontations took place in the area at some point prior to the destruction, but deny that their properties were used to carry out attacks. In the overwhelming majority of cases the Israeli army has not specifically accused those whose houses, land and other properties it has destroyed of having themselves been involved in attacks, and it has not attempted to arrest or prosecute them.

According to the Israeli army's reasoning, the fact that a suspect may have fired from, or run through, someone's land or near someone's house, factory or shop is enough for the property and everything around it to be destroyed—even though the owners or inhabitants played no part in the attack, had no knowledge of it and could not have prevented it. Palestinians whose homes and properties are near Israeli settlements, army positions or other sensitive locations find themselves in an impossible situation. Their movements in and around their properties are severely restricted by the Israeli army. Anyone, be they the owners of the property or trespassers, spotted in these areas at night, and in certain areas even during the day, risks being shot by the army. Therefore the army makes it nearly impossible, even for those inclined to do so, for property owners to protect their land from intruders who may carry out attack against Israelis. Yet, if someone carries out an attack from or near their property, they are punished by having their property destroyed.

Israeli officials have acknowledged to Amnesty International that it is often difficult to pinpoint the point of origin of armed attacks. This acknowledgment concerned mostly sources of Palestinian gunfire, which is easier to establish than the source of mortar fire, which has a variable trajectory and range. Indeed, Israeli soldiers have repeatedly been proved to have been mistaken in identifying sources of fire, even of gunfire at a very short distance. Hundreds of unarmed Palestinians, including children, women and elderly people, as well as foreign journalists and humanitarian workers have been killed in situations where the Israeli army wrongly claimed to have targeted sources of fire.[36]

In addition, the Israeli army has generally not conducted ballistics, forensic or on-site investigations to determine the source of gunfire, mortar or other attacks. At times uncertainty is explicit in official Israeli statements, for example describing destroyed properties as being "thought to hide tunnels".[37]

To date the Israeli army has not accounted for the exact number and location of properties it has destroyed, nor has it provided evidence that the specific properties were used to carry out attacks and were destroyed while being used for such a purpose. Amnesty International delegates, international humanitarian and human rights workers, journalists and others have repeatedly witnessed Israeli soldiers destroying and damaging houses, land and other properties at times when there were no disturbances or confrontations with Palestinians.

In this respect, it is significant that the Israeli authorities have consistently and vigorously opposed the presence of international human rights monitors, despite repeated calls by the international community, Israeli, Palestinian and international human rights organizations and representatives of civil society.[38] Amnesty International believes that international human rights monitors could help reduce violations by both sides and could play an important role to establish the veracity of the claims made by

[36] Such examples include the cases of Iain Hook, a British national working for the UN who was shot dead by Israeli soldiers in his office in Jenin refugee camp in November 2002; British peace activist Tom Hurndall and British journalist James Miller, shot dead by Israeli soldiers in Rafah in April and May 2003; American peace activist Brian Avery, who was shot in the head by Israeli soldiers in Jenin in April 2003; and Yusuf Bashir, who was shot in the back by Israeli soldiers in the presence of UN staff members in February 2004.

[37] "IDF Activity Against the Palestinian Terrorist Infrastructure," 23 October 2002, IDF Website, http://www.idf.il/newsite/english/021023-2.stm.

[38] The Palestinian Authority has supported the dispatch of international observers.

each side concerning the actions of the other side—including keeping an accurate record of the scale and circumstances of destructions carried out by Israel and of attacks by Palestinian armed groups.

IV. 6. Claims that the Destroyed Properties were "Abandoned"

The Israeli authorities generally underplay the extent of the destruction and the number of people affected by it. They have remained evasive as to whether the army even keeps statistics on the numbers of houses they destroy (other than for the punitive demolitions) and of Palestinians they forcibly evict and make homeless. In most cases the Israeli authorities do not issue statements about demolition operations, and when they do, the announcements provide very few details and usually do not contain even the most basic information such as the number, type and location of the destroyed properties. The destroyed homes are not usually referred to as houses, but rather as "abandoned" or "unpopulated" "buildings" or "structures". The authorities also tend to avoid the word demolition to describe the destruction of houses and land, using instead expressions such as "engineering works" to "expose" or "clear" certain areas.[39] The destruction of agricultural land is hardly ever mentioned.

Amnesty International and other international organizations and journalists have frequently visited recently demolished homes. The sight of pots of cooked food, half-full bottles of soft drinks or shampoo, pieces of newspapers from the previous day, smashed fridges and television sets, clothes, children's toys and schoolbooks lying amongst the rubble stood in stark contrast with Israeli army claims that the houses were "unpopulated" or "abandoned".

Although at times the inhabitants of the destroyed houses were not in their homes at the time of the destruction, this cannot be construed as abandonment. Palestinians who live in areas that regularly come under Israeli army fire, notably around settlements and army positions avoid using the rooms facing these positions if they can. However, many do not have rooms protected from the source of fire. Metal sheets against windows and doors, and thin corrugated roofing material offer little or no protection against frequent Israeli army shelling. Hence people in those areas often leave their homes when army raids, shooting or clashes intensify, and they return home when the tension decreases, usually the following day. However, leaving one's home for a few hours or a few days to seek safe shelter elsewhere cannot be considered as having abandoned it.

[39] See IDF and other official statements quoted throughout this report in relation to the specific cases mentioned. Also see the IDF website: http://www.idf.il/english/news/main.stm (Spokesperson news/announcements).

In the Gaza Strip the very extensive damage caused by Israeli army gunfire and shelling to thousands of Palestinian houses facing Israeli army positions and settlements, and the manner and timing of much of the damage and destruction, suggests the Israeli army has responded disproportionately, and at times unnecessarily, to threats posed by armed Palestinians operating in these areas. Any destruction or damage aimed at forcing the civilian population in these areas to leave their homes violates international law.

IV. 7. The Failure of the Israeli Supreme Court to protect the Internationally Guaranteed Right to Housing

In the case of demolitions for "military/security needs" classified as not in the course of combat activities, the Israeli Supreme Court ruled in 2002 that affected families must be given the right to appeal unless doing so would "endanger the lives of Israelis or if there are combat activities in the vicinity."[40] However, in a subsequent ruling, the Supreme Court ruled that advance notice did not need to be given if it would hinder the success of the demolition,[41] a virtual green light for demolitions to go forward without the possibility of appeal for those affected. This is what happens in most cases.

In cases of advance notification of intended destruction where the owners of the targeted properties have appealed, the Israeli Supreme Court has usually accepted the Israeli army's arguments and assessment of what constitutes military/security needs, and has permitted the demolitions. For example in a factory owner's appeal against demolition to enable the construction of a new road near the Netzarim settlement in the Gaza Strip, the Supreme Court accepted a long list of past security incidents in the area, as well as vaguely worded and unspecified intelligence that there was "intent" to use the property again as a base for attacks.[42]

Amnesty International believes these rulings suggest that the Israeli Supreme Court has too readily accepted the Israeli army's overly broad definition of what is militarily necessary (see legal section below). By endorsing this interpretation, the Supreme Court has failed to protect Palestinians in the Occupied Territories from arbitrary destruction of their homes and property and from forced evictions, leaving open the door for Israeli demolitions for almost *any* ostensible military purpose.

---

[40] Israeli Supreme Court decision in the case 2002/2264, *Yihiye Suleiman al Mutayeb et al v. State of Israel;* 2002/2329, *Basel al Wuhaidi et. al. v. State of Israel;* 2002/2332, *Rafiq Musullem Mutaweh et al v. State of Israel,* and 2002/2333, *Anwar Awadh et al v. State of Israel,* 19 March 2002, as cited in "Israeli Supreme Court Issues Guidelines on House Demolitions," Palestinian Center for Human Rights (PCHR) Press Release 42/2002, 19 March 2002.

[41] See Israeli Supreme Court decision 4219/02, 6 August 2002.

[42] *Ibid.*

V. Demolitions of Unlicensed Houses: Discriminatory Planning and Building Policies and Enforcement Measures

"We have to begin to educate the Arab public to build high. We live in a small and crowded country and I see that in other Arab countries they build high. There is no reason that everyone in the Arab sector should live in houses"

Israeli Interior Minister Abraham Poraz, 21 January 2004

V. 1. Background to the Demolition of Unlicensed Houses

The Israeli authorities have for decades pursued a policy of demolishing houses and destroying land and other properties inside Israel and the Occupied Territories. In the overwhelming majority of cases those whose homes and properties have been destroyed are Palestinians and Israeli citizens of Palestinian origin. The situation of house demolition inside Israel differs greatly, both in law and in practice, from that prevailing in the Occupied Territories, and it is in the latter that Israel has carried out the most extensive destruction of homes and property in recent years. However, there are also similarities between the two situations, notably the main underlying causes for the demolition of homes for lack of building permits, a phenomenon which exists both in the Arab sector in Israel and in parts of the Occupied Territories.

The expropriation/confiscation of large areas of Palestinian land has significantly diminished the reserves of available land on which Palestinians and Israeli Arabs can build to accommodate the natural growth of their communities. Planning and building regulations in these areas further restrict the amount of privately owned land on which Israeli Arabs and Palestinians can build.

In the Occupied Territories Palestinians are barred from leasing or building on land which has been declared state land because state land is not for leasing or building on by "alien persons", and the whole of the local Palestinian population of the Occupied Territories are defined as aliens.[43] Palestinians have not been allowed to build on, or make other use of, most of the land, which has been available for housing, farming and commercial use by Jewish settlers, whose presence in the Occupied Territories is in violation of international law.

In Israel, since the establishment of the state more than 700 Jewish towns and villages have been established but not a single Arab one. Furthermore

---

[43] An alien person is defined as one who is *not* in one of the following categories:

(1) An Israeli citizen;
(2) One who has immigrated (to Israel) under the (Israeli) Law of Return;
(3) One who is entitled immigrant status under the Law of Return—that is a Jew by descent or religion;
(4) A company controlled by (1), (2) or (3).

dozens of Arab villages which existed prior to the establishment of the state were subsequently re-classified as non-residential and remain unrecognized and under the threat of demolition.

Some 93% of the land in Israel is state land, but some of it is administered through the Jewish National Fund, the Jewish Agency or other bodies which do not lease land to non Jews and do not accept them in the housing projects/communities they establish and other housing projects on state land have been developed specifically for new Jewish immigrants. Other measures which restrict access of Israeli Arabs to land and housing include housing subsidies, which are only available to Israelis who have completed Israeli army service. This excludes Israeli Arabs, who are not conscripted into the Israeli army.

The building plans for many Arab towns and villages in Israel have not been completed, thus restricting or blocking the issuing of building permits, whereas building plans were promptly drawn up for new Jewish towns or villages. Many Arab villages in Israel do not have their own local councils—while smaller Jewish villages do—and depend on Jewish town/village councils, where they have no representation. Privately owned land in Arab villages has been zoned as agricultural and/or placed under the jurisdiction of adjacent Jewish village councils, making it difficult or impossible for Arabs to obtain building permits.

V. 2. Planning and Building Policies

At the root of the problem of demolition of unlicensed houses in the Arab sector in Israel and in parts of the Occupied Territories lie Israel's land and planning policies and the manner in which they are enforced. These policies have been characterized by discrimination against Israeli Arabs and Palestinians both in the use of state land, including land previously expropriated from Palestinians, and in the manner in which plans are drawn up for the use of privately owned land, as well as in the enforcement of planning and building regulations. Concerns about discriminatory regulations and practices have long been recognized, including by the Or Commission of Inquiry in its report published in 2002.[44]

Excerpts from the Or Commission report (September 2003)

36. In the first 50 years of the state's existence the Arab population has grown seven-fold and at the same time the amount of land allocated for housing construction has remained almost unchanged. Thus the population density in the Arab sector grew considerably and the lack of available land harmed young couples looking for housing. Public building did not assist them substantially, new localities were

[44] The Or Commission was set up by the Israeli authorities to investigate events surrounding the killing by Israeli security forces of 13 Palestinian citizens of Israel in protest demonstrations in October 2000 (the excerpts cited above are translated by Amnesty International).

not established, except the Bedouin settlements (townships), and Israel Lands Administration [ILA] land was not usually allocated for building in the Arab sector. Residents of the Arab sector who wish to build on land which they own but which is placed under the jurisdiction of neighbouring Jewish local authorities were blocked by the regulation of these authorities.

37. A major obstacle facing construction for housing purposes in the Arab sector has been the lack of outline and master plans. The preparation and updating of such plans always requires time, yet in the Arab sector there were unreasonable delays. Added to that was the problem of the lack of effective representation of the Arab sector in planning and building committees. In the national and district commissions there was token representation or no representation of the Arab sector. In many cases local commissions were not established in Arab localities and instead, these localities were placed under the jurisdiction of commissions managed by Jews. As a result the decisions regarding the developments of the Arab sector have not been sensitive enough to the needs of the Arab population.

Even after the preparation of plans had been speeded up during the 1990s, by the end of the century half of the Arab localities still did not have approved master plans that enabled the expansion of built up areas and many of them did not have approved outline plans. As a result in large parts of the areas of jurisdiction (of the Arab localities) private land owners could not build houses legally. A widespread phenomenon of unlicensed buildings has developed which partly stems from the inability to obtain building permits. Unlicensed buildings usually consist of single family houses. Demolition orders were issued for houses of Arabs in the Galilee, Negev, Triangle and the mixed cities. It has been claimed that behind the legal situation are political and ideological motives and that a situation of double standards has been created towards the Arab citizens. The citizens began preparing to oppose house demolition; public figures took active part in mobilizing the public in this opposition, encouraging them to defend the houses with their bodies and even called for violence to be used against policemen.

On 18 June 2003 Israeli security forces demolished the home of 25-year-old Hani Zbeida, who is paraplegic and wheelchair bound. Hani lives in Lod with his parents and siblings in a house which the families rents from the Amidar (the Israeli authority which administers the houses and properties which belonged to Palestinians who were expelled or forced to flee in the war which followed the establishment of the state of Israel in 1948, and which were declared as "abandoned" and taken over by the state). The house has a garden and a small piece of land adjacent to the house.

On this piece of land there used to be two small storage wide doors and an en suite bathroom for Hani, so that he could move more easily in his wheelchair, have some privacy and space to work. Even though he cannot use his hands, Hani works with computers, typing with his head, by means of a stick which he attaches to his forehead. He told Amnesty International that he had been very happy when his family built him his own home next to the family home because it was spacious and more comfortable. His parents stated that when the security forces came to demolish Hani's home and the family protested, the police beat Hani's father and his brother, who had a leg

> in a cast following a car accident. Shortly after the demolition, the family rebuilt Hani's home but when it was almost complete they received a new demolition order and were forced to halt the work.

The newly built home of Amal and Zuhair Hajji in Majd al-Krum (in the north of Israel) was demolished as soon as they had finished building it on 14 April 2002. Amal's father gave her a piece of land in the west of the village but it is impossible to obtain a building permit because the land is zoned as agricultural. Amal told Amnesty International: *"We have the land but cannot build on it, there is no way of getting a permit; so many people are in the same situation; and so we have no other way than to build our homes without a permit. We have five children, we need a home; we can't keep building on top of existing houses, it is not safe, and even that is not allowed anyway. So what can we do, do we have no right to have a home?"* In Majd al-Krum, like in other villages in the Arab sector in Israel, house density in the area of the village zoned for building has increased dramatically and there is now a shortage of land for building. Part of the village's land was seized for "military needs" decades ago. Although it has not been used for military purposes it has never been returned to the villagers and is reportedly intended to be used for the expansion of the nearby Jewish town of Karmiel.

V.3. Building Restrictions in the Occupied Territories Since the Oslo Accords

"Our policy is not to approve building in Area C"

Israeli Army spokesperson to Amnesty International delegates in 1999

". . . practically speaking, it doesn't exist as an issue. There are no more construction permits for Palestinians".

Israeli army Legal Advisor Colonel Shlomo Politus, speaking about Area C of the West Bank to the Constitution, Justice and Law Committee of the Israeli Parliament on 13 July 2003

The Oslo Accords divided the West Bank in three areas: Areas, A, B and C. The Palestinian Authority (PA) was given responsibility for civil affairs (such as health, education and building permits) in Areas A and B, which covered only 40% of the West Bank territory but contained 97.6% of the Palestinian population. Israel retained responsibility of both civil affairs and security in Area C, which covered 60% of the West Bank and included most of the unpopulated Palestinian land, the Israeli settlements and the main roads. Areas A and B are not contiguous but are fragmented into some 227 separate enclaves each surrounded by Area C, under Israeli military and civil control.

The Gaza Strip was similarly divided, with the most densely populated areas under PA jurisdiction and the unpopulated or less populated land under full Israeli control. The latter, referred to as "Yellow Areas" (similar to

Area C in the West Bank), cover more than 30% of the Gaza Strip, including Israeli settlements.

As a result Palestinians have continued to be prevented from building in most of the West Bank. Those who, unable to obtain permits, built their homes in these areas without a permit had their homes demolished by the Israeli army. According to figures given by the Israeli military authorities to the Israeli human rights organization B'Tselem, in 2001–2002 the army demolished 419 structures for lack of building permits in Area C of the West Bank. Up to date statistics are not available but Amnesty International has received information on scores of houses and other properties destroyed in Areas C of the West Bank for lack of permits in the past year and a half.

At the same time Israel dramatically accelerated the establishment and expansion of illegal settlements in and around East Jerusalem, in Area C of the West Bank and in the Yellow Areas in the Gaza Strip, and built an extensive network of roads throughout the Occupied Territories to connect these settlements to each other and to Israel. In the seven years of the Oslo peace process, from 1993 to the outbreak of the *intifada* in 2000, Israel increased the number of settlers in the West Bank and Gaza Strip by more than 50%. The expansion of Israeli settlements in the Occupied Territories continues. According to figures published on 2 March 2004 by the Israeli Central Bureau of Statistics (CBS), in 2003 housing construction in Israel fell by 8%, but increased by 35% in the settlements in the Occupied Territories

Israeli settlements and settlers' roads continue to be built on Palestinian land progressively confiscated or "temporarily" seized by the Israeli military authorities since the beginning of the occupation in 1967.[45] In theory the "temporary" seizure of land on grounds of (unspecified) "security needs" is for a set period only, but can be extended indefinitely. In practice "temporary" land seizures have invariably become permanent.

At present the Israeli army continues to seize Palestinian land on grounds of "military/security needs" in order to build permanent structures to benefit the Israeli settlements in the Occupied Territories.

> On the morning of 13 August 2003 five homes were demolished by the Israeli army and border guards in al-Walaja village, to the south-west of Jerusalem. Some 80 people were made homeless by the demolition. Among the destroyed houses was the home of the Shahadeh family: the parents, two daughters and two sons, one of them married with a child. The family had built their house in 1999 and had been living in it since then.

[45] The exact amount of Palestinian land confiscated by Israel has never been revealed. In the West Bank alone more than 70% of the land is estimated to have been confiscated. Often Palestinians learned that their land had been confiscated only when the Israeli army started to build a new Israeli settlement or a new road, even though the land had been confiscated years earlier.

Badria Shahadeh told Amnesty International: *"Some time after moving into the house we received a demolition order and we appealed to the court. The last court session was in June 2003 and we received a fine of 18,000 Shekels, of which we paid the first two monthly installments before the house was demolished. The court also decided that we must seal all the windows by January 2004, but no decision to destroy the house. The border guards came early in the morning and did not want to listen to anything we had to say and refused to even look at the court papers which we wanted to show them. They told us that they had an order to demolish our house but never showed us any order or any other papers. They gave us no time; we rushed to take out whatever we could; my sister broke her hand trying to take out furniture. My parents are old and they were still asleep; six soldiers took my father from his bed and put him outside the house."*

V. 4. The Impact of Israeli Settlements on Building Restrictions for Palestinians

26. . . . Furthermore, the Committee is gravely concerned about the continuing practice of expropriation of Palestinian properties and resources for the expansion of Israeli settlements in the occupied territories (ibid, para. 24).

Concluding Observations of the Committee on Economic, Social and Cultural Rights: Israel. 23 May 2003, E/C.12/1/Add.90.7.

During the 37 years of occupation the Israeli authorities have employed a variety of measures to prevent and restrict Palestinian planning, development and building in the West Bank and Gaza Strip. At the same time, successive Israeli governments have pursued with varying degrees of intensity a policy of establishing Jewish settlements on large areas of confiscated Palestinian land all over the Occupied Territories, in violation of international law.[46] Generous financial incentives have made moving to the settlements in the Occupied Territories attractive to Israelis and new Jewish immigrants who would not necessarily have chosen to move there for ideological reasons.

After it occupied the West Bank and Gaza Strip, Israel froze planning in Palestinian towns and villages. Planning schemes dating back several decades and no longer suitable to cater for the needs of a growing population were used as the basis for rejecting Palestinians' applications for building permits. Palestinians, facing a situation where prolonged, complicated and costly permit applications to build on their land were invariably refused, were left with no option but to build their homes without permits. Rather than considering allowing the development of more adequate planning and building procedures to allow for the development of Palestinian

[46] For more details on Israel's settlement policy in the Occupied Territories see Amnesty International's paper: *Israel and the Occupied Territories: The issue of settlements must be addressed according to international law*, 8 September 2003 (AI Index: MDE 15/085/2003).

towns and villages, Israel adopted a policy of mass demolition of Palestinian houses.

At the same time, Israel developed comprehensive and efficient planning schemes for more than 150 Jewish settlements it established throughout the Occupied Territories. Despite this, thousands of houses were built in these settlements without permits. Israel refrained from demolishing these houses, and instead issued retroactive building permits for thousand of houses constructed without permits and for entire settlements established without government authorization.

V. 5. Land Confiscation/Expropriation

In Israel, after the establishment of the state, large areas of land were also seized under emergency regulations. The areas were declared closed military zones and the inhabitants/landowners were expelled. Even though the land was officially seized only temporarily, in several cases the owners were never allowed to return.[47]

Israel has expropriated large areas of land both in Israel and in the Occupied Territories by declaring that land which was not officially registered or under continuous cultivation is not in private ownership but is in fact 'state' land. The justification for this is the Ottoman Land Law which defined the *miri* class of ownership under which most Palestinian agricultural land is held by virtue of use. *Miri* land includes pasture and range lands; land not cultivated for three years could be auctioned to a villager prepared to cultivate (or, if there are no claimants, given to a needy villager); cultivation for 10 years entitles the cultivator to *tabu* (deed of ownership). Possession without title deeds was the norm in Palestine prior to the settlement of title deeds process initiated by the British Mandate authorities but which was not completed before the end of the British Mandate.[48] Many Palestinians had not registered their land under either the Ottoman or British administration in order to avoid taxation and because it was not necessary, as their right to the land was never disputed.

After the establishment of the state of Israel (and after 1967 in the Occupied Territories) land shown by aerial photo not to have been cultivated each year for a 10 year period became liable to be forfeit—not to the village but to the state. Notification of an area being declared as state land could be given to a village representative, or posted on the land (for example left

[47] Such cases include the villages of Iqrit and Bir'im (in northern Israel, near the border with Lebanon), whose inhabitants were temporarily expelled but have never been allowed to return, in spite of a Supreme Court ruling in their favour, and the villages were subsequently destroyed by the Israeli army. Subsequent appeals to the Supreme Court by the inhabitants of these villages to be allowed to return to their properties are still ongoing and unresolved—55 years after their temporary expulsion.

[48] The process started in the north of the country, which is where most land was registered in private ownership by the end of the British Mandate.

under a stone), or the declaration could be made orally. The onus of proof is on the owner to commission a cadastral survey and submit an appeal within a limited period of time. Many owners never received the notification and few have had the resources to mount a legal claim. Hardly any of those who did have been successful.

Under the Absentee Property Law (enacted by Israel in 1950) land, houses and other properties of Palestinians who were defined as absentees was expropriated and declared state land. The law defined as absentees all Palestinians who were outside the country or away from their place of residency after 29 November 1947. More than 800,000 Palestinians who were expelled or fled the country in the war were dispossessed of their land and property under this law, as were about a quarter of the 150,000 Palestinians who remained in the country but who had become internally displaced on account of the war.

Land belonging to Palestinian citizens of Israel was also expropriated through the Land Acquisition for Public Purpose Ordinance (Public Purposes Ordinance). This law, introduced by the British Mandate administration in 1943, allows the authorities to take permanent or temporary ownership of land for public purposes. A public purpose is one defined as such by the authorities who are not required to provide details of the purpose.[49]

V. 6. Discriminatory Enforcement of Planning and Building Regulations

The Jewish town of Kamon was established in 1980 around the land of the Sawad family. The family has previously had some land confiscated and has been battling for their rights in Israeli court for decades. The Sawad's family land was included in the 1984 plan of the Misgav Regional Council for the town of Kamon as land zoned for building (included within the blue line of the Kamon plan). However, the Kamon plan was subsequently re-drawn so as to exclude the Sawad family land from the blue line defining the area which can be built developed. When the family challenged the amendment to the plan they were informed that the amendment did not alter the status of their land, which remains zoned for building. However, when the family obtained the plan they learned that their land had been parceled into seven plots each including also some land belonging to the Regional Council. Hence, building permits are subject to the agreement of the Council, even though the family's ownership of the land is not contested and the requested building permits only concern the part of the plots which belong to the family and not those parts belonging to the state. The procedure for parcelation of land can take years and in this case the re-parcelation of the Sawad's family land into plots comprising only their own land would require the agreement

[49] Several areas of Palestinian land expropriated under this law between the 1950s and 1970s were subsequently used to build Jewish towns and villages, including Karmiel and Upper Nazareth.

of the Council, which has not been forthcoming. Therefore the family has not succeeded in obtaining the necessary building permits for their land.

In the Arab sector in Israel and in the East Jerusalem area much of the privately owned land has been zoned as green land, on which it is not permitted to build. Attempts to have such land re-zoned so that it can be used for building homes have invariably failed. However, in the Jewish sector it has been possible to re-zone agricultural land not just for building houses but also for the construction of commercial properties. Over the years the Israel Lands Administration (ILA) readily approved the re-zoning of land in *moshavim* and *kibbutzim* (agricultural farms in the Jewish sector) from agricultural to commercial use.[50]

> *"A 1997 survey by the Planning Authorities of the Agricultural Ministry found 7,400 commercial activities in Moshavs, of which 3,000 were in the central district of the country. This is probably an underestimate since according to data from the Supervision Unit of the Planning and Building Committee in the central district alone there were 7,250 cases of exceptional use of agricultural land. The survey did not show if these were legal or not but according to a letter of December 1997 from the Director of the Planning Authorities to the Agriculture Ministry, most of them did not have statutory status. Exceptional use of agricultural land is also found in urban localities. For example, the Supervision Unit of the District Planning and Building Committee of the central district found that in February 1998 there were 25 structures built without permit on agricultural land in the Petah Tikva area".*
> State Controller report 2000[51]

Planning and building regulations, both in Israel and in the Occupied Territories, are enforced in a manner that, in the overwhelming majority of cases, discriminates against Israeli Arabs and Palestinians. Violations of these regulations also occur in the Jewish sector in Israel and in Jewish settlements in the Occupied Territories. However demolitions of homes of Israeli Jews are virtually unheard of. Information from official sources about demolitions is not disaggregated into separate statistics for the Jewish and Arab sectors.[52] However, according to available information only rarely are properties demolished in the Jewish sector and usually these are extensions to existing buildings, rather than entire homes. The practice in the

[50] In some cases concerning agricultural land in the Jewish sector being used for commercial purposes, rather than for housing, appeals seeking to invalidate ILA's decisions are currently pending before the Supreme Court.

[51] Report 52 B of the State Comptroller, section on "Use of agricultural land for commercial purposes", page 418, points 2 and 3.

[52] On 19 January 2004 Deputy Minister of the Interior Victor Brilovsky responded to a parliamentary question that: *"The National Supervision Unit of Buildings at the Interior Ministry does not differentiate between the demolition of Jewish or Arab structures. However, it should be mentioned that most of the illegal constructions in open areas are in the Arab sector."* (www.knesset.gov.il). The latter assertion contradicts information from official sources according to which unlicensed buildings on agricultural land in the Jewish sector are a widespread phenomenon.

Jewish sector has tended to be retroactive granting of permits and tolerance of unlicensed buildings, rather than demolition.

In the Occupied Territories the establishment by Israel of Israeli settlements is illegal under international law. In addition, the settlements established without government authorization have usually been granted authorization retroactively and have been provided with services such as water and electricity, even prior to being granted authorization. A widely publicized government decision to dismantle a few unauthorized settlement outposts (consisting of mostly uninhabited caravans) in 2003 was not eventually carried out. In some cases the outposts were not removed and in other cases they were removed but were promptly reestablished by the settlers and left in place by the authorities.

> *16. The Committee is deeply concerned about the continuing difference in treatment between Jews and non-Jews, in particular Arab and Bedouin communities, with regard to their enjoyment of economic, social and cultural rights in the State party's territory. . . . This discriminatory attitude is apparent in the continuing lower standard of living of Israeli Arabs as a result, inter alia, of . . . lack of access to housing, water, electricity and health care and a lower level of education, despite the State party's efforts to close the gap. In this regard, the Committee expresses its concern that the State party's domestic legal order does not enshrine the general principles of equality and non-discrimination.*
>
> Concluding Observations of the Committee on Economic, Social and Cultural Rights: Israel. 23 May 2003, E/C.12/1/Add.90.
>
> On 21 August 2003, on the morning of his wedding, As'ad Mu'yin had his house demolished; the house of his cousin Ziad As'ad, who had married a week earlier, was demolished at the same time. The two adjacent houses had been built over the past five years and were located in the West Bank town of Nazla 'Issa (area C according to the Oslo Agreements). As'ad Mu'yin had been living on the ground floor of the house with his parents and three brothers and had furnished and prepared the second floor to move in with his wife. The house was demolished before he could do so. The new furniture and the wedding gifts disappeared under the rubble, along with the content of the family home on the ground floor. All he has left is a pack of photographs of his house as it was on the eve of the demolition; completely furnished and ready for him to move in with his new bride.
>
> He told Amnesty International: *"The army came early in the morning, at about 7am. I was getting ready for the wedding, for a very happy day. They had bulldozers and there were also border guards and police with them and they gave us 15 minutes to leave the house. We had no time to salvage anything. They said that we did not have building permits and that we needed building permits because this is Area C. But everyone knows that Israel does not give building permits in Area C. Within an hour both our houses were destroyed. There was nothing we could do".*

Ziad As'ad's house was also on two floors, one for him and one for his brother. He had been living in his half of the house, the upper floor, since his wedding a week before the demolition.

V. 7. The Unrecognized Bedouin Villages in the Negev Region: Trespassers in their Homes

"The police poisoned the fields with airplanes; they must have used something very strong, poison, because we got sick. At first we thought it was a chemical attack from Iraq; the television had talked a lot about Iraq launching a chemical attack on Israel in the American war in Iraq; I hadn't thought much about it but when the planes came to throw this gas, this poison, I don't know what it was, I was terrified; my husband was not here, he was in Be'er Sheva and I was alone with the children and I was very scared. The children got really sick; I got very dizzy . . . Some people vomited and even fainted. I didn't know what to do. I though that's it, it is the chemical attack; then later I learned that it was the police, to kill our crops. Why do they do such things? To bring airplanes to kill our crops? We have nothing here, you see; we don't get water to irrigate our fields; you can't cultivate the land without water; and even that little bit we manage to do they destroy; why?"

A resident of an unrecognized Bedouin village on the destruction of crops in March 2003.

Some 60,000–70,000 Bedouins live in some 45 "unrecognized villages" in the Negev, Israel's southern region. Although they have lived in the Negev for generations and were the main population of the region before the establishment of the state of Israel, their villages have never been recognized by the authorities and are not provided with basic services, such as running water, electricity, sewage, schools, health facilities and paved roads. Health problems and child mortality rates in these villages are the highest in the country. The inhabitants of these villages are not permitted by the Israeli authorities to build houses nor to farm the land, and live in constant fear that their homes will be demolished. In the past two years alone the security forces have demolished scores of homes in these villages and have destroyed the Bedouins' crops by helicopter spraying on seven occasions. In the last such incident, on 11 March 2004, the ILA confirmed that the chemical used to spray the fields is the herbicide *Roundup*, produced by the Monsanto Corporation. According to the manufacturer's instructions, this product should not be used with aerial spraying equipment and even when sprayed at ground level, people and animals should not be allowed in the treated area for seven days.[53] However, the Israeli authorities gave no warning to the local Bedouin population to evacuate the area before spraying the area. A number of people were affected by the crop spraying and had to seek hospital treatment as a result.

---

[53] See press release of 24 March 2004 about the petition to the Israeli Supreme Court by the Israeli human rights organization Adalah: http://www.adalah.org/eng/index.php.

Since more permanent constructions in the unrecognized Bedouin villages are more likely to be destroyed by the Israeli authorities, many Bedouins are forced to live in shed-like homes with corrugated iron roofs, which offer little protection against the extreme desert climate. Even so, most of their homes and animal sheds are under the threat of demolition. The ILA puts the number of unlicensed (and thus liable to demolition) structures in these villages at 60,000, of which 25,000 are houses, and the Israeli Interior Ministry gives a figure of 30,000.[54]

The authorities have prohibited the Bedouins from building homes and cultivating the land in an effort to prevent them from formally establishing a permanent presence and acquiring land rights through continuous cultivation. Up to the late 1940s the Bedouins held a much larger area of the Negev.[55] After the establishment of the state the authorities forcibly confined the Arab population of the Negev to an area which was declared a closed military zone and became known as the *Siyag* (the *Siyag* is a triangular area between Rahat in the north, Yerucham in the south and Arad in the East). After Israeli military rule over the Arab population ended in 1966, the Bedouins were never allowed to return to the land they previously held. Today they remain in the *Siyag*, on an area which constitutes about 2% of the Negev.[56]

The Bedouins claim that the land of the unrecognized villages belongs to them and that in fact it is only a small percentage of their land even though they do not have deeds of ownership.[57] The Israeli authorities contend that this land is state land, even though it was not registered as state land. In spite of their contention that the Bedouins of the unrecognized villages are trespassers on public land, for years the Israeli authorities have been putting pressure on the Bedouins living in the unrecognized villages (including by destroying their homes and crops and denying them basic services) to sign agreements renouncing their claims to this land and move to urbanized townships being planned by the authorities for them.

In past decades about half of the Bedouin population has given in to government pressures and moved to five townships lacking in infrastructure and opportunities for work and economic development, which were set up by the Israeli authorities especially for the Bedouins. These Bedouin townships remain amongst the poorest localities in the country and have high

[54] Figures quoted by the State Comptroller in his report 52B of 2000 (section on The Bedouin Diaspora in the Negev, page 111, paragraph 2).

[55] Historically the Negev region in southern Israel had been inhabited almost exclusively by Bedouins. According to the British Mandate Survey of Palestine carried out in 1945–46 by the Anglo-American Committee of Inquiry, some 15% of the land in the Negev was used by Arabs, 0.5% was owned by Jews, 0.2% was public land and the remaining 84% had no defined ownership.

[56] The Negev makes up 60% of Israel's total surface and is sparsely populated.

[57] For details about land registration and acquisition of deeds of ownership see the chapter on Land confiscation/expropriation on page 39.

rates of unemployment and crime. The 60–70,000 Bedouins who continue to live in the unrecognized villages have resisted the government's pressures to give up their land and traditional lifestyle of farming and animal-grazing and to move to such townships.

While stepping up efforts to concentrate the Bedouin population into small townships with little or no employment or development prospects, the authorities have encouraged and sponsored the establishment of new Jewish villages and single farms in the region. According to the State Comptroller report (52B) of 2000 the ILA has leased 66,000 dunums of state land to some 35 Jewish single family farms in the Negev. This makes a striking comparison with the situation of the 60–70,000 Bedouins of the unrecognized villages who are not allowed to build homes or farm the land on which they have lived for generations. Isolated Jewish single family farms in the Negev receive services such as electricity and water, while Bedouin villages (even those located near the electricity and water plants) are denied these services.

> *The Committee continues to be concerned about the situation of Bedouins residing in Israel, and in particular those living in villages that are still unrecognized. . . . Despite measures by the State party to close the gap between the living conditions of Jews and Bedouins in the Negev, the quality of living and housing conditions of the Bedouins continue to be significantly lower, with limited or no access to water, electricity and sanitation. Moreover, Bedouins continue to be subjected on a regular basis to land confiscations, house demolitions, fines for building "illegally", destruction of agricultural crops, fields and trees, and systematic harassment and persecution by the Green Patrol, in order to force them to resettle in "townships".* Concluding Observations of the Committee on Economic, Social and Cultural Rights: Israel. 23 May 2003, E/C.12/1/Add.90(27).

In recent years the Negev has been designated by the government as a priority area for development and for absorption of new Jewish immigrants and the authorities have often restated their determination to remove the Bedouins from the unrecognized villages to seven townships being planned for them.[58]

The government is also taking steps to strengthen eviction laws. A new draft law, called "removal of intruders" law, aims to strengthen the procedures and mechanisms for the *"eviction/removal [from public land] of every person, cattle, everything which is built and planted on them, and of everything else which is permanently connected [to the land]"*.[59] Notably, it provides for a

[58] See for example Interior Minister Poraz's statement at the Knesset's debate on the issue of the master plan in the Arab sector, on 21 January 2004 (www.knesset.gov.il).

[59] *The Public Land [Removal of Intruders] Law [Amendment] 2002*, amending the primary 1981 law by the same name, was submitted by the government to the Knesset (parliament) in 2002 and is pending approval.

substantially increased budget for security services to carry out more evictions/removals, in a more timely and effective manner.

On 4 August 2003 Israeli security forces demolished the home of 'Ali and Sara Abu Sbeit and their six children, aged between 13 and two and a half years, in Sa'wa, one of the unrecognized Bedouin villages. 'Ali Abu Sbeit told Amnesty International:

"The police and border guards came at about 7am. We were still asleep. There were more than 200 of them and they had bulldozers. They tied my hands behind my back and took me, my wife and the children out. They did not allow us time to take anything out of the house. Some policemen took out a few things but most of what we had remained in the house. They started to hit the house with the bulldozer and demolished it very quickly, then some of them clapped and they all left. It was a terrible day, my wife and the children were very sad, we were all very upset. Since our home was destroyed we have been staying with our relatives, but not all together because there are a lot of us. My wife was very affected by the demolition of our home and she needed looking after to recover, so she and our little daughter are staying with her parents in Ramle, our two oldest daughters are staying with my brother, and me and the three boys are staying with my mother. My children have not seen their mother and their little sister for three weeks. We are going to visit them in Ramle later today; but how can we live like this, we are a family and need our own home.

This is the second time that my home has been demolished. The first time was in 1997 and I had to demolish the house myself; or else the authorities were going to make me pay the cost of the bulldozer and everything for the demolition. At that time there was a court order that said that I had to demolish the house and I did. I have always been a law-abiding citizen. I have been serving in the Israeli army for 13 years;[60] every year I do my reserve service; I just finished my reserve duty a few weeks ago, and two weeks after I came home from reserve duty the police came to demolish my home; without warning, I never received any court order or anything. We can't build anywhere, where are we supposed to live? After my house was demolished in 1997 my family and I lived with my mother for three years, but now there isn't space for all of us there. Then in 1999 I built this home, and now we are homeless again".

On the same day Israeli security forces demolished nine other homes in the same village. The house which was demolished immediately after 'Ali Abu Sbeit's belonged to his cousin, who is married with four children.

[60] Bedouins, like Israeli Arabs, are not conscripted into the Israeli army but some of them enlist voluntarily for army service, whereas Israeli Arabs never serve. Fewer Bedouins serve in the Israeli army now than in previous decades, reportedly because of increasing grievances amongst Bedouins about discrimination and unequal treatment by the state.

V. 8. Planning and Building Restrictions in East Jerusalem

Salim and 'Arabia Shawamreh's house has been demolished four times since July 1998. After the last demolition, on 2 April 2003, the house was rebuilt with the help of volunteers from several Israeli human rights groups as a peace centre in memory of Noha Maqadmeh, a mother of 10 children who was crushed to death under the rubble of her destroyed home in Gaza in March 2003 (see page 11), and of Rachel Corrie, a 23-year-old American peace activist who was crushed to death by an Israeli army bulldozer in March 2003 as she tried to prevent the demolition of a house in Rafah refugee camp in the Gaza Strip.

Salim and 'Arabia have seven children aged between 2 and 21 years. They are from Palestinian refugee families who lost their homes when their village in the northern Negev was destroyed by Israel after the establishment of the state in 1948. They lived in the overcrowded Shu'fat refugee camp in Jerusalem, and eventually bought a plot of land in the nearby village of 'Anata. After having spent more than four years and a lot of money trying to obtain a permit, they lost hope and built their home without a permit.

They told Amnesty International:

"The authorities gave us different justifications for refusing us the building permit: that the land was too steep, that it was zoned as agriculture, that signatures were missing from the property deed, that a highway was planned nearby, that their application had been lost. Each time we succeeded to challenge or disprove the reason they had given us for the refusal, our application was rejected on different grounds. We spent thousands of dollars on this process and in the end we understood that it was hopeless and we built our home without a permit".

'Arabia told Amnesty International about the repeated demolition of their home:

"The first time they demolished our home it was on 9 July 1998; we had been living in our home for fsive year. They came in the morning without warning. There were a lot of soldiers and police, with bulldozers. I locked the door but the soldiers threw teargas through the window and broke down the door. They tied Salim's hands so tight they swelled and they beat him and our oldest son, who was 14 at the time. They hit me on the head with a gun butt and ill-treated the children. Some female soldiers grabbed my little girls by the hair and dragged them. I was taken to hospital. We were living in a tent on our land and started to rebuild the house immediately. A month later, when the house was almost finished the army and police came again, in the middle of the night and threatened to shoot anyone who moved, including the Israeli peace activists who were staying with us and helping us. They demolished the house again. The children were terrified and remained disturbed and the little ones wet the bed for a long time after that. The children were traumatized and so was I; I could not even speak for some time; I became very depressed. It was very difficult for all of us"

The family started to rebuild their house in 1999 and finished it and moved in on 3 April 2001. The following day the Israeli security forces again came to demolish the house and this time they also destroyed the foundations. In the summer of 2002 the family once again started to rebuild their home and on 3 April 2003, as the inside of the house was being finished, the house was destroyed once more. Since the house was rebuilt in the summer of 2003 as a peace centre, the Israeli security forces have again threatened to destroy but at the time of writing this report it had not been demolished.

Hundreds of homes have been demolished in East Jerusalem[61] on the ground that they had been constructed without building permits in recent years, and thousands more are at risk of demolition. Many Palestinian residents of Jerusalem find it impossible to obtain permits to build homes on their land because most of the Palestinian land has been classified by the Israeli authorities as green land.

When Israel occupied the West Bank in 1967 it immediately annexed East Jerusalem and the land of 28 surrounding towns and villages,[62] and expropriated more than a third (24.5 km^2) of the total land annexed (71 km^2). Most of the expropriated land was privately owned by Palestinians. According to the Israeli human rights organization B'Tselem:

"By the end of 2000, on the land expropriated in East Jerusalem, close to 44,000 housing units had been built for Jews, while not even one housing unit was built for Palestinians". . . . "82 percent of the housing units built [in the whole of Jerusalem], were for Jews; 18 percent were for Palestinians. The disparity has been greater in recent years: of the units completed between 1990 and the end of 2000, only 11.4 percent were constructed in Palestinian neighborhoods".[63]

Since annexing East Jerusalem Israel has severely limited new construction in the Palestinian neighbourhoods. The expropriation of large areas of land near Palestinian neighbourhoods and villages left most Palestinian neighbourhoods with little or no land on which to build, and where there is land it is not permitted to build on it. Whereas in the rest of the West Bank the Israeli authorities have cited ancient plans which give no opportunity for development, in East Jerusalem they have done the opposite. Shortly after annexation in 1967 the Israeli authorities cancelled the (Jordanian) development plan which had been approved in 1966 and which gave extensive opportunity for development. A planning vacuum was thus created pending the approval of new plans and in the interim period only rare *ad hoc* building permits were issued to Palestinians and only in extremely restricted areas.

---

[61] According to international law East Jerusalem is part of the Occupied Territories and its annexation by Israel is in violation of international law. However, because of the annexation, East Jerusalem is governed under Israeli civil laws, and not under military laws like the rest of the Occupied Territories. It is to avoid confusion that the situation in East Jerusalem is detailed on its own in this chapter.

[62] The boundaries of the annexed Palestinian land were drawn to include as much land and as few Palestinians as possible, mostly leaving out the urban areas of these towns and villages.

[63] See the section on Discrimination in Planning, Building, and Land Expropriation, on B'Tselem's website: www.btselem.org.

Since the 1980s outline plans have been drawn up for most of the Palestinian neighbourhoods of East Jerusalem. A striking feature of these plans is the extraordinary amount of land, some 40%, zoned as "open landscape" (*shetah nof patuah*), where any form of development is prohibited. The plans approved by the end of 1999 only allow building on little over 11% of the land in the East Jerusalem area which is privately owned by Palestinians, and this land is mainly within already built-up areas. Separate outline plans are issued for Jewish settlements and for Palestinian neighbourhoods, with manifestly different standards adopted. The plans for Palestinian neighbourhoods are geographically restrictive, have insufficient capacity and do not take into account the needs of the Palestinian population.

Geographically, the plans establish a 'blue line' boundary around most existing developed areas, within which land is zoned to allow 'infill' development on empty plots between existing buildings. No significant allocation of new development land has ever been made. The need to confine the boundaries so as not to exceed the 'quota' is cited in Israeli records as justification for the tight development boundaries. Land outside the blue line is zoned as "open landscape", on which no development is permitted, which in practice often precludes even agriculture.

The zoning of land as "open landscape" has been frequently used to freeze development of land until later confiscation for Jewish settlements (as at Reches Shu'fat, Beit Safafa and the most recent major settlement at Jabal Abu Ghneim/Har Homa). For example, land at Shu'fat which had been zoned for Palestinian housing in the 1966 Jordanian plan, was later re-zoned by Israel as "open landscape" and planted with cypress trees; in 1994 it was allocated to the Jewish National Fund for Jewish housing which has since been built.

The procedures used are also a source of problems. Even though Palestinians normally only build on land in family ownership, no attempt has been made to take ownership patterns into account in formulating the plans. There has been no attempt to devolve local decision making to the local Palestinian neighbourhoods. Even when outline plans are approved it is often then necessary for a detailed plan to be approved, and larger plots require an approved parcelation plan (the subdivision of land into different ownership plots)—a process which can take years to approve.

Due to these and other factors, thousands of Palestinians and Israeli Arabs have found it impossible to obtain building permits even after lengthy and costly application procedures. Many have turned to the courts, incurring further expenses, but in most cases their appeals have been unsuccessful. Others, knowing that they have no chance of obtaining a building permit, have built their homes without applying for a permit. As a result, thousands of homes have been demolished and thousands more are under the threat of demolition.

Many who built their homes without a permit subsequently received heavy fines, in some cases up to the cost of the houses themselves. They believed payment of the fine would result in the building permit being granted or at least in the threat of demolition being removed or suspended until a hoped-for review of the building permit system. However, after paying part of the fine, in some cases most of the fine, they nevertheless received demolition orders.

VI. Applicable International Legal Standards

Both in Israel and in the Occupied Territories, Israel is bound by international human rights law, including the international human rights treaties to which Israel is a State Party. The most relevant to the concerns addressed in this report include: The International Covenant on Economic, Social and Cultural Rights (ICESCR), the International Covenant on Civil and Political Rights (ICCPR), the International Convention on the Elimination of All Forms of Racial Discrimination (ICERD), the UN Convention on the Elimination of All Forms of Discrimination against Women (the Women's Convention) and the UN Convention on the Rights of the Child (CRC).

In the Occupied Territories two sets of complementary legal frameworks apply: international human rights law and international humanitarian law. Hence, in addition to the above-mentioned international human rights treaties, Israel's conduct as the occupying power in the Occupied Territories must also comply with the provisions of international humanitarian law applicable to belligerent occupation, including:

- The Hague Convention (IV) respecting the Laws and Customs of War on Land and its annexed Regulations respecting the Laws and Customs of War on Land of 18 October 1907 (hereafter Hague Regulations);
- The Fourth Geneva Convention relative to the Protection of Civilian Persons in Time of War of 12 August 1949 (hereafter Fourth Geneva Convention);
- Rules of customary international law, including Article 75 of the 1977 Protocol Additional to the Geneva Conventions relating to the Protection of Victims of International Armed Conflicts (Protocol I);

VI. 1. Applicability of International Law in the Occupied Territories

International human rights law: Israel has consistently denied that it is under any obligation to apply the UN human rights treaties to which it is a State Party in the West Bank and Gaza Strip. Israel has argued that under international law it is not required to apply these treaties to areas that are not part of its sovereign territory. It takes the position that limited provisions of humanitarian law should be applied in the Occupied Territories to the exclusion of international human rights law. However, it is a basic principle of human rights law that international human rights treaties are applicable in all areas in which states parties exercise effective control, regardless of whether or not they exercise sovereignty in that area.

In addition, Israel contends that it cannot be internationally responsible for ensuring the implementation of these treaties in these areas because the majority of civil powers and responsibilities have been transferred to the PA under the Oslo Accords. The Oslo Agreements envisage that the PA should exercise extensive powers and responsibilities in the Occupied Territories. However, the PA is clearly dependent on Israel's cooperation to exercise these powers and responsibilities. Israel can and does control the access of the Palestinian population of the Occupied Territories to vital resources such as land and water. Israel always retained overall effective control of the Occupied Territories. And as stipulated by Article 47 of the Fourth Geneva Convention:

> *"Protected persons who are in occupied territory shall not be deprived, in any case or in any manner whatsoever, of the benefits of the present Convention by any change introduced as the result of the occupation of a territory, into the institutions or government of the said territory, nor by any agreement concluded between the authorities of the occupied territory and the Occupying power, nor by any annexation by the latter of the whole or part of the occupied territory."*

Moreover, in recent years Israel has redeployed its forces in towns and villages which according to the Oslo Agreements are under PA jurisdiction and where most Palestinians live. Indeed most of the Palestinian homes, land and other properties which have been destroyed in the past three years were located in areas under the jurisdiction of the PA. There can be no doubt that Israel continues to exercise effective control over the Occupied Territories and is therefore responsible for implementing its obligations under international human rights law.

Israel's position on the applicability of the UN human rights conventions in the Occupied Territories has not been accepted by any of the UN human rights treaty bodies. For example, the UN Committee on Economic, Social and Cultural Rights (CESCR), in its conclusions on Israel's initial report in 2000, stated: *"The Committee is of the view that the State's obligations under the Covenant apply to all territories and populations under its effective control."*[64] The Committee requested Israel to provide it with additional information on the realization of economic, social and cultural rights in the Occupied Territories *"in order to complete the State party's initial report and thereby ensure*

[64] CESCR, E/C.12/1/Add.27, para. 8.

full compliance with its reporting obligations."[65] The Committee has reconsidered this issue in the past two years and in 2001 maintained its position that the International Covenant on Economic, Social and Cultural Rights is applicable in the Occupied Territories. It stated that: *"Even during armed conflict, fundamental human rights must be respected and . . . basic economic, social and cultural rights as part of the minimum standards of human rights are guaranteed under customary international law and are also prescribed by international law."*[66]

International humanitarian law: Even though Israel has argued before the UN human rights treaty bodies that the appropriate legal regime to be applied in the Occupied Territories is humanitarian law only, it has refused to accept that many of these norms are applicable. While recognizing the *de jure* applicability of the Hague Regulations, Israel has consistently rejected the applicability of the Fourth Geneva Convention to the West Bank and Gaza Strip. Israel maintains that it applies *de facto* unspecified "humanitarian provisions" contained in the Fourth Geneva Convention, while arguing that it is not required to do so by international law.

Israel stands alone in contending that the Fourth Geneva Convention does not apply to its occupation of the West Bank and Gaza Strip. The UN, the International Committee of the Red Cross (ICRC) and the international community have consistently maintained that the Fourth Geneva Convention fully applies to the Occupied Territories and that the Palestinians are a protected population under the terms of the Convention.

VI. 2. International Human Rights Law

VI. 2.1 The Right to Housing

The right to housing is a basic right, which is a fundamental component of the right to an adequate standard of living and central to the enjoyment of other human rights. The imperative for all people "of housing for personal security, privacy, health, safety, protection from the elements and many other attributes of a shared humanity"[67] has lead the international community to enshrine the right in a number of human rights instruments, including Article 25 of the Universal Declaration of Human Rights and international human rights treaties to which Israel is a party.

[65] CESCR, E/C.12/1/Add.27, para. 32.

[66] E/C.12/1/Add.69, para. 12.

[67] *Housing Rights Legislation, Review of international and national legal instruments*, United Nations Housing Rights Programme, Report No.1, UN Human Settlements Programme (UN-HABITAT) and the Office of the High Commissioner for Human Rights (OHCHR), 2002, p 1.

For example, the International Covenant on Economic, Social and Cultural Rights (ICESCR) guarantees the right to adequate housing in Article 11(1):

> *"The States Parties to the present Covenant recognize the right of everyone to an adequate standard of living for himself and his family, including adequate food, clothing and housing, and to the continuous improvement of living conditions. States Parties will take appropriate steps to ensure the realization of this right . . ."*

The UN Committee on Economic, Social and Cultural Rights (CESCR), the expert body which monitors states' implementation of the ICESCR, in its General Comment 3 concerning State Parties' obligations under the ICESCR, clarifies that:

> *". . . while the full realization of the relevant rights may be achieved progressively, steps towards that goal must be taken within a reasonably short time after the Covenant's entry into force for the States concerned. Such steps should be deliberate, concrete and targeted as clearly as possible towards meeting the obligations recognized in the Covenant."*[68]

The right to housing encompasses the right to live somewhere in peace, security and dignity, as well as the right to *adequate* housing. The right to adequate housing not only includes adequate privacy, space, security, protection from the elements and threats to health, ventilation at a reasonable cost, but also, among other things legal security of tenure—including protection against forced eviction, harassment and threats; sustainable access to: safe drinking water, heating, lighting, sanitation and washing facilities, refuse disposal, emergency services.[69]

Under Article 12 of the International Covenant on Civil and Political Rights (ICCPR), all persons lawfully on a territory are guaranteed the right to freedom to choose one's residence.

The right of children to adequate housing is enshrined in Principle 4 of the Declaration of the Rights of the Child. The obligation of States Parties including Israel, in cases of need to provide material assistance and support programmes to families and children, particularly with regard to housing, is set out in Article 27(3) of the Convention on the Rights of the Child (CRC).

The obligation of states, including Israel, to eliminate discrimination against women in rural areas in order to ensure that they enjoy adequate living conditions, particularly in relation to housing, is enshrined in Article 14(2)(h) of the Women's Convention.

---

[68] CESCR, General Comment 3, Art. 2, para. 1.
[69] CESCR, General Comment 4, paras 7 and 8.

The CESCR clarifies State Parties' obligations under Article 11 of the ICESCR in its General Comment 4:

> *". . . the right to housing should not be interpreted in a narrow or restrictive sense which equates it with, for example, the shelter provided by merely having a roof over one's head or views shelter exclusively as a commodity. Rather it should be seen as the right to live somewhere in security, peace and dignity. . . . the reference in article 11(1) must be read as referring not just to housing but to* ***adequate*** *housing".*[70] (emphasis added).

> *"In addition, the full enjoyment of other rights—such as the right to freedom of expression, the right to freedom of association . . . the right to freedom of residence and the right to participate in public decision making—is indispensable if the right to adequate housing is to be realized and maintained by all groups in society. Similarly, the right not to be subjected to arbitrary or unlawful interference with one's privacy, family, home or correspondence constitutes a very important dimension in defining the right to adequate housing".*[71]

> *"Regardless of the state of development of any country, there are certain steps which must be taken immediately. As recognized in the Global Strategy for Shelter and in other international analyses, many of the measures required to promote the right to housing would only require the abstention by the Government from certain practices and a commitment to facilitating "self-help" by affected groups . . ."* [72]

In its concluding observations in May 2003 the CESCR expressed serious concerns about Israel's practices which violate the right to housing of Israeli Arabs, including Bedouins in Israel, and of Palestinians in the Occupied Territories.[73]

The Committee also expressed regret that a number of the concerns it had raised in 1998 remained outstanding and reiterated its concerns about these issues.[74]

Among other things, in 1998 the Committee had expressed

> *". . . grave concern that the Status Law of 1952 authorizes the World Zionist Organization/Jewish Agency and its subsidiaries, including the Jewish National Fund, to control most of the land in Israel, since these institutions are chartered to benefit Jews exclusively. Despite the fact that the institutions are chartered under private law, the State of Israel nevertheless has a decisive influence on their policies and thus remains responsible for their activities. A State party cannot divest itself of its obligations under the Covenant by privatizing governmental functions. The Committee takes the view that large-scale and systematic confiscation of Palestinian land and property by the State and the transfer of that property to these agencies*

[70] CESCR, General Comment 4, para 7.
[71] CESCR, General Comment 4, para 9.
[72] CESCR General Comment 4, para 10.
[73] Concluding Observations of the CESCR: Israel, 23/05/2003; UN Doc: E/C.12/1/Add.9, paras 16, 26 and 27.
[74] Ibid, UN Doc: E/C.12/1/Add.9, paras 12, 26, 27 and 28.

constitute an institutionalized form of discrimination because these agencies by definition would deny the use of these properties to non-Jews".[75]

The Committee also expressed its

"... deep concern that a significant proportion of Palestinian Arab citizens of Israel continue to live in unrecognized villages without access to water, electricity, sanitation and roads ... In addition, these villagers are continuously threatened with demolition of their home and confiscation of their land. ... In this connection, the Committee takes note that while Jewish settlements are constructed on a regular basis, no new Arab villages have been built in the Galilee".[76]

In addition, in 1998, the Committee expressed

"... grave concern about the situation of the Bedouin Palestinians settled in Israel. ... They have no access to water, electricity and sanitation and are subjected on a regular basis to land confiscations, house demolitions, fines for building 'illegally', destruction of agricultural fields and trees ...".[77]

VI. 2.2 Discrimination

The fundamental duty of a State to guarantee rights without discrimination is enshrined in the international human rights treaties, including the ICCPR (Article 2(1) and Article 26) and the ICESCR (Article 2(2)).

The International Convention on the Elimination of All Forms of Racial Discrimination (ICERD) forbids any discrimination in the exercise of the various rights, including the right to housing. Under Article 5(e)(iii):

"... States Parties undertake to prohibit and to eliminate racial discrimination in all its forms and to guarantee the right of everyone, without distinction as to race, colour, or national or ethnic origin, to equality before the law, notably in the enjoyment of ... economic, social and cultural rights, in particular ... the right to housing ..."

The CESCR has made clear that the duty to ensure the right to adequate housing applies to everyone without discrimination is not progressive, it is immediate. The Committee also clarified that:

"States must give due priority to those social groups living in unfavourable conditions by giving them particular consideration. Policies and legislation should correspondingly not be designed to benefit already advantaged social groups at the expense of others."[78]

Israel's housing and land policies violate the right of Israeli Arab citizens and of Palestinians in the Occupied Territories to non-discrimination.

In March 1998 the UN Committee on the Elimination of Racial Discrimination (CERD) called *"... for a halt to the demolition of Arab properties in East Jerusalem and for respect for property rights irrespective of the ethnic origin of*

[75] Ibid, UN Doc: E/C.12/1/Add.27, para 11.
[76] Ibid, UN Doc: E/C.12/1/Add.27, para 26.
[77] Ibid, UN Doc: E/C.12/1/Add.27, para 28.
[78] CERD, General Comment 4, paras 11 and 6; General Comment 3, para 1.

the owner." and expressed concern ". . . about ethnic inequalities, particularly those centring upon what are known as "unrecognized" Arab villages [in Israel]."[79]

VI. 2.3 Forced Eviction

Forced eviction is the *"permanent or temporary removal against their will of individuals, families and/or communities from the homes and/or land which they occupy, without the provision of, and access to appropriate forms of legal or other protections. The prohibition on forced evictions does not, however, apply to evictions carried out by force in accordance with the law and in conformity with the provisions of the International Convenants on Human Rights."*[80]

As mentioned, the right to adequate housing includes the right to security of tenure, including legal guarantees against forced eviction, harassment and other threats.[81]

Through forced eviction and the mass demolition of homes in the Occupied Territories and, to a lesser extent in Israel, the Israeli authorities have deliberately made tens of thousands of Palestinians and thousands of Israeli Arabs homeless just in the past few years.

Whether it justifies such action on grounds of "military/security needs" or whether such action is imposed as a form of collective punishment, or whether carried out in enforcement of planning regulations such large-scale forced evictions are inconsistent with the realization of the right to adequate housing. The obligation of the state under international law is that it must refrain from forced evictions.

The CESCR, in its General Comment 4 on the right to adequate housing, has clarified that it:

> *". . . considers that instances of forced eviction are prima facie incompatible with the requirements of the Covenant and can only be justified in the most exceptional circumstances, and in accordance with the relevant principles of international law."*[82]

In its General Comment 7, the Committee makes it clear that forced eviction and house demolition as a punitive measure are also inconsistent with the norms of the Covenant and with the provisions of the Geneva Conventions prohibiting the displacement of the civilian population and the destruction of private property.[83]

According to the Committee:

> *"States parties shall ensure, prior to carrying out any evictions, and particularly those involving large groups, that all feasible alternatives are explored in consultation*

[79] CERD/C/304/Add.45, paras.11 and 19.
[80] CESCR, General Comment 7, para 3.
[81] CESCR, General Comment 4, para 8(a).
[82] CESCR, General Comment 4, para 18.
[83] CESCR, General Comment 7, para 12.

with the affected persons, with a view to avoiding, or at least minimizing, the need to use force . . ."[84]

Forced evictions also constitute a violation of the privacy of the home. Article 17(1) and (2) of the ICCPR stipulates that:

1. No one shall be subjected to arbitrary or unlawful interference with his privacy, family, home or correspondence . . .

2. Everyone has the right to the protection of the law against such interference or attacks.

The issue of legal tenure is particularly relevant to the situation of the unrecognized Bedouin villages in the Negev, where the Israeli authorities dispute the Bedouins' claims to ownership of the land. A basic protection against forced eviction is to take measures to confer legal security of tenure on people who lack such protection.

Both the CESCR and the UN Commission on Human Rights (CHR) have called on states to provide legal tenure to those threatened with forced eviction.

The Committee lists various types of tenure, including informal settlements, and adds:

"notwithstanding the type of tenure, all persons should possess a degree of security of tenure which guarantees legal protection against forced eviction, harassment and other threats. States parties should consequently take immediate measures aimed at conferring legal security of tenure upon those persons and households currently lacking such protection, in genuine consultation with affected persons and groups."[85]

In its resolution on Forced Evictions in 1993, the CHR, stated that: *"the practice of forced eviction constitutes a gross violation of human rights, in particular the right to adequate housing"* and urged governments to *"confer legal security of tenure on all persons currently threatened with forced eviction and to adopt all necessary measures giving full protection against forced eviction, based upon effective participation, consultation and negotiation with affected persons or groups."*[86]

Forced evictions and demolitions of homes have not only violated the right to adequate housing, the rights to privacy, family and home and the right to the peaceful enjoyment of their possessions, but also have resulted in violations of the rights to life and to security of persons, guaranteed by Article 6 and 9 of the ICCPR. Several people have been killed or injured in the demolition of their homes or of nearby buildings or while protesting the demolitions.

---

84 CESCR, General Comment 7, para 13.
85 CESCR, General Comment 4, para 8(a).
86 CHR Resolution 1993/77: Forced Evictions, paras 1 and 3.

The UN Committee against Torture has expressed concern about Israeli policies on house demolitions which may, in certain instances, amount to cruel, inhuman or degrading treatment or punishment, in violation of Article 16 of the Convention against Torture and Other Cruel, Inhuman or Degrading Treatment or Punishment. The Committee called on the Israeli government to desist from the policy of such house demolition.[87]

VI. 2.4 Due Process and Right to Effective Remedy

Article 26 of the ICCPR stipulates that:

> *"All persons are equal before the law and are entitled without any discrimination to the equal protection of the law. In this respect, the law shall prohibit any discrimination and guarantee to all persons equal and effective protection against discrimination on any ground such as race, colour, sex, language, religion, political or other opinion, national or social origin, property, birth or other status."*

Article 17 of the ICCPR guarantees the right not to be subjected to arbitrary or unlawful interference with privacy, family and home, and the right to the protection of law against such interference.

The CESCR has stated that the right to adequate housing is at least consistent with the provision of legal remedies such as:

a) legal appeals aimed at preventing planned evictions or demolitions through the issuance of court-ordered injunctions;

b) legal procedures seeking compensation following an illegal eviction;. . .[88]

Article 2(3) of the ICCPR requires that States Parties, including Israel, ensure that any person whose rights or freedoms are violated has a right to an effective remedy, determined by a competent authority.

In the rare cases where advance warning of the intended eviction and demolition of a home or property has been given by Israeli authorities, in the overwhelming majority of cases lengthy and costly legal cases did not result in protection against demolition or redress for victims of house demolition. In most cases demolition of houses and destruction of land and other property is carried out without prior notice, leaving little if any recourse for the victims. Israeli courts, including the Supreme Court, have repeatedly sanctioned the Israeli army's demolition of homes as a measure of "deterrence", and the mass destruction of homes, land and other property on grounds of "military/security needs". In ruling that the Israeli army need not give advance warning before demolishing homes or other properties the Supreme Court has undermined the victims' right to due

[87] Conclusions and Recommendations of the Committee against Torture: Israel. 23/11/2001. CAT/C/XXVII/Concl.5 (paras 6.j and 7.g).

[88] CESCR, General Comment 4, para 17.

process. In cases of demolition of homes on grounds of lack of building permits, the courts have consistently failed to address discriminatory laws, planning regulations and enforcement practices which have resulted in house demolition.

VI. 3. International Humanitarian Law

As the Occupying Power, Israel is bound by the rules of the Fourth Geneva Convention. Israel retains and exercises effective control over the Occupied Territories. For example, Israeli soldiers carry out frequent arrests and searches in houses and other buildings throughout the Occupied Territories, in rural or urban areas, refugee camps, towns or villages, during the day or at night. The Israeli army routinely subjects the Palestinian population of the West Bank and Gaza Strip to curfews and other restrictions, and in the past three and a half years it has imposed a degree of control over the movement of Palestinians and foreigners throughout the West Bank and Gaza Strip unprecedented in the 37 years of occupation.

Israel is prohibited from attacking civilians and civilian objects. Palestinian residents of the West Bank and Gaza Strip are civilians benefiting from the protection of the Fourth Geneva Convention. Armed Palestinians who directly participate in hostilities—for example by shooting at Israeli soldiers or civilians—lose their protected status for the duration of the attack. Article 51(3) of Protocol I Additional to the Geneva Conventions of 1949, relating to the Protection of Victims of International Armed Conflicts (Protocol I) explains how civilian status can be temporarily lost. *"Civilians shall enjoy the protection afforded by this Section, unless and for such time as they take direct part in hostilities."* Palestinians engaged in armed clashes with Israeli forces are not combatants. They are civilians who lose their protected status for the duration of the armed engagement. They cannot be killed at any time other than while they are firing upon or otherwise posing an immediate threat to Israeli troops or civilians. Because they are not combatants, the fact that they participated in an armed attack at an earlier point cannot justify targeting them for death later on.

Similarly, there are no Palestinian objects in the Occupied Territories that meet the criteria of military objectives. Certain objects may be attacked while they are being used for firing upon Israeli forces. But they revert to their status as civilian objects as soon as they are no longer being used for launching attacks.

There has been considerable debate as to whether the violence in Israel and the Occupied Territories has reached a scale and intensity whereby the rules of international humanitarian law on the conduct of hostilities in international armed conflicts should apply, and if so to what extent. It may be argued that a few instances of fighting, such as the prolonged military operations in Jenin and Nablus in the spring of 2002, reached the requisite threshold. In such situations, international humanitarian law sets out standards of humane conduct applicable to both state forces and armed groups. These rules are codified in Protocol I, which applies to international armed conflicts including *"armed conflicts in which people are fighting against colonial domination and alien occupation and against racist regimes in the exercise of their rights of self-determination"* (Article 1(4) of Protocol I). The provisions of Protocol I concerning the protection of the civilian population are regarded as norms of customary international law. In the overwhelming majority of situations of destruction of property and eviction in the Occupied Territories, the applicable legal regime is the Fourth Geneva Convention and human rights standards—not conduct of hostilities standards.

In countering any armed attacks by Palestinians, Israeli forces are prohibited from responding with disproportionate force. The standards that should be applied in determining whether security forces have responded appropriately are those relevant to the use of firearms against members of the public.

VI. 3.1 Prohibition on Destruction of Property and Disproportionate Use of Force

As the Occupying Power, Israel is forbidden from destroying the property of Palestinians in the West Bank and Gaza Strip, unless it is militarily necessary to do so. Article 53 of the Fourth Geneva Convention stipulates that:

> *"Any destruction by the occupying power of real or personal property belonging individually or collectively to private persons, or to the State, or to other public authorities, or to social or co-operative organizations, is prohibited, except where such destruction is rendered absolutely necessary by military operations."*

The Commentary to the Convention is clear that the provision specifically applies to occupied territory.[89]

A similar provision is contained in Article 23(g) of the 1907 Hague Regulations. This Article stipulates that it is forbidden *"to destroy or seize the enemy's property unless such destruction or seizure be imperatively demanded by the necessities of war."*[90]

---

[89] "In order to dissipate any misconception in regard to the scope of Article 53, it must be pointed out that the property referred to is not accorded general protection; the Convention merely provides here for its protection in occupied territory."

[90] The Israeli army has referred to this article in its responses to Palestinian and Israeli NGOs (such as the Gaza-based Palestinian Center for Human Rights and the Jerusalem-based B'Tselem) about cases of destruction and seizure of Palestinian houses, land and other property. See copy of the Israeli army response to B'Tselem in the report *Israel's Policy of House Demolition and Destruction of Agricultural Land in the Gaza Strip*, February 2002, www.btselem.org.

The commentary to Article 53 of the Fourth Geneva Convention specifically notes that the Hague Regulations apply to situations that would not be covered under Article 53.[91]

And according to Article 147 of the Fourth Geneva Convention, *"extensive destruction and appropriation of property, not justified by military necessity and carried out unlawfully and wantonly"* is a grave breach, and hence, a war crime.

Military necessity *"means the necessity for measures which are essential to attain the goals of war, and which are lawful in accordance with the laws and customs of war.*[92] *. . . based on four foundations: urgency, measures which are limited to the indispensable, the control (in space and time) of the force used, and the means which should not infringe on an unconditional prohibition."*[93]

It should not be interpreted in a broad and vague manner which would undermine the fundamental norms of international human rights and humanitarian law, and measures intended to have long term preventative effects would thus not be justifiable on the grounds of absolute military necessity.

In the case of long-held occupied territory over which the occupying power exercises effective control, military necessity must be read extremely narrowly—in light of the concept of proportionality inherent in policing standards, rather than conduct of hostilities standards which should only apply in the course of actual armed conflict. As there are no permanent military objectives in the Occupied Territories, property can only be destroyed when it is absolutely unavoidable in the course of fighting or when absolutely necessary for lawful military purposes. Such purposes could include the removal of imminent threats to life, but would not include measures aimed at facilitating the expansion and consolidation of Israeli settlements in the Occupied Territories, which are illegal under international law. Even in cases where destruction or eviction may be justified on grounds of absolute necessity for military operations, Israel should consider less drastic alternatives. Demolitions and evictions should never be anything but a last resort. In the past three and half years the Israeli army has carried out extensive destruction of homes and properties throughout the West Bank and Gaza which is not justified by military necessity. Some of these acts of destruction amount to grave breaches of the Fourth Geneva Convention and are war crimes.

---

[91] "It will be remembered that Article 23(g) of the Hague Regulations forbids the unnecessary destruction of enemy property; since that rule is placed in the section entitled "hostilities," it covers all property in the territory involved in a war; its scope is therefore much wider than that of the provision under [Article 53]."

[92] ICRC, Commentary on Protocol I, p. 393.

[93] Ibid, p. 396.

VI. 3.2 Prohibition on Collective Punishment

The Fourth Geneva Convention specifically prohibits collective punishment. Its Article 33 stipulates: *"No protected person may be punished for an offence he or she has not personally committed. Collective penalties and likewise all measures of intimidation or of terrorism are prohibited."* As explained in the authoritative commentary of the ICRC: *"This paragraph then lays a prohibition on collective penalties . . . penalties of any kind inflicted on persons or entire groups of persons, in defiance of the most elementary principles of humanity, for acts that these persons have not committed."*[94]

The *Handbook of Humanitarian Law in Armed Conflict*, a respected interpretative guide to international humanitarian law, interprets the prohibition on collective punishment as follows:

> *"Collective penalties and all measures of intimidation and terrorism carried out by the occupying power have only one purpose: to make the population of the occupied territory submissive. Such measures may take different forms, such as a curfew preventing the inhabitants from fulfilling their daily duties, punishment or detention of several members of a group or family for an alleged offense by one member, or the destruction of the house belonging to the family of an alleged offender. Such acts are prohibited, without exception, by Article* 33 [of the Fourth Geneva Convention]".[95]

The prohibition on collective punishment is also a cardinal rule of human rights law.[96] The recently accelerated Israeli practice of demolishing houses owned by relatives of suicide bombers or other Palestinian armed attackers is a blatant form of collective punishment, but the phenomenon also is expressed in other ways. Collective penalties include such measures as attacking an entire community in retaliation for acts committed by members of that community, or arbitrarily restricting the movement of an entire population. The logic of collective punishment is encapsulated by the words of Major-General Doron Almog of the Israeli army who, when reporting that houses in the Rafah refugee camp had been destroyed in retaliation for an attack on an Israeli army post, explained: *"most of our operations have focused on the Rafah area, as that is where the two Hamas terrorists came from."*[97]

[94] ICRC, Commentary: IV Geneva Convention Relative to the Protection of Civilian Persons in Time of War, p. 225. (Geneva: ICRC, 1958).

[95] Dieter Fleck (ed.), *The Handbook of Humanitarian Law in Armed Conflict*, p. 249.

[96] Notably General Comment 29 on Article 4 of the ICCPR.

[97] Major-General Doron Almog. Officer Commander (OC) Southern Command (Gaza Strip), speaking to the Israeli TV Channel 2's "Meet the Press", as quoted by the Jerusalem Post of 13 January 2002.

VII. Recommendations

TO THE ISRAELI AUTHORITIES:

Concerning punitive house demolition, described as "deterrent"

- The demolition of the homes of relatives of Palestinians known or suspected of involvement in suicide bombings or other attacks against Israeli civilians and soldiers violates international law and should stop immediately.
- All those whose homes have been demolished on such grounds should receive full reparation, including adequate compensation, as should those whose homes have been incidentally demolished or damaged in the course of such demolition operations.

Concerning destruction of properties claimed to be for other "military/ security needs"

- The destruction of houses, land, and other properties without absolute military necessity as prescribed by international humanitarian law should stop immediately.
- The law must be amended in a manner so as to require that, except during the actual conduct of military operations or armed confrontations which make the destruction absolutely necessary, no demolition should be carried out without prior notification to the concerned parties, who should be given adequate time and opportunity to challenge before an independent and impartial court of law any order for the demolition of a house or the destruction of land or other property. Legal aid must be provided to those unable to afford counsel. The current practice of destruction and eviction without prior notice must stop immediately.
- All those whose properties have been unlawfully destroyed without adequate prior notification and the effective opportunity to challenge the decision before a court of law should receive reparation and be allowed, where possible, to rebuild their properties in the same place.
- The creation and expansion of Israeli civilian settlements in the Occupied Territories and infrastructure to support them, including roads, violates international law. Israel must cease and prohibit the destruction of houses, land or other properties for these purposes.
- Measures must be taken to evacuate Israeli civilians living in settlements in the Occupied Territories, in such a manner as to ensure the human rights of Palestinians are respected, in particular their rights to free movement and to an adequate standard of living. Such measures

should include respect for the rights of the Israeli citizens evacuated, including adequate compensation.

- Israel must stop construction of the wall/fence *within* the Occupied Territories, remove what has already been constructed within the Occupied Territories, restore seized property, and ensure reparation for land and property seized, confiscated or destroyed.
- The Israeli army should keep and publish accurate records of property destroyed or damaged. Such reporting should be part of the required operational debrief following any military operation. The records should also include detailed information about the circumstances of the damage or destruction of each property.
- A judicial commission of inquiry should be established to investigate all the cases of destruction, confiscation and damage to property carried out by the Israeli army in the Occupied Territories since October 2000, in order to establish the extent of the damage caused and the necessary reparation. The commission should also investigate the legality, according to international law, of the grounds that the army claims rendered the destruction necessary.
- Israel should invite the international community to deploy qualified and experienced observers in the Occupied Territories to monitor the conduct of the Israeli army, Palestinian armed groups and Palestinian security forces. Such independent, expert observers should report publicly on the conduct of all parties in light of international law, including in relation to destruction of and damage to property. The observers should be granted free and unhindered access within the Occupied Territories and to relevant documentation in order to conduct thorough and impartial investigations, including forensic investigation.

Concerning the demolition of unlicensed houses in the Occupied Territories

- Israel should cancel all demolition orders of unlicensed houses in the Occupied Territories.
- Responsibility for planning and building policies and regulations in the Occupied Territories should be removed from the Israeli authorities and placed solely with the local Palestinian communities.
- All those whose properties have been destroyed in violation of international law should be granted effective redress. Israel should ensure reparation to those whose houses were unlawfully destroyed.

Concerning the demolition of unlicensed houses in Israel

- All outstanding orders for forced evictions and demolitions should be cancelled and a moratorium should be placed on future forced evictions and demolitions until such time as the law is amended in a manner that complies with international standards.

- Laws and policies governing the zoning and allocation of land must be amended immediately. Provisions which are discriminatory must be repealed or amended. Laws and policies must be implemented in a manner that respects the prohibition on discrimination on grounds including race, religion, national or ethnic origin and descent.
- Legal recognition/status should be granted immediately to the unrecognized villages. Legal security of tenure should be afforded to the residents of these unrecognized villages. Sustainable access to safe, potable drinking water, electricity, sanitation, sewage, refuse disposal, emergency services, medical care and education must be guaranteed to all residents. Efforts to forcibly remove the inhabitants of unrecognized villages should be immediately halted.
- Israel should ensure access to effective redress and reparation to those who have had their homes demolished.

TO THE PALESTINIAN AUTHORITY:

- The PA should take all possible measures to prevent attacks by Palestinian armed groups and individuals against Israeli civilians in the Occupied Territories and inside Israel.
- The PA should take all possible measures to ensure that Palestinian armed groups and individuals do not initiate armed confrontations from residential civilian areas.
- The PA should support the call on the international community to deploy qualified and experienced observers in the Occupied Territories to monitor the conduct of the Israeli army, Palestinian armed groups and Palestinian security forces, and should undertake to grant full cooperation to any observers who may be deployed in the areas of the Occupied Territories which are under its jurisdiction, including access to relevant documentation necessary for any investigations, including forensic investigation.

TO THE INTERNATIONAL COMMUNITY:

- The International community and states parties to international human rights and humanitarian law treaties to which Israel is a party must take steps to ensure Israel's compliance with its obligations under international law.
- States, particularly the USA, should stop the sale or transfer of weaponry and equipment that are used to commit unlawful destruction of homes and other serious violations of international human rights and

humanitarian law, until they secure guarantees that Israeli forces will not use the equipment to commit violations.

- Governments and agencies which have been involved in funding or carrying out development projects and emergency assistance should carry out and make public assessments to determine if and to what extent their projects/programs have been adversely affected by the Israeli policy of destruction of properties.

TO CATERPILLAR Inc.

- Caterpillar Inc., the US company which produces the bulldozers used by the Israeli army, should take measures—within the company sphere of influence—to guarantee that its bulldozers are not used to commit human rights violations, including the destruction of homes, land and other properties.
- Caterpillar should adopt a code of conduct which complies with the UN Human Rights Norms for Business and should respect and ensure the application of Article 3 of the UN Norms, which states that Trans National Corporations and other business enterprises shall not engage in, nor benefit from, war crimes, crimes against humanity and other violation of international humanitarian law. In particular commentary (a) to Article 3 also states that Trans National Corporations and other business enterprises shall take stringent measures to prevent any products or services which they produce or supply from being used to commit violations of international human rights or humanitarian law and to comply with evolving best practices in this regard.

DOCUMENT NO. 12

TWO YEARS AFTER LONDON: RESTARTING PALESTINIAN ECONOMIC RECOVERY

World Bank Report

September 24, 2007

Acronyms

AHLC	Ad-Hoc Liaison Committee
AMA	Agreement on Movement and Access
CG	Consultative Group
COGAT	Coordinator of Government Activities in the Palestinian Territories
EC	European Commission
EU	European Union
GDP	gross domestic product
GNP	gross national product
GoI	Government of Israel
ICA	Investment Climate Assessment
IMF	International Monetary Fund
LACS	Local Aid Coordination Secretariat
MENA	Middle East and North Africa
MOF	Ministry of Finance
MOP	Ministry of Planning
MTEF	Medium-Term Expenditure Framework
MTIT	Ministry of Telecommunications and Information Technology
NGO	non-governmental organization
ODA	official development assistance
PA	Palestinian National Authority
PCBS	Palestinian Central Bureau of Statistics
PRDP	Palestinian Reform and Development plan

PER	Public Expenditure Review
PLC	Palestinian Legislative Council
PMA	Palestinian Monetary Authority
PWA	Palestinian Water Authority
QR	Quartet Representative
SWG	Sector Working Group
TA	technical assistance
UNRWA	United Nations Relief and Works Agency
UNSCO	Office of the United Nations Special Coordinator
VAT	Value-Added Tax
WB&G	West Bank and Gaza

Acknowledgements

This Economic Monitoring Note derives as much from its economic analysis as from the consultative process through which it was prepared. To ensure that the report reflects to the extent possible the views of all involved parties, approximately two months of intensive consultations were carried out with a vast spectrum of Palestinian, Israeli and international officials and agencies. Where possible, their inputs have been incorporated into the analysis. And where the World Bank's analysis and conclusions differed, every effort was made to reflect these varying views in the footnotes to the text.

We are grateful for the inputs and guidance of H.E. Prime Minister Salam Fayyad and the Ministries of Finance and Planning, as well as the Office of H.E. President Mahmoud Abbas. In addition, the feedback of the following institutions is gratefully acknowledged: Palestinian Investment Fund (PIF), Palestinian Monetary Authority (PMA), PLO Negotiations Affairs Department (NAD), Palestinian Federation of Industries (PFI), PalTrade, Palestinian Private Sector Coordination Council (PSCC), Palestinian Shippers' Council (PSC), various Palestinian private sector leaders in Gaza, Palestinian Central Bureau of Statistics (PCBS), Palestinian Center for Policy and Survey Research (PSR), and the Public Administration and Civil Service Reform Project Team (PACSR).

The inputs and feedback of the Israeli authorities also greatly benefited this report. We are grateful to the Ministry of Foreign Affairs, the Ministry of Justice, and the Office of the Coordinator of Government Activities in the Territories (COGAT) for their cooperation throughout the drafting of this report.

Last but not least, we gratefully acknowledge the inputs and feedback of the following international and donor agencies, and NGOs, with particular thanks to the International Monetary Fund (IMF) and the UN Office of the

Coordinator of Humanitarian Affairs (OCHA) who provided significant analysis for this report. In addition, we note with appreciation the inputs of the European Commission (EC), EU Temporary International Mechanism (TIM), UK Department for International Development (DfID), Office of the Quartet Representative, U.S. Consulate General, U.S. Agency for International Development (USAID), Norwegian Representative's Office, Canadian International Development Agency (CIDA), UN Special Coordinator (UNSCO), UN Relief and Works Agency (UNRWA), Portland Trust, Development Alternatives Inc. (DAI), International Crisis Group (ICG), Oxfam International, B'Tselem, Bimkom, and Campaign for the Right of Entry/ Re-Entry.

Executive Summary

1. At the 2005 AHLC meeting in London, the World Bank issued a report examining progress over the previous year, and reiterating the already-known preconditions for growth without which donor assistance would not yield lasting results. These are: (1) a drastic improvement in the security environment; (2) dismantling restrictions on the movement of Palestinian people and goods; and (3) clear progress on Palestinian reform and institution-building. In recognition of these widely accepted preconditions, the AHLC called for parallel and reinforcing actions by the Palestinian Authority (PA), the Government of Israel (GoI) and the donors.

2. This report evaluates the progress made since London in meeting the preconditions for a virtuous cycle of growth, and the changing circumstances in which these preconditions continue to apply. It also seeks to reflect some of the lessons learned over the past few years in the hope of influencing the concrete policies that are necessary, looking forward to the proposed Donor Conference in December, to revive the Palestinian economy and the overall peace process.

Economic and Fiscal Events

3. The decline of the Palestinian economy since the Second *Intifada* has left per capita GDP at $1,129 in 2006, about a third less than its level of $1,612 in 1999. The emerging recovery in 2003–2005 was again reversed in 2006 as a result of the fiscal crisis following the Palestinian Legislative Council (PLC) elections.

4. More troubling than the negative growth rates over the past few years is the changing composition of the economy, as GDP is being increasingly driven by government and private consumption from remittances and donor aid, while investment has fallen to exceedingly low levels, leaving little productive base for a self-sustaining economy.

5. Furthermore, the West Bank and Gaza (WB&G) faces an expanding labor force and a shrinking private sector. Thus, the public sector has become the only alternative for jobs. With few options at its disposal, and despite an unsustainable wage bill, the PA has resorted to absorbing workers as a way to alleviate poverty. At the same time, many workers have been hired as part of a trend to bolster political support. As a result, public sector employment has grown by 60% since 1999 and by 2006 stood at about 157,800. The current Caretaker Government has sought to roll this back by not paying 31,000 civil servants and security personnel hired illegally since the end of 2005. However, the PA may find it politically challenging to reduce the workforce any further.

6. Thus, while the public sector has expanded, the economy's productive capability has begun to hollow out making it increasingly donor dependent. While borrowing, remittances and increased aid outside key institutions of the PA managed to prevent a collapse in GDP in 2006, output in the productive sectors declined. Public investment to maintain or add infrastructure has nearly ceased and in the last two years almost all government funds have been used to pay salaries and cover operating costs. The IMF estimates that already-low private investment declined by over 15% between 2005 and 2006.

7. Adding to this, unpredictability of the border crossings and chechpoints has prevented Palestinian businesses from importing inputs and exporting products in a timely and planned manner. In response, enterprises have closed and large amounts of financial and human capital have fled. The pace of capital flight has reached an all-time high in the last two years with almost no foreign direct investment and most local capital being kept abroad or invested in real estate or short term trading activities.

8. The social impacts of the past few years are no less significant. Health indicators have seen a steady drop over the last three years. Chronic diseases have surged 31% since 2005. Chronic malnutrition among children under five jumped 3% between 2004 and 2006. The number of households with safe drinking water has also dropped by over 8% between 2000 and 2007. The quality of education and enrollment are also declining. The increasing insecurity, especially in the Gaza strip, is impacting the performance of students: failure rates in mathematics and Arabic are nearly 80% and 40%, respectively. Furthermore, the continuing conflict is perpetuating an internal cycle of violence, fragmenting social cohesion and affecting psychosocial well-being. A 2006 survey concluded that nearly three quarters of Palestinians suffer from severe depression. Women, who historically play a key role as income providers, are increasingly relegated to the informal market as a result of movement and access restrictions. Their participation in the labor market, at 15.2%, is amongst the lowest in the world. Also, since September 2000, youth have been caught literally and figuratively

in the crossfire of the conflict. Nearly 75% of the injured during the second *Intifada* were between 10 to 29 years old. Youth also suffer from high rates of unemployment (60%).

9. The PA has sought to deliver services to an increasingly dependent population, and to compensate for a dwindling private sector. The PA's longstanding fiscal crisis deepened in 2006 as a result of GoI's withholding of Palestinian clearance revenues and the aid boycott, resulting in a deficit of over $1 billion. Yet, wages and non-wage operating costs, transfers, and spending on utilities and energy continued to grow despite the drop in funding. The PA's financial position continues to deteriorate at an increasing rate in 2007. In the first half of 2007, the deficit was $100 million a month. Even after Israel's decision in June 2007 to release withheld clearance revenues, the wage bill currently exceeds government revenues. This is further impacted by the PA's limited ability to increase domestic revenues given the loss in value-added tax (VAT) and customs duties from the suspension of Gaza trade.

10. As such, nearing the end of 2007, the PA finds itself with a large deficit, a significant stock of arrears and falling revenues. External assistance has been unusually high in 2007; nearly $450 million has been received in the first half of the year. Looking forward, the PA forecasts a need for at least $1.62 billion in donor assistance per year to close the fiscal gap, of which 94% will go to meet recurrent expenditure needs as opposed to development aid.

A Note on Gaza

11. From the outset, Gaza has been hit harder by closures and economic crises. Gaza's economic backbone and private sector vitality risks collapse if the current closure policy after Hamas' June 14th takeover of the Strip continues. Recent calls by various parties for the entry of solely humanitarian goods are a necessary but insufficient condition for the survival of the Gaza economy. However, a sustainable solution must include commercial imports and exports, considering that over 54% of employment in Gaza is private sector-driven (representing more than 100,000 jobs). Of these, 35,000 workers—18,000 skilled—operate the industrial sector. According to the Palestinian Private Sector Coordination Council (PSCC), the current restrictions have led to the suspension of 90% of Gaza's industrial operations.

12. The likely lay-off of over 30,000 industrial workers, resulting from the current restrictions, would translate into an unprecedented private sector-driven unemployment level of about 44% in Gaza. The impacts of these closures will become more difficult to reverse. Most Gaza industries are export-oriented and have purchase and supply contracts with Israeli and other firms. Gaza manufacturers import 95% of their inputs. About 76% of their furniture products, 90% of their garments and 20% of their food products

are exported to Israel, and some to the West Bank. Employment in construction and building has also been impacted by the suspension and cancellation of most construction projects due to lack of construction materials. Also, 5,000 Gazan farmers depend on the export of cash crops. Israeli and other suppliers and purchasers needing to maintain their operations will soon cancel contracts and seek alternative supply chains elsewhere.

13. At the same time, the Hamas control of Gaza is incurring a direct negative impact on the economy. Without delving into the political context of the current stalemate, it is evident that Hamas also bears responsibility for creating a political and logistical environment in which all sides can reengage in Gaza. Furthermore, it must be noted that attacks on the crossings continue to take place, greatly undermining any efforts to shield Gaza's population and private sector from the impacts of the current situation.

Progress Since the 2005 AHLC: Revisiting the Preconditions

Movement and Access

14. The main challenge for Palestinian economic recovery remains the comprehensive restrictions on movement and access imposed by GoI, which go beyond concrete and checkpoints to a complex matrix of restrictive policies and administrative procedures that combine to stunt Palestinian economic growth. Beyond movement within and across the Palestinian Territories, these policies and procedures also restrict access to domestic and international markets, water and other natural resources, and donor-financed projects for approximately 60% of the West Bank (Areas C).

15. While there is consensus on the legitimacy of Israel's security concerns, it is difficult to reconcile this with the clear correlation between access restrictions and the protection and expansion of Israeli settlement activity in the West Bank. The commitments entered into by Israel under the 2005 Agreement on Movement and Access (AMA) remain as unfulfilled as they are critical. The AMA must be implemented immediately; the loosening of restrictions on people and products is a long-term source of stability, not a consequence of it.

Palestinian Governance

16. The combined shocks of the last two years have endangered many Palestinian institutional gains. The refusal of the Hamas-led PA to meet the Quartet conditions, and the international reaction to the PLC elections have marginalized the legislative branch as a potential multi-party platform for policy-setting and for balance with the executive branch. Also, efforts at imposing law and order, reforming the executive and judicial branches of

government and conducting the normal day-to-day operation of government have been frustrated by factional fighting and paralysis of the PLC.

17. However, the formation of the June 14th Emergency Government and later the Caretaker Government has opened the door to return to a path of reform. In terms of law and order, the resumption of high-level security coordination between the Caretaker Government and the GoI offers an opportunity for coordinated approaches.

18. On the fiscal front, the Caretaker Government has begun to reverse the impacts of 2006–07 and the legacy of its past spending practices. The PA has successfully rehabilitated parts of the Public Financial Management system, including reconsolidating the Single Treasury Account (STA), preparing a budget for 2007 and reversing some staffing additions of early 2005 and onward. The preparation of the 2008–10 Palestinian Reform and Development Plan will begin to address longstanding disconnects in policy-making, planning and budgeting processes.

19. Moving forward, the Government's prospects for success will depend on the credibility of its national policy agenda, including pragmatic plans to put the PA on the path to fiscal sustainability. These include re-linking PA institutions between the West Bank and Gaza, reforming its human resources, tackling intergovernmental fiscal relations and the spiraling municipal needs and rationalizing spending in the social sectors to ensure the sustainability of these services to the population. Reform of the pension system is a key priority in this regard. The August 27th, 2007 decree modifying previous pension laws does not tackle an insolvent pension system with substantial implicit liabilities for the PA. The PA's success will also depend on sufficient and predictable external assistance, including budget support, and a strong recovery of private economic activity. Both Israel and donors have a role to play.

The Donor Response and Strategies

20. Aid flows into the WB&G have been considerable, but remain fragmented and focused on bilateral arrangements with donors based on short-term political positions rather than a collective, longer-term view on broader economic and governance fundamentals. Thus, aid has not been governed by a longer-term Palestinian development agenda, nor has it been matched by parallel actions by the PA and the GoI to create an environment where funds translate into sustainable growth.

21. Aid has been reactive and lacking levers to encourage or enable institution-building or to create powerful incentives to reform. In addition, the hollowing out of the Palestinian economy has risked reversing the benefits of over $10 billion in past aid, and has diverted funds to recurrent expenditures

and basic lifeline humanitarian support rather than to an investment in building effective Palestinian institutions and infrastructure.

22. Donors have long been aware of this issue, hence the establishment of multilateral financing mechanisms and new aid coordination bodies at the last AHLC in London. However, the effectiveness of these structures was undermined by the aid boycott. Going forward, these aid coordination bodies must be revitalized. The presence of the new Quartet Representative, and his leveraging of these structures, could strengthen them considerably. Also, donor commitment to the Palestinian Reform and Development Plan 2008–10 will be a key test of their support of Palestinian-driven institution-building, recovery and growth.

The Way Forward

23. Moving forward, the restoration of growth and peace will require all sides not only to return to the preconditions for economic recovery, but to take actions collectively and in parallel, in view of the longer-term benefits and not only the short-term costs. Experience over the past 15 years has shown that only parallel actions on the issues outlined in this report will lead to tangible results.

24. The viability of the PA is a precondition for a lasting recovery and peace. For the PA to be viable, it must restore law and order and become fiscally self-sufficient. Continued donor investment in and through PA institutions must be based on economic considerations and bolster a commitment by the Government to the reforms noted in this report, not be conditioned on it. Similarly, the PA's reform agenda must clearly and realistically reflect a finite horizon of aid dependency.

25. GoI actions on Palestinian movement and access must also reflect a clear policy on settlement activity, and a view of the removal of these restrictions as a major catalyst for stability, and not a consequence of it. In addition to the private sector, Israeli restrictions also impede the functions of the Palestinian public sector. The PA is obliged to administer a series of isolated territories despite complex obstacles in coordinating government policy, administrative procedures, service delivery and law enforcement.

26. However, any discussion on economic recovery and peace is incomplete without the Gaza Strip. Gaza represents about 40% of the population and a quintessential part of the Palestinian territory, economy and identity. Thus, any serious options for a private-sector led and export-oriented Palestinian economy must include Gaza. Without it, the collective investments and commitments advocated in this report are unlikely to materialize due to continued uncertainties about the sustainability and inclusiveness of Palestinian institutions.

27. Whether practical or not under the current circumstances, the need for these parallel steps is evident. These are the fundamentals of economic growth, and draw on the basics that guide all economies. Without them, all well-intentioned and creative solutions, policies and investments are undermined. The implication of this view is that all parties will need to expend more resources and assume more risks than they have done in the past. Perhaps this is best referred to as an investment in peace. The costs are subjective to each side, and are beyond the scope of this report. But the benefits of success make this an investment worth making.

1. Introduction

1. *On December 14th, 2005, the members of the Ad-Hoc Liaison Committee (AHLC) gathered in London to take stock of progress since the previous meeting in Oslo, and to chart a path for Palestinian economic development* to underpin a lasting peace in the region.[1] There, the World Bank issued a report examining progress over the previous year, and reiterating the already-known preconditions for growth without which donor assistance would not yield lasting results. These are: (1) a drastic improvement in the security environment; (2) dismantling restrictions on the movement of Palestinian people and goods; and (3) clear progress on Palestinian reform and institution-building. These were outlined in a matrix of Indicators of Economic Revival to anchor these preconditions in a qualitative analysis.

2. *Much analysis has been devoted to the events since 2005. And deservedly so, as their impacts on a frail Palestinian economy are clear and acute.* However, they also represent a new digression since the Second *Intifada* that masks the persistent challenge facing the three partners to Palestinian recovery and the peace process. The key remains the parallel fulfillment by the Palestinian Authority (PA), the Government of Israel (GOI) and the donors of commitments and investments towards viable Palestinian institutions and a healthy private sector.

3. *The path of Palestinian economic recovery has been at risk long before the events of the last two years, with a confluence of policies and actions that have unraveled many successes, and that are stripping the Palestinian economy of any capacity of self-sufficiency and growth.* In 1968, an average Israeli citizen was 10 times wealthier than an average Palestinian in the West Bank and Gaza (WB&G). Today, Israeli per capita GDP is more than 20 times that of the Palestinians. Two-thirds of Palestinians are below the poverty line. Even within the Palestinian Territories, Gaza is witnessing a dramatic drop in incomes and well-being, amplifying an economic rift.

[1] See Annex 1 for the statement of the 2005 AHLC Chair.

To claim that this growing rift among two worlds separated by a wall is a result of intentional Israeli or donor actions, or that Palestinian and Israeli development are a 'zero-sum' game, would be false. What is true, however, is that the investment in peace and prosperity has been far from complete.

4. *The calling together of the AHLC coincides with a time of new momentum for the restoration of Palestinian recovery, and for a revisiting of the practices of the past.* The continued commitment of donors to the Palestinian people is evident, and the current positive steps taken by the Israeli and Palestinian Governments towards a return to the peace agenda are commendable. As such, the AHLC offers an opportunity to explore the preconditions for a return to sustainable development driven by Palestinian institutions.

5. *The good news is that all sides are aware of what is needed. The less positive news is that this involves much financial and political capital. The precondition for success is that parallel actions must be taken by all sides to trigger a virtuous cycle of growth and peace.* This fact is embedded in the view that the actions of one side directly impact the success of the others. Hence, the previous and politically simpler concept of sequencing will need revisiting. The success of Palestinian reform and political stability relies on immediate and free movement and access, a healthy private sector, and predictable donor assistance. The impact of donor assistance depends on critical PA reforms. Israel's facilitation of Palestinian movement requires realistic assurances of law and order. Another precondition relates to the situation in Gaza, without which a discussion of Palestinian restoration would at best be incomplete if not temporary.

6. *This report evaluates the progress made since 2005 in creating the preconditions for a virtuous cycle of growth* without which actions will yield few lasting results.

2. Events since London

2.1 Economic and Fiscal Events

7. *The past two years since the London AHLC have witnessed a sequence of events that have at best retarded—and at worst, reversed—the precarious course of Palestinian institutional development and economic growth.* The international response to the victory of Hamas in Parliamentary elections in early 2006 heralded an almost instant drop in services and incomes, and a polarizing effect on the populations of Gaza and the West Bank as access to incomes, donor assistance and crossings diverged (See Annex 6 for a summary of events since January 2006). At the same time, Gaza saw the brunt of Israeli restrictions and military action after the abduction of an Israeli soldier in the summer of 2006. Since London, Palestinians killed in

conflict-related incidents rose from 210 in 2005 to 673 in 2006, and another 146 by June 2007. This does not include a new figure—400 Palestinians dead in 2007 from internecine fighting between Palestinian factions—more than double those killed by the conflict with Israel. Over the same period, Israel witnessed 25 deaths in 2006 and 6 deaths in 2007, from various attacks including Qassam Rockets which have exceeded 2,700 since 2004. Palestinians injured over the two years reached more than 4,200, and Israelis injured more than 500.[2]

8. ***The decline of the Palestinian economy triggered by the Second Intifada in 2000 and compounded by recent events has left per capita GDP at $1,129 by the end of 2006, about a third less than it is level of $1,612 in 1999.*** The emerging recovery in 2003–2005 was again reversed in 2006 as a result of the fiscal crisis, and movement and access restrictions, following the Hamas victory in the PLC elections (Figure 1). GDP contracted by nearly 8.8% in 2006, and by a further 4.2% in the first quarter of 2007. This trend appears to be continuing in the second half of 2007.

9. ***More troubling than the negative growth rate is the changing composition of the economy, as GDP*** is being increasingly driven by government and private consumption from remittances and donor aid, while investment has fallen to exceedingly low levels, leaving little of the productive base needed for a self-sustaining economy.

10. ***From the outset, Gaza has been hit harder by closures and economic crisis.*** Since Israel's disengagement from Gaza in September 2005, its borders

Figure 1: Economic Growth 1999–2007

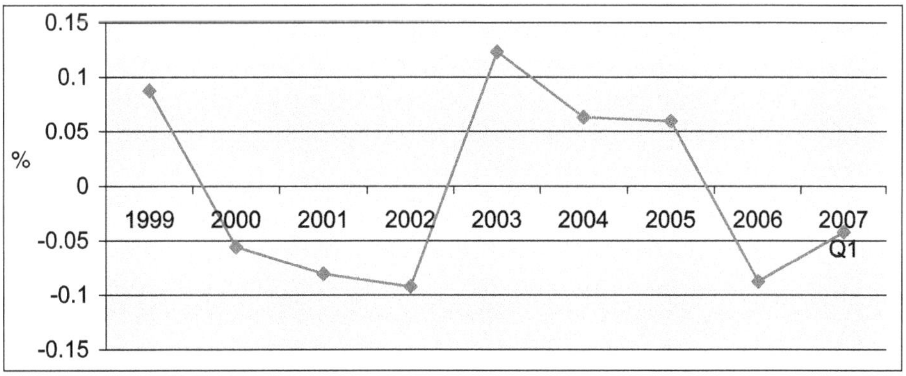

Source: PCBS and World Bank Staff Calculations.

[2] Source: OCHA, oPt Protection of Civilians Summary, June 2007.

Figure 2: Official Unemployment WB and Gaza

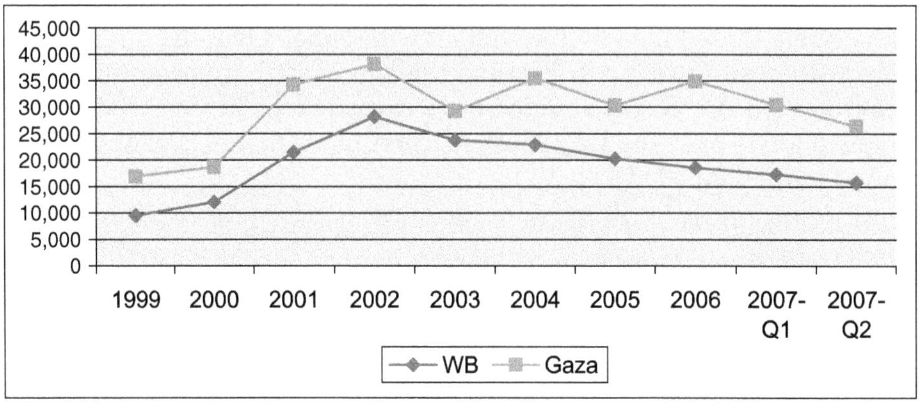

Source: PCBS Labor Force Servey.

have been closed for extended periods, inhibiting trade and the movement of people. Unemployment in Gaza rose from 30.3% in 2005 to almost 35% in 2006 (Figure 2), while unemployment in the West Bank actually fell from 20.3 to 18.6%. In the first half of 2007, unemployment fell in both regions. But these figures are misleading. First, as a result of the fiscal crisis and its impacts on both public sector employees and private sector contractors, employment did not always translate into a regular salary payment. Furthermore, Gaza's unemployment rates were mitigated by temporary employment programs by UNRWA and others, which inject badly-needed funds but also conceal structural problems in the job market. Also, official unemployment data excludes workers who turn to unpaid family labor or seasonal agriculture to make up for lost jobs.[3] Thirdly, the figures do not include many discouraged workers who have left the labor market because they can not find employment. PCBS estimates that adding discouraged and underemployed workers would raise the 2006 unemployment rate in the West Bank to 28% and over 39% in Gaza.

11. A better measure of the extent of the crisis is the poverty rate, which has dramatically increased in the last two years. Despite large inflows of aid, the percentage of Gazans who live in deep poverty has been steadily increasing, rising from 21.6% in 1998 to nearly 35% in 2006.[4] With the continued economic decline in 2007 and the implementation of even more strict closures on Gaza the current poverty rate is almost certainly higher.

[3] In 2006 PCBS estimates that 11.1% of employed workers were unpaid family members.

[4] PCBS constructed the deep poverty line to reflect a budget for food, clothing and housing. For a family of six the deep poverty line in 2006 was NIS 1,837.

This rate reflects actual consumption, which implies that without remittances and food aid the poverty rate is closer to *67%*. The increase in poverty in the West Bank has been lower but still significant (Figure 3).

12. ***Adding to the downturn in the Palestinian economy is the reduction in the number of workers allowed in Israel.*** Population growth in WB&G is around 3.3% per annum; making it one of the highest rates in the world and creating an ever larger labor force. Israeli closure policies and political instability have discouraged investment in WB&G, making Palestinian private sector absorption of the labor force impossible. As such, the large surplus of Palestinian labor flocked to the Israeli economy where, throughout most of the last 40 years, they have received relatively higher wages than in WB&G. However, since the *Second Intifada,* Israel has been steadily reducing the number of permits for Palestinians to work in Israel, with the expressed goal of eliminating them in the near future.[5] The number of Palestinians working in Israel or its settlements has thus declined by nearly 55%

Figure 3: Deep Proverty 1998–2006

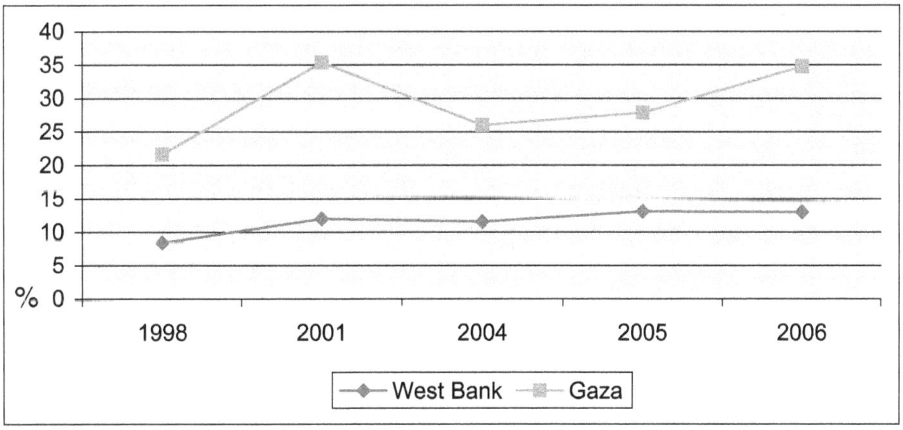

Source: PCBS unpublished estimates based on 6th Palestinian Expenditure and Consumption Servey.

[5] The Israeli Ministry of Justice asserts that "The report notes that Palestinian links to the Israeli economy have driven up labor costs, without referring to the need to examine alternatives to these links, such as Palestinian employment in other regional states. In some of its previous reports, the World Bank began to recommend that Palestinian economy and labor look outside the Israeli market, and suggested that these options be examined. However, these states have systematically refused to employ Palestinians or establish joint industrial areas. It is strongly suggested that this report to the donors follow up on this broader and more realistic economic view, and enhance these recommendations." This assertion, however, does not address the impacts of Israel's policies on the mobility of Palestinian labor and on its growing dependence on Israeli labor markets since 1967. As such, a phased approach is required for such fundamental structural changes, matched with removal of restrictions against labor mobility.

Figure 4: Share of WB&G Labor Force in Israel or Settlement

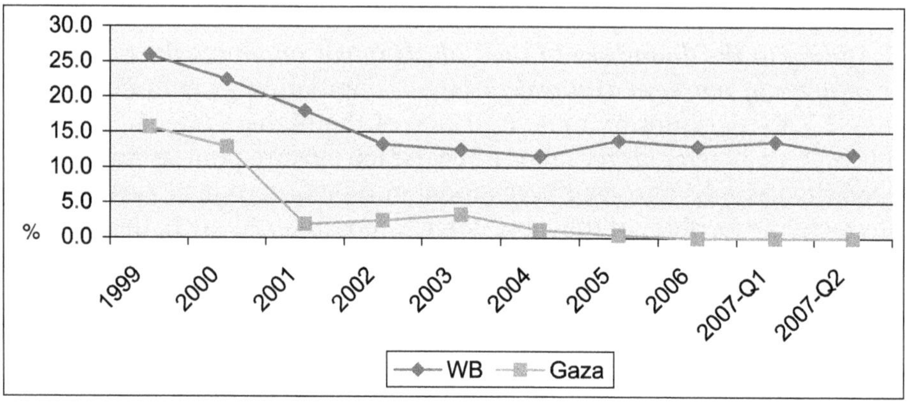

Source: PCBS 2006 Labor Force Servey.

since 1999.[6] The share of the work force employed in Israel has fallen from 23% to less than 10%.[7] All of these are from the West Bank as Gaza is now completely closed and no workers from Gaza are allowed into Israel (Figure 4). The loss of these relatively high paying jobs has been a devastating blow to the Palestinian economy and is a major factor in the growing poverty.

13. ***The WB&G faces an expanding labor force and a shrinking private sector. Thus, the civil service and security forces have become the only alternative for jobs.*** With few options at its disposal, and despite an unsustainable wage bill, the PA has resorted to absorbing workers as a way to alleviate poverty. At the same time, many workers have historically been hired to bolster political support. As a result, the public sector has grown by 60% since 1999 and in May 2007 stood at 168,319. The Caretaker Government has sought to roll this back by not paying 31,000 workers hired illegally since the end of 2005. However, the PA may find it politically challenging to reduce the work force any further. Unless the economy improves and the private sector is energized by a removal of movement and access restrictions, there remains little alternative to public sector jobs.

14. ***The economy's productive capability is diminishing making it increasingly donor dependent.*** GDP did not decline as much as expected after

[6] These are PCBS figures taken from the 2006 Labor Force Survey. The number of workers includes both those that have permits to work in Israel and those that are working illegally.

[7] The Israeli Coordinator of Government Activities in the Palestinian Territories (COGAT) has disputed this figure, noting that 42,000 Palestinians were allowed to work in Israel or the settlements by August 2007, up from 24,000 in May 2005.

donors suspended direct aid to the Hamas—led PA in 2006 (See Table 1). A combination of borrowing, remittances and increased aid that circumvented the PA allowed consumption to remain strong. PCBS estimates that despite the crisis, household consumption dropped by only 0.6% in 2005 and 2006. Nevertheless, output in the productive sectors declined in 2006.[8] The construction sector was the hardest hit, falling by nearly 13%. Industry fell by over 6% and services by nearly 4%. The IMF estimates that the public sector declined by 10 percent.

15. Investment has fallen to precariously low levels, endangering the prospects for long-term growth. Public investment to maintain or add infrastructure has nearly ceased and in the last two years almost all government funds have been used to pay salaries and cover operating costs. Already-low private investment is estimated by the IMF to have fallen by over 15% between 2005 and 2006. A recent World Bank Investment Climate Assessment found that less than a quarter of private sector firms made any investments in 2005/2006 and that manufacturing equipment were on average over 10 years old. Managers had access to finance, but were operating at less than 50% capacity, and saw few opportunities for investment under the current closure regime. Gross capital formation in the private sector fell by over 60% between 1999 and 2005 (See Table 1). The lack of investment in public infrastructure and private firms is eliminating any residue of the Palestinian productive base, making the economy more aid-dependent. When conditions improve, large investments will be needed just to rehabilitate assets let alone create new wealth.

Table 1: Composition of Real GDP in WB&G

	1999	2000	2001	2002	2003	2004	2005	2006
	(percentage change)							
Real GDP	8.9	−5.4	−15.4	−9.4	5.8	6.0	6.0	**−8.0**
Consumption	8.3	−1.9	−6.7	−7.7	4.5	8.6	5.6	**−4.8**
Private	8.3	−4.4	−5.4	−8.5	6.0	8.5	5.6	**−3.8**
Public	8.4	9.4	−11.6	−4.3	−1.6	9.5	5.7	**−9.4**
Investment	33.9	−27.0	−44.6	9.4	18.0	0.6	2.0	**−24.8**
Private	36.0	−26.5	−52.1	8.7	16.9	0.4	1.4	**−15.0**
Public	25.5	−29.4	−9.9	11.1	20.6	1.2	3.3	**−47.1**
Exports	3.7	−6.8	−34.7	−13.0	−4.0	13.5	8.2	**−11.6**
Imports	19.1	−13.9	−18.1	−2.0	4.8	9.9	4.4	**−8.5**

[8] The exception was agriculture where a large olive harvest allowed agriculture to post a 7% gain.

	1999	2000	2001	2002	2003	2004	2005	2006
				(percentage change)				
Change in inventories	62.3	−73.5	−8.9	−36.7	—	—	—	—
Real GDP/capita	4.4	−9.3	−18.7	−12.6	2.1	2.5	2.5	**−10.9**
Real GDI/capita	3.4	−7.4	−8.1	−7.2	−3.8	0.9	1.8	**−3.2**

Source: PCBS and IMF Staff Estimates.

16. ***The unpredictability of the border openings has prevented firms from importing inputs and exporting products in a planned and profitable way.*** In response, enterprises have closed and large amounts of financial and human capital have fled. The pace of capital flight reached an all-time high in the last two years. Investors have always been wary of investing in WB&G, with almost no foreign direct investment in the past few years and most local capital is kept abroad or invested in real estate or short term trading activities. Now local entrepreneurs are closing existing operations and moving them to neighboring countries. This capital and the entrepreneurial and technical talent that go with it are irreplaceable and unlikely to return unless conditions dramatically improve.

17. ***Despite the economic downturn, bank deposits continue to grow reflecting the continued inflows of aid and remittances.*** Private sector deposits increased by about 8% in 2006, and 6% in early 2007, compared to 2% in 2005. While a breakdown between businesses and households is not available, this expansion seems to reflect continued inflows from abroad, which are being used for consumption rather than investment. No comprehensive data are available on remittances, but interviews with commercial banks indicated that private inflows from abroad picked up in 2006 and continued to grow in 2007. Despite the crisis, banks continued to extend credit to the private sector, albeit at a much slower pace than in 2005.

18. ***Trade data indicate a significant decline in exports from WB&G but a smaller fall in imports.*** Most trade takes place with Israel and much of that is done informally and not reported. While trade data are not readily available, the Palestinian Monetary Authority (PMA) publishes estimates that indicate a significant economic slowdown. In 2006 imports declined by 10% but exports fell by close to 16%. The fall in trade in Gaza overshadowed the decline in West Bank. For most of 2006 and 2007 the borders there have rarely been open. Since the June 2007 events, these borders have been completely shut and there have been no commercial imports or exports.

19. ***The social impacts of the current crisis are no less significant, but are often overlooked.*** Health indicators in the WB&G have seen a steady drop over the last three years. Chronic diseases have surged 31% since 2005. Chronic malnutrition among children under five jumped 3% between 2004 and 2006. Ten out of every 100 children under 5 are stunted (13% in the Gaza strip and 8% in the West Bank).[9] The number of households with safe drinking water has also dropped by more than 8% between 2000 and 2007.[10] In the education sector, school enrolment is high but declining. The quality of education is also suffering because schools lack textbooks and other materials. The increasing insecurity, especially in the Gaza strip, is having a devastating effect on the performance of students: failure rates in mathematics are nearly 80% and 40% in Arabic.[11] In the West Bank, closures and restrictions on movement and access, especially due to the Separation Barrier are preventing many students and teachers from reaching their schools.

20. ***Furthermore, the continuing conflict is perpetuating an internal cycle of violence, fragmenting social cohesion and affecting psychosocial well-being.*** A 2006 survey concluded that nearly three quarters of Palestinians suffer from severe depression as a result of the current situation.[12] Women, who historically play a key role as income providers, are increasingly relegated to the informal market as a result movement and access restrictions. Their participation in the labor market, at 15.2%,[13] is amongst the lowest in the world. Also, since September 2000, youth have been caught literally and figuratively in the crossfire of the conflict. Nearly 75% of the injured during the second *Intifada* were between 10 to 29 years old.[14] Youth have also been active participants in the *Intifada* and have therefore suffered both violence and imprisonment with its consequent impact on mental health and physical disability. They also suffer from high rates of unemployment (60 percent[15]) and are excluded from formal mechanisms of decision making.

The Fiscal Spiral

21. ***The PA's longstanding fiscal crisis deepened further in 2006 as a result of Israel's withholding of Palestinian clearance revenues and the aid boycott, resulting in a deficit of over $1 billion.*** Many donors cut off direct aid

[9] Palestinian Family Health Survey, 2006.
[10] PCBS, "Special Report on the 59th Anniversary of the Nakba," May 14, 2007.
[11] UN News Service, "With Education Standards in Gaza Plummeting, UN Launches New Action Plan," 5 September 5, 2007
[12] Near East Consulting, "Depression in the Occupied Palestinian Territories," Sept 2006.
[13] PCBS, Labor Force Survey, April – June 2007.
[14] PCBS, "Palestinian Youth: Facts and Figures," 2001. http://www.unfpa.org/adolescents/opportunities/palestina/docs/facts+figures%20Palestine.pdf.
[15] PCBS, Labor Force Survey April – June 2007.

to the PA, but continued providing funds through the EU TIM, the Office of President Abbas, and other mechanisms. The IMF estimates that external aid towards recurrent operations reached $740 million in 2006; over double the amount in 2005. Yet, total resources for recurrent expenditures fell by a third. About $0.9 billion in expenditure arrears were accumulated, including $385 million in arrears on net wages (excluding those related to pensions and other wage deductions), $175 million in arrears on pension contributions (employees' and government's contributions), and $200 million in arrears to the private sector (including Israeli suppliers and unpaid domestic tax refunds).

22. ***Of an estimated $770 million in Palestinian clearance revenues collected by Israel in 2006, only about $344 million was released to the PA due to deductions to for the payment of utilities.*** In addition, domestic revenues fell from $476 million in 2005 to around $395 million in 2006. Tax revenues remained about the same despite the fall in economic activity and government strike.

23. ***The PIF's assets continued to be depleted with about $190 million being used to pay dividends and to finance the PA in 2006.*** This was largely used to pay for fuel imports and cover debt service obligations to banks. Banks, fearing foreign anti-terrorism laws, sharply reduced lending to the PA and liquidated PIF assets held as collateral.

24. ***Non-wage operating costs, transfers, and spending on utilities and energy continued to grow despite the decrease in funding.*** The fiscal crisis meant that spending had to be prioritized, wages being the highest. However, as of the second quarter of 2006, wages could only be partially paid. Overall, including TIM payments, civil servants received about 60–65 percent of their wages. Yet these payments absorbed nearly half of the available resources. Social benefits and spending on utilities and energy took up the rest. Payments to cover production and consumption of energy and utilities, including subsidies of domestic petroleum products, reached almost $400 million.

25. ***The PA's underlying financial position has continued to deteriorate at an increasing rate in 2007.*** In the first half of 2007 the deficit was likely above $100 million a month. The largest expense is the wage bill, which on a commitment basis grew by nearly 20 percent in 2006 (See Annex 3).[16] Despite the Government's recent efforts to limit the growth in the public sector, the payroll remains at an unsustainable level. Even taking into account Israel's decision in June to release withheld clearance revenues,[17]

[16] To some extent this reflects the full-year effect of wage increases granted in 2005 but it is also due to the increased number of government workers.

[17] The GOI decided to release the withheld clearance revenue and resume monthly transfers with a first installment of NIS 500 million on July 2nd through the Single Treasury Account. The total stock

and even with a recovery of domestic tax revenues, the wage bill due now exceeds total government revenues. This implies that all non-wage expenditures such as energy and infrastructure would have to be covered from other sources.

26. ***The PA has only a limited ability to increase domestic revenues.*** PIF assets have been depleted and the PIF cannot be expected to maintain its previous level of funding. There is room for increased efficiency in tax collection, but this will not offset the loss in VAT and customs duty from the suspension of Gazan trade.[18] Thus, with deteriorating domestic revenues, most of the clearance revenues will go towards funding recurrent costs, and the PA will continue to accumulate arrears.

27. ***Nearing the end of 2007, the PA finds itself with a large current deficit and a significant stock of arrears.*** External assistance has been unusually high in 2007; about $560 million in the first half of the year. In the absence of equal or greater amounts of assistance, the year 2008 may herald an extremely precarious fiscal situation for the PA, with a large deficit, a substantial stock of arrears and falling domestic revenues. Looking forward, the PA forecasts a need for at least $1.62 billion in donor assistance per year to achieve fiscal sustainability.[19] Of this amount, 94% will need to go to meet recurrent expenditure needs, as opposed to development assistance. The PA will soon unveil a three-year Palestinian Reform and Development Plan (PRDP 2008–10) based on a Medium Term Expenditure Framework (MTEF) approach. The will begin to address longstanding disconnects in policy-making, planning and budgeting processes. Its success will depend partly on the credibility of the reform agenda and pragmatic plans to achieve fiscal sustainability. However, these steps must be matched with predictable donor assistance and a growing private sector that will provide a larger tax base and alternatives to public sector employment. The removal of movement and access restrictions, and the ability of the Palestinian private sector to exploit its trade potential, will both increase the PA's revenues and allow it to reduce its expenditures.

of revenues collected as of July, net of deductions for payments of utilities (and net of the transfers made) was preliminarily estimated at NIS 2.7 billion. Of that amount, close to NIS 400 million has been attached by Israeli courts. The Israeli MoF agreed to release monthly installments of NIS 370 million until the stock of withheld revenues is fully repaid. Regular monthly transfers started in early August.

[18] It is unclear how the drop in Gazan trade will affect tax revenues from West Bank enterprises. On the one hand, Gaza is an important market for a number of West Bank enterprises. On the other, many West Bank enterprises are reporting an increase in business as Israeli and other firms shift away from Gazan enterprises.

[19] Ministry of Finance, Budget Directorate.

2.2 A Note on the Gaza Strip

28. ***It is difficult to make definitive statements on Gaza without appearing to encroach on the politics of the current Hamas-PA conflict*** following the June violent takeover of Gaza by Hamas militants. However, all actors have expressed a desire to shield Gaza's 1.5 million people from the effects of the current standoff. Unfortunately, action on one relates to progress on the other. Similarly, any practical discussion on reducing the hardships on Gaza's population must confront the current policy of restricting entry of all but humanitarian commodities and consumables as a way to affect a political outcome.

29. ***Thus, the calls for the entry of solely humanitarian goods are a necessary but insufficient condition for the survival of the Gazan economy, which is already in dire straits after two years of restrictions.*** A sustainable solution must include commercial imports and exports at the very least at levels similar to those pre-crisis which were already deemed insufficient and not meeting the minimum targets set in the AMA.

30. ***Without prejudice to the legality of the events of June 2007, or of the position of the Caretaker Government, the observable fact is that any economic backbone and private sector vitality in Gaza risks collapse if the current closure policy continues.*** As a policy measure, this is a blunt instrument that can neither be regulated nor fully reversed. At best, it risks amplifying the economic disparities across borders.

31. ***In 2005 the Bank had already warned of dire impacts on the Palestinian economy if commercial trade continued to be impeded.*** Unfortunately, these projections are gradually being realized. PCBS notes that the percentage of Gazans who live in deep poverty has been steadily increasing, rising from 21.6% in 1998 to nearly 35% in 2006.[20] With the continued economic decline in 2007 and the recent closures on Gaza the current poverty rate is almost certainly higher. This rate reflects actual consumption, which implies that without remittances and food aid the poverty rate is closer to *67%*. The increase in poverty in the West Bank has been lower but still significant.

32. ***In Gaza, the impact of two years of closures since disengagement and the most recent restrictions on imports and exports create a new extreme scenario.*** Over 54%[21] of employment in Gaza is private sector-driven, representing more than 100,000 jobs. Of these, 35,000 workers—18,000 skilled—operate the industrial sector. Recent data on Gaza's GDP are not readily available, but Gaza contributed $1.3 billion to Palestinian GDP in 2003 (44%), of which the private sector is the main economic driver. According

[20] PCBS constructed the deep poverty line to reflect a budget for food, clothing and housing. For a family of six the deep poverty line in 2006 was NIS 1,837.

[21] Q1 2007 as reported by PCBS Labor Force Press release, July 2007.

to the Palestinian Private Sector Coordination Council (PSCC), the current restrictions have led to the suspension of 90% of Gaza's industrial operations, including domestic and export-oriented manufacturing and agriculture, and services.[22] They can access neither the inputs for production nor the crossings to export what they would produce. Also observable is the emergence of a black market for consumer goods, and price hikes. Employment in construction and building has also been impacted by the suspension and cancellation of most construction projects, including USD $160 million in projects funded by UNRWA, UNDP, and others due to lack of construction materials.

33. ***The likely lay-off of over 30,000 industrial workers alone[23] resulting from the restrictions would lead to an unprecedented private sector driven-unemployment level of about 44% in Gaza. Recent employment generation schemes may reduce this figure, but these are temporary fixes that do not alter the emerging structural crisis in Gaza's labor market.*** Interestingly, the continued payment of civil servant salaries in the Strip—a welcome event—will still generate income to drive some degree of local demand for finished goods. Therefore, the end result would be a closure regime that serves little in the short-term, but would in the medium-term hollow out the Gazan economy of any residual production potential, transforming it into a consumer economy driven by public sector salaries and humanitarian assistance—both directly and indirectly financed by the donors.

34. ***The impacts of the closures will become less reversible with time.*** Most Gazan industries are export-oriented and have purchase and supply contracts with Israeli and other firms.[24] Gazan manufacturers import 95% of

Table 2: Industrial Decline in Gaza

	June 2005 (pre-disengagement)	Week 1, July 2007
Number of Working Establishments[1]	3,900	780
Number of Employees[1]	35,000	4,200
Exports from Gaza (truckloads)[2]	748	0

Source: PalTrade Presentation to PSCC, July 2007.
1 Source: original data from Industrial associations in Gaza reported to PalTrade.
2 Source: PalTrade.

[22] At the time of writing this report, PSCC figures showed that 780 of 3,900 industries maintained operations in Gaza, and 4,200 of 35,000 remained employed.
[23] This does not include labor in the agriculture, construction and service sectors.
[24] Private Sector Coordination Council (PSCC), Effect on Private Sector in Gaza, July 12, 2007.

their inputs. About 76% of their furniture products, 90% of their garments and 20% of their food products are exported to Israel, and some to the West Bank. By mid July, the Palestinian Shippers' Council estimated an accrued $3,000,000 in storage and demurrage fees, with 1,600 containers worth over $130,000,000 waiting at the freight terminals and the ports.[25] Naturally, Israeli and other suppliers and purchasers must maintain their operations and will soon cancel contracts and seek alternative supply chains elsewhere,[26] lest they also risk bankruptcy.[27] Experience has shown that the repair of business relationships, and the return of capital and skilled labor, takes time. And in the case of Israel and the Palestinian Territories, such business relationships are an important pillar of an eventual scenario of peace and cohabitation. Sadly, informal estimates suggest that nearly 100 enterprises have moved from Gaza within the last two years.[28]

35. ***The agriculture sector has also been badly hit. Nearly 5,000 farmers depend on the export of cash crops for Gaza.*** Production in 2007 was expected to be around $12m all of which will be lost due to the border closures. In addition, the agriculture sector is completely dependent upon imports of fertilizer, pesticides, packaging material and other inputs. Without these inputs private sector organizations estimate suggest that agriculture output will decline by fifty percent in 2007.

36. ***To arrive at a speedy and workable solution, it is important to analyze the dynamics of the closure regime.*** While the Karni Crossing has been closed since June, a pre-screened set of goods has been entering through the Sufa and Kerem Shalom Crossings. However, unlike Karni these crossings lack the infrastructure and the capacity to accommodate all goods, primarily inputs (e.g., piped products such as CO2 gas, steel, stone, etc.).[29] Thus, only limited types of goods enter. The reason cited for the closure of Karni by the GOI relates to the lack of security and logistics counterparts on the Gazan side.[30] However, the fact that creative ways have been found for the other crossings would imply that options exist for Karni. Gazan private sector officials have sought the PA's approval to explore a workable

[25] Palestinian Shipper's Council, Importers in Gaza: Edge Towards Crisis, July 2007. Palestinian firms are fully dependent of Israeli ports. 80% of Gaza importers use Ashdod port. The remaining 20% use Haifa port or Ben Gurion airport.

[26] At the time of this note, 1,000,000 finished garments and 400 containers of furniture were in storage, awaiting export to Israel.

[27] According to PFI, as of July the confirmed business losses were $20.6 million, in addition to stoppage of $160 million in construction contracts.

[28] From interviews with local private sector organizations, government officials and development agencies. One organization has a confidential list of over 70 enterprises that have moved operations out of Gaza.

[29] In rare cases, Karni has accommodated up to 400 truckloads per day. Gazan private sector representatives state that both Sufa and Kerem Shalom can accommodate up to 120 truckloads per day.

[30] Israel maintains its no-contact policy with Hamas.

solution for the operation of the Crossing, and continue to seek a PA policy and dialogue with GOI for the entry of commercial goods into Gaza.

37. ***Inaddition, the goods allowed in have excluded inputs for manufacturing operations in Gaza.*** Finished goods are allowed to enter, but not those that would trigger commercial activity. Recently, the GOI allowed finished books to enter Gaza for use by UNRWA students, but excluded paper to produce the goods in Gaza. Similarly, World Bank surveys of Gazan industrialists indicate that while soda drinks are allowed to enter Gaza, the CO2 required to produce them in Gazan factories are forbidden. Notebooks are entering, but not the paper to make notebooks locally. Many other cases abound, including inputs for tissue paper, bottled water, etc. This issue must be addressed urgently at the level of the joint security committees of the PA and GOI.

38. ***A recent trial export of seven truckloads of potatoes out of Kerem Shalom into Israel on August 28th was a welcome first step.*** It is also a testament to the possibility, if the political will exists, to allow for the movement of commercial supplies in some form or another. At the same time, the costs and organizational complexities of that shipment also attest to the need for a quick opening of the Karni Crossing as it can accommodate a greater flow of goods than the other crossings.

39. ***At the same time, the Hamas control of Gaza is incurring a direct negative impact on the economy.*** Without delving into the political context of the current stalemate, it is evident that the current position in Gaza is also a function of Hamas' political and de facto security policies. Hence, it is a party that also bares responsibility for creating a political and logistical environment in which all sides can reengage in Gaza. It must be noted that attacks on the crossings continue to take place, greatly undermining any efforts to shield Gaza's population and private sector from the impacts of the current situation.

40. ***The demographic trends in Gaza need to be recognized, not only in terms of unshackling commerce but also in terms of donor assistance.*** It is noteworthy yet often overlooked that 50% of the Gaza's population is under the age of 15 and will soon be thrust into a barely-existing labor market. Thus, the work of donors and the PA to create the basis for sustainable jobs in Gaza is as critical as ever. Clearly, there are practical and legitimate concerns by the international community on the *modus operandi* of donor-financed project implementation in Gaza, including the flow of funds. However, recent effective steps by the PA to develop 'direct payment' mechanisms to contractors and laborers in Gaza offer a critical window for donors to explore.

3. Progress Since the 2005 AHLC: Revisiting the Preconditions

41. *At the 2005 AHLC Meeting, the World Bank suggested the need for progress in lifting Israeli closures, Palestinian governance and security, and donor coordination as prerequisites for Palestinian economic recovery.* The following section takes stock of the progress on these preconditions since the AHLC meeting, and revisits the previous recommendations to assess their continuing validity. This section is not intended to offer a complete analysis of all of the relevant sectors or reforms, many of which fall outside of the mandate and competency of the World Bank. Rather, the goal is to provide sufficient analytical background to assist the PA, GOI and donors in the hope of informing the concrete policies that are necessary, looking forward to the proposed Donor Conference in December, to revive the Palestinian economy, and the overall peace process.

3.1 Movement and Access and the 'Private Sector Potential'

Summary: **The main challenge for Palestinian recovery remains the comprehensive restrictions on movement and access imposed by Israel, which go beyond concrete and checkpoints to a set of collective policies that combine to stunt economic growth. Beyond movement within and across Palestinian Territories, these policies also restrict access to domestic and international markets, land, water and other natural resources, and donor-financed projects for 60% of the West Bank (Areas C). While there is consensus on the legitimacy of Israel's security concerns, it is difficult to reconcile this with the clear correlation between access restrictions and the protection and expansion of Israeli settlement activity in the West Bank. The commitments entered to by Israel under the 2005 Agreement on Movement and Access (AMA) remain as unfulfilled as they are critical. The AMA must be implemented immediately. Moving forward, the full implementation of the AMA must be seen as an important step towards stability, not a consequence of it.**

42. *The Agreement on Movement and Access (AMA) signed in November 2005 sought to unshackle the movement of Palestinian goods and people (See Annex 5).* But the main challenge for Palestinian businesses remains the closure regime.[31] The World Bank's 2006 Investment Climate Assessment (ICA) revealed that shrinking market access and hindered movement are the main constraints for Palestinian enterprises, as uncertainties in the delivery of inputs and products hike up costs. That, combined with increasingly limited available markets, has stunted the investment potential of Palestinian entrepreneurs.

[31] The closure system effectively partitions the West Bank into a northern, a central and a southern economic zone, bounded on three sides by the Separation Barrier and to the east by a Jordan Valley that is increasingly difficult for Palestinians to access.

43. ***While the Israeli economy has evolved from agricultural and low-value manufacturing to high-end, high-technology products, the WB&G remain unindustrialized,*** with most businesses having fewer than 5 employees. And even under these circumstances, the prospects for relatively competitive low-end Palestinian goods are grim. The Palestinian links to the Israeli economy have driven up labor costs, making it an anomaly, a third word economy with first world wage rates.

44. ***As such, Israel's review of the current restrictions regime is critical, including recognition that these restrictions go beyond concrete walls and checkpoints,*** towards a confluence of policies that combine to stunt the prospects of Palestinian self-sufficiency. And the term 'access' goes beyond the physical movement of person or good- it includes access to a wide range of resources needed for sustenance and growth.

45. ***It is recognized that Israeli security concerns are valid and undeniable.*** The impacts of Qassam rocket attacks on Sderot, and other past or potential attacks on Israel, are not disputed. However, as noted by the UK Economic Secretary to the Treasury at a June 19 speech, ". . . a viable economic roadmap will not be possible unless a better balance can be struck between short-term security on one hand and on allowing movement and access on the other, necessary to promote both security and prosperity for the medium term . . ."[32] This implies a revision of Israel's approach to security as a balance between short and long-term gains, matched with PA policies that recognize the potentially devastating impacts of short-term breaches in security that have halted previous attempts at reconciliation, and that have also impacted Palestinian economic recovery.

46. ***Analysis of movement and access restrictions suggests that they primarily serve to expand and protect settlement activity***[33] and the movement of settlers and other Israelis in and out of the West Bank. There are currently 149 settlements in the West Bank, including East Jerusalem, and roughly 100 "illegal outposts" that lack Israeli government approval, but that nevertheless remain.[34] The approximately 450,000 settlers living there are 63% more than at the time of the Oslo Accord period in 1993. [35][36] Some 38% of the West Bank has been confiscated for current or future settlements,

[32] Lecture by the Economic Secretary to the UK Treasury, Ed Balls MP, on "Towards a Middle East Economic Roadmap" given at the Royal Society of Arts, London, June 19, 2007.

[33] COGAT asserts that these restrictions are also based on security considerations, and 'not necessarily' the growth of settlements in the West Bank, adding that many of the restrictions would be removed once the security environment improved.

[34] PCBS Settlements Annual Report, "Israeli Settlements in the Palestinian Territory," July 2007.

[35] OCHA, Humanitarian Impact of Israeli Settlements and other Infrastructure in the West Bank, June 2007.

[36] COGAT disputes these figures. They assert that there are 120 settlements in the Judea & Samaria region, accounting for 275,248 inhabitants. However, these figures do not include parts of municipal Jerusalem, which is the basis for OCHA's calculation.

outposts, closed military areas, municipal boundaries, and settlement regional jurisdiction. [37]

47. ***The result of this is that a vast amount of Palestinians cannot access homes and services, land, domestic and international markets, water and other natural resources, and even donor finance in areas C.*** These are analyzed in greater detail below.

Access through the Separation Barrier and to the Seam Zone

48. ***To provide security for Israel and settlements and closed areas in the West Bank, Israel has constructed the Separation Barrier,***[38] three-quarters of which departs from the 1949 Armistice Line into the West Bank,[39] creating a "seam zone"—a closed military area between the barrier and the Green Line—that consumes 8.5% the West Bank. As a further defense measure, Israel requires a "buffer zone" of 150–200 meters east of the wall.[40] [41] Another 3.4% of the West Bank to the east of the Barrier is completely or partially surrounded, creating small Palestinian enclaves where permits are needed even by those living there.[42] The Barrier and Seam Zone have thus created additional Palestinian lands that are inaccessible to Palestinians. Eventually, about 50,000 residents of 38 villages will be in the Seam Zone[43] or the enclaves created by it.[44] About 61,000 Palestinian residents of East Jerusalem—as well as half a million Palestinians within 1 km outside of the Barrier—will be separated from family and trade networks, and municipal services.[45]

Access to Domestic Markets

49. ***Israel's withdrawal from Gaza on September 12, 2005 resolved the internal movement restrictions there. However, access between the West Bank and Gaza and movement within the West Bank remain restricted.*** In

---

37 Ibid. page 9.

38 Bimkom—Planners for Planning Rights and B'Tselem, "Under the Guise of Security—Routing the Separation Barrier to Enable the Expansion of Israeli Settlements in the West Bank", (December 2005).

39 COGAT has noted that this is a temporary barrier for security purposes. The Barrier, and the security zones, are to be re-declared periodically based on the security environment.

40 UN OCHA, "Preliminary Analysis of the Humanitarian Implications of the April 2006 Barrier Projections".

41 COGAT asserts that the buffer zone serves critical security requirements, ensuring that no new construction is higher than the Barrier and therefore undermines its protective nature.

42 B'Tselem, "Separation Barrier", www.btselem.org.

43 Recent figures from OCHA's Humanitarian Impact of Israeli Settlements and other Infrastructure in the West Bank, June 2007 (p. 46) assert that 60,500 residents of 42 villages will be in the Seam Zone.

44 COGAT asserts that only 7,000 Palestinian residents are within the Seam Zone.

45 The Israeli Ministry of Justice has noted that this section only addresses the ". . . negative impact of the Security Fence on the Palestinian economy. However, it does not make mention of the fact that the Security Fence allows Israel to ease checkpoints and restrictions on movement within the West Bank. Furthermore, the relative security the fence provides, and its clear assistance in lowering terrorist activities, allows for an environment where mutual trust can be regained, and economic projects re-started, including foreign investments . . ."

Figure 5: Breakup of Economic Space West Bank Fragmentation Map

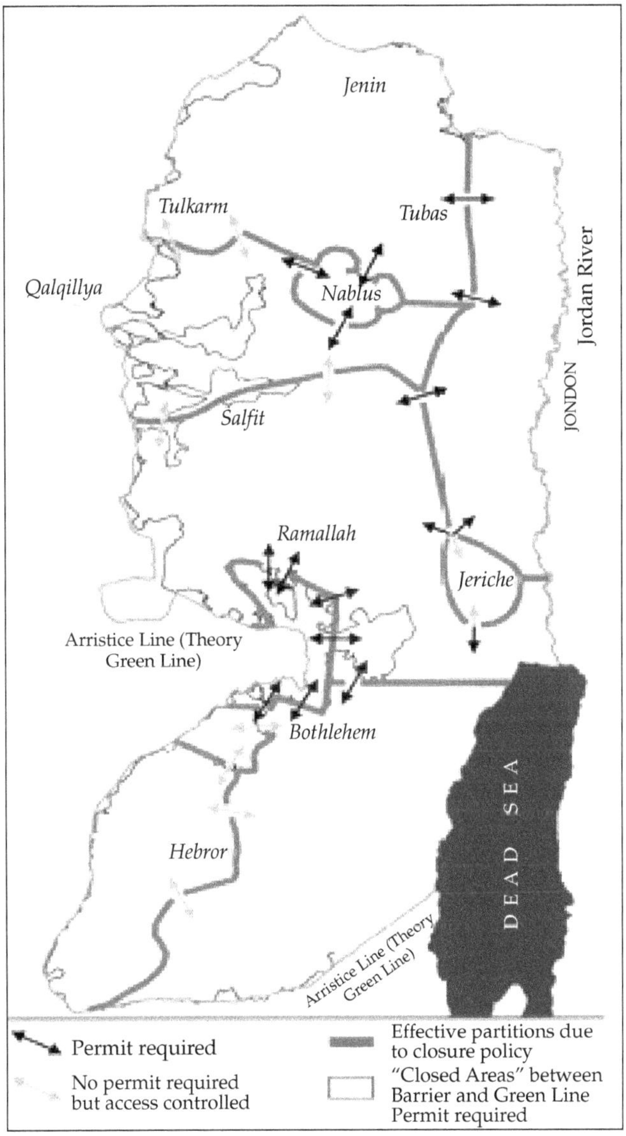

Source: OCHA oPt, 2007.

the West Bank, a confluence of policies, administrative practices, and physical impediments have fragmented the territory into ever smaller and more disconnected cantons (see figure 5).

50. ***In addition to a two-tiered road system where 1,661 km is reserved for Israelis and settlers,***[46] ***the UN estimates that the number of fixed physical impediments (checkpoints, roadblocks and gates) has gone from 376 in August 2005 to 541 in July 2007.*** Likewise, flying checkpoints have increased from 272 in June 2005 to 524 in June 2007.[47] The Israeli authorities assert that there are only 442 impediments, of which 71 are manned.[48] Whatever the number may be, these impediments, along with the permit policies in pace, present a critical constraint to the survival of the Palestinian economy. These administrative obstacles, rooted in military orders associated with the occupation of WB&G, have created uncertainty, raised transaction costs, and have shrunk markets. World Bank analysis suggests that, between 2000 and 2006, the number of Palestinian enterprises in the West Bank that sell to customers outside their local metropolitan area declined by 30%.[49]

51. ***GOI has recently committed to removing some impediments and providing several hundred permits to categories of Palestinian businessmen.*** While this is a welcome initiative, incremental steps are unlikely to lead to sustainable improvements as they have historically lacked permanence, and have been withdrawn or replaced by other restrictions. Moreover, economic recovery will remain elusive if large areas of the West Bank are inaccessible for economic exploitation and restricted movement remains the norm for the most Palestinians, their products, and their investment funds.

52. ***While East Jerusalem has historically been a hub of Palestinian economic and social activity, administrative obstacles, settlement expansion and the Barrier are severing it from the WB&G.*** The World Bank's analysis shows that the percentage of West Bank firms selling into East Jerusalem dropped from 21% to 18% between 2000 and 2005.[50] Gazan businesses are almost entirely shut out of the Jerusalem economy. There are also humanitarian impacts to this, involving a 50% drop in access by WB&G residents to critical tertiary health care in East Jerusalem's six hospitals.

53. ***Moreover, much of the Jordan Valley- a source of valuable agribusiness and tourism potential-has been off-limits to most Palestinians*** per military orders issued in August 2006. Despite the reversal of some orders in

[46] COGAT notes that the Israeli authorities have invested NIS 1 billion in 'fabric of life' roads intended to provide adequate and effective solutions for Palestinians impacted by the current closures.

[47] See the OCHA website for movement monitoring notes that track impediments; URL: www.ochaopt.org.

[48] COGAT also notes that, of these 71 manned checkpoints, half are in areas bordering Israel, and the other half are in high security areas in the West Bank.

[49] See West Bank and Gaza Investment Climate Assessment, World Bank, March 2007 URL: www.worldbank.org/ps.

[50] Ibid.

May 2007, Palestinians who do not have residency permits still cannot enter the Jordan Valley by vehicle.[51]

54. ***This stranglehold is augmented by recent practices on the issuance of temporary visas to eligible foreign nationals*** for family, tourism, humanitarian, investment and academic visits. Many documented cases abound regarding citizens from North America, Latin America, and the European Union being denied visas or issued ones for extremely short duration. These effectively discourage individuals from traveling to the Territories to tour, visit or work. A June 2007 survey by the Campaign for the Right of Entry/Re-Entry found that 30% of applicants were denied visa extensions to the West Bank. Also, foreign nationals continue to face difficulties in acquiring residency, particularly for family reunification. The same NGO noted that 500,000 to 750,000 applicants to Family Reunification may be forced to leave the West Bank as a result. This has had a direct impact on the Palestinian economy by reducing consumption and investment, as well as by eliminating the injection of foreign expertise and skills to upgrade the productivity of local businesses. [52]

Access to Israeli and International Markets

55. ***Gaza's post-2005 disengagement economy has seen a sharp reduction in external access.*** With the exception of aggregates and fuel through Nahal Oz, Gaza has a single access point at the Karni/Al-Montar Border Crossing to sustain nearly 1.5 million people. Even prior to the June 2007 events in Gaza, the operation of Karni was suboptimal from a trade perspective. Throughout 2006, its openings were erratic and involved varying hours, and inefficient screening.[53] Despite the AMA provision for continuous operations and for 150/day truck exports by January 2006 and 400/day truck exports by end 2006, an average of 16 trucks crossed daily in 2006. By end July 2007, the average had increased to 32 a day.[54] Since June 2007, Karni is no longer used except for limited imports of grains and animal feed.[55]

---

[51] COGAT informed the World Bank that the key obstacles to movement and access in the Jordan Valley had been resolved, comprising the opening of the Tayseer, Beka'ot and Hamra Crossings, and the ability of Palestinians to enter the Jordan Valley 'on foot'.

[52] In response, COGAT noted that foreigners from countries with visa agreements with Israel are able to enter freely, unless there are 'security or other prohibitions', adding that there are also 54,000 foreigners who entered with visas prior to the 2000 change in policy, and who now reside illegally in the WB&G. COGAT also added that 800 permits were allocated for 'senior businessmen' to enter the WB&G, although *697* were issued based on demand. Another 14,000 permits were allocated towards applications by local traders with Israel. However, COGAT confirmed that since 2000, family reunification has been frozen based on a decision of the Israel High Court of Justice.

[53] According to the World Bank and OCHA, Karni was closed for most of 2006. The Israeli authorities dispute this figure, noting that Karni was closed for 104 out of 203 operating days. COGAT also asserts that the improvements made in the Karni Crossing added 210,000 jobs to Gaza's economy over the course of one year.

[54] Paltrade, Al Montar/Karni Terminal Movement Monitoring Monthly Report—August 14, 2007.

[55] Since the incidents at Gaza, the Israeli Customs Authority cancelled the customs code for all products to Gaza, so goods destined there can no longer be imported through Israeli ports.

Currently, the Sufa and Kerem Shalom are being used for the import of humanitarian goods into Gaza. These crossings are neither well equipped nor prepared to handle any large trade capacity, and are not opened regularly.

56. ***West Bank trade with and through Israel is administered by six "back-to-back" commercial crossings.***[56] Once the Barrier is complete, all trade with and through Israel will have to pass through them.[57] The crossings will have a total capacity of around 2,000 trucks per day (4,000 if operated with two shifts) for both imports and exports.[58] Beyond this, most Palestinian trade to international markets goes through Israeli ports (Haifa, Ashdod, or Ben Gurion Airport).

57. ***As such, Palestinians are dependent on Israel for access to markets.*** Alternative trade routes are effectively non-existent, thus inhibiting the 'healthy competition' in routes that virtually all economies enjoy. Palestinian traders must turn to Israeli middlemen and service providers to facilitate imports and exports, making them vulnerable to changes in border policies. For example, recent requirements at Ashdod Port for Palestinian goods to be held for 48 hours caused many goods to miss sailings and remain at the port for several days. Air cargo originating in the Territories cannot be shipped on passenger airlines out of Ben Gurion, thereby limiting the frequency of services for high-value, time-sensitive goods. The only remaining possibilities for trade route alternatives are either from Gaza to Egypt through Rafah, or from the West Bank to Jordan through Allenby. Even before the events in Gaza, there had been no progress on a Palestinian port or airport as planned under the AMA.

58. ***Until the June events in Gaza, efforts were underway to open Rafah as an export gate for Palestinian products to and through Egypt.*** World Bank analysis had shown this to be logistically and financially competitive with Israeli ports, and critical for Palestinian goods to take direct advantage of favorable treatment in Arab and other markets. Since November 2005, Rafah was successfully operated by the PA, with third party monitoring by the EU Border Assistance Mission (EUBAM) with additional scrutiny

---

[56] The main commercial crossings are Jalameh (north of Jenin), Bisan/Bardala (northern Jordan Valley), Irtah/"Sha'ar Efrayim" (south of Tulkarem; referred to as Taybeh), Beitunya (southwest of Ramallah), Tarqumia (northwestern Hebron district), and Terminal 300 (near Bethlehem).

[57] Recently, the UN and other agencies were informed of new Israeli requirements once the Barrier is complete for moving aid goods through a fewer number of crossings using a 'back-to-back' system. This will raise costs as twice as many trucks will be needed, and as goods will have to be palletized. OCHA predicts a resulting tenfold increase in costs. Furthermore, local staff of all agencies will soon be restricted from entering the Seam Zone without permits, or from driving there for the conduct of their business.

[58] According to a briefing by the Israeli Civil Administration to the Economic Advisor to the Palestinian President on January 22, 2007. Later, COGAT informed the Bank of plans to hand over management of the crossings to a civilian firm, and implement new inspection mechanisms, in order to enhance efficiency. COGAT also noted recent statistics by the Israeli and Jordanian Bureaus of Statistics and the Israel Airports Authority noting an increase in trade of 1.3% between the West Bank and Israel, and of 7.7% with Jordan.

through CCTV cameras accessible to Israeli security. The crossing was fully operational until the abduction of an Israeli soldier near the Gazan border, after which it would open only intermittently. And after June 2007, the topic of exports through Rafah would be suspended indefinitely. However, the underlying economics of the Rafah crossing continue to hold, and its opening for exports remains a key step in the optimization of a Palestinian trade route.

59. ***By the same token, the West Bank economy is larger than Gaza's, and producers there also need direct access to the world market.*** An efficient and reliable crossing to and through Jordan would provide similar advantages of direct market access from the West Bank. Given that the Damieh Crossing with Jordan has been closed since September 2005 and can no longer be used for Palestinian trade, the only option for Palestinians for direct access to international markets is Allenby Bridge. But Israel's removal of access restrictions on Palestinians into the Jordan Valley is a necessary precondition to develop a Jordan trade corridor.

Access to Donor Finance-Development in Area C

60. ***The Oslo Accords grant the GoI military and civilian control over Area C,*** representing about 60% of the West Bank, and which represents the only fully contiguous area there-. This area surrounds and divides Areas A[59] (full PA military and civilian control) and B (PA civilian control, GOI military control). Area C also represents a key resource to accommodate the natural expansion of Palestinian demographics and economic base needs.

61. ***Alas, the extent of land in Area C available to Palestinians is very limited, transforming most of the West Bank into a geographic oddity*** where many Palestinian towns in Areas A or B cannot access agricultural land in Area C, and where Palestinian population densities are often double that of parts of Area C slated for settlement use.

62. ***Given the lack of space and the difficulties in obtaining a permit in Area C, many families are building without permission, resulting in house demolitions by the Israeli military.*** Donor projects in area C face similar constraints. Obtaining permits for Area C, whether for private, humanitarian or developmental purposes, is time consuming if not unattainable.[60] Any projects in any village in Area C require both a permit and a masterplan prepared by the Israeli authorities for that area. Yet, the Israeli Civil Administration has not yet prepared master plans for most towns.[61]

[59] Area A covers about 17 percent of the West Bank.

[60] The Israeli Civil Administration requires an Israeli Master plan to grant a permit for any construction or development project, but has not completed Master plans for the vast majority of village in Area C.

[61] COGAT has responded to this assertion that once a Master plan is developed, Permits are usually given without delay. However, this does not resolve the absence of Masterplans for many villages in

Consequently, most NGOs report not having received construction permits since 2005. Particularly in the Jordan Valley, the lack of construction permits prevents several communities from developing or upgrading utilities (electricity, water) and social infrastructure (schools, clinics). According to the Oslo Agreements, solid infrastructure requires approval by the Israeli authorities, but humanitarian programs and temporary structures do not. Yet, several agencies have reported being forced to remove infrastructure for basic services (electricity, water, schools clinics), including temporary structures. Approximately 82 structures in area C were destroyed in the Jordan Valley in 2006.[62]

63. ***A Task Force for Project Implementation (TFPI), comprising the UN, USAID, EC and the World Bank, undertook a survey and tour of some villages in Area C.*** One village surveyed, Al Jiftlik, had a masterplan. However, only 55% of its residents are located inside the masterplan, leaving 2,000 of the 5,500 inhabitants without electricity.[63] Another case is Furush Bet Dajan, which despite a population of 1,200 has no master plan and has thus been unable to develop since the 1990s. There is no electricity, and the main road needs paving. An application for a temporary clinic (i.e. in a container) has been pending for seven months (with funding from JICA). These are only two of many cases.

Access to Resources: Water, Telecommunications and Electricity

64. ***The Palestinian recovery formula is not complete without increased access to water, telecommunications, energy and other resources for domestic, industrial, and agricultural use.*** Palestinian use of water in the West Bank—most of which lies in Area C—is limited to 17% of total water in the aquifers. Israel uses the remaining 83% either through its settler population or pumping from the shared aquifers for consumption in Israel. This is despite the fact that 10%–14% of Palestinian GDP comes from agriculture, as opposed to 3% of Israel's GDP. Only 10% of Palestinian agriculture uses irrigation; the rest is rain-fed. Israel irrigates more than 50% of its land.[64] In the Jordan Valley, Palestinian allocations from wells are restricted with rare approvals for new wells and or increasing outputs from existing wells dug before 1967. Gaza, on the other hand, relies on wells that are increasingly infiltrated by seawater due to over-pumping by all parties. As a result, the

Area C. Recently, 16 Materplans were prepared by the Israeli authorise, of which 10 were cleared for further review by IDF Central Command.

62 OCHA update to the Task Force for Project Implementation, 2007.

63 COGAT notes that many of those left outside the mater plan are not permanent residents of Jiftlik, but seasonal migrants form nearby Tubas. Nevertheless, this implies an inability of Palestinians to move and reside freely within the Jordan Valley.

64 Sources: PWA Statistics: World Health Organization, *Health Conditions of, and Assistance to the Arab Population in the Occupied Arab Territories, including Palestine*, 58th World Health Assembly, May 17, 2005; and PLO Negotiations Affairs Department, *Presentation on water and the Two State Solution*, July 2007.

UN estimates that Gaza will have no drinking water in the next 15 years.[65] Yet, regardless of the final resolution on water rights, the scarcity of this common resource requires the Palestinian Water Authority (PWA) to minimize water losses and rationalize its use of potable water. As such, the PWA must develop alternatives such as infrastructure for water treatment and reuse, and improved irrigation techniques in Palestinian agriculture.[66]

65. ***The same principle applies for telecommunications, where several impediments face the sector.*** This includes the PA's inability, under the Oslo Agreements, to have its own international gateways, to access the needed frequency spectrum, or to easily expand infrastructure in Area C. In addition, Palestinian operators claim that several Israeli mobile operators that, under the Oslo agreements are allowed to serve Israeli settlements in the West Bank, have been able to expand coverage more easily, and have as a result captured 20% of the Palestinian market. However, internal factors have also impacted the sector, including the need to strengthen governance and regulatory oversight in the sector for existing operators and to allow new entrants into the market. Effective competition between telecommunications operators can provide a very strong tax base, but will require a transparent system to generate tax revenues, as well as a clear policy to deal with unauthorized operators.[67]

66. ***In terms of energy, three-quarters is consumed by house holds and the service sector; illustrating the weakening industrial backbone of the Palestinian economy.*** Yet since 1999, energy demand increased annually by 6% in the West Bank and 10% in Gaza. Energy supply struggles to keep up with domestic demand. Nearly all energy is provided by electricity and petroleum products purchased from Israel.[68] The only substantial domestic energy resource is Gaza's offshore Marine gas field which is currently

[65] Unfortunately, plans to enhance water availability and wastewater reuse in Gaza have been delayed by the suspension or postponement of several donor projects. Examples of key projects include: USAID's $140 million for the Gaza Seawater desalination plant and the Gaza North-South carrier, and KfW's approx Euro 70 for the Central Wastewater Treatment Plant. The World Bank-financed North Gaza Emergency Sewage Treatment Plant is facing delays due to the lack of entry of urgent supplies and equipment to complete the work. Wastewater reuse is at risk, and all poorly treated sewage generated from 70 million cubic meters of water supply is now pumped into the sea.

[66] In a formal response on this issue, the Government of Israel asserts that ". . . all actions relating to water issues are undertaken according to the 1995 Water Agreement between Israel and the Palestinians. Israel fulfills all of its obligations and more (diverting 60 million cubic meters instead of 23 to the Palestinians), and has offered the Palestinians to assist in countering water shortages in various ways." GOI adds that since 1967, the water quantity drawn by Israel from the Mountain aquifer is diminishing in favor of the Palestinians. Thirdly, GOI notes that it has offered the PA several options to access more water, including a donor-financed desalination plant to be built in Hadera, Israel that would then sell desalinated water to the Palestinians. Lastly, GOI notes that it has reduced by 50% the use of potable water in Israeli agriculture, while the Palestinian side has not, thus raising the need for potable water.

[67] Sources: (1) Findings of recent World Bank Technical Assistance to the Ministry of Telecommunications and IT, and (2) World Bank, West Bank and Gaza Infrastructure Assessment, December 2004.

[68] The PA imports a small amount of electricity from Egypt to Gaza and has negotiated an agreement to import some power from Jordan to Jericho in the West Bank.

unexploited.[69] In the West Bank, the electricity system consists of isolated distribution systems operated by municipalities and village councils, with little generation or transmission capacity. In Gaza, electricity is partly provided by the Gaza Power Plant (GPP).

67. ***Thus, the WB&G will need to diversify energy sources beyond Israel which itself needs to meet its future energy needs.*** The West Bank is landlocked but borders Jordan which can serve as a source of energy. Gaza has substantial offshore gas, can receive supplies by sea, and borders Egypt which can become a major supplier. All this requires outside investment which is difficult given the constraints caused by Palestinian access restrictions. At the same time, the PA has to address incentives for electricity retailers, especially the municipalities and councils, to collect bills from their customers. Otherwise, the PA will continue to dedicate about 20% of its total budget to meeting outstanding amounts owed to the Israeli Electric Corporation (IEC). However, any increase in bill collection is tied to the ability of a typical Palestinian family to earn income—a cycle previously addressed as directly linked to movement and access.

3.2 Palestinian Governance

Summary: **The combined political and financial shocks of the last two years have endangered many Palestinian institutional gains. The refusal of the Hamas-led PA to meet the Quartet conditions, and the international reaction to the PLC elections have marginalized the legislative branch as a forum for multi-party policy making and legislation and as a mechanism for oversight of the executive branch. Also, efforts at imposing law and order and reforming the judiciary were overtaken by factional fighting and a paralysis of the PLC. The recent resumption of high-level security coordination between the Caretaker Government and the GOI offers an opportunity for a coordinated approach to law and order.**

On the fiscal front, the PA has little time to reverse the fiscal and institutional impacts of 2006–07 and the legacy of its past spending practices. The PA has successfully rehabilitated parts of the Public Financial Management system. The preparation of a three-year Palestinian Reform and Development Plan (PRDP) will begin the process of addressing longstanding weaknesses and disconnects in policy-making, planning and budgeting processes. Its success will depend partly on the credibility of the national policy agenda, including pragmatic plans to improve the PA's performance in delivering services to the Palestinian public and putting it on the path to fiscal sustainability. But, its success also depends

[69] Discussions towards a gas production deal have been underway through the concessionaire, British Gas.

on sufficient and predictable external assistance and a strong recovery of private economic activity. Both GOI and donors have a role to play.

68. ***As mentioned earlier, the PA currently faces a large current deficit, a significant stock of arrears, and a precarious horizon of aid dependence.*** While this was amplified by the events of the past two years and the drastic drop in local and aid resources, the PA and the international community have long recognized for governance reform on several fronts, including law and order, judicial reform, public sector management, and others. This report covers some of the areas of priority.

Law and Order, and Judicial Reform

69. ***Internal security, access to justice and corruption were regarded by the PA and donors as key reform priorities in 2005. They were also decisive issues in the 2006 PLC elections. Ironically, progress on these areas has since been impossible as a result of the prevailing environment.*** Israel's incarceration of 46 PLC members, and the ongoing factional rivalry, left the PLC unable to muster a quorum and the PA in a state of policy and legislative paralysis. New aid channels fragmented the PA's Public Financial Management System, also constraining the PA's service delivery functions including security.

70. ***During 2006 and 2007, several attempts at establishing organizational arrangements to lead and coordinate security sector reform faltered.*** At the time of the Unity Government, the Presidency sought to establish an Office of National Security as a step towards consolidation of the various security apparatuses. However, these efforts foundered amid the factional fighting that culminated in the declaration of a State of Emergency. The PA's efforts to reform the justice sector has been similarly disappointing, due to continued lack of clarity in the respective roles of the Ministry of Justice and the High Judicial Council (HJC) in the administration of courts and other issues.

71. ***There have been recent positive steps by the Caretaker Government to impose law and order in the West Bank, and to begin the process of disarming militias. This was matched by incremental steps by Israel, including the reinstatement of security coordination with the PA, the granting of amnesty to a select number of militants, and the release of mostly-Fatah militants.*** However, these steps will need to be expanded in depth and scope in order to create comprehensive incentives for disarmament. The revived GOI/PA Joint Security Committee—one of the more positive events since the Second *Intifada*—must lead to tangible gains on the ground for the entire population and not just a subset, lest it leads to further factional tensions. Efforts by the PA Ministry of Interior to restructure and unify the security services are most likely to succeed if the ultimate struc-

ture is seen as fully representative and divorced from any affiliations that have embroiled it in factional fighting in the past. And also here, Israel has a key role to play in restricting further incursions into Palestinian territory, and attacks on PA security organizations that provide a powerful disincentive to disarm.

72. ***The Caretaker Government has also taken some positive steps on Judicial Reform, but these can only be complete once a broader solution is found to reintegrate Gaza.*** There have been recent observable improvements in coordination between the new Ministry of Justice and the Higher Judicial Council, with clear consensus on sector reform priorities. This is best illustrated by the recent arrangements for joint management of justice sector capacity building projects. Of course, justice derives its value by its reach and scope. Hence, these steps are regarded as necessary but insufficient conditions in the absence of a resolution to the situation in Gaza. At the same time, the strengthening of formal and credible judicial systems can counteract the emergence of tribal and other systems for conflict resolution.

Rebuilding the Public Financial Management System

73. ***The PA Public Finance Management (PFM) system became increasingly fragmented in 2006*** due to the decision of donors and banks not to transact with the government. The Single Treasury Account was suspended, and without a proper budget framework and adequate control, transparency and accountability were substantially reduced. The new situation in Gaza has brought a number of new challenges and risks for the PFM system. The fact that the vast majority of administrative capacity for budget preparation as well as the main database servers of the MoF are in Gaza is a particular concern.

74. ***However, the Caretaker Government has made successful strides in rehabilitating some of the basic elements of the PFM system,***[70] including: (a) reconsolidating the Single Treasury Account (STA), following the Arab Bank's account suspension in 2006 and the creation of separate accounts in the Bank of Palestine; (b) preparing a budget for the remainder of 2007 and beginning work on a budget for 2008;[71] (c) reversing some of the staffing additions of 2005 and onward. Initially, 31,000 of the 170,000 civil and security personnel—half of whom were recruited prior to the 2006 PLC elections—were removed by MOF subject to a closer review of their status; (d) investigating the PA's bank accounts in the West Bank and Gaza after the

[70] These issues were identified by a World Bank mission in early 2007, and further analyzed and articulated by an IMF mission in July that assessed the PA's PFM system.

[71] Since 2005 and to date, the authorities are the using 1/12 monthly budgeting The Organic Budget Law allows the 1/12 mechanism for the first three months of the year only. However, the Palestinian Legislative Council (PLC) provided repeated approvals for its extension since early 2006.

State of Emergency, and reopening accounts in the West Bank but allowing for direct payments to contractors and beneficiaries in Gaza.[72] This will allow for a workable solution for donors to ensure that urgent services continue in Gaza, through an 'acceptable' flow of funds; (e) preparing financial statements for 2006, despite the fragmentation of 2006 and the need to consolidate the aid data from the President's Office, the various donors, etc.;[73] and (f) reestablishing the MOF's control systems. Prior to 2006 the MOF set up a unit to manage central payments and deployed MOF officers in line ministries. The MOF also developed a separate internal audit function.

On a Path of PFM Reform

75. ***The current crisis provides an opportunity to take a longer term and more strategic view of Palestinian finances.*** Throughout 2005 and prior to the crisis, the PA was running an average monthly deficit in excess of $60 million, nearly 60% above its average monthly revenues. The 2007 budget prepared by the MOF now projects an average monthly deficit of about $130 million.

76. ***The Ministry of Planning, in collaboration with the Ministry of Finance, is preparing a three-year Palestinian Reform and Development Plan (PRDP) 2008–10 based on the international standard Medium-Term Expenditure Framework (MTEF) approach.*** This will begin the process of addressing longstanding weaknesses and disconnects in policy-making, planning and budgeting processes, with a view to delivering a Palestinian-owned plan for allocating resources to national policy priorities. The PRDP will be submitted to the AHLC in December 2007.

77. ***This PRDP is a welcome reform step in and of itself.*** The processes by which the PA produced its annual recurrent budget have so far been disconnected from the planning processes that yielded the Medium Term Development Plan (MTDP). Clearly, the success of the PRDP relies as much in the process as in the end result. Recognizing the time required to fully implement a new MTEF methodology, it is critical to begin the process of allowing greater participation and consultation across the PA and with NGOs and other service providers. The PRDP will set out an overall Palestinian national policy agenda, provide estimates of government revenues, provide estimates of the amount of capital and recurrent expenditure required to finance the policy agenda and, hence, provide an estimate of external financing required over the medium-term. The PA will also use

[72] The only exception has been for the Ministry of Education to pay those supervising end of year exams last June (where specific instructions were given to the bank as to the nature of payments that could be accepted), for the Courts dealing with trust money, and the pension fund.

[73] The World Bank's 2006 Public Expenditure Review (PER) noted the lack of audited financial statements, with the last aggregate financial statement in 2004. Please visit www.worldbank.org/ps.

this process to identify necessary reform in the policy, planning and financial management systems over the medium-term in order to realize the full benefits of the MTEF approach. As such, donors can assist in balancing incentives for a quick reform plan that shows progress by the Caretaker Government, with one that is pragmatic, locally-owned and sustainable.

78. ***Thus, to add to the PA's challenges, an unavoidable reality and politically difficult measures must be embedded in the fiscal framework for 2008–10.*** Areas include the wage bill, the collection of utility fees, the subsidization of petroleum products, and social transfers. To succeed, the PA's efforts must be matched by significant amounts of external assistance and a strong recovery of private economic activity. As such, a commitment from the donor community to provide budget support over the medium-term, and to comply with the provisions of the Paris Declaration on Aid Effectiveness more generally, will be critical to the success of the MTEF initiative.

Short-Term Reforms of the Public Sector

79. ***In the near-term, the PA should continue consolidating all funds around the STA, to allow the PA to effectively manage its cash and budget planning, and to set the stage for a coherent and manageable budget support operation linked to reforms.*** An optimal configuration would be the merger of the STA, PLO, Office of the President, TIM and other donor accounts. In addition, MOF can continue to strengthen confidence by resuming timely fiscal reports for the remainder of 2007. The 2006 report should be subject to external audit.

80. ***Another short-term priority is to re-link institutions in the West Bank and Gaza.*** This is an acute need given that budget preparation and the accounting system have historically been centralized in Gaza. The MOF is taking steps to create parallel systems, which is a reasonable step. However, it does not provide confidence in terms of the long-term stability of the system, nor of the broader issue of the role of Palestinian institutions. At the end of 2004,[74] 44% of public sector employees were located in Gaza. While some ministries distribute staff equally across the two areas, others do not. For example, about 75% of Ministry of Justice employees were located in Gaza and, in the case of the Ministry of Planning, the reverse applies. The impact on the PA's conduct of business is clear. For example, the Minister of Justice in the Caretaker Government has had to draw on resources from various governmental and nongovernmental organizations. If the separation persists, there will be pressure to recruit new employees and hence add further to the public sector wage bill. And even in ministries

[74] This is the last date at which reliable records of the number of public sector workers employed by individual PNA organizations located in the West Bank and Gaza Strip are available.

where the distribution of employees was roughly equal (e.g., MOF) there are still disparities in staffing levels among directorates.

Longer-Term Reforms of the Public Sector

81. The path to a sustainable fiscal footing also requires an early start on longer-term reforms. In consultation with the World Bank,[75] IMF and others, the PA has identified a number of priorities that will have a proportional impact on the budget. These include:

82. ***Human Resources Management (HRM), and Civil and Security Service Reform.*** While there is ample evidence of efforts by the Cabinet formed immediately after the PLC elections in 2006 to effect organizational changes based on political rather than technical considerations,[76] this issue has long preceded Hamas' victory in the PLC elections. Prior to the elections, the PA had already approved public sector pay increases,[77] promotions[78] and hiring that reversed earlier commitments to contain the wage bill.[79] In the current environment, aggressive reforms (e.g., staff retrenchment and/ or demobilization and reintegration of security personnel) may risk further destabilization. But there remains a menu of critical yet less dramatic steps, including a moratorium on recruitment and wage rises, and/or restrictions on overtime payments to only those in front-line delivery in the Ministry of Health. Other options can also yield immediate savings. For example, the World Bank's 2006 Public Expenditure Review suggested that a roll-back of the 2005 salary increases may save the PA about $300 million annually over two years. A voluntary retirement packages to civil and security servants may save the PA about $400 to $700 million over five years.

83. This menu would need to be accompanied by steps to tackle deeper structural problems of overstaffing and poor performance (e.g., upgrading HRM systems and procedures to facilitating payroll and performance audits, launching a pay and grading review). Unfortunately, the severing of public institutions between the West Bank and Gaza is likely to lead to more hiring to compensate for the loss of accessible staff.

---

[75] The World Bank Public Expenditure Review, 2006, www.worldbank.org/ps.

[76] An analysis of the 10th Cabinet's 210 formal decisions up to September 2006 revealed that 32% relate to appointments or promotions of civil servants, 21% relate to changes in organizational structures of government and 18% directly reverse previous government decisions. The remaining decisions relate to various administrative matters; none of them set out policies or programs.

[77] Average pay increases under the new Civil Service Law in July 2005: security services, 28%; civil service – 13%. These large pay increases awarded to the public sector were significantly out of line with the general labor market, and in particular, wage levels at the lower grades now exceed those in the private sector.

[78] Between May–October 2005, 14% of category 2 employees and 10% of category 1 employees were promoted.

[79] The wage bill increased to $1 billion in 2005 from $871 million in 2004; a rise of approx. 15%.

84. ***Local Government, Intergovernmental Fiscal Relations and Municipalities.*** WB&G has one of the more vibrant local government sectors in the region, as municipalities and village councils enjoy a relatively high degree of financial, administrative and operational autonomy from the central government. Yet the second intifada has heralded the problem of spiraling municipal financial arrears, heavy reliance on utility service surcharges for revenues, and an alarming shift of expenditures away from capital investments toward administration and wages. There is a need to consolidate the legal framework for decentralization, to ensure greater coordination among national and local agencies, and to rationalize the rising number of local governments. More encouraging are the recent attempts to improve revenue recovery by introducing pre-paid metering for utility services and the establishment of the Municipal Development and Lending Fund (MDLF) which acts as a financial intermediary in the sector and can, over time, become an important policy instrument in promoting reforms through performance-based grants to municipalities.

85. ***Health, Education and Social Services.*** The functions of the public sector were severely undermined by the financial boycott, as unpredictable finances and the public sector strike contributed to the drop in public services, particularly in the West Bank. In the education sector, 35 school days were lost. In the health sector, facilities stopped providing services beyond emergency treatment between August 2006 and May 2007. Nevertheless, the social ministries showed remarkable resilience in cushioning citizens from the impact of the boycott. For example, the Ministry of Education implemented measures to compensate for the loss of classroom time caused by the strike. Ultimately, the 2007Tawjihi (12th grade) exams were conducted successfully, though results in the West Bank show a slight decline in the percentage of students passing the exam in 2006–2007 compared with 2005–2006.[80]

86. This is not surprising given the accomplishments within the health and education systems over the years. The expansion and access in the education sector is comparable with most middle-income countries, although quality varies widely. Health indicators are generally higher than others in MENA. However, there is scope for savings across these sectors, which represent very large shares of the wage bill, often at the expense of pharmaceuticals, medical supplies and operations and maintenance. As for social services, some are operating in a limited form despite the recent financial crisis. Yet reforms are needed in this sector. PA public sector pension schemes are among the most generous in the world, Moreover, the PA's pension fund obligations have in recent years been left unpaid in favor of monthly salary payments, leaving the PA in arrears to the Gaza

[80] 59% of students passed this year in contrast to 63% of students in the previous year.

Box 1: Municipal Development & Lending Fund (MDLF)

The genesis of the MDLF dates back to 2002 when the Ministers of Local Government, Finance and Planning agreed on the need to establish a more rationalized and transparent approach to intergovernmental fiscal transfers, aid coordination in the municipal sector, and financial management at the local level. They also sought to create a policy instrument to instill fiscal discipline and increased accountability and transparency in budget preparation and reporting at the local level. With support from the European Union, Denmark, Agence Français de Développement, GTZ, KFW and the World Bank, the MDLF was established in 2005 to: (i) introduce a rules-based framework for intergovernmental fiscal transfers; (ii) mobilize PA and donor aid for capital investments and emergency assistance at the municipal level; (iii) improve aid coordination in the sector and develop a municipal finance database; and (iv) promote innovation through new programs and learning exchanges based on global best practice. Despite its emergence during a period of uncertainty and crisis, the MDLF has proven to be resilient and responsive to many of the most urgent needs of municipalities by channeling emergency and development assistance to them through various programs over the past two years. Over time and as the political situation stabilizes, the MDLF aims to restore financial solvency at the municipal level through the use of performance-based grants intended to help municipalities graduate to credit worthy status and thus be able to attract financial from the commercial banking sector.

Pension Corporation (GPIC) and further endangering the system.[81] Reforms would include revising the Unified Pension Law to ensure sustainability. The pension law for security services, passed in 2005, is excessive and simply unaffordable. The August 27th, 2007 decree modifying these laws creates a pension system that is insolvent from the start, and increases the implicit liabilities of the PA which is the guarantor. Beyond pension reform, there is scope for significant savings through better social safety net program coordination and targeting. Currently the West Bank & Gaza uses

[81] In January 2005 a Security Services Pension Law was approved covering all security personnel 45 years and above. The Law's provisions were over-generous and unsustainable. Subsequently, a Unified Pension Law (UPL) covering civil service and security employees under 45 came into force in May 2005 was also unsustainable and added to the PA's liabilities. On August 23rd, 2007 a Presidential decree modified these laws, making minor changes in the security services law but retaining fiscally unattainable provisions that increase the PA's implicit liabilities as guarantor. For example, the bylaws allow workers to collect a pension at 55 with only 15 years of service. They also link pensions to current salary scales rather than indexing these to the cost of living. Thirdly, the bylaws now cover the entire formal sector (including the private sector) under the same unaffordable parameters, including PLC members and other elected officials.

several ad-hoc programs often operating independently of each other and covering overlapping beneficiaries.

3.3 The Donor Response and Strategies

Summary: **With more than 40 donors, aid flows into the WB&G have been considerable, including in the last two years where many donors sought creative ways to assist despite their boycott of the PA. Yet, aid remains fragmented and focused on bilateral arrangements with donors based on individual political positions rather than a collective longer-term view on broader economic and governance fundamentals. This has undermined aid effectiveness and created a "shopping list" approach to development planning where projects are more aligned with the donor's requirements than with local priorities.**

Furthermore, aid has not been matched by parallel GOI and PA actions to create an environment where funds translate into sustainable growth. Aid has been reactive, and has not fully enabled institution-building or created incentives to reform. The hollowing out of the Palestinian economy has risked reversing the benefits of over $10 billion in past aid, and has diverted funds to recurrent expenditures and basic humanitarian support rather than to an investment in Palestinian institutions and infrastructure. Donors have long been aware of this issue, hence the establishment of multilateral financing mechanisms and new aid coordination bodies. Going forward, these aid structures must be revitalized. The presence of the new Quartet Special Envoy, and his leveraging of these coordination structures, could strengthen them considerably. Also, donor commitment to the Palestinian Reform and Development Plan 2008–10 will be a key test of the support to Palestinian-driven recovery and growth.

87. ***Looking back, donor assistance can be said to have slowed the pace of Palestinian economic deterioration in bad times, and contributed to growth in good times.*** When permitted by the prevailing circumstances, donors abided by their collective understanding of the links between economic opportunities and the peace process, and on their role in building Palestinian institutions to underpin this peace. However, in reality donor funds have mostly gone to offsetting the impacts declines rather than underwriting growth (See Table 3 and Figure 6).

88. ***A 1999 joint report by the Government of Japan and the World Bank estimated that donor assistance since Oslo had contributed an additional 6–7% per annum to the growth of Palestinian GNP per capita.***[82] At the same time, the downturn of the economy since the Second *Intifada* was

[82] Aid Effectiveness in the West Bank & Gaza, World Bank/Government of Japan, 1999, AHLC Report, p. 1.

Table 3: Aid Disbursements grants and loans (in USD)[4]

Type of Aid	2002	2003	2004	2005	2006
Development[1]	$310,931,454	$448,917,192	$368,106,060	$381,358,856	$252,777,407
Humanitarian Aid[2]	$351,431,666	$339,063,715	$377,034,035	$490,987,126	$412,890,057
Budget support[3]	$497,200,000	$250,980,000	$361,080,000	$349,000,000	$738,210,000
Total	$1,159,563,120	$1,038,960,907	$1,106,220,095	$1,221,345,982	$1,403,877,464

Sources:
1- Development disbursements from Ministry of Planning PAMS database. Some humanitarian aid may be misclassified in this category, particularly in the health sector.
2- Humanitarian aid disbursements from Ministry of Planning PAMS database and includes UNRWA support and is adjusted by inputs from some key donors.
3- Budget support disbursements from Ministry of Finance and IMF.
4- These figures were compiled by the World Bank based on Ministry of Planning, Ministry of Finance, IMF, and donor data. The accuracy of these figures may be in question due to the lack of harmonized and consistent reporting on aid disbursements.

matched with a large injection of donor funds. In reality, these donor funds seem to have prevented a complete collapse in the economy, and mitigated the effects of the drop in GDP, employment, etc. As such, the amount of donor funds in recent times can be regarded as the quantification of the costs of mobility restrictions and other external shocks.

89. *From the outset, the objective was to move from humanitarian assistance and basic services to setting long-term infrastructure for Palestinian-driven*

Figure 6: External Assistance to the WB&G

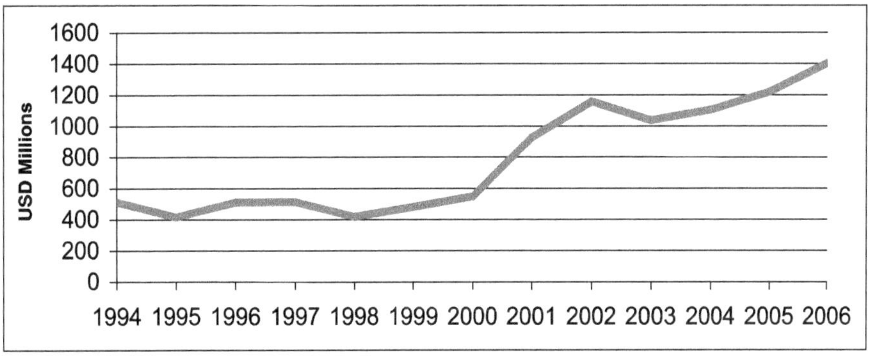

Source: 1994–1997: Report on Aid Effectiveness, WB and Japan, 1999; 1998–2001: Four Years of Intifada and Economic Crisis, WB; 2002–2006: WB compliation of MOP, MOF, and IMF data.

development supported by local institutions.[83] However, from a technical perspective, the actual course has been erratic and bound by a series of shocks that prevented local institutions from achieving any lasting momentum. Strategies and policies were delayed, and predictable signals of donor commitment to reform were suspended.

90. ***The past two years have been a particularly challenging episode in donor-PA relations.*** Political considerations led to the near cessation of direct relations between most bilateral donors and the PA, with only some multilateral agencies and a few donors continuing direct contact and project administration.[84]

91. ***The impact of the donor boycott on the PA has been discussed at length.*** Despite collective efforts to provide humanitarian assistance and basic services to the population, the PA was forced to operate at about 66% of its 2005 expenditures.[85] The alternative mechanisms employed by donors centered on direct implementation or the Office of the President as a counterpart. The EU TIM injected badly-needed funds directly to beneficiaries. Arab funds were also paid directly to the OoP for disbursement. While the OoP made a valiant effort in managing these funds, their best efforts could not substitute for years of capacity and systems development at the Ministry of Finance.

Aid Trends

92. ***Despite the boycott and Israel's freezing of clearance revenues, total donor assistance reached a record $1.4 billion*** in 2006, over half of which was in a form of budgetary support.[86] Arab donors provided nearly $600 million in budgetary support from January 2006 – June 2007, a quarter of which was transferred in 2007. The EU TIM provided over $520 million through July 2007 in essential supplies and running costs for health, education and social services (through the World Bank run ESSP program, or Window I), power and fuel for sanitation and health services (Window II), and allowances for some public servants and social hardship cases (Window III).

93. ***Thus, 2006 saw a doubling of budgetary support to $738 million. While budget support is in itself desirable as it relies on local prioritization and***

[83] World Bank analysis shows that growth rates are twice as high in countries with effective institutions. There, assistance of 1%of GDP produces a sustained increase of 0.5% in GDP growth, reduces poverty by 1%, and increases private investment by 1.9%. But in the absence of good policies and institutions, aid has little or no effect on long-term economic growth, and negative effects on private investment (World Bank 1998a).

[84] Some donors maintained contact with the PA government officials at a technical level and allowed the continuation of ongoing projects. Others allowed only humanitarian projects. Some countries altered their policies somewhat with the formation of the unity government. Overall, the particulars of donor policy during this period were by no means homogeneous and varied over time.

[85] West Bank and Gaza: Fiscal Performance 2006, IMF, March 2007.

[86] This includes direct financing to the Office of the President, the PA, and the EU TIM.

Figure 7: Budget Support to the WB&G

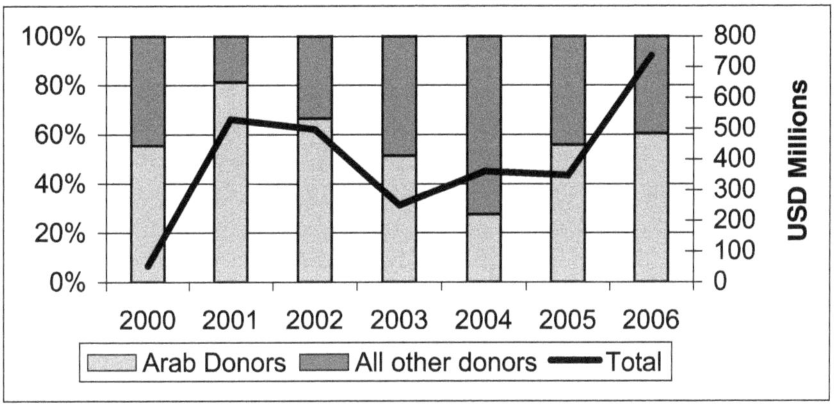

Source: MOF and IMF data.

implementation, the aid given in 2006–07 flowed away from the PA and from development projects. This trend, combined with the hollowing out of the Palestinian economy's productive base, risks thrusting the WB&G into a protracted period of aid dependence for recurrent spending and humanitarian assistance. The injection of massive budget support did not offset the effects of the frozen clearance revenues, nor the reductions in tax revenues resulting from a depressed economy. Equally damaging was the fact that the doubling of external budget support was accompanied by a comparably sharp decline in aid for development projects (See Figures 7

Figure 8: Budget Support versus Development Assistance

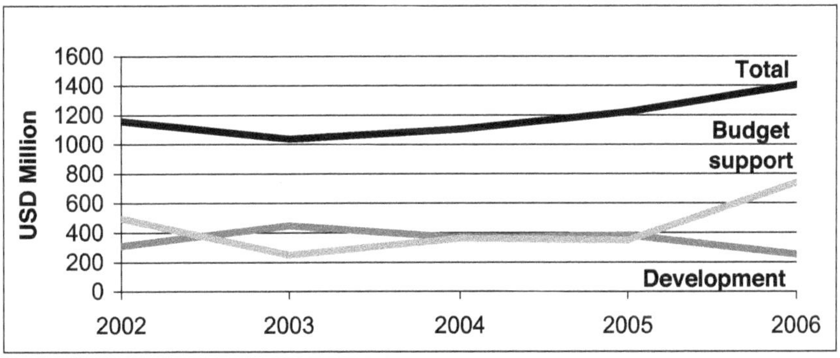

Source: Budget support from MOF and IMF; Development figures from MOP; Total is a complication from MOF, IMF, MOP, and donors and includes budgets, development, and humanitarian aid.

and 8). For the 2008 budget, about 94% of the required donor funds will go towards recurrent expenditures as opposed to development assistance.

94. ***According to the Ministry of Planning, development aid dropped by at least one third from its $381 million level in 2005.***[87] Coming at a time of little to no public investment, and a very limited appetite for private investment under an excessive movement and access regime, this has and will continue to diminish any residue of productive capital in the economy. Thus, the sheer amount of donor money injected into the economy may have buffered any catastrophic effects of the boycott and restrictions, but it did not trigger any development 'multiplier effect' that is the normal standard for aid elsewhere.

PA Management of Donor Assistance

95. ***The 'bypass financing routes' used by most donors undermined the PA's ability to plan or allocate funds.*** The lack of donor contact with PA officials in the Ministries of Planning, Finance, and others limited the latter's influence on funding decisions. While this approach may have been a practical response to political constraints, it was neither cost-effective nor aligned with the PA's broader priorities.

96. ***While this problem was particularly acute in 2006, the lack of PA ownership in planning and prioritization is a longer standing issue.*** At the core of this issue is the PA's Medium Term Development Planning (MTDP) process which intended to provide a framework for the prioritization and selection of projects. However, there was no actual commitment to the MTDP within the PA or among donors, including the need to abide by the MOP's mandate to endorse projects and programs, and provide accurate and comprehensive information on their activities to the MOP's database.

97. ***The Palestinian Reform and Development Plan 2008–10 to be presented to the AHLC in December intends to marry budgetary and development planning,*** and will be an impetus for greater Palestinian ownership. As such, donor support to this process and to a predictable flow of aid would be an unmistakable signal of an underlying commitment to Palestinian institution-building.[88] Also, donors should actively support the MOP's efforts towards a Palestinian Harmonization and Aid Effectiveness Action Plan.

[87] These figures are only estimates and are subject to error due to lack of harmonization in classification of aid projects and other inconsistencies.

[88] The PA's recognition of the need to interface with donors is imbedded in the PRDP preparation process, whereby PA sub-teams were created on economic development, infrastructure, governance and social and humanitarian policy. The setup of these teams mirrors the structure of the Local Strategy Groups.

Developments in Aid Coordination

98. *Recognizing the challenges described above, a new aid coordination structure was approved at the London AHLC in 2005, creating the Local Development Forum and four strategy groups to coordinate aid at the local level and report to the AHLC.* The key features of this new formula were the leadership of the PA and its partnership with donors in four Strategy Groups (economic development, governance, infrastructure, and social and humanitarian issues). Unfortunately, the boycott of the PA made it difficult to fully implement this structure. Three out of the four Strategy Groups actually convened, in addition to a number of sector working sub-groups.[89] There were however gaps in either PA or donor representation in various groups and, more importantly, the ability of these groups to engage in a meaningful strategic planning and coordination. Some plans were presented, including the PA's 2007 Operational Plan, a recovery plan for 2007, and the Private Sector Recovery and Resilience Plan. With the exception of the latter, which did influence some donor initiatives, there was little donor engagement with these plans.

99. *There has been substantial progress since June 2007 in reactivating these strategy groups with the full participation of the PA, and with the first meeting of the Infrastructure Group on September 11, 2007.* Moving forward, the sustained value-added of these groups will depend on the active participation of donors, PA ministries, and the new Quartet Representative. As most donors operating in the WB&G are signatories to the Paris Declaration on Aid Effectiveness, this would be a continuation of commitments and practices observed elsewhere.

4. The Way Forward

100. *Sadly, lost within this story are some important strides by the PA, Israel and the donors over the years to enable Palestinian economic recovery.* The PA's past reforms in public financial management, municipal governance, education and health were impressive. The commitment of donors to support the Palestinian people throughout a series of unprecedented political crises is also notable, as is Israel's efforts to balance peace with a legitimate goal of protecting its citizens.

101. *Moving forward, the restoration of growth and peace will require all sides not only to return to the now well-known preconditions for economic recovery, but to take actions collectively and in parallel, with a view to longer-term benefits and not only the short-term costs.* Experience over

[89] Donors operating in the WB&G are signatories to the March 2005 Paris Declaration on Aid Effectiveness, which requires reciprocal actions by the partner and donors to improve partner ownership of development agenda, donor alignment with partner priorities, and harmonization among donors.

the past 15 years has shown that only parallel actions on the recommendations of this report will lead to tangible results. The interactions among PA, GOI and donor policies are tied to such an extent that there is no recourse but to parallel steps and reforms—the absence of one greatly undermines the success of the other.

102. ***There is little doubt that parallel actions in a situation of conflict and political uncertainty are risky and politically costly. But experience to date has provided no substitute.*** The viability of the PA is a precondition for a lasting recovery and peace. For the PA to be viable, it must take bold steps to restore law and order and become fiscally self-sufficient. To date, it has not been able to do without predictable access to its clearance revenues, predictable donor financing over the medium-term, and a revitalized private sector that can generate tax revenues and absorb current and future labor. The PA's first priority of security and the disarming of militias is challenged by the absence of alternative jobs and the uncertainty about a future peace arrangement, making most unwilling to give up the only tangible item at their disposal—the gun.

103. As such, continued donor investment in and through PA institutions must bolster a commitment by the Government to carry out key reforms noted in this report, not be conditioned on it. Similarly, the PA's reform agenda must clearly and realistically reflect a finite horizon of aid dependency. Clearly, donors must expect reasonable assurances of transparency and due diligence in the use of their funds, as well as a reform trajectory. Yet, the complexity of the current situation may have shifted most donor requirements, creating scenarios where political conditions for aid may lead the PA to adapt in a way that is inconsistent with the economic conditions for aid (e.g., wage bill containment versus security sector consolidation). Of course, donors are not oblivious to this fact, which is consistent with the Paris Declaration on Aid Effectiveness that nearly all have adopted. But they have not been able to fully practice what they promote without efforts by the PA to ensure internal political stability, or by GOI to create the environment for a shift away from humanitarian support.

104. ***Israel's actions on Palestinian movement and access must also reflect a clear policy on settlement activity, and a view of the removal of these restrictions as a major catalyst for stability, and not merely a consequence of it.*** In addition to the private sector, Israeli restrictions also impede the functions of the Palestinian public sector. The PA is obliged to administer series of isolated territories despite complex obstacles in coordinating government policy, administrative procedures, service delivery,[90] and law

[90] Government authority and administrative procedures in the West Bank and Gaza continue to be based on a plethora of laws, regulations and military orders issued by a succession of occupying forces. Progress towards eliminating discrepancies and replacing these legal instruments with unified laws and regulations has been hampered by territorial fragmentation.

enforcement. Even in the delivery of basic services, the PA is unable to exploit economies of scale as a means of controlling the cost of service delivery.[91] As such, the movement restrictions have shaped the Palestinian Territories into a series of micro-territories each requiring their only health facilities, waste sites, etc. Thus, the case for the removal of restrictions is clear, and requires a revision of Israel's approach to security as a balance between short and long term gains, in parallel with PA policies at disarmament of militias and reform of the security services, recognizing the devastating impacts of short-term breaches in security on previous attempts at reconciliation, and on the Palestinian economy itself.

105. ***Of course, any discussion on economic recovery and the prospects for peace is incomplete without the Gaza Strip.*** Gaza represents about 40% of the population, and a quintessential part of the Palestinian territory, economy and identity. Thus, any serious options for a private-sector led and export-oriented Palestinian economy must include Gaza. Without it, the collective investments and commitments advocated in this report are unlikely to materialize due to continued uncertainties about the sustainability and inclusiveness of Palestinian institutions.

106. Whether practical or not under the circumstances, the need for these parallel steps is evident. These are the fundamentals of economic growth, and draw on the basics that guide all economies. Without them, all well-intentioned and creative solutions, policies and investments are undermined. As the past years have shown, there is no prosthetic for an economy whose basic building blocks—people, natural resources and entrepreneurial spirit- are unable to move freely. The implication of this view is that all parties will need to expend more resources and assume more risks than done in the past. Perhaps this is best referred to as an investment in peace. The costs are subjective to each side, and are beyond the scope of this report. But the benefits of success make this an investment worth making.

[91] Fragmentation of communities creates demand for more schools and healthcare facilities than is ordinarily required to serve a similar-sized population that is free to travel across a similar-sized territory.

DOCUMENT NO. 13

OCCUPIED PALESTINIAN TERRITORIES TORN APART BY FACTIONAL STRIFE

Amnesty International Report
MDE 21/020/2007

October 24, 2007

Glossary

al-Aqsa Brigades al-Aqsa Martyrs' Brigades	armed wing of Fatah
Executive Force Security	force set up in 2006 by the then Hamas government
Fatah	Main party of the PLO, formerly headed by the first PA President Yasser Arafat
Hamas	Islamic Resistance Movement
ICRC	International Committee of the Red Cross
al-Mezan	A Palestinian human rights organization
Mukhabarat	General Intelligence
OPT	Occupied Palestinian Territories
PA	Palestinian Authority
PCHR	Palestinian Centre for Human Rights
PICCR	Palestinian Independent Commission for Citizens' Rights
PLO	Palestine Liberation Organization
Qassam Brigades 'Izz al-Din al-Qassam Brigades	armed wing of Hamas
RPGs	Rocket-propelled grenades

Chronology

January 2006 Hamas wins PA elections in the West Bank and Gaza Strip, defeating Fatah party of President Mahmoud Abbas.

March 2006 Hamas forms a government led by Prime Minister Isma'il Haniyeh.

February 2007 Fatah and Hamas leaders meet in Saudi Arabia to negotiate an end to inter-factional fighting and agree to form a national unity government.

17 March 2007 Fatah and Hamas form a unity government led by Prime Minister Haniyeh.

March-May 2007 Sporadic inter-factional clashes and attacks continue between security forces and armed groups loyal to Fatah and Hamas.

May 2007 Fatah-Hamas inter-factional clashes escalate.

June 2007 Hamas forces and armed groups attack and take control (by 14 June) of all Fatah-controlled PA security installations and government buildings in the Gaza Strip. On 14 June President Abbas dismisses Prime Minister Haniyeh's government, declares a state of emergency and establishes an emergency government based in the West Bank headed by outgoing Finance Minister, now Prime Minister Salam Fayyad. Hamas refuses to recognize the emergency government and sets up a Hamas de-facto administration in the Gaza Strip.

1. Introduction

Unprecedented levels of political violence between Palestinian factions in the Gaza Strip during the past year, which culminated in June 2007 when Hamas seized control of Palestinian Authority (PA) security institutions in the territory, took a heavy toll on the civilian population and compounded the devastating impact of decades of Israeli occupation and military campaigns, causing a further deterioration in living conditions and prompting greater international isolation.

In all, some 350 people were killed and more than 2,000 were injured in the first half of 2007 as a direct result of the inter-factional armed clashes and attacks in the Gaza Strip between rival security forces and armed militias loyal to PA President Mahmoud Abbas' Fatah party and to (the now deposed) Prime Minister Isma'il Haniyeh's Hamas party. Many of the dead and injured were bystanders who had taken no part in the fighting; others were militants of one side or another, including many who were killed in cold blood.

Both Fatah and Hamas security forces and armed groups committed grave human-rights abuses and displayed a flagrant disregard for the safety of the civilian population. Rival security forces whose responsibility it was to uphold and enforce the law, and to protect the population, betrayed this responsibility and instead acted as partisans, in concert with armed groups that serve as their proxy militias, and themselves broke the law and committed gross abuses with complete impunity.

Both sides killed captured rivals and abducted scores of members of rival groups and held them hostage, to be exchanged for friends and relatives held by their rivals. Indiscriminate attacks and reckless gun battles in residential neighbourhoods left a beleaguered civilian population virtual prisoners in their own homes. Roadblocks set up by gunmen from both sides further endangered the safety of residents and impeded their movements.

Much of the fighting took place in, from and around residential buildings, endangering both residents and passers by. Hamas gunmen commandeered the roofs of tall buildings from which they launched attacks against PA security forces, while Fatah gunmen made similar use of buildings from which to attack Hamas positions. Gunmen fired rocket-propelled grenades (RPGs) and other missiles at and from residential buildings in which civilians were present causing large-scale damage and starting fires that resulted in further destruction. They also mounted attacks in and around hospitals, directly targeting and launching attacks from hospital buildings, putting patients and staff in danger, impeding the work of medical staff and hindering access to healthcare for those in need. At times, they directly targeted patients in their hospital beds.

In its visit to the Occupied Palestinian Territories (OPT) in June/July, Amnesty International heard harrowing accounts from victims of both sides and from residents who were directly affected by the waves of armed clashes which took place in the Gaza Strip in June and previous months. Although accounts of gun battles and other attacks in which both gunmen and uninvolved bystanders were killed and injured are often contested, there is incontrovertible evidence that both sides acted with reckless disregard for the safety of local residents and committed grave human rights abuses.

The situation that has emerged since Hamas' violent takeover in the Gaza Strip in June has further undermined the rule of law. President Abbas' decision to suspend all operations of PA security forces and judicial institutions in the Gaza Strip created a legal and institutional vacuum which Hamas has filled by establishing an alternative security and law enforcement apparatus which lacks appropriately-trained personnel or adequate accountability mechanisms or safeguards. Hamas' Executive Force and the 'Izz al-Din al-Qassam Brigades (Qassam Brigades, Hamas' armed wing), operating outside the legal framework, continue to target Fatah activists and other critics. They routinely use violence to break up demonstrations and other gatherings, carry out arbitrary arrests and frequently subject detainees to beatings, torture or other ill-treatment. Undertakings by deposed Prime Minister Haniyeh and other Hamas leaders to investigate such abuses, hold those responsible to account and prevent the abuses from recurring have been ineffective. If anything, abuses have increased.

In the West Bank, the emergency government appointed by President Abbas in June has done little to hold to account the Fatah gunmen who reacted to the Hamas attacks in Gaza by attacking and abducting Hamas supporters and burning down their houses and businesses as well as the offices of charities believed to be linked to Hamas. Even though attacks targeting Hamas members and supporters mostly ceased after a few days, Fatah's armed wing, the al-Aqsa Martyrs' Brigades (al-Aqsa Brigades), continue to operate outside the law and to attack and intimidate Hamas supporters with impunity. Hundreds of known or presumed Hamas supporters and other Fatah critics have been arrested by PA security forces, and violations of arrest and detention procedures have been frequent. The space for freedom of speech and non-violent political activities in both the West Bank and Gaza Strip has shrunk significantly, both due to harassment and intimidation by militias acting outside the legal framework, and as a result of direct measures taken by the PA to silence their opponents.

Amnesty International is greatly concerned about the conduct of the PA security forces and Fatah-controlled armed groups and that of Hamas-controlled forces and armed groups, in particular at:

reckless use of force by all parties in the armed clashes, which resulted in the killing and wounding of unarmed bystanders, including children;

deliberate killings of political opponents and of hostages, and of armed men who had been captured or incapacitated;

the use by all parties to the armed clashes of hospitals, schools and civilian residential buildings from which to carry out attacks against their opponents, including attacks carried out against and within such buildings, including hospitals;

abductions, hostage-taking and arbitrary detention;

torture and other ill-treatment of detainees and hostages;

denial of detainees' access to legal counsel;

use of excessive, unnecessary and even deadly force against peaceful demonstrators;

systematic impunity for members of the security forces and armed groups responsible for these grave human rights abuses in the West Bank and Gaza Strip.

In the Gaza Strip Amnesty International is concerned at:

political killings and the re-emergence of a situation of lawlessness;

the targeting of Fatah supporters and other political opponents by the Executive Force and the Qassam Brigades in a politically-motivated campaign of arbitrary detentions and abductions;

torture and other ill-treatment of detainees and hostages;

arbitrary detention of detainees in locations not authorized by law for this purpose, where detainees are at risk;

the establishment by the Hamas de-facto administration of agencies and mechanisms to enforce the law and administer justice, but which lack the requisite independence, skills and accountability to discharge this role and to ensure that the rule of law is respected for both victims and accused, that human-rights abuses are not committed, that victims have access to effective mechanisms to obtain redress, and that those accused of crimes are afforded due process;

the impunity enjoyed by perpetrators of crimes and the lack of political will on the part of the Hamas de-facto administration to hold such perpetrators to account and to respect fundamental human rights, including the rights to freedom of expression, assembly and association.

In the West Bank Amnesty International is concerned at:

the targeting of Hamas supporters by PA security forces in a politically-motivated campaign of arbitrary detentions and intimidation;

torture and other ill-treatment of detainees held arbitrarily by the PA security forces;

systematic breaches of the procedures laid down by Palestinian law relating to arrest, detention and prosecution of suspects; arrests are carried out by security forces who have no authority under the law to do so and detainees are held arbitrarily in security-force facilities that are not designated by law for such purpose;

the failure of the security forces to bring detainees before prosecutors and judges within the legally-stipulated period, and the continued arbitrary detention of detainees whose release has been ordered by a judge;

attacks by members of al-Aqsa Brigades against Hamas supporters and others;

the impunity enjoyed by members of the security forces and al-Aqsa Brigades and the lack of political will on the part of the PA administration to hold such perpetrators to account; to respect fundamental human rights, including the rights to freedom of expression, assembly and association; and to afford due process and redress to the victims.

2. Background

In January 2006 Hamas won the Palestinian legislative elections, defeating the Fatah party of President Mahmoud Abbas which had been in power continuously since the establishment of the PA in 1994. Hamas formed a government in March 2006, led by Prime Minister Isma'il Haniyeh.

Over the following months, political tensions between the rival parties and their supporters developed into armed confrontations in which security forces and militia-type armed groups loyal to Fatah were pitted against security forces and similar militia-type armed groups loyal to Hamas. These clashes became increasingly frequent and intensified as repeated attempts to reach a compromise and form a Fatah-Hamas coalition government failed, and a new wave of inter-factional fighting broke out after President Abbas announced in December 2006 that he intended to call new presidential and parliamentary elections in the PA.

In February 2007, leaders of the two parties met in Mecca, under the auspices of King Abdallah of Saudi Arabia, and reached what became known as the "Mecca Agreement".[1] Essentially, this was a pledge to end the inter-factional fighting and form a national unity government: crucially, the agreement failed to spell out the concrete measures the two sides would take to achieve the stated goal.

The unity government was then established on 17 March 2007. Prime Minister Haniyeh remained in place as its head but it included ministers from Fatah and Hamas, as well as independents and representatives of small parties. It failed to bring any improvement, however, and the continuing involvement of Hamas led the international community largely to maintain its boycott and the sanctions it had imposed on the Hamas-led government following its election in 2006, and to continue to limit its contacts and funding to the PA to President Abbas and non-Hamas ministers. Hamas resented its continuing international isolation but persisted in its refusal to comply with the conditions laid down by the Quartet (USA, European Union, Russia and the UN), namely that it should recognize the State of Israel, renounce violence in its struggle against Israeli occupation and accept agreements previously signed by the Palestine Liberation Organization (PLO) with Israel.

Tensions continued to mount particularly in the Gaza Strip, where the Hamas leadership remained confined and became increasingly resentful

---

[1] *http://www.jmcc.org/new/07/feb/meccaagree.htm.*

that its ministers and institutions continued to be isolated by the international boycott and sanctions while the mostly West Bank-based Fatah leadership enjoyed international recognition and continued to receive foreign financial support.

As the level of distrust between Fatah and Hamas grew, the viability of the new unity government was increasingly called into question and both sides accused the other of seeking to undermine it. At the same time, the security situation deteriorated, marked by abductions and attacks against foreigners, and Hamas alleged that certain individuals within Fatah were deliberately fomenting chaos in the Gaza Strip in order to force the collapse of the unity government.

In May 2007, armed clashes between the two sides resumed with renewed intensity. A series of ceasefires were agreed by the Fatah and Hamas leadership, but these collapsed within days or even hours. Each time, the ensuing casualties and damage engendered further resentment and mistrust between the two sides, so exacerbating the divisions between them and increasing the likelihood of further violent clashes. As lawlessness spread, the distinctions between politically-motivated attacks and score-settling by sub-groups on each side, attacks by other political groups and long-standing family feuds became increasingly blurred. In May, unity government Interior Minister Talab al-Qawasmi resigned amid mounting tension between Fatah and Hamas and actions by both sides which undermined his position.[2] Then, after the Israeli government authorized the entry into the Gaza Strip from Egypt of hundreds of Fatah fighters newly trained under a US-funded programme and Hamas gunmen ambushed a convoy which they alleged was carrying weapons newly delivered to Fatah, both sides accused the other of plotting a coup. Widespread and intensive armed clashes ensued.

Hamas forces and armed groups attacked and took over all the PA security forces positions and other institutions, and effectively took control of internal affairs in the Gaza Strip. In response, on 14 June, President Abbas dismissed Prime Minister Haniyeh's unity government, declared a state of emergency and appointed outgoing Finance Minister Salam Fayyad as Prime Minister of a new emergency government based in the West Bank. The emergency government was appointed on 17 June for a 30-day period, as stipulated by the Palestinian Basic Law,[3] but has remained in place to date, without the approval of the Palestinian Legislative Council (parliament). [4]This violates the Basic Law, which stipulates: *"The state of emergency*

---

[2] See: *http://news.bbc.co.uk/1/hi/world/middle_east/6653437.stm.*

[3] The Basic Law of 2003, amended in 2005, acts as a sort of constitution pending the establishment of a Palestinian state.

[4] Basic Law, Article 110(1): "The President of the National Authority may declare a state of emergency by decree when there is a threat to national security caused by war, invasion, armed insurrection or in times of natural disaster, for a period not to exceed thirty (30) days."

may be extended for another period of thirty (30) days if a two-thirds majority of the members of the Legislative Council vote in favor of the extension."[5]

Hamas has refused to recognize the West Bank-based emergency government, insisting that the deposed Prime Minister Haniyeh is the legitimate, democratically-elected Prime Minister and calling for a resumption of dialogue with Fatah. President Abbas, Fatah and the emergency government insist that Hamas relinquish control of all PA security installations and other institutions in the Gaza Strip before any political dialogue can be considered. Other political parties represented in the Palestinian Parliament have abstained from participating in the emergency government, except for the Third Way party of Prime Minister Fayyad, but some have backed President Abbas' call for a return to the *status quo ante* in the Gaza Strip.

3. Legal Framework

Palestinian and International Human Rights Law

During a few brief periods, up to 14 June 2007, when the violence between Fatah and Hamas security forces and armed groups in the Gaza Strip reached the requisite scale and intensity, the relevant rules of international humanitarian law[6] on the conduct of hostilities also applied, alongside human rights standards.

International humanitarian law sets out standards of humane conduct applicable to all parties in armed conflicts, including armed groups. In the words of the International Committee of the Red Cross (ICRC), the foremost authority on international humanitarian law, "whenever armed force is used the choice of means and methods is not unlimited." This basic rule is explicitly reflected in a number of international humanitarian law treaties. Article 3 common to the four Geneva Conventions of 1949 and their Additional Protocol 2 are the instruments most directly relevant to non-international armed conflict. These treaties increasingly are supplemented by customary international law. The authoritative ICRC study of customary international humanitarian law has determined that many of the rules of international humanitarian law that were codified for international conflict now apply to non-international conflicts as well. These customary rules[7] include the prohibition of direct attacks on civilians; the prohibition

[5] Basic Law, Article 110(2).

[6] The law of occupation, which is part of international humanitarian law, continues to apply in the OPT. Palestinians in Gaza and the West Bank are protected persons under the Fourth Geneva Convention. Despite the removal of Israeli settlements from the Gaza Strip, it remains occupied territory as Israel exercises de-facto control over many aspects of life in Gaza. As the Occupying Power, Israel has a responsibility for the welfare of the civilian populations in the West Bank and Gaza. In the years after the Oslo agreement, the PA exercised some state-like functions, including operating a justice system, police and security forces and it undertook to respect and uphold human rights law.

[7] ICRC, Customary International Humanitarian Law, Vol. I: rules.

of indiscriminate attacks—attacks which fail to take necessary precautions to distinguish between civilians and fighters; and the prohibition of disproportionate attacks—attacks which may be expected to cause incidental loss of civilian life, injury to civilians, damage to civilian objects, or a combination thereof, which would be excessive in relation to the concrete and direct military advantage anticipated. And it is long established that willful killings and torture; the taking of hostages, and attacks against those who are *hors de combat* are prohibited by international humanitarian law of non-international armed conflict.[8]

International criminal law provides that individuals who perpetrate serious violations of international humanitarian law are individually responsible and should be brought to justice. Serious violations of international humanitarian law are war crimes.

The right to life, liberty and security of person is enshrined in the Universal Declaration of Human Rights (UDHR - Article 3).

Although not fully in line with internationally recognized human rights standards, Palestinian laws contain numerous provisions, which—if implemented—would provide important safeguards for detainees against arbitrary detention, torture and other ill-treatment.

Article 13 of the Basic Law categorically prohibits the use of torture or duress against detainees and stipulates that statements or confessions obtained as a result of such abuses are considered null and void.

The obligation not to subject people to torture or other ill-treatment is a rule of customary international law and the prohibition of torture is absolute. The absolute prohibition has been codified in the Universal Declaration of Human Rights (UDHR), as well as several human rights treaties, notably the Convention Against Torture and Other Cruel, Inhuman or Degrading Treatment, and in non-treaty human rights standards. The Body of Principles for the Protection of All Persons under Any Form of Detention or Imprisonment (hereafter The Body of Principles)[9] stipulates in Principle 6: *"No person under any form of detention or imprisonment shall be subjected to torture or to cruel, inhuman or degrading treatment or punishment.*[10] *No circumstance whatever may be invoked as a justification for torture or other cruel, inhuman or degrading treatment or punishment."*

[8] International humanitarian law defines those hors de combat as including: those who are in the power of an adverse party, those who clearly expresses an intention to surrender, and those who have been rendered unconscious or are otherwise incapacitated by wounds or sickness, and who are therefore unable to defend themselves - provided that in any of these cases they abstain from any hostile act and do not attempt to escape.

[9] Adopted by the UN General Assembly in 1988.

[10] See: *http://www.ohchr.org/english/law/bodyprinciples.htm* - wp1025564#wp1025564.

Torture and other ill-treatment is also prohibited by international humanitarian law, as a grave breach of the Geneva Conventions and a war crime.

Article 9 of the UDHR prohibits arbitrary arrest or detention. The prohibition of arbitrary deprivation of liberty is also considered a norm of customary international law.[11] This prohibition is also enshrined in the Body of Principles. Principle 2 of the Body of Principles states: "*Arrest, detention or imprisonment shall only be carried out strictly in accordance with the provisions of the law and by competent officials or persons authorized for that purpose.*"

Principle 36 (2) states: "*The arrest or detention of such a person pending investigation and trial shall be carried out only for the purposes of the administration of justice on grounds and under conditions and procedures specified by law. The imposition of restrictions upon such a person which are not strictly required for the purpose of the detention or to prevent hindrance to the process of investigation or the administration of justice, or for the maintenance of security and good order in the place of detention, shall be forbidden.*"

Furthermore, international standards require that all detentions be ordered by and subject to challenge before and supervision by an independent judicial authority. Principle 4 of the Body of Principles states:

> "*Any form of detention or imprisonment and all measures affecting the human rights of a person under any form of detention or imprisonment shall be ordered by, or be subject to the effective control of, a judicial or other authority.*"

Principle 11 states: "A person shall not be kept in detention without being given an effective opportunity to be heard promptly by a judicial or other authority. A detained person shall have the right to defend himself or to be assisted by counsel as prescribed by law."

The same Principle also requires that a detained person and his counsel "*receive prompt and full communication of any order of detention, together with the reasons therefore*" and that "*a judicial or other authority shall be empowered to review as appropriate the continuance of detention.*" The right to challenge the lawfulness of detention may not be suspended, even during times of emergency.[12]

Similar provisions are contained in Palestinian law: Article 11 of the Basic Law makes it unlawful to arrest and imprison any person except by judicial order in accordance with the provisions of the law, and requires that detainees are held only in places authorized by the laws relating to the organization of prisons. Article 29 of the Penal Procedures Law states: "*No person may be arrested or imprisoned except by order of the competent authority*

[11] See, e.g., Human Rights Committee General Comment 29 on States of Emergency (Article 4 of the ICCPR) UN Doc CCPR/C/21/Rev.1/Add.11, at paragraph 11.

[12] See, e.g. Human Rights Committee General Comment 29 on States of Emergency (Article 4 of the ICCPR) UN Doc CCPR/C/21/Rev.1/Add.11, at para 16.

as designated by law. He must be treated in a manner that will preserve his dignity and may not be physically or morally harmed."

Further, both international standards[13] and Palestinian law prohibit holding people in unofficial places of detention. Article 68 of the Penal Procedures Law states: *"No person may be detained or confined except in a correctional and rehabilitation centre [a prison] and in the places of detention designated by law."* The failure to abide by the above-mentioned Palestinian law and/or these international standards renders a detention or arrest arbitrary under international human rights standards.

The Body of Principles states that the detaining authorities *"shall exercise only the powers granted to them under the law and the exercise of these powers shall be subject to recourse to a judicial or other authority"* (Principle 9), that detentions must be promptly reviewed by a judicial or other authority (Principle 11) and that detainees must be given prompt access to their families and legal counsel (Principle 15).

Similar provisions are contained in the Palestinian Penal Procedures Law, according to which the detention of any individual prior to their being charged with an offence must be reviewed within 24 hours by a prosecutor (Article 34), who may extend the detention for an additional 48 hours. After 72 hours of detention, the case must be reviewed by a judge (Article 51), who may extend the pre-charge detention by 15 days (Articles 62 and 63), renewable by a judge every 15 days to a maximum of 45 days.[14] The law also grants detainees prompt and unhindered access to legal counsel (Article 46). Further, Article 12 of the Basic Law requires that detainees be charged and brought to trial without delay.

Palestinian Justice System

The **legal system** in the areas of the OPT under PA jurisdiction comprises a body of laws and decrees which include those remaining from previous centuries when the area was ruled by other powers—Ottoman, British, Jordanian (in the West Bank), Egyptian (in the Gaza Strip) and Israeli—and legislation introduced since 1994, notably decrees issued by former President Yasser 'Arafat and current President Mahmoud 'Abbas, and laws passed by the Palestinian parliament, the Palestinian Legislative Council (PLC). The first elections to the PLC, which comprises 132 members, were held in 1996. Laws passed by the PLC come into force once ratified by the PA President. The PLO Revolutionary Code of 1979 (developed by PLO structures in exile prior to the establishment of the PA) is also still in force and is the basis of the military justice system. The Basic Law of 2003,

[13] Article 10 of the UN Declaration on Enforced Disappearance.

[14] The 45-day maximum may be further extended by an additional 45 days on application by the prosecutor to a higher court than that which authorized the first 45 days of detention.

amended in 2005, acts as a form of constitution pending the establishment of a Palestinian state.

The **court system** consists of *Sulh* (Conciliation/Magistrate) courts, which hear cases of misdemeanors; *Bidaya* (First Instance) courts, which hear cases of more serious crimes and appeals against judgments handed down by *Sulh* courts; Appeal Courts, which hear appeals against judgments of the First Instance Court; and the High Court, which provides the highest level of appeal and hears petitions for cassation challenging procedural breaches. A Supreme Criminal Court was set up in 2006 to try crimes including murder, abduction, rape, so-called honour crimes and attacks on public finance and national security. Military Courts hear cases involving members of the security forces and apply the 1979 PLO Revolutionary Code. In 2006 a law was passed establishing a High Constitutional Court, but it has not yet been set up in practice.[15] Civil courts hear civil cases and *Shari'a* (religious) courts hear cases under family and personal status law (such as marriage and divorce). The State Security Courts were abolished by the Minister of Justice in 2003.[16]

The Attorney General and prosecutors investigate and prosecute crimes, oversee the legality of detentions and investigate complaints by detainees. The Attorney General and the judges are nominated by the Higher Judicial Council, which is headed by the President of the High Court, but appointed by the PA President.

A traditional ***'Urf* (customary) system** of conciliation and mediation by clan/tribal leaders and other respected figures in the community has continued to exist and to function in parallel to the court system; for many Palestinians, this remains the preferred means through which to resolve family/clan feuds and other disputes, ranging from issues affecting family "honour" to murder, injury or financial issues. This mediation system has also been used as a basis for addressing clashes between political factions, including brokering cease-fires, negotiating safe passage for militants/leaders in danger, and resolving other cases of disputes between Fatah and Hamas which arose in the course of the bloody clashes which occurred in the Gaza Strip in the first half of 2007.[17]

[15] Law No.3 of 17 February 2006.

[16] The State Security Courts were set up by the late President 'Arafat in 1995 and were used to try the political opponents detained in the waves of arrests in the 1990s in notoriously unfair trials. Palestinian jurists have argued that since these courts were set up by Presidential Decree, a decision by the Minister of Justice is not sufficient to abolish them and another Presidential Decree is required.

[17] Fatah and Hamas militants in the Gaza Strip told Amnesty International that the interventions and mediation efforts by other political factions, such as the Islamic Jihad and the Popular Front for the Liberation of Palestine (PFLP), in many cases avoided further bloodshed.

Institutional and Judicial Vacuum in the Gaza Strip

After Hamas took control of the PA security installations in the Gaza Strip in June, President Abbas instructed the police and security forces not to report for duty in Gaza, on penalty of losing their salaries. On 10 July the Attorney General, who is responsible for investigating and prosecuting criminal cases,[18] confirmed to Amnesty International that his office had not undertaken any activity in the Gaza Strip since mid-June.[19]

On 2 July the Chief Justice and President of the Higher Judicial Council and of the Supreme Court issued the following instructions to the presidents of the *bidaya* and *sulh* courts:

> *"Due to the current situation in the Gaza Strip and due to the lack of a police force to assist and safeguard the implementation of judicial decisions, we request all judges and workers in the directorates responsible for implementing judicial decisions to suspend all decisions requiring police assistance for their implementations, in order to protect the independence and dignity of the judiciary and protect it from any interference that would threaten its independence".*[20]

Only the Sharia courts continued to function, but rulings which required action by the police could not be implemented due to the absence of a police force following President Abbas' order to the police to stand down.

This exacerbated what was already a lawless situation. For several years, virtually none of those responsible for political killings and abductions—mostly carried out by armed groups linked to Fatah, and more recently also by Hamas' armed wing and other groups, have been brought to justice. With security forces and successive attorney generals and prosecutors mostly unable or unwilling to prosecute political cases, arrests and prosecutions tended to be limited to common-law cases, while crimes committed in the context of political and intra-clan/families clashes tended to be tackled through informal mediation efforts between the concerned parties conducted by respected community leaders, or else they were simply left unaddressed. This signal failure on the part of the PA, its security forces and the judiciary to investigate and bring to justice perpetrators of human rights abuses, contributed to a large extent to the lawlessness which became increasingly entrenched in the Gaza Strip, as well as in the West Bank.[21]

---

[18] According to the Penal Procedure Law No.3 of 2001: "The right to file and conduct a penal action is vested exclusively in the Public Prosecution" (Article 1) and "The Attorney General shall prosecute the penal action himself or through one of the members of the Public Prosecution" (Article 2).

[19] PICCR quotes the Attorney General confirming on 11 July that since the end of armed clashes in the Gaza Strip the office of the Attorney General had not taken up any cases there. See: PICCR Special Report 58: Arrests outside the legal framework in the Gaza Strip; issued on 10 September 2007 (in Arabic).

[20] Decision of the Chief Justice, Head of the Higher Judicial Council, dated 2 July 2007, addressed to the Presidents of First Instance and Arbitration (sulh) courts (translation of Arabic original).

[21] In the Gaza Strip the more limited presence of Israeli forces in the main population centres has allowed the PA greater operational capability to administer internal affairs.

These long-standing failures and short-comings underscored the need for urgent and far-reaching reforms—such as the appointment of non-partisan police and other officials, better training, the establishment of effective oversight and accountability mechanisms that could help stamp out abuses by the security forces, and measures to empower the judiciary and enhance its independence. Instead, President Abbas' decision to freeze the activities of the police and the judiciary in the Gaza Strip resulted in an institutional and judicial vacuum that left the 1.5 million inhabitants of the Gaza Strip effectively without any law enforcement institution to which they could turn.[22] It also opened the way for the Hamas de-facto administration to put in place alternative systems to fill this judicial and policing vacuum, which, however, lack adequate independence, impartiality, training, oversight and public accountability.

Prior to June 2007, the Gaza Strip's residents faced great difficulties in obtaining justice or redress from the malfunctioning judicial institutions and mechanisms of the PA. Since the Hamas takeover, however, the situation has deteriorated further. Gazans now have no chance at all to obtain justice or redress through the law because the official institutions are absent. In the past, while the police and the courts of the PA rarely took action against security forces and armed militias responsible for "political" crimes such as killings and abductions, they did act in other types of cases, such as common law crimes, as well as to enforce the rulings of civil and religious courts.

Since June, the absence of PA institutions has left the residents of the Gaza Strip with no choice other than to take the law into their own hands or to turn to the politically-partisan security and law enforcement apparatus set up by Hamas. Ultimately, the vacuum encouraged Hamas to develop parallel systems and to take ad hoc measures outside the judicial and institutional framework.

Since July members of the security forces in the Gaza Strip have been receiving their salaries in full from the West Bank-based PA emergency government after many months, during which their salaries were paid only partly or not at all. However, the payment of salaries is conditional on the personnel not reporting for duty—in effect, they are paid not to work. Those who continued to work under the Hamas de-facto administration had their salaries stopped.[23] Thus, whereas for more than a year the security forces were expected to carry out their duties without receiving their

[22] In fact, some members of the police who support Hamas defied President Abbas' orders and continued to work alongside the Executive Force.

[23] Only some members of the police who support Hamas defied President Abbas' orders and continued to work, under the command of the Executive Forces.

salaries, they are now required not to work as a condition for receiving their salaries.

Proliferation of Parallel Systems Outside the Legal Framework in the Gaza Strip

Hamas filled the void by deploying the Executive Force throughout the Gaza Strip. The rank and file members of this force are drawn from Hamas' Qassam Brigades (see Chapter 4), who are trained to carry out attacks against Israeli targets and to fight Israeli forces during their incursions into the Gaza Strip—not to act as law enforcement officers. As was the case in the past, when political and personal loyalties—rather than skills and competence—were often the determining factor in the recruitment of members of the Fatah-dominated PA security forces and judicial apparatus, the Hamas de-facto administration has been recruiting Hamas supporters into its forces and other public institutions.

The Qassam Brigades have participated in attacks against demonstrators alongside the Executive Force and have also abducted people independently of the Executive Force and run two detention centers in the Gaza Strip. Neither the Qassam Brigades nor the Executive Force have any legal authority to arrest and detain people; the Qassam Brigades is an armed group which exists outside the framework of the law and the Executive Force is a force which is not authorized by law to carry out arrests and detain people. Such detentions are arbitrary, and violate both Palestinian law and international standards.

Since July 2007, Hamas has announced a series of new bodies or mechanisms to replace the PA security forces and judicial institutions that have refused to operate under or alongside the Hamas de-facto administration. According to the Palestinian Independent Commission for Citizens' Rights (PICCR—the national human rights body),[24] the Executive Force set up a committee on 9 July to deal with the cases of detainees who had been held in Gaza central prison in al-Saraya security compound prior to the Hamas takeover of the compound.[25]

On 21 July the Executive Force spokesman announced that Hamas had formed a legal committee to address the lack of functioning judicial institutions

[24] PICCR Special Report 58: Arrests outside the legal framework in the Gaza Strip, p.7, 10 September 2007 (in Arabic).

[25] Some 500 detainees were released from Gaza central prison when Hamas stormed the al-Saraya security compound on 13 June and dozens of them gave themselves up to the Executive Force in the following days and returned to the prison, seemingly out of fear that if they remained free the families of their victims would kill them in revenge. Subsequently Amnesty International learned from other former inmates, who had fled the central prison on 13 June and who had been detained there without trial, that they had been summoned by the Executive Force for questioning about their case and released within 24–48 hours.

in the Gaza Strip and stated that this committee replaces the PA prosecution service "and prevents it from interfering in cases of the Palestinian public".[26] However, it was not until 16 August that the Executive Force took over the offices of the PA Attorney General in Gaza City. Shortly afterwards, the General Director for Legal Affairs in the Justice Ministry of the Hamas de-facto administration announced that it had appointed eight prosecutors and 20 assistant prosecutors to replace those who had stopped working in mid-June.[27]

On 16 August the Executive Force arrested the Attorney General, who had been in the West Bank since the beginning of the crisis and had recently returned to Gaza. In a testimony to the Palestinian Centre for Human Rights (PCHR), he said he had been taken from his office and beaten while being taken to the central prison, where he was told to sign an undertaking not to exercise any prosecution-related duties, travel to the West Bank or make statements to the media, and to stop "incitement" against the Hamas administration. He refused to sign the statement but was released after a short time. The Executive Force spokesman informed PCHR that the Attorney General had been detained for one hour on suspicion of smuggling legal files on cases of corruption and murder, an allegation which the Attorney General denied. Executive Force members also body-searched the Attorney General's assistants, erased pictures from their mobile telephones and threatened them at gunpoint. A lawyer with the Palestinian human rights organization al-Mezan was likewise briefly detained by the Executive Force when he attempted to photograph Executive Force members surrounding the Attorney General's office. He was also taken to al-Saraya security compound and held there for an hour before being released

The head of the Executive Force, Jamal Jarrah, announced on 18 August that a new rapid response force was being formed and would be deployed imminently to deal with "collaborators" and with security issues requiring rapid intervention, such as drug smuggling. On 27 August, the Secretary General of the Hamas de-facto administration, Muhammad Awad, announced the creation of three new Palestinian police forces—an internal security force, a beach force and a female force.

On 4 September the Hamas de-facto administration announced the establishment of the Supreme Justice Council, which is to be responsible for appointing judges, in co-operation with the Justice Department. This Council is intended to replace the Higher Judicial Council, which nominates the Attorney General and judges, for appointment by the PA President,

[26] As quoted by Maan News on 21 July 2007.
[27] As quoted by Paltimes.Net on 30 August 2007, in Arabic: http://www.paltimes.net/arabic/?action=detile&detileid=7258.

and trains the judges. Such moves are inconsistent with the principle of the independence of the judiciary and are in breach of numerous Palestinian laws—notably the Judicial Authority Law.[28]

Amnesty International is concerned that the bodies and mechanisms set up by the Hamas de-facto administration to carry out law enforcement and the administration of justice lack the necessary skills, independence, oversight and accountability to ensure that the rule of law is respected for both victims and accused; that human rights abuses are not committed; that victims have access to effective mechanisms to obtain redress; and that accused persons are afforded due process. To the contrary, it appears clear that perpetrators of human rights abuses continue to enjoy impunity, and that the Hamas de-facto administration lacks the political will to hold perpetrators of crimes to account, especially Hamas members, and to respect fundamental human rights, including the rights to freedom of expression, assembly and association. Essentially, the Hamas de-facto administration in the Gaza Strip is fast replicating and, indeed, exceeding many of the abuses and shortcomings for which it formerly denounced, on good grounds, the Fatah-dominated PA institutions, notably disregard of human rights by security forces and lack of political will to enforce the rule of law, leading to widespread lawlessness.

4. Security Forces and Armed Groups—Blurred Lines

Security Forces

Some 10 different security forces were set up by the PA in the second half of the 1990s, including the Preventive Security Service, Force 17, General Intelligence, Military Intelligence and Civil Police, comprising more than 30,000 members in all. For years, torture by PA security forces, notably the Preventive Security, was common against political detainees and detainees accused of "collaboration" with Israeli intelligence services.[29] Each security force ran its own detention centres, outside the legal framework, and in some cases detainees were held for years without trial or any effective means of remedy or redress.[30]

In 2005 President Abbas consolidated the security forces into three branches: National Security, Internal Security and General Intelligence, each

[28] The Judiciary Authority Law No.1 of 2002 was amended in 2005 by Law No.15, but the latter was ruled as unconstitutional in November 2005 by the High Court, in its capacity as the Constitutional Court. However, Law No.15 was never formally repealed.

[29] Large-scale arrests of political opponents by PA security forces were common until 2000, and virtually stopped after the outbreak of the intifada at the end of 2000.

[30] For example, in May 2005 the PA released several detainees who had been held for up to 10 years without trial or in spite of court orders for their release in a section of Gaza City Prison run by Major-General Musa Arafat, the head of Military Intelligence, who was assassinated four months later. See: *http://web.amnesty.org/report2006/pse-summary-eng.*

comprising several forces.[31] General Intelligence includes Military Intelligence and the Military Police and is under the direct control of the PA President, as is the Presidential Guard/Force 17.[32] National Security is defined as "a regular military body"[33] and includes several forces. Internal Security includes the Preventive Security, the Police and the Civil Defense. National Security and Internal Security are under the jurisdiction of the Ministers of National Security and the Interior respectively, but the heads of the two forces are appointed by the PA President.[34]

After Hamas won the legislative elections and established a government in early 2006, it was not able to gain any measure of control over the security forces, some of which, notably the Presidential Guard/Force 17 and the Preventive Security, openly challenged the authority of the new government and carried out assassinations and other attacks against Hamas members.

The **Executive Force** was set up in April-May 2006 by the then Interior Minister in the Hamas government, who maintained that with no control over existing PA security forces, which remained essentially Fatah structures, the government had no law enforcement mechanism under its command and could not fulfil its duty and tackle the growing lawlessness and frequent abductions. The Executive Force is composed of members of the 'Izz al-Din al-Qassam Brigades (Qassam Brigades) and Hamas supporters, and its leadership includes Major-General Tawfik Jaber, a former police chief under a Fatah government.

President Abbas objected to the creation of the Executive Force and called for it to be disbanded, but for more than a year he took no measures to force the then Hamas government to comply with this instruction.[35] Meanwhile the Hamas government made no efforts to have the parliament, in which it held a majority, to introduce legislation to establish formally the Executive Force and to regulate its operation.[36] The Executive Force, therefore, continues to operate outside the framework of the law.

---

[31] Defined in Article 3 of the Service in the Palestinian Security Forces Law No.8 of June 2005 as: "The National Security Forces and the Palestine National Liberation Army; the Internal Security Forces; the General Intelligence; and any other force or forces that are existent or to be established and which shall be within one of the three forces."

[32] Force 17 was established in the early 1970s as a special unit of the Fatah movement. When the PA was established in the early 1990s it became an official PA security force, reputed to be the most loyal and trusted by the late President Arafat. In 2005 it was renamed Presidential Security/Force 17 (Amn al-Ri'asa–Quwwa 17), but in English translations it is commonly referred to simply as the Presidential Guard in an apparent effort to discard the poor reputation of Force 17 at the international level.

[33] Article 7 of Law No.8 of 2005.

[34] Articles 8 and 11 of Law No.8 of 2005.

[35] The PA President did not refer the matter to the courts nor did he issue a Presidential Decree outlawing the Executive Force, a measure which he took in June 2007, after Hamas seized control of the Gaza Strip.

[36] Since it was established after the passing of Law No.8 of June 2005, regulating the Palestinian Security Forces, the Executive Force's existence and role is not detailed in any laws.

According to reports, there were negotiations between Fatah and Hamas about possibly merging the Executive Force with existing PA security forces, but no agreement to do this was ever reached. Assassinations, abductions and intermittent armed clashes between rival Fatah and Hamas gunmen became increasingly frequent, with Fatah's al-Aqsa Brigades and Hamas' Qassam Brigades acting as auxiliary militias to certain PA security forces and to the Executive Force.

Only after Hamas' Executive Force and the Qassam Brigades seized control of the PA security installations and other institutions in the Gaza Strip, did President Abbas issue a Presidential Decree outlawing the Executive Force.[37]

Armed Groups

Most Palestinian political factions have an armed wing or armed groups affiliated to them.[38] However, the inter-factional armed clashes and attacks have been almost exclusively between the armed wing of Fatah, the al-Aqsa Brigades, and the armed wing of Hamas, the Qassam Brigades, which are also the two largest armed groups.

The al-Aqsa Brigades were created by Fatah activists, including members of the PA security forces, notably Force 17 and the Preventive Security,[39] in late 2000/early 2001, shortly after the outbreak of the intifada (the Palestinian uprising against Israel's military occupation of the West Bank and Gaza Strip).[40] They first became known in Nablus, which has remained one of their main strongholds in the West Bank, and later became established in other towns, notably Jenin and Ramallah, as well as in the Gaza Strip. Their stated aim is armed resistance to Israeli occupation, including through the use of suicide bombings and other attacks against Israelis, including Israeli civilians, in Israel and in the OPT. However, in recent years, notably since 2004-05, they have been increasingly responsible for abductions of fellow Palestinians and foreign nationals mostly with the aim of extracting concessions from the PA—such as obtaining jobs, securing the release of friends and relatives detained by the PA for criminal activities, or to register their disagreement with positions taken by the PA leadership in their negotiations with Israel. The al-Aqsa Brigades have also

37 President Abbas issued two Presidential Decrees outlawing the Executive Force, on 16 June and 12 August 2007.

38 Notably Islamic Jihad, the Popular Front for the Liberation of Palestine and the Democratic Front for the Liberation of Palestine. Other smaller armed groups have emerged in recent years in the Gaza Strip, such as the Abu al-Rish Brigades, a Fatah splinter faction, and the Army of Islam, an off-shoot of the Dughmush clan.

39 Some members of the security forces also joined the Popular Resistance Committees, an umbrella group composed of militants from different Palestinian factions, mostly present in the Gaza Strip.

40 Al-Aqsa Brigades claimed their first civilian victim in February 2001—Lior Attiah, a 23-year-old Israeli resident of Afula, who was shot dead near the Palestinian village of Jalame in the West Bank.

been responsible for the vast majority of killings of fellow Palestinians accused of "collaboration" with Israeli intelligence services and have also abducted and tortured people to force them to pay ransoms. The al-Aqsa Brigades have consistently been afforded impunity for human rights abuses—whether against Palestinians, foreign nationals or Israeli civilians.

Although Fatah and the PA have never formally recognized the al-Aqsa Brigades as the armed wing of Fatah, the Brigades have consistently identified themselves as Fatah's armed wing and have never been disavowed—either by the current or former PA President, or by the Fatah leadership. On the contrary, PA Fatah leaders have often granted concessions and recognition to the al-Aqsa Brigades. For example, during his 2005 presidential election campaign, President Abbas was photographed being carried on the shoulders of Zakaria Zubeidi, the al-Aqsa Brigades leader in Jenin.[41] Shortly after his election, President Abbas ordered the integration of al-Aqsa Brigades' members into the PA security forces, where they would obtain official status and be paid by the PA.[42] On 12 July 2007, President Abbas issued a Presidential Decree granting the Jerusalem Medal to Samih al Madhoun, a colonel in the Presidential Guard/Force 17 and leader of al-Aqsa Brigades in the Gaza Strip, who was brutally killed in June 2007 by Hamas gunmen, a day after he had boasted in a radio interview about burning 20 houses of Hamas supporters.[43]

An unspecified number of al-Aqsa Brigades members have been integrated into the PA security forces over the years, notably into the Presidential Guard/Force 17; others have become members of the Brigades while already serving in the PA security forces. The ambiguous situation took on an added complexity from 2004 onwards, with the emergence of splinter groups within the ranks of the Brigades and their involvement in inter-factional fighting, first within Fatah itself and later against Hamas. Attacks by the al-Aqsa Brigades against Hamas members increased after Hamas gained control of several municipalities in the first Palestinian municipal elections in 2005 and prior to the January 2006 legislative elections,[44] and escalated further after Hamas' victory in those legislative elections.

---

[41] See photograph, dated 5 January, at: *http://www.standwithus.com/news_post.asp?NPI=200.*

[42] See AFP report: Abbas calls for militants to be incorporated into security services, 16 January 2005.

[43] Presidential Decree (Arabic) at: *www.wafa.ps/arabic/printnews.asp?id=55895.*

[44] Hamas' participation in the municipal election was a departure from Hamas' previous refusal to participate in PA institutions. After its relative success in the first two rounds of municipal elections in December 2004 and May 2005, attacks by al-Aqsa Brigades caused disruption and cancellation of the third and fourth rounds in late 2005 in some areas. The fifth and sixth rounds, scheduled for 2006, never took place due to the increase in Fatah-Hamas armed confrontation after Hamas' victory in the legislative elections.

The Qassam Brigades were established in the early 1990s,[45] reportedly under the leadership of Yahia Ayash, who was later assassinated by the Israeli army. Their stated aim is armed resistance to Israeli occupation, including through the use of suicide bombings and other attacks against Israelis, including Israeli civilians, in Israel and in the OPT. However, in recent years, notably since 2005, they have increasingly been involved in armed clashes with and attacks against Fatah members, notably in the Gaza Strip. They have also been responsible for some killings of fellow Palestinians accused of "collaboration" with Israeli intelligence services.

Unlike the members of the al-Aqsa Brigades, members of the Qassam Brigades and of Hamas have been periodically targeted by the PA and its security forces—notably in the mid- to late-1990s. In this period, hundreds of Qassam Brigades and Hamas supporters were arrested by the PA; many were tortured or otherwise ill-treated and imprisoned after unfair trials or held for prolonged periods without charge or trial. These detentions appeared to be motivated essentially by political considerations—intended to stifle dissent against the PA and also to respond to Israeli and international pressure on the PA to act against armed groups—rather than by a genuine desire to bring perpetrators of serious crimes to justice. From the beginning of the intifada in late 2000 until the Hamas takeover in Gaza in mid-June 2007, however, the PA generally failed to take action against the al-Aqsa Brigades, the Qassam Brigades or any other armed groups that carried out attacks against Israeli civilians, although such attacks against civilians constituted gross breaches of international law.

Proliferation of Unlicensed Weapons—a Root Cause of Lawlessness

The unchecked proliferation and misuse of firearms and explosives has contributed greatly to the growing lawlessness and insecurity in the West Bank and Gaza Strip, and has had a disastrous impact on the lives of the civilian population. Hundreds of Palestinians, including children, have been killed by other Palestinians using firearms and explosives, either deliberately or by accident, in recent years.

The armed clashes in the Gaza Strip and the attacks in the West Bank were facilitated by the ready availability of firearms and explosives, which armed groups claim to use only in the context of armed resistance to the Israeli occupation, but which have been used with increasing frequency against other Palestinians, notably by Fatah's and Hamas' armed groups. Over the years, the growing lawlessness and the inaction of the PA security forces in the face of such violence has led many Palestinians not linked to armed groups to acquire weapons for their own protection. Such proliferation of

[45] The Qassam Brigades carried out the first suicide bomb attack on civilians in Israel in 1994, an attack that killed five people on a bus in Hadera.

firearms has in turn fuelled violence within Palestinian society and aggravated the consequences of confrontations, with minor disputes between neighbours often escalating into prolonged gun battles that endanger the lives of residents of entire neighbourhoods.

The Firearms and Ammunition Law (2) of 1998 requires that no person may be in possession of a firearm unless they have obtained authorization from the Ministry of the Interior (Articles 2 and 3); that no one aged under 21 may possess or carry firearms (Article 5.a); that no one may own more than one firearm (Article 11); that firearms may not be carried in public areas, at conference, meetings, ceremonies or at wedding parties; and that it is absolutely prohibited to show off firearms (Article 14).

In practice, this law has rarely been applied. Adults and even children routinely carry and use unauthorized firearms in public places, including hospitals and schools. Busy streets in densely populated residential areas have frequently been the scene of gun battles between armed groups, rival security forces or feuding families, and armed individuals and members of the security forces frequently fire live ammunition in crowded public areas in celebration or protest, or simply to display their weapons. Such proliferation of weapons is unjustified and presents a real and continuing threat to the human rights of many Palestinians.

5. Abuses in the Gaza Strip

Unlawful Killings and Abductions

Both during and after the clashes that ended with Hamas' de-facto takeover in the Gaza Strip, Hamas gunmen have hunted down members of the PA's security forces and of the al-Aqsa Brigades, which they accused of being part of a group which had ordered and carried out assassinations of Hamas members.[46] High-ranking members of this target group who were captured by members of the Executive Force and Qassam Brigades were killed, while less prominent members or helpers were often shot in the legs in a deliberate policy to exact revenge and intimidate others.

Testimony of **F.H.**, a mechanic working with the Presidential Guard/Force 17:

> *"On Sunday 10 June in the late morning, at about 10.30-11am, I and my colleague,* **Mohammed Swerki**, *who worked as a cook, were sent to deliver food to our colleagues who were in the Bacri Tower [a tall residential building in Gaza City]. However, we went to the wrong building by mistake; we went to the nearby Ghifari tower, where there was a Hamas group. When they opened the door downstairs we*

[46] The group was reportedly led by Fatah's strongman in Gaza, Muhammad Dahlan, who was appointed as President Abbas' National Security Advisor earlier in 2007 but resigned after the June events in Gaza. He had led the crackdown on Hamas members in the mid-1990s, as head of the notorious Preventive Security Service in Gaza, where detainees were routinely tortured and some died as a result.

told them we were from Force 17 and they took us in and tied our hands and blindfolded us and took us upstairs; I don't know if it was the top floor or one below. I don't know if they were Qassam Brigades or Executive Force; they were dressed in black and masked. They asked me for names and telephone numbers of officers in Force 17 and which weapons they had and I said I didn't know; I am a mechanic and my job was to repair cars and Mohammed was a cook; we were not involved in security issues. Then very quickly they left me and went to fight because they were being attacked by Force 17. Me and Mohammed were kept separate. At about 4 or 5 pm I heard screaming and the Hamas group came back to me and told me that Mohammed had fallen off the roof. They gave me water and allowed me to wash and pray. In the meantime some of my relatives had been alerted and there was intervention and someone came to get me and I was allowed to leave. Mohammed's body was found in the street below the building; his hands were tied and he was blindfolded. He was 26 years old; he was married but did not yet have children."

As the news of Mohammed Swerki's death spread it was rumoured that he had been thrown off the roof by Hamas gunmen, and masked Fatah gunmen quickly surrounded the home of Dr Ala' al-Rifati, dean of the business faculty at the Islamic University in Gaza City and abducted his brother, **Mohammed al-Rifati**, a 35-year-old imam and reported Hamas supporter. He was later found dead, his body riddled with bullets, near the PA security compound in the Ansar area of Gaza City.

Later that evening masked gunmen abducted **Husam Abu Qinas** when he was in a shared taxi returning home from work in Khan Yunis. They bundled him into a jeep reportedly belonging to the Presidential Guard/Force 17 and took him to the Mhanna tower (a tall residential building) in Gaza City and threw him off the roof, handcuffed. He had been shot in the head first, but it is not known whether he was still alive when he was thrown from the roof. Husam Abu Qinas, a 35-year-old tiler, married and expecting his first child, was religious but reportedly not a Hamas member. Both attacks were believed to have been carried out in revenge for the killing of Mohammed Swerki.

Gun battles lasting hours took place in residential neighbourhoods around the houses of leading figures of the al-Aqsa Brigades, PA security services and Fatah. The reckless use of rocket-propelled grenades (RPGs), rockets and other heavy weapons gravely endangered the safety of residents and passers by. Some of those involved in the fighting who were captured were summarily killed when they were *hors de combat*—including in and around hospitals. Others not involved in the fighting were abducted and deliberately killed while being held hostage.

Testimony of a relative of **Jamal Abu Jedian (Abu Maher)**, the 52-year-old Secretary-General of Fatah in the north of Gaza, a colonel in the Presidential Guard/Force 17 and leading commander of the al-Aqsa Brigades in the north of Gaza and a close associate of Muhammad Dahlan, the former head of the Preventive Security and President Abbas' strong man in the Gaza Strip:

> *"At about 4pm on 11 June Hamas gunmen besieged our house; there are six apartments in the house and some 50 people live here; many women and children. They took over the house diagonally opposite and used it to attack our house. They launched RPGs and rockets, which caused all this destruction and fire. Jamal was injured in the face by the explosion of a rocket and other relatives and bodyguards were also injured. We managed to get out from the back to go to the Kamal 'Adwan hospital, nearby. When we reached the hospital Hamas gunmen attacked us there. They shot Abu Maher many times in the head.*[47] *Then they took 10 relatives and bodyguards [all young men] outside, near the hospital and shot them all in the legs. Two of them, Shadi Ahmed and Bassam Abu Ruqbeh, had both legs amputated; Samed Abu Jedian and Ala' Odeh had to have one leg amputated; others sustained fractures as the shooting was at close range."*

A Hamas gunman was also killed and tens of people, including two women, were reported to have been injured during the battle around Jamal Abu Jedian's house.

On the afternoon of the same day, 11 June, armed clashes broke out between members of Hamas' Executive Force and members of the al-Masri clan, a well-armed clan that has been involved in bloody family feuds for many years. The clan is headed by the Head of the *Mukhabarat* (General Intelligence) in the Gaza Strip. The clashes took place at the family compound in Beit Hanoun, in the north of the Gaza Strip. After the killing of one of their members in the clashes, Executive Force members chased members of the al-Masri clan and caught up with them at Beit Hanoun hospital.

Testimony of **F A**, aged 24, mother of five young children:

> *"There was shooting outside the hospital and then Hamas gunmen went inside the hospital looking for my relatives. They took 'Id, a father of 20, his son Brahim, aged 21, and his nephew Faraj, aged 22, to a separate room and shot them dead; they shot them in the head and chest. When the gunmen shot and threw grenades outside the hospital my cousin Taghreed [aged 17 and in her second year at high school] was seriously injured in the hip and lower back. She may remain disabled from her injury. When I found Faraj and saw that he had been shot dead I ran after the gunmen, I screamed at them and one of them kicked me. I picked up a stone to throw at him and he shot at me; I was injured in the stomach; I am recovering now but it will take some time."*

[47] Jamal Abu Jedian was reportedly shot 41 times in the head. A doctor at the hospital was quoted by Reuters as saying: "Everybody is shooting at everybody", at: *http://news.bbc.co.uk/1/hi/world/middle_east/6739691.stm.*

Children and Bystanders Caught in the Crossfire

During the clashes several bystanders, including children, were killed or injured in the crossfire. **Shahed Thamer Miqdad**, a child aged 18 months, and her aunt, **Nida' Ahmad Miqdad**, 22, were seriously wounded on two consecutive days in their fourth-floor apartment in the Maggousi housing project in Gaza City as reckless armed clashes took place around the house of a Fatah spokesman, Maher Miqdad, between Hamas and Fatah gunmen.

Testimony of **Shahed's grandmother:**

> *"On 13 June at about 6pm Shahed was in this room with her mother; they were sitting down; then Shahed asked her mother for something sweet [habba] and her mother got up to get a sweet from the cupboard, while Shahed was standing in the middle of the room. At that point a bullet came through the window and hit Shahed in the head. The bullet hit her by her left eye and exited at the back of her head. She lost her left eye and is still in a serious condition. She still does not speak or move; we don't know if she will survive. The following morning at 9am Nida' was in the same room and a bullet came through the same window and hit her in the lower back. She is now recovering."*

It is not clear whether the bullets that injured Shahed and Nida' were stray bullets from the clashes or whether the apartment was deliberately targeted, possibly by mistake or because other family members worked in the security forces.

Many students risked their lives to take key exams that began on 11 June, passing through checkpoints erected by gunmen and areas where armed clashes were taking place. For some, the journey cost them their lives.

Testimony of a relative of **'Aisha Maher Al-Shawwa**, aged 17:

> *"'Aisha was on her way to school in a minibus; she was in her last year of secondary school and always had very high marks and school was very important for her. That morning she was scared but she did not want to miss her exams; and she went. The minibus was in the area near the Rasha al-Shawa centre (in Gaza City) and when it reached the corner of the Abu Qas Supermarket two Qassam members on the corner told the driver to take care because there were snipers from the Preventive Security and the National Security on the Soussi building on Thalatini Street. As soon as the minibus turned a bullet came through the window from high above and hit 'Aisha in the back, travelling down and damaging vital internal organs. All the information we have obtained shows that the bullet was fired from the top of the Soussi building, where a squad of the Preventive Security and some of their colleagues from the National Security had taken position."*

Musa Ahmad Abu 'Oda, aged nine, was fatally wounded by shrapnel from a rocket that exploded in the street near his house on 13 June. His 12-year-old sister, **Khouloud**, was injured in the left leg. The two children had taken advantage of a lull in the clashes to go out to buy sweets. Another passer by, 20-year-old **Ra'ed Muhammad Abu 'Obeid**, was also killed and 13-year-old **Mahmoud Mousa al-Sisi** was injured in the legs. According to the families of the three victims, the rocket had been fired from the *Mukhabarat* centre and was aimed at a jeep belonging to the Executive Force, but the car turned a corner and the rocket exploded in the street. According to other sources, the rocket was more likely to have been fired by Hamas militants at the *Mukhabarat* centre, and the stray bullet that killed 'Aisha Maher al-Shawwa could just as likely have been fired by Hamas gunmen. In these, as in many other cases, the reckless conduct of both sides ended in tragedy for uninvolved bystanders.

Peaceful Demonstrators Under Fire

A peaceful march against the Fatah-Hamas confrontation, calling on both sides to stop the fighting, came under fire on the morning of 13 June in Gaza City. Amnesty International has been unable to establish whether the demonstrators were deliberately targeted or, rather, were also victims of the reckless use of fire which characterized the armed clashes. The demonstration had been organized by left-wing parties, the local *mukhtars* (notables), Islamic Jihad and the Egyptian delegation in Gaza.[48] It started from the Shaja'iya district and continued past the parliament building and along 'Omar al-Mukhtar Street, where it came under fire. Two demonstrators were killed and more than 20 injured, including 19-year-old **Mohammad Mahmoud Adas**, who was reported to have later died. **Taghreed Salah al-'Alia**, a 31-year-old clerk, was wounded and died shortly after, and 22-year-old **Shadi Tayseer al-'Ijla**, a psychology student and peace activist, was injured and died two days later.

Testimony of **Shadi Tayseer al-'Ijla's mother:**

> *"Shadi was very active in the community; he wanted to contribute to building a better society and to the peaceful resolution of conflicts. Last year he participated in another demonstration in Rafah calling for an end to violence. He was involved in workshops and teaching for children. Two days after he died UNRWA [the UN Relief and Works Agency] called to invite him to participate in activities in a summer camp for children. He was shot in the chest as he was helping another demonstrator who had been injured."*

Testimony of **Taghreed Salah al-'Alia's mother:**

> *"Taghreed always wanted to do good. She had recently taken a first aid course, because of the events, so that she could help treat the injured; she was able to help the doctor in the clinic at the Navy, where she worked as a clerk. That morning she was worried about going on the demonstration but she believed it was a good*

[48] Left-wing parties, the Islamic Jihad, local notables and well respected figures, and the Egyptian delegation were all involved in mediating between Fatah and Hamas, negotiating repeated ceasefires and intervening to defuse tensions in many confrontations.

initiative. I told her that if I had not been feeling unwell due to my recent eye operation I would have gone with her. When she was shot she was bent over another demonstrator who had been injured. She was taken to the Shifa hospital nearby but after waiting for 45 minutes without getting any treatment her friend took her in a taxi to al-Quds hospital, but she died shortly after arriving there."

University students **M.** and his brother **A.** were both injured in the demonstration. M, aged 19, was hit by a bullet in his right leg and sustained a broken shin, and 20-year-old A received a bullet in the back. They told Amnesty International that they did not know whether the shot came from Hamas or Fatah gunmen or whether the shots were directed at the demonstrators or at the gunmen who were near the demonstrators.[49]

'Punitive' Shootings Spread Fear

As well as assassinations and abductions, both Fatah and Hamas security forces and gunmen attacked each other's members or supporters to exact revenge or instil fear. Such attacks were especially widespread between late 2006 and June 2007. Abducting their opponents and shooting them in the legs became an increasingly common practice by both Fatah and Hamas gunmen. During and immediately after the last wave of armed clashes, throughout June 2007, such attacks were most commonly perpetrated by Hamas gunmen against hostages and survivors of armed clashes who were *hors de combat*. Earlier in the year, such attacks were often perpetrated by PA security forces and Fatah gunmen against Hamas members. In most cases investigated by Amnesty International, the shots were fired at very close range, clearly deliberately and intended to maximize injury, causing multiple fractures of the shin and thigh bones. In several cases the damage was so serious that the limbs had to be amputated.

Testimony of **T A,** a 25-year-old bodyguard to his uncle, the head of a Preventive Security regional division:

"On the morning of Tuesday 12 June 2007 I was going from my sister's house, where I had spent the night, to my family home with a relative who my mother had sent to pick me up because she wanted me to go home. I had my Kalashnikov and a grenade with me. When we reached the al-Garara junction (in the south of the Gaza Strip) a group of Qassam Brigades members, 20 or so of them, stopped our car and said to me 'you are the guard of XX'. They told me to get out of the car and made me spread my legs and said 'we have not even started with the Preventive Security.' They beat me up on the spot and then took me away from the side of the road, into a field and made me lie face down and asked me my name, my position and who I work

[49] See photo of Fatah gunman adjusting a high-calibre machine gun mounted on a pick-up truck near the demonstration, at: *http://www.mctcampus.com/visuals/preview.htm?doc=KRT%2Fkrtphotos%2Fdocs%2F341%2F532* photo of Fatah gunmen near the demonstrators, at: *http://www.mctcampus.com/visuals/preview.htm?doc=KRT%2Fkrtphotos%2Fdocs%2F341%2F533* and photo of demonstrators marching past Fatah gunmen manning a checkpoint, at: *http://www.mctcampus.com/visuals/preview.htm?doc=KRT%2Fkrtphotos%2Fdocs%2F341%2F529.*

for, etc. Then they put me in a car, a white Subaru, and once in the car they blindfolded me. They took me to a house or a building, I could not see. There they asked me why I had stopped working for the National Security Service and moved to the Preventive Security. They asked if I had other weapons and I said no but they kept insisting that I had. They asked me what my boss did and I said that I did not know but they did not believe me and kept insisting. They wanted to know about the RPGs and the rockets which had been used on the day of the clashes at my boss' house. I said that I did not know. They started to pinch my armpits with pliers and it was very painful. One of them told the others to kill me. Then they put me in the car again and put the barrel of the Kalashnikov into my mouth and pretended to shoot. Then they took me out of the car and took off my blindfold; we were opposite Nasser hospital in Khan Yunis. They put me on the ground face down and shot me twice in the right leg, one shot in the calf and one in the thigh. As they were going to shoot me in the other leg a woman who was passing with a child threw herself on top of my left leg and told them they would have to kill her before shooting me and they left. She was very brave and saved me. A couple of days after Hamas took control of Gaza (15 or 16 June) they sent me a paper at home asking for weapons and summoning me to bring any weapons to the 'Abdallah Bin Messa'oud mosque in al-Garara. I could not move and my father went in my place and challenged them for what their gunmen had done to me and they apologized. Since then they haven't come to bother me at home and I have not gone out; I will not be able to walk for weeks."

Testimony of **Mahmoud Abu Kersh**, 23, who worked in the family restaurant:

"On Friday 18 May 2007 at about 5pm I was with my brother Mohammed. He is 26 years old, married with a little daughter and also worked in our family's restaurant. We had come out from Shifa Hospital (in Gaza City) and were going on to al-Quds Hospital, to visit children with cancer, an activity we do for a charity. We were in a taxi in Mujamma al-Wuzara' Street when we were stopped by a group of members of the Preventive Security and Presidential Guards. They were in two white Velox Jeeps with dark windows, were masked and armed with Kalashnikovs and machine guns. There were about 20 of them and others arrived shortly after. They asked our family names and then took us first to the Presidential Guard centre. We were beaten for some time; they banged our heads against the wall and put our heads in the toilet. They were saying to my brother 'ukfur' [ordering him to blaspheme or renounce God] but he refused. Then they took us to the Preventive Security centre in Tal al-Hawa; we were blindfolded but I could see a little from under the blindfold. There we were put in separate cells; it was very dirty. The following day they put us both out in the sun for a bit but said that if we talked together we would be shot. They had beaten my brother with a shovel on the head and banged his head against the metal door and he was bleeding but they did not allow him to wash. They said they were going to kill one of us and shoot the other in the legs and we could choose; I said they should kill me because my brother has a child and I am not married. The day after, on Sunday, they put us both in the boot of a car; we were still blindfolded and with our hands tied. At one of their checkpoints we heard them say they were going to kill us. When they stopped and got us out of the boot they told us to walk, but my brother could not walk; his legs seemed broken. They started to shoot near us and at us. One bullet ricocheted and broke one of my front teeth and

then I was hit by a high velocity bullet in my left calf, one in my [outer] left thigh, one in my left knee, one in my right foot and three in my left shin; these three could not be taken out and will remain inside. My brother got at least five bullets in each leg; at the hospital they could not tell exactly how many bullets had gone through his left leg because there was virtually no flesh left and the bone was shattered. After a few days in Shifa hospital he was taken to a hospital in Egypt and he is still there. While we were detained our parents called my mobile phone and the Preventive Security replied that they were from the Qassam Brigades, but my parents knew it was not true because the taxi driver had been taken to the Presidential Guard centre and then released and he had alerted my parents. I think that they did this to us for revenge because one of our relatives killed a member of the Preventive Security."

Testimony of **S A**, an officer in the National Security Forces, Special Force, aged 21:

"I went with a group of colleagues to the headquarters of the Preventive Security in Tal al-Hawa (in Gaza City) to help them to defend the position which was under attack by Hamas. When the place fell into the hands of the Hamas gunmen, on 14 June, they came in and most of us surrendered; only some kept shooting. We were about 25 in all. They put us all against the wall and told us to come forward and shot at us, especially aiming at the legs but as people fell they were hit in other parts of the body. I saw my colleagues fall to the ground; I didn't know who was dead and who was injured; it was a massacre. Then the gunmen left and we stayed there, I don't know for how long, until help arrived and we were taken to hospital. I heard that 17 of my colleagues died and the others were all injured."

S A was hit by three bullets in the left leg, just above the knee. One of the bullets hit a main artery and his leg had to be amputated. As his medical condition worsened, he was taken to a hospital in Israel. He told Amnesty International that he intends to return to Gaza once he has recovered: *"I am not afraid of going back home to Gaza. I have already been punished, so what else can they do to me?"*

Testimony of a member of the **'Ashour family:**

"On 16 May at 6am a group of 40 members of the Preventive Security came to the house; most were in uniform and some were masked; all were armed. They asked for our son 'Ali and we said that he was sleeping upstairs. They went up and took 'Ali, who is 21 years old and in his second year at university studying social science, and then also took our other son, Mohammed, who is barely 18; he is in his last year of secondary school. They took them both to the Preventive Security headquarters nearby. Mohammed was released the following day at noon but was beaten to a pulp; he had injuries on his face, head, arms, legs and back, the back was especially bad; he couldn't move for days. While they were detained we contacted everyone, including high level people in the Preventive Security, asking them to intervene."

'Ali 'Ashour added:

"As soon as we were brought into the Preventive Security headquarters they beat us with Kalashnikovs on our heads; then they shot me in the right leg, just above the knee, from a distance of one and a half metres; I dropped to the ground. They took me

to another room, blindfolded me and put me on the floor face down and questioned me for hours; they wanted names of Hamas gunmen but I didn't know any and they kept hitting the leg where they had shot me. Then I collapsed and a nurse came from al-Quds hospital, who said they had to take me to hospital immediately and they did. At the hospital they took off my blindfold. The hospital was full of armed men, many from the Preventive Security. The doctor who looked at my leg said it was too serious and they should take me to Shifa hospital. They didn't want to take me and sent me there in an ambulance."

Testimony of **N A,** 30, a bodyguard of Fatah leader Maher Miqdad:

"On 26 May at 7.15am I took a shared taxi to go to work as usual and on Jala' Street (in Gaza City) a white Mitsubishi cut in front of us and four armed and masked men got out; three of them had Kalashnikovs and one had a gun, but I don't know if they were from the Executive Force or the Qassam Brigades. I was sitting at the back and they came to me directly and said 'good morning N., can you please get out of the car.' When I got out they put a bag over my head and put me in their car without saying anything to me or to the people who were in the taxi with me. They told me to give them whatever I had on me and I gave them my telephone and 8 shekels (US $2). They said 'how is Maher Miqdad and his guards? Do not worry, we have nothing against you, you are one of the respected people in Fatah and we will let you go soon.' After a while we stopped in Nafak road and we got out of the car. They said 'we are in front of your house, you will go in and close the door and don't say anything and nothing will happen to you.' Then two of them held me one on each side and another shot me twice in my left leg and once in my right leg. Then they took the bag off my head and left without saying a word, leaving me on the ground. They kept my telephone, which contained some 200 telephone numbers. None of the other guards of Maher Miqdad went anywhere since earlier in May, when the clashes intensified; Later one of them was killed and another one injured during the clashes. After that Maher Miqdad left Gaza."

Testimony of **Dr Samir Musallam al-Akhras,** aged 49, father of seven children:

"I am a dentist and work as administrative director in primary dental care in a governmental clinic in Khan Yunis (in the south of the Gaza Strip), and also have a private clinic in the evening. On 29 January 2007 I was on holiday that day and went into the centre of Khan Yunis. I was driving in my car and approaching the Force 17 centre; there was no checkpoint but there was a group of men, some masked, wearing Mukhabarat (Intelligence Services) uniforms and armed, near the door of the centre. There were several cars in front of mine but they came straight to me. I told them 'I am a doctor, what do you want from me?' One of the masked men told me to get out of the car and I said that I wouldn't. They opened the door and tried to pull me out and pulled my hands off the steering wheel and the car [automatic] moved forward a bit. They fired at the back of my legs, just below the knees and at my lower back. That bullet exploded inside my stomach and caused internal damage. They left me there and a passing car took me to hospital. The doctors predicted that I would not survive because the internal damage in my stomach was so serious. I have still not recovered. The civil police came to take a statement and a picture of the car, but they never did any follow-up."

Silencing Dissent

The days and weeks following Hamas' seizure of the PA security installations in the Gaza Strip, in mid-June 2007, saw a marked improvement in the overall security situation in the territory. Armed clashes ended, groups of masked armed men no longer filled the streets and the previously ever-present threat of abductions subsided. Hamas secured the release of the two longest-held hostages:[50] BBC correspondent **Alan Johnston**, a British national abducted four months earlier by the Dughmush clan and the Army of Islam group, and **Salim Sabra**, a Palestinian engineer from Gaza City who had been held hostage for more than a year by members of the Abu Khousa clan, one of whose members was a senior official in the PA government, who demanded a large ransom in exchange for his release. Both were released unharmed.

However, the lawlessness which reigned previously in Gaza was soon replaced by increasing repression, as the Executive Force and the Qassam Brigades continued to target members of PA security forces and the al-Aqsa Brigades, as well as other Fatah activists. Initially, such attacks appeared to target individuals against whom Hamas bore grudges, as well as to confiscate weapons. However, within weeks the Executive Force and the Qassam Brigades began breaking up demonstrations and gatherings of Fatah activists. They used undue force to break up protests organized by Fatah activists, and raided wedding or other celebrations where participants allegedly chanted the praises of Fatah or the al-Aqsa Brigades. People were harassed for displaying Fatah flags on the roofs of their homes or for having posters or video clips on their mobile telephones of leaders of Fatah and/or the al-Aqsa Brigades, notably of Samih al Madhoun. Journalists covering protest demonstrations and other incidents were attacked on several occasions and had their footage or equipment damaged or destroyed, to prevent them from reporting the violent attacks and arrests of demonstrators. Hamas spokespersons alleged that Fatah activists used violence against the Executive Force during the demonstrations, but the evidence indicates that the demonstrations were peaceful, except for some minor scuffles, and that the attacks by the Executive Force and Qassam Brigades were unwarranted and ostensibly intended to silence opposition to Hamas and to prevent reporting of the repression by the media.

Hundreds of activists, most of them Fatah members, were detained for participating in non-violent protests and demonstrations. Most were released within 24 to 48 hours but were required as a condition of their

[50] The two longest-held hostages in the context of the inter-factional violence and lawlessness in the Gaza Strip. Hamas' armed wing and another Gaza-based Palestinian armed group are still holding an Israeli soldier, Gilad Shalit, whom they captured from an Israeli military base near the Gaza Strip in June 2006.

release to sign pledges not to participate in demonstrations or other protest activities. In many cases the Executive Force demanded that detainees pay fines or made the release conditional on the payment or promise of payment of up to US $4,000 if they participated in future protest activities. Such conditions were first used by PA security services in the West Bank in June 2007 and were subsequently adopted by the Executive Force in Gaza.

One of the most serious attacks took place on 7 September, when the Executive Force and Qassam Brigades broke up large gatherings of people who were holding Friday prayers in open areas in the Gaza Strip following a call by Fatah and other PLO factions that the prayers should be held outside mosques in protest against what they alleged was Hamas' propaganda and control of Gaza's mosques. Demonstrators and journalists covering the event were assaulted with sticks and rifle butts, leaving scores injured. Members of the Executive Force fired in the air, apparently to intimidate those present. Journalists were targeted as they filmed, took photographs or interviewed Fatah activists; some had their tapes confiscated and their equipment damaged. Although some demonstrators reportedly threw stones at the Executive Force, the gatherings were mostly peaceful and the level of force used by the Executive Force was unwarranted and excessive. However, despite the Executive Force's efforts to prevent media reporting of its repressive actions, these were widely publicised in both Palestinian and foreign news media and prompted yet further protests by Palestinian and international media organizations. On 9 September deposed Prime Minister Haniyeh publicly expressed regret at the attacks on journalists by the Executive Force and stated that he had ordered an investigation into the incidents. Other Hamas officials similarly pledged their commitment to ensuring press freedom.[51] However, no measures are known to have been taken to investigate the attacks and bring those responsible to account.

Hamas has sought to justify the crackdown by accusing Fatah activists of responsibility for bomb and shooting attacks against Hamas members, which have increased since August 2007. For example, on 1 September a bomb exploded in the car of Hamas member **Firas Taysis Abu 'Ida** near his home in Gaza City; the explosion did not cause any injuries. During the night of 3–4 September, another bomb exploded in the car of **Talal al-Dahshan**, a member of the Executive Force and aide to the former foreign minister in the Hamas government, outside his home in Gaza City. The explosion damaged several nearby houses, injuring a toddler in the head, but Talal al-Dahshan escaped injury. The same day another bomb exploded outside a building under construction in Rafah.

[51] See: *http://www.maannews.net/en/index.php?opr=ShowDetails&ID=25257.*

In addition to the bomb attacks, abductions and deliberate killings by unknown gunmen have also increased since August, targeting Hamas and Fatah members and others, though not with the same frequency as in the first half of 2007. On 6 September, unknown gunmen abducted **Tarzan** and **Ibrahim Dughmush**, two members of Preventive Security and of the Dughmush clan, which had been involved in the abduction of BBC journalist Alan Johnston. Ibrahim Dughmush managed to flee and was shot in the back, but Tarzan Dughmush's body was later found south of Gaza City; he had been shot in the head. Such attacks have provoked fears that widespread lawlessness such as prevailed in the Gaza Strip prior to June 2007 may be about to recur.

Armed confrontations have also repeatedly occurred when Executive Force members have attempted to carry out arrests, in some cases leading to bystanders being injured apparently because of excessive and reckless use of force by the Executive Force. According to the UN Code of Conduct for Law Enforcement Officials, security forces *"may use force only when strictly necessary and to the extent required for the performance of their duty."* Further, according to the 1990 UN Basic Principles on the Use of Force and Firearms by Law Enforcement Officials, *"intentional lethal use of firearms"* is only to be made *"when strictly unavoidable in order to protect life"*. The Executive force has disregarded these standards and the Hamas leadership has done nothing to put an end to such violent and dangerous behaviour; its inaction, effectively, has encouraged such abuses to continue.

Arbitrary Detentions, Abductions and Torture by Hamas Forces

Since mid-June the Executive Force has detained more than 1,000 people in the context of a politically-motivated detention campaign.[52] In some cases, the Qassam Brigades have also abducted and detained people, operating alongside the Executive Force or on their own. Most of those detained were released within a few hours or days but some have been held for longer—in some cases reportedly for more than two weeks.

As stated in chapter 4, the Executive Force is not authorized by law to arrest and detain people, and therefore any detention by this force is arbitrary. The prohibition of arbitrary detention is considered a norm of customary international law (as detailed in chapter 3).

Moreover, Hamas forces have been holding detainees in least 23 different locations in the Gaza Strip, most of them former PA security installations which are not authorized by law as detention facilities, in breach of the law which regulates prisons and detention centres.[53] By so doing, the Hamas

[52] The scope of this report does not include the detention of people accused of common law crimes.

[53] Law No.6 of 1998. The only authorized detention facility in the Gaza Strip is the central prison in Gaza City, which is used by Hamas forces to house common law detainees.

de-facto administration in Gaza is perpetuating the long-standing practice of the PA security forces, which until June 2007 similarly flouted the law by holding detainees in a multitude of unauthorized sites.

According to information received by Amnesty International from released detainees and families of detainees, the International Committee of the Red Cross (ICRC) has been allowed access to places of detention across the Gaza Strip since the first days of the Hamas' takeover in Gaza. The PICCR and other Palestinian human rights organizations have also been allowed to visit detention centres.[54]

Former detainees testified to Amnesty International that they were subjected to torture and other ill-treatment during their detention, and such abuses are common, with detainees routinely being subjected to severe beatings. The PICCR and other Palestinian human rights organizations, including the PCHR, al-Mezan and al-Dameer, have all reported receiving complaints of beatings and torture or other ill-treatment from released detainees who still bore injuries and bruises consistent with the abuses alleged. Other forms of torture or ill-treatment have also been reported, including forcibly shaving detainees' heads, tying detainees in painful positions (*shabeh*), and threatening them, including that they will be killed or shot in the legs.

Testimony of **A B**, 21 years old:

> *"I was arrested by the Executive Force on 26 June in Khan Yunis. There were several of them in two blue police jeeps. They took me to their headquarters in the former Israeli settlement of Gush Katif near the Tuffah area. There they beat me badly, all over the body. On the first day they just beat me and did not ask me any questions. Then they asked me what I did and I told them that I worked in the police. They beat me so badly that the day after my arrest they had to take me to the hospital for treatment. The ICRC came to visit the centre on 27 June but I was in another room and did not see them. I was released after three days. They dropped me off near my home in the middle of the night. I still don't know why they arrested and beat me. There were nine others detained in the same place, mostly common law cases; one of them was accused of stealing a mobile phone and another was there because they wanted information about his brother who is accused of killing someone in a dispute between families."*

Some people have been detained and tortured to force them to hand over their weapons. Immediately after its takeover in the Gaza Strip, Hamas announced that the Executive Force would remove all "unauthorized"

---

[54] On 10 September 2007 the PICCR issued a report detailing 23 places of detention visited by the organization's lawyers and fieldworkers, and expressed concern about the detention by the Executive Force of Palestinians in locations which are not authorized for this purpose. According to the PICCR report, as of 3 September there were some 300 detainees in the Gaza Strip, of whom 80 had been in detention since before 14 June 2007, having been detained by the PA. The remainder included both common law and political detainees arrested after 14 June.

weapons from the streets and collect all weapons used for inter-Palestinian fighting and gang rule, but that they would not confiscate "personal" weapons (which people may keep for self-defence purposes) or weapons used for "resistance against the occupation."[55]

Testimony of **Tariq Mohammed Asfour**, aged 43, former policeman, father of 11, from Khan Yunis:

> *"The Executive Force and the Qassam Brigades came to my home at the end of June and told me to get dressed and took me to a field and tied my hands behind my back. None of them were masked. The beat me for six hours with metal wires, sticks and a shovel. They beat me for 10 minutes at a time and told me 'Dahlan and Madhoun, where are they now, they can't help you now.' They said that I had shot at Hamas people and killed them and I said it was not true. They kept asking about my brother's weapons and I told them that I didn't have them. My brother was in the al-Aqsa Martyrs' Brigades and he had left Gaza before that. In the end they put 10 nails into my legs (shin) with a hammer. I admitted that I had one gun which I had buried in the garden where the dog is kept and I called my son to dig it out and bring it. When I collapsed they gave me cold water and rushed me to Nasser Hospital and told the doctor to make me better and send me home."*

On 7 July the Palestinian news agency Maan News reported that its editor-in-chief had received a threatening telephone call from a Hamas spokesperson after publishing an article in Arabic detailing the case of Tariq Mohammed Asfour.[56]

Testimony of **M A**, aged 25, unemployed:

> *"I was arrested in the evening of 29 September in the street near my house (in the south of the Gaza Strip) with a friend and we were taken to the Executive Force centre nearby. They said they wanted the weapons I have but I told them that I don't have any. They insisted that I do and accused me of making trouble against them. They told me to take down the Fatah flag on top of my house. They beat me with sticks and ropes and one of them kicked me and punched me. They continued beating me for a long time, maybe half an hour. When I couldn't move any more they put me in a cell on my own. The day after they asked me again about the same things and beat me again; I was bruised and in pain from the previous day and I collapsed quickly and they left me and then they released me and told me to watch out and that I had been warned."*

At least two detainees have died while being detained by the Executive Force in the Gaza Strip since 15 June. **Walid Abu Dalfa**, 45, was arrested

[55] The crackdown seems to have targeted a small percentage of armed groups and individuals. Several people, including Fatah supporters and members of the PA security forces told Amnesty International that they had been allowed to keep their weapons or that their weapons had been confiscated but returned after checking their provenance, or that they had been asked to hand over weapons but were left alone after they were able to prove that they no longer had these weapons. Others reported that they or their relatives managed to hold on to some of their weapons by hiding them and lying about what was in their possession.

[56] See: *http://www.maannews.net/en/index.php?opr=ShowDetails&ID=23728.*

with his brother on 9 July 2007 from their home and was detained in al-Mashtal security compound (formerly the General Intelligence compound), controlled by the Qassam Brigades. On 15 July his body was brought to Gaza City's Shifa hospital, bearing marks of torture. His brother, who was arrested with him, and a second brother arrested three days later, testified to the PCHR that all three had been tortured in detention and that Walid had died as a result. According to the PCHR, whose representative was present at the post mortem examination, the body bore "bruises on the hands and the legs, haematomas in the legs and signs of stranglehold on the neck."[57]

On 10 July **Fadhel Dahmash**, 31, died in the custody of the Executive Force in Gaza central prison, where he had been held since 6 July on suspicion of "collaborating" with Israeli intelligence services. Fadhel Dahmash was first abducted on 5 July by members of the al-Quds Brigades, the armed wing of Islamic Jihad, which released a video showing a man getting out of an Israeli military jeep, taking off his military uniform and putting on civilian clothes. The PCHR called on the al-Quds Brigades not to harm Fadhel Dahmash and to hand him over to the PA. Fadhel Dahmash's brother informed the PCHR that his brother had been released by the al-Quds Brigades the same day, after he had been tortured, but that he was arrested by the Executive Force the following day, 6 July. Later that morning, according to hospital records, while in the custody of the Executive Force, Fadhel Dahmash was briefly admitted to hospital. On 10 July his body was taken to Gaza City's hospital, accompanied by a letter from the director of Gaza central prison stating that Fadhel Dahmash had suffered heart failure and difficulties in breathing.[58] According to the PICCR, Fadhel Dahmash's body bore marks of torture; however, to date Amnesty International has been unable to obtain information about the cause of death.

After persistent reports of torture and other ill-treatment of detainees by the Executive Force, its leader, Jamal Jarrah, acknowledged that members had used violence and committed abuses. In an interview with Palestinian media on 19 August, he was quoted as saying:

> *"We try to minimize violations and avoid them through the training of our members . . . there were some minor cases [of torture], which we have admitted and we condemn any such practices . . . The Executive Force has formed investigation committees in order to investigate all the violations and seriously address all the cases in the prisons."*

However, no information has been made public by the Executive Force or by the Hamas de-facto administration in Gaza about the findings of any investigations that have been conducted or any measures that have been

[57] See: *http://pchrgaza.org/files/PressR/English/2007/60.2007.htm.*
[58] See: *http://pchrgaza.org/files/PressR/English/2007/57.2007.htm.*

taken to prevent further abuses, and reports of torture and other ill-treatment of detainees have continued to be received by Amnesty International and by Palestinian human rights organizations.[59]

6. Abuses in the West Bank

Crackdown on Hamas Supporters

The armed confrontations between Fatah and Hamas in the Gaza Strip have had severe repercussions throughout the West Bank. The al-Aqsa Brigades, Fatah's armed wing, which have had stronger structures in the West Bank than their Hamas counterparts for years, carried out scores of attacks on Hamas supporters and presumed sympathizers in the West Bank in revenge for Hamas' attacks on Fatah in the Gaza Strip. Attacks included killings, abductions, arson and shooting attacks on houses, businesses, charities and media outlets linked to Hamas, as well as on others whom they considered to be critical of Fatah. Most attacks took place at the same time and immediately following the last round of bloody clashes between Fatah and Hamas in the Gaza Strip, in the second week of June 2007, but sporadic attacks against both people and property have continued.

As the wave of the al-Aqsa Brigades revenge attacks against Hamas was under way, in mid-June, PA security forces launched a crackdown on Hamas supporters and presumed sympathizers, and arrested hundreds. The PA alleged that those arrested were planning to set up an Executive Force and launch attacks against PA security installations in the West Bank, as had happened in the Gaza Strip. However, the aim of the arrest campaign, which targeted Hamas sympathizers, not activists, seems to have been mainly to intimidate Hamas supporters. In mid-July senior PA security officials told Amnesty International that virtually all those detained in the previous four weeks, some 300 to 400 people, had been released within a few days after pledging not to get involved with Hamas—an indication that they were not being investigated for any crimes. People detained in the same period told Amnesty International that they had not been subjected to any serious questioning about their activities, but rather were told to condemn the Hamas takeover in Gaza and warned or threatened that they should not get involved with Hamas and/or the Executive Force.

Arrests of known or presumed Hamas supporters have continued, reaching more than 1,000 by early October. Reports of torture or other ill-treatment of detainees, rare in the first weeks, subsequently increased, as did violations of the laws regulating detention.

[59] See: PCRH's statement of 27 August 2007, at: *http://www.pchrgaza.org/files/PressR/English/2007/109-2007.html* and PICCR Special Report No. 58 of 10 September 2007 (in Arabic).

The ongoing campaign of arrests of Hamas supporters by PA security forces has shown that when the PA deems it necessary it can secure the necessary cooperation of the Israeli security forces to allow its PA security forces to arrest, detain and move detainees between towns and villages throughout the West Bank. For years, the PA has claimed that the presence of Israeli forces in and around Palestinian towns and villages made it impossible to detain Palestinians involved in attacks against Israeli civilians.[60]

In addition to the large-scale arrests of Hamas supporters, the PA took other measures against Hamas supporters in the West Bank, including a decision by the PA emergency government to close more than 100 charities linked to Hamas,[61] and PA security forces used violence against protest demonstrations and at public gatherings of Hamas sympathisers. On 9 September PA security forces violently broke up a large gathering of Hamas students outside Hebron University, beating students and journalists and preventing the latter from documenting the incident and confiscating equipment. Several journalists and students were injured and some 10 students were arrested. On 22 September the police used tear gas to break up a demonstration in the centre of Ramallah by women calling for the release of their relatives who were being held as detainees in PA custody. Some of the women also complained that they had been forcibly pushed back by the police.

As well, the PA government and security forces have failed to take action against members of the al-Aqsa Brigades who have been responsible for abductions, killings and attacks against Hamas supporters and their property and against news media linked to Hamas.

Continued Impunity for Fatah Armed Groups

President Abbas issued two decrees outlawing "the Executive Force and militias belonging to the Hamas movement."[62] A third decree outlaws "all armed militias and military and para-military groups of any kind,"[63] but does not mention the al-Aqsa Brigades—the largest and most active armed group in the West Bank which has been responsible for the vast majority of

[60] Though true to a varying degree, depending on the extent of the presence of Israeli forces in a given area at a given time, the curtailment of PA security forces' ability to operate in the West Bank has often been used by the PA as a pretext for its failure to act against Palestinian armed groups responsible for attacks on Israeli civilians, abductions and other attacks against Palestinians, Israelis and foreigners.

[61] On 28 August 2007 PA Prime Minister Salam Fayyad, announced his government's decision to close 103 charitable associations linked to Hamas, alleging that they has committed "legal, administrative, or financial violations" of the law on Benevolent Societies and Non-governmental Institutions (Law No. 1 of 2000). The total number of Palestinian non-governmental organizations (NGOs) in the West Bank and Gaza is reported to be well in excess of 2,000, and the fact that the NGOs affected were linked to Hamas raised concerns that the law was applied selectively in order to target Hamas.

[62] Presidential Decrees issued on 16 June and 12 August 2007.

[63] Presidential Decrees issued on 26 June 2007.

intra-Palestinian killings and attacks within the West Bank—or any other armed groups.[64]

The PA's arrest and detention of more than 1,000 presumed Hamas supporters who, PA security forces have acknowledged, are mostly not accused of any crime, stands in stark contrast to its failure to arrest and bring to justice members of al-Aqsa Brigades responsible for unlawful killings, hostage-taking, arson and other attacks against people and property. Even though those responsible for such attacks were often known in their communities, acted in full view of the security forces and often boasted about their actions in the media, they have not been arrested and no legal proceedings are known to have been brought against them.

In meetings with an Amnesty International delegate in June and July 2007, senior officials in the Military Intelligence, Preventive Security and Presidential Guard/Force 17 could not provide any information about a single case of arrest or other measures taken against members of the al-Aqsa Brigades for deliberate killings, hostage-taking, or other attacks against people and property, nor did they seem interested in pursuing such cases. They acknowledged that some members of the al-Aqsa Brigades are also members of the security forces, notably of the Presidential Guard/Force 17.

The impunity enjoyed by the al-Aqsa Brigades increased the atmosphere of fear and intimidation among people who are not members of Hamas but who are or may be perceived as sympathizers. Several victims of attacks by the al-Aqsa Brigades told Amnesty International that they did not wish it to become known that they had reported the attacks or that they had identified the perpetrators. Some said that they had not lodged complaints with the security forces because they considered it to be pointless or because doing so could expose them to retaliation by the Brigades. Others said that the security forces were present when the attacks occurred but did not act to stop the attacks or apprehend the perpetrators. Other still said that gunmen had obstructed the fire-fighters' interventions. A university lecturer whose car was shot at some 60 times by members of the al-Aqsa Brigades in June in Nablus told Amnesty International that when he reported the attack to the police he gave the names of the two members of the group who carried out the attack, but the police refused to write down the names in the complaint report.

Armed attacks against presumed Hamas supporters

Anis Hisham Anis Sal'us, a 37-year-old tailor from Nablus, married with two young children, was abducted by a group of armed masked men as he

64 Other armed groups in the West Bank, all of which are small and generally not involved in inter-factional Palestinian violence, include the Islamic Jihad, the PFLP, the DFLP, and the PRC.

was leaving the mosque near his home in Nablus on 14 June 2007, after the evening prayer. He was driven to a place between the old and new Askar refugee camp and shot dead. His family was first alerted by witnesses that he had been abducted and shot, and later heard on television that he had been killed. When the family went to the morgue to identify the body they saw that he had been shot in the head, chest and stomach. According to the family, no autopsy was carried out. The family took the death certificate from the hospital to the police but were not contacted for any follow up and are not aware of any investigation.

Jamal Salim 'Arif al-Usta, a 46-year-old father of four, was abducted by a group of armed masked men as he was coming out of a mosque in Nablus on 16 June 2007. He was bundled into a car and taken to a location where he was beaten before being set free. The following day four armed masked men went to his workplace and shot him in the head and left him for dead. He was reported to have died but, in fact, he was seriously injured and went into a coma and survived.

Munir Abdallah Abd al-Majid Umar, head of the Ministry of Higher Education office in Tulkarem, aged 49, married and father of six:

> *"In the morning of 3 July 2007 I was kidnapped from my office by masked gunmen. At about 11.30am four armed masked men in civilian dress entered my office by force and asked for my ID. They smashed up things in the office and asked me to stand against a wall, beating me and insulting me all the while. They warned me not to come to my office again and not to do my job. They told me to leave within five minutes and then changed their minds and took me away in a plain car without number plate. In the car they beat me repeatedly on the back of the neck and threatened to kill me while pointing a gun at me. About 500m down the road they threw me out of the car and fired just above my head, and then drove off. Usually there are two policemen outside the office but on that morning they weren't there. I have contacted the Preventive Security and asked them to carry out an investigation."*[65]

Shaher Sa'ed, Secretary-General of the Federation of Palestinian Labor Unions and President of the Institutions Committee in Nablus:

> *"At approximately 2.30pm on Tuesday 10 July 2007, I accompanied a group of Italian union activists, on a visit to witness the conditions of Palestinian workers, to eat lunch at Asfoura Restaurant in Rafidya Quarter in the west of Nablus. As we were sitting in the restaurant, I was surprised by four masked gunmen demanding at gunpoint that I leave the guests and accompany them. They took me in their car to an area near Melehes Shoe Factory in Tunisia Street in Rafidya. They told me that they are a militia that isn't affiliated with any party. They demanded that I resign from the Union and Institutions Committee in the city. They accused me of collaborating with Hamas, and of working with Hamas. I was abducted for about 90 minutes with the purpose of delivering this message."*

[65] Testimony given to PCHR.

Ahmad Khaldi, former Justice Minister (in the Hamas government) and lecturer at al-Najah University in Nablus, was similarly abducted and threatened on 22 June 2007 by gunmen who accused him of being close to Hamas.

Testimony of **Rabi'a Hussein Rabi'a**, lawyer and member of Ramallah municipal council:[66]

> *"During the night of 13–14 June at about 1am I was at home with my family and I received an alarm call about my office; the alarm system is connected to the police, so they are alerted as soon as the alarm goes off. I telephoned the police and they said that they would check and call me back and shortly after they called and asked me to go to my office. My wife came with me. There were police cars in the street outside the building. The door into the building was open and in the stairs there was smoke and no light. We went upstairs to my office and found that the metal door which protects the front door had been taken off but the front door remained in place and locked but inside the office was on fire. The arsonists had seemingly not been able to break down the door and had thrown petrol under the door and set fire that way. The surveillance cameras inside the office recorded the fire, which caused significant damage. Almost immediately five masked armed men appeared and said they were from the al-Aqsa Martyrs' Brigades and told me to go with them. When I asked why and where they told me to shut up. They took me downstairs and to the car park across the road, forced me into the back of a car and put a bag over my head and held me on each side. There were other cars, both official security forces' cars and unmarked ones and there was shooting in the air. They took me to a place somewhere in the open air and a man who sounded and smelled drunk asked me what I thought of the events in Gaza and I said that both sides were wrong. They asked me to condemn Hamas and I said I didn't know enough about the details of what happened in Gaza. Then they asked me to call my wife and tell her that I was OK, which I did. Then they tied my hands and put me in the boot of a car and took me to another place and said it was a place to investigate collaborators. They asked me why I was elected to the municipal council on the Change and Reform electoral list [the name of the party under which Hamas ran in the elections]. I said that I had proposed a joint list but it didn't happen and I ran on the Change and Reform list because there were good and moderate people and wanted to do something good at the municipal level. I am clearly not a Hamas member. Then they put me in a car again and put my head down. They were speaking on walkie-talkie, saying to be careful as there were Israeli forces in the area. We arrived at a building and walked up three or four floors; I still had a bag over my head and could not see. There they took my belt, watch, wallet and also my glasses, without which I cannot see. By then it must have been 4 or 4.30am. They told me to go to sleep. Other detainees were brought into the room and I heard the voice of my younger brother. He had gone to my office to look for me after my wife called him and had been taken from there. Me and the others in the room were allowed to take off the hoods to pray but had to put them back after. My brother complained of a headache and they asked him if he wanted to be shot in the head or*

[66] He notes that he ran for the council on a Hamas list because he wanted to be involved in local politics but has never been a member of Hamas.

> *in the legs. There was another man in the same room and five others in the next room. They brought us water and some food. I was blindfolded, not hooded anymore. They were dressed in plain clothes except one who was in uniform. Some were polite and said they had orders to detain us, while others were aggressive. They said that they had killed Zahar and Siyam [two Hamas leaders in Gaza]. The following day, a Friday, we were allowed to pray together and that afternoon they gave us food. They told us we would be released and gave us our stuff back, but as they were taking me downstairs they roughed me up; held me by the neck and pushed me against the wall and pointed a gun to the back of my head. Another detainee was sick and he fainted and they [the jailers] took some money from me to send him to hospital . . . When we got downstairs they took the blindfold off and I was in a very dirty room with four bunk beds. We were again searched and our belongings were again taken from us but this time we filled in forms stating what was taken from us. On the form it was written "Istikhbarat" [military intelligence]. I realized the other six and I had been the whole time in the Istikhbarat building in the Um Shraib area of Ramallah. We were not blindfolded and officers in plain clothes said we were at the Istikhbarat station and were safe but said we had to stand when they entered the room. It was dirty and we asked for water and we cleaned the room. Then I wrote a list of things I needed from the shop, toothbrush, soap, etc and they brought us some of the things. I was told by the head of the centre that those who had taken him were not officials. I was released with another detainee that day [15 June] at 11pm. During my detention my wife had contacted high level officials to alert them about my case. My brother and another detainee were released the following day. The last one of our group was released on 25 June. But while I was detained there I heard others being brought in. And after my release I heard about others. One is a young man who is supposed to get married next month, who was arrested on 16 June [the latter was released on 1 July]."*

Several weeks later Rabi'a Hussein Rabi'a reported that he had resigned from the Hamas-run municipal council due to repeated threats.

The head of the Military Intelligence centre in Ramallah confirmed to Amnesty International that Rabi'a Hussein Rabi'a was abducted by members of al-Aqsa Brigades but maintained that he was handed over to Military Intelligence officers before reaching the Military Intelligence compound. He stated that the identity of the gunmen who abducted Rabi'a Hussein Rabi'a was not known and that therefore no measures could be taken against them.

Testimony of **Hassan al-Titi**, a journalist and owner of the main foreign media centre in Nablus:

> *"On 17 June 2007, just after 9pm a group of masked gunmen stormed my house and burned the first floor of the house, which houses the Palestine Media Center, an independent media centre that is part of Palestinian Telecommunication Group. All the equipment was destroyed. Upstairs from the office is my home and luckily my wife and children were out or they could have been hurt in the fire. My office is the only place with the facilities for live transmission and everyone uses it. The office is not linked to any one satellite channel; rather, it provides media services to all news agencies and satellite channels. The attack was obviously the result of incitement*

against al-Jazeera Satellite Channel, which has been accused of pro-Hamas bias. However, I am a correspondent of al-Jazeera; at times I report to al-Jazeera on incidents in Nablus, as I report to many other media."

In the same week, more than a dozen attacks on the pro-Hamas news media were carried out, ranging from burning down and destroying premises, to seizing and burning newspapers before they could be distributed, and attacking and threatening journalists.

Testimony of **S A,** President of a Women's vocational centre in Nablus (presumed to be linked to Hamas):

"Armed men came at about 11.30 on the evening of 14 June; they were in three cars and set fire to the centre. A colleague who lives upstairs from the centre saw everything but could do nothing to stop them or the fire. By the time the fire brigade arrived everything had burned down. There was mostly embroidery and papers and it burned quickly. This was a women's centre which has existed since 1998. We trained women in embroidery, which was then sold, or prepared food for companies and government institutions for Ramadhan parties and other celebrations, ran courses in self-confidence and communication skills for girls aged 14 to 18, and ran a crèche for babies in the area. The centre provided income for some 90 women and families, poor women for whom the income made a difference."

Testimony of **Ali Dado,** owner of a large carpet shop in Tulkarem (formerly active in Hamas, some 14 years ago):

"On 12 June 2007 at around 12.30am, armed men shot at the shop and broke some windows. On 14 June at around 10.30pm a group of armed masked men in uniform came to the house when only my mother and youngest son were at home, while I was in hospital in Ramallah. Ten of them entered the house and eight official cars surrounded the house. They wanted to detain me and in my absence searched the house and threatened to kill my son. A few hours later, at around 3am a group of seven or eight masked men went to my carpet shop and set it on fire, while shooting in the air. The fire brigade was prevented from putting out the fire immediately by the men shooting at it, but were subsequently allowed to put out the fire which had spread to neighbouring shops. My brother received a call that our shop was on fire and on his way there he passed armed masked men who warned him not to go to the shop. He waited a while before going and by the time he got there everything had burnt down. He called the fire brigade and they told him they had been prevented from putting out the fire by armed masked men. He called the police and they said it was not their responsibility and told him to call the General Security. The Police and Preventive Security came past but later, at around 5am. The loss is an estimate US $1–1.5million. I have lodged a complaint but am not aware of any investigation.

The PA has sought to minimize the scale and seriousness of attacks perpetrated by the al-Aqsa Brigades against Hamas supporters or other Fatah critics and their property, seemingly justifying them as an understandable reaction to the attacks by Hamas on Fatah in the Gaza Strip. No investigations are known to have been carried out into such attacks, which have continued with impunity.

On 24 July 2007 Muhammad Raddad, a 21-year-old student and member of the student council at al-Najah university in Nablus, and a Hamas supporters, was reportedly shot in the head at very close range by a member of a Fatah youth group some of whose members are involved with al-Aqsa Brigades in the course of a scuffle between Fatah and Hamas students at the university campus. He died three days later.

Between 7 and 10 September, the al-Aqsa Brigades carried out three separate attacks in Nablus and Tulkarem. In the evening of 7 September, masked gunmen blew up two ambulances at the Zakat Hospital in Tulkarm. The previous day two gunmen had threatened the hospital and ordered the administrators to dismiss any staff hired by the Hamas government.

In the evening of 9 September, four masked gunmen wearing al-Aqsa Brigades T-shirts abducted **Abd al-Fattah Fayez Sa'id**, a merchant from Tulkarem, and took him to a nearby field. They threw him to the ground and questioned him about his relationship with Hamas, beating him with sticks and gun butts during the interrogation. The gunmen then took his ID card, house keys and money, and left him.

On 10 September at around midday gunmen from the al-Aqsa Brigades forcibly closed the office of the Prisoners' Club (*Nadi al-Asir*) in Nablus. The Director of the Club, Ra'ed Amer, told PCHR that some 20 gunmen stormed into the office and ordered it closed, telling him that the closure was a message to the PA and other parties whom they accused of neglecting their duties towards prisoners.

Arbitrary Detentions, Torture and Other Ill-Treatment

In the first weeks after the arrest campaign began in June credible reports of torture were rare. Reports of ill-treatment were also infrequent and mostly related to the time of arrest and transfer to the place of detention rather than during interrogation. However, there was a discernible pattern of intimidation, with detainees unwilling to discuss their arrest and detention citing fear of repercussions. By the end of July, reports of torture and other ill-treatment during detention had increased and by early October in every case reported to Amnesty International there was credible evidence that detainees had been subjected to torture or other ill-treatment.

Most of the detentions were arbitrary because they were carried out by security forces, notably Preventive Security, who are not authorized by law to detain suspects;[67] because detainees were held in locations that are not authorized by law as places of detention; and because the detentions were

[67] The security forces authorized to carry out arrest are the Police (Article 21, Part 2 Chapter 1 of the Penal Procedures Law No. 3 of 2001 defines the "Officers invested with judicial powers") and the Military Intelligence (Article 12, Chapter 2 of the General Intelligence Law No.17 of 2005). Since June most arrests have been carried out by forces other than the Police.

not authorized by the prosecutors and judges within the timeframe stipulated by Palestinian law.

At the end of June an Amnesty International delegate met the head of the Jneid Presidential Guard/Force 17 compound in Nablus, where most of those arrested in the Nablus area were detained. Colonel Abu 'Ali al-Turk gave Amnesty International a copy of a form which detainees were asked to sign before being released, which states:

> *"In the name of God, the compassionate and merciful, I the undersigned . . . have no relation, from close or afar, with the organization of the Hamas movement and will not get involved in it in the future. I condemn the criminal actions which were committed by the 'Izz al-Din al-Qassam Brigades and the Executive Force belonging to Hamas in the Gaza Strip against our people and against the PA installations, and I consider them criminal and murderous gangs against the Palestinian cause."*[68]

Similar forms, with slightly different wording, were in use throughout the West Bank. The demand that a detainee, often held outside the framework of the law, should sign an undertaking not to have any relation with Hamas—which has never been outlawed by the PA—and should condemn events which they had not witnessed as a condition for being released, is but one indication of the arbitrary nature of such detentions.

The PICCR and some Palestinian human rights organizations have been given access to most of the detention centres, but only a minority of the hundreds of detainees held there have been interviewed by these organizations in detention due to time and resource constraints, and to the quick turnover of detainees. The ICRC has also visited detention centres. Former detainees told Amnesty International that they had not revealed that they had suffered torture or ill-treatment, either to visitors or to prosecutors, for fear that their treatment would worsen. Many of those contacted by Amnesty International either refused to speak about their treatment in detention or spoke only on condition that their details would not be made public, saying that they feared being re-arrested or otherwise targeted.

In none of the cases known to Amnesty International were the families of the detainees informed of their relatives' arrest and whereabouts. Detainees' families either guessed because they knew which security force had carried out the arrests, or were informed unofficially by friends or relatives in the security forces or by released detainees. In some cases detainees held for longer periods have been allowed to receive visits from their families, mostly arranged through personal contacts rather than through established visiting procedures.

[68] Original in Arabic on file at Amnesty International.

Testimony of **O H**, aged 21, from Nablus:

> *"On 18 June, I received a call from Preventive Security summoning me. I contacted a neighbour who is an officer in Preventive Security and was taken to the Preventive Security building, where I spent the first night. They told me to hand in my weapons and asked some basic questions. The next morning I was transferred in an unmarked car to Jneid security compound. The treatment in Jneid was completely different. On arrival I was hit on the head and shoulder with a Kalashnikov and made to stand for about an hour on one leg with my arms raised [shabeh]. I was held alone in a filthy cell with no light. The first night I slept on the concrete floor with no mattress. I was forced to stand on one leg with my arms raised every night. At night the guards banged on the doors to prevent us from sleeping and insulted us and Hamas leaders. Guards also entered my cell, which had no light, and shone a blue light in my eyes. I was questioned twice in all, in a washroom. I sat facing the wall and they took off my blindfold and they sat behind me so I didn't see them. They asked if I am Hamas, if I am Executive Force, about Gaza events, about my relations with some individuals, and if he has weapons. They asked about my job in a local Hamas TV station and then I was told to sign a paper denouncing Hamas and the Gaza events. I signed in order to get out and was released two days later, on 23 June. When I was released they threatened me saying that they may call me back and that they can't protect me from masked men. During my detention I saw the prison doctor for an eye problem, the ICRC visited but only to take down the name and telephone number of my family, and an AP journalist also visited."*

Another detainee who was held in the same place during the same period told Amnesty International that he had been subjected to similar torture or other ill-treatment, but others who had been held there told the organization that they had not been beaten or ill-treated.

N A, 36-year-old father of two held at Jneid detention centre from 19 to 24 June 2007, said:

> *"On arrival in Jneid they hit me on the head and shoulder with a Kalashnikov and made me stand for about an hour on one leg with my arms raised. I was held alone in a cell which was filthy with faeces, cockroaches and no light. The situation made me ill; I became very tense and broke down. I suffered from this once before. I was taken to hospital and kept there for a day and a night. Some 10 masked gunmen accompanied me to the hospital. Then I was taken back to Jneid and to the filthy cell. They cleaned the cell before the ICRC came; the ICRC only took names and contact details for the families. Once a guard came in and pressed his boot down on my head. At night the guards kept banging on the doors so I couldn't sleep; they cursed Hamas leaders and I also cursed Hamas in order to get rid of the guard and be able to sleep. They called me a kafir [infidel] several times. They told me that to get released I must sign a paper denouncing Hamas and what they did in Gaza and I signed so I could get out. Before releasing me they told me they can't protect me from masked gunmen."*

N E, a Hamas supporter who was released on 15 August after 47 days of detention by the Preventive Security in Bethlehem and Ramallah, told Amnesty International that he was tied in an uncomfortable position, forced to stand for several hours at a time, and subjected to sleep deprivation in order to pressure him to "confess" to activities in which he had not been involved—notably the creation of an Executive Force in the West Bank and possession of weapons. Upon his release he was hospitalized and found to have internal bleeding. He required treatment for other injuries too, notably to his limbs. He was never taken to court, as required by Palestinian law, and in the last days of his detention, when he was eventually due to appear before a judge, he was transferred by Preventive Security in Bethlehem to another Preventive Security post in the Betounia area of Ramallah. While there a judge in Bethlehem ordered his release but he was not freed until several days later. After his release he stopped receiving his salary from the Ministry where he worked. He was told he had been dismissed because of his arrest, even though he was not charged with any offence.

Violation of Laws Regulating Detention

Amnesty International has learned of several other cases where Preventive Security have moved detainees from the north and south of the West Bank to the Preventive Security centre in Betounia (Ramallah), instead of complying with the judges' orders to release them, or to prevent them from appearing before a judge. The security forces' refusal to comply with judges' release orders have become increasingly frequent since August. As well, most detainees have not been brought before a judge within the 72-hour period stipulated by Palestinian law, if at all.

Pre-charge detention is regulated by the Penal Procedures Law.[69] This law requires detention to be reviewed by a prosecutor within 24 hours of the arrest (Article 34). The prosecutor may then extend the individual's detention for a further 48 hours. If the detainee is not released after this 72-hour period, a judge must review the case (Article 51). The judge may extend pre-arraignment detention initially for up to 15 days (Articles 62–63) and thereafter any further extension up to a maximum of period of 45 days must be reviewed by a judge every 15 days. Upon request of a prosecutor to a higher court, the detention of an individual may be extended further for a period not exceeding an additional 45 days. The law also grants detainees prompt and unhindered access to legal counsel (Article 46).

However, in the 30-day period during which the state of emergency declared by President Abbas was in force, from 14 June to 13 July 2007, detention was regulated by Article 112 of the Basic Law, which stipulates: *"Any detention done in accordance with the decree of the emergency situation, shall be reviewed by the Attorney General or by the concerned court during a*

[69] Penal Procedure Law No. 3 of 2001.

period not exceeding fifteen (15) days from the date of detention." The application of Article 112 of the Basic Law over this 30-day period, if it had been implemented, would have supplanted the provisions of the Penal Procedures Law to the extent that the first review of the detention would have taken been conducted by the Attorney General by the fifteenth day of detention (rather than by a prosecutor after the first 24 hours and a judge after the first 72 hours of detention and thereafter). However, according to information available to Amnesty International, several people detained prior to 13 July and for longer than 15 days were not brought before the Attorney General.[70]

Ibrahim Yousef al-Sheikh, an 18-year-old student was arrested on 4 September at the Salesian college where he studies in Bethlehem and taken to the Preventive Security centre in the town. He was not brought before a judge until 16 September, nine days after the expiry of the 72-hour period at the end of which detainees must appear before a judge or be released. The judge ordered his release but he remained in detention at the time of writing, 40 days after his arrest, in violation of Palestinian law. Two of his relatives, Brahim Qasem al-Sheikh and Bakir 'Ali Qasem al-Sheikh, were arrested on 8 and 6 September, respectively. They did not appear in front of a judge until 23 September, a delay of at least 10 days, and were both ordered released by the judge but remained in detention at the time of writing, more than three weeks later, and were reported to have been tortured.

Isma'il 'Abdelkarim Mohammed Isma'il, a 31-year-old house painter and father of five young children, was arrested from his home in Beit Iba, near Nablus, on 25 August; he had still not appeared before a judge more than six weeks later. He remained in detention at the time of writing and was reported to have been tortured.

A fourth relative, **Hussein al-Sheikh**, a lawyer working with *Nadi al-Asir*, the Prisoners' Club, a NGO which provides support and legal counsel for Palestinians detained by the Israeli authorities, was detained on 14 September by Preventive Security in Bethlehem; three days later he appeared before a judge who ordered his release, but he was not released until 30 September, after several colleagues intervened on his behalf. After his release he told

[70] On 6 July 2007 President Abbas issued a presidential decree placing all crimes against internal and public security under the jurisdiction of the military courts. The decree stipulated that it was applicable from the date of issue. However, on 10 July 2007 the Attorney General told Amnesty International that any cases related to the Fatah-Hamas infighting which occurred after the declaration of the State of Emergency on 14 June 2007 were no longer within his brief and were to be dealt with by the Military Attorney General—indicating that the decree was being applied retroactively, even though there is no provision in the Basic Law or any other laws allowing such a measure. In any case, the validity of this decree expired on 13 July 2007, when the State of Emergency ended and the provisions of the above-mentioned Penal Procedure Law No. 3 of 2001 became once again applicable—though in practice routinely ignored.

Amnesty International that during his detention he had been subjected to sleep deprivation and *shabeh* and that he had lost 14 kilos in weight during the two weeks in detention. On 11 October he was arrested by Israeli forces and remained in Israeli custody at the time of writing. A fifth member of the family, **Mustapha Taha al-Sheikh**, a 19-year-old student, was similarly arrested by Israeli forces on 11 October, two days after having been released from the Preventive Security centre in Bethlehem, where he had been detained without charge or trial for two weeks. Several other people were similarly arrested by Israeli forces shortly after Preventive Security was compelled to release them, after periods of arbitrary detention. By mid-October, a pattern was emerging in which a number of people who had been detained by PA security forces beyond the limits of Palestinian law and in breach of judges' orders to release them, were detained by Israeli forces after their release from PA custody, suggesting a degree of increased "security" cooperation between the PA's Preventive Security and Israeli forces.

Conclusion And Recommendations

The lawlessness which has increasingly gripped the West Bank and Gaza Strip in recent years, culminating in the unprecedented inter-factional violence which occurred in the first half of 2007, is to a large extent the result of the prolonged and systematic failure of the PA to uphold and enforce the law, to curb the proliferation of unlicensed weapons in the hands of private individuals and groups, and to hold both armed groups and members of the PA security forces who commit human rights abuses accountable for their crimes. Lawlessness has been stimulated by an increasingly entrenched climate of impunity, which has served only to fuel abuses and to bring the PA's law enforcement and judicial institutions and mechanisms into disrepute within the wider Palestinian community they are supposed to serve.

Amnesty International recognizes that the PA's ability to fulfill its law-enforcement and administration of justice duties has been severely constrained by outside factors resulting from the ongoing Israeli occupation of the West Bank and Gaza Strip, including repeated attacks by the Israeli army against PA security installations and other institutions and restrictions imposed by Israel on the movement and operational capability of the PA security forces in the areas under the PA jurisdiction. Notwithstanding this reality, the organization believes that the PA has too often used these constraints as a pretext to justify its lack of political will and its failure to act against Palestinian armed groups and powerful interest groups responsible for serious crimes—whether against other Palestinians or against Israeli civilians and foreigners.

Amnesty International considers that urgent, concrete steps are now needed to address this systematic failure and to begin to impose respect for the rule of law in the areas of the Occupied Palestinian Territories which fall under the jurisdiction of the PA. In particular, Amnesty International makes the following recommendations:

To the PA and the Hamas de-facto administration in the Gaza Strip:

Establish a Commission of experts

- Agree to the establishment of an independent, impartial and non-partisan commission of experts to investigate human rights abuses committed by both parties, their forces and armed groups in the context of the inter-factional clashes which have been occurring since the beginning of 2006.
- Undertake to cooperate with such a commission and to facilitate its mission.
- Undertake to take the necessary steps to address the findings and recommendations of the investigation, which should be made public.

To the PA:

End impunity

- End the impunity which persists, including by issuing clear instructions requiring all PA security forces to uphold the law and respect human rights, and by instructing them that members of armed groups and others who commit offences are to be apprehended and brought to justice regardless of what political faction or clan to which they belong.

End arbitrary arrests and detentions

- Ensure that all those arbitrarily detained are released, that arbitrary arrests cease immediately and that no one is deprived of their liberty except in accordance with procedures and on grounds prescribed by law. Notably, arrests and detention should only be carried out by security forces which are authorized to do so by law.

End torture and other ill-treatment

- Ensure that all detainees are treated humanely and held only in detention centres authorized by law, and that their detention is promptly reviewed by a judge, in compliance with Palestinian law and in line with internationally recognized standards, and that they are either charged with a recognizably criminal offence and promptly brought to trial in line with international standards for fair trial and without recourse to the death penalty, or released;
- ensure that the families of those detained are informed promptly of the place of detention of their relatives and that detainees are allowed prompt access to their families and lawyers;

- require that all detainees are examined by an independent doctor as soon as possible after they are arrested and regularly thereafter throughout their detention;
- ensure that those making a complaint of torture or other ill-treatment and any witnesses to such abuse are adequately protected against possible reprisals, intimidation or harassment, and take firm action if such harassment or other abuses takes place;
- ensure that all allegations of torture or other ill-treatment of detainees are investigated promptly and independently, that anyone found responsible is brought to justice, and provide reparation to the victims;
- put in place urgently a mechanism to ensure independent, impartial and non-partisan oversight and accountability of the security forces, including regular inspections of detention centres without advance notice to the detaining authorities;
- issue clear instructions to all members of the security forces that anyone who abuses their power or fails to carry out their duty to enforce the law, taking into account their duty to protect and uphold human rights, will be subject to disciplinary measures or criminal prosecution.

Investigate and ensure justice for other abuses

- Ensure that all unlawful killings, abductions and any other attacks against civilians, be they Palestinians, Israelis or nationals of other countries, are investigated promptly, thoroughly and impartially, and that those responsible for such crimes are brought to justice in proceedings which comply with internationally recognized standards for fair trial and without recourse to the death penalty.

End the proliferation of weapons used to commit human rights abuses

- Take measures to ensure that no groups or individuals, including the al-Aqsa Martyrs' Brigades, are allowed to use or carry firearms or ammunition in a manner that may jeopardize the security of the civilian population.

Restore the rule of law in the Gaza Strip

- Instruct the Attorney General, prosecutors, judges and police force to resume discharging their duties in the Gaza Strip.

De-politicize PA security forces

- Establish clearly defined criteria and procedures for the recruitment and training of members of the PA's security forces to ensure that they are free from partisan political control, effective and accountable to the community they serve, receive appropriate training and operate according to appropriate professional principles and standards, and deliver an impartial criminal justice system which conforms to human rights standards. Anyone who does not uphold these principles should be held accountable.

Strengthen judicial independence

- Take measures to ensure the independence of the judiciary, including that members of the judiciary are protected from political or other pressure or physical attacks, that they receive adequate training and resources to enable them to fulfil their professional duties, and that they are appointed solely on the basis of their training or qualifications in law, professional competence and integrity, without discrimination on grounds of their political or other opinions or other prohibited grounds.

Review and improve systems for the administration of justice

- Establish a review mechanism to examine the role of the General Prosecution and security forces and the reasons underlying their failure to adequately carry out their responsibilities to maintain law and order, taking fully into account their duty to protect and uphold human rights, and recommending measures to address these failures; such a mechanism should be composed of independent and impartial experts with the necessary skills, experience and credibility.

To the Hamas de-facto administration in the Gaza Strip:

End abuses

- End the widespread abuses which continue to be committed in the Gaza Strip by the Executive Force and the Qassam Brigades, including by issuing clear instructions requiring all members of the Hamas security forces to uphold the law and respect human rights.

End arbitrary arrests and detentions

- Ensure that all those arbitrarily detained are released, that arbitrary arrests cease immediately and that no one is deprived of their liberty except in accordance with procedures and on grounds prescribed by law. Notably, arrests and detention should not be carried out by forces which are not authorized to do so by law.

End torture and other ill-treatment

- Ensure that all detainees are treated humanely and held only in detention centres authorized by law, and that their human rights are fully respected;
- ensure that the families of those detained are informed promptly of the place of detention of their relatives and that detainees are allowed prompt access to their families and lawyers;

- require that all detainees are examined by an independent doctor as soon as possible after their detention and regularly thereafter throughout their detention;
- ensure that those making a complaint of torture or other ill-treatment and any witnesses to such abuse are adequately protected against possible reprisals, intimidation or harassment, and take firm action if such harassment or other abuses takes place;
- ensure that all allegations of torture or other ill-treatment of detainees are investigated promptly and independently and that anyone found responsible is held accountable, and provide reparation to the victims;
- allow unhindered access to independent, impartial and non-partisan monitors to all places of detention, including regular inspections without advance notice;
- issue clear instructions to all members of the Hamas forces that anyone who commits human rights abuses will be held accountable.

Restore the rule of law in the Gaza Strip

- reverse with immediate effect any measures aimed at replacing the Attorney General, prosecutors, judges and the Higher Judicial Council; allow these officials to resume their functions immediately; and issue a clear and unambiguous pledge to ensure that their security will not be at risk, that they will be protected, and that they will not be obstructed in the independent, impartial and professional discharge of their duties.

End the proliferation of weapons used to commit human rights abuses

- Take measures to ensure that no groups or individuals, including the 'Izz al-Din al-Qassam Brigades, are allowed to use or carry firearms or ammunition in a manner that may jeopardize the security of the civilian population.

To the al-Aqsa Brigades and Qassam Brigades:

- Immediately end unlawful killings, abductions, hostage-taking, torture or other ill-treatment of captives, attacks on people and property, threats and intimidations against individuals.

To the International Community:

- Immediately cease the sale or transfer of weapons to any parties until guarantees can be secured that such equipment will not be used to violate human rights and international humanitarian law.
- Put respect for human rights at the core of the agenda in discussions with all the Palestinian parties and hold all of them accountable to the same human rights standards.

- Ensure that emergency assistance essential to fulfilling fundamental human rights is never used as a bargaining tool to further political goals. Notably, refrain from imposing sanctions that negatively affect the provision of humanitarian assistance and ensure that the Palestinian population in the Gaza Strip is not punished for the positions and actions of the Hamas de-facto administration.
- Ensure that Israel, as the Occupying Power, fulfils its obligation to provide for the protection and welfare of the Palestinian population and refrains from imposing sanctions which violate their human rights.

C. THE SECURITY WALL

DOCUMENT NO. 14

LEGAL CONSEQUENCES OF THE CONSTRUCTION OF A WALL IN THE OCCUPIED PALESTINIAN TERRITORY

Advisory Opinion from the International Court of Justice

July 9, 2004

Jurisdiction of the Court to give the advisory opinion requested.

Article 65, paragraph 1, of the Statute—Article 96, paragraph 1, of the Charter—Power of General Assembly to request advisory opinions—Activities of Assembly.

Events leading to the adoption of General Assembly resolution ES-10/14 requesting the advisory opinion.

Contention that General Assembly acted ultra vires *under the Charter—Article 12, paragraph 1, and Article 24 of the Charter—United Nations practice concerning the interpretation of Article 12, paragraph 1, of Charter—General Assembly did not exceed its competence.*

Request for opinion adopted by the Tenth Emergency Special Session of the General Assembly—Session convened pursuant to resolution 377 A (V) ("Uniting for Peace")—Conditions set by that resolution—Regularity of procedure followed.

Alleged lack of clarity of the terms of the question—Purportedly abstract nature of the question—Political aspects of the question—Motives said to have inspired the request and opinion's possible implications—"Legal" nature of question unaffected.

Court having jurisdiction to give advisory opinion requested.

* *

Discretionary power of Court to decide whether it should give an opinion.

Article 65, paragraph 1, of Statute—Relevance of lack of consent of a State concerned—Question cannot be regarded only as a bilateral matter between Israel and Palestine but is directly of concern to the United Nations—Possible effects of opinion *on a political, negotiated solution to the Israeli-Palestinian conflict—Question representing only one aspect of Israeli-Palestinian conflict—Sufficiency of information and evidence available to Court—Useful purpose of opinion—*Nullus commodum capere potest de sua injuria propria*—Opinion to be given to the General Assembly, not to a specific State or entity.*

No "compelling reason" for Court to use its discretionary power not to give an advisory opinion.

* *

"Legal consequences" of the construction of a wall in the Occupied Palestinian Territory, including in and around East Jerusalem—Scope of question posed—Request for opinion limited to the legal consequences of the construction of those parts of the wall situated in Occupied Palestinian Territory—Use of the term "wall".

Historical background.
Description of the wall.

* *

Applicable law.

United Nations Charter—General Assembly resolution 2625 (XXV)—Illegality of any territorial acquisition resulting from the threat or use of force—Right of peoples to self-determination.

International humanitarian law—Regulations annexed to the Fourth Hague Convention of 1907—Fourth Geneva Convention of 1949—Applicability of Fourth Geneva Convention in the Occupied Palestinian Territory—Human rights law—International Covenant on Civil and Political Rights—International Covenant on Economic, Social and Cultural Rights—Convention on the Rights of the Child—Relationship between international humanitarian law and human rights law—Applicability of human rights instruments outside national territory—Applicability of those instruments in the Occupied Palestinian Territory.

* *

Settlements established by Israel in breach of international law in the Occupied Palestinian Territory—Construction of the wall and its associated régime create a "fait accompli" on the ground that could well become permanent—Risk of situation tantamount to de facto *annexation—Construction of the wall severely impedes the exercise by the Palestinian people of its right to self-determination and is therefore a breach of Israel's obligation to respect that right.*

Applicable provisions of international humanitarian law and human rights instruments relevant to the present case—Destruction and requisition of properties—Restrictions on freedom of movement of inhabitants of the Occupied Palestinian Territory—Impediments to the exercise by those concerned of the right to work, to health, to education and to an adequate standard of living—Demographic changes in the Occupied Palestinian Territory—Provisions of international humanitarian law enabling account to be taken of military exigencies—Clauses in human rights instruments qualifying rights guaranteed or providing for derogation—Construction of the wall and its associated régime cannot be justified by military exigencies or by the requirements of national security or public order—Breach by Israel of various of its obligations under the applicable provisions of international humanitarian law and human rights instruments.

Self-defence—Article 51 of the Charter—Attacks against Israel not imputable to a foreign State—Threat invoked to justify the construction of the wall originating within a territory over which Israel exercises control—Article 51 not relevant in the present case.

State of necessity—Customary international law—Conditions—Construction of the wall not the only means to safeguard Israel's interests against the peril invoked.

Construction of the wall and its associated régime are contrary to international law.

* *

Legal consequences of the violation by Israel of its obligations.

Israel's international responsibility—Israel obliged to comply with the international obligations it has breached by the construction of the wall—Israel obliged to put an end to the violation of its international obligations—Obligation to cease forthwith the works of construction of the wall, to dismantle it forthwith and to repeal or render ineffective forthwith the legislative and regulatory acts relating to its construction, save where relevant for compliance by Israel with its obligation to make reparation for the damage caused—Israel obliged to make reparation for the damage caused to all natural or legal persons affected by construction of the wall.

*Legal consequences for States other than Israel—*Erga omnes *character of certain obligations violated by Israel—Obligation for all States not to recognize the illegal situation resulting from construction of the wall and not to render aid or assistance in maintaining the situation created by such construction—Obligation for all States, while respecting the Charter and international law, to see to it that any impediment, resulting from the construction of the wall, to the exercise by the Palestinian people of its right to self-determination is brought to an end—Obligation for all States parties to the Fourth Geneva Convention, while respecting the Charter and international law, to ensure compliance by Israel with international humanitarian law as embodied in that Convention—Need for the United Nations, and especially the General Assembly and the Security Council, to consider what further action is required to bring to an end the illegal situation resulting from the construction of the wall and its associated régime, taking due account of the Advisory Opinion.*

* *

Construction of the wall must be placed in a more general context—Obligation of Israel and Palestine scrupulously to observe international humanitarian law—Implementation in good faith of all relevant Security Council resolutions, in particular resolutions 242 (1967) and 338 (1973)—"Roadmap"—Need for efforts to be encouraged with a view to achieving as soon as possible, on the basis of international law, a negotiated solution to the outstanding problems and the establishment of a Palestinian State, with peace and security for all in the region.

Advisory Opinion

Present: President SHI; *Vice-President* RANJEVA; *Judges* GUILLAUME, KOROMA, VERESHCHETIN, HIGGINS, PARRA-ARANGUREN, KOOIJMANS, REZEK, AL-KHASAWNEH, BUERGENTHAL, ELARABY, OWADA, SIMMA, TOMKA; *Registrar* COUVREUR.

On the legal consequences of the construction of a wall in the Occupied Palestinian Territory,

THE COURT,

composed as above,

gives the following Advisory Opinion:

1. The question on which the advisory opinion of the Court has been requested is set forth in resolution ES-10/14 adopted by the General Assembly of the United Nations (hereinafter the "General Assembly") on 8 December 2003 at its Tenth Emergency Special Session. By a letter dated 8 December 2003 and received in the Registry by facsimile on 10 December 2003, the original of which reached the Registry subsequently, the Secretary-General of the United Nations officially communicated to the Court the decision taken by the General Assembly to submit the question for an advisory opinion. Certified true copies of the English and French versions of resolution ES-10/14 were enclosed with the letter. The resolution reads as follows:

> "*The General Assembly,*
>
> *Reaffirming* its resolution ES-10/13 of 21 October 2003,
>
> *Guided* by the principles of the Charter of the United Nations,
>
> *Aware* of the established principle of international law on the inadmissibility of the acquisition of territory by force,
>
> *Aware also* that developing friendly relations among nations based on respect for the principle of equal rights and self-determination of peoples is among the purposes and principles of the Charter of the United Nations,
>
> *Recalling* relevant General Assembly resolutions, including resolution 181 (11) of 29 November 1947, which partitioned mandated Palestine into two States, one Arab and one Jewish,
>
> *Recalling also* the resolutions of the tenth emergency special session of the General Assembly,

Recalling further relevant Security Council resolutions, including resolutions 242 (19671 of 22 November 1967, 338 (1973) of 22 October 1973, 267 (1969) of 3 July 1969, 298 (1971) of 25 September 1971, 446 (1979) of 22 March 1979, 452 (1979) of 20 July 1979, 465 (1980) of 1 March 1980, 476 (1980) of 30 June 1980, 478 (1980) of 20 August 1980, 904 (1994) of 18 March 1994, 1073 (1996) of 28 September 1996, 1397 (2002) of 12 March 2002 and 1515 (2003) of 19 November 2003,

Reaffirming the applicability of the Fourth Geneva Convention[1] as well as Additional Protocol I to the Geneva Conventions[2] to the Occupied Palestinian Territory, including East Jerusalem,

Recalling the Regulations annexed to the Hague Convention Respecting the Laws and Customs of War on Land of 1907,[3]

Welcoming the convening of the Conference of High Contracting Parties to the Fourth Geneva Convention on measures to enforce the Convention in the Occupied Palestinian Territory, including Jerusalem, at Geneva on 15 July 1999,

Expressing its support for the declaration adopted by the reconvened Conference of High Contracting Parties at Geneva on 5 December 2001,

Recalling in particular relevant United Nations resolutions affirming that Israeli settlements in the Occupied Palestinian Territory, including East Jerusalem, are illegal and an obstacle to peace and to economic and social development as well as those demanding the complete cessation of settlement activities,

Recalling relevant United Nations resolutions affirming that actions taken by Israel, the occupying Power, to change the status and demographic composition of Occupied East Jerusalem have no legal validity and are null and void,

Noting the agreements reached between the Government of Israel and the Palestine Liberation Organization in the context of the Middle East peace process.

Gravely concerned at the commencement and continuation of construction by Israel, the occupying Power, of a wall in the Occupied Palestinian Territory, including in and around East Jerusalem, which is in departure from the Armistice Line of 1949 (Green Line) and which has involved the confiscation and destruction of Palestinian land and resources, the disruption of the lives of thousands of protected civilians and the de facto annexation of large areas of territory, and underlining the unanimous opposition by the international community to the construction of that wall,

1 United Nations, *Treaty Series*, Vol. 75, No. 973.
2 *Ibid.*, Vol. 1125, No. 17512.
3 See Carnegie Endowment for International Peace, *The Hague Conventions and Declarations of 1899 and 1907* (New York, Oxford University Press, 1915).

Gravely concerned also at the even more devastating impact of the projected parts of the wall on the Palestinian civilian population and on the prospects for solving the Palestinian-Israeli conflict and establishing peace in the region,

Welcoming the report of 8 September 2003 of the Special Rapporteur of the Commission on Human Rights on the situation of human rights in the Palestinian territories occupied by Israel since 1967,[4] in particular the section regarding the wall.

Affirming the necessity of ending the conflict on the basis of the two-State solution of Israel and Palestine living side by side in peace and security based on the Armistice Line of 1949, in accordance with relevant Security Council and General Assembly resolutions,

Having received with appreciation the report of the Secretary-General, submitted in accordance with resolution ES-10/13,[5]

Bearing in mind that the passage of time further compounds the difficulties on the ground, as Israel, the occupying Power, continues to refuse to comply with international law vis-à-vis its construction of the above-mentioned wall, with all its detrimental implications and consequences,

Decides, in accordance with Article 96 of the Charter of the United Nations, to request the International Court of Justice, pursuant to Article 65 of the Statute of the Court, to urgently render an advisory opinion on the following question:

What are the legal consequences arising from the construction of the wall being built by Israel, the occupying Power, in the Occupied Palestinian Territory, including in and around East Jerusalem, as described in the report of the Secretary-General, considering the rules and principles of international law, including the Fourth Geneva Convention of 1949, and relevant Security Council and General Assembly resolutions?

Also enclosed with the letter were the certified English and French texts of the report of the Secretary-General dated 24 November 2003, prepared pursuant to General Assembly resolution ES-10/13 (A/ES-10/248), to which resolution ES-10/14 makes reference.

2. By letters dated 10 December 2003, the Registrar notified the request for an advisory opinion to all States entitled to appear before the Court, in accordance with Article 66, paragraph 1, of the Statute.

3. By a letter dated 11 December 2003, the Government of Israel informed the Court of its position on the request for an advisory opinion and on the procedure to be followed.

[4] E/CN.4/2004/6.
[5] A/ES-10/248."

4. By an Order of 19 December 2003, the Court decided that the United Nations and its Member States were likely, in accordance with Article 66, paragraph 2, of the Statute, to be able to furnish information on all aspects raised by the question submitted to the Court for an advisory opinion and fixed 30 January 2004 as the time-limit within which written statements might be submitted to it on the question in accordance with Article 66, paragraph 4, of the Statute. By the same Order, the Court further decided that, in the light of resolution ES-10/14 and the report of the Secretary-General transmitted with the request, and taking into account the fact that the General Assembly had granted Palestine a special status of observer and that the latter was co-sponsor of the draft resolution requesting the advisory opinion, Palestine might also submit a written statement on the question within the above time-limit.

5. By the aforesaid Order, the Court also decided, in accordance with Article 105, paragraph 4, of the Rules of Court, to hold public hearings during which oral statements and comments might be presented to it by the United Nations and its Member States, regardless of whether or not they had submitted written statements, and fixed 23 February 2004 as the date for the opening of the said hearings. By the same Order, the Court decided that, for the reasons set out above (see paragraph 4), Palestine might also take part in the hearings. Lastly, it invited the United Nations and its Member States, as well as Palestine, to inform the Registry, by 13 February 2004 at the latest, if they were intending to take part in the above-mentioned hearings. By letters of 19 December 2004, the Registrar informed them of the Court's decisions and transmitted to them a copy of the Order.

6. Ruling on requests submitted subsequently by the League of Arab States and the Organization of the Islamic Conference, the Court decided, in accordance with Article 66 of its Statute, that those two international organizations were likely to be able to furnish information on the question submitted to the Court, and that consequently they might for that purpose submit written statements within the time-limit fixed by the Court in its Order of 19 December 2003 and take part in the hearings.

7. Pursuant to Article 65, paragraph 2, of the Statute, the Secretary-General of the United Nations communicated to the Court a dossier of documents likely to throw light upon the question.

8. By a reasoned Order of 30 January 2004 regarding its composition in the case, the Court decided that the matters brought to its attention by the Government of Israel in a letter of 31 December 2003, and in a confidential letter of 15 January 2004 addressed to the President pursuant to Article 34, paragraph 2, of the Rules of Court, were not such as to preclude Judge Elaraby from sitting in the case.

9. Within the time-limit fixed by the Court for that purpose, written statements were filed by, in order of their receipt: Guinea, Saudi Arabia, League

of Arab States, Egypt, Cameroon, Russian Federation, Australia, Palestine, United Nations, Jordan, Kuwait, Lebanon, Canada, Syria, Switzerland, Israel, Yemen, United States of America, Morocco, Indonesia, Organization of the Islamic Conference, France, Italy, Sudan, South Africa, Germany, Japan, Norway, United Kingdom, Pakistan, Czech Republic, Greece, Ireland on its own behalf, Ireland on behalf of the European Union, Cyprus, Brazil, Namibia, Malta, Malaysia, Netherlands, Cuba, Sweden, Spain, Belgium, Palau, Federated States of Micronesia, Marshall Islands, Senegal, Democratic People's Republic of Korea. Upon receipt of those statements, the Registrar transmitted copies thereof to the United Nations and its Member States, to Palestine, to the League of Arab States and to the Organization of the Islamic Conference.

10. Various communications were addressed to these latter by the Registry, concerning in particular the measures taken for the organization of the oral proceedings. By communications of 20 February 2004, the Registry transmitted a detailed timetable of the hearings to those of the latter who, within the time-limit fixed for that purpose by the Court, had expressed their intention of taking part in the aforementioned proceedings.

11. Pursuant to Article 106 of the Rules of Court, the Court decided to make the written statements accessible to the public, with effect from the opening of the oral proceedings.

12. In the course of hearings held from 23 to 25 February 2004, the Court heard oral statements, in the following order, by:

for Palestine:

H.E. Mr. Nasser Al-Kidwa, Ambassador, Permanent Observer of Palestine to the United Nations,

Ms Stephanie Koury, Member, Negotiations Support Unit, Counsel,

Mr. James Crawford, S.C., Whewell Professor of International Law, University of Cambridge, Member of the Institute of International Law, Counsel and Advocate,

Mr. Georges Abi-Saab, Professor of International Law, Graduate Institute of International Studies, Geneva, Member of the Institute of International Law, Counsel and Advocate,

Mr. Vaughan Lowe, Chichele Professor of International Law, University of Oxford, Counsel and Advocate,

	Mr. Jean Salmon, Professor Emeritus of International Law, Université libre de Bruxelles, Member of the Institute of International Law, Counsel and Advocate;
for the Republic of South Africa:	H.E. Mr. Aziz Pahad, Deputy Minister for Foreign Affairs, Head of Delegation,
	Judge M. R. W. Madlanga, S.C.;
for the People's Democratic Republic of Algeria:	Mr. Ahmed Laraba, Professor of International Law
for the Kingdom of Saudi Arabia:	H.E. Mr. Fawzi A. Shobokshi, Ambassador and Permanent Representative of the Kingdom of Saudi Arabia to the United Nations in New York, Head of Delegation;
for the People's Republic of Bangladesh:	H.E. Mr. Liaquat Ali Choudhury, Ambassador of the People's Republic of Bangladesh to the Kingdom of the Netherlands;
for Belize:	Mr. Jean-Marc Sorel, Professor at the University of Paris I (Panthéon-Sorbonne);
for the Republic of Cuba:	H.E. Mr. Abelardo Moreno Fernández, Deputy Minister for Foreign Affairs;
for the Republic of Indonesia:	H.E. Mr. Mohammad Jusuf, Ambassador of the Republic of Indonesia to the Kingdom of the Netherlands, Head of Delegation;
for the Hashemite Kingdom of Jordan:	H.R.H. Ambassador Zeid Ra'ad Zeid Al-Hussein, Permanent Representative of the Hashemite Kingdom of Jordan to the United Nations, New York, Head of Delegation,
	Sir Arthur Watts, K.C.M.G., Q.C., Senior Legal Adviser to the Government of the Hashemite Kingdom of Jordan;
for the Republic of Madagascar:	H.E. Mr. Alfred Rambeloson, Permanent Representative of Madagascar to the Office of the United Nations at Geneva and to the Specialized Agencies, Head of Delegation;
for Malaysia:	H.E. Datuk Seri Syed Hamid Albar, Foreign Minister of Malaysia, Head of Delegation;
for the Republic of Senegal:	H.E. Mr. Saliou Cissé, Ambassador of the Republic of Senegal to the Kingdom of the Netherlands, Head of Delegation;

for the Republic of the Sudan:	H.E. Mr. Abuelgasim A. Idris, Ambassador of the Republic of the Sudan to the Kingdom of the Netherlands;
for the League of Arab States:	Mr. Michael Bothe, Professor of Law, Head of the Legal Team;
for the Organization of the Islamic Conference:	H.E. Mr. Abdelouahed Belkeziz, Secretary General of the Organization of the Islamic Conference,
	Ms Monique Chemillier-Gendreau, Professor of Public Law, University of Paris VII-Denis Diderot, as Counsel.

* * *

13. When seised of a request for an advisory opinion, the Court must first consider whether it has jurisdiction to give the opinion requested and whether, should the answer be in the affirmative, there is any reason why it should decline to exercise any such jurisdiction (see *Legality of the Threat or Use of Nuclear Weapons, Advisory Opinion, I.C.J. Reports 1996 (I)*, p. 232, para. 10).

* *

14. The Court will thus first address the question whether it possesses jurisdiction to give the advisory opinion requested by the General Assembly on 8 December 2003. The competence of the Court in this regard is based on Article 65, paragraph 1, of its Statute, according to which the Court "may give an advisory opinion on any legal question at the request of whatever body may be authorized by or in accordance with the Charter of the United Nations to make such a request". The Court has already had occasion to indicate that:

> "It is . . . a precondition of the Court's competence that the advisory opinion be requested by an organ duly authorized to seek it under the Charter, that it be requested on a legal question, and that, except in the case of the General Assembly or the Security Council, that question should be one arising within the scope of the activities of the requesting organ." (*Application for Review of Judgement No. 273 of the United Nations Administrative Tribunal, Advisory Opinion, I.C.J. Reports 1982*, pp. 333–334, para. 21.)

15. It is for the Court to satisfy itself that the request for an advisory opinion comes from an organ or agency having competence to make it. In the present instance, the Court notes that the General Assembly, which seeks the advisory opinion, is authorized to do so by Article 96, paragraph 1, of the Charter, which provides: "The General Assembly or the Security Council may request the International Court of Justice to give an advisory opinion on any legal question."

16. Although the above-mentioned provision states that the General Assembly may seek an advisory opinion "on any legal question", the Court has sometimes in the past given certain indications as to the relationship between the question the subject of a request for an advisory opinion and the activities of the General Assembly *(Interpretation of Peace Treaties with Bulgaria, Hungary and Romania, I.C.J. Reports 1950*, p. 70; *Legality of the Threat or Use of Nuclear Weapons, I.C.J. Reports 1996 (I)*, pp. 232 and 233, paras. 11 and 12).

17. The Court will so proceed in the present case. The Court would observe that Article 10 of the Charter has conferred upon the General Assembly a competence relating to "any questions or any matters" within the scope of the Charter, and that Article 11, paragraph 2, has specifically provided it with competence on "questions relating to the maintenance of international peace and security brought before it by any Member of the United Nations . . . " and to make recommendations under certain conditions fixed by those Articles. As will be explained below, the question of the construction of the wall in the Occupied Palestinian Territory was brought before the General Assembly by a number of Member States in the context of the Tenth Emergency Special Session of the Assembly, convened to deal with what the Assembly, in its resolution ES-10/2 of 25 April 1997, considered to constitute a threat to international peace and security.

* *

18. Before further examining the problems of jurisdiction that have been raised in the present proceedings, the Court considers it necessary to describe the events that led to the adoption of resolution ES-10/14, by which the General Assembly requested an advisory opinion on the legal consequences of the construction of the wall in the Occupied Palestinian Territory.

19. The Tenth Emergency Special Session of the General Assembly, at which that resolution was adopted, was first convened following the rejection by the Security Council, on 7 March and 21 March 1997, as a result of negative votes by a permanent member, of two draft resolutions concerning certain Israeli settlements in the Occupied Palestinian Territory (see, respectively, S/1997/199 and S/PV.3747, and S/1997/241 and S/PV.3756). By a letter of 31 March 1997, the Chairman of the Arab Group then requested "that an emergency special session of the General Assembly be convened pursuant to resolution 377 A (V) entitled 'Uniting for Peace'" with a view to discussing "Illegal Israeli actions in occupied East Jerusalem and the rest of the Occupied Palestinian Territory" (letter dated 31 March 1997 from the Permanent Representative of Qatar to the United Nations addressed to the Secretary-General, A/ES-10/1, 22 April 1997, Annex). The majority of Members of the United Nations having concurred in this request, the first meeting of the Tenth Emergency Special Session of the General Assembly took place on 24 April 1997 (see A/ES-10/1, 22 April 1997). Resolution ES-10/2

was adopted the following day; the General Assembly thereby expressed its conviction that:

> "the repeated violation by Israel, the occupying Power, of international law and its failure to comply with relevant Security Council and General Assembly resolutions and the agreements reached between the parties undermine the Middle East peace process and constitute a threat to international peace and security",

and condemned the "illegal Israeli actions" in occupied East Jerusalem and the rest of the Occupied Palestinian Territory, in particular the construction of settlements in that territory. The Tenth Emergency Special Session was then adjourned temporarily and has since been reconvened 11 times (on 15 July 1997, 13 November 1997, 17 March 1998, 5 February 1999, 18 October 2000, 20 December 2001, 7 May 2002, 5 August 2002, 19 September 2003, 20 October 2003 and 8 December 2003).

20. By a letter dated 9 October 2003, the Chairman of the Arab Group, on behalf of the States Members of the League of Arab States, requested an immediate meeting of the Security Council to consider the "grave and ongoing Israeli violations of international law, including international humanitarian law, and to take the necessary measures in this regard" (letter of 9 October 2003 from the Permanent Representative of the Syrian Arab Republic to the United Nations to the President of the Security Council. S/2003/973, 9 October 2003). This letter was accompanied by a draft resolution for consideration by the Council, which condemned as illegal the construction by Israel of a wall in the Occupied Palestinian Territory departing from the Armistice Line of 1949. The Security Council held its 4841st and 4842nd meetings on 14 October 2003 to consider the item entitled "The situation in the Middle East, including the Palestine question". It then had before it another draft resolution proposed on the same day by Guinea, Malaysia, Pakistan and the Syrian Arab Republic, which also condemned the construction of the wall. This latter draft resolution was put to a vote after an open debate and was not adopted owing to the negative vote of a permanent member of the Council (S/PV.4841 and S/PV.4842).

On 15 October 2003, the Chairman of the Arab Group, on behalf of the States Members of the League of Arab States, requested the resumption of the Tenth Emergency Special Session of the General Assembly to consider the item of "Illegal Israeli actions in Occupied East Jerusalem and the rest of the Occupied Palestinian Territory" (A/ES-10/242); this request was supported by the Non-Aligned Movement (A/ES-10/243) and the Organization of the Islamic Conference Group at the United Nations (A/ES-10/244). The Tenth Emergency Special Session resumed its work on 20 October 2003.

21. On 27 October 2003, the General Assembly adopted resolution ES-10/13, by which it demanded that

> "Israel stop and reverse the construction of the wall in the Occupied Palestinian Territory, including in and around East Jerusalem, which is in departure of the Armistice Line of 1949 and is in contradiction to relevant provisions of international law" (para. 1).

In paragraph 3, the Assembly requested the Secretary-General

> "to report on compliance with the . . . resolution periodically, with the first report on compliance with paragraph 1 [of that resolution] to be submitted within one month . . .".

The Tenth Emergency Special Session was temporarily adjourned and, on 24 November 2003, the report of the Secretary-General prepared pursuant to General Assembly resolution ES-10/13 (hereinafter the "report of the Secretary-General") was issued (A/ES-10/248).

22. Meanwhile, on 19 November 2003, the Security Council adopted resolution 1515 (2003), by which it "*Endorse[d]* the Quartet Performance-based Roadmap to a Permanent Two-State Solution to the Israeli-Palestinian Conflict". The Quartet consists of representatives of the United States of America, the European Union, the Russian Federation and the United Nations. That resolution

> "*Call[ed] on* the parties to fulfil their obligations under the Roadmap in cooperation with the Quartet and to achieve the vision of two States living side by side in peace and security."

Neither the "Roadmap" nor resolution 1515 (2003) contained any specific provision concerning the construction of the wall, which was not discussed by the Security Council in this context.

23. Nineteen days later, on 8 December 2003, the Tenth Emergency Special Session of the General Assembly again resumed its work, following a new request by the Chairman of the Arab Group, on behalf of the States Members of the League of Arab States, and pursuant to resolution ES-10/13 (letter dated 1 December 2003 to the President of the General Assembly from the Chargé d'affaires a.i. of the Permanent Mission of Kuwait to the United Nations, A/ES-10/249, 2 December 2003). It was during the meeting convened on that day that resolution ES-10/14 requesting the present advisory opinion was adopted.

*

24. Having thus recalled the sequence of events that led to the adoption of resolution ES-10/14, the Court will now turn to the questions of jurisdiction that have been raised in the present proceedings. First, Israel has alleged that, given the active engagement of the Security Council with the situation in the Middle East, including the Palestinian question, the General

Assembly acted *ultra vires* under the Charter when it requested an advisory opinion on the legal consequences of the construction of the wall in the Occupied Palestinian Territory.

25. The Court has already indicated that the subject of the present request for an advisory opinion falls within the competence of the General Assembly under the Charter (see paragraphs 15–17 above). However, Article 12, paragraph 1, of the Charter provides that:

> "While the Security Council is exercising in respect of any dispute or situation the functions assigned to it in the present Charter, the General Assembly shall not make any recommendation with regard to that dispute or situation unless the Security Council so requests."

A request for an advisory opinion is not in itself a "recommendation" by the General Assembly "with regard to [a] dispute or situation". It has however been argued in this case that the adoption by the General Assembly of resolution ES-10/14 was *ultra vires* as not in accordance with Article 12. The Court thus considers that it is appropriate for it to examine the significance of that Article, having regard to the relevant texts and the practice of the United Nations.

26. Under Article 24 of the Charter the Security Council has "primary responsibility for the maintenance of international peace and security". In that regard it can impose on States "an explicit obligation of compliance if for example it issues an order or command . . . under Chapter VII" and can, to that end, "require enforcement by coercive action" *(Certain Expenses of the United Nations (Article 17, paragraph 2, of the Charter), Advisory Opinion, I.C.J. Reports 1962*, p. 163). However, the Court would emphasize that Article 24 refers to a primary, but not necessarily exclusive, competence. The General Assembly does have the power, *inter alia*, under Article 14 of the Charter, to "recommend measures for the peaceful adjustment" of various situations *(ibid.)*.

> "[T]he only limitation which Article 14 imposes on the General Assembly is the restriction found in Article 12, namely, that the Assembly should not recommend measures while the Security Council is dealing with the same matter unless the Council requests it to do so." *(I.C.J. Reports 1962*, p. 163.)

27. As regards the practice of the United Nations, both the General Assembly and the Security Council initially interpreted and applied Article 12 to the effect that the Assembly could not make a recommendation on a question concerning the maintenance of international peace and security while the matter remained on the Council's agenda. Thus the Assembly during its fourth session refused to recommend certain measures on the question of Indonesia, on the ground, *inter alia*, that the Council remained seised of the matter (*Official Records of the General Assembly, Fourth Session*, Ad Hoc *Political Committee, Summary Records of Meetings, 27 September–7 December*

1949, 56th Meeting, 3 December 1949, p. 339, para. 118). As for the Council, on a number of occasions it deleted items from its agenda in order to enable the Assembly to deliberate on them (for example, in respect of the Spanish question *(Official Records of the Security Council, First Year: Second Series, No. 21*, 79th Meeting, 4 November 1946, p. 498), in connection with incidents on the Greek border *(Official Records of the Security Council, Second Year, No. 89*, 202nd Meeting, 15 September 1947, pp. 2404–2405) and in regard to the Island of Taiwan (Formosa) (*Official Records of the Security Council, Fifth Year, No. 48*, 506th Meeting,'29 September 1950, p. 5)). In the case of the Republic of Korea, the Council decided on 31 January 1951 to remove the relevant item from the list of matters of which it was seised in order to enable the Assembly to deliberate on the matter *(Official Records of the Security Council, Sixth Year*, S/PV.531, 531st Meeting, 31 January 1951, pp. 11–12, para. 57).

However, this interpretation of Article 12 has evolved subsequently. Thus the General Assembly deemed itself entitled in 1961 to adopt recommendations in the matter of the Congo (resolutions 1955 (XV) and 1600 (XVI)) and in 1963 in respect of the Portuguese colonies (resolution 1913 (XVIII)) while those cases still appeared on the Council's agenda, without the Council having adopted any recent resolution concerning them. In response to a question posed by Peru during the twenty-third session of the General Assembly, the Legal Counsel of the United Nations confirmed that the Assembly interpreted the words "is exercising the functions" in Article 12 of the Charter as meaning "is exercising the functions at this moment" (General Assembly, Twenty-third Session, Third Committee, 1637th meeting, A/C.3/SR.1637, para. 9). Indeed, the Court notes that there has been an increasing tendency over time for the General Assembly and the Security Council to deal in parallel with the same matter concerning the maintenance of international peace and security (see, for example, the matters involving Cyprus, South Africa, Angola, Southern Rhodesia and more recently Bosnia and Herzegovina and Somalia). It is often the case that, while the Security Council has tended to focus on the aspects of such matters related to international peace and security, the General Assembly has taken a broader view, considering also their humanitarian, social and economic aspects.

28. The Court considers that the accepted practice of the General Assembly, as it has evolved, is consistent with Article 12, paragraph 1, of the Charter.

The Court is accordingly of the view that the General Assembly, in adopting resolution ES-10/14, seeking an advisory opinion from the Court, did not contravene the provisions of Article 12, paragraph 1, of the Charter. The Court concludes that by submitting that request the General Assembly did not exceed its competence.

29. It has however been contended before the Court that the present request for an advisory opinion did not fulfil the essential conditions set by resolution

377 A (V), under which the Tenth Emergency Special Session was convened and has continued to act. In this regard, it has been said, first, that "The Security Council was never seised of a draft resolution proposing that the Council itself should request an advisory opinion from the Court on the matters now in contention", and, that specific issue having thus never been brought before the Council, the General Assembly could not rely on any inaction by the Council to make such a request. Secondly, it has been claimed that, in adopting resolution 1515 (2003), which endorsed the "Roadmap", before the adoption by the General Assembly of resolution ES-10/14, the Security Council continued to exercise its responsibility for the maintenance of international peace and security and that, as a result, the General Assembly was not entitled to act in its place. The validity of the procedure followed by the Tenth Emergency Special Session, especially the Session's "rolling character" and the fact that its meeting was convened to deliberate on the request for the advisory opinion at the same time as the General Assembly was meeting in regular session, has also been questioned.

30. The Court would recall that resolution 377 A (V) states that:

> "if the Security Council, because of lack of unanimity of the permanent members, fails to exercise its primary responsibility for the maintenance of international peace and security in any case where there appears to be a threat to the peace, breach of the peace, or act of aggression, the General Assembly shall consider the matter immediately with a view to making appropriate recommendations to Members for collective measures . . .".

The procedure provided for by that resolution is premised on two conditions, namely that the Council has failed to exercise its primary responsibility for the maintenance of international peace and security as a result of a negative vote of one or more permanent members, and that the situation is one in which there appears to be a threat to the peace, breach of the peace, or act of aggression. The Court must accordingly ascertain whether these conditions were fulfilled as regards the convening of the Tenth Emergency Special Session of the General Assembly, in particular at the time when the Assembly decided to request an advisory opinion from the Court.

31. In the light of the sequence of events described in paragraphs 18 to 23 above, the Court observes that, at the time when the Tenth Emergency Special Session was convened in 1997, the Council had been unable to take a decision on the case of certain Israeli settlements in the Occupied Palestinian Territory, due to negative votes of a permanent member; and that, as indicated in resolution ES-10/2 (see paragraph 19 above), there existed a threat to international peace and security.

The Court further notes that, on 20 October 2003, the Tenth Emergency Special Session of the General Assembly was reconvened on the same basis as in 1997 (see the statements by the representatives of Palestine and Israel, A/ES-10/PV.21, pp. 2 and 5), after the rejection by the Security Council, on

14 October 2003, again as a result of the negative vote of a permanent member, of a draft resolution concerning the construction by Israel of the wall in the Occupied Palestinian Territory. The Court considers that the Security Council again failed to act as contemplated in resolution 377 A (V). It does not appear to the Court that the situation in this regard changed between 20 October 2003 and 8 December 2003, since the Council neither discussed the construction of the wall nor adopted any resolution in that connection. Thus, the Court is of the view that, up to 8 December 2003, the Council had not reconsidered the negative vote of 14 October 2003. It follows that, during that period, the Tenth Emergency Special Session was duly reconvened and could properly be seised, under resolution 377 A (V), of the matter now before the Court.

32. The Court would also emphasize that, in the course of this Emergency Special Session, the General Assembly could adopt any resolution falling within the subject-matter for which the Session had been convened, and otherwise within its powers, including a resolution seeking the Court's opinion. It is irrelevant in that regard that no proposal had been made to the Security Council to request such an opinion.

33. Turning now to alleged further procedural irregularities of the Tenth Emergency Special Session, the Court does not consider that the "rolling" character of that Session, namely the fact of its having been convened in April 1997 and reconvened 11 times since then, has any relevance with regard to the validity of the request by the General Assembly. The Court observes in that regard that the Seventh Emergency Special Session of the General Assembly, having been convened on 22 July 1980, was subsequently reconvened four times (on 20 April 1982, 25 June 1982, 16 August 1982 and 24 September 1982), and that the validity of resolutions or decisions of the Assembly adopted under such circumstances was never disputed. Nor has the validity of any previous resolutions adopted during the Tenth Emergency Special Session been challenged.

34. The Court also notes the contention by Israel that it was improper to reconvene the Tenth Emergency Special Session at a time when the regular session of the General Assembly was in progress. The Court considers that, while it may not have been originally contemplated that it would be appropriate for the General Assembly to hold simultaneous emergency and regular sessions, no rule of the Organization has been identified which would be thereby violated, so as to render invalid the resolution adopting the present request for an advisory opinion.

35. Finally, the Tenth Emergency Special Session appears to have been convened in accordance with Rule 9 *(b)* of the Rules of Procedure of the General Assembly, and the relevant meetings have been convened in pursuance of the applicable rules. As the Court stated in its Advisory Opinion of 21 June 1971 concerning the *Legal Consequences for States of the Continued Presence of*

South Africa in Namibia (South West Africa) notwithstanding Security Council Resolution 276 (1970), a

> "resolution of a properly constituted organ of the United Nations which is passed in accordance with that organ's rules of procedure, and is declared by its President to have been so passed, must be presumed to have been validly adopted" (*I.C.J. Reports 1971*, p. 22, para. 20).

In view of the foregoing, the Court cannot see any reason why that presumption is to be rebutted in the present case.

*

36. The Court now turns to a further issue related to jurisdiction in the present proceedings, namely the contention that the request for an advisory opinion by the General Assembly is not on a "legal question" within the meaning of Article 96, paragraph 1, of the Charter and Article 65, paragraph 1, of the Statute of the Court. It has been contended in this regard that, for a question to constitute a "legal question" for the purposes of these two provisions, it must be reasonably specific, since otherwise it would not be amenable to a response by the Court. With regard to the request made in the present advisory proceedings, it has been argued that it is not possible to determine with reasonable certainty the legal meaning of the question asked of the Court for two reasons.

First, it has been argued that the question regarding the "legal consequences" of the construction of the wall only allows for two possible interpretations, each of which would lead to a course of action that is precluded for the Court. The question asked could first be interpreted as a request for the Court to find that the construction of the wall is illegal, and then to give its opinion on the legal consequences of that illegality. In this case, it has been contended, the Court should decline to respond to the question asked for a variety of reasons, some of which pertain to jurisdiction and others rather to the issue of propriety. As regards jurisdiction, it is said that, if the General Assembly had wished to obtain the view of the Court on the highly complex and sensitive question of the legality of the construction of the wall, it should have expressly sought an opinion to that effect (cf. *Exchange of Greek and Turkish Populations, Advisory Opinion, 1925, P.C.I.J., Series B, No. 10*, p. 17). A second possible interpretation of the request, it is said, is that the Court should assume that the construction of the wall is illegal, and then give its opinion on the legal consequences of that assumed illegality. It has been contended that the Court should also decline to respond to the question on this hypothesis, since the request would then be based on a questionable assumption and since, in any event, it would be impossible to rule on the legal consequences of illegality without specifying the nature of that illegality.

Secondly, it has been contended that the question asked of the Court is not of a "legal" character because of its imprecision and abstract nature.

In particular, it has been argued in this regard that the question fails to specify whether the Court is being asked to address legal consequences for "the General Assembly or some other organ of the United Nations", "Member States of the United Nations", "Israel", "Palestine" or "some combination of the above, or some different entity".

37. As regards the alleged lack of clarity of the terms of the General Assembly's request and its effect on the "legal nature" of the question referred to the Court, the Court observes that this question is directed to the legal consequences arising from a given factual situation considering the rules and principles of international law, including the Geneva Convention relative to the Protection of Civilian Persons in Time of War of 12 August 1949 (hereinafter the "Fourth Geneva Convention") and relevant Security Council and General Assembly resolutions. The question submitted by the General Assembly has thus, to use the Court's phrase in its Advisory Opinion on *Western Sahara*, "been framed in terms of law and raise[s] problems of international law"; it is by its very nature susceptible of a reply based on law; indeed it is scarcely susceptible of a reply otherwise than on the basis of law. In the view of the Court, it is indeed a question of a legal character (see *Western Sahara, Advisory-Opinion, I.C.J. Reports 1975*, p. 18, para. 15).

38. The Court would point out that lack of clarity in the drafting of a question does not deprive the Court of jurisdiction. Rather, such uncertainty will require clarification in interpretation, and such necessary clarifications of interpretation have frequently been given by the Court.

In the past, both the Permanent Court and the present Court have observed in some cases that the wording of a request for an advisory opinion did not accurately state the question on which the Court's opinion was being sought *(Interpretation of the Greco-Turkish Agreement of 1 December 1926 (Final Protocol, Article IV), Advisory Opinion, 1928, P.C.I.J., Series B, No. 16 (I)*, pp. 14-16), or did not correspond to the "true legal question" under consideration (*Interpretation of the Agreement of 25 March 1951 between the WHO and Egypt, Advisory Opinion, I.C.J. Reports 1980*, pp. 87–89, paras. 34–36). The Court noted in one case that "the question put to the Court is, on the face of it, at once infelicitously expressed and vague" *(Application for Review of Judgement No. 273 of the United Nations Administrative Tribunal, Advisory Opinion, I.C.J. Reports 1982*, p. 348, para. 46).

Consequently, the Court has often been required to broaden, interpret and even reformulate the questions put (see the three Opinions cited above; see also *Jaworzina, Advisory Opinion, 1923, P.C.I.J., Series B, No. 8; Admissibility of Hearings of Petitioners by the Committee on South West Africa, Advisory Opinion, I.C.J. Reports 1956*, p. 25; *Certain Expenses of the United Nations (Article 17, paragraph 2, of the Charter), Advisory Opinion, I.C.J. Reports 1962*, pp. 157–162).

In the present instance, the Court will only have to do what it has often done in the past, namely "identify the existing principles and rules, interpret them and apply them . . ., thus offering a reply to the question posed based on law" *(Legality of the Threat or Use of Nuclear Weapons, I.C.J. Reports 1996 (I)*, p. 234, para. 13).

39. In the present instance, if the General Assembly requests the Court to state the "legal consequences" arising from the construction of the wall, the use of these terms necessarily encompasses an assessment of whether that construction is or is not in breach of certain rules and principles of international law. Thus, the Court is first called upon to determine whether such rules and principles have been and are still being breached by the construction of the wall along the planned route.

40. The Court does not consider that what is contended to be the abstract nature of the question posed to it raises an issue of jurisdiction. Even when the matter was raised as an issue of propriety rather than one of jurisdiction, in the case concerning the *Legality of the Threat or Use of Nuclear Weapons*, the Court took the position that to contend that it should not deal with a question couched in abstract terms is "a mere affirmation devoid of any justification" and that "the Court may give an advisory opinion on any legal question, abstract or otherwise" *(I.C.J. Reports 1996 (I)*, p. 236, para. 15, referring to *Conditions of Admission of a State to Membership in the United Nations (Article 4 of the Charter), Advisory Opinion, 1948, I.C.J. Reports 1947–1948*, p. 61; *Effect of Awards of Compensation Made by the United Nations Administrative Tribunal, Advisory Opinion, I.C.J. Reports 1954*, p. 51; and *Legal Consequences for States of the Continued Presence of South Africa in Namibia (South West Africa) notwithstanding Security Council Resolution 276 (1970), Advisory Opinion, I.C.J. Reports 1971*, p. 27, para. 40). In any event, the Court considers that the question posed to it in relation to the legal consequences of the construction of the wall is not an abstract one, and moreover that it would be for the Court to determine for whom any such consequences arise.

41. Furthermore, the Court cannot accept the view, which has also been advanced in the present proceedings, that it has no jurisdiction because of the "political" character of the question posed. As is clear from its long-standing jurisprudence on this point, the Court considers that the fact that a legal question also has political aspects,

> "as, in the nature of things, is the case with so many questions which arise in international life, does not suffice to deprive it of its character as a 'legal question' and to 'deprive the Court of a competence expressly conferred on it by its Statute' *(Application for Review of Judgement No. 158 of the United Nations Administrative Tribunal, Advisory Opinion, I.C.J. Reports 1973*, p. 172, para. 14). Whatever its political aspects, the Court cannot refuse to admit the legal character of a question which invites it to discharge an essentially judicial task, namely, an assessment of the legality of the possible conduct of States with regard to the obligations imposed upon them by international law

(cf. *Conditions of Admission of a State to Membership in the United Nations (Article 4 of the Charter), Advisory Opinion, 1948, I.C.J. Reports 1947–1948*, pp. 61–62; *Competence of the General Assembly for the Admission of a State to the United Nations, Advisory Opinion, I.C.J. Reports 1950*, pp. 6–7; *Certain Expenses of the United Nations (Article 17, paragraph 2, of the Charter), Advisory Opinion, I.C.J. Reports 1962*, p. 155)." *(Legality of the Threat or Use of Nuclear Weapons, Advisory Opinion, I.C.J. Reports 1996 (I)*, p. 234, para. 13.)

In its Opinion concerning the *Interpretation of the Agreement of 25 March 1951 between the WHO and Egypt*, the Court indeed emphasized that,

> "in situations in which political considerations are prominent it may be particularly necessary for an international organization to obtain an advisory opinion from the Court as to the legal principles applicable with respect to the matter under debate . . ." *(I.C.J. Reports 1980*, p. 87, para. 33).

Moreover, the Court has affirmed in its Opinion on the *Legality of the Threat or Use of Nuclear Weapons* that

> "the political nature of the motives which may be said to have inspired the request and the political implications that the opinion given might have are of no relevance in the establishment of its jurisdiction to give such an opinion" *(I.C.J. Reports 1996 (I)*, p. 234, para. 13).

The Court is of the view that there is no element in the present proceedings which could lead it to conclude otherwise.

*

42. The Court accordingly has jurisdiction to give the advisory opinion requested by resolution ES-10/14 of the General Assembly.

* *

43. It has been contended in the present proceedings, however, that the Court should decline to exercise its jurisdiction because of the presence of specific aspects of the General Assembly's request that would render the exercise of the Court's jurisdiction improper and inconsistent with the Court's judicial function.

44. The Court has recalled many times in the past that Article 65, paragraph 1, of its Statute, which provides that "The Court *may* give an advisory opinion . . ." (emphasis added), should be interpreted to mean that the Court has a discretionary power to decline to give an advisory opinion even if the conditions of jurisdiction are met *(Legality of the Threat or Use of Nuclear Weapons, Advisory Opinion, I.C.J. Reports 1996 (I)*, pp. 234–235, para. 14). The Court however is mindful of the fact that its answer to a request for an advisory opinion "represents its participation in the activities of the Organization, and, in principle, should not be refused" *(Interpretation of Peace Treaties with Bulgaria, Hungary and Romania, First Phase, Advisory Opinion, I.C.J. Reports 1950*, p. 71; see also, for example, *Difference Relating to Immunity from Legal Process of a Special Rapporteur of the Commission on*

Human Rights, Advisory Opinion, I.C.J. Reports 1999 (I), pp. 78–79, para. 29.) Given its responsibilities as the "principal judicial organ of the United Nations" (Article 92 of the Charter), the Court should in principle not decline to give an advisory opinion. In accordance with its consistent jurisprudence, only "compelling reasons" should lead the Court to refuse its opinion *(Certain Expenses of the United Nations (Article 17, paragraph 2, of the Charter), Advisory Opinion, I.C.J. Reports 1962*, p. 155; see also, for example, *Difference Relating to Immunity from Legal Process of a Special Rapporteur of the Commission on Human Rights, Advisory Opinion, I.C.J. Reports 1999 (I)*, pp. 78-79, para. 29.)

The present Court has never, in the exercise of this discretionary power, declined to respond to a request for an advisory opinion. Its decision not to give the advisory opinion on the *Legality of the Use by a State of Nuclear Weapons in Armed Conflict* requested by the World Health Organization was based on the Court's lack of jurisdiction, and not on considerations of judicial propriety (see *I.C.J. Reports 1996 (I)*, p. 235, para. 14). Only on one occasion did the Court's predecessor, the Permanent Court of International Justice, take the view that it should not reply to a question put to it *(Status of Eastern Carelia, Advisory Opinion, 1923, P.C.I.J., Series B, No. 5)*, but this was due to

> "the very particular circumstances of the case, among which were that the question directly concerned an already existing dispute, one of the States parties to which was neither a party to the Statute of the Permanent Court nor a Member of the League of Nations, objected to the proceedings, and refused to take part in any way" *(Legality of the Threat or Use of Nuclear Weapons, I.C.J. Reports 1996 (I)*, pp. 235–236, para. 14).

45. These considerations do not release the Court from the duty to satisfy itself, each time it is seised of a request for an opinion, as to the propriety of the exercise of its judicial function, by reference to the criterion of "compelling reasons" as cited above. The Court will accordingly examine in detail and in the light of its jurisprudence each of the arguments presented to it in this regard.

*

46. The first such argument is to the effect that the Court should not exercise its jurisdiction in the present case because the request concerns a contentious matter between Israel and Palestine, in respect of which Israel has not consented to the exercise of that jurisdiction. According to this view, the subject-matter of the question posed by the General Assembly "is an integral part of the wider Israeli-Palestinian dispute concerning questions of terrorism, security, borders, settlements, Jerusalem and other related matters". Israel has emphasized that it has never consented to the settlement of this wider dispute by the Court or by any other means of compulsory adjudication; on the contrary, it contends that the parties repeatedly agreed that these issues are to be settled by negotiation, with the possibility

of an agreement that recourse could be had to arbitration. It is accordingly contended that the Court should decline to give the present Opinion, on the basis *inter alia* of the precedent of the decision of the Permanent Court of International Justice on the *Status of Eastern Carelia.*

47. The Court observes that the lack of consent to the Court's contentious jurisdiction by interested States has no bearing on the Court's jurisdiction to give an advisory opinion. In an Advisory Opinion of 1950, the Court explained that:

> "The consent of States, parties to a dispute, is the basis of the Court's jurisdiction in contentious cases. The situation is different in regard to advisory proceedings even where the Request for an Opinion relates to a legal question actually pending between States. The Court's reply is only of an advisory character: as such, it has no binding force. It follows that no State, whether a Member of the United Nations or not, can prevent the giving of an Advisory Opinion which the United Nations considers to be desirable in order to obtain enlightenment as to the course of action it should take. The Court's Opinion is given not to the States, but to the organ which is entitled to request it; the reply of the Court, itself an 'organ of the United Nations', represents its participation in the activities of the Organization, and, in principle, should not be refused." *(Interpretation of Peace Treaties with Bulgaria, Hungary and Romania, First Phase, Advisory Opinion, I.C.J. Reports 1950,* p. 71; see also *Western Sahara, I.C.J. Reports 1975,* p. 24, para. 31.)

It followed from this that, in those proceedings, the Court did not refuse to respond to the request for an advisory opinion on the ground that, in the particular circumstances, it lacked jurisdiction. The Court did however examine the opposition of certain interested States to the request by the General Assembly in the context of issues of judicial propriety. Commenting on its 1950 decision, the Court explained in its Advisory Opinion on *Western Sahara* that it had "Thus . . . recognized that lack of consent might constitute a ground for declining to give the opinion requested if, in the circumstances of a given case, considerations of judicial propriety should oblige the Court to refuse an opinion." The Court continued:

> "In certain circumstances . . . the lack of consent of an interested State may render the giving of an advisory opinion incompatible with the Court's judicial character. An instance of this would be when the circumstances disclose that to give a reply would have the effect of circumventing the principle that a State is not obliged to allow its disputes to be submitted to judicial settlement without its consent." *(Western Sahara, I.C.J. Reports 1975,* p. 25, paras. 32–33.)

In applying that principle to the request concerning *Western Sahara,* the Court found that a legal controversy did indeed exist, but one which had arisen during the proceedings of the General Assembly and in relation to matters with which the Assembly was dealing. It had not arisen independently in bilateral relations (*ibid.*, p. 25, para. 34).

48. As regards the request for an advisory opinion now before it, the Court acknowledges that Israel and Palestine have expressed radically divergent views on the legal consequences of Israel's construction of the wall, on which the Court has been asked to pronounce. However, as the Court has itself noted, "Differences of views . . . on legal issues have existed in practically every advisory proceeding" (*Legal Consequences for States of the Continued Presence of South Africa in Namibia (South West Africa) notwithstanding Security Council Resolution 276 (1970), Advisory Opinion, I.C.J. Reports 1971*, p. 24, para. 34).

49. Furthermore, the Court does not consider that the subject-matter of the General Assembly's request can be regarded as only a bilateral matter between Israel and Palestine. Given the powers and responsibilities of the United Nations in questions relating to international peace and security, it is the Court's view that the construction of the wall must be deemed to be directly of concern to the United Nations. The responsibility of the United Nations in this matter also has its origin in the Mandate and the Partition Resolution concerning Palestine (see paragraphs 70 and 71 below). This responsibility has been described by the General Assembly as "a permanent responsibility towards the question of Palestine until the question is resolved in all its aspects in a satisfactory manner in accordance with international legitimacy" (General Assembly resolution 57/107 of 3 December 2002). Within the institutional framework of the Organization, this responsibility has been manifested by the adoption of many Security Council and General Assembly resolutions, and by the creation of several subsidiary bodies specifically established to assist in the realization of the inalienable rights of the Palestinian people.

50. The object of the request before the Court is to obtain from the Court an opinion which the General Assembly deems of assistance to it for the proper exercise of its functions. The opinion is requested on a question which is of particularly acute concern to the United Nations, and one which is located in a much broader frame of reference than a bilateral dispute. In the circumstances, the Court does not consider that to give an opinion would have the effect of circumventing the principle of consent to judicial settlement, and the Court accordingly cannot, in the exercise of its discretion, decline to give an opinion on that ground.

*

51. The Court now turns to another argument raised in the present proceedings in support of the view that it should decline to exercise its jurisdiction. Some participants have argued that an advisory opinion from the Court on the legality of the wall and the legal consequences of its construction could impede a political, negotiated solution to the Israeli-Palestinian conflict. More particularly, it has been contended that such an opinion could undermine the scheme of the "Roadmap" (see paragraph 22 above), which requires

Israel and Palestine to comply with certain obligations in various phases referred to therein. The requested opinion, it has been alleged, could complicate the negotiations envisaged in the "Roadmap", and the Court should therefore exercise its discretion and decline to reply to the question put.

This is a submission of a kind which the Court has already had to consider several times in the past. For instance, in its Advisory Opinion on the *Legality of the Threat or Use of Nuclear Weapons*, the Court stated:

> "It has . . . been submitted that a reply from the Court in this case might adversely affect disarmament negotiations and would, therefore, be contrary to the interest of the United Nations. The Court is aware that, no matter what might be its conclusions in any opinion it might give, they would have relevance for the continuing debate on the matter in the General Assembly and would present an additional element in the negotiations on the matter. Beyond that, the effect of the opinion is a matter of appreciation. The Court has heard contrary positions advanced and there are no evident criteria by which it can prefer one assessment to another." *(I.C.J. Reports 1996 (I)*, p. 237, para. 17; see also *Western Sahara, I.C.J. Reports 1975*, p. 37, para. 73.)

52. One participant in the present proceedings has indicated that the Court, if it were to give a response to the request, should in any event do so keeping in mind

> "two key aspects of the peace process: the fundamental principle that permanent status issues must be resolved through negotiations; and the need during the interim period for the parties to fulfil their security responsibilities so that the peace process can succeed".

53. The Court is conscious that the "Roadmap", which was endorsed by the Security Council in resolution 1515 (2003) (see paragraph 22 above), constitutes a negotiating framework for the resolution of the Israeli-Palestinian conflict. It is not clear, however, what influence the Court's opinion might have on those negotiations: participants in the present proceedings have expressed differing views in this regard. The Court cannot regard this factor as a compelling reason to decline to exercise its jurisdiction.

54. It was also put to the Court by certain participants that the question of the construction of the wall was only one aspect of the Israeli-Palestinian conflict, which could not be properly addressed in the present proceedings. The Court does not however consider this a reason for it to decline to reply to the question asked. The Court is indeed aware that the question of the wall is part of a greater whole, and it would take this circumstance carefully into account in any opinion it might give. At the same time, the question that the General Assembly has chosen to ask of the Court is confined to the legal consequences of the construction of the wall, and the Court would only examine other issues to the extent that they might be necessary to its consideration of the question put to it.

*

55. Several participants in the proceedings have raised the further argument that the Court should decline to exercise its jurisdiction because it does not have at its disposal the requisite facts and evidence to enable it to reach its conclusions. In particular, Israel has contended, referring to the Advisory Opinion on the *Interpretation of Peace Treaties with Bulgaria, Hungary and Romania,* that the Court could not give an opinion on issues which raise questions of fact that cannot be elucidated without hearing all parties to the conflict. According to Israel, if the Court decided to give the requested opinion, it would be forced to speculate about essential facts and make assumptions about arguments of law. More specifically, Israel has argued that the Court could not rule on the legal consequences of the construction of the wall without enquiring, first, into the nature and scope of the security threat to which the wall is intended to respond and the effectiveness of that response, and, second, into the impact of the construction for the Palestinians. This task, which would already be difficult in a contentious case, would be further complicated in an advisory proceeding, particularly since Israel alone possesses much of the necessary information and has stated that it chooses not to address the merits. Israel has concluded that the Court, confronted with factual issues impossible to clarify in the present proceedings, should use its discretion and decline to comply with the request for an advisory opinion.

56. The Court observes that the question whether the evidence available to it is sufficient to give an advisory opinion must be decided in each particular instance. In its Opinion concerning the *Interpretation of Peace Treaties with Bulgaria, Hungary and Romania (I.C.J. Reports 1950,* p. 72) and again in its Opinion on the *Western Sahara,* the Court made it clear that what is decisive in these circumstances is

> "whether the Court has before it sufficient information and evidence to enable it to arrive at a judicial conclusion upon any disputed questions of fact the determination of which is necessary for it to give an opinion in conditions compatible with its judicial character" *(Western Sahara, I.C.J. Reports 1975,* pp. 28–29, para. 46).

Thus, for instance, in the proceedings concerning the *Status of Eastern Carelia,* the Permanent Court of International Justice decided to decline to give an Opinion *inter alia* because the question put "raised a question of fact which could not be elucidated without hearing both parties" *(Interpretation of Peace Treaties with Bulgaria, Hungary and Romania, I.C.J. Reports 1950,* p. 72; see *Status of Eastern Carelia, P.C.I.J., Series B, No. 5,* p. 28). On the other hand, in the *Western Sahara* Opinion, the Court observed that it had been provided with very extensive documentary evidence of the relevant facts *(I.C.J. Reports 1975,* p. 29, para. 47).

57. In the present instance, the Court has at its disposal the report of the Secretary-General, as well as a voluminous dossier submitted by him to

the Court, comprising not only detailed information on the route of the wall but also on its humanitarian and socio-economic impact on the Palestinian population. The dossier includes several reports based on on-site visits by special rapporteurs and competent organs of the United Nations. The Secretary-General has further submitted to the Court a written statement updating his report, which supplemented the information contained therein. Moreover, numerous other participants have submitted to the Court written statements which contain information relevant to a response to the question put by the General Assembly. The Court notes in particular that Israel's Written Statement, although limited to issues of jurisdiction and judicial propriety, contained observations on other matters, including Israel's concerns in terms of security, and was accompanied by corresponding annexes; many other documents issued by the Israeli Government on those matters are in the public domain.

58. The Court finds that it has before it sufficient information and evidence to enable it to give the advisory opinion requested by the General Assembly. Moreover, the circumstance that others may evaluate and interpret these facts in a subjective or political manner can be no argument for a court of law to abdicate its judicial task. There is therefore in the present case no lack of information such as to constitute a compelling reason for the Court to decline to give the requested opinion.

*

59. In their written statements, some participants have also put forward the argument that the Court should decline to give the requested opinion on the legal consequences of the construction of the wall because such opinion would lack any useful purpose. They have argued that the advisory opinions of the Court are to be seen as a means to enable an organ or agency in need of legal clarification for its future action to obtain that clarification. In the present instance, the argument continues, the General Assembly would not need an opinion of the Court because it has already declared the construction of the wall to be illegal and has already determined the legal consequences by demanding that Israel stop and reverse its construction, and further, because the General Assembly has never made it clear how it intended to use the opinion.

60. As is clear from the Court's jurisprudence, advisory opinions have the purpose of furnishing to the requesting organs the elements of law necessary for them in their action. In its Opinion concerning *Reservations to the Convention on the Prevention and Punishment of the Crime of Genocide*, the Court observed: "The object of this request for an Opinion is to guide the United Nations in respect of its own action." *(I.C.J. Reports 1951*, p. 19.) Likewise, in its Opinion on the *Legal Consequences for States of the Continued Presence of South Africa in Namibia (South West Africa) notwithstanding Security Council Resolution 276 (1970)*, the Court noted: "The request is put forward

by a United Nations organ with reference to its own decisions and it seeks legal advice from the Court on the consequences and implications of these decisions." (*I.C.J. Reports 1971*, p. 24, para. 32.) The Court found on another occasion that the advisory opinion it was to give would "furnish the General Assembly with elements of a legal character relevant to its further treatment of the decolonization of Western Sahara" (*Western Sahara, I.C.J. Reports 1975*, p. 37, para. 72).

61. With regard to the argument that the General Assembly has not made it clear what use it would make of an advisory opinion on the wall, the Court would recall, as equally relevant in the present proceedings, what it stated in its Opinion on the *Legality of the Threat or Use of Nuclear Weapons*:

> "Certain States have observed that the General Assembly has not explained to the Court for what precise purposes it seeks the advisory opinion. Nevertheless, it is not for the Court itself to purport to decide whether or not an advisory opinion is needed by the Assembly for the performance of its functions. The General Assembly has the right to decide for itself on the usefulness of an opinion in the light of its own needs." (*I.C.J. Reports 1996 (I)*, p. 237, para. 16.)

62. It follows that the Court cannot decline to answer the question posed based on the ground that its opinion would lack any useful purpose. The Court cannot substitute its assessment of the usefulness of the opinion requested for that of the organ that seeks such opinion, namely the General Assembly. Furthermore, and in any event, the Court considers that the General Assembly has not yet determined all the possible consequences of its own resolution. The Court's task would be to determine in a comprehensive manner the legal consequences of the construction of the wall, while the General Assembly—and the Security Council—may then draw conclusions from the Court's findings.

*

63. Lastly, the Court will turn to another argument advanced with regard to the propriety of its giving an advisory opinion in the present proceedings. Israel has contended that Palestine, given its responsibility for acts of violence against Israel and its population which the wall is aimed at addressing, cannot seek from the Court a remedy for a situation resulting from its own wrongdoing. In this context, Israel has invoked the maxim *nullus commodum capere potest de sua injuria propria*, which it considers to be as relevant in advisory proceedings as it in contentious cases. Therefore, Israel concludes, good faith and the principle of "clean hands" provide a compelling reason that should lead the Court to refuse the General Assembly's request.

64. The Court does not consider this argument to be pertinent. As was emphasized earlier, it was the General Assembly which requested the advisory opinion, and the opinion is to be given to the General Assembly, and not to a specific State or entity.

* *

65. In the light of the foregoing, the Court concludes not only that it has jurisdiction to give an opinion on the question put to it by the General Assembly (see paragraph 42 above), but also that there is no compelling reason for it to use its discretionary power not to give that opinion.

* * *

66. The Court will now address the question put to it by the General Assembly in resolution ES-10/14. The Court recalls that the question is as follows:

> "What are the legal consequences arising from the construction of the wall being built by Israel, the occupying Power, in the Occupied Palestinian Territory, including in and around East Jerusalem, as described in the report of the Secretary-General, considering the rules and principles of international law, including the Fourth Geneva Convention of 1949, and relevant Security Council and General Assembly resolutions?"

67. As explained in paragraph 82 below, the "wall" in question is a complex construction, so that that term cannot be understood in a limited physical sense. However, the other terms used, either by Israel ("fence") or by
the Secretary-General ("barrier"), are no more accurate if understood in the physical sense. In this Opinion, the Court has therefore chosen to use the terminology employed by the General Assembly.

The Court notes furthermore that the request of the General Assembly concerns the legal consequences of the wall being built "in the Occupied Palestinian Territory, including in and around East Jerusalem". As also explained below (see paragraphs 79–84 below), some parts of the complex are being built, or are planned to be built, on the territory of Israel itself; the Court does not consider that it is called upon to examine the legal consequences arising from the construction of those parts of the wall.

68. The question put by the General Assembly concerns the legal consequences of the construction of the wall in the Occupied Palestinian Territory. However, in order to indicate those consequences to the General Assembly the Court must first determine whether or not the construction of that wall breaches international law (see paragraph 39 above). It will therefore make this determination before dealing with the consequences of the construction.

69. To do so, the Court will first make a brief analysis of the status of the territory concerned, and will then describe the works already constructed or in course of construction in that territory. It will then indicate the applicable law before seeking to establish whether that law has been breached.

* *

70. Palestine was part of the Ottoman Empire. At the end of the First World War, a class "A" Mandate for Palestine was entrusted to Great Britain by

the League of Nations, pursuant to paragraph 4 of Article 22 of the Covenant, which provided that:

> "Certain communities, formerly belonging to the Turkish Empire have reached a stage of development where their existence as independent nations can be provisionally recognized subject to the rendering of administrative advice and assistance by a Mandatory until such time as they are able to stand alone."

The Court recalls that in its Advisory Opinion on the *International Status of South West Africa*, speaking of mandates in general, it observed that "The Mandate was created, in the interest of the inhabitants of the territory, and of humanity in general, as an international institution with an international object—a sacred trust of civilization." *(I.C.J. Reports 1950*, p. 132.) The Court also held in this regard that "two principles were considered to be of paramount importance: the principle of non-annexation and the principle that the well-being and development of . . . peoples [not yet able to govern themselves] form[ed] 'a sacred trust of civilization' " *(ibid*, p. 131).

The territorial boundaries of the Mandate for Palestine were laid down by various instruments, in particular on the eastern border by a British memorandum of 16 September 1922 and an Anglo-Transjordanian Treaty of 20 February 1928.

71. In 1947 the United Kingdom announced its intention to complete evacuation of the mandated territory by 1 August 1948, subsequently advancing that date to 15 May 1948. In the meantime, the General Assembly had on 29 November 1947 adopted resolution 181 (II) on the future government of Palestine, which "*Recommends* to the United Kingdom . . . and to all other Members of the United Nations the adoption and implementation . . . of the Plan of Partition" of the territory, as set forth in the resolution, between two independent States, one Arab, the other Jewish, as well as the creation of a special international régime for the City of Jerusalem. The Arab population of Palestine and the Arab States rejected this plan, contending that it was unbalanced; on 14 May 1948, Israel proclaimed its independence on the strength of the General Assembly resolution; armed conflict then broke out between Israel and a number of Arab States and the Plan of Partition was not implemented.

72. By resolution 62 (1948) of 16 November 1948, the Security Council decided that "an armistice shall be established in all sectors of Palestine" and called upon the parties directly involved in the conflict to seek agreement to this end. In conformity with this decision, general armistice agreements were concluded in 1949 between Israel and the neighbouring States through mediation by the United Nations. In particular, one such agreement was signed in Rhodes on 3 April 1949 between Israel and Jordan. Articles V and VI of that Agreement fixed the armistice demarcation line between Israeli and Arab forces (often later called the "Green Line" owing

to the colour used for it on maps; hereinafter the "Green Line"). Article III, paragraph 2, provided that "No element of the . . . military or para-military forces of either Party . . . shall advance beyond or pass over for any purpose whatsoever the Armistice Demarcation Lines . . . " It was agreed in Article VI, paragraph 8, that these provisions would not be "interpreted as prejudicing, in any sense, an ultimate political settlement between the Parties". It was also stated that "the Armistice Demarcation Lines defined in articles V and VI of [the] Agreement [were] agreed upon by the Parties without prejudice to future territorial settlements or boundary lines or to claims of either Party relating thereto". The Demarcation Line was subject to such rectification as might be agreed upon by the parties.

73. In the 1967 armed conflict, Israeli forces occupied all the territories which had constituted Palestine under British Mandate (including those known as the West Bank, lying to the east of the Green Line).

74. On 22 November 1967, the Security Council unanimously adopted resolution 242 (1967), which emphasized the inadmissibility of acquisition of territory by war and called for the "Withdrawal of Israel armed forces from territories occupied in the recent conflict", and "Termination of all claims or states of belligerency".

75. From 1967 onwards, Israel took a number of measures in these territories aimed at changing the status of the City of Jerusalem. The Security Council, after recalling on a number of occasions "the principle that acquisition of territory by military conquest is inadmissible", condemned those measures and, by resolution 298 (1971) of 25 September 1971, confirmed in the clearest possible terms that:

> "all legislative and administrative actions taken by Israel to change the status of the City of Jerusalem, including expropriation of land and properties, transfer of populations and legislation aimed at the incorporation of the occupied section, are totally invalid and cannot change that status".

Later, following the adoption by Israel on 30 July 1980 of the Basic Law making Jerusalem the "complete and united" capital of Israel, the Security Council, by resolution 478 (1980) of 20 August 1980, stated that the enactment of that Law constituted a violation of international law and that "all legislative and administrative measures and actions taken by Israel, the occupying Power, which have altered or purport to alter the character and status of the Holy City of Jerusalem . . . are null and void". It further decided "not to recognize the 'basic law' and such other actions by Israel that, as a result of this law, seek to alter the character and status of Jerusalem".

76. Subsequently, a peace treaty was signed on 26 October 1994 between Israel and Jordan. That treaty fixed the boundary between the two States "with reference to the boundary definition under the Mandate as is shown in Annex I *(a)* . . . without prejudice to the status of any territories that came under Israeli military government control in 1967" (Article 3, paragraphs 1

and 2). Annex I provided the corresponding maps and added that, with regard to the "territory that came under Israeli military government control in 1967", the line indicated "is the administrative boundary" with Jordan.

77. Lastly, a number of agreements have been signed since 1993 between Israel and the Palestine Liberation Organization imposing various obligations on each party. Those agreements *inter alia* required Israel to transfer to Palestinian authorities certain powers and responsibilities exercised in the Occupied Palestinian Territory by its military authorities and civil administration. Such transfers have taken place, but, as a result of subsequent events, they remained partial and limited.

78. The Court would observe that, under customary international law as reflected (see paragraph 89 below) in Article 42 of the Regulations Respecting the Laws and Customs of War on Land annexed to the Fourth Hague Convention of 18 October 1907 (hereinafter "the Hague Regulations of 1907"), territory is considered occupied when it is actually placed under the authority of the hostile army, and the occupation extends only to the territory where such authority has been established and can be exercised.

The territories situated between the Green Line (see paragraph 72 above) and the former eastern boundary of Palestine under the Mandate were occupied by Israel in 1967 during the armed conflict between Israel and Jordan. Under customary international law, these were therefore occupied territories in which Israel had the status of occupying Power. Subsequent events in these territories, as described in paragraphs 75 to 77 above, have done nothing to alter this situation. All these territories (including East Jerusalem) remain occupied territories and Israel has continued to have the status of occupying Power.

*

79. It is essentially in these territories that Israel has constructed or plans to construct the works described in the report of the Secretary- General. The Court will now describe those works, basing itself on that report. For developments subsequent to the publication of that report, the Court will refer to complementary information contained in the Written Statement of the United Nations, which was intended by the Secretary-General to supplement his report (hereinafter "Written Statement of the Secretary-General").

80. The report of the Secretary-General states that "The Government of Israel has since 1996 considered plans to halt infiltration into Israel from the central and northern West Bank . . . " (para. 4). According to that report, a plan of this type was approved for the first time by the Israeli Cabinet in July 2001. Then, on 14 April 2002, the Cabinet adopted a decision for the construction of works, forming what Israel describes as a "security fence", 80 kilometres in length, in three areas of the West Bank.

The project was taken a stage further when, on 23 June 2002, the Israeli Cabinet approved the first phase of the construction of a "continuous fence" in the West Bank (including East Jerusalem). On 14 August 2002, it adopted the line of that "fence" for the work in Phase A, with a view to the construction of a complex 123 kilometres long in the northern West Bank, running from the Salem checkpoint (north of Jenin) to the settlement at Elkana. Phase B of the work was approved in December 2002. It entailed a stretch of some 40 kilometres running east from the Salem checkpoint towards Beth Shean along the northern part of the Green Line as far as the Jordan Valley. Furthermore, on 1 October 2003, the Israeli Cabinet approved a full route, which, according to the report of the Secretary-General, "will form one continuous line stretching 720 kilometres along the West Bank". A map showing completed and planned sections was posted on the Israeli Ministry of Defence website on 23 October 2003. According to the particulars provided on that map, a continuous section (Phase C) encompassing a number of large settlements will link the north-western end of the "security fence" built around Jerusalem with the southern point of Phase A construction at Elkana. According to the same map, the "security fence" will run for 115 kilometres from the Har Gilo settlement near Jerusalem to the Carmel settlement south-east of Hebron (Phase D). According to Ministry of Defence documents, work in this sector is due for completion in 2005. Lastly, there are references in the case file to Israel's planned construction of a "security fence" following the Jordan Valley along the mountain range to the west.

81. According to the Written Statement of the Secretary-General, the first part of these works (Phase A), which ultimately extends for a distance of 150 kilometres, was declared completed on 31 July 2003. It is reported that approximately 56,000 Palestinians would be encompassed in enclaves. During this phase, two sections totalling 19.5 kilometres were built around Jerusalem. In November 2003 construction of a new section was begun along the Green Line to the west of the Nazlat Issa-Baqa al-Sharqiya enclave, which in January 2004 was close to completion at the time when the Secretary-General submitted his Written Statement.

According to the Written Statement of the Secretary-General, the works carried out under Phase B were still in progress in January 2004. Thus an initial section of this stretch, which runs near or on the Green Line to the village of al-Mutilla, was almost complete in January 2004. Two additional sections diverge at this point. Construction started in early January 2004 on one section that runs due east as far as the Jordanian border. Construction of the second section, which is planned to run from the Green Line to the village of Taysir, has barely begun. The United Nations has, however, been informed that this second section might not be built.

The Written Statement of the Secretary-General further states that Phase C of the work, which runs from the terminus of Phase A, near the Elkana settlement, to the village of Nu'man, south-east of Jerusalem, began in December 2003. This section is divided into three stages. In Stage Cl, between *inter alia* the villages of Rantis and Budrus, approximately 4 kilometres out of a planned total of 40 kilometres have been constructed. Stage C2, which will surround the so-called "Ariel Salient" by cutting 22 kilometres into the West Bank, will incorporate 52,000 Israeli settlers. Stage C3 is to involve the construction of two "depth barriers"; one of these is to run north-south, roughly parallel with the section of Stage Cl currently under construction between Rantis and Budrus, whilst the other runs east-west along a ridge said to be part of the route of Highway 45, a motorway under construction. If construction of the two barriers were completed, two enclaves would be formed, encompassing 72,000 Palestinians in 24 communities.

Further construction also started in late November 2003 along the south-eastern part of the municipal boundary of Jerusalem, following a route that, according to the Written Statement of the Secretary-General, cuts off the suburban village of El-Ezariya from Jerusalem and splits the neighbouring Abu Dis in two.

As at 25 January 2004, according to the Written Statement of the Secretary-General, some 190 kilometres of construction had been completed, covering Phase A and the greater part of Phase B. Further construction in Phase C had begun in certain areas of the central West Bank and in Jerusalem. Phase D, planned for the southern part of the West Bank, had not yet begun.

The Israeli Government has explained that the routes and timetable as described above are subject to modification. In February 2004, for example, an 8-kilometre section near the town of Baqa al-Sharqiya was demolished, and the planned length of the wall appears to have been slightly reduced.

82. According to the description in the report and the Written Statement of the Secretary-General, the works planned or completed have resulted or will result in a complex consisting essentially of:

(1) a fence with electronic sensors;

(2) a ditch (up to 4 metres deep);

(3) a two-lane asphalt patrol road;

(4) a trace road (a strip of sand smoothed to detect footprints) running parallel to the fence;

(5) a stack of six coils of barbed wire marking the perimeter of the complex.

The complex has a width of 50 to 70 metres, increasing to as much as 100 metres in some places. "Depth barriers" may be added to these works.

The approximately 180 kilometres of the complex completed or under construction as of the time when the Secretary-General submitted his report included some 8.5 kilometres of concrete wall. These are generally found where Palestinian population centres are close to or abut Israel (such as near Qalqiliya and Tulkarm or in parts of Jerusalem).

83. According to the report of the Secretary-General, in its northernmost part, the wall as completed or under construction barely deviates from the Green Line. It nevertheless lies within occupied territories for most of its course. The works deviate more than 7.5 kilometres from the Green Line in certain places to encompass settlements, while encircling Palestinian population areas. A stretch of 1 to 2 kilometres west of Tulkarm appears to run on the Israeli side of the Green Line. Elsewhere, on the other hand, the planned route would deviate eastward by up to 22 kilometres. In the case of Jerusalem, the existing works and the planned route lie well beyond the Green Line and even in some cases beyond the eastern municipal boundary of Jerusalem as fixed by Israel.

84. On the basis of that route, approximately 975 square kilometres (or 16.6 per cent of the West Bank) would, according to the report of the Secretary-General, lie between the Green Line and the wall. This area is stated to be home to 237,000 Palestinians. If the full wall were completed as planned, another 160,000 Palestinians would live in almost completely encircled communities, described as enclaves in the report. As a result of the planned route, nearly 320,000 Israeli settlers (of whom 178,000 in East Jerusalem) would be living in the area between the Green Line and the wall.

85. Lastly, it should be noted that the construction of the wall has been accompanied by the creation of a new administrative régime. Thus in October 2003 the Israeli Defence Forces issued Orders establishing the part of the West Bank lying between the Green Line and the wall as a "Closed Area". Residents of this area may no longer remain in it, nor may non-residents enter it, unless holding a permit or identity card issued by the Israeli authorities. According to the report of the Secretary-General, most residents have received permits for a limited period. Israeli citizens, Israeli permanent residents and those eligible to immigrate to Israel in accordance with the Law of Return may remain in, or move freely to, from and within the Closed Area without a permit. Access to and exit from the Closed Area can only be made through access gates, which are opened infrequently and for short periods.

* *

86. The Court will now determine the rules and principles of international law which are relevant in assessing the legality of the measures taken by Israel. Such rules and principles can be found in the United Nations Charter and certain other treaties, in customary international law and in the relevant resolutions adopted pursuant to the Charter by the General Assembly and the Security Council. However, doubts have been expressed by Israel as to the applicability in the Occupied Palestinian Territory of certain rules

of international humanitarian law and human rights instruments. The Court will now consider these various questions.

87. The Court first recalls that, pursuant to Article 2, paragraph 4, of the United Nations Charter:

> "All Members shall refrain in their international relations from the threat or use of force against the territorial integrity or political independence of any State, or in any other manner inconsistent with the Purposes of the United Nations."

On 24 October 1970, the General Assembly adopted resolution 2625 (XXV), entitled "Declaration on Principles of International Law concerning Friendly Relations and Co-operation among States" (hereinafter "resolution 2625 (XXV)"), in which it emphasized that "No territorial acquisition resulting from the threat or use of force shall be recognized as legal." As the Court stated in its Judgment in the case concerning *Military and Paramilitary Activities in and against Nicaragua (Nicaragua* v. *United States of America)*, the principles as to the use of force incorporated in the Charter reflect customary international law (see *I. C. J. Reports 1986*, pp. 98–101, paras. 187–190); the same is true of its corollary entailing the illegality of territorial acquisition resulting from the threat or use of force.

88. The Court also notes that the principle of self-determination of peoples has been enshrined in the United Nations Charter and reaffirmed by the General Assembly in resolution 2625 (XXV) cited above, pursuant to which "Every State has the duty to refrain from any forcible action which deprives peoples referred to [in that resolution] . . . of their right to self-determination." Article 1 common to the International Covenant on Economic, Social and Cultural Rights and the International Covenant on Civil and Political Rights reaffirms the right of all peoples to self-determination, and lays upon the States parties the obligation to promote the realization of that right and to respect it, in conformity with the provisions of the United Nations Charter.

The Court would recall that in 1971 it emphasized that current developments in "international law in regard to non-self-governing territories, as enshrined in the Charter of the United Nations, made the principle of self-determination applicable to all [such territories]". The Court went on to state that "These developments leave little doubt that the ultimate objective of the sacred trust" referred to in Article 22, paragraph 1, of the Covenant of the League of Nations "was the self-determination . . . of the peoples concerned" *(Legal Consequences for States of the Continued Presence of South Africa in Namibia (South West Africa) notwithstanding Security Council Resolution 276 (1970), Advisory Opinion, I.C.J. Reports 1971*, p. 31, paras. 52–53). The Court has referred to this principle on a number of occasions in its jurisprudence (*ibid.*; see also *Western Sahara, Advisory Opinion, I.C.J. Reports*

1975, p. 68, para. 162). The Court indeed made it clear that the right of peoples to self-determination is today a right *erga omnes* (see *East Timor (Portugal* v. *Australia), Judgment, I.C.J. Reports 1995*, p. 102, para. 29).

89. As regards international humanitarian law, the Court would first note that Israel is not a party to the Fourth Hague Convention of 1907, to which the Hague Regulations are annexed. The Court observes that, in the words of the Convention, those Regulations were prepared "to revise the general laws and customs of war" existing at that time. Since then, however, the International Military Tribunal of Nuremberg has found that the "rules laid down in the Convention were recognised by all civilised nations, and were regarded as being declaratory of the laws and customs of war" (Judgment of the International Military Tribunal of Nuremberg, 30 September and 1 October 1946, p. 65). The Court itself reached the same conclusion when examining the rights and duties of belligerents in their conduct of military operations *(Legality of the Threat or Use of Nuclear Weapons, Advisory Opinion, I.C.J. Reports 1996 (I)*, p. 256, para. 75). The Court considers that the provisions of the Hague Regulations have become part of customary law, as is in fact recognized by all the participants in the proceedings before the Court.

The Court also observes that, pursuant to Article 154 of the Fourth Geneva Convention, that Convention is supplementary to Sections II and III of the Hague Regulations. Section III of those Regulations, which concerns "Military authority over the territory of the hostile State", is particularly pertinent in the present case.

90. Secondly, with regard to the Fourth Geneva Convention, differing views have been expressed by the participants in these proceedings. Israel, contrary to the great majority of the other participants, disputes the applicability *de jure* of the Convention to the Occupied Palestinian Territory. In particular, in paragraph 3 of Annex I to the report of the Secretary-General, entitled "Summary Legal Position of the Government of Israel", it is stated that Israel does not agree that the Fourth Geneva Convention "is applicable to the occupied Palestinian Territory", citing "the lack of recognition of the territory as sovereign prior to its annexation by Jordan and Egypt" and inferring that it is "not a territory of a High Contracting Party as required by the Convention".

91. The Court would recall that the Fourth Geneva Convention was ratified by Israel on 6 July 1951 and that Israel is a party to that Convention. Jordan has also been a party thereto since 29 May 1951. Neither of the two States has made any reservation that would be pertinent to the present proceedings.

Furthermore, Palestine gave a unilateral undertaking, by declaration of 7 June 1982, to apply the Fourth Geneva Convention. Switzerland, as depositary State, considered that unilateral undertaking valid. It concluded, however, that it "[was] not—as a depositary—in a position to decide whether" "the request [dated 14 June 1989] from the Palestine Liberation Movement in the name of the 'State of Palestine' to accede" *inter alia* to the Fourth Geneva Convention "can be considered as an instrument of accession".

92. Moreover, for the purpose of determining the scope of application of the Fourth Geneva Convention, it should be recalled that under common Article 2 of the four Conventions of 12 August 1949:

> "In addition to the provisions which shall be implemented in peacetime, the present Convention shall apply to all cases of declared war or of any other armed conflict which may arise between two or more of the High Contracting Parties, even if the state of war is not recognized by one of them.
>
> The Convention shall also apply to all cases of partial or total occupation of the territory of a High Contracting Party, even if the said occupation meets with no armed resistance.
>
> Although one of the Powers in conflict may not be a party to the present Convention, the Powers who are parties thereto shall remain bound by it in their mutual relations. They shall furthermore be bound by the Convention in relation to the said Power, if the latter accepts and applies the provisions thereof."

93. After the occupation of the West Bank in 1967, the Israeli authorities issued an order No. 3 stating in its Article 35 that:

> "the Military Court . . . must apply the provisions of the Geneva Convention dated 12 August 1949 relative to the Protection of Civilian Persons in Time of War with respect to judicial procedures. In case of conflict between this Order and the said Convention, the Convention shall prevail."

Subsequently, the Israeli authorities have indicated on a number of occasions that in fact they generally apply the humanitarian provisions of the Fourth Geneva Convention within the occupied territories. However, according to Israel's position as briefly recalled in paragraph 90 above, that Convention is not applicable *de jure* within those territories because, under Article 2, paragraph 2, it applies only in the case of occupation of territories falling under the sovereignty of a High Contracting Party involved in an armed conflict. Israel explains that Jordan was admittedly a party to the Fourth Geneva Convention in 1967, and that an armed conflict broke out at that time between Israel and Jordan, but it goes on to observe that the territories occupied by Israel subsequent to that conflict had not previously fallen under Jordanian sovereignty. It infers from this that that Convention is not applicable *de jure* in those territories. According however to the great majority of other participants in the proceedings, the Fourth Geneva Convention is applicable to those territories pursuant to Article 2, paragraph 1, whether or not Jordan had any rights in respect thereof prior to 1967.

94. The Court would recall that, according to customary international law as expressed in Article 31 of the Vienna Convention on the Law of Treaties of 23 May 1969, a treaty must be interpreted in good faith in accordance with the ordinary meaning to be given to its terms in their context and in the light of its object and purpose. Article 32 provides that:

> "Recourse may be had to supplementary means of interpretation, including the preparatory work of the treaty and the circumstances of its conclusion, in order to confirm the meaning resulting from the application of article 31, or to determine the meaning when the interpretation according to article 31 . . . leaves the meaning ambiguous or obscure; or . . . leads to a result which is manifestly obscure or unreasonable." (See *Oil Platforms (Islamic Republic of Iran* v. *United States of America), Preliminary Objection, Judgment, I.C.J. Reports 1996 (II)*, p. 812, para. 23; see, similarly, *KasikililSedudu Island (Botswana!Namibia), Judgment, I.C.J. Reports 1999 (II)*, p. 1059, para. 18, and *Sovereignty over Pulau Ligitan and Pulau Sipadan (Indonesia!Malaysia), Judgment, I.C.J. Reports 2002*, p. 645, para. 37.)

95. The Court notes that, according to the first paragraph of Article 2 of the Fourth Geneva Convention, that Convention is applicable when two conditions are fulfilled: that there exists an armed conflict (whether or not a state of war has been recognized); and that the conflict has arisen between two contracting parties. If those two conditions are satisfied, the Convention applies, in particular, in any territory occupied in the course of the conflict by one of the contracting parties.

The object of the second paragraph of Article 2 is not to restrict the scope of application of the Convention, as defined by the first paragraph, by excluding therefrom territories not falling under the sovereignty of one of the contracting parties. It is directed simply to making it clear that, even if occupation effected during the conflict met no armed resistance, the Convention is still applicable.

This interpretation reflects the intention of the drafters of the Fourth Geneva Convention to protect civilians who find themselves, in whatever way, in the hands of the occupying Power. Whilst the drafters of the Hague Regulations of 1907 were as much concerned with protecting the rights of a State whose territory is occupied, as with protecting the inhabitants of that territory, the drafters of the Fourth Geneva Convention sought to guarantee the protection of civilians in time of war, regardless of the status of the occupied territories, as is shown by Article 47 of the Convention.

That interpretation is confirmed by the Convention's *travaux préparatoires*. The Conference of Government Experts convened by the International Committee of the Red Cross (hereinafter, "ICRC") in the aftermath of the Second World War for the purpose of preparing the new Geneva Conventions recommended that these conventions be applicable to any armed conflict "whether [it] is or is not recognized as a state of war by the parties" and "in cases of occupation of territories in the absence of any state of war" *(Report on the Work of the Conference of Government Experts for the Study of the Conventions for the Protection of War Victims, Geneva, 14–26 April 1947*, p. 8). The drafters of the second paragraph of Article 2 thus had no intention, when they inserted that paragraph into the Convention, of restricting the latter's scope of application. They were merely seeking to provide for cases of occupation without combat, such as the occupation of Bohemia and Moravia by Germany in 1939.

96. The Court would moreover note that the States parties to the Fourth Geneva Convention approved that interpretation at their Conference on 15 July 1999. They issued a statement in which they "reaffirmed the applicability of the Fourth Geneva Convention to the Occupied Palestinian Territory, including East Jerusalem". Subsequently, on 5 December 2001, the High Contracting Parties, referring in particular to Article 1 of the Fourth Geneva Convention of 1949, once again reaffirmed the "applicability of the Fourth Geneva Convention to the Occupied Palestinian Territory, including East Jerusalem". They further reminded the Contracting Parties participating in the Conference, the parties to the conflict, and the State of Israel as occupying Power, of their respective obligations.

97. Moreover, the Court would observe that the ICRC, whose special position with respect to execution of the Fourth Geneva Convention must be "recognized and respected at all times" by the parties pursuant to Article 142 of the Convention, has also expressed its opinion on the interpretation to be given to the Convention. In a declaration of 5 December 2001, it recalled that "the ICRC has always affirmed the *de jure* applicability of the Fourth Geneva Convention to the territories occupied since 1967 by the State of Israel, including East Jerusalem".

98. The Court notes that the General Assembly has, in many of its resolutions, taken a position to the same effect. Thus on 10 December 2001 and 9 December 2003, in resolutions 56/60 and 58/97, it reaffirmed

> "that the Geneva Convention relative to the Protection of Civilian Persons in Time of War, of 12 August 1949, is applicable to the Occupied Palestinian Territory, including East Jerusalem, and other Arab territories occupied by Israel since 1967".

99. The Security Council, for its part, had already on 14 June 1967 taken the view in resolution 237 (1967) that "all the obligations of the Geneva Convention relative to the Treatment of Prisoners of War . . . should be complied with by the parties involved in the conflict". Subsequently, on 15 September 1969, the Security Council, in resolution 271 (1969), called upon "Israel scrupulously to observe the provisions of the Geneva Conventions and international law governing military occupation".

Ten years later, the Security Council examined "the policy and practices of Israel in establishing settlements in the Palestinian and other Arab territories occupied since 1967". In resolution 446 (1979) of 22 March 1979, the Security Council considered that those settlements had "no legal validity" and affirmed *"once more* that the Geneva Convention relative to the Protection of Civilian Persons in Time of War, of 12 August 1949, is applicable to the Arab territories occupied by Israel since 1967, including Jerusalem". It called *"once more upon* Israel, as the occupying Power, to abide scrupulously" by that Convention.

On 20 December 1990, the Security Council, in resolution 681 (1990), urged "the Government of Israel to accept the *dejure* applicability of the Fourth Geneva Convention . . . to all the territories occupied by Israel since 1967 and to abide scrupulously by the provisions of the Convention". It further called upon "the high contracting parties to the said Fourth Geneva Convention to ensure respect by Israel, the occupying Power, for its obligations under the Convention in accordance with article 1 thereof".

Lastly, in resolutions 799 (1992) of 18 December 1992 and 904 (1994) of 18 March 1994, the Security Council reaffirmed its position concerning the applicability of the Fourth Geneva Convention in the occupied territories.

100. The Court would note finally that the Supreme Court of Israel, in a judgment dated 30 May 2004, also found that:

> "The military operations of the [Israeli Defence Forces] in Rafah, to the extent they affect civilians, are governed by Hague Convention IV Respecting the Laws and Customs of War on Land 1907 . . . and the Geneva Convention relative to the Protection of Civilian Persons in Time of War 1949."

101. In view of the foregoing, the Court considers that the Fourth Geneva Convention is applicable in any occupied territory in the event of an armed conflict arising between two or more High Contracting Parties. Israel and Jordan were parties to that Convention when the 1967 armed conflict broke out. The Court accordingly finds that that Convention is applicable in the Palestinian territories which before the conflict lay to the east of the Green Line and which, during that conflict, were occupied by Israel, there being no need for any enquiry into the precise prior status of those territories.

*

102. The participants in the proceedings before the Court also disagree whether the international human rights conventions to which Israel is party apply within the Occupied Palestinian Territory. Annex I to the report of the Secretary-General states:

> "4. Israel denies that the International Covenant on Civil and Political Rights and the International Covenant on Economic, Social and Cultural Rights, both of which it has signed, are applicable to the occupied Palestinian territory. It asserts that humanitarian law is the protection granted in a conflict

> situation such as the one in the West Bank and Gaza Strip, whereas human rights treaties were intended for the protection of citizens from their own Government in times of peace."

Of the other participants in the proceedings, those who addressed this issue contend that, on the contrary, both Covenants are applicable within the Occupied Palestinian Territory.

103. On 3 October 1991 Israel ratified both the International Covenant on Economic, Social and Cultural Rights of 19 December 1966 and the International Covenant on Civil and Political Rights of the same date, as well as the United Nations Convention on the Rights of the Child of 20 November 1989. It is a party to these three instruments.

104. In order to determine whether these texts are applicable in the Occupied Palestinian Territory, the Court will first address the issue of the relationship between international humanitarian law and human rights law and then that of the applicability of human rights instruments outside national territory.

105. In its Advisory Opinion of 8 July 1996 on the *Legality of the Threat or Use of Nuclear Weapons*, the Court had occasion to address the first of these issues in relation to the International Covenant on Civil and Political Rights. In those proceedings certain States had argued that "the Covenant was directed to the protection of human rights in peacetime, but that questions relating to unlawful loss of life in hostilities were governed by the law applicable in armed conflict" *(I.C.J. Reports 1996 (I)*, p. 239, para. 24).

The Court rejected this argument, stating that:

> "the protection of the International Covenant of Civil and Political Rights does not cease in times of war, except by operation of Article 4 of the Covenant whereby certain provisions may be derogated from in a time of national emergency. Respect for the right to life is not, however, such a provision. In principle, the right not arbitrarily to be deprived of one's life applies also in hostilities. The test of what is an arbitrary deprivation of life, however, then falls to be determined by the applicable *lex specialis*, namely, the law applicable in armed conflict which is designed to regulate the conduct of hostilities." (*ibid.*, p. 240, para. 25.)

106. More generally, the Court considers that the protection offered by human rights conventions does not cease in case of armed conflict, save through the effect of provisions for derogation of the kind to be found in Article 4 of the International Covenant on Civil and Political Rights. As regards the relationship between international humanitarian law and human rights law, there are thus three possible situations: some rights may be exclusively matters of international humanitarian law; others may be exclusively matters of human rights law; yet others may be matters of both these branches of international law. In order to answer the question put to

it, the Court will have to take into consideration both these branches of international law, namely human rights law and, as *lex specialis*, international humanitarian law.

107. It remains to be determined whether the two international Covenants and the Convention on the Rights of the Child are applicable only on the territories of the States parties thereto or whether they are also applicable outside those territories and, if so, in what circumstances.

108. The scope of application of the International Covenant on Civil and Political Rights is defined by Article 2, paragraph 1, thereof, which provides:

> "Each State Party to the present Covenant undertakes to respect and to ensure to all individuals within its territory and subject to its jurisdiction the rights recognized in the present Covenant, without distinction of any kind, such as race, colour, sex, language, religion, political or other opinion, national or social origin, property, birth or other status."

This provision can be interpreted as covering only individuals who are both present within a State's territory and subject to that State's jurisdiction. It can also be construed as covering both individuals present within a State's territory and those outside that territory but subject to that State's jurisdiction. The Court will thus seek to determine the meaning to be given to this text.

109. The Court would observe that, while the jurisdiction of States is primarily territorial, it may sometimes be exercised outside the national territory. Considering the object and purpose of the International Covenant on Civil and Political Rights, it would seem natural that, even when such is the case, States parties to the Covenant should be bound to comply with its provisions.

The constant practice of the Human Rights Committee is consistent with this. Thus, the Committee has found the Covenant applicable where the State exercises its jurisdiction on foreign territory. It has ruled on the legality of acts by Uruguay in cases of arrests carried out by Uruguayan agents in Brazil or Argentina (case No. 52/79, *Lopez Burgos* v. *Uruguay*; case No. 56/79, *Lilian Celiberti de Casariego* v. *Uruguay*). It decided to the same effect in the case of the confiscation of a passport by a Uruguayan consulate in Germany (case No. 106/81, *Montero* v. *Uruguay*).

The *travaux preparatoires* of the Covenant confirm the Committee's interpretation of Article 2 of that instrument. These show that, in adopting the wording chosen, the drafters of the Covenant did not intend to allow States to escape from their obligations when they exercise jurisdiction outside their national territory. They only intended to prevent persons residing abroad from asserting, vis-a-vis their State of origin, rights that do not fall within the competence of that State, but of that of the State of residence (see the discussion of the preliminary draft in the Commission on Human Rights,

E/CN.4/SR.194, para. 46; and United Nations, *Official Records of the General Assembly, Tenth Session, Annexes*, A/2929, Part II, Chap. V, para. 4 (1955)).

110. The Court takes note in this connection of the position taken by Israel, in relation to the applicability of the Covenant, in its communications to the Human Rights Committee, and of the view of the Committee.

In 1998, Israel stated that, when preparing its report to the Committee, it had had to face the question "whether individuals resident in the occupied territories were indeed subject to Israel's jurisdiction" for purposes of the application of the Covenant (CCPR/C/SR.1675, para. 21). Israel took the position that "the Covenant and similar instruments did not apply directly to the current situation in the occupied territories" (*ibid.*, para. 27).

The Committee, in its concluding observations after examination of the report, expressed concern at Israel's attitude and pointed "to the long-standing presence of Israel in [the occupied] territories, Israel's ambiguous attitude towards their future status, as well as the exercise of effective jurisdiction by Israeli security forces therein" (CCPR/C/79/ Add.93, para. 10). In 2003 in face of Israel's consistent position, to the effect that "the Covenant does not apply beyond its own territory, notably in the West Bank and Gaza . . .", the Committee reached the following conclusion:

> "in the current circumstances, the provisions of the Covenant apply to the benefit of the population of the Occupied Territories, for all conduct by the State party's authorities or agents in those territories that affect the enjoyment of rights enshrined in the Covenant and fall within the ambit of State responsibility of Israel under the principles of public international law" (CCPR/CO/78/ISR, para. 11).

111. In conclusion, the Court considers that the International Covenant on Civil and Political Rights is applicable in respect of acts done by a State in the exercise of its jurisdiction outside its own territory.

112. The International Covenant on Economic, Social and Cultural Rights contains no provision on its scope of application. This may be explicable by the fact that this Covenant guarantees rights which are essentially territorial. However, it is not to be excluded that it applies both to territories over which a State party has sovereignty and to those over which that State exercises territorial jurisdiction. Thus Article 14 makes provision for transitional measures in the case of any State which "at the time of becoming a Party, has not been able to secure in its metropolitan territory or other territories under its jurisdiction compulsory primary education, free of charge".

It is not without relevance to recall in this regard the position taken by Israel in its reports to the Committee on Economic, Social and Cultural Rights. In its initial report to the Committee of 4 December 1998, Israel provided "statistics indicating the enjoyment of the rights enshrined in the Covenant by Israeli settlers in the occupied Territories". The Committee noted that, according to Israel, "the Palestinian population within the same jurisdictional areas were excluded from both the report and the protection of the Covenant" (E/C.12/1/Add.27, para. 8). The Committee expressed its concern in this regard, to which Israel replied in a further report of 19 October 2001 that it has "consistently maintained that the Covenant does not apply to areas that are not subject to its sovereign territory and jurisdiction" (a formula inspired by the language of the International Covenant on Civil and Political Rights). This position, continued Israel, is "based on the well-established distinction between human rights and humanitarian law under international law". It added: "the Committee's mandate cannot relate to events in the West Bank and the Gaza Strip, inasmuch as they are part and parcel of the context of armed conflict as distinct from a relationship of human rights" (E/1990/6/ Add.32, para. 5). In view of these observations, the Committee reiterated its concern about Israel's position and reaffirmed "its view that the State party's obligations under the Covenant apply to all territories and populations under its effective control" (E/C.12/1/Add.90, paras. 15 and 31).

For the reasons explained in paragraph 106 above, the Court cannot accept Israel's view. It would also observe that the territories occupied by Israel have for over 37 years been subject to its territorial jurisdiction as the occupying Power. In the exercise of the powers available to it on this basis, Israel is bound by the provisions of the International Covenant on Economic, Social and Cultural Rights. Furthermore, it is under an obligation not to raise any obstacle to the exercise of such rights in those fields where competence has been transferred to Palestinian authorities.

113. As regards the Convention on the Rights of the Child of 20 November 1989, that instrument contains an Article 2 according to which "States Parties shall respect and ensure the rights set forth in the . . . Convention to each child within their jurisdiction . . .". That Convention is therefore applicable within the Occupied Palestinian Territory.

* *

114. Having determined the rules and principles of international law relevant to reply to the question posed by the General Assembly, and having ruled in particular on the applicability within the Occupied Palestinian Territory of international humanitarian law and human rights law, the Court will now seek to ascertain whether the construction of the wall has violated those rules and principles.

* *

115. In this regard, Annex II to the report of the Secretary-General, entitled "Summary Legal Position of the Palestine Liberation Organization", states that "The construction of the Barrier is an attempt to annex the territory contrary to international law" and that "The de facto annexation of land

interferes with the territorial sovereignty and consequently with the right of the Palestinians to self-determination." This view was echoed in certain of the written statements submitted to the Court and in the views expressed at the hearings. *Inter alia*, it was contended that:

> "The wall severs the territorial sphere over which the Palestinian people are entitled to exercise their right of self-determination and constitutes a violation of the legal principle prohibiting the acquisition of territory by the use of force."

In this connection, it was in particular emphasized that "[t]he route of the wall is designed to change the demographic composition of the Occupied Palestinian Territory, including East Jerusalem, by reinforcing the Israeli settlements" illegally established on the Occupied Palestinian Territory. It was further contended that the wall aimed at "reducing and parcelling out the territorial sphere over which the Palestinian people are entitled to exercise their right of self-determination".

116. For its part, Israel has argued that the wall's sole purpose is to enable it effectively to combat terrorist attacks launched from the West Bank. Furthermore, Israel has repeatedly stated that the Barrier is a temporary measure (see report of the Secretary-General, para. 29). It did so *inter alia* through its Permanent Representative to the United Nations at the Security Council meeting of 14 October 2003, emphasizing that "[the fence] does not annex territories to the State of Israel", and that Israel is "ready and able, at tremendous cost, to adjust or dismantle a fence if so required as part of a political settlement" (S/PV.4841, p. 10). Israel's Permanent Representative restated this view before the General Assembly on 20 October and 8 December 2003. On this latter occasion, he added:

> "As soon as the terror ends, the fence will no longer be necessary. The fence is not a border and has no political significance. It does not change the legal status of the territory in any way." (A/ES-10/PV.23, p. 6.)

117. The Court would recall that both the General Assembly and the Security Council have referred, with regard to Palestine, to the customary rule of "the inadmissibility of the acquisition of territory by war" (see paragraphs 74 and 87 above). Thus in resolution 242 (1967) of 22 November 1967, the Security Council, after recalling this rule, affirmed that:

> "the fulfilment of Charter principles requires the establishment of a just and lasting peace in the Middle East which should include the application of both the following principles:
>
> > (i) Withdrawal of Israel armed forces from territories occupied in the recent conflict;
> >
> > (ii) Termination of all claims or states of belligerency and respect for and acknowledgement of the sovereignty, territorial integrity and political independence of every State in the area and their right to live in peace

> within secure and recognized boundaries free from threats or acts of force".

It is on this same basis that the Council has several times condemned the measures taken by Israel to change the status of Jerusalem (see paragraph 75 above).

118. As regards the principle of the right of peoples to self-determination, the Court observes that the existence of a "Palestinian people" is no longer in issue. Such existence has moreover been recognized by Israel in the exchange of letters of 9 September 1993 between Mr. Yasser Arafat, President of the Palestine Liberation Organization (PLO) and Mr. Yitzhak Rabin, Israeli Prime Minister. In that correspondence, the President of the PLO recognized "the right of the State of Israel to exist in peace and security" and made various other commitments. In reply, the Israeli Prime Minister informed him that, in the light of those commitments, "the Government of Israel has decided to recognize the PLO as the representative of the Palestinian people". The Israeli-Palestinian Interim Agreement on the West Bank and the Gaza Strip of 28 September 1995 also refers a number of times to the Palestinian people and its "legitimate rights" (Preamble, paras. 4, 7, 8; Article II, para. 2; Article III, paras. 1 and 3; Article XXII, para. 2). The Court considers that those rights include the right to self-determination, as the General Assembly has moreover recognized on a number of occasions (see, for example, resolution 58/163 of 22 December 2003).

119. The Court notes that the route of the wall as fixed by the Israeli Government includes within the "Closed Area" (see paragraph 85 above) some 80 per cent of the settlers living in the Occupied Palestinian Territory. Moreover, it is apparent from an examination of the map mentioned in paragraph 80 above that the wall's sinuous route has been traced in such a way as to include within that area the great majority of the Israeli settlements in the occupied Palestinian Territory (including East Jerusalem).

120. As regards these settlements, the Court notes that Article 49, paragraph 6, of the Fourth Geneva Convention provides: "The Occupying Power shall not deport or transfer parts of its own civilian population into the territory it occupies." That provision prohibits not only deportations or forced transfers of population such as those carried out during the Second World War, but also any measures taken by an occupying Power in order to organize or encourage transfers of parts of its own population into the occupied territory.

In this respect, the information provided to the Court shows that, since 1977, Israel has conducted a policy and developed practices involving the establishment of settlements in the Occupied Palestinian Territory, contrary to the terms of Article 49, paragraph 6, just cited.

The Security Council has thus taken the view that such policy and practices "have no legal validity". It has also called upon "Israel, as the occupying Power, to abide scrupulously" by the Fourth Geneva Convention and:

> "to rescind its previous measures and to desist from taking any action which would result in changing the legal status and geographical nature and materially affecting the demographic composition of the Arab territories occupied since 1967, including Jerusalem and, in particular, not to transfer parts of its own civilian population into the occupied Arab territories" (resolution 446 (1979) of 22 March 1979).

The Council reaffirmed its position in resolutions 452 (1979) of 20 July 1979 and 465 (1980) of 1 March 1980. Indeed, in the latter case it described "Israel's policy and practices of settling parts of its population and new immigrants in [the occupied] territories" as a "flagrant violation" of the Fourth Geneva Convention.

The Court concludes that the Israeli settlements in Occupied Palestinian Territory (including East Jerusalem) have been established in breach of international law.

121. Whilst the Court notes the assurance given by Israel that the construction of the wall does not amount to annexation and that the wall is of a temporary nature (see paragraph 116 above), it nevertheless cannot remain indifferent to certain fears expressed to it that the route of the wall will prejudge the future frontier between Israel and Palestine, and the fear that Israel may integrate the settlements and their means of access. The Court considers that the construction of the wall and its associated régime create a "fait accompli" on the ground that could well become permanent, in which case, and notwithstanding the formal characterization of the wall by Israel, it would be tantamount to *de facto* annexation.

122. The Court recalls moreover that, according to the report of the Secretary-General, the planned route would incorporate in the area between the Green Line and the wall more than 16 per cent of the territory of the West Bank. Around 80 per cent of the settlers living in the Occupied Palestinian Territory, that is 320,000 individuals, would reside in that area, as well as 237,000 Palestinians. Moreover, as a result of the construction of the wall, around 160,000 other Palestinians would reside in almost completely encircled communities (see paragraphs 84, 85 and 119 above).

In other terms, the route chosen for the wall gives expression *in loco* to the illegal measures taken by Israel with regard to Jerusalem and the settlements, as deplored by the Security Council (see paragraphs 75 and 120 above). There is also a risk of further alterations to the demographic composition of the Occupied Palestinian Territory resulting from the construction of the wall inasmuch as it is contributing, as will be further explained in paragraph 133 below, to the departure of Palestinian populations from certain areas. That construction, along with measures taken previously, thus severely impedes the exercise by the Palestinian people of its right to self-determination, and is therefore a breach of Israel's obligation to respect that right.

*

123. The construction of the wall also raises a number of issues in relation to the relevant provisions of international humanitarian law and of human rights instruments.

124. With regard to the Hague Regulations of 1907, the Court would recall that these deal, in Section II, with hostilities and in particular with "means of injuring the enemy, sieges, and bombardments". Section III deals with military authority in occupied territories. Only Section III is currently applicable in the West Bank and Article 23 *(g)* of the Regulations, in Section II, is thus not pertinent.

Section III of the Hague Regulations includes Articles 43, 46 and 52, which are applicable in the Occupied Palestinian Territory. Article 43 imposes a duty on the occupant to "take all measures within his power to restore, and, as far as possible, to insure public order and life, respecting the laws in force in the country". Article 46 adds that private property must be "respected" and that it cannot "be confiscated". Lastly, Article 52 authorizes, within certain limits, requisitions in kind and services for the needs of the army of occupation.

125. A distinction is also made in the Fourth Geneva Convention between provisions applying during military operations leading to occupation and those that remain applicable throughout the entire period of occupation. It thus states in Article 6:

> "The present Convention shall apply from the outset of any conflict or occupation mentioned in Article 2.
>
> In the territory of Parties to the conflict, the application of the present Convention shall cease on the general close of military operations.
>
> In the case of occupied territory, the application of the present Convention shall cease one year after the general close of military operations; however, the Occupying Power shall be bound, for the duration of the occupation, to the extent that such Power exercises the functions of government in such territory, by the provisions of the following Articles of the present Convention: 1 to 12, 27, 29 to 34, 47, 49, 51, 52, 53, 59, 61 to 77, 143.
>
> Protected persons whose release, repatriation or re-establishment may take place after such dates shall meanwhile continue to benefit by the present Convention."

Since the military operations leading to the occupation of the West Bank in 1967 ended a long time ago, only those Articles of the Fourth Geneva Convention referred to in Article 6, paragraph 3, remain applicable in that occupied territory.

126. These provisions include Articles 47, 49, 52, 53 and 59 of the Fourth Geneva Convention.

According to Article 47:

> "Protected persons who are in occupied territory shall not be deprived, in any case or in any manner whatsoever, of the benefits of the present Convention by any change introduced, as the result of the occupation of a territory, into the institutions or government of the said territory, nor by any agreement concluded between the authorities of the occupied territories and the Occupying Power, nor by any annexation by the latter of the whole or part of the occupied territory."

Article 49 reads as follows:

> "Individual or mass forcible transfers, as well as deportations of protected persons from occupied territory to the territory of the Occupying Power or to that of any other country, occupied or not, are prohibited, regardless of their motive.
>
> Nevertheless, the Occupying Power may undertake total or partial evacuation of a given area if the security of the population or imperative military reasons so demand. Such evacuations may not involve the displacement of protected persons outside the bounds of the occupied territory except when for material reasons it is impossible to avoid such displacement. Persons thus evacuated shall be transferred back to their homes as soon as hostilities in the area in question have ceased.
>
> The Occupying Power undertaking such transfers or evacuations shall ensure, to the greatest practicable extent, that proper accommodation is provided to receive the protected persons, that the removals are effected in satisfactory conditions of hygiene, health, safety and nutrition, and that members of the same family are not separated.
>
> The Protecting Power shall be informed of any transfers and evacuations as soon as they have taken place.
>
> The Occupying Power shall not detain protected persons in an area particularly exposed to the dangers of war unless the security of the population or imperative military reasons so demand.
>
> The Occupying Power shall not deport or transfer parts of its own civilian population into the territory it occupies."

According to Article 52:

> "No contract, agreement or regulation shall impair the right of any worker, whether voluntary or not and wherever he may be, to apply to the representatives of the Protecting Power in order to request the said Power's intervention.
>
> All measures aiming at creating unemployment or at restricting the opportunities offered to workers in an occupied territory, in order to induce them to work for the Occupying Power, are prohibited."

Article 53 provides that:

> "Any destruction by the Occupying Power of real or personal property belonging individually or collectively to private persons, or to the State, or to other public authorities, or to social or co-operative organizations, is prohibited, except where such destruction is rendered absolutely necessary by military operations."

Lastly, according to Article 59:

> "If the whole or part of the population of an occupied territory is inadequately supplied, the Occupying Power shall agree to relief schemes on behalf of the said population, and shall facilitate them by all the means at its disposal.
>
> Such schemes, which may be undertaken either by States or by impartial humanitarian organizations such as the International Committee of the Red Cross, shall consist, in particular, of the provision of consignments of foodstuffs, medical supplies and clothing.
>
> All Contracting Parties shall permit the free passage of these consignments and shall guarantee their protection.
>
> A Power granting free passage to consignments on their way to territory occupied by an adverse Party to the conflict shall, however, have the right to search the consignments, to regulate their passage according to prescribed times and routes, and to be reasonably satisfied through the Protecting Power that these consignments are to be used for the relief of the needy population and are not to be used for the benefit of the Occupying Power."

127. The International Covenant on Civil and Political Rights also contains several relevant provisions. Before further examining these, the Court will observe that Article 4 of the Covenant allows for derogation to be made, under various conditions, to certain provisions of that instrument. Israel made use of its right of derogation under this Article by addressing the following communication to the Secretary-General of the United Nations on 3 October 1991:

> "Since its establishment, the State of Israel has been the victim of continuous threats and attacks on its very existence as well as on the life and property of its citizens.
>
> These have taken the form of threats of war, of actual armed attacks, and campaigns of terrorism resulting in the murder of and injury to human beings.
>
> In view of the above, the State of Emergency which was proclaimed in May 1948 has remained in force ever since. This situation constitutes a public emergency within the meaning of article 4 (1) of the Covenant.
>
> The Government of Israel has therefore found it necessary, in accordance with the said article 4, to take measures to the extent strictly required by the exigencies of the situation, for the defence of the State and for the

> protection of life and property, including the exercise of powers of arrest and detention.
>
> In so far as any of these measures are inconsistent with article 9 of the Covenant, Israel thereby derogates from its obligations under that provision."

The Court notes that the derogation so notified concerns only Article 9 of the International Covenant on Civil and Political Rights, which deals with the right to liberty and security of person and lays down the rules applicable in cases of arrest or detention. The other Articles of the Covenant therefore remain applicable not only on Israeli territory, but also on the Occupied Palestinian Territory.

128. Among these mention must be made of Article 17, paragraph 1 of which reads as follows: "No one shall be subjected to arbitrary or unlawful interference with his privacy, family, home or correspondence, nor to unlawful attacks on his honour and reputation."

Mention must also be made of Article 12, paragraph 1, which provides: "Everyone lawfully within the territory of a State shall, within that territory, have the right to liberty of movement and freedom to choose his residence."

129. In addition to the general guarantees of freedom of movement under Article 12 of the International Covenant on Civil and Political Rights, account must also be taken of specific guarantees of access to the Christian, Jewish and Islamic Holy Places. The status of the Christian Holy Places in the Ottoman Empire dates far back in time, the latest provisions relating thereto having been incorporated into Article 62 of the Treaty of Berlin of 13 July 1878. The Mandate for Palestine given to the British Government on 24 July 1922 included an Article 13, under which:

> "All responsibility in connection with the Holy Places and religious buildings or sites in Palestine, including that of preserving existing rights and of securing free access to the Holy Places, religious buildings and sites and the free exercise of worship, while ensuring the requirements of public order and decorum, is assumed by the Mandatory . . ."

Article 13 further stated: "nothing in this mandate shall be construed as conferring . . . authority to interfere with the fabric or the management of purely Moslem sacred shrines, the immunities of which are guaranteed".

In the aftermath of the Second World War, the General Assembly, in adopting resolution 181 (II) on the future government of Palestine, devoted an entire chapter of the Plan of Partition to the Holy Places, religious buildings and sites. Article 2 of this Chapter provided, in so far as the Holy Places were concerned:

> "the liberty of access, visit and transit shall be guaranteed, in conformity with existing rights, to all residents and citizens [of the Arab State, of the

Jewish State] and of the City of Jerusalem, as well as to aliens, without distinction as to nationality, subject to requirements of national security, public order and decorum".

Subsequently, in the aftermath of the armed conflict of 1948, the 1949 General Armistice Agreement between Jordan and Israel provided in Article VIII for the establishment of a special committee for "the formulation of agreed plans and arrangements for such matters as either Party may submit to it" for the purpose of enlarging the scope of the Agreement and of effecting improvement in its application. Such matters, on which an agreement of principle had already been concluded, included "free access to the Holy Places".

This commitment concerned mainly the Holy Places located to the east of the Green Line. However, some Holy Places were located west of that Line. This was the case of the Room of the Last Supper and the Tomb of David, on Mount Zion. In signing the General Armistice Agreement, Israel thus undertook, as did Jordan, to guarantee freedom of access to the Holy Places. The Court considers that this undertaking by Israel has remained valid for the Holy Places which came under its control in 1967. This undertaking has further been confirmed by Article 9, paragraph 1, of the 1994 Peace Treaty between Israel and Jordan, by virtue of which, in more general terms, "Each party will provide freedom of access to places of religious and historical significance."

130. As regards the International Covenant on Economic, Social and Cultural Rights, that instrument includes a number of relevant provisions, namely: the right to work (Arts. 6 and 7); protection and assistance accorded to the family and to children and young persons (Art. 10); the right to an adequate standard of living, including adequate food, clothing and housing, and the right "to be free from hunger" (Art. 11); the right to health (Art. 12); the right to education (Arts. 13 and 14).

131. Lastly, the United Nations Convention on the Rights of the Child of 20 November 1989 includes similar provisions in Articles 16, 24, 27 and 28.

*

132. From the information submitted to the Court, particularly the report of the Secretary-General, it appears that the construction of the wall has led to the destruction or requisition of properties under conditions which contravene the requirements of Articles 46 and 52 of the Hague Regulations of 1907 and of Article 53 of the Fourth Geneva Convention.

133. That construction, the establishment of a closed area between the Green Line and the wall itself and the creation of enclaves have moreover imposed substantial restrictions on the freedom of movement of the inhabitants of the Occupied Palestinian Territory (with the exception of Israeli citizens and those assimilated thereto). Such restrictions are most marked

in urban areas, such as the Qalqiliya enclave or the City of Jerusalem and its suburbs. They are aggravated by the fact that the access gates are few in number in certain sectors and opening hours appear to be restricted and unpredictably applied. For example, according to the Special Rapporteur of the Commission on Human Rights on the situation of human rights in the Palestinian territories occupied by Israel since 1967, "Qalqiliya, a city with a population of 40,000, is completely surrounded by the Wall and residents can only enter and leave through a single military checkpoint open from 7 a.m. to 7 p.m." (Report of the Special Rapporteur of the Commission on Human Rights, John Dugard, on the situation of human rights in the Palestinian territories occupied by Israel since 1967, submitted in accordance with Commission resolution 1993/2 A and entitled "Question of the Violation of Human Rights in the Occupied Arab Territories, including Palestine", E/CN.4/2004/6, 8 September 2003, para. 9.)

There have also been serious repercussions for agricultural production, as is attested by a number of sources. According to the Special Committee to Investigate Israeli Practices Affecting the Human Rights of the Palestinian People and Other Arabs of the Occupied Territories

> "an estimated 100,000 dunums [approximately 10,000 hectares] of the West Banks most fertile agricultural land, confiscated by the Israeli Occupation Forces, have been destroyed during the first phase of the wall construction, which involves the disappearance of vast amounts of property, notably private agricultural land and olive trees, wells, citrus grows and hothouses upon which tens of thousands of Palestinians rely for their survival" (Report of the Special Committee to Investigate Israeli Practices Affecting the Human Rights of the Palestinian People and Other Arabs of the Occupied Territories, A/58/311, 22 August 2003, para. 26).

Further, the Special Rapporteur on the situation of human rights in the Palestinian territories occupied by Israel since 1967 states that "Much of the Palestinian land on the Israeli side of the Wall consists of fertile agricultural land and some of the most important water wells in the region" and adds that "Many fruit and olive trees had been destroyed in the course of building the barrier" (E/CN.4/2004/6, 8 September 2003, para. 9). The Special Rapporteur on the Right to Food of the United Nations Commission on Human Rights states that construction of the wall "cuts off Palestinians from their agricultural lands, wells and means of subsistence" (Report by the Special Rapporteur of the United Nations Commission on Human Rights, Jean Ziegler, "The Right to Food", Addendum, Mission to the Occupied Palestinian Territories, E/CN.4/ 2004/10/Add.2, 31 October 2003, para. 49). In a recent survey conducted by the World Food Programme, it is stated that the situation has aggravated food insecurity in the region, which reportedly numbers 25,000 new beneficiaries of food aid (report of the Secretary-General, para. 25).

It has further led to increasing difficulties for the population concerned regarding access to health services, educational establishments and primary sources of water. This is also attested by a number of different information sources. Thus the report of the Secretary-General states generally that "According to the Palestinian Central Bureau of Statistics, so far the Barrier has separated 30 localities from health services, 22 from schools, 8 from primary water sources and 3 from electricity networks." (Report of the Secretary-General, para. 23.) The Special Rapporteur of the United Nations Commission on Human Rights on the situation of human rights in the Palestinian territories occupied by Israel since 1967 states that "Palestinians between the Wall and Green Line will effectively be cut off from their land and workplaces, schools, health clinics and other social services." (E/CN.4/2004/6, 8 September 2003, para. 9.) In relation specifically to water resources, the Special Rapporteur on the Right to Food of the United Nations Commission on Human Rights observes that "By constructing the fence Israel will also effectively annex most of the western aquifer system (which provides 51 per cent of the West Bank's water resources)." (E/CN.4/2004/10/Add.2, 31 October 2003, para. 51.) Similarly, in regard to access to health services, it has been stated that, as a result of the enclosure of Qalqiliya, a United Nations hospital in that town has recorded a 40 per cent decrease in its caseload (report of the Secretary-General, para. 24).

At Qalqiliya, according to reports furnished to the United Nations, some 600 shops or businesses have shut down, and 6,000 to 8,000 people have already left the region (E/CN.4/2004/6, 8 September 2003, para. 10; E/CN.4/2004/10/Add.2, 31 October 2003, para. 51). The Special Rapporteur on the Right to Food of the United Nations Commission on Human Rights has also observed that "With the fence/wall cutting communities off from their land and water without other means of subsistence, many of the Palestinians living in these areas will be forced to leave." (E/CN.4/2004/10/Add.2, 31 October 2003, para. 51.) In this respect also the construction of the wall would effectively deprive a significant number of Palestinians of the "freedom to choose [their] residence". In addition, however, in the view of the Court, since a significant number of Palestinians have already been compelled by the construction of the wall and its associated régime to depart from certain areas, a process that will continue as more of the wall is built, that construction, coupled with the establishment of the Israeli settlements mentioned in paragraph 120 above, is tending to alter the demographic composition of the Occupied Palestinian Territory.

134. To sum up, the Court is of the opinion that the construction of the wall and its associated régime impede the liberty of movement of the inhabitants of the Occupied Palestinian Territory (with the exception of Israeli

citizens and those assimilated thereto) as guaranteed under Article 12, paragraph 1, of the International Covenant on Civil and Political Rights. They also impede the exercise by the persons concerned of the right to work, to health, to education and to an adequate standard of living as proclaimed in the International Covenant on Economic, Social and Cultural Rights and in the United Nations Convention on the Rights of the Child. Lastly, the construction of the wall and its associated régime, by contributing to the demographic changes referred to in paragraphs 122 and 133 above, contravene Article 49, paragraph 6, of the Fourth Geneva Convention and the Security Council resolutions cited in paragraph 120 above.

135. The Court would observe, however, that the applicable international humanitarian law contains provisions enabling account to be taken of military exigencies in certain circumstances.

Neither Article 46 of the Hague Regulations of 1907 nor Article 47 of the Fourth Geneva Convention contain any qualifying provision of this type. With regard to forcible transfers of population and deportations, which are prohibited under Article 49, paragraph 1, of the Convention, paragraph 2 of that Article provides for an exception in those cases in which "the security of the population or imperative military reasons so demand". This exception however does not apply to paragraph 6 of that Article, which prohibits the occupying Power from deporting or transferring parts of its own civilian population into the territories it occupies. As to Article 53 concerning the destruction of personal property, it provides for an exception "where such destruction is rendered absolutely necessary by military operations".

The Court considers that the military exigencies contemplated by these texts may be invoked in occupied territories even after the general close of the military operations that led to their occupation. However, on the material before it, the Court is not convinced that the destructions carried out contrary to the prohibition in Article 53 of the Fourth Geneva Convention were rendered absolutely necessary by military operations.

136. The Court would further observe that some human rights conventions, and in particular the International Covenant on Civil and Political Rights, contain provisions which States parties may invoke in order to derogate, under various conditions, from certain of their conventional obligations. In this respect, the Court would however recall that the communication notified by Israel to the Secretary-General of the United Nations under Article 4 of the International Covenant on Civil and Political Rights concerns only Article 9 of the Covenant, relating to the right to freedom and security of person (see paragraph 127 above); Israel is accordingly bound to respect all the other provisions of that instrument.

The Court would note, moreover, that certain provisions of human rights conventions contain clauses qualifying the rights covered by those provisions.

There is no clause of this kind in Article 17 of the International Covenant on Civil and Political Rights. On the other hand, Article 12, paragraph 3, of that instrument provides that restrictions on liberty of movement as guaranteed under that Article

> "shall not be subject to any restrictions except those which are provided by law, are necessary to protect national security, public order *(ordre public)*, public health or morals or the rights and freedoms of others, and are consistent with the other rights recognized in the present Covenant".

As for the International Covenant on Economic, Social and Cultural Rights, Article 4 thereof contains a general provision as follows:

> "The States Parties to the present Covenant recognize that, in the enjoyment of those rights provided by the State in conformity with the present Covenant, the State may subject such rights only to such limitations as are determined by law only in so far as this may be compatible with the nature of these rights and solely for the purpose of promoting the general welfare in a democratic society."

The Court would observe that the restrictions provided for under Article 12, paragraph 3, of the International Covenant on Civil and Political Rights are, by the very terms of that provision, exceptions to the right of freedom of movement contained in paragraph 1. In addition, it is not sufficient that such restrictions be directed to the ends authorized; they must also be necessary for the attainment of those ends. As the Human Rights Committee put it, they "must conform to the principle of proportionality" and "must be the least intrusive instrument amongst those which might achieve the desired result" (CCPR/C/21/Rev.l/Add.9, General Comment No. 27, para. 14). On the basis of the information available to it, the Court finds that these conditions are not met in the present instance.

The Court would further observe that the restrictions on the enjoyment by the Palestinians living in the territory occupied by Israel of their economic, social and cultural rights, resulting from Israel's construction of the wall, fail to meet a condition laid down by Article 4 of the International Covenant on Economic, Social and Cultural Rights, that is to say that their implementation must be "solely for the purpose of promoting the general welfare in a democratic society".

137. To sum up, the Court, from the material available to it, is not convinced that the specific course Israel has chosen for the wall was necessary to attain its security objectives. The wall, along the route chosen, and its associated régime gravely infringe a number of rights of Palestinians residing in the territory occupied by Israel, and the infringements resulting from that route cannot be justified by military exigencies or by the requirements of national security or public order. The construction of such a wall accordingly constitutes breaches by Israel of various of its obligations

under the applicable international humanitarian law and human rights instruments.

*

138. The Court has thus concluded that the construction of the wall constitutes action not in conformity with various international legal obligations incumbent upon Israel. However, Annex I to the report of the Secretary-General states that, according to Israel: "the construction of the Barrier is consistent with Article 51 of the Charter of the United Nations, its inherent right to self-defence and Security Council resolutions 1368 (2001) and 1373 (2001)". More specifically, Israel's Permanent Representative to the United Nations asserted in the General Assembly on 20 October 2003 that "the fence is a measure wholly consistent with the right of States to self-defence enshrined in Article 51 of the Charter"; the Security Council resolutions referred to, he continued, "have clearly recognized the right of States to use force in self-defence against terrorist attacks", and therefore surely recognize the right to use non-forcible measures to that end (A/ES-10/PV.21, p. 6).

139. Under the terms of Article 51 of the Charter of the United Nations:

> "Nothing in the present Charter shall impair the inherent right of individual or collective self-defence if an armed attack occurs against a Member of the United Nations, until the Security Council has taken measures necessary to maintain international peace and security."

Article 51 of the Charter thus recognizes the existence of an inherent right of self-defence in the case of armed attack by one State against another State. However, Israel does not claim that the attacks against it are imputable to a foreign State.

The Court also notes that Israel exercises control in the Occupied Palestinian Territory and that, as Israel itself states, the threat which it regards as justifying the construction of the wall originates within, and not outside, that territory. The situation is thus different from that contemplated by Security Council resolutions 1368 (2001) and 1373 (2001), and therefore Israel could not in any event invoke those resolutions in support of its claim to be exercising a right of self-defence.

Consequently, the Court concludes that Article 51 of the Charter has no relevance in this case.

140. The Court has, however, considered whether Israel could rely on a state of necessity which would preclude the wrongfulness of the construction of the wall. In this regard the Court is bound to note that some of the conventions at issue in the present instance include qualifying clauses of the rights guaranteed or provisions for derogation (see paragraphs 135 and 136 above). Since those treaties already address considerations of this kind within their own provisions, it might be asked whether a state of necessity as recognized in customary international law could be invoked with regard

to those treaties as a ground for precluding the wrongfulness of the measures or decisions being challenged. However, the Court will not need to consider that question. As the Court observed in the case concerning the *Gabčíkovo-Nagymaros Project (Hungary/Slovakia)*, "the state of necessity is a ground recognized by customary international law" that "can only be accepted on an exceptional basis"; it "can only be invoked under certain strictly defined conditions which must be cumulatively satisfied; and the State concerned is not the sole judge of whether those conditions have been met" *(I.C.J. Reports 1997*, p. 40, para. 51). One of those conditions was stated by the Court in terms used by the International Law Commission, in a text which in its present form requires that the act being challenged be "the only way for the State to safeguard an essential interest against a grave and imminent peril" (Article 25 of the International Law Commission's Articles on Responsibility of States for Internationally Wrongful Acts; see also former Article 33 of the Draft Articles on the International Responsibility of States, with slightly different wording in the English text). In the light of the material before it, the Court is not convinced that the construction of the wall along the route chosen was the only means to safeguard the interests of Israel against the peril which it has invoked as justification for that construction.

141. The fact remains that Israel has to face numerous indiscriminate and deadly acts of violence against its civilian population. It has the right, and indeed the duty, to respond in order to protect the life of its citizens. The measures taken are bound nonetheless to remain in conformity with applicable international law.

142. In conclusion, the Court considers that Israel cannot rely on a right of self-defence or on a state of necessity in order to preclude the wrongfulness of the construction of the wall resulting from the considerations mentioned in paragraphs 122 and 137 above. The Court accordingly finds that the construction of the wall, and its associated régime, are contrary to international law.

* * *

143. The Court having concluded that, by the construction of the wall in the Occupied Palestinian Territory, including in and around East Jerusalem, and by adopting its associated régime, Israel has violated various international obligations incumbent upon it (see paragraphs 114–137 above), it must now, in order to reply to the question posed by the General Assembly, examine the consequences of those violations.

* *

144. In their written and oral observations, many participants in the proceedings before the Court contended that Israel's action in illegally constructing this wall has legal consequences not only for Israel itself, but also for other States and for the United Nations; in its Written Statement, Israel,

for its part, presented no arguments regarding the possible legal consequences of the construction of the wall.

145. As regards the legal consequences for Israel, it was contended that Israel has, first, a legal obligation to bring the illegal situation to an end by ceasing forthwith the construction of the wall in the Occupied Palestinian Territory, and to give appropriate assurances and guarantees of non-repetition.

It was argued that, secondly, Israel is under a legal obligation to make reparation for the damage arising from its unlawful conduct. It was submitted that such reparation should first of all take the form of restitution, namely demolition of those portions of the wall constructed in the Occupied Palestinian Territory and annulment of the legal acts associated with its construction and the restoration of property requisitioned or expropriated for that purpose; reparation should also include appropriate compensation for individuals whose homes or agricultural holdings have been destroyed.

It was further contended that Israel is under a continuing duty to comply with all of the international obligations violated by it as a result of the construction of the wall in the Occupied Palestinian Territory and of the associated régime. It was also argued that, under the terms of the Fourth Geneva Convention, Israel is under an obligation to search for and bring before its courts persons alleged to have committed, or to have ordered to be committed, grave breaches of international humanitarian law flowing from the planning, construction and use of the wall.

146. As regards the legal consequences for States other than Israel, it was contended before the Court that all States are under an obligation not to recognize the illegal situation arising from the construction of the wall, not to render aid or assistance in maintaining that situation and to co-operate with a view to putting an end to the alleged violations and to ensuring that reparation will be made therefor.

Certain participants in the proceedings further contended that the States parties to the Fourth Geneva Convention are obliged to take measures to ensure compliance with the Convention and that, inasmuch as the construction and maintenance of the wall in the Occupied Palestinian Territory constitutes grave breaches of that Convention, the States parties to that Convention are under an obligation to prosecute or extradite the authors of such breaches. It was further observed that

> "the United Nations Security Council should consider flagrant and systematic violation of international law norm[s] and principles by Israel, particularly . . . international humanitarian law, and take all necessary measures to put an end [to] these violations",

and that the Security Council and the General Assembly must take due account of the advisory opinion to be given by the Court.

* *

147. Since the Court has concluded that the construction of the wall in the Occupied Palestinian Territory, including in and around East Jerusalem, and its associated régime, are contrary to various of Israel's international obligations, it follows that the responsibility of that State is engaged under international law.

148. The Court will now examine the legal consequences resulting from the violations of international law by Israel by distinguishing between, on the one hand, those arising for Israel and, on the other, those arising for other States and, where appropriate, for the United Nations. The Court will begin by examining the legal consequences of those violations for Israel.

*

149. The Court notes that Israel is first obliged to comply with the international obligations it has breached by the construction of the wall in the Occupied Palestinian Territory (see paragraphs 114–137 above). Consequently, Israel is bound to comply with its obligation to respect the right of the Palestinian people to self-determination and its obligations under international humanitarian law and international human rights law. Furthermore, it must ensure freedom of access to the Holy Places that came under its control following the 1967 War (see paragraph 129 above).

150. The Court observes that Israel also has an obligation to put an end to the violation of its international obligations flowing from the construction of the wall in the Occupied Palestinian Territory. The obligation of a State responsible for an internationally wrongful act to put an end to that act is well established in general international law, and the Court has on a number of occasions confirmed the existence of that obligation *(Military and Paramilitary Activities in and against Nicaragua (Nicaragua* v. *United States of America), Merits, Judgment, I.C.J. Reports 1986*, p. 149; *United States Diplomatic and Consular Staff in Tehran, Judgment, I.C.J. Reports 1980*, p. 44, para. 95; *Hay a de la Torre, Judgment, I.C.J. Reports 1951*, p. 82).

151. Israel accordingly has the obligation to cease forthwith the works of construction of the wall being built by it in the Occupied Palestinian Territory, including in and around East Jerusalem. Moreover, in view of the Court's finding (see paragraph 143 above) that Israel's violations of its international obligations stem from the construction of the wall and from its associated régime, cessation of those violations entails the dismantling forthwith of those parts of that structure situated within the Occupied Palestinian Territory, including in and around East Jerusalem. All legislative and regulatory acts adopted with a view to its construction, and to the establishment of its associated régime, must forthwith be repealed or rendered ineffective, except in so far as such acts, by providing for compensation or other forms of reparation for the Palestinian population, may continue to be relevant for compliance by Israel with the obligations referred to in paragraph 153 below.

152. Moreover, given that the construction of the wall in the Occupied Palestinian Territory has, *inter alia*, entailed the requisition and destruction of homes, businesses and agricultural holdings, the Court finds further that Israel has the obligation to make reparation for the damage caused to all the natural or legal persons concerned. The Court would recall that the essential forms of reparation in customary law were laid down by the Permanent Court of International Justice in the following terms:

> "The essential principle contained in the actual notion of an illegal act—a principle which seems to be established by international practice and in particular by the decisions of arbitral tribunals—is that reparation must, as far as possible, wipe out all the consequences of the illegal act and reestablish the situation which would, in all probability, have existed if that act had not been committed. Restitution in kind, or, if this is not possible, payment of a sum corresponding to the value which a restitution in kind would bear; the award, if need be, of damages for loss sustained which would not be covered by restitution in kind or payment in place of it—such are the principles which should serve to determine the amount of compensation due for an act contrary to international law." (*Factory at Chorzow, Merits, Judgment No. 13, 1928, P.C.I.J., Series A, No. 17*, p. 47.)

153. Israel is accordingly under an obligation to return the land, orchards, olive groves and other immovable property seized from any natural or legal person for purposes of construction of the wall in the Occupied Palestinian Territory. In the event that such restitution should prove to be materially impossible, Israel has an obligation to compensate the persons in question for the damage suffered. The Court considers that Israel also has an obligation to compensate, in accordance with the applicable rules of international law, all natural or legal persons having suffered any form of material damage as a result of the wall's construction.

*

154. The Court will now consider the legal consequences of the internationally wrongful acts flowing from Israel's construction of the wall as regards other States.

155. The Court would observe that the obligations violated by Israel include certain obligations *erga omnes*. As the Court indicated in the *Barcelona Traction* case, such obligations are by their very nature "the concern of all States" and, "In view of the importance of the rights involved, all States can be held to have a legal interest in their protection" (*Barcelona Traction, Light and Power Company, Limited, Second Phase, Judgment, I.C.J. Reports 1970*, p. 32, para. 33). The obligations *erga omnes* violated by Israel are the obligation to respect the right of the Palestinian people to self-determination, and certain of its obligations under international humanitarian law.

156. As regards the first of these, the Court has already observed (paragraph 88 above) that in the *East Timor* case, it described as "irreproachable"

the assertion that "the right of peoples to self-determination, as it evolved from the Charter and from United Nations practice, has an *erga omnes* character" *(I.C.J. Reports 1995*, p. 102, para. 29). The Court would also recall that under the terms of General Assembly resolution 2625 (XXV), already mentioned above (see paragraph 88),

> "Every State has the duty to promote, through joint and separate action, realization of the principle of equal rights and self-determination of peoples, in accordance with the provisions of the Charter, and to render assistance to the United Nations in carrying out the responsibilities entrusted to it by the Charter regarding the implementation of the principle . . ."

157. With regard to international humanitarian law, the Court recalls that in its Advisory Opinion on the *Legality of the Threat or Use of Nuclear Weapons* it stated that "a great many rules of humanitarian law applicable in armed conflict are so fundamental to the respect of the human person and 'elementary considerations of humanity' . . .", that they are "to be observed by all States whether or not they have ratified the conventions that contain them, because they constitute intransgressible principles of international customary law" *(I.C.J. Reports 1996 (I)*, p. 257, para. 79). In the Court's view, these rules incorporate obligations which are essentially of an *erga omnes* character.

158. The Court would also emphasize that Article 1 of the Fourth Geneva Convention, a provision common to the four Geneva Conventions, provides that "The High Contracting Parties undertake to respect and to ensure respect for the present Convention in all circumstances." It follows from that provision that every State party to that Convention, whether or not it is a party to a specific conflict, is under an obligation to ensure that the requirements of the instruments in question are complied with.

159. Given the character and the importance of the rights and obligations involved, the Court is of the view that all States are under an obligation not to recognize the illegal situation resulting from the construction of the wall in the Occupied Palestinian Territory, including in and around East Jerusalem. They are also under an obligation not to render aid or assistance in maintaining the situation created by such construction. It is also for all States, while respecting the United Nations Charter and international law, to see to it that any impediment, resulting from the construction of the wall, to the exercise by the Palestinian people of its right to self-determination is brought to an end. In addition, all the States parties to the Geneva Convention relative to the Protection of Civilian Persons in Time of V/ar of 12 August 1949 are under an obligation, while respecting the United Nations Charter and international law, to ensure compliance by Israel with international humanitarian law as embodied in that Convention.

160. Finally, the Court is of the view that the United Nations, and especially the General Assembly and the Security Council, should consider what further

action is required to bring to an end the illegal situation resulting from the construction of the wall and the associated régime, taking due account of the present Advisory Opinion.

* * *

161. The Court, being concerned to lend its support to the purposes and principles laid down in the United Nations Charter, in particular the maintenance of international peace and security and the peaceful settlement of disputes, would emphasize the urgent necessity for the United Nations as a whole to redouble its efforts to bring the Israeli-Palestinian conflict, which continues to pose a threat to international peace and security, to a speedy conclusion, thereby establishing a just and lasting peace in the region.

162. The Court has reached the conclusion that the construction of the wall by Israel in the Occupied Palestinian Territory is contrary to international law and has stated the legal consequences that are to be drawn from that illegality. The Court considers itself bound to add that this construction must be placed in a more general context. Since 1947, the year when General Assembly resolution 181 (II) was adopted and the Mandate for Palestine was terminated, there has been a succession of armed conflicts, acts of indiscriminate violence and repressive measures on the former mandated territory. The Court would emphasize that both Israel and Palestine are under an obligation scrupulously to observe the rules of international humanitarian law, one of the paramount purposes of which is to protect civilian life. Illegal actions and unilateral decisions have been taken on all sides, whereas, in the Court's view, this tragic situation can be brought to an end only through implementation in good faith of all relevant Security Council resolutions, in particular resolutions 242 (1967) and 338 (1973). The "Roadmap" approved by Security Council resolution 1515 (2003) represents the most recent of efforts to initiate negotiations to this end. The Court considers that it has a duty to draw the attention of the General Assembly, to which the present Opinion is addressed, to the need for these efforts to be encouraged with a view to achieving as soon as possible, on the basis of international law, a negotiated solution to the outstanding problems and the establishment of a Palestinian State, existing side by side with Israel and its other neighbours, with peace and security for all in the region.

* * *

163. For these reasons,

The Court,

(1) Unanimously,

Finds that it has jurisdiction to give the advisory opinion requested;

(2) By fourteen votes to one,

Decides to comply with the request for an advisory opinion;

IN FAVOUR: *President* Shi; *Vice-President* Ranjeva; *Judges* Guillaume, Koroma, Vereshchetin, Higgins, Parra-Aranguren, Kooijmans, Rezek, Al-Khasawneh, Elaraby, Owada, Simma, Tomka;

AGAINST: *Judge* Buergenthal;

(3) *Replies* in the following manner to the question put by the General Assembly:

A. By fourteen votes to one,

The construction of the wall being built by Israel, the occupying Power, in the Occupied Palestinian Territory, including in and around East Jerusalem, and its associated régime, are contrary to international law;

IN FAVOUR: *President* Shi; *Vice-President* Ranjeva; *Judges* Guillaume, Koroma, Vereshchetin, Higgins, Parra-Aranguren, Kooijmans, Rezek, Al-Khasawneh, Elaraby, Owada, Simma, Tomka;

AGAINST: *Judge* Buergenthal;

B. By fourteen votes to one,

Israel is under an obligation to terminate its breaches of international law; it is under an obligation to cease forthwith the works of construction of the wall being built in the Occupied Palestinian Territory, including in and around East Jerusalem, to dismantle forthwith the structure therein situated, and to repeal or render ineffective forthwith all legislative and regulatory acts relating thereto, in accordance with paragraph 151 of this Opinion;

IN FAVOUR: *President* Shi; *Vice-President* Ranjeva; *Judges* Guillaume, Koroma, Vereshchetin, Higgins, Parra-Aranguren, Kooijmans, Rezek, Al-Khasawneh, Elaraby, Owada. Simma, Tomka;

AGAINST: *Judge* Buergenthal;

C. By fourteen votes to one,

Israel is under an obligation to make reparation for all damage caused by the construction of the wall in the Occupied Palestinian Territory, including in and around East Jerusalem;

IN FAVOUR: *President* Shi; *Vice-President* Ranjeva; *Judges* Guillaume, Koroma, Vereshchetin, Higgins, Parra-Aranguren, Kooijmans, Rezek, Al-Khasawneh, Elaraby, Owada, Simma, Tomka;

AGAINST: *Judge* Buergenthal;

D. By thirteen votes to two,

All States are under an obligation not to recognize the illegal situation resulting from the construction of the wall and not to render aid or assistance in maintaining the situation created by such construction; all States parties to the Fourth Geneva Convention relative to the Protection of Civilian Persons in Time of War of 12 August 1949 have in addition the obligation, while respecting the United Nations Charter and international law, to ensure compliance by Israel with international humanitarian law as embodied in that Convention;

IN FAVOUR: *President* Shi; *Vice-President* Ranjeva; *Judges* Guillaume, Koroma, Vereshchetin, Higgins, Parra-Aranguren, Rezek, Al-Khasawneh, Elaraby, Owada, Simma, Tomka;

AGAINST: *Judges* Kooijmans, Buergenthal;

E. By fourteen votes to one,

The United Nations, and especially the General Assembly and the Security Council, should consider what further action is required to bring to an end the illegal situation resulting from the construction of the wall and the associated régime, taking due account of the present Advisory Opinion.

IN FAVOUR: *President* Shi; *Vice-President* Ranjeva; *Judges* Guillaume. Koroma, Vereshchetin, Higgins, Parra-Aranguren, Kooijmans, Rezek, Al-Khasawneh, Elaraby, Owada, Simma, Tomka;

AGAINST: *Judge* Buergenthal.

Done in French and in English, the French text being authoritative, at the Peace Palace, The Hague, this ninth day of July, two thousand and four, in two copies, one of which will be placed in the archives of the Court and the other transmitted to the Secretary-General of the United Nations.

(Signed) Shi Jiuyong,
President.

(Signed) Philippe COUVREUR,
Registrar.

Judges Koroma, Higgins, Kooijmans and Al-Khasawneh append separate opinions to the Advisory Opinion of the Court; Judge BUER-GENTHAL appends a declaration to the Advisory Opinion of the Court; Judges Elaraby and Owada append separate opinions to the Advisory Opinion of the Court.

(Initialled) J.Y.S.
(Initialled) Ph.C.

DOCUMENT NO. 15

ESTABLISHMENT OF THE UNITED NATIONS REGISTER OF DAMAGE CAUSED BY THE CONSTRUCTION OF THE WALL IN THE OCCUPIED PALESTINIAN TERRITORY

General Assembly Resolution A/RES/ES-10/17

January 24, 2007

The General Assembly,

Guided by the principles enshrined in the Charter of the United Nations and the rules and principles of international law, including international humanitarian law and human rights law,

Reaffirming the permanent responsibility of the United Nations towards the question of Palestine until it is resolved in all its aspects in a satisfactory manner on the basis of international legitimacy,

Recalling the relevant resolutions of the Security Council,

Recalling also its relevant resolutions, including the resolutions of its tenth emergency special session on illegal Israeli actions in Occupied East Jerusalem and the rest of the Occupied Palestinian Territory,

Recalling further the advisory opinion rendered on 9 July 2004 by the International Court of Justice on the *Legal Consequences of the Construction of a Wall in the Occupied Palestinian Territory,*[1] and recalling in particular the Court's reply to the question put forth by the General Assembly in resolution ES-10/14 of 8 December 2003, as set forth in the *dispositif* of the advisory opinion,[2]

Recalling in this regard the Court's conclusion that, inter alia, "Israel is under an obligation to make reparation for all damage caused by the construction

[1] See A/ES-10/273 and Corr.1.
[2] Ibid., para. 163.

of the wall in the Occupied Palestinian Territory, including in and around East Jerusalem",

Reaffirming its resolution ES-10/15 of 20 July 2004 entitled "Advisory opinion of the International Court of Justice on the legal consequences of the construction of a wall in the Occupied Palestinian Territory, including in and around East Jerusalem",

Recalling the request made in resolution ES-10/15 for the Secretary-General to establish a register of damage caused to all natural or legal persons concerned in connection with paragraphs 152 and 153 of the advisory opinion,

Noting in this connection the Court's conclusion whereby, inter alia:

> Israel is accordingly under an obligation to return the land, orchards, olive groves and other immovable property seized from any natural or legal person for purposes of construction of the wall in the Occupied Palestinian Territory. In the event that such restitution should prove to be materially impossible, Israel has an obligation to compensate the persons in question for the damage suffered. The Court considers that Israel also has an obligation to compensate, in accordance with the applicable rules of international law, all natural or legal persons having suffered any form of material damage as a result of the wall's construction,[3]

Deploring the continuing construction, contrary to international law, by Israel, the occupying Power, of the wall in the Occupied Palestinian Territory, including in and around East Jerusalem, against the conclusions of the International Court of Justice in its advisory opinion of 9 July 2004 and resolution ES-10/15 and in breach of the applicable rules and principles of international law,

Recognizing the necessity of accurately documenting the damage caused by the construction of the wall for the purpose of fulfilling the obligation to make the above-mentioned reparations, including restitution and compensation, in accordance with the rules and principles of international law, and noting that the act of registration of damage, as such, does not entail, at this stage, an evaluation or assessment of the loss or damage caused by the construction of the wall,

Taking note with appreciation of the report of the Secretary-General of 17 October 2006 pursuant to resolution ES-10/15,[4]

1. *Reaffirms* its resolution ES-10/15 entitled "Advisory opinion of the International Court of Justice on the legal consequences of the construction of a wall in the Occupied Palestinian Territory, including in and around East Jerusalem", and reiterates the demands made therein, inter alia, the

[3] Ibid., para. 153.
[4] A/ES-10/361.

demand that Israel, the occupying Power, comply with its legal obligations as mentioned in the advisory opinion;

2. *Takes note with appreciation* of the report of the Secretary-General submitted pursuant to resolution ES-10/15;[4]

3. *Establishes* the United Nations Register of Damage Caused by the Construction of the Wall in the Occupied Palestinian Territory:

(a) To serve as a record, in documentary form, of the damage caused to all natural and legal persons concerned as a result of the construction of the wall by Israel, the occupying Power, in the Occupied Palestinian Territory, including in and around East Jerusalem;

(b) To be referred to henceforth in brief as the "Register of Damage";

4. *Decides* to set up an office of the Register of Damage, which will be:

(a) Responsible for the establishment and comprehensive maintenance of the Register of Damage;

(b) Composed of a three-member Board and a small secretariat, headed by an Executive Director and consisting of substantive, administrative and technical support staff;

(c) A subsidiary organ of the General Assembly operating under the administrative authority of the Secretary-General;

(d) Established at the site of the United Nations Office at Vienna;

5. *Requests* the Secretary-General to appoint the three-member Board of the Office of the Register of Damage, according to the selection criteria in the above-mentioned report, at the earliest practicable date;

6. *Decides* that the responsibilities assumed by the Board of the Office of the Register of Damage shall be as follows:

(a) The Board shall have overall responsibility for the establishment and maintenance of the Register of Damage;

(b) The Board shall establish the rules and regulations governing the work of the Office of the Register of Damage;

(c) The Board shall determine the eligibility criteria, bearing in mind varying circumstances with regard to the title and residency status of the claimants, for the inclusion of damages and losses caused in the Register of Damage with an established causal link to the construction of the wall;

(d) The Board shall, guided by the relevant findings of the advisory opinion, general principles of international law and principles of due process of law, also determine the criteria of damage and the procedure for the collection and registration of damage claims;

(e) The Board, on the recommendation of the Executive Director, shall have the ultimate authority in determining the inclusion of damage claims in the Register of Damage;

(f) The Board shall meet at least four times each year at the Office of the Register of Damage to determine which claims should be included in the Register of Damage, based on the established objective criteria defined in the rules and regulations;

(g) The Board shall engage, periodically and as deemed necessary, the expertise of technical specialists in relevant fields, inter alia, agriculture, land law, topography and assessment and compensation, to assist it in establishing and maintaining the Register of Damage;

(h) The Board shall render progress reports periodically to the Secretary-General for transmission to the General Assembly, including, as appropriate, possible further steps in connection with paragraphs 152 and 153 of the advisory opinion;

7. *Requests* the Secretary-General to appoint, at the earliest practicable date, the Executive Director of the Office of the Register of Damage, who shall:

(a) Have responsibility for overseeing and administrating the work of the secretariat of the Office of the Register of Damage;

(b) Be responsible for forwarding all damage claims to the Board for its approval for inclusion in the Register of Damage and serve in an advisory capacity to the Board in this regard;

8. *Decides* that the secretariat of the Office of the Register of Damage shall provide substantive, technical and administrative support for the establishment and maintenance of the Register of Damage by undertaking, inter alia, the following functions:

(a) Designing the format of the damage claims;

(b) Administering a public awareness programme to inform the Palestinian public about the possibility of and the requirements for filing a damage claim for registration, including an extensive community outreach programme to explain the purpose of the Register of Damage and provide guidance on how to fill out and submit the claim forms;

(c) Receiving and processing all damage claims and establishing the credibility of the causal link of those claims to the construction of the wall for registration in the Register of Damage;

(d) Submitting all processed damage claims through the Executive Director to the Board for inclusion in the Register of Damage;

(e) Aggregating and maintaining the records of damage claims approved by the Board, including both hard copies of the claims and their electronic version, which shall be maintained at the Office of the Register of Damage;

(f) Providing legal advice regarding the operations of the Office of the Register of Damage and the submitted claims;

9. *Resolves* that the Register of Damage shall remain open for registration for the duration of existence of the wall in the Occupied Palestinian Territory, including in and around East Jerusalem;

10. *Resolves also* that the Office of the Register of Damage shall remain active for the duration of the process of registration and shall carry out the specific functions and directives ascribed to it by the Secretary-General in his report, as set out in the present resolution, and such additional functions as request-ed by the General Assembly upon recommendation by the Secretary-General;

11. *Calls for* the establishment and operation of the Office of the Register of Damage and the establishment of the Register of Damage itself within six months of the adoption of the present resolution and the immediate undertaking thereafter of the process of registration of damage claims;

12. *Instructs* the Office of the Register of Damage, immediately upon its establishment, to seek the cooperation of the concerned Governments and authorities so as to facilitate its work in connection with the collection, submission and processing of damage claims in the Occupied Palestinian Territory, including East Jerusalem;

13. *Calls upon* the Government of Israel and the Palestinian Authority and relevant Palestinian institutions to cooperate with the Office of the Register of Damage;

14. *Calls upon* the Secretary-General to instruct the United Nations agencies and offices present on the ground in the Occupied Palestinian Territory to lend their support and expertise to the Office of the Register of Damage, upon its request, so as to facilitate its work;

15. *Requests* the Secretary-General to provide the necessary staff and facilities and to make appropriate arrangements to provide the necessary funds required to carry out the terms of the present resolution;

16. *Also requests* the Secretary-General to report to the General Assembly within six months on the progress made with regard to the establishment

and operation of the Office of the Register of Damage and the establishment of the Register of Damage;

17. *Decides* to adjourn the tenth emergency special session temporarily and to authorize the President of the General Assembly at its most recent session to resume the meeting of the special session upon request from Member States.

31st plenary meeting
15 December 2006

D. HAMAS-RELATED CASES IN U.S. COURTS

DOCUMENT NO. 16

UNITED STATES OF AMERICA
v.
MOUSA MOHAMMED ABU MARZOOK

N.D. III. 2003

COURT OPINION

Count One

The SPECIAL AUGUST 2003-2 GRAND JURY charges:

1. At times material to this indictment:

The Islamic Resistance Movement ("Hamas") ("Harakat al Muqawama al Islamiyya")

A. From at least as early as 1988 and up until the date of the filing of this indictment, there existed an international organization known as *Harakat al Muqawama al Islamiyya,* which translates as the Islamic Resistance Movement and is commonly referred to as "Hamas." Hamas has, among its publicly stated purposes, the establishment of a Palestinian/Islamic state in the lands that comprise the State of Israel ("Israel") and the West Bank and Gaza Strip, including Jerusalem.

B. Hamas has pursued the objective of a Palestinian/Islamic state by fostering support among Palestinians through community building activities in the West Bank and Gaza Strip. The West Bank and Gaza Strip are disputed territories often referred to as the Occupied Territories. While Hamas has undertaken social welfare activities, in order to obtain its objective it has also engaged in numerous terrorist attacks aimed at Israeli military personnel, police officers and civilians. These terrorist activities, for which Hamas has repeatedly and publicly claimed credit, have as their broadly represented purpose the undermining of the Israeli-Palestinian peace process, and, more generally, forcing the State and citizens of Israel to cede physical and political control over the lands comprising Israel, the West

Bank, and the Gaza Strip, and replacing the Israeli political authority over these lands with an Islamic government. In or about 1988, Hamas published a charter calling for such violent terrorist attacks. According to the Hamas Charter, the means of confronting the "usurpation of Palestine by the Jews" is proclaimed to be *"jihad"* (holy war). Hamas defines *jihad* as violent activities with such violent activities being carried out by Hamas's so-called military wing, commonly known as the Izz Al-Din Al-Qassam Brigades ("Al-Qassam Brigades").

C. Hamas has maintained offices throughout the world, including headquarters in Damascus, Syria. In addition, Hamas has maintained a worldwide network of members who donate money to support the goals of Hamas. Much of the fundraising was done by and through individuals as well as various non-profit organizations that collect money.

D. Hamas has included members and affiliated organizations situated throughout the United States. Hamas's members and affiliated organizations in the United States have served two primary purposes: (1) recruitment of members and donors to Hamas; and (2) financing directly and indirectly the activities of Hamas including the terrorist activities carried out by the Al-Qassam Brigades.

E. Hamas has been comprised of various committees or bureaus, including among others, a political committee, a military committee, and a social/charitable committee, all of which worked together to achieve the goals of Hamas.

F. Hamas placed members of its leadership in countries in the Middle East and elsewhere, with these leaders being referred to by members of Hamas as the "outside," while Hamas also maintained leadership members, cells and committees inside the West Bank and Gaza Strip, with these elements being referred to by members of Hamas as the "inside."

G. On January 24, 1995, pursuant to Executive Order 12947, the Department of Treasury, Office of Foreign Assets Control, designated Hamas as a Specially Designated Terrorist organization. This designation makes it illegal for any United States person or entity to engage in any unlicensed transactions or dealings involving the property or interests of Hamas. Hamas's designation as a Specially Designated Terrorist organization has remained in place since January 24, 1995.

H. On October 8, 1997, the Secretary of State, pursuant to the laws of the United States, designated Hamas as a "foreign terrorist organization." As a result of this designation, it became illegal for any person within the United States or subject to its jurisdiction to provide material support or resources to Hamas. Because "foreign terrorist organization" designations lapse every two years unless renewed, Hamas has been redesignated three times as a "foreign terrorist organization," most recently on October 2, 2003.

Defendants

I. Defendant MOUSA MOHAMMED ABU MARZOOK, a/k/a "Abu Omar," "Tareq," and "Abu Rizq," is a member of Hamas. ABU MARZOOK formerly held the position of Chief of the Hamas Political Bureau. He presently lives in Damascus, Syria, and is the Deputy Chief of the Hamas Political Bureau. The Political Bureau functioned as the highest ranking leadership body in the Hamas organization, setting policies and guidelines regarding Hamas's activities, including directing and coordinating terrorist acts by Hamas and the Al-Qassam Brigades. From in or about 1988 until in or about February 1993, while living in the United States, ABU MARZOOK coordinated and financed the activities of Hamas within the United States and elsewhere, first from Louisiana and then from Northern Virginia. During that period, ABU MARZOOK traveled throughout the United States to meet with other American-based Hamas members, as well as foreign-based Hamas members traveling to the United States for organizational purposes. ABU MARZOOK additionally maintained constant phone contact with Hamas membership and leadership in the United States and abroad. During this time period, ABU MARZOOK also maintained and shared numerous bank accounts through which substantial sums of money were transferred from bank accounts located outside the United States to other accounts within the United States, including bank accounts controlled by or associated with defendant MUHAMMAD HAMID KHALIL SALAH, for ultimate disbursal to accounts and individuals outside the United States for use in furtherance of Hamas.

J. MUHAMMAD HAMID KHALIL SALAH, a/k/a "Muhammad Abd Al-'Hamid Salah," and "Abu Ahmad," was a member of Hamas who lived in or around Chicago. Between in or about 1989 and in or about January 1993, SALAH traveled throughout the United States and to London, England, Israel and the West Bank and Gaza Strip on behalf of Hamas, meeting with Hamas representatives as well as leaders and members of the Al-Qassam Brigades, recruiting and training new members of Hamas in the United States, and disbursing money from the United States to directly support Hamas members and activities of Hamas and the Al-Qassam Brigades. In approximately January 1993, SALAH, while in Israel to assist Hamas, was arrested and, thereafter, incarcerated until approximately November 1997. Nonetheless, SALAH carried on his membership in Hamas and, subsequent to his return to the United States, continued his activities in support of Hamas, including directing and financing travel to Israel and the West Bank in or about October 1999 of a Chicago-based associate.

K. ABDELHALEEM HASAN ABDELRAZIQ ASHQAR, a/k/a "Abu Hasan," "Abu Ali Hasan," and "Samir," initially entered the United States as a graduate student at the University of Mississippi in Oxford,

Mississippi, and currently resides in the Washington, D.C. area. From at least as early as 1989, ASHQAR functioned as a conduit of money for Hamas members both in the United States and abroad. In this role, ASHQAR opened various bank accounts in and around Oxford, Mississippi which he utilized as a clearinghouse for Hamas funds from defendant ABU MARZOOK as well as other Hamas members and organizations in the United States and abroad. ASHQAR furthered these financial activities both through the use of his personal bank accounts as well as through his establishment of the Al-Aqsa Educational Fund, Inc. ASHQAR also served as a communications conduit for Hamas both through his participation in and linking of telephone calls between various Hamas members in the United States and abroad, as well as his storing and disseminating numerous Hamas-related documents that concerned both the public activities of Hamas as well as the internal operation of Hamas. In this role, ASHQAR had contact with numerous co-conspirators.

Hamas Co-Conspirators

L. The activities of the defendants were carried out and supported through the assistance of other Hamas members located in the United States and abroad who provided communications, logistical, and financial support in furtherance of Hamas. At times material to this indictment, these members included but were not limited to:

i. Khalid Mish'al, a/k/a "Khalid Abdulqader," and "Abu Walid;" Abdel Aziz Al-Rantisi, a/k/a "Abu Mohammad," "Abu Ahmad," and "Abu Ayas;" and Imad Al-Alami, a/k/a "Abu Hamman," were all high-ranking members and officers of Hamas who had significant input into the direction and activities of Hamas. Defendant ASHQAR had contact with various of these individuals to discuss Hamas issues and to facilitate these individuals' communication with individuals in the West Bank and Gaza Strip.

ii. Mohammed Qassem Sawalha, a/k/a "Muhammad Khadhem Sawalha," "Abu Obeida," "Abu Ubada," "Abu Ubaydah," and "Abu Ubeida," was initially a Hamas leader in the West Bank until he relocated to London, England in the early 1990s. Defendants SALAH and Co-conspirator A met with Sawalha in London while en route from the United States to Israel in 1992 and 1993. During these meetings, defendant SALAH and Co-conspirator A received instructions from Sawalha regarding particular Hamas-related activities they were to carry out while in Israel, the West Bank, and the Gaza Strip.

iii. Adel Ahmed Awadallah, a/k/a "Aadil Awadallah" and "The Engineer 3," was a high-ranking Hamas military leader who was responsible for facilitating several deadly terrorist attacks carried out in

Israel. During trips to the Middle East in 1992 and 1993, defendant SALAH met with Awadallah to discuss Hamas issues and to provide Awadallah funds to be used in furtherance of Hamas activities. On approximately September 10, 1998, Awadallah was killed during a shootout with Israeli defense forces in the town of Hebron in the West Bank.

iv. Salah Al-Arouri, a/k/a "Salih Suleiman," and "Salih Dar Sulaiman," was a high-ranking Hamas military leader dating back to his role as a Hamas student cell leader at Hebron University in the early 1990s. In his capacity as a Hamas military leader, Al-Arouri met with and received from defendant SALAH tens of thousands of dollars for Hamas-related activities. Al-Arouri used the funds provided by defendant SALAH for the purchase of weapons that were to be used in terrorist attacks.

v. Sheik Jamil Hamami, a/k/a "Jamil Hamimi" and "Abu Hamza," was a Hamas leader active in the West Bank who, on occasion, traveled to the United States to conduct Hamas business and raise funds for Hamas. In particular, in March 1994, Hamami met with defendant ASHQAR in Mississippi to discuss a variety of issues related to Hamas.

vi. Hassan Salameh was a Hamas member who initially worked under the command of Hamas bomb builder and co-conspirator Yihye Ayash, a/k/a "The Engineer," and "The Engineer 1," until Ayash's death, at which time Ayash's position in Hamas was filled by co-conspirator Adel Awadallah. Salameh, with the assistance of other Hamas co-conspirators, was responsible for a string of bus bombings in approximately February and March 1996 that killed numerous civilians. After his arrest, Salameh continued his work on behalf of Hamas by publicizing his actions carried out for Hamas and Hamas's goal of pursuing terrorist activities to force the State and citizens of Israel to cede physical and political control over the lands comprising Israel, the West Bank, and the Gaza Strip.

vii. Ismael Selim Elbarasse, a/k/a "Ismael Selim El-barasse," from at least as early as 1990, worked as an assistant to defendant ABU MARZOOK. Elbarasse maintained a joint bank account with defendant ABU MARZOOK that was used to transfer substantial sums of money to Hamas members, including defendant SALAH.

viii. Co-conspirator A was a member of Hamas who lived in or around Chicago. Beginning no later than in or about January 1993, Co-conspirator A traveled to London and to Israel and the West Bank on behalf of Hamas, meeting with Hamas representatives as well as leaders and members of the Al-Qassam Brigades in support of Hamas members and activities in the Middle East. In approximately May 1993, Co-conspirator

A was convicted in an Israeli military court of crimes related to his association with Hamas. Nonetheless, Co-conspirator A carried on his membership in Hamas. Subsequent to his return to the United States, Co-conspirator A briefed Hamas leadership in the United States regarding his mission with defendant SALAH, and received compensation for his involvement with Hamas.

ix. Co-conspirator B was a Hamas member who has lived in Louisiana. Coconspirator B traveled between the United States and West Bank on numerous occasions over the past 15 years using approximately 14 passports. During the early 1990s, Co-conspirator B relayed messages between defendant SALAH and high-ranking Hamas military leaders, including Adel Awadallah and Salah Al-Arouri. On one occasion, Co-conspirator B relayed a message and passport photographs from Adel Awadallah to defendant SALAH in order for defendant SALAH to obtain a false passport for Awadallah so that Awadallah could travel outside of the West Bank without detection by the Israeli government. In addition, in the early 1990s Co-conspirator B received approximately $140,000 in a wire transfer from overseas in relation to his Hamas activities.

x. Co-conspirator C was recruited by defendant SALAH during the early 1990s to become a member of Hamas. After his recruitment by defendant SALAH, defendant SALAH and other Hamas members trained Co-conspirator C in various Hamas methods. After his arrest by Israeli authorities in January 1993, defendant SALAH attempted to use consular officials from the American Embassy in Israel, unbeknownst to the consular officials, to pass messages to Co-conspirator C.

xi. Co-conspirator D was recruited by defendant SALAH during the early 1990s to become a member of Hamas. After his recruitment by defendant SALAH, defendant SALAH and other Hamas members trained Co-conspirator D in various Hamas methods. After his arrest by Israeli authorities in January 1993, defendant SALAH attempted to use consular officials from the American Embassy in Israel, unbeknownst to the consular officials, to pass messages to Co-conspirator D.

xii. Co-conspirator E, Co-conspirator F, Co-conspirator G, Co-conspirator H, and Co-conspirator I, among others, received transfers of funds from defendants ABU MARZOOK and ASHQAR and other co-conspirators and disbursed these funds, frequently in smaller amounts, to foreign accounts and individuals, including defendant SALAH, for ultimate disbursal to Hamas members in the West Bank and Gaza Strip.

xiii. Co-conspirator J was a Hamas member in the West Bank with whom defendant SALAH met in approximately January 1993 and who further traveled to the United States and established bank accounts to hold Hamas funds from defendant ABU MARZOOK and co-conspirator Elbarasse to be utilized for Hamas purposes.

The Hamas Enterprise

2. At times material to this indictment, Hamas constituted an "enterprise" as that term is defined in Title 18, United States Code, Section 1961(4); that is, a group of individuals associated in fact, and which enterprise was engaged in, and the activities of which affected, interstate and foreign commerce. This enterprise is hereby referred to for purposes of this count as "Hamas" or the "enterprise." Hamas constituted an ongoing organization whose members functioned as a continuing unit for a common purpose of achieving the objectives of the enterprise. Defendants ABU MARZOOK, SALAH, and ASHQAR participated in the operation and management of the enterprise. The objectives of Hamas were the forcing of the State and citizens of Israel to cede physical and political control over the lands comprising Israel, the West Bank, and the Gaza Strip, and the replacement of the Israeli political authority over these lands with an Islamic government, through means that included the promotion and execution of acts of terrorism.

The Racketeering Conspiracy

3. Beginning no later than 1988 and continuing to the present, in Chicago, Bridgeview, and other locations in the Northern District of Illinois, Eastern Division, and elsewhere:

MOUSA MOHAMMED ABU MARZOOK,
a/k/a "Abu Omar,"
a/k/a "Tareq,"
a/k/a "Abu Rizq,"
MUHAMMAD HAMID KHALIL SALAH,
a/k/a "Muhammad Abd Al-'Hamid Salah,"
a/k/a "Abu Ahmad," and
ABDELHALEEM HASAN ABDELRAZIQ ASHQAR,
a/k/a "Abu Hasan,"
a/k/a "Abu Ali Hasan,"
a/k/a "Samir,"

defendants herein, along with Khalid Mish'al, Abdel Aziz Al-Rantisi, Imad Al-Alami, Mohammed Qassem Sawalha, Adel Ahmed Awadallah, Salah

Al-Arouri, Sheik Jamil Hamami, Yihye Ayash, Hassan Salameh, Ismael Selim Elbarasse, Co-conspirator A, Co-conspirator B, Co-conspirator C, Co-conspirator D, Co-conspirator E, Co-conspirator F, Co-conspirator G, Co-conspirator H, Co-conspirator I, Co-conspirator J, and others both known and unknown, being persons employed by and associated with an enterprise, namely Hamas, which engaged in and the activities of which affected interstate and foreign commerce, did conspire to violate Title 18, United States Code, Section 1962(c), that is, to conduct and participate, directly and indirectly, in the conduct of the affairs of the enterprise through a pattern of racketeering activity, that is, through multiple acts indictable under the following federal provisions or involving murder and chargeable under the following State laws, namely:

(a) 720 ILCS 5/8-2 and 720 ILCS 5/9-1 (first degree murder and conspiracy to commit first degree murder);

(b) 720 ILCS 5/8-1.1 (solicitation of first degree murder);

(c) 18 U.S.C. § 956(a)(1) (conspiracy to kill, kidnap, maim or injure persons in a foreign country);

(d) 18 U.S.C. § 1956 (money laundering and attempt and conspiracy to do so);

(e) 18 U.S.C. § 1503 (obstruction of justice);

(f) 18 U.S.C. § 2339B (providing material support or resources to designated foreign terrorist organizations and attempt and conspiracy to do so);

(g) 18 U.S.C. § 1203 (hostage taking and attempt and conspiracy to do so);

(h) 18 U.S.C. § 1543 (forgery or false use of passport and attempt to do so); and

(i) 18 U.S.C. § 1952 (travel in aid of racketeering enterprises).

4. It was a part of the conspiracy that defendants ABU MARZOOK, SALAH, and ASHQAR agreed amongst themselves and with other co-conspirators that a conspirator would commit at least two acts of racketeering in the conduct of the affairs of the enterprise.

Methods and Means of the Conspiracy

5. It was part of the conspiracy that Hamas members solicited, organized, and carried out acts of violence, intimidation, and threats against Israel, its inhabitants and others, including murders, suicide bombings, and kidnappings, and solicited and caused others to do so, with the intent to establish a Palestinian/Islamic state in the lands comprising Israel, the West Bank,

and Gaza Strip, and to derail peace initiatives between the government of Israel and Palestinian representatives.

6. It was further part of the conspiracy that Hamas arranged to make videotaped statements and wills of Hamas members who were planning to personally participate in acts of violence, including suicide attacks, to be disseminated, after the deaths of those members, as tools to promote the goals of the enterprise and to increase and further the public perception of Hamas as a terrorist organization with its goal to establish a Palestinian/ Islamic state in the lands that comprise Israel, the West Bank, and Gaza Strip, and to derail peace initiatives between the government of Israel and Palestinian representatives.

7. It was further part of the conspiracy that Hamas members made public statements and issued public declarations which, among other things: (a) proclaimed and acknowledged that specific acts of violence had been committed by Hamas; (b) threatened future acts of violence if Hamas's demands were not met; and (c) were intended to promote and foster the prestige and standing of Hamas among the Palestinian people and others.

8. It was further part of the conspiracy that Hamas members secretly established cells or sections of Hamas in different countries, including the United States, and, within the United States, used various means, including corporate structures and financial institutions, to conceal the activities of Hamas and the movement of money for Hamas activities.

9. It was further part of the conspiracy that Hamas members actively raised money both in the United States and elsewhere in order to fund the activities of the enterprise, including the violent acts of the enterprise.

10. It was further part of the conspiracy that Hamas members routinely moved money into the United States through wire transfers and other means from locations outside the United States in order to eventually move the money to the West Bank and Gaza Strip, including for the funding of violent activities to be committed by Hamas.

11. It was further part of the conspiracy that Hamas provided funds to the families of Hamas detainees, deportees, and suicide bombers.

12. It was further part of the conspiracy that Hamas members infiltrated various universities and other academic and social institutions in the West Bank and Gaza Strip in order to control the educational directives of the universities and institutions and use the universities and institutions for recruitment of additional enterprise members, some of whom were tasked with committing violent acts on behalf of the enterprise.

13. It was further part of the conspiracy that Hamas members worked with terrorist and other organizations including, but not limited to, Fatah, the Popular Front for the Liberation of Palestine, the Democratic Front for the

Liberation of Palestine, the Palestinian Islamic Jihad, and the Palestinian Liberation Organization, to achieve the goals of the enterprise.

14. It was further part of the conspiracy that Hamas arranged to have enterprise members in the United States serve as facilitators of communications between other enterprise members within Israel, the West Bank, the Gaza Strip, and various other countries.

15. It was further part of the conspiracy that Hamas arranged for the creation of false passports and other travel documents for its members.

16. It was further part of the conspiracy that Hamas members purchased weapons and explosives for use in terrorist activities.

17. It was further part of the conspiracy that Hamas trained its military operatives in the use of weapons, explosives, and military strategies.

18. It was further part of the conspiracy that Hamas members were trained and instructed to refuse to provide information to authorities trying to investigate the enterprise in order to ensure the enterprise could continue to function and so that other members of the enterprise would not be apprehended.

19. It was further part of the conspiracy that Hamas members who had been apprehended by Israeli authorities continued to work on behalf of the enterprise while detained by: (a) attempting to provide to Hamas members who had not been apprehended an accounting of the detained member's activities on behalf of the enterprise so that the detained member's activities could be continued; (b) attempting to trade with Israeli authorities information about the activities of Hamas, such as the location of the bodies of individuals killed by Hamas, in exchange for various concessions from the government of Israel, such as the release of other detainees; (c) continuing to direct the affairs of Hamas members who had not been apprehended; and (d) making statements publicizing and glorifying Hamas's actions and Hamas's goal of pursuing terrorist activities to force the State and citizens of Israel to cede physical and political control over the lands comprising Israel, the West Bank, and the Gaza Strip.

20. It was further part of the conspiracy that Hamas, for the purpose of assessing and minimizing disruption to the enterprise: (a) maintained lists of Hamas members detained or otherwise arrested for activities undertaken on behalf of the enterprise; (b) obtained and analyzed copies of confessions provided by apprehended enterprise members to Israeli authorities; and (c) monitored proceedings against those enterprise members who had been apprehended by Israeli authorities.

21. It was further part of the conspiracy that Hamas utilized instrumentalities and facilities of interstate and foreign commerce including telephones, telephone facsimiles, private commercial carriers, computers, mail, and

wire facilities, to communicate and promote and conduct the affairs of the enterprise.

22. It was further part of the conspiracy that Hamas members utilized codes and aliases in conversations and written communication to conceal and disguise the activities of the enterprise and the identities of members of the enterprise.

23. It was a further part of the conspiracy that defendants ABU MARZOOK, SALAH, and ASHQAR, and others misrepresented, concealed and hid, and caused to be misrepresented, concealed and hidden the purposes of, and acts done, in furtherance of the conspiracy.

Overt Acts

24. In furtherance of the conspiracy and to accomplish the objects of the conspiracy, the defendants and their co-conspirators committed, among others, the following overt acts within the Northern District of Illinois and elsewhere:

A. In or about August 1988, an organization which came to be known as Hamas issued an organizational charter setting forth as its purpose and objective the transformation of Israel, the West Bank, and Gaza Strip into an Islamic state, and specified *jihad*, to include killing Israelis, as a means by which the enterprise's objectives were to be achieved.

B. Beginning no earlier than in or about August 1988, defendants ABU MARZOOK, SALAH, and ASHQAR, as well as others known and unknown, began working on behalf of Hamas.

C. Beginning no later than 1990, defendants ABU MARZOOK and SALAH were members of a United States-based Hamas security committee. The activities of the security committee included, among other things, the identification of Palestinian men studying in the United States, for the purpose of attempting to recruit those Palestinian men into Hamas. The security committee generally, and defendant SALAH specifically, compiled information on the Palestinian men which included their fields of study, the projected completion dates of their study, the projected dates of their return to the West Bank and Gaza Strip, and their capacity to participate in terrorist activities against Israel. This process produced numerous names which the security committee sorted based on their knowledge of chemistry, physics, computer science, and military operations.

D. Sometime in the early 1990s, the individuals identified by the security committee were tested and eventually narrowed down to a small number of individual candidates for operational roles in Hamas terrorist activities. Those candidates, including Co-conspirator C and Co-conspirator

D, were provided with advanced training in military operations and bomb-making.

E. In or about September 1992, to facilitate the training of Co-conspirator C and Co-conspirator D, defendant SALAH, while in Chicago, Illinois, purchased airline tickets for travel between the United States and locations in the Middle East for Co-conspirator C and Co-conspirator D. Both Co-conspirator C and Co-conspirator D traveled to the Middle East with the tickets provided by defendant SALAH and received advanced training in bomb-making from, among others, Hamas military operatives.

F. In approximately August 1992, defendant SALAH met and conferred with defendant ABU MARZOOK and co-conspirator Mohammed Qassem Sawalha regarding the need to revitalize Hamas terrorist operations in the West Bank. During the meeting, Sawalha, who had previously been in charge of Hamas terrorist operations within the West Bank, identified specific Hamas members still residing in the West Bank who could be used to revitalize Hamas's terrorist activities. Among these individuals were co-conspirators Adel Ahmed Awadallah and Salah Al-Arouri.

G. To further the objective of revitalizing Hamas's terrorist operations in the West Bank, in approximately September 1992, defendant SALAH traveled from Chicago, Illinois, to the West Bank. While in the West Bank, defendant SALAH, who used the name Abu Ahmad, met with Awadallah on several occasions. During these meetings, defendant SALAH and Awadallah discussed both Hamas terrorist activities and political activities in the West Bank and Gaza Strip. Awadallah informed defendant SALAH that Awadallah would need several months to reorganize Hamas's terrorist cells in the West Bank because Awadallah, after an arrest by Israeli authorities, had directed Hamas members to burn Hamas organizational documents containing information about Hamas cells in the West Bank. Defendant SALAH and Awadallah also discussed whether Hamas should murder Victim A, a Palestinian leader regarded as a leading proponent of peace with Israel.

H. Also while in the West Bank in approximately September 1992, defendant SALAH met with co-conspirator Salah Al-Arouri, a Hamas member headquartered at Hebron University in the West Bank. Al-Arouri informed defendant SALAH that Hamas needed money to purchase weapons to carry out terrorist activities. Defendant SALAH agreed to provide Al-Arouri money for the purchase of weapons and other military supplies and, thereafter, provided Al-Arouri at least approximately $50,000 for these purposes. Defendant SALAH was able to provide the money to Al-Arouri by making withdrawals from one of his Chicago bank accounts of ten $5,000 checks which were cashed in Israel on or about September 8, 1992.

I. Also in approximately September 1992, defendant SALAH met with Hamas leader Sheik Jamil Hamami a/k/a Abu Hamza.

J. Also in approximately September 1992, defendant SALAH met with Hamas leader Abu Saeb, a/k/a Abu Saab, who was involved in Hamas terrorist operations in the Gaza Strip. Abu Saeb informed defendant SALAH that he had approximately fifty-three Hamas recruits who were prepared to carry out terrorist attacks, but that funding was needed to help carry out the attacks. Abu Saeb informed defendant SALAH that Hamas was having problems with individuals collaborating and providing information about Hamas activities to Israeli authorities. Abu Saeb informed defendant SALAH that certain collaborators needed to be killed. Defendant SALAH agreed to and did pass on the information provided by Abu Saeb and Abu Saeb's request for money to defendant ABU MARZOOK and others.

K. After his return to Chicago from the Middle East in approximately September 1992, defendant SALAH received a $50,000 check from the bank account of defendant ABU MARZOOK as repayment for funds that defendant SALAH provided to Hamas members in the West Bank and Gaza Strip.

L. From approximately September 18, 1992, to approximately December 13, 1992, Hamas members publicly claimed credit for eight different terrorist actions that resulted in the deaths of numerous Israeli civilians and military personnel. In the December 13, 1992 terrorist operation, members of the Al-Qassam Brigades kidnaped Israeli soldier Nissam Toledano and offered to release Toledano in exchange for the release of jailed Hamas founder and leader Sheik Ahmed Yassin. Hamas members publicly stated that if Sheik Yassin was not released then Toledano would be killed. Hamas members publicly claimed that when Sheik Yassin was not released they killed Toledano. Toledano's body was found on approximately December 15, 1992, on the Jerusalem-Jericho highway.

M. From at least as early as 1989 through January 1993, defendants ABU MARZOOK, ASHQAR, co-conspirator Elbarasse, Co-conspirator E, Co-conspirator H, Co-conspirator I, Co-conspirator J, and others utilized various accounts at financial institutions throughout the United States to transfer large sums of money from various sources abroad through the United States to Israel and elsewhere. These transfers included, but are not limited to, the following:

i. In approximately November 1990, Co-conspirator H received into his Cleveland-based account approximately $130,000 from the Louisiana-based account of defendant ABU MARZOOK, approximately $40,000 from the Mississippi-based account of defendant ASHQAR, and approximately $54,000 from the Louisiana-based account of Co-conspirator E, a portion of which funds were thereafter sent to Israel and Switzerland.

ii. In approximately February 1991, Co-conspirator I, an associate of defendant ABU MARZOOK, received a wire transfer of approximately $480,000 from a bank in Saudi Arabia to his Virginia-based account. Co-conspirator I, in turn, wired approximately $99,000 to the Cleveland-based account of Co-conspirator H who, in turn, wrote approximately 16 checks worth $100,000 to Co-conspirator F, which checks were negotiated in Israel.

iii. In approximately May 1991, defendant ABU MARZOOK and co-conspirator Elbarasse transferred approximately $40,000 from a Virginia-based bank account to a Cleveland-based account held by Co-conspirator H who, in turn, signed five checks each in the amount of $8,500, several of which were written to Co-conspirator F, which checks were negotiated in Israel.

iv. From approximately August 1991 to approximately November 1991, Co-conspirator H received into his Cleveland-based account approximately $50,000 from the Louisiana-based account of defendant ABU MARZOOK, approximately $125,000 from the Mississippi-based account of defendant ASHQAR, and approximately $100,000 from the Louisiana-based account of Co-conspirator E, a portion of which funds were thereafter sent to Israel.

v. In approximately December 1991, defendant ABU MARZOOK and co-conspirator Elbarasse received a wire transfer of approximately $100,000 into their Virginia-based account from an account in Geneva, Switzerland. In turn, defendant ABU MARZOOK and co-conspirator Elbarasse thereafter transferred $50,000 from their Virginia-based account to the Cleveland-based account of Co-conspirator H who, in turn, wrote five $10,000 checks to Co-conspirator F or to cash, all five of which were negotiated in Israel in January 1992.

vi. In approximately January 1992, Co-conspirator E received wire transfers of approximately $613,000 into his Virginia-based account from an account in Saudi Arabia. Soon thereafter, Co-conspirator E made a series of wire transfers to accounts in the United States and abroad, including a transfer of approximately $100,000 to the Cleveland-based account of Co-conspirator H.

vii. In approximately June 1992, defendant ABU MARZOOK and co-conspirator Elbarasse received approximately $900,000 in multiple wire-transfers into their Virginia-based bank account. Soon thereafter, defendant ABU MARZOOK and co-conspirator Elbarasse wire transferred approximately $350,000 to four accounts domestically and overseas, including $100,000 into the Milwaukee-based account of Co-conspirator J.

viii. In approximately October 1992, Co-conspirator E received a wire transfer of approximately $150,000 into his Virginia-based account. The day following the receipt of the funds, Co-conspirator E wire transferred approximately $150,000 to Geneva, Switzerland.

ix. On approximately December 21, 1992, defendant ABU MARZOOK and co-conspirator Elbarasse received a wire transfer of approximately $100,000 into their Virginia-based account from an account in New York in the name of "Gazi Abu Samah."

x. On approximately January 4, 1993, defendant ABU MARZOOK and co-conspirator Elbarasse received a wire transfer of approximately $100,000 into their Virginia-based account from an account in New York in the name of "Gazi Abu Samah."

N. In approximately December 1992, Co-conspirator B came to Chicago, Illinois, and provided two pictures of co-conspirator Adel Awadallah to defendant SALAH so that defendant SALAH could have a false passport made for Awadallah. Defendant SALAH and co-conspirator Mohammed Qassem Sawalha attempted to have the false passport manufactured.

O. In approximately December 1992, in response to Israel's deportation of over 400 Hamas members and other radicals from Israel, the West Bank, and the Gaza Strip, defendant ABU MARZOOK contacted Hamas members throughout the Middle East and elsewhere to discuss how to deal with the deportation of the Hamas members. Among those individuals defendant ABU MARZOOK called to discuss the issue of the Hamas deportees was defendant SALAH.

P. In approximately late December 1992 and early January 1993, in response to Israel's deportation of over 400 Hamas members and other radicals from Israel, the West Bank, and the Gaza Strip, Hamas leadership, including defendant ABU MARZOOK as the chairman of the Hamas delegation, met with leadership of the anti-Israeli Fatah organization. Leadership from Hamas and Fatah discussed how to deal with the deported Hamas members, whether the Palestinian Liberation Organization ("PLO") should break off then ongoing peace discussions with Israel, and whether to limit terrorist attacks to Israeli settlers in the West Bank and Gaza Strip and Israeli soldiers. During the meetings, defendant ABU MARZOOK stated a willingness and readiness to escalate the acts of violence against Israel. Discussions also covered changes in organizational Q. structures with the purpose of best promoting "armed struggle against the Zionist enemy."

Q. In approximately late December 1992, at the request of Hamas leadership, and defendant ABU MARZOOK specifically, defendant SALAH agreed to travel from Chicago to the West Bank and Gaza Strip to assess the ability of Hamas to function after the deportations and to deliver money to Hamas members in the individual regional cells within the West Bank and Gaza Strip. In particular, defendant SALAH was directed to assess Hamas's abilities to continue to carry out terrorist attacks.

R. Beginning on or about December 29, 1992, and continuing until on or about January 25, 1993, defendant SALAH received into his Chicago based bank accounts a series of wire transfers, totaling approximately $985,000, from accounts associated with defendant ABU MARZOOK, to be distributed to Hamas members in the West Bank and Gaza Strip. Those transfers included:

i. On or about December 29, 1992 the wire transfer of approximately $300,000 from a Virginia-based bank account held in the name of defendant ABU MARZOOK and co-conspirator Elbarasse, which money had previously entered the Virginia-based account in two wire transfers, one originating from Geneva, Switzerland, and a second received from an account in New York held in the name of "Gazi Abu Samah."

ii. On or about January 20, 1993, the wire transfer of approximately $135,000 from a Virginia-based bank account held in the name of defendant ABU MARZOOK and co-conspirator Elbarasse, a portion of which money had previously entered the Virginia-based account in a wire transfer received from an account in New York held in the name of "Gazi Abu Samah."

iii. On or about January 21, 1993, the wire transfer of approximately $50,000 from a Virginia-based bank account held in the name of defendant ABU MARZOOK and co-conspirator Elbarasse.

iv. On or about January 21, 1993, the wire transfer of approximately $30,000 from a Virginia-based bank account held in the name of Co-conspirator E.

v. On or about January 22, 1993, the wire transfer of approximately $170,000 from a Virginia-based bank account held in the name of Co-conspirator E, which money had previously entered the Virginia-based account on approximately January 21, 1993, from the Virginia-based account of defendant ABU MARZOOK and co-conspirator Elbarasse.

vi. On or about January 25, 1993 the wire transfer of approximately $300,000 from a Virginia-based bank account held in the name of defendant ABU MARZOOK and co-conspirator Elbarasse.

S. On or about January 13, 1993, defendant SALAH left the United States en route to the West Bank and Gaza Strip for the purpose of assessing the ability of Hamas to function after the deportation and to deliver money to Hamas members.

T. While en route to the Middle East, defendant SALAH stopped in London, England and met with co-conspirator Mohammed Qassem Sawalha. Sawalha directed defendant SALAH to provide money to various Hamas members in the West Bank and Gaza Strip, and provided contact information for meetings with, among others, co-conspirator Adel Awadallah, Abu Hasam a/k/a Abu Hussam, and Abu Majahad a/k/a Abu Majhad.

U. Between on or about January 17, 1993, to on or about January 19, 1993, after arriving in Israel, defendant SALAH arranged to have approximately $230,000 of the money in his Chicago bank accounts transferred to him through a money changer in Ramallah. Defendant SALAH transferred $30,000 of that amount by executing three $10,000 checks and providing them to the money changer. The transfer of the additional $200,000 was effected by means of a wire transfer made by defendant SALAH's wife from one of his Chicago accounts directly to a Chicago account associated with the money changer. Defendant SALAH collected the $230,000 in cash from the money changer for distribution to Hamas members in the West Bank and Gaza Strip.

V. After arriving in Israel, defendant SALAH met with co-conspirator Adel Awadallah. Defendant SALAH and Awadallah conferred on Hamas personnel issues and specific planned terrorist attacks. Defendant SALAH arranged for $60,000 to be provided to Awadallah for various Hamas needs.

W. While in Israel, defendant SALAH also traveled to the Gaza Strip and met with Hamas member Abu Majahad. Defendant SALAH provided Abu Majahad money for various Hamas organizational needs. Defendant SALAH agreed to carry messages from Abu Majahad to Hamas members abroad.

X. While in Israel, defendant SALAH also met with Hamas member Abu Saeb a/k/a Abu Saab. Defendant SALAH and Abu Saeb discussed various terrorist attacks carried out by Hamas and the state of the Al-Qassam Brigades in the Gaza Strip. Abu Saeb informed defendant SALAH that Hamas now had eight underground shelters for hiding fugitives and that Hamas members in Rahat had: (1) three M-16 rifles; (2) three Kalishnikov rifles; and (3) two Uzi machine guns. Abu Saeb informed defendant SALAH that there would be an increase in terrorist activity during the month of Ramadan. Abu Saeb asked defendant SALAH for additional money to continue terrorist activity and to purchase weapons. Defendant SALAH agreed to provide additional money.

Y. On or about January 25, 1993, defendant SALAH was arrested by Israeli authorities based on his involvement in Hamas. After his arrest, defendant SALAH continued to attempt to assist Hamas. In particular, defendant SALAH attempted to trade information given to him by defendant ABU MARZOOK and Co-conspirator G regarding the burial location of an Israeli soldier, Ilan Sa'adon, who was murdered in a Hamas terrorist attack in 1989, in return for the release of numerous Hamas members.

Z. On or about March 19, 1993, defendant SALAH attempted to use consular officials from the American Embassy in Israel, unbeknownst to the consular officials, to pass messages to Co-conspirator C and Co-conspirator D, who had recently returned from the Middle East. Further, defendant SALAH falsely denied to consular officials any association with defendant MARZOOK or Hamas.

AA. After his arrest, defendant SALAH attempted to provide information to his co-conspirators regarding how to avoid capture in the future and how to deal with the negative publicity of his arrest in the United States.

BB. In or about August 1993, after Co-conspirator A returned from Israel to the United States, defendant ASHQAR debriefed Co-conspirator A regarding Co-conspirator A's and defendant SALAH's mission to the Middle East on behalf of Hamas culminating with their arrests by Israeli authorities.

CC. In or about August 1993, Co-conspirator A reported to Hamas co-conspirators in the United States including, among others, defendant ASHQAR, that Co-conspirator A believed that Co-conspirator A and defendant SALAH had been caught by the Israeli authorities because, among other reasons, other Hamas members had confessed about Co-conspirator A's and defendant SALAH's roles in Hamas and because defendant SALAH had withdrawn large sums of money. Co-conspirator A further detailed specific physical evidence relating to Hamas operations seized at the time of defendant SALAH's arrest, including documents and records listing names of Hamas operatives, codes and money to be used in Hamas operations. Based on this information, specific recommendations for future Hamas operations were generated.

DD. In or about the Fall of 1993, defendant ASHQAR facilitated Co-conspirator A's reintegration into the community and Hamas in the United States. These efforts included the transfer of over $15,000 to Co-conspirator A, as well as a proposal to other Hamas members that

Coconspirator A be included in a secret meeting of Hamas members to take place in Philadelphia, Pennsylvania.

EE. Further, as part of his role as a Hamas administrator, defendant ASHQAR produced, collected, and disseminated numerous documents and information in furtherance of Hamas's goals in the United States and abroad, including goals related to the Hamas command and control structure, recruitment of new members for Hamas, progress reports of Hamas plans and activities, and control and minimization of damage to Hamas from the arrest and loss of members involved in terrorist actions. In particular, defendant ASHQAR collected and, at times, disseminated documents related to:

i. Hamas members' aliases, phone numbers, and addresses, including information for defendants SALAH and ABU MARZOOK, as well as other co-conspirators.

ii. The death or capture of various Hamas members.

iii. Hamas terrorist attacks.

iv. Security training and directives, including counter-surveillance techniques, secrecy protocols, and interrogation issues.

v. Confessions provided by captured Hamas members, including several of defendant SALAH's confessions to Israeli authorities.

vi. Assessments and analysis on the state of Hamas within the West Bank and Gaza Strip as well as abroad.

vii. Minutes or summaries of meetings between Hamas members and other organizations and groups, including the Palestinian Liberation Organization ("PLO"), Fatah, the Palestinian Front for the Liberation of Palestine ("PFLP"), and the Palestinian Islamic Jihad ("PIJ"), as well as meetings between Hamas members and foreign countries.

viii. Information the Israelis obtained regarding Hamas membership and activities, including a document detailing information defendant SALAH provided to the Israelis and the circumstances under which the information was provided.

ix. Israeli indictments against various Hamas members, including the indictment against Co-conspirator A.

x. The movement of money for Hamas activities.

xi. The Hamas deportees who were deported to Lebanon in December 1992, including statements by defendant ABU MARZOOK on the issue of the deportees.

xii. Opposition to peace attempts between the State of Israel and Palestinians.

xiii. A secret meeting of Hamas members in Philadelphia, Pennsylvania.

xiv. Resistance to Israeli occupation of the West Bank and Gaza Strip and Hamas's relationship with other pro-Palestinian organizations.

xv. Policies and activities of various terrorist organizations or anti-Israeli groups.

xvi. Hamas statements distributed by the Islamic Association for Palestine ("IAP").

FF. As part of his role as a Hamas administrator, defendant ASHQAR participated in a number of phone conversations related to Hamas activity both in the United States and abroad. These phone conversations sometimes occurred in code. These phone calls were in furtherance of Hamas's goals in the United States and abroad, including goals related to the Hamas command and control structure, recruitment of new members for Hamas, progress reports of Hamas plans and activities, and control and minimization of damage to Hamas from the arrest and loss of members involved in terrorist actions. In particular, defendant ASHQAR participated in phone conversations related to:

i. Hamas members' contacts with the United States government.

ii. Hamas's need for financial assistance in order to further its goals.

iii. The movement of money for Hamas.

iv. The Hamas members who were deported to Lebanon in December 1992.

v. Management of Hamas and Hamas personnel within the Gaza Strip and West Bank, including specific conversations related to:

1. Killing a Hamas member who was not obeying orders.

2. Hamas members collaborating with Israelis.

vi. Management of Hamas and Hamas members in the United States.

vii. Meetings defendant ASHQAR was to have with Co-conspirator G and Sheik Jamil Hamami in January and March 1994.

viii. A secret meeting of Hamas members in Philadelphia, Pennsylvania in October 1993.

ix. The affairs and activities of Co-conspirator A.

x. Hamas terrorist operations and terrorists.

xi. Hamas organizational initiatives in the United States.

xii. Opposition to peace attempts between the State of Israel and Palestinians.

xiii. Hamas founder Sheik Ahmed Yassin.

xiv. Hamas's views on the PLO, Yasir Arafat, and anti-Israeli organizations.

xv. The affairs and activities of defendant SALAH.

GG. In or about October 1993, defendant ASHQAR met with various Hamas members in Philadelphia, including co-conspirator Elbarasse, to discuss Hamas issues including, but not limited to, Hamas activities inside the United States and abroad and lessons learned from the capture of defendant SALAH.

HH. In or about March 1994, defendant ASHQAR met in Oxford, Mississippi, with two other Hamas members, including co-conspirator Sheik Jamil Hamami, to discuss Hamas issues and the transfer of money for Hamas activities overseas.

II. Throughout the mid-1990s, Hamas members publicly claimed credit for various terrorist actions that resulted in the death of numerous civilians and military personnel in Israel. These included, but are not limited to: (1) an April 6, 1994 terrorist operation in which Hamas members publicly claimed responsibility for driving a car bomb into a public bus in Afula, Israel, killing eight Israelis; (2) an October 19, 1994 terrorist operation, in which Hamas members publicly claimed responsibility for a suicide bombing on a public bus in Tel Aviv, Israel, that killed thirteen Israelis and a Dutch national; (3) a February 26, 1996 terrorist operation in which Hamas members publicly claimed responsibility for a suicide bombing on a public bus in Jerusalem that killed twenty-four Israelis and two Americans; (4) a March 3, 1996 terrorist operation in which Hamas members publicly claimed responsibility for a suicide bombing on a public bus in Jerusalem that killed eight Israelis, an Ethiopian, and seven Romanians; (5) a May 13, 1996 terrorist operation in which Hamas members publicly claimed responsibility for a drive-by shooting at students waiting at a public bus stop in Beit El in the West Bank that resulted in the death of American student David Boim; and (6) a July 30, 1997 terrorist operation in which Hamas members publicly claimed responsibility for two suicide bombings in a market in Jerusalem that killed sixteen Israelis.

JJ. In approximately Fall 1997, co-conspirator Hassan Salameh, after his arrest for participation in various Hamas terrorist attacks, continued his work on behalf of Hamas by publicizing his actions carried out for Hamas and Hamas's goal of pursuing terrorist activities to force the State and citizens of Israel to cede physical and political control over the lands comprising Israel, the West Bank, and the Gaza Strip.

KK. In or about February 1998, defendant ASHQAR, despite a grant of immunity, refused to testify before a federal Grand Jury sitting in New York, New York, and continued to refuse to testify into August 1998, in an effort to hide his and co-conspirators' activities on behalf of Hamas, and to continue his activities on behalf of Hamas undetected.

LL. In or about March 1998, co-conspirator Elbarasse, despite a grant of immunity, refused to testify before a federal Grand Jury sitting in New York, New York, and continued to refuse to testify into September 1998, in an effort to hide his and co-conspirators' activities on behalf of Hamas, and to continue his activities on behalf of Hamas undetected.

MM. In or about July 1999, Co-conspirator C, despite a grant of immunity, refused to testify before a federal Grand Jury sitting in Chicago, Illinois, and continued to refuse to testify into August 2000, in an effort to hide his and co-conspirators' activities on behalf of Hamas, and to continue his activities on behalf of Hamas undetected.

NN. In or about November 2000, Co-conspirator D, having been served with a subpoena requiring his appearance before a federal Grand Jury, fled the United States to Jordan and has not returned to the United States since that time, in an effort to hide his and co-conspirators' activities on behalf of Hamas, and to continue his activities on behalf of Hamas undetected.

OO. Upon his return to the United States in approximately November 1997, defendant SALAH continued his activities on behalf of Hamas within the United States. Among other things, this included the recruitment of Individual A to join Hamas and make trips to the Middle East in order to conduct Hamas activities. As part of the recruitment of Individual A, defendant SALAH discussed with Individual A defendant SALAH's prior activities and actions on behalf of Hamas.

PP. In or about October 1999, defendant SALAH assisted Individual A with travel arrangements to Israel to conduct business on behalf of Hamas.

QQ. In or about October 1999, at the direction of defendant SALAH, Individual A traveled to Israel and the West Bank. At defendant SALAH's direction, Individual A was to: (1) contact and meet with various Hamas members to convey messages and assess various Hamas needs in the West Bank; (2) deliver money to the family of imprisoned co-conspirator Salah Al-Arouri; (3) meet with co-conspirator Salah Al-Arouri in

Ashkelon prison; and (4) scout specific locations in and around Jerusalem for suitability as targets for Hamas terrorist attacks.

RR. In or about October 1999, after arriving in Israel, at the direction of defendant SALAH, Individual A provided money previously given to him by defendant SALAH to the family of imprisoned co-conspirator Salah Al-Arouri.

SS. In or about October 1999, after arriving in Israel, at the direction of defendant SALAH, Individual A attempted to meet with co-conspirator Salah Al-Arouri in Ashkelon prison.

TT. In or about October 1999, after arriving in Israel, at the direction of defendant SALAH, Individual A scouted specific locations in and around Jerusalem for suitability as targets for Hamas terrorist attacks.

UU. In or about October 1999, after arriving in Israel, at the direction of defendant SALAH, Individual A attempted to enter the Gaza Strip to visit with Hamas leader Sheik Ahmed Yassin.

VV. In or about October 1999, after arriving in Israel, at the direction of defendant SALAH, Individual A met with various Hamas members.

WW. In or about October 1999, after arriving in Israel, defendant SALAH and Individual A periodically discussed the progress that Individual A was making during his trip to Israel.

XX. In or about October 1999, defendant SALAH discussed Individual A's trip to Israel with Hamas members in the West Bank with whom Individual A met.

YY. In approximately October 1999, upon Individual A's return to the United States, defendant SALAH debriefed Individual A regarding Individual A's trip to Israel and the West Bank.

ZZ. In approximately October 1999, upon Individual A's return to the United States, defendant SALAH told Individual A he was pleased with the success of Individual A's trip and informed Individual A that Individual A would be asked to take additional trips in furtherance of Hamas activities.

AAA. In approximately October 1999, upon Individual A's return to the United States, defendant SALAH obtained from Individual A a photograph of defendant SALAH with co-conspirators Salah Al-Arouri and Adel Awadallah which Individual A had received from co-coconspirator Salah Al-Arouri's mother.

BBB. In or about April 2001, defendant SALAH, in a civil suit filed in federal court in Chicago, Illinois (*Boim v. Quranic Literacy Institute, et al.*, 00 C 2905), alleging that defendants SALAH and ABU MARZOOK, among others, as members of Hamas, were responsible for the death of David Boim who was murdered in a drive-by shooting in the West Bank in May 1996, in an attempt to avoid liability and thereby protect funds entrusted to him by defendant ABU MARZOOK and others, to hide his activities on behalf of Hamas, and to continue his activities on behalf of Hamas undetected, provided sworn answers to interrogatories in the *Boim* civil suit that he knew to be false. In the sworn answers to interrogatories, among other falsehoods, defendant SALAH: (1) falsely represented that he never provided or delivered funds for the purpose of supporting Hamas; (2) falsely represented that he had only provided funds to a very limited number of individuals and failed to include a variety of fund transfers in which he had participated; (3) failed to disclose that he was a member of Hamas; (4) falsely represented that he had never met with defendant ABU MARZOOK; (5) falsely represented that he had never trained or attended training sessions of Hamas members; and (6) failed to disclose that he had transferred funds in excess of $1,000 to defendant ABU MARZOOK and others.

CCC. In or about June 2003, defendant ASHQAR, despite a grant of immunity, refused to testify before a Grand Jury sitting in Chicago, Illinois, and continued to refuse to testify into October 2003, in an effort to hide his and co-conspirators' activities on behalf of Hamas, and to continue his activities on behalf of Hamas undetected.

All in violation of Title 18, United States Code, Sections 1962(d) and 2.

Count Two

————The SPECIAL AUGUST 2003-2 GRAND JURY further charges:

1. Paragraphs 24OO through 24AAA of Count One are incorporated and realleged as though fully set forth herein.

2. In or about October 1999, in the Northern District of Illinois, Eastern Division, and elsewhere:

MUHAMMAD HAMID KHALIL SALAH,

a/k/a "Muhammad Abd Al-'Hamid Salah,"

a/k/a "Abu Ahmad,"

knowingly provided and attempted to provide material support and resources, specifically currency and personnel, to a foreign terrorist organization, specifically Hamas;

In violation of Title 18, United States Code, Section 2339B.

Count Three

————The SPECIAL AUGUST 2003-2 GRAND JURY further charges:

1. Paragraph 24BBB of Count One is incorporated and realleged as though fully set forth herein.

2. In or about April 2001, in the Northern District of Illinois, Eastern Division, and elsewhere:

MUHAMMAD HAMID KHALIL SALAH,
a/k/a "Muhammad Abd Al-'Hamid Salah,"
a/k/a "Abu Ahmad,"

corruptly endeavored to influence, obstruct and impede the due administration of justice by submitting to the United States District Court, through lawyers acting under the authority of the court, false and misleading verified answers to interrogatories propounded on defendant SALAH in a civil suit filed against defendant SALAH and others which answers falsely stated, among other things, that defendant SALAH had never provided or delivered funds for the purpose of supporting Hamas;

In violation of Title 18, United States Code, Section 1503.

Count Four

————The SPECIAL AUGUST 2003-2 GRAND JURY further charges:

1. At times material to this indictment:

(a) A federal grand jury investigation was occurring before the Special April 2002 Grand Jury (02 GJ 369) in which the grand jury was actively involved in the investigation of the organization known as Hamas and members of Hamas for violation of various federal statutes, including, among others, the following provisions of Title 18 of the United States Code: Sections 1961 and 1962 (racketeering); Section 2339A (material support to terrorists); Section 2339B (material support to designated foreign terrorist organizations); Section 2339C (financing of terrorism); Section 956 (conspiracy to kill, kidnap, maim or injure persons or damage property in a foreign country); Section 2332 (killing of a United States national); Sections 1956 and 1957 (money laundering); Section 1341 (mail fraud); Section 1343 (wire fraud); Section 1001 (false statements to a government official); and Section 1512 (obstruction of justice).

(b) On or about June 25, 2003, defendant ABDELHALEEM HASAN ABDELRAZIQ ASHQAR appeared before Chief Judge Charles P. Kocoras. Chief Judge Kocoras entered an order compelling defendant ASHQAR to testify before the Special April 2002 Grand Jury, pursuant to Title 18, United States Code, Sections 6002 and 6003 (the "Compulsion Order"), and further ordering that no testimony provided by defendant ASHQAR or any information directly or indirectly derived from such testimony could be used against him in any criminal case except a prosecution for perjury, giving a false statement or otherwise failing to comply with the Compulsion Order.

(c) On or about June 25, 2003, defendant ASHQAR appeared before the Special April 2002 Grand Jury and was asked a series of questions, including, among others, questions about Hamas and members of Hamas, as well as questions regarding defendant ASHQAR's personal and professional background, including his place of birth, his employment history in the United States, and whether he personally was a member of Hamas. Defendant ASHQAR refused to answer those questions.

2. On or about June 25, 2003, at Chicago, in the Northern District of Illinois, Eastern Division,

ABDELHALEEM HASAN ABDELRAZIQ ASHQAR,

a/k/a "Abu Hasan,"

a/k/a "Abu Ali Hasan,"

a/k/a "Samir,"

defendant herein, did knowingly and willfully disobey and resist a lawful order and command of the Court, namely, to testify before the Special April 2002 Grand Jury (02 GJ 369), in that, after being granted immunity pursuant to the Compulsion Order, he refused to answer questions put to him during his grand jury appearance;

In violation of Title 18, United States Code, Section 401(3).

Count Five

————The SPECIAL AUGUST 2003-2 GRAND JURY further charges:

1. Paragraph 1 of Count Four is incorporated and realleged as though fully set forth herein.

2. From June 25, 2003, and continuing to October 9, 2003, defendant ASHQAR continued to refuse to answer questions before the Special April 2002 Grand Jury (02 GJ 369) despite the Compulsion Order.

3. Beginning on or about June 25, 2003 and continuing until October 9, 2003, at Chicago, in the Northern District of Illinois, Eastern Division,

ABDELHALEEM HASAN ABDELRAZIQ ASHQAR,

a/k/a "Abu Hasan,"

a/k/a "Abu Ali Hasan,"

a/k/a "Samir,"

defendant herein, corruptly influenced, obstructed, and impeded the due administration of justice, and endeavored to do so, by refusing to testify before the Special April 2002 Grand Jury (02 GJ 369) which was investigating Hamas and members of Hamas, after having been ordered and compelled to do so;

In violation of Title 18, United States Code, Section 1503.

Forfeiture Allegation

The SPECIAL AUGUST 2003-2 GRAND JURY further charges:

1. The allegations contained in Count One of the indictment are realleged and incorporated by reference for the purposes of alleging forfeiture pursuant to Title 18, United States Code, Section 1963.

2. As a result of the violation of Title 18, United States Code, Section 1962(d), as alleged in the foregoing indictment,

MOUSA MOHAMMED ABU MARZOOK,

a/k/a "Abu Omar,"

a/k/a "Tareq,"

a/k/a "Abu Rizq,"

MUHAMMAD HAMID KHALIL SALAH,

a/k/a "Muhammad Abd Al-'Hamid Salah,"

a/k/a "Abu Ahmad," and

ABDELHALEEM HASAN ABDELRAZIQ ASHQAR,

a/k/a "Abu Hasan,"

a/k/a "Abu Ali Hasan,"

a/k/a "Samir,"

defendants herein:

(a) have acquired and maintained interests in violation of Title 18, United States Code, Section 1962, which interests are subject to forfeiture to the United States pursuant to Title 18, United States Code, Section 1963(a)(1);

(b) have interests in, securities of, claims against, and property and contractual rights affording sources of influence over, the enterprise described in Count One which defendants established, operated, controlled, conducted, and participated in the conduct of, and conspired to do so, in violation of Title 18, United States Code, Section 1962, thereby making all such interests, securities, claims, and property and contractual rights subject to forfeiture to the United States of America pursuant to Title 18, United States Code, Section 1963(a)(2);

(c) have property constituting and derived from proceeds obtained, directly and indirectly, from racketeering activity in violation of Title 18, United States Code, Section 1963(a)(3).

3. The interests of the defendants, jointly and severally subject to forfeiture to the United States pursuant to Title 18, United States Code, Section 1963(a)(1), (a)(2), and (a)(3) include but are not limited to:

(a) Approximately $2, 700, 000.00;

(b) All Funds in Standard Bank & Trust Account No. 5580349268;

(c) All Funds in Standard Bank &Trust Account No. 239328806;

(d) All Funds in LaSalle Bank, F.S.B. Account No. 022034532; and

(e) As to defendant MUHAMMAD HAMID KHALIL SALAH only:

Residential real property commonly known as 9229 S.

Thomas, Bridgeview, Illinois, with Cook County,

Illinois PIN 23-01-404-012.

4. To the extent that the proceeds and property described above as being subject to forfeiture pursuant to Title 18, United States Code, Section 1963, as a result of any acts or omission by any defendant:

(a) cannot be located upon the exercise of due diligence;

(b) has been transferred or sold to, or deposited with, a third party;

(c) has been placed beyond the jurisdiction of the Court;

(d) has been substantially diminished in value; or

(e) has been commingled with other property which cannot be subdivided without difficulty;

it is the intent of the United States of America, pursuant to Title 18, United States Code, Section 1963(m), to seek forfeiture of any other property of the defendants up to the value of the proceeds and property described above as being subject to forfeiture such substitute property to include, but not being limited to:

All Funds in First National Bank of Chicago Account No. 8060700;

All pursuant to Title 18, United States Code, Section 1963.

Sentencing Allegations

The SPECIAL AUGUST 2003-2 GRAND JURY further alleges:

1. In and during the course of the commission of the conduct alleged in Count One of the Indictment (racketeering conspiracy):

a. Defendants MOUSA MOHAMMED ABU MARZOOK, MUHAMMAD HAMID KHALIL SALAH, and ABDELHALEEM HASAN ABDELRAZIQ ASHQAR were organizers and leaders of five or more participants. USSG §3B1.1(a).

b. The offense was a felony that involved, or was intended to promote, a federal crime of terrorism. USSG § 3A1.4(a).

c. Defendants MOUSA MOHAMMED ABU MARZOOK, MUHAMMAD HAMID KHALIL SALAH, and ABDELHALEEM HASAN ABDELRAZIQ ASHQAR intentionally selected victims or property as the object of the offense because of the actual or perceived religion, national origin, and ethnicity of any person. USSG § 3A1.1(a).

d. Defendant ABDELHALEEM HASAN ABDELRAZIQ ASHQAR willfully obstructed and impeded, or attempted to obstruct or impede, the administration of justice during the course of the investigation. USSG § 3C1.1.

e. The amount of laundered funds involved more than $2,500,000. USSG § 2S1.1(a)(1); USSG § 2B1.1(b)(1)(J).

f. The defendants believed the laundered/structured funds were intended to promote a crime of violence or unlawful activity. USSG § 2S1.1(b)(1); USSG § 2S1.3(b)(1)(A).

g. The offense involved sophisticated laundering. USSG § 2S1.1(b)(3).

h. The offense was part of a pattern of unlawful activity involving more than $100,000 in a 12-month period. USSG § 2S1.3(b)(2)(B).

i. The offense resulted in substantial interference with the administration of justice. USSG § 2J1.2(b)(2).

j. The offense involved a ransom demand or a demand upon government. USSG § 2A4.1(b)(1).

k. A victim sustained permanent or life-threatening bodily injury. USSG § 2A4.1(b)(2)(A)

l. A dangerous weapon was used. USSG § 2A4.1(b)(3).

2. In and during the course of the commission of the conduct alleged in Count Two (material support) of the Indictment:

a. Defendant MUHAMMAD HAMID KHALIL SALAH was an organizer and leader of five or more participants. USSG §3B1.1(a).

b. The offense was a felony that involved, or was intended to promote, a federal crime of terrorism. USSG § 3A1.4(a).

c. Defendant MUHAMMAD HAMID KHALIL SALAH intentionally selected victims or property as the object of the offense because of the actual or perceived religion, national origin, and ethnicity of any person. USSG § 3A1.1(a).

3. In and during the course of the commission of the conduct alleged in Count Three (obstruction of justice) of the Indictment:

a. Defendant MUHAMMAD HAMID KHALIL SALAH was an organizer and leader of five or more participants. USSG §3B1.1(a).

b. The offense was a felony that involved, or was intended to promote, a federal crime of terrorism. USSG § 3A1.4(a).

4. In and during the course of the commission of the conduct alleged in Counts Four (criminal contempt) and Five (obstruction of justice) of the Indictment:

a. Defendant ABDELHALEEM HASAN ABDELRAZIQ ASHQAR was an organizer and leader of five or more participants. USSG §3B1.1(a).

b. The offense was a felony that involved, or was intended to promote, a federal crime of terrorism. USSG § 3A1.4(a).

c. The offense resulted in substantial interference with the administration of justice. USSG § 2J1.2(b)(2).

A TRUE BILL:

____

FOREPERSON

____

UNITED STATES ATTORNEY

DOCUMENT NO. 17

EFRAT UNGAR, ET AL.
v.
THE PALESTINE LIBERATION ORGANIZATION, ET AL.

1st Cir., March 31, 2005

COURT OPINION

Before: Selya, *Circuit Judge*, Campbell, *Senior Circuit Judge*, and Lipez, *Circuit Judge*.

Ramsey Clark, with whom *Lawrence W. Schilling, Deming E. Sherman*, and *Edwards & Angell, LLP* were on brief, for appellants.

David J. Strachman, with whom *McIntyre, Tate, Lynch & Holt* was on brief, for appellees.

Daniel J. Popeo, Richard A. Samp, Joel J. Sprayregen, and *Jared M. Wayne* on consolidated brief for Washington Legal Foundation and Allied Educational Foundation, amici curiae.

March 31, 2005

SELYA, ***Circuit Judge***. This appeal raises exceptionally important questions of justiciability and sovereignty, emblematic of unsettled political conditions that have plagued the Middle East for many years. In it, the Palestinian Authority (PA) and the Palestine Liberation Organization (PLO) ask us to countermand the district court's refusal to dismiss the action against them. They contend that the case hinges on a nonjusticiable political question and that, at any rate, the defendants enjoy sovereign immunity. In the event that these arguments do not carry the day, the defendants seek vacation of two $116,000,000-plus default judgments, one entered against each of them, on the ground that they were entitled to a binding determination of sovereign immunity (including appellate review of any unfavorable decision) before being forced to bear the burdens of litigation.

After careful consideration of the relevant legal authorities and perscrutation of an amplitudinous record, we conclude that this case is justiciable;

that the defendants have not established an entitlement to sovereign immunity; and that the defendants' strategic litigation choices undercut their arguments as to the sequencing of the litigation. Consequently, we affirm the judgment below.

I. Background

This case had its genesis in a terrorist attack that occurred in Israel on June 9, 1996. On that date, Yaron Ungar (a citizen of the United States), his wife Efrat, and their infant son Yishai were driving home from a wedding. Near Beit Shemesh, a car approached the Ungars' vehicle and loosed a salvo of machine-gun fire, killing both Yaron and Efrat. The three occupants of the attacking vehicle were all members of the Hamas Islamic Resistance Movement (Hamas), a group designated as a terrorist organization by the United States Department of State. *See* 8 U.S.C. § 1189; Redesignation of Foreign Terrorist Organizations, 68 Fed. Reg. 56,860, 56,861 (Oct. 2, 2003). The authorities apprehended the three assailants and, soon after, arrested a fourth Hamas member as an accessory. An Israeli court convicted all four men.

David Strachman was appointed as the administrator of the estates of Yaron and Efrat Ungar. On March 13, 2000, Strachman and other plaintiffs filed suit in the United States District Court for the District of Rhode Island pursuant to the Anti-Terrorism Act (ATA), 18 U.S.C. §§ 2331–2338. That statute provides a cause of action in favor of any "national of the United States injured in his or her person, property, or business by reason of an act of international terrorism, or his or her estate, survivors, or heirs." *Id.* § 2333(a). Venue for such an action may be laid in, inter alia, "any district where any plaintiff resides," *id.* § 2334(a), and the plaintiff(s) may recover treble damages, costs, and attorneys' fees, *id.* § 2333(a).

The original complaint set forth both ATA and state law claims. It was brought by numerous plaintiffs against numerous defendants. We need not call the roll; for all practical purposes, the case boils down to a suit involving the estate and heirs of Yaron Ungar as plaintiffs and the PA and the PLO as defendants.[1] The centerpiece of the complaint was an allegation that the defendants had engaged in international terrorism within the purview of the ATA. *See id.* § 2331(1).

On an ensuing motion to dismiss, the district court rejected an assertion that the PA and the PLO were immune from service of process. *Estates of*

[1] On the plaintiffs' side, the claims brought by the estate and heirs of Efrat Ungar were dismissed because she was not a United States national. *Estates of Ungar ex rel. Strachman* v. *Palestinian Auth.*, 153 F. Supp. 2d 76, 97 (D.R.I. 2001). On the defendants' side, a number of Hamas defendants were sued, but none of them entered an appearance and, accordingly, the district court defaulted them. *See id.* at 85 n.2. The court dismissed the action as to several other defendants for want of in personam jurisdiction. *Id.* at 95. For present purposes, then, it simplifies matters to think of this case as a suit by Yaron Ungar's estate and heirs against the PA and the PLO.

Ungar ex rel. Strachman v. *Palestinian Auth.*, 153 F. Supp. 2d 76, 90–91 (D.R.I. 2001) (*Ungar I*). However, the court dismissed the state law claims, finding that Rhode Island choice-of-law principles favored the application of Israeli law. *Id.* at 98–99.

The plaintiffs served an amended complaint on August 23, 2001, asserting one claim under the ATA and three Israeli law claims, all on behalf of the estate and heirs of Yaron Ungar. The PA and the PLO moved to dismiss the amended complaint on essentially the same grounds as previously urged, adding only that the claims were nonjusticiable. Alternatively, they sought to have the district court certify, pursuant to 28 U.S.C. § 1292(b),[2] various questions, including a question as to whether the defendants were entitled to a non-specific "functional" immunity "arising from the peculiar status of the PA as a functioning governmental entity." At that point, the defendants were not claiming statehood; they argued only that the policy considerations underlying the ATA's recognition of immunity for foreign states "appl[ied] equally" to them.

The PA and the PLO later changed their position. On January 30, 2002—during the pendency of their motion to dismiss the amended complaint—they jointly moved for "leave to assert defenses." In the memorandum accompanying that motion, they for the first time claimed an immunity from suit based on sovereignty. They explained that they initially had chosen not to seek immunity on the basis of statehood and suggested that emergent political events in their region had caused a change of plan. The motion for leave to assert defenses was a curiosity—the defendants had not yet answered the amended complaint and were free to assert, by motion to dismiss or otherwise, any colorable defense—and the district court never acted on it.

In the same time frame, the defendants moved for a stay of discovery and the plaintiffs moved for an order compelling discovery. The court granted the requested stay pending resolution of the motion to dismiss the amended complaint. On November 4, 2002, the district court denied the dismissal motion and dissolved the stay. The court flatly rejected the claim of nonjusticiability. *Estates of Ungar ex rel. Strachman* v. *Palestinian Auth.*, 228 F. Supp. 2d 40, 44–47 (D.R.I. 2002) (*Ungar II*). It also determined that the amended complaint stated claims upon which relief could be granted both

[2] This statute provides in pertinent part:

> When a district judge, in making in a civil action an order not otherwise appealable . . ., shall be of the opinion that such order involves a controlling question of law as to which there is substantial ground for difference of opinion and that an immediate appeal from the order may materially advance the ultimate termination of the litigation, he shall so state in writing in such order. The Court of Appeals . . . may thereupon, in its discretion, permit an appeal to be taken from such order, if application is made to it within ten days after the entry of the order. . . .

28 U.S.C. § 1292(b).

under the ATA and under Israeli law. *Id.* at 47–48. Finally, the court reiterated its earlier rejection of the defendants' claim of immunity from service of process and added that the PA, as a governmental entity, was not a sovereign state immune from suit under the ATA. *Id.* at 48–49. Finally, the court declined the defendants' invitation to certify questions for interlocutory review. *Id.* at 49–51 (citing *Klinghoffer* v. *S.N.C. Achille Lauro*, 937 F.2d 44, 47–49 (2d Cir. 1991)).

The PA and the PLO moved for reconsideration and again asked for a stay. Some two months later, the district court granted the plaintiffs' outstanding motion to compel discovery, giving the defendants additional time to respond due to their overseas location. The defendants nonetheless moved for reconsideration of the discovery order and submitted a letter from Palestine's permanent observer at the United Nations, which stated that the defendants could not be expected to respond to discovery due to the unremitting violence in the region. The letter suggested that the defendants should be allowed to wait until there was a final decision on the jurisdictional question before being forced to attend to the discovery requests.

On February 7, 2003, the plaintiffs moved for an entry of default based on the defendants' failure to answer the amended complaint. Six weeks later, the district court denied the defendants' pending motion to reconsider the order compelling discovery. On April 11, the court held a hearing on the defendants' outstanding motion to reconsider its decision in *Ungar II*. The court indicated from the bench that it would deny both that motion and the concomitant request for a stay, but it did not actually enter such an order until April 22, 2003. Meanwhile, a magistrate judge entered the requested default, concluding that the defendants' failure to answer the amended complaint and their refusal to participate in discovery were the result of a deliberate strategic choice. The default was posted on the docket on April 21, 2003.

The defendants filed a notice of appeal to this court on April 23, 2003, in which they sought interlocutory review of both the lower court's decision in *Ungar II* and that court's refusal to reconsider that decision. They averred that they had been deprived of the opportunity to make a showing of sovereign immunity because the district court failed to take action on their motion for leave to assert a sovereign immunity defense, yet proceeded to determine that the defendants had no entitlement to immunity. We summarily affirmed the orders appealed from, noting that the defendants had neither moved to dismiss on the ground of sovereign immunity nor attempted, in the lower court, to make the evidentiary showing required to sustain such a defense. *Ungar* v. *Palestinian Liberation Org.*, No. 03-1544, 2003 WL 21254790, at *1 (1st Cir. May 27, 2003) (per curiam) (unpublished). We added that the defendants' motion for leave to assert a defense was wholly gratuitous, as they did not need the court's permission to raise the sovereign immunity issue at that stage of the case. *See id.*

We issued our order without prejudice to the defendants' future efforts to press their newly asserted sovereign immunity defense in an appropriate fashion. *See id.* (admonishing that the defendants "must adhere to the rules that govern all litigants"). The next pleading, however, came from the plaintiffs, who moved for a default judgment. The defendants responded by filing their third motion to dismiss. This time, they predicated the motion on three bases, namely, (i) that the case centered around nonjusticiable political questions; (ii) that the defendants were entitled to sovereign immunity under the Foreign Sovereign Immunities Act (FSIA), 28 U.S.C. §§ 1602–1611; and (iii) that section 2337(2) of the ATA, which provides that a suit under section 2333 may not be maintained against "a foreign state [or] an agency of a foreign state," independently divested the district court of jurisdiction.

The parties were like ships passing in the night. Pursuing the plaintiffs' path, the magistrate judge, on March 31, 2004, recommended the entry of default judgments against the PA and the PLO in amounts exceeding $116,000,000.[3] The defendants interposed timely objections to the report and recommendation, reasserting their nonjusticiability and sovereign immunity points and contending, for the first time, that they were entitled to a final determination on sovereign immunity (including appellate review) before being required either to answer the complaint or to submit to discovery.

Meanwhile, the district court had been pursuing the course charted by the defendants. On April 23, 2004, it denied the defendants' renewed motion to dismiss the amended complaint. *Estates of Ungar* v. *Palestinian Auth.*, 315 F. Supp. 2d 164, 187 (D.R.I. 2004) (*Ungar III*). The court hewed to its earlier rejection of the defendants' nonjusticiability thesis. *See id.* at 173–74 (referencing *Ungar II*, 228 F. Supp. 2d at 44–47). Next, the court held that the FSIA and section 2337(2) of the ATA were two sides of the same coin with respect to sovereign immunity. *Id.* at 174–75. This left only a single question: "whether the PA and/or the PLO represent or constitute a foreign State and are thus entitled to sovereign immunity." *Id.* at 175. The court answered that question in the negative. *Id.* at 176–87. The plaintiffs immediately moved to amend the court's order pursuant to Fed. R. Civ. P. 59(e), arguing that the sovereign immunity defense had been waived. The defendants did nothing.

On July 12, 2004, the district court went down the plaintiffs' path. It adopted the magistrate judge's "default judgment" report and recommendation in its totality, overruled the defendants' objections thereto, and denied the

[3] The amounts differed slightly. The recommended judgment against the PA was for $116,421,048 and the recommended judgment against the PLO was for $116,415,468. The reasons for this minor disparity are not material to the issues on appeal.

plaintiffs' motion to amend *Ungar III*. *See Estates of Ungar & Ungar ex rel. Strachman* v. *Palestinian Auth.*, 325 F. Supp. 2d 15, 21–22, 26–28 (D.R.I. 2004) (*Ungar IV*). In the course of that decision, the court rebuffed the defendants' claim that they were entitled to a full review of their sovereign immunity defense before being required to answer the complaint or proceed further. *Id.* at 23–24. The court then ordered judgment for the plaintiffs in the recommended amounts. *Id.* at 28. This appeal ensued.

II. Justiciability

The defendants maintain that the complaint against them should have been dismissed because it presents a non-justiciable political question. We find this argument unconvincing.

In *Baker* v. *Carr*, 369 U.S. 186 (1962), the Supreme Court provided guidance as to the attributes of a nonjusticiable political question. The Court explained that "it is the relationship between the judiciary and the coordinate branches of the Federal Government . . . which gives rise to the 'political question.'" *Id.* at 210. Withal, not "every case or controversy which touches foreign relations lies beyond judicial cognizance." *Id.* at 211. Determining justiciability requires an "analysis of the particular question posed, in terms of the history of its management by the political branches, of its susceptibility to judicial handling in light of its nature and posture in the specific case, and of the possible consequences of judicial action." *Id.* at 211–12. The Court then set forth six tests designed to confirm or negate the existence of a political question:

> [1] a textually demonstrable constitutionalcommitment of the issue to a coordinate political department; or [2] a lack of judicially discoverable and manageable standards for resolving it; or [3] the impossibility of deciding without an initial policy determination of a kind clearly for nonjudicial discretion; or [4] the impossibility of a court's undertaking independent resolution without expressing lack of the respect due coordinate branches of government; or [5] an unusual need for unquestioning adherence to a political decision already made; or [6] the potentiality of embarrassment from multifarious pronouncements by various departments on one question.

Id. at 217. The Court explained, in a later case, that "[t]hese tests are probably listed in descending order of both importance and certainty." *Vieth* v. *Jubelirer*, 124 S. Ct. 1769, 1776 (2004).

The defendants assert with little elaboration that the central issue in this case fails each of the six tests. Most of their argumentation presumes that the district court intruded into forbidden territory when it interpreted an array of United Nations resolutions and Israeli-PLO agreements in a politically controversial manner. To this they add that the default judgment entered by the district court was so huge that it amounted to a political statement.

The defendants' position rests on a misunderstanding of the fundamental nature of this action. This is a tort suit brought under a legislative scheme that Congress enacted for the express purpose of providing a legal remedy for injuries or death occasioned by acts of international terrorism. The defendants are organizations that allegedly violated the statute. They have attempted to avoid liability by wrapping themselves in the cloak of sovereign immunity. The question we must answer, then, is whether the defendants have set forth sufficient evidence to support their claim of immunity—no more and no less.

On this view of the case, the plaintiffs easily clear the six *Baker* hurdles. To begin, the lower court's immunity decision neither signaled an official position on behalf of the United States with respect to the political recognition of Palestine nor amounted to the usurpation of a power committed to some other branch of government. After all, Congress enacted the ATA, and the President signed it. The very purpose of the law is to allow the courts to determine questions of sovereign immunity under a legal, as opposed to a political, regime.[4] Seen in this light, the district court's decision denying immunity did not impede the constitutional prerogatives of the political branches over foreign policy. *See generally Baker*, 369 U.S. at 211 & n.31 (noting that the Constitution commits foreign relations to the executive and legislative branches, thus permitting them to determine what "may be done in the exercise of this political power").

The second and third *Baker* hurdles present no insuperable obstacles here. The district court had access to judicially manageable standards for resolving the issue before it, *see infra* Part III(A), and those standards did not require the court to make nonjudicial policy determinations. Both sides agreed that the definition of a "state" under the relevant statutes was informed by an objective test rooted in international law and articulated in the Restatement (Third) of Foreign Relations. Under these circumstances, the determination of whether the defendants have adduced sufficient evidence to satisfy that definition is quintessentially appropriate for a judicial body. *See Kadic* v. *Karadzic*, 70 F.3d 232, 249 (2d Cir. 1995).

The final three hurdles need not concern us. These tests are "relevant only if judicial resolution of a question would contradict prior decisions taken by a political branch in those limited contexts where such contradiction

---

[4] The FSIA operates in the same fashion. *See* 28 U.S.C. § 1602 ("The Congress finds that the determination by United States courts of the claims of foreign states to immunity from the jurisdiction of such courts would serve the interests of justice and would protect the rights of both foreign states and litigants in United States courts."); H.R. Rep. No. 94-1487, at 7 (1976), *reprinted in* 1976 U.S.C.C.A.N. 6604, 6606 ("A principle purpose of [the FSIA] is to transfer the determination of sovereign immunity from the executive branch to the judicial branch, thereby reducing the foreign policy implications of immunity determinations and assuring litigants that these often crucial decisions are made on purely legal grounds. . . .").

would seriously interfere with important governmental interests." *id.* Here, the political branches have enacted a law that leaves undiminished their ability either to recognize or withhold recognition from foreign states, while leaving to the courts the responsibility of determining the existence vel non of statehood for jurisdictional purposes. Moreover, the district court's resolution of that question is not incompatible with any formal position thus far taken by the political branches. By the same token, its jurisdictional decision does not turn a blind eye to any position expressed by those responsible for conducting the nation's foreign relations. *Cf. Republic of Austria* v. *Altmann,* 124 S. Ct. 2240, 2255 (2004) (noting that the State Department has retained authority to file "statements of interest suggesting that courts decline to exercise jurisdiction in particular cases implicating foreign sovereign immunity"). As a result, the decision did not signify a lack of respect for, or conflict with, the wishes of the political branches. No more is exigible for this purpose. *See Baker,* 369 U.S. at 212–13 (endorsing judicial competence in matters touching on foreign relations in the absence of any "conclusive governmental action" or "recognizedly authoritative executive declaration") (citation and internal quotation marks omitted).

The defendants make a number of specific arguments, but these are largely derivative of their disagreement with the result reached by the district court. Their unhappiness is understandable, but legally irrelevant. The reality is that, in these tempestuous times, any decision of a United States court on matters relating to the Israeli-Palestinian conflict will engender strong feelings. Be that as it may, the capacity to stir emotions is not enough to render an issue nonjusticiable. For jurisdictional purposes, courts must be careful to distinguish between political questions and cases having political overtones. *See Klinghoffer,* 937 F.2d at 49.

The one remaining argument that warrants particularized attention is the defendants' assertion that the district court made a political statement in calibrating the size of the award. That assertion is wholly unsupported. The judgment reflects the wrongful death of a youthful man and includes a trebling of damages as mandated by law. *See* 18 U.S.C. § 2333(a). It also includes attorneys' fees. *See id.* The defendants have not challenged either the measure of damages utilized by the lower court or the integrity of its mathematical computations. We add, moreover, that even if the court erred on the side of generosity—a matter on which we take no view—a mere error in the calculation of a damages award would not implicate the propriety of federal subject matter jurisdiction. We therefore reject the defendants' "political statement" assertion as meritless.

To say more on this aspect of the case would be supererogatory. The short of it is that the political question doctrine does not preclude judicial resolution of the plaintiffs' case. We turn, therefore, to the merits of the sovereign immunity defense.

III. Sovereign Immunity

We divide our discussion of the defendants' sovereign immunity defense into segments, starting with the legal framework and historical background. We then proceed to the merits.

A. The Legal Landscape

The FSIA, with exceptions not relevant here, provides that "a foreign state shall be immune from the jurisdiction of the courts of the United States." 28 U.S.C. § 1604. Although the statute does not define the term "foreign state," it makes pellucid that the term includes "a political subdivision of a foreign state or an agency or instrumentality of a foreign state." *Id.* § 1603 (a). It also defines what constitutes an agency or instrumentality of a foreign state. *Id.* § 1603(b).

The ATA contains analogous language. It provides that no civil action thereunder may be maintained against "a foreign state, an agency of a foreign state, or an officer or employee of a foreign state or an agency thereof acting within his or her official capacity or under color of legal authority." 18 U.S.C. § 2337(2). Like the FSIA, the ATA contains no definition of the term "foreign state."

Because the two statutory regimes use language that is similar but not identical, the first—and most obvious—question is whether there are substantive differences in the meaning of the term "foreign state" as used in the FSIA and the ATA, respectively. The district court concluded that the two statutes were to be read in pari materia. *See Ungar III*, 315 F. Supp. 2d at 175. We agree with that conclusion.

We recognize, of course, that even identical terms can have divergent meanings when used in different statutes. *See, e.g., Hanover Ins. Co.* v. *United States*, 880 F.2d 1503, 1504 (1st Cir. 1989); *United States* v. *Sterling Nat. Bank & Trust Co.*, 494 F.2d 919, 923 (2d Cir. 1974). Generally speaking, however, that phenomenon occurs only when the purpose, history, and structure of the statutes make manifest a principled basis for interpreting the words differently. *See, e.g., Perez-Arellano* v. *Smith*, 279 F.3d 791, 794 (9th Cir. 2002). Here, however, the Supreme Court has observed that "the text and structure of the FSIA demonstrate Congress' intention that the FSIA be the sole basis for obtaining jurisdiction over a foreign state in our courts." *Argentine Republic* v. *Amerada Hess Shipping Corp.*, 488 U.S. 428, 434 (1989). Nothing in either the language or legislative history of the ATA gives any indication that Congress intended the newer statute to supercede, rather than to mirror, the detailed jurisdictional framework described in the FSIA. To cinch matters, the Supreme Court, in a post-ATA case, recently repeated its admonition that "courts should decide claims of sovereign immunity in conformity with the [FSIA's] principles." *Altmann*, 124 S. Ct. at 2249. Consequently, we regard an assertion of sovereign immunity under the ATA, 18 U.S.C. § 2337(2), as being functionally equivalent to an assertion of sovereign immunity under the FSIA, 28 U.S.C. § 1604.

This brings a second question into focus. Since neither the FSIA nor the ATA define the term "foreign state" as it relates to a sovereign power, we must determine the intended meaning of that term. There is no controlling precedent in this circuit as to the essential attributes of statehood in this context. The parties, however, find common ground in their shared conviction that the definition should be derived by application of the standard set forth in the Restatement (Third) of Foreign Relations. This standard deems a state to be "an entity that has a defined territory and a permanent population, under the control of its own government, and that engages in, or has the capacity to engage in, formal relations with other such entities." Restatement (Third) of Foreign Relations § 201 (1987). Under the Restatement standard, political recognition—typically thought of as "a formal acknowledgment by a nation that another entity possesses the qualifications for nationhood," *N.Y. Chinese TV Programs, Inc.* v. *U.E. Enters., Inc.*, 954 F.2d 847, 853 (2d Cir. 1992)—is not a prerequisite to a finding of statehood. *See* Restatement (Third) of Foreign Relations § 202 cmt. b (explaining that "[a]n entity that satisfies the requirements of § 201 is a state whether or not its statehood is formally recognized by other states").

Using the Restatement standard as the rule of decision is a colorable position. In this regard, the Restatement tracks the historical standard found in international law. *See Nat'l Petrochem. Co. of Iran* v. *M/T Stolt Sheaf*, 860 F.2d 551, 553 (2d Cir. 1988); *see also* Convention on Rights and Duties of States (Montevideo Convention), Dec. 26, 1933, art. 1, 49 Stat. 3097, 3100, 165 L. N.T.S. 19, 25.[5] In addition, the FSIA's legislative history is itself replete with congressional references to sovereign immunity's roots in international law. *See, e.g.*, H.R. Rep. No. 94–1487, at 7 (1976), *reprinted in* 1976 U.S.C.C.A.N. 6604, 6605 (noting that the objective of the bill was to codify sovereign immunity doctrine as recognized by international law and to ensure that this international standard would be applied in federal litigation). The legislative history goes on to recount that the very foundation of foreign sovereign immunity in federal jurisprudence rests on the Supreme Court's recognition of that doctrine in *The Schooner Exchange* v. *McFaddon*, 11 U.S. (7 Cranch) 116 (1812). There, the Court established that the federal courts generally have no jurisdiction over suits involving foreign sovereigns with whom the United States is at peace, deriving such an immunity from the custom and practice of international law. *Id.* at 135–46.

[5] The Montevideo Convention is still in effect and the United States is a party to it. *See* United States Dep't of State, *Treaties in Force* 480 (2004).

Over time, the federal courts came to rely less on international law and more on the actions of the State Department in determining whether to grant immunity in individual cases. H.R. Rep. No. 94-1487, at 8, *reprinted in* 1976 U.S.C.C.A.N. at 6606. The committee report that accompanied the FSIA noted that this practice was generally at odds with the views of the international community; indeed, in "virtually every country . . . sovereign immunity is a question of international law to be determined by the courts." *Id.* at 9, *reprinted in* 1976 U.S.C.C.A.N. at 6607–08. To that end, Congress endeavored to bring the United States back into conformity with the world community by taking immunity decisions out of the hands of the executive branch and depositing them in the judicial branch. *Id.* at 12, *reprinted in* 1976 U.S.C.C.A.N. at 6610. The committee report unequivocally restates the "central premise of the bill" as being that "decisions on claims by foreign states to sovereign immunity are best made by the judiciary on the basis of a statutory regime which *incorporates standards recognized under international law.*" *Id.* at 14, *reprinted in* 1976 U.S.C.C.A.N. at 6613 (emphasis supplied).

This legislative history offers strong support for the proposition that courts should look to international law to determine statehood for purposes of the FSIA. The case law that has evolved in the lower federal courts, while scanty, pushes in the same direction. *See, e.g., Morgan Guar. Trust Co.* v. *Republic of Palau*, 924 F.2d 1237, 1243–47 (2d Cir. 1991) (using Restatement standard to determine whether Palau qualified as a foreign state); *Klinghoffer*, 937 F.2d at 47–49 (same with respect to PLO). Consequently, for purposes of this case, we accept the parties' agreement that the Restatement standard controls the statehood question.[6]

B. The Historical Background

Following World War I, the League of Nations placed the region of Palestine, formerly a part of the Ottoman Empire, under a mandate. The mandate system grew out of the idea that some former colonies of nations defeated in World War I were "not yet able to stand by themselves" and should be placed under the tutelage of "advanced nations." League of Nations Covenant art. 22, paras. 1, 2. Palestine was among those territories deemed to

[6] We caution that the Restatement standard, though embraced by both sides in this case, is not inevitably correct. It may be argued that a foreign state, for purposes of the FSIA, is an entity that has been recognized as a sovereign by the United States government. *See, e.g., Ungar III*, 315 F. Supp. 2d at 186–87 (alternate holding); *cf.* 13B Charles Alan Wright, Arthur R. Miller, & Edward H. Cooper, Federal Practice & Procedure § 3604 (2d ed. 1984) (noting that for purposes of former 28 U.S.C. § 1332(a)(2)(1970)—a statute modified by the FSIA—federal courts generally had held that a foreign state was one that had been recognized as such by the United States government, in either a de jure or de facto capacity (collecting cases)). Here, however, all roads lead to Rome. The defendants' sovereign immunity defense fails the Restatement test. *See infra* Part III(C). If recognition were the test, the result would be the same. After all, the United States has not recognized Palestine as a sovereign nation. Thus, we need not probe the point too deeply.

"have reached a stage of development where their existence as independent nations [could] be provisionally recognized," subject to "administrative advice and assistance" from more mature governments. *Id.* at para. 4. The United Kingdom held the mandate over Palestine. Rather than "advice and assistance," however, the powers conferred were more akin to rule. Subject to implicit limitations not relevant here, the mandate gave the United Kingdom "full powers of legislation and of administration" over the region, as well as "control of the foreign relations of Palestine." *Mandate for Palestine* arts. 1, 12, League of Nations Doc. C.529 M.314 1922 VI (1922). The mandate also made the United Kingdom responsible for "placing [Palestine] under such political, administrative and economic conditions as will secure the establishment of the Jewish national home." *Id.* art. 2.

Heavy Jewish immigration to the region followed, owing in large part to the persecution of Jews in Europe. Tension between the Jewish and Arab populations led to violence and civil unrest. *See* United Nations Dep't of Pub. Info., The Question of Palestine & The United Nations at 3, U.N. Doc. DPI/2276, U.N. Sales No. 04.I.15 (2003) (Question of Palestine). By 1947, the United Kingdom's patience had worn thin. It took steps to divest itself of the mandate and dump the problem into the lap of the United Nations. *Id.*

The United Nations rose to the occasion. It formulated a plan that involved the creation of two independent states within the mandate territory: one Jewish, the other Arab. This plan also purposed to make Jerusalem an international enclave administered by the United Nations. *See Future Gov't of Palestine*, G.A. Res. 181(II), U.N. GAOR, 2d Sess., at 131, U.N. Doc. A/519 (1947). The plan delineated the boundaries of the two states and the Jerusalem enclave, *id.* at 142–46; established a timetable for the withdrawal of British forces; and proposed to end the existing mandate no later than August 1, 1948. *Id.* at 132–33. As the British withdrew, power would temporarily vest in a United Nations commission pending the establishment of provisional governments by each of the two putative states. *Id.* at 133. At that point, the provisional governments would "progressively receive" full administrative responsibility. *Id.* at 134. When the independence of a state had "become effective," that state would be accorded "sympathetic consideration" for admission to the United Nations. *Id.* at 142.

The plan never took effect. Although Jewish leaders accepted it, Palestinian leaders did not. *See* Question of Palestine at 10. The Palestinians, still representing two-thirds of the population of the affected territory, argued vociferously against partition. *Id.* at 7, 10. Faced with a steadily deteriorating situation, the British abandoned the mandate and withdrew from the region. *Id.* at 11. On the same date—May 14, 1948—Jewish leaders announced the establishment of the State of Israel, using the territorial boundaries delineated in G.A. Res. 181(II) to demarcate its borders. *Id.*

The next day, armed forces of the surrounding Arab states entered the former mandate territory. *Id.* The Arab League notified the U.N.'s Secretary-General that they intended to fill the vacuum left by the abrupt departure of the British forces and to restore law and order in the region. *See* United Nations, The Origins and Evolution of the Palestine Problem 137–38 (1990).

The Arab invasion precipitated the first Arab-Israeli war. Question of Palestine at 11. During the conflict, nearly three-quarters of a million Palestinian refugees fled Israeli- controlled territory. *Id.* at 81. By the time of the eventual armistice, Egypt had taken control of the Gaza Strip, Jordan was in control of the West Bank (including East Jerusalem), and Israel had taken control of the remainder of the former mandate territory. *Id.* at 12.

This division persisted until 1967, when war again broke out between Israel, on the one hand, and Egypt, Jordan, and Syria, on the other hand. *Id.* at 18. Israel prevailed. Its spoils included occupation of the Gaza Strip and the West Bank, as well as the Sinai peninsula (previously under Egyptian rule) and the Golan Heights region of Syria. *Id.*

The U.N.'s Security Council attempted to undo these gains by diplomatic means. It issued a resolution that called for the "[w]ithdrawal of Israeli armed forces from territories occupied in the recent conflict" and beseeched the protagonists to respect and acknowledge "the sovereignty, territorial integrity and political independence of every State in the area." S.C. Res. 242, U.N. SCOR, 22d Sess., Resolutions and Decisions, at 8, U.N. Doc. S/INF/22/Rev.2 (1967). The document did not directly address the question of Palestine. The PLO, which had been formed in 1964, strongly criticized the resolution for that reason. Question of Palestine at 19.

In 1968, the PLO declared that the international community had failed to secure the rights of Palestinian Arabs and vowed to take up the struggle. *Id.* at 31. In 1973, a third Arab- Israeli war led the Security Council to renew its call for implementation of the terms of Resolution 242. *See* S.C. Res. 338, U.N. SCOR, 28th Sess., Resolutions and Decisions, at 10, U.N. Doc.S/INF/29 (1973). The following year, the United Nations General Assembly adopted two resolutions: one affirming the rights of Palestinians to "self-determination without external interference" and to "national independence, and sovereignty," and the other granting the PLO observer status at the United Nations. G.A. Res. 3236 & 3237, U.N. GAOR, 29th Sess., Supp. No. 31, at 4, U.N. Doc. A/9631 (1974).

Over the next decade, the PLO provided municipal services to Palestinians in the West Bank and other refugee-dominated areas. By the early 1980s, these activities had put into place "an extensive rival bureaucratic structure." 25 *Encyclopaedia Britannica* 423 (15th ed. 2003). PLO attacks against

Israel grew in intensity, eventually leading to Israel's invasion of Lebanon and the expulsion of a large PLO contingent. Question of Palestine at 26–28.

On July 31, 1988, Jordan gave up its claims to the West Bank. *See* Jordan: Statement Concerning Disengagement from the West Bank and Palestinian Self-Determination, 27 I.L.M. 1637 (1988). Within a few weeks thereafter, the PLO, speaking from exile in Algeria, issued a "Declaration of Independence" that proclaimed the "establishment of the State of Palestine in the land of Palestine with its capital at Jerusalem." Palestine Nat'l Council: Political Communique & Decl. of Indep., 27 I.L.M. 1660, 1670 (1988). In response, the United Nations decided to use the term "Palestine" instead of "Palestine Liberation Organization" within the United Nations system, but expressly stated that this redesignation did not enhance the group's observer status. G.A. Res. 43/177, U.N. GAOR, 43d Sess., Supp. No. 49, at 62, U.N. Doc. A/43/49 (1988).

In 1993, the United States helped to broker the first agreement between Israel and the PLO. Under its terms, Israel accepted the PLO as the representative of the Palestinian people and the PLO acknowledged Israel's statehood. Question of Palestine at 47. This rapprochement culminated in the signing of the first of the Oslo Accords: the Declaration of Principles on Interim Self-Government Arrangements (DOP), Sept. 19, 1993, Isr.-P.L.O., 32 I.L.M. 1525. The DOP's stated purposes included the establishment of a Palestinian interim self-governing authority (the PA) as a precursor to a permanent arrangement based on Security Council Resolutions 242 and 338. *Id.* art. I, 32 I.L.M. at 1527. The DOP treated the West Bank and the Gaza Strip as a single territorial unit and stated that, when certain conditions had been achieved, Israel would transfer authority over "education and culture, health, social welfare, direct taxation, and tourism" in those areas to the PA. *Id.* art. VI, 32 I.L.M. at 1529. The DOP also set forth a framework for negotiating the structure of the PA. *Id.* art. VII, 32 I.L.M. at 1530–31. And, it specified that while the PA, when created, would be responsible for self-policing, Israel would remain responsible for external security (including the overall safety of Israelis), in the affected territory. *Id.* art. VIII, 32 I.L.M. at 1531.

The protagonists reached agreement as to the structure of the PA in 1994, and the PA then became a reality. *See* Agreement on the Gaza Strip and the Jericho Area, May 4, 1994, Isr.-PLO, art. IV, 33 I.L.M. 622, 628. On September 28, 1995, Israel and the PLO signed the interim agreement called for in the DOP, aspiring to reach a permanent agreement within five years. *See* Interim Agreement on the West Bank & the Gaza Strip, Sept. 28, 1995, Isr.- P.L.O., pmbl., 36 I.L.M. 551, 558. The interim agreement enumerated those powers and responsibilities to be transferred to the PA. For example, it granted executive responsibility to the PA with respect to "all matters within its jurisdiction," including the formulation of policies, the issuance of rules and regulations, and the making of contracts. *Id.* art. IX, 36 I.L.M. at 560–61. The PA was, however, denied authority over foreign relations, including the establishment of embassies, the hiring of diplomatic staff, and the exercise of diplomatic functions.[7] *Id.* Moreover, the interim agreement took pains to note that Israel would "continue to exercise powers and responsibilities not so transferred." *Id.* art. I, 36 I.L.M. at 558.

The drafters of the interim agreement considered the West Bank and the Gaza Strip as a single territorial unit. Nevertheless, they subdivided the land within that unit into three main zones, each under a different level of PA control. *Id.* art. XI, 36 I.L.M. at 561–62. The overall framework required the PA to police the Palestinian populace but continued Israeli responsibility over external threats and border defense. *Id.* arts. XII-XIV, 36 I.L.M. at 562–63. Israel also retained jurisdiction over all Israeli settlers living in the territory. *Id.*

The PA's legislative powers were similarly restricted. The interim agreement specified that any law that "amends or abrogates existing laws or military orders, which exceeds the jurisdiction of the Council or which is otherwise inconsistent with the provisions of the DOP, this Agreement, or of any other agreement that may be reached between the two sides during the interim period, shall have no effect and shall be void *ab initio.*" *Id.* art. XVIII, 36 I.L.M. at 564–65.

In January of 1996, the PA held an election. Question of Palestine at 51. Negotiations on a permanent settlement began shortly thereafter, but terrorist attacks stalled the process. *Id.* at 51–52. The events giving rise to this case occurred during this period.

In August of 1998, the United Nations enhanced the PLO's observer status, granting it the right to participate in General Assembly debate, albeit without a vote. G.A. Res. 52/250, U.N. GAOR, 52d Sess., Supp. No. 49, at 4, U.N. Doc. A/52/49 (1998). That October, Israel and the PLO signed the Wye River Memorandum (a document expressly subject to the terms of both the DOP and the interim agreement). *See* Wye River Memorandum (Interim Agreement), Oct. 23, 1998, Isr.-P.L.O., 37 I.L.M. 1251. This marked a restarting of the peace process. The following year, the parties negotiated a similar sort of interim agreement. *see* Sharm El- Sheikh Memorandum, Sept. 4, 1999, Isr.-P.L.O., 38 I.L.M. 1465. In 2000, however, the two sides failed in an effort to reach a final agreement. Question of Palestine at 54. A firestorm of Palestinian attacks and Israeli reprisals ensued. *Id.* at 55.

[7] The interim agreement permitted the PLO to conduct limited foreign affairs activities on behalf of the PA. Those activities pertained only to economic, cultural, scientific, and educational matters. Interim Agreement on the West Bank & the Gaza Strip art. IX, 36 I.L.M. at 560–61.

In 2003, the Quartet—a group comprised of representatives of the United States, the European Union, the Russian Federation, and the United Nations—presented a "road map" setting forth a series of aspirational steps designed to break the impasse and move toward a permanent two-state solution in the region. *See Letter Dated 7 May 2003 from the Secretary-General Addressed to the President of the Security Council*, U.N. Doc. S/2003/529 (2003).

To date, Israel and the PLO have not traveled down the newly mapped road. Peace negotiations have been virtually non- existent since 2000, and the violence continues. There is, however, a glimmer of hope: the recent election of a new PA president has thawed relations between the two sides and created a sense of anticipation that a meaningful peace process will resume. *See* Steven Erlanger, *Abbas Declares War With Israel Effectively Over*, N.Y. Times, Feb. 14, 2005, at A1.

C. The Merits

We now reach the merits of the sovereign immunity defense. In scrutinizing a district court's resolution of a foreign sovereign immunity issue, we review factual findings for clear error and legal conclusions de novo. *Karaha Bodas Co.* v. *Perusahaan Pertambangan Minyak Dan Gas Bumi Negara*, 313 F.3d 70, 80 (2d Cir. 2002). Here, the defendants' claim to sovereign immunity derives from their assertion that Palestine is a state, and the evidence presented to the district court in support of that assertion consisted entirely of indisputably authentic international legal documents. The district court's determination that Palestine was not a state was premised on a legal conclusion: the court determined that the defendants' documentary proffer did not satisfy the legal standard derived from international law. Our review of that decision is de novo. *Id.*

International law defines a state as "an entity that has a defined territory and a permanent population, under the control of its own government, and that engages in, or has the capacity to engage in, formal relations with other such entities." Restatement (Third) of Foreign Relations § 201. This definition derives from the Montevideo Convention of 1933. *See supra* Part III(A). In applying this definition, some courts have subdivided the analysis into four parts, asking whether the putative state (i) has a defined territory and (ii) a permanent population, which (iii) is under the control of its own government, and (iv) has the capacity to engage in foreign relations. *See, e.g., Klinghoffer*, 937 F.2d at 47–48.

In practice, the third element is the most salient factor in the statehood calculus. *See Knox* v. *PLO*, 306 F. Supp. 2d 424, 434 (S.D.N.Y. 2004); *See also* James Crawford, The Creation of States in International Law 42 (1979) (Creation of States). The Restatement's explanation of this element is rather sparse; it notes only that "[a] state need not have any particular form of government, but there must be some authority exercising governmental functions and able to represent the entity in international relations." Restatement (Third) of Foreign Relations § 201 cmt. d. To satisfy these requirements, a state's government must, at a bare minimum, be independent and in general control of its territory, maintaining at least a modicum of law and order.[8] *See* Creation of States at 45–46; *See also* Nii Lante Wallace-Bruce, Claims to Statehood in International Law 54 (1994) (explaining that what is required "is a coherent system of authority structures regulating . . . the territory under that government's control"). In short, the existence of a state demands a community integrated and organized as a political unit. *See* 1 Robert Jennings & Arthur Watts, Oppenheim's International Law 122 (9th ed. 1992). Its government must speak for the state as a whole; the mere presence of independent tribes or factions within a territory, lacking common institutions, cannot constitute a government in control. *See Western Sahara*, 1975 I.C.J. 12, 63 (Oct. 16).

The first, second, and fourth elements are dependent on (or, sometimes, subsumed by) the third. As to the first—defined territory—the "only requirement is that the State must consist of a certain coherent territory effectively governed." Creation of States at 40. As such, this element is merely a function of independence and governmental control. *Id.* So too the second element, which typically is satisfied by showing a permanent population within the defined territory. *See id.* at 40–42. The relationships of these elements with the all-important third element is readily evident. As one court put it, the question is essentially whether the entity claiming statehood has a "defined territory *under its control*" and a "permanent population *under its control*." *Knox*, 306 F. Supp. 2d at 434 (emphasis in original).

The fourth element—"capacity to engage in foreign relations"—focuses on "competence, within [a state's] own constitutional system, to conduct international relations with other states, as well as the political, technical, and financial capabilities to do so." Restatement (Third) of Foreign Relations § 201 cmt. e. Again, this is a function of independence and effective government control. *See* Creation of States at 47–48. In that sense, then, it too is dependent on the third element.

We add that the party who alleges sovereign immunity has the burden of proving that status. *See Drexel Burnham Lambert Group, Inc.* v. *Comm. of Receivers*, 12 F.3d 317, 325 (2d Cir. 1993); *Alberti* v. *Empresa Nicaraguense de la Carne*, 705 F.2d 250, 253 (7th Cir. 1983). With this in mind, we move from the general to the specific.

[8] Of course, if statehood exists at a finite point in time, it is not terminated by belligerent occupation, without more. *See* Restatement (Third) of Foreign Relations § 201, reporter's note 3 (explaining that "[m]ilitary occupation, whether during war or after an armistice, does not terminate statehood").

The defendants argue that the state of Palestine exists; that they constitute core elements of that state; and that, therefore, they are immune from suit under the FSIA (and, thus, under the ATA). This argument has a quicksilver quality: it is hard to pin down exactly when or how the defendants assert that Palestine achieved statehood. At various points in their briefs, they hint at three possibilities: (i) the period from the beginning of the mandate through the 1967 Arab-Israeli war; (ii) the period from the end of that war up until the creation of the Palestinian Authority (1994); and (iii) the period from 1994 forward. In an abundance of caution, we consider whether the defendants have made a prima facie showing of statehood at any such juncture.

For each of the three periods, the defendants' proffer is much the same anent the first and second elements of the test for statehood. With respect to the first, the defendants consistently claim that Palestine comprises the territory defined by Security Council Resolution 242, that is, those portions of the once and former mandate territory occupied by Israel during the 1967 war (including the West Bank, the Gaza Strip, and East Jerusalem). With respect to the second element, the defendants asseverate that this territory has had a permanent population from time immemorial (and, thus, that it had such a population throughout the three periods with which we are concerned). Assuming, arguendo, the accuracy of these averments, the focus shifts to the third prong of the test for statehood. At that stage, the question becomes whether the defendants have shown that the identified territory and population are self-governing. In answering this question, we look separately at each period.

1. The Initial Period

As to the pre-1967 period, the defendants' argument seems to be that the territory that comprised the Palestinian portion of the mandate was a state prior to, during, and after the mandate. Their support for this thesis is very weak; they assert only that throughout this interval there were local governmental institutions in place that catered to the Palestinian populace.

This assertion is manifestly insufficient to make the defendants' prima facie case of statehood. The third element of the test requires governmental independence and control of a defined territory. That element plainly was not satisfied while the defined territory was part of the Ottoman Empire; even if the Palestinian people exercised operating control over domestic governmental functions in the region—and the defendants offer nothing to support such a claim—that would not be sufficient to show the existence of an independent political unit that *controlled* the territory.

The same is true for the latter portions of the period. During the currency of the mandate, the United Kingdom exercised suzerainty over the administration and laws of the defined territory. *See Klausner* v. *Levy*, 83 F. Supp.

599, 600 (E.D. Va. 1949). Following the United Kingdom's relinquishment of the mandate and the onset of the 1967 Arab-Israeli war, the Israelis occupied much of the land designated for a future Arab state, and the Egyptians and Jordanians seized the rest. The net result is that, at all times, other states had control over the defined territory.

The defendants resist the obvious conclusion. In particular, they rely upon United Nations General Assembly Resolution 181(II), noting that it called for an independent Arab state to come into existence no later than October 1, 1948, and that this became a reality in the sense that "Palestinian government institutions continued to function under Egyptian and Jordanian occupation much as they had under the Mandate." Appellants' Br. at 21. These assertions are insufficient to show that a political unit was in control of the defined territory and populace. The mere fact that the United Nations conceived an aspirational plan for Palestinian statehood does not establish the existence of a state. Nor does the fact that the Egyptians and Jordanians occupied and controlled a significant portion of the defined territory immediately following the end of the mandate aid the defendants' cause. To the contrary, the fact is a stark reminder that no state of Palestine could have come into being at that time. *See Knox*, 306 F. Supp. 2d at 437 (noting that under "international law, a state will *maintain* its statehood during a belligerent occupation . . . but it would be anomalous indeed to hold that a state may *achieve* sufficient independence and statehood in the first instance while subject to and laboring under the hostile military occupation of a separate sovereign").

2. The Middle Period

The interval following the occupation of the West Bank and the Gaza Strip by Israel in 1967 is no more promising. With respect to this time span, the defendants rely heavily on Security Council Resolution 242 and its hortatory call for Israeli withdrawal from "territories occupied in the recent conflict" and for all states to respect and acknowledge "the sovereignty, territorial integrity and political independence of every State in the area." That reliance is mislaid. There is a vast difference between what should be and what is; the fact that some political leaders recognize that particular territory should comprise a state does not make that territory a state under the prevailing principles of international law.

What counts is that the defendants have not presented *any* evidence indicating that Palestine actually became a state following Israel's conquest of the lands previously occupied by Jordan and Egypt. The one circumstance to which the defendants advert—that the Israelis did not dismantle the local governmental institutions in the region—is wholly inadequate to show that there was a Palestinian state underlying the Israeli occupation.

The territory went directly from Jordanian/Egyptian control to Israeli control, thus undermining the defendants' statehood argument. *See id.*

To be sure, the defendants point proudly to the U.N.'s 1974 recognition of the PLO. We do not minimize the political significance of that event. The fact remains, however, that neither political recognition of the PLO nor United Nations support for self-governance is sufficient to signify that the Restatement's conditions for statehood have been met. *See Klinghoffer*, 937 F.2d at 48 (noting that the PLO did not satisfy the objective requirements for statehood despite its political recognition by some foreign states).

3. The Most Recent Period

The defendants' argument for current statehood posits that Palestine's changing status over the last decade marked the emergence of the defined territory from Israeli control and the establishment of a Palestinian government in its place. The PLO's 1988 declaration of independence adumbrated the inception of this period. The period itself commenced, however, in 1994, the signal event being the creation of the PA as an entity having some lawful authority in the West Bank and Gaza. The defendants suggest that this development signified the birth of a government sufficiently in control of the defined territory to satisfy the third element of the Restatement test. We reject the suggestion.

Undoubtedly, the agreements to which the defendants allude vested some autonomy in the newly created PA. But the authority so transferred was limited and, during and after that transition, Israel explicitly reserved control over all matters not transferred. *See* Interim Agreement art. I, 36 I.L.M. at 558. Several of these reserved powers are incompatible with the notion that the PA had independent governmental control over the defined territory. To illustrate, the interim agreement expressly denied the PA the right to conduct foreign relations, *id.* art. IX, 36 I.L.M. at 561; left Israel with an undiminished ability to defendand control the territorial borders, *id.* art. XII, 36 I.L.M. at 562; denied the PA the right to create or maintain either an army or a navy,[9] *id.* art. XIV, 36 I.L.M. at 563; retained Israeli control over the territorial airspace, *id.* at Annex I, art. XIII, 36 I.L.M. at 586; and placed severe restrictions on the PA's lawmaking ability (declaring, inter alia, that any laws passed in contravention of the DOP would be void ab initio), *id.* art. XVIII, 36 I.L.M. at 565. These restrictions remain in effect. It is, therefore, transparently clear that the PA has not yet exercised sufficient governmental control over Palestine to satisfy the third element of the Restatement test. *See* Geoffrey R. Watson, The Oslo Accords 68–72 (2000) (concluding that "there was no Palestinian state at the time of the signing of the Interim Agreement"); D.J. Harris, Cases and Materials on International Law 226

[9] The PA was permitted to organize a police force, but this had no jurisdiction over Israeli citizens within the territory. *See* Interim Agreement at Annex I, art. XI, 36 I.L.M. at 585.

(5th ed. 1998) (concluding that the interim agreement "fall[s] short of [achieving] statehood for the Palestinian people"); United Nations Comm'n on Human Rights, *Question of the Violation of Human Rights in the Occupied Arab Territories, Including Palestine* at 12, U.N. Doc. E/Cn.4/2001/121 (2001) (noting that, as of 2001, Palestine "still falls short of the accepted criteria of statehood").[10]

The defendants do not deny that these limitations are incompatible with statehood, but, rather, contend that they were imposed by force and that the Israeli occupation is all that is preventing the full exercise of the prerogatives of statehood. The problem with this contention is that it presupposes that Palestine was a state *before* the Israeli occupation—and the defendants have not shown that it was. *See Knox*, 306 F. Supp. 2d at 437.

We recognize that the status of the Palestinian territories is in many ways sui generis. Here, however, the defendants have not carried their burden of showing that Palestine satisfied the requirements for statehood under the applicable principles of international law at any point in time. In view of the unmistakable legislative command that sovereign immunity shall only be accorded to states—a command reflected in both the FSIA and the ATA—the defendants' sovereign immunity defense must fail.

IV. The Default Judgment

We come now to the defendants' protest that they were entitled to a final determination on the sovereign immunity question (including appellate review) before they could be required to bear any of the burdens of litigation. In mounting this protest, the defendants place great weight on *In re Papandreou*, 139 F.3d 247 (D.C. Cir. 1998). There, the Greek governmental entities and officials moved to dismiss claims against them on grounds of lack of in personam jurisdiction, forum non conveniens, and sovereign immunity. *Id.* at 249. The plaintiffs sought discovery for the limited purpose of determining whether FSIA's "commercial activity" exemption applied. *See* 28 U.S.C. § 1605(a)(2). The defendants objected and asked the district court to adjudicate their other non-merits-based defenses before allowing any discovery. *Papandreou*, 139 F.3d at 254. The district court authorized the jurisdictional discovery, including the depositions of several Greek cabinet ministers. *Id.* at 249. The defendants petitioned for a writ of mandamus and the court of appeals obliged. The court held (i) that there

[10] Indeed, this conclusion dovetails with the conclusion reached by a prominent legal advisor to the PLO during the 1999–2000 peace talks. *See* Omar M. Dajani, *Stalled Between Seasons: The International Legal Status of Palestine During the Interim Period*, 26 Denv. J. Int'l L. & Pol'y 27, 86 (1997) (remarking that "the interim character and extraordinarily limited powers of the PA make it impossible to characterize that body as the 'effective government' of the [territory]"; *see also* Omar Dajani, *On a Better Road This Time in the Mideast?*, Wash. Post, May 4, 2003, at B1.

were less intrusive ways of determining the applicability of the FSIA exemption, and (ii) that the trial court should have grappled with the non-merits-based defenses before subjecting the defendants to jurisdictional discovery. *Id.* at 254.

We do not lightly dismiss the reasoning behind *Papandreou*. Had the defendants in this case raised their sovereign immunity defense in a timely manner, their argument that they were entitled to adjudication of that defense before proceeding with the merits of the litigation might have some force. After all, a district court's denial of a motion to dismiss a complaint on the ground of foreign sovereign immunity is immediately appealable under the collateral order doctrine. *See Price* v. *Socialist People's Libyan Arab Jamahiriya*, 389 F.3d 192, 196 (D.C. Cir. 2004); *S & Davis Int'l, Inc.* v. *Republic of Yemen*, 218 F.3d 1292, 1295 (11th Cir. 2000); *Transatlantic Shiffahrtskontor GmbH* v. *Shanghai Foreign Trade Corp.*, 204 F.3d 384, 387 (2d Cir. 2000); *Jungquist* v. *Sheikh Sultan Bin Khalifa Al Nahyan*, 115 F.3d 1020, 1025 (D.C. Cir. 1997). And such an appeal ordinarily divests the district court of jurisdiction to proceed with the litigation pending its resolution. *See Rivera-Torres* v. *Ortiz Velez*, 341 F.3d 86, 93 (1st Cir. 2003); *Apostol* v. *Gallion*, 870 F.2d 1335, 1338 (7th Cir. 1989); *see also Eckert Int'l, Inc.* v. *Gov't of Sovereign Democratic Republic of Fiji*, 834 F. Supp. 167, 175 (E.D. Va. 1993) (noting that foreign state's non-frivolous interlocutory sovereign immunity appeal divests district court of jurisdiction).

These principles are not absolute. None of the cited cases stand for the proposition that sovereign immunity is a trump card that may be held in reserve until a defendant sees fit to play it, thus enabling the defendant to stop the litigation in its tracks at a time of its choosing. That is simply not the law. As we have explained in a related context, "in exchange for the defendant's right to interrupt the judicial process, the court may expect a reasonable modicum of diligence in the exercise of that right." *Guzmán-Rivera* v. *Rivera-Cruz*, 98 F.3d 664, 668–69 (1st Cir. 1996) (quoting *Kennedy* v. *City of Cleveland*, 797 F.2d 297, 301 (6th Cir. 1986)). Demanding such diligence is "virtually essential to orderly judicial management of the vexing procedural problems" that accompany assertions of immunity.[11] *Fisichelli* v. *City Known as Town of Methuen*, 884 F.2d 17, 19 (1st Cir. 1989).

[11] Of course, an entity alleging an entitlement to sovereign immunity may choose to ignore an action or court order directed at it, accept a default, and then assert its immunity at a later state of the litigation. But such a choice represents a rather risky gamble. If the assertion of immunity is valid, the defendant wins the entire pot (i.e., it walks away from the suit unscathed) but if the assertion of immunity fails, the defendant loses outright (i.e., it must live with the default). There is no need to engage in such high-stakes wagering. A defendant may both assert sovereign immunity and defend on the merits. *See MCI Telecomm. Corp.* v. *Alhadhood*, 82 F.3d 658, 662 (5th Cir. 1996); *Practical Concepts, Inc.* v. *Republic of Bolivia*, 811 F.2d 1543, 1547 (D.C. Cir. 1987).

The defendants, for whatever reason, elected not to assert sovereign immunity in either of their first two motions to dismiss. By the time that the district court ordered the entry of a default, the defendants still had not moved to dismiss on the ground of sovereign immunity. The district court found, and the defendants' own words appear to confirm, that this recalcitrance was intentional and designed to accomplish some obscure strategic aim. *See Ungar IV*, 325 F. Supp. 2d at 23–24.

Given this sequence of events, the defendants' arguments are unpersuasive. Here, as contemplated in *Papandreou*, discovery was stayed until the defendants had a full determination of the non-merits-based defenses that they initially chose to assert (including insufficiency of process, forum non conveniens, and lack of in personam jurisdiction). After rejecting those defenses and denying two motions to dismiss, the district court in effect ordered the litigation to proceed. The defendants—who to that point had not raised a sovereign immunity defense—nonetheless refused either to answer the amended complaint or to comply with the court's discovery orders. In view of this history, we believe that the district court acted well within the encincture of its discretion in entering the default. *See Compania Interamericana Export-Import, S.A.* v. *Compania Dominicana de Aviacion*, 88 F.3d 948, 951–52 (11th Cir. 1996) (permitting entry of default against foreign state due to its willful failure to comply with court orders). The defendants deliberately chose to hold off on asserting a sovereign immunity defense—and they must live with the consequences of that choice.[12]

V. Conclusion

We need go no further. The defendants have not shown that this case involves nonjusticiable political questions. By like token, they have not shown that Palestine is a state and, as a consequence, they do not have available to them the buckler of sovereign immunity. Consequently, they cannot set aside the judgment on that ground. And, finally, they have failed to show that the district court acted precipitously either in entering a default or in reducing the default to judgment. Accordingly, we reject their appeal.

Affirmed.

[12] We recognize, of course, that the existence vel non of foreign sovereign immunity implicates federal subject matter jurisdiction. Thus, the failure to raise the defense in a timely manner cannot result in a waiver. *See, e.g., Haven* v. *Polska*, 215 F.3d 727, 733 (7th Cir. 2000). Nevertheless, a failure of that kind can appropriately affect the trial court's management of the litigation. *See, e.g., Bolduc* v. *United States*, ___ F.3d ___, ___ (1st Cir. 2005) [No. 03-2081, slip op. at 9] (explaining that "the belated filing of a motion to dismiss for want of subject matter jurisdiction can have consequences in terms of a court's case-management decisions"). That is the situation here.

E. EUROPEAN APPROACH TO THE PALESTINIAN PROBLEM

DOCUMENT NO. 18

PALESTINIAN AUTHORITY OF THE WEST BANK AND GAZA STRIP

Commission of the European Communities
SEC(2004) 565

Brussels, May 12, 2004

1. Introduction

1.1. The European Neighbourhood Policy

On 1 May 2004, the enlargement of the European Union took place with the accession of ten new Member States. It has brought changes to the EU's political geography offering new opportunities to deepen existing relations between the Union and its neighbours to the East and to the South. The Union is determined to further develop partnerships with its neighbours to mutual benefit, promoting security as well as stability and prosperity. The EU's external borders will not become new dividing lines but the focus of enhanced co-operation.

The European Neighbourhood Policy sets ambitious objectives for partnership with neighbouring countries based on strong commitments to shared values and political, economic and institutional reforms. Partner countries are invited to enter into closer political, economic and cultural relations with the EU, to enhance cross border co-operation and to share responsibility in conflict prevention and resolution. The Union offers the prospect of a stake in its Internal Market and of further economic integration. The speed and intensity of this process will depend on the will and capability of each partner country to engage in this broad agenda. The policy builds upon and reinforces the existing framework of co-operation.

In the present report, the Commission provides an assessment of bilateral relations between the Union and the Palestinian Authority. The report reflects progress in relations under the Interim Association Agreement, and describes the current situation in selected areas of particular interest for this partnership: the development of political institutions based on the values—democracy, the rule of law, human rights—underlined in the Agreement, structural and fiscal reforms that will create new opportunities for development and modernisation, for further liberalisation of trade and for gradual participation in the Internal Market. The report provides guidance for the preparation of a joint action plan, and may also serve as a basis for assessing future progress in the Union's relations with the Palestinian Authority.

The report reflects the particular circumstances created by the Middle East conflict. This has a major impact on political and economic conditions in the West Bank and Gaza Strip.

1.2. Relations Between the European Union and the Palestinian Authority

The European Institutions and the Member States have been working closely with the Palestinian Authority to build up the institutions of a future democratic, independent and viable Palestinian State in peace and security with Israel and its neighbours.

The **Interim Association Agreement** on Trade and Co-operation between the European Community and the PLO (for the benefit of the Palestinian Authority) was signed on 24 February 1997 and entered into force on 1 July 1997. The primary objective of this Agreement is to establish the conditions for increased liberalisation of trade and to provide an appropriate framework for a comprehensive dialogue between the EU and the PA. These measures are aimed at integrating the Palestinians into the Euro-Mediterranean Process.

Since the outbreak of the second Intifada in September 2000, implementation of the Interim Association Agreement has proven extremely difficult. A Joint Committee meeting of the Interim Association Agreement was held in Ramallah on 26 June 2003. This meeting was the second of its kind and the first in over three years. The meeting discussed ways in which to facilitate trade between the EU and the West Bank and Gaza Strip and means to fully implement the Interim Association Agreement, including provisions related to the Palestinian reform programme.

European Community assistance to the Palestinians began in 1971, when the first contribution was made to the regular budget of the United Nations Relief and Works Agency for Palestine Refugees in the Near East (UNRWA).

Community Assistance 2000–2003

Budget Heading	Commitment Appropriations (million €)			
	2000	2001	2002	2003
MEDA	119.60	0.00	104.50	92.75
Community operations in connection with the Peace Agreement	20.40	43.05	87.75	47.00
Contribution to the UNRWA	40.24	57.25	55.00	57.75
Humanitarian aid (ECHO)	18.20	26.26	35.00	38.00
Food aid/Food security	16.06	17.10	35.00	20.28
Total	**214.5**	**143.66**	**317.25**	**255.78**

The EU is the most important financial donor to the Palestinians, providing humanitarian assistance, support to refugees, development assistance and support to the Palestinian Authority. EU and other international donor assistance to the Palestinian Authority have been essential for the PA to carry out basic public services in times of crisis. Total assistance from the European Community budget in support of the reform process and in response to the worsening economic and humanitarian crisis stands at €570 million for 2002–2003. This covers assistance to the PA, an emergency fund for the Palestinian private sector, rehabilitation of municipalities, preparations for elections, assistance to refugees, food aid, support for the health sector, institution building and judicial reform.

The EU attaches a number of conditions to its financial support with the aim of advancing Palestinian reform efforts including **administrative and judicial reform**, and **financial accountability**. Particular importance has been put on improving the management of public finances by the PA and strengthening the system of financial control.

The Palestinian Authority participates in a range of Euro-Med programmes promoting people-to-people contacts, cultural cooperation and co-operation between actors of civil society, youth associations and NGOs. The PA is eligible for participation in the Community programmes in the field of higher education, namely Tempus and Erasmus Mundus.

West Bank/Gaza has been one of about 30 "focus countries" for the European Initiative for Democracy and Human Rights for the year 2002-4 and has benefited of support amounting to 2,5 ME. The EIDHR supports civil society initiatives that aim to promote democracy and human rights.

The EU continues to support initiatives to further the peace process, in particular through civil society, to promote a culture of tolerance and mutual understanding, and to strengthen democratic principles and respect for human rights.

2. Political Issues

2.1. Political Situation

In September 1993, the Palestinian Liberation Organisation (PLO) and Israel signed the Palestinian Declaration of Principles establishing the framework for an interim period of Palestinian self rule in the Gaza Strip and Jericho. This was the first in a series of steps known as the "**Oslo Peace process**".

A transfer of powers and responsibilities from Israeli to Palestinian control took place following the Israel–PLO Cairo Agreement of 4 May 1994 on the Gaza Strip and the Jericho Area. As an immediate result of this agreement, the head of the PLO, Yasser Arafat returned from exile in Tunisia to take over as Chairman of the newly established Palestinian Authority.

The transfer of civil government and partial security responsibilities from Israel to the Palestinian Authority took place in other areas of the West Bank pursuant to the Israel-PLO September 28, 1995 Interim Agreement, the January 17, 1997 Protocol Concerning Redeployment in Hebron and the September 4, 1999 Sharm el Sheikh Agreement. Pursuant to the Interim Agreement, the Palestinian Territory was divided into Areas A, B, and C indicating differing levels of Palestinian and Israeli control, although the effective exercise of responsibilities in these areas has been blurred since the onset of the Intifada.

In January 1996, Palestinians held their first and only presidential and legislative elections for an interim 88-member Palestinian Legislative Council and President (Ra'is) of the Palestinian Authority.

The Declaration of Principles under the Oslo accords had established a two-phased timetable. After the interim period, the second phase was expected to address "permanent status" or "final status" issues, and resolve "remaining issues", including: Jerusalem, refugees, settlements, security arrangements, borders, relations and cooperation with other neighbours, and other issues of common interest. A final status agreement would mark the official peace agreement between Israel and the Palestinian Authority, including the possible establishment of a sovereign Palestinian state. These negotiations were postponed on a number of occasions and the Camp David summit in July 2000 failed to reach an accord.

Developments since September 2000: with the onset of the second Intifada in late September 2000, the region has experienced unprecedented levels of violence and bloodshed. Official negotiations between Israel and the Palestinian Authority for a peaceful resolution to the conflict collapsed soon after the Taba talks in January 2001 and violence and terrorist attacks increased dramatically. In particular, a campaign of suicide bombings was launched primarily by groups rejecting the Oslo peace accords and the right of existence of the state of Israel. As a result, there have been regular Israeli incursions into and reoccupation of a large part of Palestinian controlled towns and villages, curfew and severe restrictions imposed on the movement of persons, in both the West Bank and the Gaza Strip. The Intifada and violence associated with the conflict had, by the beginning of 2004, claimed the lives of over 3300 people and over 24,000 persons had sustained injuries.

Closures and curfew, restricting movement of both goods and people, have led to a worsening humanitarian situation and the Palestinian economy has experienced an unprecedented decline since September 2000.

Israel has begun to construct a "separation barrier" in the West Bank on the grounds that this will provide greater security against attacks and suicide bombings inside Israel. The Israeli Government has argued that this is a temporary measure and that the barrier can be taken down once the security outlook has improved. However, Palestinians have argued that the barrier, by deviating from the "Green line" and cutting deep into the West Bank, undermines the possibility of a negotiated settlement and a lasting peace based on a viable Palestinian state. The United Nations and the World Bank have also reported to the international community on the negative social and economic consequences of the barrier for the Palestinian population.

The **Quartet** (UN, US, EU and Russia) **Roadmap**, published in April 2003, sets out the steps which need to be taken towards a comprehensive settlement to the Israel-Palestinian conflict by 2005, by which time an independent, democratic and viable Palestinian state should emerge, living side by side in peace and security with Israel and its neighbours. The political horizon set in the Roadmap was confirmed at the Aqaba Summit in June 2003. The European Union, along with the international community, has supported this process.

Reform of the Palestinian Authority: the need to **strengthen and reform Palestinian public institutions** was first addressed in a comprehensive and systematic manner in 1999 by the EU-supported Independent Task Force led by former Prime Minister Michel Rocard under the auspices of the Council on Foreign Relations.

In June 2002, the Palestinian Authority, in response to increasing domestic and international pressure, adopted a wide-ranging programme on reform. A number of important measures were taken, such as the adoption and entry into force of the Basic Law, and legislation on the independence of the judiciary. In February 2003 the Palestinian Legislative Council (PLC) adopted the 2003 budget which was, for the first time, made public, and more generally, important efforts were made to strengthen financial control.

In March 2003 the PLC revised the Basic Law establishing a post of Prime Minister of the PA. In his inaugural address to the PLC on 29 April 2003, the first PA Prime Minister, Mahmoud Abbas stated that further progress on reform would be a high priority for the new government. He made a number of commitments to establish rule of law, to halt incitement, to respect human rights and to prepare for free and democratic elections. He also announced a detailed PA reform programme for 2003 and a new administrative reform strategy. Following the resumption of violence after a period of cease-fire, Mahmoud Abbas resigned in September 2003, and a new cabinet under a new Prime Minister, Ahmed Qurei, was endorsed by the PLC in November 2003.

2.2. Democracy and the Rule of Law

The **general constitutional order** of the Palestinian Authority arises from the interim agreements, on the basis of which the Basic Law was approved by the Palestinian Legislative Council in 1997, and belatedly enacted by President Arafat in 2002.

The Basic Law provides for the establishment of three separate branches: the executive, the legislature (embodied in the 88-member Palestinian Legislative Council), and the judiciary.

The post of Prime Minister was instituted following an amendment to the Basic Law in 2003. The cabinet was placed, thereafter, under the authority of the Prime Minister.

International representation is still the responsibility of the Palestine Liberation Organisation, and the Palestinian National Council is the forum comprising representatives from both the Diaspora and the West Bank and Gaza Strip.

The Basic Law provides for a **parliamentary democracy**, political and party pluralism and fundamental freedoms. The system of government could be further defined as semi-presidential. Whilst the PLC is accorded with a number of important powers to control the executive (e.g. approving laws, adoption of the budget), one of the main characteristics of the Palestinian Basic Law is the important role it gives to the President who is responsible for appointing a Prime Minister, signing laws after their approval by the PLC, issuing decrees that have the power of law, as well as overall control of security forces.

The PLC's legal term expired in 1999 and no new elections have been held since then. This has, according to opinion surveys and civil rights groups, weakened the legitimacy of PLC members in the eyes of the Palestinian population. Movement restrictions have prevented members of PLC in Gaza and within the West Bank from travelling to plenary sessions in Ramallah and Gaza respectively.

In January 1996 presidential **elections** were held. Mr Yasser Arafat was elected "Ra'is" (Arabic for chairman or president) of the Palestinian Authority, with 88.1 percent of the vote. His main opponent, Samiha Yusuf Khalil gained 9.3% of the vote.

For the PLC elections, the majority of the 88 seats were won by Fatah or independents affiliated with Fatah. The elections were officially boycotted by groups rejecting the Oslo peace accords such as Hamas and the Popular Front for the Liberation of Palestine.

In October 2002, following a commitment by the PA to carry out wide-ranging reform, an independent Central Elections Commission was established. Prime Minister Ahmed Qurei's Government Programme includes a commitment to hold elections in the course of 2004.

There are a number of difficulties in organising elections to the Palestinian Authority. There are the practical questions of updating the voter register and freedom of movement to allow for canvassing, work of election officials, and eventually, voting; and there are sensitive issues such as the framework for elections, participation in East Jerusalem in accordance with the interim agreement and the participation of Palestinian refugees in local council elections.

There is currently no legislation regulating **political parties**. Draft legislation from 1998 has never been adopted by the Palestinian Authority.

The main political groups and factions within the West Bank and Gaza Strip and in the Diaspora fall under umbrella of the Palestinian Liberation Organisation (PLO). These include the majority faction Fatah which is led by the chairman of the PLO, Yasser Arafat, the Palestinian People's Party, the Palestinian Democratic Union (FIDA), the Popular Front for the Liberation of Palestine; and the Democratic Front for the Liberation of Palestine. Other major Palestinian groups outside the PLO which are active both in the Palestinian Territory and the region include the Islamic Resistance Movement (Hamas) and the Palestinian Islamic Jihad. Both the Palestinian Islamic Jihad and Hamas are classified as terrorist organisations by the EU.

At the centre of **government** are the institutions of the President's Office, the Council of Ministers, and the ministries. The President assumes the presidency of the Palestinian Authority and the Executive Committee of the Palestine Liberation Organisation. Until the Basic Law was amended in early 2003, the President also headed the Cabinet of Ministers. Each PLC member or the Cabinet can introduce draft bills. The President can issue decrees with the power of law in exceptional cases, and while the PLC is not in session. The validity of such decrees is however subject to subsequent PLC approval.

According to the amended version of the Basic Law of March 2003, there may not be more than 24 ministers in the cabinet in addition to the prime minister, while the previous version of the law envisaged only 19. The Cabinet was formed twice in 2002 (in June and October) and three times in 2003 (in March, October and November) including the formation of an emergency restricted Cabinet.

The **central administration** within the West Bank and Gaza Strip is divided into sixteen governorates: ten in the West Bank, five in Gaza and Jerusalem. Governors are appointed by the President.

There is a single tier of local government in the Palestinian territories, the units being either "municipalities" or "village councils". The Local Government Law, which was amended in 1997, sets out the formation, financing and responsibilities of elected local authorities. In the absence of local elections since 1976 the Ministry of Local Government has appointed mayors and council members.

Since its establishment, there has been a proliferation of public institutions and agencies within or attached to the Palestinian Authority. The civil service payroll has grown and now exceeds 70,000, not including the various PA security services. Without clear division of responsibilities, job profiles and unclear lines of reporting, the Palestinian public administration lacks efficiency and effectiveness. This problem is compounded by the absence of any coherent human resource development programme and training for civil servants.

Public institutions have, furthermore, been severely affected since the outbreak of the Intifada and the resulting violence by Israeli incursions into the West Bank and Gaza Strip, curfews and damage to physical infrastructure which have weakened the capacity of the Palestinian Authority to carry out basic functions.

Comprehensive public administration and civil service reform has become a priority in the overall reform programme of the Palestinian Authority. There has, however, been limited progress in implementing this programme. The Civil Service Law from 1998 has not been fully implemented.

Of the measures which have been taken, a Cabinet paper was drawn up in February 2003 and a pilot project was launched in June 2003 involving five ministries—Labour, Local Government, Social Affairs, Culture and Planning. A number of institutions have been brought under the control of ministries. The petroleum and tobacco monopolies have, for instance, been brought under the direct responsibility of the Ministry of Finance and all monopolies and investments have been incorporated into the Palestinian Investment Fund.

The Palestinian Authority, upon its establishment, set about putting in place a new **judicial system**. In addition to new and unified PA laws which apply to the whole Palestinian Territory, the West Bank relies on civil or French-influenced Jordanian law, while the Gaza Strip relies on Egyptian and British laws. Some Ottoman and Israeli laws and decrees continue to be applied in both areas, as well as laws used by the PLO prior to the establishment of the PA.

The key legal bases for the PA judicial system are the Basic Law and the Judicial Authority Law which provide for separation of powers and regulate the formation of courts, delineation of jurisdictions and enforcement of judicial rulings. Most of the legislation applying to the functioning of courts in the West Bank and Gaza Strip has now been unified.

Much of the legislation has not been implemented and the judicial system is far from being fully operational. The division of responsibilities between the Ministry of Justice and the Higher Judicial Council remains unclear. There are also major challenges in implementing the newly unified legal framework under current Israeli movement restrictions and closures. The court infrastructure is extremely poor. Courts are unable to hold sessions most days of the year, resulting in an increased backlog of court cases. There are insufficient resources for proper training within the judiciary. Judges and court personnel also suffer from lack of communication between courts, ineffective procedures and poor management of records. This is once again compounded by movement restrictions between the West Bank and Gaza Strip.

The independence of the judiciary has, according to human rights organisations, been undermined by interference from the executive.

Whilst in principle the State Security Courts were formally abolished in 2003, the military courts, established in 1995, remain active, including some competence in civilian cases. Military Courts jurisdiction applies to police and security force personnel as well as crimes by civilians against security forces.

The Oslo Accords provided for the establishment of a PA police force. At least ten largely autonomous police and security forces now operate in the PA, including civil police, criminal investigation, preventive security, general intelligence, and military intelligence. Efforts to unify the various security services have been unsuccessful.

Prisons, known as reform and rehabilitation centres, come under the police directorate. The various security forces operate their own detention and interrogation centres, access to which has often been denied to outside bodies or international human rights organisations.

Towards the end of 2003, there were increasing signs of a deterioration of law and order in the West Bank and Gaza Strip. Central commands have been de-connected from local units, and forces are unable to move, due to closures. Police and Preventive Security commanders have often been unable or unwilling to carry out arrests of criminals and armed militants, since this often results in armed confrontations with radical groups or large family clans.

The Transparency International **Corruption** Perceptions index included the Palestinian Authority for the first time in 2003 with a ranking of 78 out of 133. Recent polls have indicated a general perception of lack of public confidence in Palestinian public institutions.

Since its announcement of a comprehensive reform programme in June 2002, the Palestinian Authority has set about addressing shortcomings and improving its overall system of public finances. Progress has since been achieved in the area of financial transparency and important achievements have been recognised by the International Monetary Fund.

2.3. Human Rights and Fundamental Freedoms

Palestinian legislation includes a number of provisions for the **protection of human rights and basic civil liberties**, without explicit reference to international texts and conventions. The Palestinian Authority has made the political commitment to respect International Human Rights standards. Human rights organisations have, however, reported numerous violations.

The Palestinian Basic Law prohibits **torture, force against detainees and illegal arrests**. However, there have been numerous reports of cases of torture and ill-treatment in PA detention centres, namely those operated by the security services. According to human rights organisations, security services arbitrarily detain persons and use excessive force. Despite PA declarations condemning such practices, the security services do not appear to have clear procedures for investigating complaints effectively and impartially and there is limited control over their interrogation methods.

The Basic Law guarantees **freedom of expression**. In practice, however, freedom of expression remains highly restricted. **Freedom of association** is also provided for in the Basic Law relating to the establishment of trade unions, guilds, associations, societies, clubs and public institutions. The general right of association is stated in the Non-Governmental and Benevolent Organisations Law.

The printing and publication Law provides for **freedom of the press and media**. Despite legal guarantees, freedom of the press is, in practice, restricted and there is government censorship on the Palestinian mass media. Several journalists and human rights activists have been arrested or interrogated. There are also several cases where newspapers, magazines or TV/radio stations have been closed. Court orders to reopen media centres closed by the security branches are often ignored. According to human rights organisations, harassment has led to self-censorship of the press and media.

The main religious groups within the Palestinian Territory are Muslims (92%), Christians (7.5%) and Samaritans (0.3%). According to the Basic Law, Islam is the official religion of the West Bank and Gaza Strip. **Freedom of other religions** is guaranteed insofar as they do not violate public order or public morals. Freedom of religion is generally respected within Palestinian society.

Women account for only 13% of the formal labour force, mostly concentrated in the services sector such as health and education. Whilst **equality of rights** has not been given highest priority in the past, there has recently been some change in public attitudes. Discussions on issues such as violence against women, rape (including marital rape and so-called "honour crimes") and woman's shelters have been held and in November 2003, a Ministry for Women Affairs was established.

Civil society organisations play an important role in the Palestinian society. As the worsening situation on the ground impairs the Palestinian authorities to provide basic services, NGO's often are the only organisations capable of delivering these services to the population in a wide range of areas, such as health, education, vocational training, culture, children and youth, women, agriculture, water and small businesses.

In addition, in the current context of the PA reform process, the involvement of Palestinian civil society has increased. The National Reform Committee, which was established in May 2003 to oversee the reform agenda, includes representative of civil society organisations.

A Law on NGOs entered into force in 2000. Relations however, between the PA and civil society are generally poor, with the PA closely monitoring the activities of several civil society organisations, in particular those promoting greater reform and protection of human rights. Organisations are also faced with excessive delays in registering as NGOs with the Ministry of Interior.

A number of NGOs promotes intercultural dialogue based on equality and reciprocity between Arabs and Israelis, including the Arab Palestinian minority in Israel with the aim of working together for mutual benefit and tangible results. These initiatives are designed to help re-create the conditions among civil society for relaunching the peace process.

The Basic Law and the law on NGOs regulate the establishment of **unions and rights of association**. The Palestinian General Federation for Trade Unions (PGFTU) represents the workers movement in Palestinian Territory. Its board and chairman are appointed by the President of the Palestinian Authority. There are reports of acts of intimidation and arbitrary arrests of strike leaders by security services.

Equality of all Palestinians under the Law and Judiciary is affirmed in the Basic Law which does not permit **discrimination** on the basis of race, sex, colour, religion, political views, or disability. The Palestinian Electoral law sets a quota of representatives of religious minorities at the PLC.

3. Economic and Social Situation

3.1. Macroeconomic and Social Developments

3.1.1. Recent Sector Developments

Since the beginning of the Intifada at the end of 2000, the Palestinian economy has gone into severe decline. The conflict and Israeli closure policy have hit the Palestinian economy through several channels, including collapse of tourism, the inability of Palestinian workers to work in Israel, and the inability of Palestinians within the territories to undertake basic economic activities. Transaction costs have significantly increased and lower incomes have forced the population to use savings to finance daily expenditures, thereby negatively impacting upon the level of investment. All these factors have had a negative impact on domestic demand, with estimates of the decline in real income ranging from 30%–50% over three years to the end of 2003.

In 2002, real GDP was estimated to have dropped by around 15%, with consumption down by around 8% in real terms, investment down by over 30%, and exports dropped by over 20%. In 2003, the economy stabilised somewhat and a modest pick-up in economic activity could be recorded due to several positive factors. The launching of the Roadmap improved the political situation, and violence diminished in the first part of 2003. In addition, Israel began to repay arrears on tax revenues (clearance) collected on behalf of the PA, providing a stimulus for domestic demand. There was also some easing in the closure policy, allowing a recovery of the number of Palestinian workers in Israel. Despite some deterioration in the second half of 2003, these factors have led to a positive real growth of around 4.5% in 2003, albeit from a low base.

The standard of living of a large proportion of the population has fallen dramatically. GNI per capita (which includes workers remittances from abroad) fell by around 26% in 2002, and poverty levels increased dramatically, with those living on less than US$ 2 per day tripling to 60% of the population since the beginning of the Intifada. This per capita level has improved only slightly during 2003. Health and food consumption indicators have also declined.

The close monetary and economic ties, particularly trade links, between West Bank and Gaza Strip and Israel mean that overall price movements are highly correlated, and tend to be linked to shekel/US dollar rate movements. However, recent price developments in Gaza and in the West Bank have shown different trends due to the different impact of the Intifada and closure policy. For example, in Gaza, the recession has been much more pronounced than in the West Bank, and domestic demand has been more subdued. The tighter closure policy in the West Bank has had a much greater impact upon transportation costs, which has to a large extent offset the dampening effect of the recession. As a result, price increases in the West Bank in 2002 reached around 6%, compared to 2.7% in the Gaza strip, broadly 5.7% overall. In 2003, prices are expected to have risen by around 1.1% in the West Bank and Gaza Strip.

3.1.2. Fiscal Management, Monetary and Exchange Rate Policy

Palestinian revenues collapsed as Israeli transfer payments, accounting for broadly two-thirds of the PA's pre-Intifada revenues (derived mainly from indirect taxes, VAT, import taxes, and excise taxes), were stopped at the beginning of the Intifada and only resumed on a regular basis in 2003. Against this background, the PA has implemented a series of austerity expenditure plans to limit spending and allocating resources to areas that are crucial to maintain the viability of the Palestinian Authority.

In 2002, domestically collected revenues reached US$ 225 million, with some clearance payments made by Israel totalling US$ 29 million. With expenditures limited to US$ 90 million per month, there was a financing gap of US$ 773 million for the whole year. This was filled through external donor support and some domestic bank financing and through arrears accumulation. By the end of 2002, total gross revenues withheld by Israel amounted to over US$ 700 million or US$ 450 million, netting out PA payments due to Israel for electricity, water and other services.

The 2003 budget maintained a tight expenditure stance of broadly US$ 90 million per month, assuming continued donor support around the same level as in 2002. Although domestic revenues increased in 2003, as a result of transfer revenues received from Israel, external donor support and Israeli transfers from the stock of arrears was less than expected. The PA cleared much of its arrears to the private sector, but it was unable to reduce its bank debt. As a result, in 2003, the deficit totalled US$ 527.4 million (an average of US$ 44.0 million per month).

The Palestine Monetary Authority (PMA), established in 1994, has only limited functions, as set out in the Paris Economic Protocol. It is responsible for licensing, supervising and inspecting banks; determining the liquidity requirements on all deposits held by banks operating in the self-rule areas; and managing foreign exchange reserves and foreign currency transactions. The PMA also has the power to regulate and supervise capital activities in the self-rule areas, including the licensing of capital market institutions, finance companies and investment funds.

Despite the stresses caused by the Intifada, the financial system continues to function, and provides basic services to the population. This is to a large extent due to rapid growth in bank deposits between the mid-1990s and the second Intifada, which have been mostly re-invested overseas. Furthermore, the banks have adopted a cautious lending policy due to the risky political and security environment, as well as the difficulty in enforcing contracts. Nevertheless, during the period of the Intifada, non-performing loans have increased from around 8% to around 30% in 2002 (given the nature of banks' balance sheets, this represents less than 10% of assets).

3.1.3. Social Situation and Human Development Policies

Using a **poverty** line of US$2 per day, the World Bank estimated that 21% of the Palestinian population were poor in 1999; this figure increased to 60% by 2003. Average daily consumption of a poor person has also dropped from US$1.47 per day in 1998 to US$1.32 in 2002.

As a result of external closures nearly 100 000 Palestinian workers (or two thirds of the Palestinian workers formerly employed in Israel) have lost their jobs in Israel since September 2000. This decrease had direct consequences on the income of Palestinian households as workers' remittances from Israel represented some 18% of their total disposable incomes.

The unemployment rate in the West Bank has fallen to 20.7% (115,000 persons) in the fourth quarter of 2003 (down from 31.4% in the first quarter of 2003):. In Gaza, fourth quarter 2003 unemployment stood at 31.9% (83,000 persons).

In 1994, authority in the **education** sector was transferred from the Israeli civil authorities to the Palestinian Authority. The Palestinian Ministry of Higher Education was officially established in June 1996 in response to the need to create a centralised public body to develop and co-ordinate Palestinian higher education. The Ministry of Higher Education has now been merged with the Ministry of Education. There are several Palestinian universities and technical colleges in the West Bank and Gaza Strip. All were established after 1967, and two of them as late as the 1990s.

3.2. Structural and fiscal reforms

In June 2002, the PA released a new reform agenda, in which it expressed its commitment to a broad programme of reforms, including the promotion of transparency and accountability in the public sector, and the creation of a supportive environment for private sector development. Towards the end of 2003, the PA formulated a Medium Term Plan setting out the financing needs for the Palestinian economy in 2004 and 2005.

The regulatory framework for the Palestinian economy is in the process of being developed and key laws still need to be adopted, including the Capital Markets Authority Law, the Income Tax Law amendments, the Competition Law, the Foreign Trade Act, the Intellectual Property Law, Insurance and Securities Laws and revisions to the Customs Law and tariffs.

Since the beginning of the Intifada, several reforms have been implemented to improve effectiveness, efficiency and transparency in the context of EU and other donor budget support operations. On the revenue side, all revenues are now transferred to the Single Treasury Account (STA) at the Ministry of Finance, including the transfer of income from PA commercial activities. After an independent evaluation, PA assets have been transferred into the newly created Palestinian Investment Fund (PIF), with consideration now being given to privatisation of those assets.

On the expenditure side, control has been improved through various measures. PA employment is more tightly controlled after the transfer of the payroll in August 2002 to the Ministry of Finance. While this has had a positive effect, PA employment levels continued to increase. The move towards bank account payments for security service personnel has been a step towards further tightening in this area by allowing for greater control through a full data base. Other measures have included the development of modern and effective internal and external audit services.

In order to improve transparency, extensive budget data is now published on a regular basis, and the 2003 and 2004 budgets are more comprehensive than in previous years, including the macroeconomic framework, comparisons with previous years outturns, information on employment, PIF activities and bank borrowing. Progress has been made on establishing modern internal and external audit capabilities within the administration.

In the last few years, but particularly in 2003, reform of the pension system was examined with assistance from international financial organisations, including steps to unify pensions schemes and including security staff within the scheme, while putting it on a more sustainable footing.

3.3. Trade, Market and Regulatory Reform

Despite trade and co-operation agreements with Jordan, Egypt, Saudi Arabia, the European Union, the United States and others, which all provide preferential access for Palestinian exports, there has been almost no geographical diversification of trade. West Bank and Gaza trade remains dominated by Israel, according to World Bank data, which amounts for more than 70% of Palestinian imports, and some 90% of Palestinian exports, in the context of an overall compression of Palestinian trade since 2000.

Imports account for around 85% of GDP, while exports account for around 15% of GDP. The Palestinian Authority's chronic trade deficit (60–75% of GDP) reflects trade orientation towards Israel, a narrow export base and the substantial import dependence of the economy. Furthermore, the disadvantage of narrow industrial and agricultural production bases has been exacerbated by Israeli restrictions on the use of natural resources, as well as occasional border closures. Although earnings by Palestinian workers in Israel and remittances from abroad partly offset the large trade deficits, resulting in current account deficits of around 30% of GDP, international donor support has been needed to meet the remaining financing requirement. In 2002–03, these financial assistance flows have allowed to compress the current account deficit below 20% despite an increase of the trade deficit to close to 80% of GDP.

According to World Bank data, exports dropped by around 35% in value terms between the beginning of the Intifada and the end of 2003, while imports fell by around 31% over the same period.

The Paris Protocol on Economic Relations of April 1994 governs the trade relations between the PA and Israel. It also defines responsibilities for the PA in a number of economic spheres, including the movement of goods. In the area of **technical regulations and standards for industrial products**, according to the Paris Protocol, standards for Palestinian imports should be in conformity with Israeli standards, with the exception of certain goods under the PA's authority. Palestinian standards are set through the Palestinian Standard Institute.

The movement of Palestinian goods has been severely affected in recent years by restrictions imposed by the Israeli authorities on security grounds, which apply to the movement of both goods and persons within the West Bank and Gaza Strip.

The need to restructure the Palestinian economy has been addressed within a wider Economic Recovery Strategy for the PA. Several issues, resulting mostly from the crisis, need to be addressed to set solid foundations for economic stabilization and recovery, including private sector institutional reform, access to financing, enhanced competitiveness and private-public dialogue.

Customs legislation in the West Bank and Gaza Strip derives from Jordanian or Israeli law/Israeli military orders. In addition to this, the Paris Economic Protocol of 1994 governs economic and trade relations between the PA and Israel. Most customs procedures and tariff measures are based on Israeli norms, and to a large extent, Israeli controlled. However, on the basis of the Paris Economic Protocol, certain products fall under the authority of the PA, which can determine increases or decreases in tariff rates. Other products fall under the PA's authority but are still subject to quantitative restrictions or Israeli standards.

The PA has established directorates for VAT, and Customs and Excise, unified under the Customs and Excise General Directorate of the Ministry of Finance. In terms of administrative capacity, it is necessary to ensure the existence of a strong customs law and codes and that the Customs Directorate the necessary powers to effectively fulfill its functions.

The Palestinian Authority, as a partner to the Barcelona Process, endorsed the new Protocol on rules of origin in July 2003 allowing for the extension of the Pan-European system of cumulation of origin to the Barcelona Partners. The next stage aims at amending the origin protocol in the relevant Euro-Mediterranean Agreement in order to insert the changes necessary for the application of diagonal cumulation. This could help fostering economic integration and allow for a better use of the complementarities and the economics of scale in the Euro-mediterranean area.

In the area of **taxation**, the Palestinian Authority has put in place a system of VAT, income tax, purchase tax, property tax and excise taxes. VAT was introduced in 1976 and is covered by two separate but identical military orders issued by the Israeli Occupation authorities in the West Bank and Gaza Strip. In March 1999, the PA passed new legislation on income tax brackets for individuals and companies. Property tax is covered by the Property Tax Laws of 1967.

The Ministry of Finance currently has three major departments, which are responsible for the administration of tax laws: the Customs and VAT Department, the Income Tax Departments and the Property Tax Department. Due to the absence of any formal fiscal or customs borders with Israel, Israel continues to be the major collector of Palestinian revenue, receiving two thirds of the tax for later transfer to the PA.

Work is underway to introduce a modern tax system and to establish a regulatory framework on the basis of international best practices. The fragmentation of the tax administration has been exacerbated by the absence of coordination between West Bank and Gaza treasuries and tax administrations. Effective enforcement of legislation is still lagging behind.

In the area of **competition policy**, regulatory structures are in transition. Many of them have been inherited from Jordan or the British Mandate.

Applicable legislation may differ between West Bank and Gaza Strip, however unification is in progress. A new basic regulatory framework, including a new Competition Law, has not yet been adopted.

The Civil Claim Law of 1993 in Gaza and the Commercial Law of 1953 and Patent Law of 1953 in the West Bank currently govern **intellectual property**. Registration is done at the Ministry of Economy and Trade. In the area of **public procurement**, the General Procurement Law was adopted in 1998 and has since been modified by the PLC in May 2003.

Regarding **provision of services and right of establishment**, the Law on Encouragement of Investments promotes capital investment in all sectors of the Palestinian economy by both local and foreign corporations registered to do business in the West Bank and Gaza Strip. Two other laws govern investment in the Industrial Estates and Free Zones: the 'Industrial Estates and Free Zones Law' and the 'Encouragement of Investment in Palestine Law'. A foreign investor can fully own a company without any local partnership requirements. Investors may invest in any sector of the Palestinian economy under the free admission principle. Transfers of foreign currency are free and there is freedom of repatriation of income generated from investment in Palestine. The Palestinian Investment Promotion Agency (PIPA) is the implementing agency.

The Jordanian Companies Law of 1964 governs the registration of companies in the West Bank, with the exception of companies doing business in non-autonomous areas of the West Bank which is governed by the Israeli Military Order of 1970. The prevailing legal framework for registering a company in Gaza is the British Mandatory Companies Law of 1929. In the West Bank, registration of companies falls within the purview of the Ministry of Economy and Trade and in Gaza, under the Ministry of Justice, which is also responsible for administering the company law.

As regards financial services, despite the decline in economy, the Palestinian financial system remains upright, functioning and liquid.

The **Banking Law** of 1997, revised in 2002, and was approved by the PLC and entered into force in 2003; however it is not fully implemented. The Law was revised to bring it more in line with Basle core principles. It stipulates that locally incorporated banks and foreign branches must set aside 10% of net annual profits to a local reserve, up until a maximum of its capital base. The revised law also details guidelines for both internal and external auditing of banks, data obligations to the Monetary Authority and sets out the guidelines for on- and off-site inspection, penalties, liquidations and mergers. The regulatory framework for the banking sector is in general further advanced than those for the securities and insurance sector. The **insurance law**, at the moment under the supervision of an inter-ministerial committee (National Economy, Finance and Justice) has been drafted and is awaiting approval by the Palestinian Legislative Council. The Security law is expected to pass a first reading in 2004. At present the Ministry of Finance acts also on a temporary basis as supervisor of security exchanges. Eventually, both lows should fall under the permanent supervision of the Capital Market Authority; the CMA Law is awaiting the signature of the President, who asked the Cabinet for an opinion and, in addition, regulations and forms still need to be prepared.

Financial control over the PA's public finances has been developed over the past years, both on the revenue and the expenditure side. Revenue management was developed following the Oslo agreements and the subsequent transfer of clearance revenue from the Israeli authorities to the PA with the establishment of a Single Treasury Account (STA). Revenues, including those stemming from PA commercial activities, excise duties, and revenues from PA monopolies, have been gradually consolidated under the direct control of the Ministry of Finance. In a further step, all commercial activities were consolidated in a newly created Palestinian Investment Fund (PIF). The PIF assets have been audited by an international auditing firm. In 2003, the Petroleum Authority was brought fully under the responsibility of the Ministry of Finance, leading to an increase in revenues.

On the expenditure side, two main issues were pursued following the appointment of Finance Minister Salaam Fayyad: the consolidation of expenditure management in the West Bank and Gaza, and the limitation of recruitment in the civil service. All expenditure requests are checked for corresponding budgetary appropriations, accounting systems in the West Bank and Gaza are unified, and advances from commercial banks are no longer possible. Reporting on revenues and expenditure is made public. The integration of the whole payroll under the Ministry of Finance was achieved in August 2002.

In the field of internal audit, reform has started with the establishment of an Internal Audit Department (IAD) in the Ministry of Finance. A General Control Institute (GCI) which operates under the direct supervision of the President has been established in 1994 as the external audit institution of the PA. However, the GCI has not submitted any annual reports to the PLC, as stipulated by the Basic Law and both its effectiveness and independence have been called into question. A new law is required to bring the legal framework for external audit in line with international standards.

Despite the positive developments of the last few years, there remain shortcomings in the Palestinian financial control system, which require further reform and capacity building to bring it up to international best practices.

3.4. Transport, Energy, Environment and Research and Innovation

The Palestinian **transport sector** is under the responsibility of the PA Ministry of Transport. In practice, transport operations within the West Bank and Gaza Strip are dictated by the closure policy which is enforced by Israel as a result of the worsening conflict. The Gaza seaport and airport are not functioning, due to Israeli security concerns and much of their infrastructure has been destroyed by the Israeli army. Road transport has been highly restricted as a result of permanent and flying Israeli checkpoints throughout the West Bank and Gaza Strip. Road freight and passenger transport operations are highly restricted and freight transport within the West Bank is subject to a cumbersome back-to-back transportation system.

The Palestinian **energy sector** relies to a large extent on imported energy, either directly from Israel or under the supervision of the Israeli authorities for oil products. The domestic resources are restricted to limited production of biomass, small private electricity generation and solar energy. About 95% of the Palestinian electricity is generated by the Israel Electricity Corporation (IEC). The rest is produced privately, mainly in the remote regions. The energy institutions established are the Palestinian Energy Authority (PEA) charged with the overseeing of the energy sector policy and development and the General Petroleum Authority (GPA). The PEA in 1997 formed the Palestinian Electricity Company (PEC). The efficiency of the distribution utilities is poor and the transformation and distribution losses range from 25% to as high as 30–35%.

The restructuring process of the regulatory environment for the Palestinian energy sector is still ongoing. A Palestinian Energy Authority has been established, and draft regulations are under discussion in the PLC.

In an initiative sponsored by the EU, the Palestinian Energy Authority has signed three agreements with the Israeli Ministry of Infrastructure and the Israel Electricity Corporation to outline the principles of cooperation and to organise the sector. In this context, a number of proposals have been discussed, including the possibility of constructing a Combined Heat Power Plant and interconnections of the gas network with Israel and neighbouring countries.

The Palestinian Authority disposes of offshore gas resources and is developing a pipeline network to supply its territory.

As regards the **environment**, the Environmental Law of 1999 sets out the general legal framework. The Palestinian Authority has developed a ten-year Environmental Strategy and a National Environment Action Plan, which have adversely been affected by the ongoing conflict. In 2002, an Environmental Quality Authority was established as successor to the Ministry of Environmental Affairs and it reports to the Cabinet of the Palestinian Authority.

Most activities on environment issues have been suspended since the onset of the Intifada. The Palestinian Authority has a been beneficiary of Community support under the programmes SMAP and LIFE-Third Countries', although such support has been limited due to the conflict.

The Higher Council for **Research**, established within the Palestinian Ministry of Education, plays a central role in setting strategies and priorities for academic research. In spite of the difficulties in implementation caused by the ongoing conflict, Palestinian institutes and universities have participated in a number of projects under the EU 5th Framework Programme and have been selected for further projects under the 6th Framework Programm

DOCUMENT NO. 19

EU/PALESTINIAN AUTHORITY ACTION PLAN

January 19, 2007

1. Introduction

The enlargement of the European Union on 1 May 2004 has brought a historical shift for the Union in political, geographic and economic terms. The EU and the Palestinian Authority, as close neighbours, will reinforce their political and economic interdependence. Enlargement offers the opportunity for the EU and the Palestinian Authority to create the conditions for developing an increasingly close relationship in preparation for a future Palestinian State, going beyond co-operation, to involve a significant measure of economic integration and deepening of political cooperation.

The European Neighbourhood Policy of the European Union sets ambitious objectives based on commitments to shared values and effective implementation of political, economic, social and institutional reforms.

Achieving Palestinian statehood requires full implementation of the Quartet Roadmap and an end to violence in order to reach a fair and lasting peace in the Middle East, on the basis of the relevant UN Security Council Resolutions, and allowing for the establishment of an independent, viable, sovereign and contiguous Palestinian state, living side by side with the state of Israel in peace and security.

The Palestinian Authority welcomes the EU initiative to enter into intensified political, security, economic and cultural relations, and shared responsibility in conflict prevention and conflict resolution. The European Union and the Palestinian Authority are determined to make use of this occasion to enhance their relations and to promote stability, security and wellbeing, and to support the Palestinians in their efforts to build their own future. The approach is founded on partnership, joint ownership and differentiation.

Palestinian participation in the European Neighbourhood Policy takes place in the context of the overall political situation in the region which affects the scope of actions that can be feasibly undertaken. There are a number of constraints and limitations resulting from the ongoing Israeli-Palestinian conflict and the continuing occupation, including settlement activity, restrictions to movement as a result of the closure policy and the separation barrier. The limitations on the Palestinian Authority pending the creation of a Palestinian state must also be taken into account. Joint action will be required both to bring about the implementation of the Roadmap and to continue the preparations for statehood.

The level of ambition of the EU-PA relationship will depend on the degree of commitment to common values as well as the capacity to implement jointly agreed priorities. The pace of progress of the relationship will acknowledge fully the efforts and concrete achievements in meeting those commitments.

The European Neighbourhood Policy is part of the European Union's response to the Palestinian Authority's political and economic reform agenda. This Reform has been developed to consolidate democracy, accountability, transparency and justice in the West Bank and Gaza.

This Action Plan is a first step in this process. It covers a timeframe of three to five years. Its implementation will help fulfil the provisions in the Interim Agreement (IA) and will encourage and support the Palestinian Authority's national reform objectives and further integration into European economic and social structures. Implementation of the Action Plan will significantly advance the approximation of Palestinian legislation, norms and standards to those of the European Union. It will also build solid foundations for further economic integration based on the adoption and implementation of economic and trade-related rules and regulations with the potential to enhance trade, investment and growth. It will furthermore help to devise and implement policies and measures to promote economic growth employment and social cohesion, to reduce poverty and to protect the environment, thereby contributing to the long-term objective of sustainable development. The Palestinian Authority and the EU will cooperate closely in implementing this Action Plan.

New Partnership Perspectives

The European Neighbourhood Policy opens new partnership perspectives:

- The perspective of moving beyond cooperation to a significant degree of integration, including through a stake in the EU's Internal Market, and the possibility for the Palestinian Authority to participate progressively in key aspects of EU policies and programmes.
- An upgrade in the scope and intensity of political cooperation;
- The opportunity for convergence of economic legislation, the opening of economies to each other, and the continued reduction of trade barriers which will stimulate investment and growth;

- More targeted financial support: EU financial assistance for the Palestinian Authority will be better targeted to support the actions identified in the present document. The Commission is furthermore proposing a new European Neighbourhood and Partnership Instrument (ENPI), for this purpose, also covering the very important aspect of transnational cooperation. There may also be infrastructure investment support through the European Investment Bank;
- Possibilities of gradual opening of or reinforced participation in relevant Community programmes, promoting, inter alia, cultural, educational, environmental, technical and scientific links;
- Support including technical assistance and twinning to meet EU norms and standards, and targeted advice and support for legislative approximation through a mechanism such as Technical Assistance Information Exchange (TAIEX);
- Deepening trade and economic relations, extending them progressively to cover agriculture and the service sector, and to provide the conditions for increasing investment and exports

For the near future the Interim Association Agreement remains a valid basis for EU- Palestinian cooperation and will permit the implementation of the priorities of the Action Plan. In the light of the fulfilment of the objectives of this Action Plan and of the overall evolution of the EU-PA relations, consideration will be given to the possibility of a new contractual relationship. The Commission has suggested that this could take the form of a European Neighbourhood Agreement. Upon the establishment of an independent Palestinian State, this would include the features of a full Association Agreement.

Priorities for Action

The Action Plan sets out agreed priority objectives to be achieved, which have been jointly agreed by the both the EU and the PA. Many of these priorities are based on the ongoing Palestinian reform programme which was launched in June 2002. Given the prevailing political situation in the West Bank and Gaza Strip, it is not possible to distinguish between short and medium term actions. In this context the EU and the Palestinian Authority attach particular importance to:

- Facilitating efforts to resolve the Middle East conflict, and to alleviate the humanitarian situation
- Enhancing political dialogue and cooperation, based on shared values, including issues such as strengthening the fight against terrorism and incitement to violence, promoting the protection of human rights and the rights of minorities, improving the dialogue between cultures

and religions, co-operating in the fight against racism and xenophobia, in particular anti-Semitism and Islamophobia.

- Progress on establishing a functioning judiciary and effective enforcement of legislation; strengthening the rule of law and respect for human rights
- Strengthening institutions and further reinforcing administrative capacity
- Organisation of elections in the West Bank and Gaza Strip in accordance with international standards
- Building on progress made in establishing an accountable system of public finances
- Developing trade relations with the Palestinian Authority and progress with economic and regulatory reform plans; fully implement the Interim Association Agreement
- Enhance cooperation on transport and energy issues with the objective of strengthening Palestinian participation in Trans Euro-Mediterranean networks

Progress in meeting these priorities will be monitored in structures under the Interim Association Agreement. On this basis, the EU, together with the Palestinian Authority, will review the content of the Action Plan and decide on its adaptation and renewal. Within three years, decisions may be taken on the next step in the development of bilateral relations, including the possibility of new contractual links.

2. Actions

2.1 Political Dialogue and Reform—Building the Institutions of an Independent, Democratic and Viable Palestinian State

Development of Enhanced Political Dialogue and Cooperation

(1) Strengthen political dialogue and cooperation including on foreign and security policy issues

Regular EU-PA political dialogue is provided for in the context of the Interim Association Agreement on Trade and Cooperation. Political dialogue and cooperation should be strengthened and extended to include the following regional and international issues.

- Developments in the region and prospects for cooperation to resolve the Middle East conflict, including intensified efforts to facilitate the peace process and bring about the implementation of the Quartet Roadmap to a permanent two-state solution to the Israeli-Palestinian conflict

- Measures to facilitate improving the overall humanitarian situation
- Ensuring respect for international law, in particular international humanitarian law
- Dialogue between cultures and religions
- Measures in the fight against racism and xenophobia, including anti-Semitism and Islamophobia
- Fight against terrorism
- Strengthen EU-PA cooperation on the Palestinian reform programme

(2) *Intensify co-operation in the areas of combating terrorism, non-proliferation of weapons of mass destruction and illegal arms trade*

- Strengthen EU-Palestinian Authority co-operation on the fight against and prevention of terrorism, including the prevention of illicit funding and supply of arms;
- Co-operate to reinforce the role of the UN in the multilateral fight against terrorism, including through full implementation of UNSC Resolutions 1373/01 and 1267/99, through implementation and enforcement of the UN Convention for the Suppression of the Financing of Terrorism;
- Ensure respect of human rights in the fight against terrorism.
- Co-operation on non-proliferation of weapons of mass destruction, their means of delivery and ballistic missiles, including through implementing UNSC resolution 1540/04, ensuring full compliance with and national implementation of existing international obligations and promoting the accession to and compliance with other relevant international instruments and export control regimes
- Further develop co-operation in the prevention of and fight against the illicit trafficking of WMD-related materials
- Co-operation on establishing effective systems of national export control, controlling export and transit of WMD-related goods, including WMD end-use control on dual use technologies, and effective sanctions for breaches of export controls
- Apply the risk-based customs control ensuring safety and security of goods imported, exported or in transit, and explore possible definitions of standards for certification of operators (exporters and transporters) intervening in commercial exchanges
- Improve overall co-ordination in the non-proliferation area,and examine specific threats related to WMD which undermine regional security and the scope for cooperation in addressing them

- Promote the relevant provisions of the political and security partnership of the Barcelona Declaration with the objective of pursuing a mutually and effectively verifiable Middle East zone free of weapons of mass destruction.

Democracy and Rule of Law

(3) *Establishment of an independent, impartial and fully functioning judiciary in line with international standards and strengthen the separation of powers.*

- Adopt a coherent strategy for judicial reform
- Ensure progress on unification of the legal codes of the West Bank and Gaza Strip
- Ensure effective implementation of the Basic Law, in particular those articles relating to Citizen's Rights and Civil Liberties, and to the respect of provisions regarding the Military Courts
- Progressively improve the courts infrastructure
- Ensure full implementation of the "Law on the Judicial Authority", including the complete and transparent division of responsibilities between the Supreme Judicial Council and the Ministry of Justice and strengthen the administrative capacity
- Improve conditions for training in relevant areas (including human rights) and examine possibilities for establishing a Judicial Training Institute
- Implement reform of the PA security services

(4) *Organisation of transparent general and local elections according to international standards*

- Revise the legal framework to ensure compatibility with international standards and best practice
- Update the Voter Register for the West Bank, Gaza Strip and East Jerusalem (subject to freedom of movement within the Palestinian Territory).
- Start preparations for polling, counting, observation and party registration
- Adopt a legal framework for the registration and activities of political parties
- Ensure the independence of the elections commissions and a fair and free election process covering both general and local elections.
- Guarantee conditions for media coverage preceding and during the election campaign

(5) *Acceleration of constitutional and legislative reform*

- Finalise work on the drafting of a democratic Constitution and consultation with wider public.

(6) *Public administration and civil service reform*

- Continue implementation of the civil service and public administration reform programme, in particular making the non-ministerial public institutions operating outside the jurisdiction of the Council of Ministries and the Palestinian Legislation Council (PLC) accountable, and continuing the restructuring efforts in various Ministries, including the development of mandate, mission statements, and development programmes
- Strengthen the capacity of institutions responsible for implementing the reform programme

Human Rights and Fundamental Freedoms

(7) *Strengthen legal guarantees for freedom of speech, freedom of the press, freedom of assembly and association in accordance with international standards*

- Ensure effective freedom of the media, including journalists' rights and allow for unhindered functioning of a pluralistic media system
- Review the legal framework in view of providing for full freedom of the press in accordance with international best practices (including possibilities for establishing an independent media commission)
- Ensure full implementation of the 2000 NGO Law according to the by-laws adopted in November 2003 and the Basic Law

(8) *Ensure the respect of human rights and basic civil liberties in accordance with the principles of international law, and foster a culture of non-violence, tolerance and mutual understanding.*

- Adopt and implement an Action Plan on fostering a culture of non-violence, tolerance and mutual understanding, covering, *inter alia,* public institutions the education system and the media, including effective measures against incitement.
- Strengthen possibilities for legal redress against violations of human rights and civil liberties and access to information on citizens' rights
- Promote women's rights and ensure equal treatment and opportunities for women
- Strengthen and ensure effective enforcement of legal provisions against torture
- Provide training for the relevant Palestinian authorities on human rights issues and civil liberties

Financial Accountability and Sound Management of Public Finances

(9) *Continue efforts to establish a modern and well-functioning system of financial control in line with international best practices*

- Strengthen internal audit within the Finance Ministry and all PA spending agencies
- Provide training in modern methods of financial control (internal and external audit)
- Pursue adoption and implementation of the new law on external audit that provides for a modern and efficient Supreme Audit Institution, headed by an independent Auditor General, empowered to conduct audits on the public sector on a regular basis and accountable to the legislature.
- Submit annual reports of the General Control Institute to the Palestinian Legislative Council, in accordance with legal requirements
- Continue cooperation on exchange of information between the Palestinian Authority's law enforcement authorities and other relevant authorities (including specialised bodies at European level)
- Continue cooperation with relevant EU institutions and bodies in the case of on-the-spot checks and inspections related to the management and control of EU funds.

(10) *Continue work to improve transparency of the PA finances and to take concerted action to tackle corruption within public institutions and to fight against fraud.*

- Complete the implementation of the Palestinian Reform programme on budgetary and fiscal transparency
- Provide training for public institutions on anti-corruption measures
- Develop sufficient administrative capacity to prevent and fight against fraud and other irregularities affecting national and international funds, including the establishment of well-functioning co-operation structures involving all relevant national entities.

(11) *Ensure transparency of public procurement operations.*

- Develop conditions for open, fair and competitive award of public contracts in accordance with international best practices.
- Enforce the General Procurement Law

(12) *Put in place a modern and financially sustainable pension system.*

- Adopt an action plan for the reform of the pension system

- Establish a legal framework for a new pensions system, including the PA security services and restructuring and unifying the existing civil service pension schemes

2.2 Economic Reform and Development

(13) *Improve the conditions for the establishment and functioning of a market economy*

- Carry out necessary legislative reform and ensure adoption and implementation of a basic regulatory framework (including: Capital Market Authority Law, amended Income Tax Law, Companies Law, Competition Law)
- Strengthen the administrative capacity of the Palestinian Authority and other relevant agencies in the area of economic reform.
- Strengthen the capacity of the Land Authority

2.3 Trade-Related Issues, Market and Regulatory Reform

(14) *Develop trade relations between the European Community and the Palestinian Authority*

- Proceed with gradual liberalisation of trade in agricultural and fishery products and develop the necessary tools for trade control and management, including the gathering and analysis of data
- Implement the Palermo Action Plan approved at the July 2003 Euro-Mediterranean Conference of Trade Ministers
- Examine priorities for veterinary and phytosanitary standards in order to improve access to the EU market

(15) *Strengthen regional cooperation with neighbouring countries*

- Reinforce co-operation among the EC, the Palestinian Authority and Israel to facilitate implementation of trade-related aspects of the Interim Association Agreement
- Develop competencies, required knowledge and skills for trade negotiations
- Enable Palestinian participation in the Pan-Euro-Mediterranean cumulation of origin.

(16) *Develop the regulatory framework for a modern taxation system and institutions based on international best practices.*

- Revise the Income tax law in line with international best practices, and encompassing a single tax code for the West Bank and Gaza Strip.

- Continue efforts to unify the taxation administration in the West Bank and Gaza Strip, and to improve the overall effectiveness of revenue collection
- Improve coordination between the West Bank and Gaza treasuries and tax administrations
- Strengthen administrative capacity of the treasuries and tax administrations

(17) *Revitalise the private sector*

- Provide support for sustainable private sector development, including institution-building
- Strengthen relations between the Palestinian private sector and its institutions and EU counterparts
- Strengthen EU-PA cooperation on enterprise policy, including implementation of the EuroMed charter for enterprises
- Simplify administrative procedures for business

(18) *Further develop the statistics system based on international best practices*

- Reinforce the administrative capacity of the statistics bureau and improve overall coordination on collection of data.
- Ensure the appropriate legal framework for a modern statistics system based on impartiality, reliability, transparency and confidentiality of data

2.4 Energy, Environment, Transport and Science and Technology

(19) *Take steps to promote good environmental governance, to aim for prevention of deterioration of the environment, and to enhance co-operation on environmental issues*

- Review the PA environment policy and prioritise activities included in the Palestinian Environmental Law
- Strengthen administrative capacity and clarify responsibilities between different authorities
- Work towards improvements in the overall water and sanitation management system
- Promote enhanced regional cooperation with neighbouring countries, including on the sharing and management of water resources
- Pursue efforts to improve water supply and quality, especially in rural areas, with a view to meeting WHO standards

- Assess possibilities for participation in selected European Environment Agency activities
- Explore scope for strengthening capabilities for the safe disposal of hazardous waste

(20) *Enhance cooperation on energy and transport issues*

- Strengthen institutional capacity in the field of energy
- Develop regional cooperation on, *inter alia*, electricity and gas; energy and renewable energy sources and networks (in particular Euro-Mediterranean, and on the basis of relevant agreements, e.g. EC-Israel-Palestinian Authority)
- Strengthen cooperation on transport and promote Palestinian participation in Trans Euro-Mediterranean networks, and on other regional issues
- Promote participation of the PA in regional transport programmes, including satellite navigation

(21) *Science and technology, research and development*

- Evaluate the current situation with regard to research and development (infrastructure, human resources, institutional capacity)
- Promote improved Palestinian participation in the EU Sixth Framework Programme on Research and Development (including the establishment of national contact points)

2.5 People-to-People Contacts, Education, and Public Health Education, Training, And Youth

(22) *Develop a modern education system based on peace, tolerance and mutual understanding*

- Ensure continued progress on the new Palestinian Authority School Curriculum for all grades
- Upgrade the higher education system
- Enhance regional cooperation in the field of education and youth;
- Promote intercultural dialogue, and youth exchanges including cooperation through youth and other relevant cultural cooperation programmes
- Examine possibilities for developing sporting activities
- Reinforce participation in the EC TEMPUS programme and encourage participation in the Erasmus Mundus programme

- Examine ways to implement recommendations on bridging the knowledge gap as identified in the UNDP Arab Human Development Reports.
- Implement the national strategy for technical and vocational education and training through capacity building and human resource development

Public Health

- Upgrade the Palestinian Public health system, and examine ways to improve sustainability beyond the conflict
- Strengthen the administrative capacity of the Ministry of Health
- Strengthen coordination with relevant international organisations and health service providers, including NGOs

2.6 European Community-Palestinian Authority Cooperation

(23) *Take concrete measures to implement the Interim Association Agreement on Trade and Cooperation between the EC and the PLO (for the benefit of the Palestinian Authority)*

- Examine possibilities of greater use of the institutional framework of the Interim Association Agreement (e.g. Joint Committee meetings, working groups etc.)
- Examine prospects of negotiation of a full Association Agreement

(24) *Support the implementation of PA reform programme, focused on the priorities set out in the Action Plan.*

- Participate in the Quartet Task Force on Palestinian Reform and the Ad Hoc Liaison Committee on Assistance to Palestinians
- Provide targeted financial assistance and institution building support, focused on the priorities of the Action Plan and the overall objective of building the institutions of a Palestinian state living in peace and security with Israel

3. Monitoring

The Action Plans will be submitted for formal adoption to the Joint Committees between the EU and the Palestinian Authority. The Action Plans will guide the work between the EU and the Palestinian Authority. Should the need arise, on the EU side, for specific measures necessitating legally binding decisions, the Commission will recommend to the Council the adoption of the necessary negotiating directives.

The joint bodies established under the Interim Association Agreement will advance and monitor the implementation of the Action Plan on the basis of regular reports on its implementation.

A first review of the implementation of the Action Plan will be taken within two years of its adoption.

The Action Plans can be regularly amended, on a joint basis, and/or updated to reflect progress in addressing the priorities.

SUBJECT INDEX

Doc/Pg

Arms Proliferation

Border Security

Congressional Research Service (CRS) Reports

Counterterrorism

European Union

Human Rights

National Security – Threats to

Doc/Pg

Palestinian Authority

Terrorism Legislation – U.S.

Terrorism – Criminal Prosecution

Terrorism – Financing of

Terrorism – International

Terrorism – Military Role

Terrorism – Policy

Terrorist Incidents

Terrorist Organizations

www.ingramcontent.com/pod-product-compliance
Ingram Content Group UK Ltd.
Pitfield, Milton Keynes, MK11 3LW, UK
UKHW051048150926
475595UK00005B/171

9 780195 382778